MARCHING ORDERS

Also by Bruce Lee:
Pearl Harbor: Final Judgement

MARCHING ORDERS

THE UNTOLD STORY OF WORLD WAR II

Bruce Lee

DA CAPO PRESS

Map on page 45 copyright © 1995 by Mark Stein

Map on page 93 courtesy of U.S. National Archives

Maps on pages 346–48 reprinted with the permission of Simon & Schuster from *The
Chronological Atlas of World War II* by Charles Messenger. Copyright © 1989 by
Bloomsbury Publishing Ltd.

Design by June Bennett-Tantillo

Cataloging-in-Publication data is available from the Library of Congress.

This Da Capo paperback edition of *Marching Orders: The Untold Story of World War
II* is an unabridged republication of the edition first published in 1995. It is reprinted
by arrangement with the author.

First Da Capo Press edition 2001
ISBN 0-306-81036-0

Published by Da Capo Press
A Member of the Perseus Books Group
http://www.dacapopress.com

1 2 3 4 5 6 7 8 9—05 04 03 02 01

for
Janetta
my wife, co-skipper, resident editor and best friend . . .

PREFACE

Marching Orders is a unique book whose controversial conclusions have been tested by time and confirmed by subsequent revelations and publications.

There was one question, however, that the first edition did not address. This is: "Just how can you quantify the value to the Allies of their breaking the Ultra/Magic codes of Germany and Japan, and how much did this affect the Second World War as a whole?"

No straightforward answer can be found in old documentary records. Many military leaders of the time, such as Supreme Commander Dwight D. Eisenhower, never referred to their use of the Ultra/Magic decrypts in their public statements after the war. *Marching Orders* explains this phenomenon. But there are answers.

For example, in researching *Marching Orders*, I carefully studied more than 1.5 *million pages* of US Army records, including purchasing some 16,000 pages of Magic/Ultra summaries and conducted some 200 interviews. During all this research I found only *one* official reference of the value of the Magic/Ultra decrypts. This was the US Army's own secret report about using the information gleaned from the Ultra/Magic radio intercepts to prepare the daily

---

1. SRH–005 National Archives. This 86-page, still heavily censored document refers to the daily briefings prepared by the European Order of Battle Section for General Marshall. An extensive search for these briefings has been unsuccessful. Only a few copies have been found; they are incredible in their detailed knowledge of the daily operations of the German army. Senior archivist John E. Taylor advised me that if these briefings do, in fact, exist that they would not be released.

Magic Summary for Chief of Staff George C. Marshall. The paper is titled: "Use of CX/MSS Ultra by the United States War Department (1943–1945)".[1] The paper claims that when the Pentagon's European Order of Battle Section brought items directly to Marshall's attention, "it has been estimated that 35 percent were taken from Ultra/Magic traffic." Yet another 32 percent of information received from other intelligence sources was corroborated by Ultra/Magic sources. The remaining 32 percent of the information adjudged to be accurate came from operational cables from various Allied commands abroad. In summation then: The ability of the British and the Americans to break the enemy's Ultra/Magic radio traffic provided Marshall with information about the strategic intentions and the disposition of the Axis forces in Europe that was believed to be 67 percent correct. This is probably the greatest intelligence success in military history.

Now, let's estimate the value of the Ultra/Magic decrypts in monetary terms. What was the Ultra/Magic code breaking worth to the overall war effort? According to Henry C. Clausen, who was Secretary of War Stimson's personal investigator into the proximate causes of the Pearl Harbor disaster: "The paltry sum that Washington spent prior to 1941 to create the machine that broke the Japanese Magic ciphers produced the best return on investment in American military history."[2]

Now, let's estimate the contribution that breaking the Ultra/Magic codes made to Allied military effectiveness. Prime Minister Churchill said the results were worth many, many more divisions. Admiral Chester Nimitz rated the value of breaking Magic as the equivalent of another whole Pacific Fleet. And General Thomas Handy, Deputy Chief of Staff of the US Army during the entire war, claimed that it shortened the course of the war in Europe by a full year.

Comments such as those above have helped this book score a number of notable "firsts." Among them are: (1) This is the only book that collates and compares the actual orders issued by General Marshall with the information he received from the Magic Summaries on a daily basis during the war—and, later, into the early months of America's occupation of Japan. (2) It is the first book to point out that Generals Eisenhower and Bradley, and Field Marshall

---

2. *Pearl Harbor: Final Judgment* by Henry C. Clausen and Bruce Lee (New York: Crown Publishers, 1992), 47.

Montgomery, benefited prior to the invasion of Europe by knowing that (a) Hitler had swallowed the Allied deception plans about where they would land in Europe; (b) the Allied leaders knew the disposition of the German forces defending the beaches; (c) the Allies also knew why Hitler would not release reserve forces to defend against the Allied invasion. This gave the Allied generals the confidence to endure terrible casualties, plus the fortitude to keep committing troops even when the success of the invasion was in doubt.

Marching Orders is also the first book to explain the political and military considerations that led General Marshall to order Supreme Commander Eisenhower to halt on the Elbe River and let the Russians capture Berlin. And it is the first book to show how the use of Ultra/Magic intercepts, especially the diplomatic traffic between Tokyo and Moscow, helped the Allies reach the tragic decision to use atomic weapons on Japan and end the war in a "quick and decisive manner."

Let us examine the statement by General Handy that I quoted earlier. As Marshall's right-hand man, Handy witnessed what went on in Marshall's office, especially the use of Magic/Ultra. Thus, Handy is an impeccable source. However, not until the year 2000 did the British address the subject. Handy said it shortened the course of the war by one year. Today, British intelligence experts claim that the Allied breaking of Ultra/Magic shortened the course of the war by two years![3]

One of the sources for this estimate is Dr. David Rees, emeritus professor of mathematics at Exeter University. He claims that the new code-breaking technology of 1944, as developed by the British in the form of a computer named Colossus II, confirmed "that Hitler had swallowed the Allies' deception campaigns over where the invasion force would be landed, giving the Allies the confidence to go ahead with the invasion of Europe."

This confirmation of what I had written about the invasion of Europe in *Marching Orders* is most satisfying. But the most significant statement the British now make is that the Allied use of Ultra/Magic intercepts shortened the course of the war by *two years*! (Other American cipher experts are more inclined to emphasize the

---

3. "Colossal Code of Silence Broken" is the headline for a full-page spread by Roger Highfield. The Daily *Telegraph* (London), page 22, September 6, 2000. See also: *Enigma: The Battle for the Codes* by Hugh Sebag-Montefiore (London: Weidenfeld & Nicholson, 2000) and *The Emperor's Codes: Bletchley Park and the Breaking of Japan's Secret Ciphers* by Michael Smith (London: Bantam Press, 2000).

importance of Allied improvements in armament and personnel, as well as tactics and experience in decision-making in this regard.)

Nevertheless, the unexpected crossing of the Rhine River in March 1945, and the sudden collapse of Germany immediately thereafter, surprised British and American strategic planners. They had estimated that the war in Europe would last through the winter of 1945–46. Thus, if the war in Europe had lasted longer (as Gen. Handy and others thought it would), it is most likely then that the first atomic bomb would have been dropped on Germany and not on Japan.

And if the bomb had first been used against Germany, it is most likely that atomic weapons would not have been used against Japan, because Japan would have witnessed the devastation wrought on Germany and would have surrendered.

As it was, however, a new and uncertain President Harry S. Truman was faced with the fact, in the short period of time that the atomic bomb was first tested successfully on July 16, 1945, and the time the first bomb was dropped on Hiroshima on August 6, 1945, that Japan had *not* agreed to the Allied demand for unconditional surrender. Furthermore, Truman had no choice but to accept as valid the horrific casualties anticipated in an American invasion of Japan. And given the additional information gleaned from Magic/Ultra sources that (1) the Japanese had issued orders to kill all their Allied POW in the event of an invasion of Japan, and (2) the Japanese militarists had been given the approval of Emperor Hirohito to try to establish a new treaty between Japan and the Soviet Union that would divide China between the two nations, Truman was forced to use atomic weapons against Japan.

These facts destroy the twisted arguments used by the revisionists that the Allies held off from using the atomic bomb on Germany to use it instead on Japan, primarily for racist reasons.

It is important that we also remember the number of people *killed* in World War II. We forget how horrific these casualties were. The numbers are: United States 300,000; United Kingdom 400,000; Finland 90,000; Norway 10,000; Holland 200,000; Belgium 100,000; Denmark 7,000; France 600,000; Germany 5 million; Austria 310,00; Italy 300,000; Albania 20,000; Greece 100,000; Poland 6 million; Czechoslovakia 350,000; Hungary 400,000; Rumania 700,000; Bulgaria 17,000; Yugoslavia 1.6 million; India 36,000; the British Colonies 21,000; Australia 29,000; New Zealand 5,000;

South Africa 9,000; the Soviet Union 20 million (this figure does not include another 12 million Soviets who were murdered by Stalin to maintain control of the country during the war); China 2.5 million (this figure is believed to be conservative); Japan 2 million.

The total of wartime dead between the years 1939–1945 is *53 million*! This averages 7.5 million people killed each year of the war. Thus, if the Allied use of the Ultra/Magic decrypts helped shorten the course of the war by two years, it means the potential saving of 15 million lives!

This is a magnificent achievement. It also proves that the killing in World War II had to be stopped, no matter how tragic the use of atomic weapons might be.

Another controversial aspect of *Marching Orders* is the book's estimates of American casualties in the event we had to invade and forcibly occupy the home islands of Japan. The figures presented in early 1945 to President Truman by our Chiefs of Staff were these: The attacking American forces would suffer 833,000 casualties in the first thirty days of the two proposed invasions of Japan. If the invasion lasted sixty days, the casualties would double. If the invasion lasted ninety days, the casualty figure would triple.

The significance of the first figure—883,000 casualties—is this: The figure represents nearly three times the casualties suffered by America during the entire war. And, in 1945, this figure represented fifteen percent of our total armed forces, or nearly one percent of America's total population of the time.

The book points out that these casualty figures were unacceptable to President Truman. He could count casualties as quickly as he could count votes. He remarked to his Joint Chiefs that the proposed invasion of Japan was about to create another battle such as the one for Okinawa [one dead American soldier for every one-and-a-half dead Japanese] but on a far greater scale.

The US Army became so worried about the forthcoming invasion of Japan that it ordered the minting of so many Purple Heart medals that enough were made to see us through the Korean War, the Vietnam War and the Gulf War—with plenty left to spare.

I also noted in the first edition of *Marching Orders* that there were 300,000 Allied POW in Japanese hands on Java, plus another 100,000 American POW in Japan. It was known that all of these POW were to be killed if the Allies invaded Japan. At the time, however, the radio intercepts of Tokyo's orders to kill those POW were not available to me. Thus, I wrote that if these intercepts could be found that they would cause headlines around the world.

Five years later, in a book only published recently, Linda Goetz Holmes confirmed my prophecy. Ms. Holmes located the original orders issued by Tokyo to execute these POW. The intercepts of these orders issued by Tokyo reveal the methods to be used: "(A) Whether they are destroyed individually or in groups, or however it is done, with mass bombing, poisonous smoke, poisons, drowning, decapitation, or what, dispose of them as the situation dictates. (B) In any case it is the aim not to allow the escape of a single one, to annihilate them all, and not to leave any traces."[4]

Thus, in the process of proving that an alternative to a seaborne invasion of Japan had to be found, plus the saving of lives of the POW, it becomes clear that the use of Ultra/Magic decrypts saved more than one *million* American lives.

When I published these estimates in May, 1995, revisionists challenged them. A debate raged for many months, and it was finally put to rest by a review of *Marching Orders* written that November by the British historian M. R. D. Foot. He wrote: "The most interesting and topical passages of the book deal with the concluding stage of the war between the United States and Japan. They demonstrate conclusively the hold that the naval and military chiefs had over Japanese state policy, and the overwhelming argument about impending casualties for the seaborne invasion of Japan. (To this point the reviewer can testify; he helped make the calculations, which totalled about 1,500,000 service dead, not counting civilians.) Had the first atomic bombs not demonstrated vastly superior power to the Japanese, so they could 'honorably' surrender, the butchers bill would have been a great deal worse."[5]

I wrote to Michael Foot, thanking him and asking if he could speak further about his projections of invasion casualties. He replied that it was not until May 1945 that the British had begun to study casualty estimates for the invasion and forcible occupation of Japan. Foot and another RNVR officer named Rich were given all the casualty figures for the invasions made during the war, from Dieppe to

4. *Unjust Enrichment: How Japan's Companies Built Postwar Fortunes Using American Prisoners of War* by Linda Goetz Holmes (Mechanicsburg, PA: Stackpole Books, 2001), manuscript page 231.
5. *Times Literary Supplement* (London), November 3. 1995.

Okinawa, and were told to work out a probable casualty rate for a seaborne invasion of Japan. In his letter Foot said: "I have never been able to forget our conclusion. The invasion would have cost 600,000 Allied dead, plus 900,000 Japanese dead. We specified that we counted service dead only, taking no account of civilian casualties."

I also had concluded in *Marching Orders* that if we had not dropped the atomic bombs on Japan, and if we had merely continued our already scheduled fire bombings of 140 Japanese cities—in which from 100,000 to 300,000 civilians were already being killed in each attack—that the continued conventional bombing of Japan would have cost more than 14 million Japanese civilian dead!

It took months for this issue to fade from the public eye. Finally, historian Arthur Schlesinger, Jr., wrote a *New York Times* op-ed article in which he said the decision to drop the atomic bomb "was the most tragic decision in our history." He then said that he had "problems in seeing how a responsible President [Truman] could have done otherwise."

The argument can also be made that if Truman had *not* used the bomb, and if the invasion of Japan had cost a million American casualties, that when the public learned of his failure to use atomic weapons Truman would have been impeached.

Also, during the time *Marching Orders* was published, Washington was the focus of a bitter argument about how the Smithsonian Museum should commemorate the war in the Pacific with its proposed *Enola Gay* exhibit. The revisionists who supported the original anti-bomb exhibit fought tooth-and-nail against various veterans associations, or the men and women who were present during the war and knew first-hand what the war was about. Some revisionists wrote featured articles for Japanese newspapers apologizing for their inability to deliver a pro-Japanese *Enola Gay* exhibit at the Smithsonian.

The tragedy of the Smithsonian situation becomes apparent when one considers that *Marching Orders* was the first book to reveal how, in 1945, the US Army fooled the Japanese into believing we had never broken their diplomatic codes. This deception allowed the occupation government of General Douglas MacArthur to stay one step ahead of the new Japanese government in its attempts to control its ill-gotten wartime gains by creating secret bank accounts and dummy corporations around the world. Our reading of the postwar Ultra/Magic traffic also revealed that one of the first actions taken by the new post-war Japanese government was to create and finance a world-wide propaganda campaign depicting America and Great Britain as war criminals for their use of the atomic bomb. In explaining this new Japanese program to its embassies around the world, Foreign Minister Shigemitsu said that Tokyo's reason for the campaign was to keep Emperor Hirohito from being named a war criminal, and to mitigate the Allied charges of myriad atrocities committed by the Japanese throughout the course of the Pacific war, especially their atrocities against Allied prisoners of war.

Instead of warning the American public about the forthcoming propaganda campaign, however, Washington invoked the excuse of national security. No one was to know that the Allies had broken the Japanese and German codes during the war. Meanwhile, the Japanese kept spending more and more money around the world building their anti-American, anti-British campaign. The Japanese policy of denial continued. During the 1980s, for example, Japan spent more money lobbying Washington and people of influence than did any other country or organization. One result was that politically correct American revisionists unwittingly became apologists for Japan.

This brings us to the conclusion of the argument about the *Enola Gay* exhibit. The American veterans associations finally won the fight. The Smithsonian had to recast its program. The original *Enola Gay* exhibit that effectively supported Japan's contention and was blessed by the revisionists was then moved to American University. Only later did the *Washington Post* reveal that the exhibit was funded by Tokyo.

This takes us back, once again, to the original question about the significance of the role played by the Allied interceptions of the Ultra/Magic radio traffic. As Chief of Staff Marshall viewed the world situation in January, 1942, only three weeks after Pearl Harbor, it looked like this: Nazi Germany and Italy together had invaded and occupied the following countries—Norway, Denmark, Czechoslovakia, Austria, Holland, Belgium, Luxembourg, France, Sardinia, Albania, Greece, Morocco, French West Africa, Tunisia, Libya, Syria, Abyssinia, Italian Somaliland, Madagascar, Rumania, Hungary, Iraq, Poland, Lithuania, Estonia, Latvia and all of Russia from within 30 miles of Moscow southward including the Crimea.

For its part, Japan had invaded and occupied the following: Manchuria, Korea, all of northeast China, Formosa, Hong Kong, the Philippine Islands, French Indo-China (later to be called Vietnam),

Malaya, Burma, Thailand, Sumatra, Borneo, New Guinea. In simple terms this meant that Japan controlled nearly one-quarter of the world's population at the time.

On Marshall's side of the ledger as he saw it, at the end of 1941 the American army was no larger than what had once been the combined armies of Greece and Belgium. Our Pacific battleship fleet was on the bottom at Pearl Harbor. Not only were the Allies outgunned, they were outmanned. Every soldier knows that it is easier to defend a fortified position than to attack it. The common belief was that one needed from four to eight times more attacking troops than defenders to be successful.

Marshall knew that the Allies would never be able to achieve this numerical superiority in trying to regain the territory already occupied by Axis forces. Unless, of course, we knew about the enemy's strategic and tactical intentions so we could use fewer men in attacks against relatively lightly-defended enemy positions. And this is where our ability to read the secret codes of the Axis gave us the vital edge.

Consider the following: In June 1942, only seven months after Pearl Harbor, the US Navy won the battle of Midway. This changed the course of the war in the Pacific. Then, in August 1942, General Montgomery won his first victory at the battle of Alam Halfa. This changed the course of the war in North Africa and Europe. The common denominator of these two battles was that they were won because we had broken the Japanese and German radio codes.

From this time onward the Allies always attacked successfully, often using smaller forces to defeat superior enemy forces. The net result was the most successful military campaign in history.

We can now see precisely how the accomplishments of the Allied code breakers could well have shortened the course of the war by one or two years. The breaking of the Ultra/Magic ciphers also saved untold millions of lives on both the Allied and the Axis sides of the war. The breaking of the Ultra/Magic ciphers was a prize whose value was beyond measure. As Frederick the Great once said: "If we had exact information of our enemy's dispositions, we should beat him every time."

Bruce Lee
New York City
February 2001

FOREWORD

Virtually everyone familiar with the history of the Second World War understands the meaning of the word Magic, the top secret code name for America's breaking of the Japanese diplomatic Purple ciphers. These were the intercepts that should have prevented Pearl Harbor; and these were the intercepts that heightened the controversy during the congressional hearings into what caused the disaster at Pearl Harbor. But until this book no one has revealed the wealth at the very highest level of these incredible decrypts as they flowed daily across the desk of Chief of Staff George C. Marshall throughout the war. Nor has anyone used this priceless information as an overlay on a chronology of World War II, showing how the Magic Diplomatic Summaries, as they came to be known, influenced strategy in Europe and the Pacific, as well as the way the war ended and the emergence of the postwar world.

In all honesty this book is not the one I started out to write. I had intended to write about the fall of Berlin and the end of the war in Europe. But as I dug deeper into the Magic Diplomatic Summaries, I kept finding more and more linkage of the war in Europe to Pearl Harbor, the conflict in the Pacific and the dropping of the atomic bombs on Hiroshima and Nagasaki. This meant I had to scrap everything and go back to the beginning of *America's* war—Pearl Harbor—because if one doesn't understand what went on in Marshall's office in 1941, and if one doesn't track the Magic Summaries in their proper chronological order, one cannot understand why the war in Europe ended the way it did or the reasons America and Great Britain agreed that it was necessary to employ nuclear weapons against Japan in 1945.

When I began working on this project, I agreed with the conventional wisdom, expressed so well by Gordon Craig, that America's "failure during the war against Hitler to coordinate its political with its military strategy was one of the main causes of the cold war, which it also conducted, in large part, with little regard for diplomacy and which ended with something less than a triumph.''[1] Craig also points out that Eisenhower's statement to General Marshall in 1945 that '' 'Berlin is no longer a particularly important objective'—is strikingly typical of the American leadership's stubborn denial of any vital connection between politics and war.'' Craig also makes the argument that immediately after Pearl Harbor, Anthony Eden's proposal that ''Britain and the U.S. concert their attitude toward political and territorial questions that were bound to arise in the future and then discuss them with the Soviet government was completely ignored in Washington.''

As I said, I used to agree with this conventional wisdom. But after reviewing an estimated fourteen thousand pages of Magic Diplomatic Summaries that have been declassified to date, and another estimated 1.5 million pages of U.S. Army records, I saw that this conventional wisdom no longer held true. By overlaying the Magic Summaries on American strategy and studying the resulting events, one could see that the American Army—especially Secretary of War Henry L. Stimson, Chief of Staff Marshall, Gen. Dwight D. Eisenhower—had a far better understanding of the intentions of our enemies, and of the self-serving diplomacy of our allies, i.e., the British, the Russians, the French and others, than anyone previously thought. Furthermore the U.S. Army demonstrated that it was peopled with men far cleverer than most American civilians imagine. These Army officers served their country in an exemplary fashion. They took over running the war when President Roosevelt could not make up his mind to act or was too ill to act. They won the war, but they allowed others to take the credit for much of what America achieved.

In the pages that follow, the record shows America probably achieved all she could get out of World War II given the finite limits of her military power in 1945 and the unwillingness of Congress to maintain America's dominant military position in the postwar world. Nor did America abandon the belief of its founding fathers that the British concept of colonialism, or the so-called ''political and territorial questions'' espoused by Anthony Eden, was totally unacceptable for the postwar world order. In other words, as one reads the pages that follow, it is my belief that by virtue of our being able to understand the innermost thoughts of the Axis leaders, what used to be conven-

---

1. "Looking for Order" by Gordon Craig, *The New York Review,* 12 May 1994. This review of Henry Kissinger's book *Diplomacy* is fascinating reading.

tional thinking is turned around completely. The Magic Diplomatic Summaries allow one to truly comprehend the brilliance of unelected men such as Secretary Stimson and Chief of Staff Marshall.

For example, the Magic Summaries allowed General Marshall to refuse the urgent pleas of Prime Minister Churchill that British-American troops should capture Berlin ahead of the Russians. (I used to agree with Churchill on this point.) But as my research proves, Marshall and his staff foresaw Churchill's proposal forcing American troops into potentially bloody clashes with the Russians for no valid reason. This is not widely known, but I am convinced that this is one reason Marshall ordered Eisenhower to halt his final attack through Germany on the banks of the river Elbe—and not advance on Berlin—in March 1945, before Eisenhower began the assault from the Rhine River. More important to Marshall, as the Magic Summaries reveal, was ending the war in the Pacific quickly and preventing a last-minute alliance between Russia and Japan.

Meanwhile, throughout the entire war, the Magic Summaries gave the Allies vital knowledge from Hitler's own lips about his decisions to attack or defend in Africa, Russia, Italy, France and Germany. This allowed the English and Americans to coordinate the timing of their invasions and offensives with those of the Russians on the Eastern Front. The Magic Summaries revealed Japan's hatred for Great Britain: Tokyo urged Germany to give up fighting Russia and use poison gas to subdue England. Tokyo also wanted to join hands with Germany in the Middle East so they could divide the world between them, which made the battle for Stalingrad more crucial for the Allies than previously acknowledged. Tokyo also tried to play the so-called race card in South America, Central America and Mexico in her attempts to influence these governments, and this created a relatively unknown and unstudied series of clandestine diplomatic battles between the Allies and the Axis in those countries. Perhaps most important, the Diplomatic Summaries alerted Washington and London to Stalin's postwar aim of exporting Communism throughout the world.

This brings us to perhaps the most controversial aspect of this work: In many cases I draw conclusions about Marshall's or Eisenhower's handling of a military situation based on what I know is available to them from Magic. In some cases a direct line of evidence supports my contentions, but in other cases I have had to rely on logical conclusions rather than a fact supported by direct evidence. I agree with the comment made to me by a specialist at the National Security Agency, who was kind enough to unofficially review my manuscript, that "it is often very difficult to conclude how communications intelligence was used, even in the face of overwhelming circumstantial evidence that it *must* have been used in a certain way." Thus, I am sure this work will draw criticism from certain quarters. In writing this work, however, I followed what I believed to be the rule of reasonable conclusions. In other words, if primary documentation makes a case for the linkage between supremely informative intelligence and tactical and strategic decisions that *directly* relate to that intelligence, then historians must, at the very least, consider the evidence. I am not writing from the possibly limited viewpoint of someone influenced by his or her personal experience; I have never been a government employee; I am not beholden to any general for a share of his royalties; I am not involved with a foundation that has a vested interest in protecting the name of a famous man, or a particular point of view. I may well have made errors of interpretation in this book. But they are based on unimpeachable documents and are inadvertent. I respectfully submit that unless critics can produce *documents* that refute these logical links, there should be few differing interpretations offered by either British or American intelligence experts if they weigh the evidence set forth in this book fairly and objectively. I know from experience that the standard reaction of some military and intelligence people, who would prefer that some of the information in this work remain suppressed, will be to reply to questioners: "My dear fellow, if you only knew what I know. . . ." (In researching this book, it was amazing how such people's memories were refreshed when they saw some of my documentation.) As I write these words, a new Executive Order has been signed that opens much (though definitely not all) of the archival record for 1945 and earlier. Unfortunately, this book does not contain material from these newly declassified papers. Because archival experts believe that a year or more will elapse before this new material can be catalogued and prepared for presentation to the public, this book went to press to meet its proposed publication date without my reviewing these documents.

According to Professor Warren Kimball of Rutgers University, who is chairman of the Advisory Committee on Historical Diplomatic Documentation, the material presently marked for declassification includes the Yardley collection (containing much technical information and material on the Black Room, or Chamber), all the records the NSA inherited dated prior to 1945, and an estimated 200,000 items in the "Crane Collection," which were with the National Archives and closed to researchers while I was preparing this work. This means there may be future additions or corrections to the material presented in this book, especially in reference to Pearl Harbor. Professor Kimball takes a historian's viewpoint in that he believes the final word on Pearl Harbor will not be known until the British open their files on the subject. Currently they are sealed for seventy-five years. Kimball may well be correct. I am a reporter, however, and my deadline cannot wait this long. Based on personal experience, this writer believes the British blockade on the release of such documents is a grave disservice to history. It indicates that the British Foreign Office still does not have faith in the public's ability to understand and act responsibly when it is told the truth.

I acknowledge that the communications intelligence (Comint) derived from Japanese diplomatic sources and German military messages (the former being Magic, the latter Ultra) was more important to Marshall's *tactical* decision making. The aim of this work, however, is to demonstrate the incredible impact of the Magic Diplomatic Summaries on Chief of Staff Marshall and how they influenced his *strategic* prosecution of the war. I also hope that this work will open up efforts to integrate the diplomatic and the military Ultra/Magic, i.e., the decisions made at the War Department with those of the State Department.

Only the Magic Diplomatic Summaries gave General Marshall the unique advantage of knowing precisely what the men who led the Axis were thinking just a few days after they expressed themselves in what they incorrectly assumed to be total secrecy. Magic provided Marshall with a firm foundation for discussions with President Roosevelt, Secretary of War Stimson, Secretary of State Cordell Hull, the leaders of the U.S. Navy, as well as the top American Army theater commanders, Eisenhower and MacArthur. It was the priceless value of the Magic Diplomatic Summaries that forced Marshall to beg the Republican candidate for President in 1944, Thomas E. Dewey, not to reveal the secret that we had broken the Japanese diplomatic codes prior to Pearl Harbor, because these diplomatic intercepts were the *only* source the Allies had about what Hitler and the Japanese were planning. (It was only relatively late in the war that America began to read a significant *portion* of the Japanese military and naval ciphers such as JN-25.) Fortunately for America and the Allies, Dewey kept the secret locked away, though it cost him dearly.

On the other side of the coin, America's greatest cryptologist of the time, William F. Friedman, complained that General Eisenhower never gave any credit to the men and women who broke the German and Japanese ciphers that allowed him to win his victory in Europe with fewer casualties and at a much more rapid pace than had been anticipated. As this book shows, years after the war, the U.S. Army finally put a quantifying percentage to the value of Ultra and Magic by saying that thirty-five percent of the information furnished the European Order of Battle Section came from Ultra/Magic sources. This is an incredible figure. (If anyone can hit for a .350 average, he's one heck of a baseball player, and this thirty-five percent bonus certainly helped Eisenhower carry out his mission much more effectively.) It also should be pointed out that Eisenhower wasn't allowed to mention the use of Ultra or Magic when he wrote his memoirs. Nor was anyone else. It just goes to show what I mentioned earlier: The U.S. Army is very good at the Jesuitical art of "reservation"—you don't have to tell a lie and you don't have to tell the whole truth. The Army is not happy, even today, with discussing anything other than its politically correct version of the way it fought World War II.

After the war Marshall acknowledged that American military leaders "discussed political things more than anything else. . . . But we were careful, exceedingly careful, never to discuss them with the British, and from that they took the count that we didn't observe these things at all. . . ." As Warren Kimball explains, the American military's public protests that they were not politicians were belied by their private actions.[2]

I also believe this book proves the incredible value of communications intelligence to the safety of our nation. In the glimpses that are given in this work about the secret diplomacy of our Allied partners during and after World War II (the book shows that America, and presumably the British, were reading the ciphers of at least fourteen friendly nations), one can see that today, as well as fifty years ago, America stands alone in the real world. Our allies not only want to shelter themselves under the umbrella of power offered by the American military, they also want to involve us in their self-interested stratagems to influence other nations, to say nothing about involving America in regions in which we do not belong. And I speak now only about our allies. . . . What about our enemies (and there are many of them)? How do we know what those who do not wish America well are currently planning? Communications intelligence is obviously a first line of defense. I pray that the lessons learned from reading this work will be beneficial to the collective safety of America and her people.

Bruce Lee

---

2. Warren F. Kimball, "Franklin Roosevelt: 'Dr. Win-the-War,' " in *Commanders in Chief: Presidential Leadership in Modern Wars*, Joseph Dawson, ed. (Lawrence: Univ. Press of Kansas, 1993), p. 100.

ACKNOWLEDGMENTS

Baseball players say they know their time to retire comes when they lose that half-step of speed that lets them rob someone of a base hit or steal a base. I recall interviewing Ty Cobb one day in his bedroom at the Waldorf Hotel in New York City. He proudly rolled up his trouser legs to show off a mass of scars accumulated from being spiked during the years he was on his way to the Hall of Fame. Cobb's story was simple: In his last seasons of playing ball, he wouldn't practice. He'd go to bed, in whatever city his team might be playing, and rest his legs. He wouldn't stir until game time. "When you lose your wheels, sonny, that's the time to go," he said. "Just remember to line up something to go to."

Years later, I was working for a distinguished publisher and proudly took a copy of a newly acquired manuscript about World War II, which I believed would be a best-seller, up to the publicity department. On arriving at the youthful publicist's office, I said that I had a fabulous book about the Battle of the Bulge. "Oh, no!" said the publicist. "I can't stand it. I already have two diet books on my list." The book *A Time For Trumpets* by Charles MacDonald, did become a bestseller. But I had received my own message. For me, time as an editor was running out. If I was ever going to fulfill my dream of writing, my thing "to go to," the time was near.

Retiring was hard. One doesn't like to leave one's authors, friends really, in the lurch. But choosing my editor was easy. Like picking a doctor, look for a good, younger fellow, someone who talks old yet who'll be around for a while. My agent, Lila Karpf, a longtime friend and publishing associate, agreed, and this began my professional association with James O'Shea Wade, a former competitor for acquisitions. Jim had acquired and edited one of my favorite books, the Pulitzer Prize–winning novel *The Killer Angels*. Over the years we had enjoyed many a drink and conversation. He took a risk and signed me up. Contract in hand, my wife, Janetta, and I began updating research for this work in the National Archives, where John E. Taylor helped immeasurably, as he has done for three generations of other authors. Unexpectedly, Henry Clausen telephoned and asked that I be the writer for his book *Pearl Harbor: Final Judgement,* and Wade allowed me to interrupt my contract for that work. It proved fortunate, because Henry's experiences and advice persuaded me that I had to follow the trail we'd found and return to the beginning of America's war in 1941 to effectively tell the story for which I was contracted: the fall of Berlin in 1945 and why Eisenhower had allowed the Russians to capture the capital of Germany. Meanwhile, others helped in a variety of ways. David A. Hatch, director of the NSA's Center for Cryptologic History, and his associate, Tom Johnson, were most gracious with their time and advice. Also helpful was Brigadier General Harold W. Nelson, Chief of Military History, U.S. Army, and Ms. Hannah Zeidlick, Chief of the Historical Resources Branch. Ms. Zeidlick had helped me some thirty years earlier in my research for Cornelius Ryan's best-selling *The Last Battle,* which was funded by *The Reader's Digest.* Others who helped those years past in the army's OCMH were Magda Bauer, Detmar Fincke, Charles von Luttichau, Israel Wice, and Dr. Earl Ziemke. When the U.S. Army used to keep its records in Alexandria, Virginia, I was aided on a daily basis for nearly ten months by Wilbur J. Nigh, Chief of the Records Branch, and his associates, Lois Aldridge, Morton Apperson, Joseph Avery, Richard Bauer, Nora Hinshaw, Thomas Hohmann, Hildred Livingston, V. Caroline Moore, Frances Rubright, and Hazel Ward.

For those who spoke to me on the basis of "not for attribution," I can only say thank you. Those who volunteered to go on record are named and identified with heartfelt gratitude in the appropriate place in the narrative. Most important, however, was the encouragement and advice I received from Robert T. Crowley. Bob had been involved with military intelligence in the Far East at the end of World War II. Later, he became the first and only Special Assistant to the Deputy Director/ Operations for Special Operations of the CIA (SA/DD/O/SO) and I was fortunate enough to sign him up as an author. When I told him the way I saw the research leading me for this book, Bob let out a slow whistle. I asked: Is the project viable as I explain it? "Yes," he replied. "You're the first person to think of Magic in this fashion and I agree with you completely. But what a tremendous task." Then he said: "But if anyone can do it, it's you. I'll do what I can to help." Later, when it came time to track down individuals or impress upon people the significance of the work, Bob led the charge. His help has been truly invaluable.

The staff at Crown Publishers have always made me feel at home. Jim Wade kept my spirits up, especially when I was ill, offering encouragement and consistently sound editorial advice. If Jim wasn't on deck, Associate Editor Paul Boccardi proved an excellent backstop. When I had problems with my word processor, and I am of the wrong generation for these contraptions, Lois Berkowitz, who oversees the computer problems for Crown quickly solved various crises. Steven Boldt did a fine, thorough job of copyediting, making perceptive queries in the right places. Jim Walsh, June Bennett-Tantillo, and John Sharp all sped the massive manuscript through production. Managing editor Laurie Stark did her usual magical tricks of scheduling. My publicists, Penny Simon, Nancy Maloney, and Andrew K. Martin, the head of Crown's publicity, put the finishing touches on the package. As one who knows how much caring, hard work goes into making such a project successful, for your help and support I will always be deeply grateful.

MARCHING ORDERS

No one ever called Secretary of War Henry L. Stimson indecisive.

Now, with the debacle of Pearl Harbor only three weeks old and with the Japanese believing they rule the Pacific Ocean, Stimson decides that the greatest military disaster in America's history has been caused by the failure of the system of military intelligence. "The event had been foreshadowed by the Japanese diplomatic traffic of 1941," Stimson declares. He immediately sets out to rectify the problem. The action he takes dramatically changes the way the U.S. Army runs its intelligence operations and produces unexpectedly incredible results that affect the outcome of World War II.[1]

One must read between the lines of official documents and the various biographies of Stimson and talk with men such as Henry C. Clausen, who later performed a one-man investigation into the root causes of Pearl Harbor on Stimson's orders,[2] to comprehend that Stimson never blamed the fiasco of Pearl Harbor solely on the Navy, or solely on the Army. Stimson believes the American intelligence system of the time—and both he and Marshall share blame in this—is faulty from top to bottom. The *system* must be changed lest America lose the war.

Stimson has no control over the Navy. He cannot root out the incompetent, jealous turf-protectors in Naval Intelligence or Communications. But he can, and does, force a reorganization of the Army Intelligence system from top to bottom. This old system had been ap-

---

1. SRH-005 "USE of CX/MSS Ultra" by the United States War Department (1943–45), National Archives.
2. *Pearl Harbor: Final Judgement* by Henry C. Clausen and Bruce Lee (New York: Crown Publishers, 1992).

proved by no less a personage than Chief of Staff George C. Marshall, but Stimson forever changes the way the Army views the vital, super-secret product known as signals intelligence.

To digress a moment. Why does Stimson believe that he is partially responsible for the intelligence failure that causes Pearl Harbor? The answer lies back in time, when Stimson is secretary of state, in 1929, and Under Secretary Joseph Cotton tells him that a group of code breakers, known as the Black Chamber, is operating in New York City deciphering and reading the messages sent to foreign ambassadors in Washington. According to various official documents, during the 1922 Washington Disarmament Conference, which establishes the number of capital ships that every major navy is allowed to deploy at sea, and limits their tonnage and the caliber of their guns, the American delegates to the conference are presented virtually every morning, along with their morning newspaper, the instructions sent to the Japanese, British, Italian and French delegations with whom they are negotiating.

At the time, it matters not to Stimson that this so-called Black Chamber was originally created by the U.S. Army, and to hide its operations that the Army slipped the Black Chamber into the State Department's budget (only $40,000 per year), or that the information the Black Chamber produces guarantees the supremacy of U.S. Navy battleships in the Pacific for twenty-odd years. What matters to Wall Street lawyer Stimson is that the Black Chamber, by God, is damnably unethical.

Overnight Stimson shuts the operation down. It is not right to read the traffic of "our diplomatic guests," which is how, in 1931, Stimson explains his actions in his diary.[3]

As a result of Stimson's failure to understand what is going on in the real world, the State Department withdraws its funding of the Black Chamber, and America's chief code-breaker of the time, Herbert Yardley, is fired. Yardley then goes public and writes a book that explains how the Americans have hoodwinked the Japanese about the numbers and tonnage and the caliber of guns they can use in their capital ships. Duly warned, the Japanese change their codes.

Fortunately, the Army is prepared for such weak-kneed predilections of various civilian appointees, even the secretary of state. The Army has secretly kept a second arrow in its quiver. Under the title of

---

3. In later years, working in collaboration with McGeorge Bundy on his memoirs, Stimson puts it more succinctly (but just as stupidly) when he says: "Gentlemen do not read each other's mail." Stimson forgets an old saying formulated at Seawanhaka Corinthian Yacht Club, not far from Stimson's summer house on Long Island: "It is perfectly acceptable to do business with gentlemen, but one must be very cautious in doing so."

chief signal officer, the incredible cryptographer William F. Friedman continues reading the diplomatic mail of various countries, including Japan.[4]

Friedman had been commissioned in the Army in 1918 and was immediately sent to France to seek a solution to various German codes. He succeeded and is credited with saving many American lives. He returns to America in 1921 to become head of the Signal Corps Code and Cipher Section, revising the War Department Staff Code. At the time, he and one assistant comprise the entire War Department Cryptographic section. In 1930, the U.S. Army creates the Signals Intelligence Service (SIS), which should not be confused with the British Secret Intelligence Service (or British SIS), because it is always more confusing to the enemy to have a number of different intelligence operations—all with the same initials—working against them. In 1930, the military in America and Great Britain know who their potential enemies will be: Germany, Japan and Russia. Unfortunately, the same can not be said about the British and American politicians of the time; most of them—especially the American isolationists—can't get their fingers out of their ears in this regard.

By 1934, the current secretary of war, Harry H. Woodring, hears the thunder and sees the storm clouds gathering on the world's horizons. He begins expanding the American SIS. By the time Germany invades Poland in 1939, the SIS staff is 19 in number. By the time Japan attacks Pearl Harbor in 1941, the staff has grown to 331. By the end of the war, in 1945, the total will be more than 13,000.

Meanwhile, the American Navy has been equally involved in cryptology since nearly as far back as the first radio transmission from a Navy ship in 1899. The Navy also has a code and signals section in the Naval Communications Service (NCS). In 1924, a young lieutenant, thirty-one-year-old Laurence C. Safford, is ordered to head up a radio intelligence unit, and he begins building up a radio intercept network. By the late 1930s, the U.S. Navy's cryptological organization numbers seven hundred officers and enlisted personnel (more than double the Army's manpower), and it has listening posts (intercept stations) in Washington State, Maine, Maryland, Hawaii, the Philippines, plus smaller stations in California, Florida, Guam and Long Island.

One can sense the conflict building between the Army and the Navy signals intelligence experts.

---

4. Clausen and Lee, *Pearl Harbor.*

In the midtwenties Japan is using nine cipher systems to send its coded messages to its diplomats and military around the world. The most important of these is a machine-operated system called *Angooki Taipu A,* or Cipher Machine A. The code produced for this machine is for high-level diplomatic traffic. It is unreadable.

However, after a year of intense effort, Friedman and his Army SIS team breaks the Type A code in 1936, and Friedman labels the machine that makes the decipherment possible as Red. In 1938 the Japanese change their codes. Again they are unreadable. That is until September 25, 1940, when Friedman's team creates a miracle—a machine that produces the first totally clear, ungarbled decryption of the new code, which Friedman immediately labels Purple.

All of these code designations are lumped together by the American intelligence services into one catchall word: Magic. It is a fitting name, Magic, for as it turns out, the machine that Friedman and his team have created by virtue of their intellects proves to be as efficient as the original machine the Japanese built, if not superior to it.

Meanwhile, the British have been working on the codes used by the German military. They have succeeded in breaking the so-called Enigma codes (a name derived from a special code machine used by the German armed forces). Like the Americans, the British call their product of breaking the Enigma codes by a special term: Ultra. (From now on in the text that follows, when speaking of messages derived from the American breaking of various codes, I will use the term *Magic;* when I speak of the messages derived by the codes broken by the British, I will use *Ultra.*)

As Henry Clausen told this writer: "America had the brains and ingenuity before Pearl Harbor to break the Japanese diplomatic codes. What we lacked was the common sense about how to handle this information." At the time, the British agree.

President Franklin D. Roosevelt and Prime Minister Winston S. Churchill both believe that sooner or later their countries will have to fight the Axis. In July 1940, Churchill writes Roosevelt suggesting that secret information of a technical nature be exchanged between their nations. Roosevelt concurs. Sir Henry Tizard comes to Washington to talk matters over. He meets with Gen. George Strong, the Chief of the Army's Planning Staff, and Gen. Delos C. Emmons of the Army Air Corps. It is Emmons who reveals the American breakthrough with the Purple machine. (It is unclear whether Emmons let this slip on his own, or whether he was instructed by General Marshall to do so.) Anyway, the British become very excited, and London next proposes that the exchange of information be widened to include the full exchange of cryptographic systems.

Strong and Emmons report to Marshall recommending that America should give Great Britain the matrix that will allow them to create their own machine that can break the Japanese Purple code. Taking the stance that the Army is responsible for breaking Magic, Marshall authorizes the sharing of the machine's secret with the British—without clearing the matter with the U.S. Navy. When the news reaches Admiral Anderson, the Director of Naval Intelligence, and Adm. Leigh Noyes, the Director of Naval Communications, they are furious with Marshall for not consulting them. They believe Marshall is giving up too much without getting anything in return—they want the British machine that breaks the German Enigma code.

It is believed by many in the U.S. Navy that the British failed to reciprocate and give Marshall what he desired from the deal. But according to Louis Kruh, editor of *Cryptologia,* the opposite is the case. The British answered all the questions the Americans posed. By so doing the British saved the Americans several years of organizational effort in setting up their code-breaking operations. The British also gave the Americans a paper version of the German Enigma code machine, allowing the Americans to start their own deciphering of the German ciphers. The real problem appears that Marshall's unilateral decision to trust the British causes a breach between the Chief of Staff and the Navy when it comes to future code-related matters, which makes the Army-Navy debate about who failed to do what at Pearl Harbor ever so much more bitter.

To make matters worse, the British never acknowledge that the Americans provided them with the means to read the Purple codes until November 1993, after the publication of the Clausen/Lee book *Pearl Harbor: Final Judgement,* which carries British decrypts of Japanese diplomatic messages that Clausen obtained at Bletchley Park in 1945. These decrypts match those of the U.S. Navy and Army word for word. They prove beyond reasonable doubt that Winston Churchill, for his part, remained true to *his* word and did everything in *his* power to get these decrypts to Washington so as to avoid the debacle of Pearl Harbor.

But in releasing these British decrypts without comment in late 1993, the British Public Records Office (PRO) accidentally disclosed that America had indeed given the secret of Purple to Britain. For on one British decrypt dated August 23, 1941, Churchill writes a message to Menzies, his intelligence chief. Pens Churchill in his own hand: "In view of the fact that the Americans themselves gave us the key to the

Japanese messages it seems probable the President [has seen this] already." To which Menzies replies in his own hand: "The Americans have had this message. C. 24/8/41."[5]

On another Purple decrypt of December 4, 1941, Churchill writes: "Foreign Sect. US should see. I presume this is all right."[6]

It is also important to recognize that while Friedman solves the secret of breaking the Japanese diplomatic Purple code before Pearl Harbor, we never break all of the messages we intercept. The all-important Japanese naval codes were almost never broken by *anyone* before the war. This contradicts the theories espoused by a number of British reporters and the book *Betrayal at Pearl Harbor* by Capt. Eric Nave and James Rusbridger. This coterie of conspiracy theorists claim that the JN-25 codes were being broken by the British on a regular basis and were being given the Americans before Pearl Harbor, and that Prime Minister Churchill withheld information from President Roosevelt that would have averted the disaster.

Now it's harder to put a stop to a headline-making, money-machine conspiracy theory than it is to kill a rattlesnake with a short-handled hoe. But this writer has done so. First, by interviewing Duane Whitlock, who, from November 1940 through March 16, 1942, was a radioman first class doing decryption and preparing intelligence reports based on Japanese traffic analysis for the U.S. Navy at Cavite and Corregidor. Whitlock points out that the Japanese Navy changed its code in the JN-25 series several times in 1941. Once in early August. Again on December 4.

"I know from firsthand experience," Whitlock says, "that from the fall of 1941 through the attack on Pearl Harbor we did not read any JN-25 codes. The first message we read of JN-25 on Corregidor was on March thirteenth, 1942. This message was the one in which the Japanese used the designator 'AF' to identify Midway. Nobody, including the British, with whom we worked closely, was reading JN-25 on a current basis up to the start of the war." (Whitlock later won the

---

5. PRO #094723. From Japanese Ambassador, Berlin; to Foreign Minister, Tokyo. No. 1027. 15 August 1941. This decrypt was not published in the Clausen/Lee book *Final Judgement*.

6. PRO #098541 4 December 1941. From Japanese Ambassador, Berlin; to Foreign Minister, Tokyo. No. 1393. 29 November 1941. (Chef de Mission Cipher). This decrypt is published in the Clausen/Lee book along with forty other British decrypts, which prove the British had made the same intercepts as had the Americans and that London passed on all the messages to Washington for action. These decrypts include the most important ones of all: the vital information of December 3, 1941, that Tokyo ordered its embassies and consulates around the world to destroy their codes and *code machines*. See pages 353 to 393 of *Final Judgement*.

Bronze Star for his role in breaking the Japanese codes that led to victory at the Battle of Midway.)

This writer also interviewed Capt. Albert T. Pelletier, USN (Ret.), who, in 1941, was assigned as chief yeoman to OP-20-GZ in the old Navy Building on Constitution Avenue in Washington. "In 1941 we were reading only a tiny fraction of JN-25, at the very most ten percent of a given message," he says. "More troublesome was the fact that we received the intercepts via slow boat from the Far East, about two months after they were intercepted. They were horribly out of date by the time we worked on them. I was a code breaker. I specialized in place names, dates, ship names, arrival and departure dates. I tried to put meanings into code groups. But I wasn't a linguist. We didn't have enough linguists at the time. None were assigned to our office to work on JN-25."

Capt. Prescott Currier, USN (Ret.), is the third man to confirm to this writer that the Navy was not breaking JN-25 codes prior to Pearl Harbor. He was involved in breaking codes in Washington before the Japanese attack on Pearl Harbor. Later he served in the same capacity at Pearl Harbor. "We read the occasional small message in JN-25 before the Japanese attack on Pearl Harbor," he says. "But never did we read JN-25 on a general basis, because we never had the staff to do this. Later, during the war, when we were concentrating on JN-25 full blast, we were able to read only five or six percent of the total JN-25 intercepts."

This writer asked: Did the intercepted but undecrypted JN-25 messages prior to December 7, 1941, reveal the Japanese intentions to attack Pearl Harbor?

According to Currier, in 1946, after the congressional hearings into Pearl Harbor, the Navy assigned a group of cryptologists to study some twenty thousand previously unread JN-25 intercepts. Of this number, one thousand intercepts made prior to Pearl Harbor were carefully analyzed.

"In these particular intercepts," says Currier, "there are a couple of dozen messages that give enough solid evidence to show the Japanese are going to attack Pearl Harbor."[7]

It is not until 1946, then—five years after Pearl Harbor—that the U.S. Navy knows for sure that the JN-25 codes carried specific information that could have prevented Pearl Harbor.[8]

---

7. These decrypts can be located in the SRH-406 files in the National Archives.
8. The writer conducted the interviews with Whitlock, Pelletier and Currier on February 16 and 17, 1994. They confirm the findings of the Navy's Hewitt Investigation of 1945, conducted

Perhaps the greatest failure of intelligence prior to Pearl Harbor, and let us go back in real time for this, is that in 1941 there is no central authority that reads all the intercepts in a calm fashion, analyzes them and compares them to past intercepts, correlates dates and events, and then presents them to the reader in plain English. Chief of Staff Marshall believes in 1941 that his staff must read the raw decrypt as it comes in from the field. This might have been all right for the days when Indian scouts were reading smoke signals and talking face-to-face with a company commander. But in a time of high-speed radio transmissions of worldwide significance—numbering around one hundred per day—in 1941, Marshall's concept proves to be unreasonable and unworkable.

This is the type of mental baggage that Secretary Stimson carries as he ponders how to correct matters three weeks after Pearl Harbor. He is aware of his error in shutting down Yardley's Black Chamber years earlier. He has also been a recipient of all the Purple decrypts prior to Pearl Harbor, and he knows that he failed to divine their meaning. He has to feel a strong measure of responsibility for what happened at Hawaii. This is proven later in the war when Henry Clausen tells this writer that on several occasions Stimson acknowledged that he had been wrong about the Black Chamber, and now that war is raging, Stimson is doing his best to squeeze every drop of information possible from the German and Japanese intercepts.

I asked Clausen about the appointment by Stimson of Col. Alfred McCormack on January 19, 1942, "to investigate and recommend" new procedures for handling and disseminating information derived from breaking enemy codes. McCormack's official job description is "to study the problem and to determine what had to be done in order

---

concurrently with the Army's Clausen investigation, in that we were breaking only about 10 percent of the JN-25 codes prior to 1941. More importantly, these interviews destroy the claims made by Capt. Eric Nave and James Rusbridger that the British were reading JN-25 on a regular basis before Pearl Harbor. In late February 1994, the National Security Agency authorized the writer to make the following statement: "The NSA has never made a statement saying that in 1941 the U.S. Navy was reading the JN-25 codes on a regular basis. What was said was that prior to Pearl Harbor, in cooperation with the British, we could read only a small amount of the JN-25 intercepts."

On August 3, 1994, the *New York Times* reported that Dr. Anthony Best, a lecturer in international history at the London School of Economics, had recently discovered by chance in the PRO an internal history of British naval intelligence, written in 1945, stating that "although there were warning signals about Japan's intentions, Britain did not know in early December 1941 that a Japanese force was preparing to attack the American fleet in Hawaii." (Page A11.)

to make certain that all possible useful intelligence was derived from this source."[9]

Are the SRH files accurate in describing Stimson's actions in the weeks after Pearl Harbor? I ask Clausen.

"Absolutely. But what they won't tell you is that Alfred McCormack was a favorite of Stimson's," Clausen replied. "He came from the law firm of Cravath, Swain and Moore where his partners always complained that he read too many books on military history and not enough briefs. But within a couple of months he completely revamped the Army's intelligence system, and he had his own men, civilian lawyers from Wall Street, percolating throughout G-2 (Intelligence). McCormack was top-notch. He really should have been the general in charge of Military Intelligence, and Gen. Carter Clarke should have been his deputy. Clarke was a good intelligence officer. He knew who was doing what within the entire Army. And he could make things run the Army way, quietly and smoothly. But Clarke didn't have much imagination, which is the vital ingredient necessary for McCormack's type of work. When it came to figuring out the enemy's intentions, Clarke was more like the average intelligence officer, a plodding type. What you needed were people of intellect and vision. Alfred could read the slightest scrawl on the wall and make sense out it. He was perfect for deciphering the hidden meanings in the Magic messages."

As we will see, Alfred McCormack does a magnificent job for the Army during the war. He creates a superb format for interpreting enemy intelligence and rendering it understandable to the recipient—better than anything the Army has seen before. Here is a man whose brilliance—like that of men who created the machine that breaks the Purple codes—deserves the highest honors the nation can give. But because he is a civilian, because he doesn't fit the military mold, because he thinks for himself, in the long run, the military grinds him down. "Army bureaucracy got him in the end," says Clausen. "Poor McCormack never got the thanks he deserved."

✷ ✷ ✷

One of the least understood aspects of World War II is just how much damage our breaking of the Japanese diplomatic and military ciphers did to Hitler and the Nazi dream of world conquest.

---

9. War Department, SRH-005.

It is understood that the breaking of the German Enigma ciphers (Ultra) single-handedly sealed the defeat of Germany. Not so. Official secrecy in both America and England for the fifty years since the war has prevented the public from understanding how greatly the breaking of the Japanese diplomatic codes contributed to the downfall of Third Reich.

During World War II, Tokyo assigned, to the Axis and neutral nations around the world, Japanese diplomats and military attachés, all of whom were brilliant, dedicated men. They were required to keep Tokyo informed of day-to-day events in Europe (and elsewhere in the world). In their zeal to report, these men told Tokyo all they could find out about Hitler's intentions, the planning of Hitler's top subordinates, where the Germans planned to attack, where to defend, the almost daily status of Germany's economy, her military and strategic reserves. These include the German plans for defending against an Allied invasion in Europe, the campaigns forthcoming in Russia and on the Western Front, to say nothing of the Italian Front or Africa. They reveal German hopes for espionage and diplomatic intrigue in England, the Vatican, America and South America. Reading this mass of diplomatic reports—some fifteen thousand pages of which are declassified to date—gives one an entirely different concept of the war that Japan initiated in her attempt to conquer the world as compared to what has been published to date.

These brilliant, dedicated Japanese analysts tell Tokyo *everything*.

But what these diplomats do not realize is that by the end of the war, *everything* they tell Tokyo is being read in Washington and London in about twenty-four to forty-eight hours.

In Washington, D.C., only ten men are privileged to be on the list to read the Daily Magic Summaries.[10] For the U.S. Army they are Secretary of War Henry L. Stimson, Chief of Staff George C. Marshall, the assistant chief in charge of OPD (Operations and Plans Division), the assistant chief of staff in charge of G-2 (Intelligence). At the Navy's request, a copy goes to the secretary of the navy. At the State Department's request copies go to the secretary of state and to the assistant secretary of state in charge of the Department's signals intelligence. A copy also goes to Pres. Franklin D. Roosevelt, who, unfortunately, never seems to pay much attention to the material during the course of

---

10. The British will not reveal how many men read the same Summaries in London. War Department, SRH-005.

the war, and to his military adviser, Adm. William D. Leahy, and to Adm. Ernest B. King, Chief of Naval Operations (CNO).[11]

It is interesting to note that during the war, only one elected American official is ever aware of and reads the Magic Diplomatic Summaries.

Anyway, after reading the material, all the recipients are required to return their copies to Special Branch (Army) for immediate destruction, and a careful record is kept. (This differs from what happened prior to Pearl Harbor, when no record was kept as to who saw which Japanese decrypt and the time they read it, which caused great confusion later on about who knew what about Pearl Harbor before the event and who had acted on the information concerned.)

The official records do not state how valuable the Magic Diplomatic Summaries prove to our wartime leaders. But on the basis of having read all fifteen thousand pages that have been declassified to date, and by applying the test of how a rational person would react in such a situation, it is safe to say that the mass of information provided by this material proved so vital to Stimson and Marshall—to say nothing of Eisenhower, who has his own special European Magic Diplomatic Summaries—that it changed completely the way they fought the war.

For example, the breaking of the Japanese diplomatic ciphers helps dictate the way the war ends in Europe. They provide crucial information allowing the Americans to make a strategic decision that allows Berlin to be captured by the Russians, while giving Allied forces the chance to race across Germany and seal off western Europe from the expansionist policies of Moscow. They demonstrate on a daily basis the perfidious diplomatic game that is played throughout the war by Russia and Japan. They give a different picture of what the Japanese and Germans hoped might happen if Germany had seized Stalingrad and swung southward "to shake hands with Japan" across the Persian Gulf. They alert the Americans—so naive at the beginning of the war—of the true postwar desires of the colonial powers: Great Britain, France, Spain, Holland, Portugal. They give the complete Japanese view of how to deal with China, Russia and the Far East. The list is almost endless.

Ultimately, the Magic Diplomatic Summaries can be considered something akin to federal wire taps in a Mafia crime trial. The strident, racist, warmongering words "spoken" in these supposedly "superse-

---

11. Ibid.

cret and unbreakable" Japanese communiqués provide the damning evidence of unrepentant guilt that permits America's civilian and military leaders to pronounce judgment on the leaders of Japan and drop two atomic bombs. By failing to ensure the security of its priceless communications network, Japan brings upon itself the horror of being the first victim of nuclear war.

It has taken nearly thirty years for the writer to reach this conclusion, and the logic of it seems indisputable.

✖ ✖ ✖

During the last thirty years, this author was fortunate enough to be allowed to spend nearly thirteen months, from 1962 to 1963, in the U.S. Army's archives in Alexandria, Virginia, before an estimated fourteen acres of German and U.S. Army documents, stacked in racks nearly thirty feet high in places, were broken up and redistributed to a variety of research centers around the world. (I was a White House correspondent for the *Reader's Digest* at the time and I was detached to head the Washington end of the worldwide research project for Cornelius Ryan's best-selling *The Last Battle,* which the *Digest* was funding.[12] As a well-trained *Newsweek* researcher—later editor of the "Press" section—I kept carbon copies of my transcriptions of sensitive documents, photocopies of everything I was allowed to copy, plus my interviews and correspondence for "fact-checking" of the final manuscript.) Later on, when the Army moved these records around, so I have been told, many of these documents were "lost." The people charged with "weeding and clearing" the files did not know, nor could they know, that a single piece of paper at battalion or company level might be the only surviving document of a vital divisional or corps order. Given the fact that I had discovered that many divisional, corps, and even Army-group files had previously been sanitized for security

---

12. *The Last Battle* by Cornelius Ryan (New York: Simon and Schuster, 1966). The research in the archives became so complex that I was permitted to employ two valuable freelancers: Mrs. Julia Morgan of Washington, D.C., and Dr. Julius Wildstosser, deceased. The latter examined miles of microfilm and translated thousands of German documents. All told, the three of us reviewed more than an estimated 1.4 million pages of official American and German records. From these records I chose one thousand Americans for interviews, located and sent questionnaires to seven hundred, received answers from and extensively interviewed two hundred and thirty-two. One result of this project was that I was transferred to the magazine's book department in New York and later became the first editor in chief of Reader's Digest Press.

reasons, this unintended double "weeding" has caused grave difficulties for historians.

I was also fortunate thirty years ago to interview many of the best American combat commanders before they died. But even in these interviews I learned that I could not rely solely upon their memories. The files I had read proved this. Frequently I had to "refresh" memories by using the documents I had collected. On a number of occasions, files and memories matched. Those were happy moments.

I also learned that if one is to break the seal of secrecy placed upon Ultra and Magic over the years, one cannot rely on the published memoirs of generals, field marshals, prime ministers or presidents to tell the truth. Since these memoirs fail to delve into Magic or Ultra, they do not present a fair, detached analysis of World War II strategy.

It is my hope that this work can show, in depth, in terms of real-time analysis, what America's military leaders were reading about our enemies' plans and intentions throughout World War II, and how this information influenced America's thinking about the way to fight the war.

✖ ✖ ✖

A principal reason why so-called official memoirs about World War II are flawed is that the writers, no matter what the greatness of their stature as political or military leaders, were either not allowed to write about the fact that the Allies had broken the German and Japanese codes, or else they took it upon themselves to ignore the issue.

This is understandable. No admiral or general wants his victory over the enemy to be diminished by the news that he benefited from reading the enemy's mail and had a pretty good idea what his opponent was going to do before the fighting began. It's like cheating at bridge. "The general has not been born who, after winning a battle, would admit he won thanks to a well-functioning intelligence service," claims Wilhelm F. Flicke in his manuscript *War Secrets in the Ether.*[13]

Thus, one rarely reads German historians' accounts of how the Germans defeated the Russians at the battle of Tannenburg in World War I because the Germans have superior intelligence about Russian strategy. Nor does one find in the reports of Field Marshal Rommel that he is extremely successful in his early African campaigns because

13. SRH-002, National Archives, Washington, D.C.

his intelligence is breaking the coded messages being sent by the U.S. military attaché in Cairo to "AGWAR WASH" in the Pentagon. And, of course, only recently has it been revealed that the Germans possess first-class intelligence about Allied operations throughout World War II by virtue of the fact that German intercept stations carefully monitor the radio messages of the governments in exile that reside in London during World War II.

These German intercepts are especially valuable to Berlin because the cryptographic systems used by the Allied governments in exile are of poor quality, and the messages are extremely informative. As soon as a minister for a government in exile learns something from the British government, he passes it on to his brother embassies in exile around the world. It is claimed that almost everything the British, Americans and Russians try to keep secret in London, the exiles diligently tattle. The Balkan governments and Poland are the worst offenders. This is especially true of the Polish military attaché's traffic between London and Bern, Switzerland.

Meanwhile, the Turkish government also gives the Germans excellent information in their diplomatic messages between Ankara and Moscow. The Germans can read the Turkish messages but not the Russian. Even the U.S. is guilty. Our enciphered worldwide radio net, known as WVNA, has the orders it relays intercepted on a regular basis, which gives the enemy valuable information on Allied intentions in the Far, Middle and Near East, plus Africa.[14]

The leading American expert on the paucity of intelligence-related information in official memoirs about the breaking of Japanese and German codes, and the benefits derived therefrom, is William H. Friedman, the acknowledged dean of American cryptologists. Back in April 1963, Friedman contracts with the National Security Agency (NSA) to prepare six classified lectures. In one of them, Friedman points out with considerable asperity that "there has been very little leakage with regards to the Army's cryptanalytic success except such as can be traced back to those Pearl Harbor investigations. General Eisenhower's book, *Crusade in Europe,* has not one word to say on the subjects of signals intelligence, cryptanalysis, codes, ciphers, or signals security, etc., although he does make a few rather caustic remarks about the *failures* and *errors* of his own intelligence staff."[15]

In fairness to Eisenhower, it should be pointed out that *Crusade*

---

14. Ibid.
15. SRH-004 (2) "Friedman Lectures on Cryptology," National Archives.

in Europe was published in 1948. This is after the U.S. Congress had irresponsibly allowed the secret that we had broken the Japanese diplomatic Purple code (Magic) before Pearl Harbor to become public knowledge. But other than that, in agreement with the British, Congress and our military withheld an even bigger secret: that the Allies had also broken the German codes (Ultra). Nor is anyone allowed to explain the extent to which the Magic codes had been used against Japan and Germany after Pearl Harbor. In other words, Eisenhower was under wraps when he wrote his book. This sets the stage for Friedman's being upset.

Nor does the situation improve much in the next twenty years. The British allow Frederick W. Winterbotham to break the story of how the German Enigma codes were broken and how a system was devised to allow Allied commanders to use the material in his best-selling book *The Ultra Secret*[16] in 1974. And when David Eisenhower, the general's grandson, publishes his best-seller, *Eisenhower at War, 1943–1945* in 1986,[17] when these restrictions of secrecy have been lifted, the 977-page work contains only sixteen mentions of Ultra in the index and not a single mention of Magic.

In this fashion, the impact of Ultra and Magic on the European war has been kept to a minimal level.[18]

---

16. New York: Harper and Row, 1974.

17. New York: Random House, 1986; Vintage, 1987.

18. Prior to his lectures, other books and articles that Friedman cites as mentioning the Japanese codes were:

•*The Memoirs of Cordell Hull* (New York: Macmillan Co., 1948).

•*On Active Service in Peace and War* by Henry L. Stimson and McGeorge Bundy (New York: Harper & Brothers, 1947).

•*The Road to Pearl Harbor,* Herbert Feis (Princeton, N.J.: Princeton University Press, 1950).

•*Admiral Kimmel's Story,* Husband E. Kimmel (Chicago, Ill.: Henry Regnery Co., 1954).

•"Pearl Harbor in Retrospect," Sherman Miles, *The Atlantic Monthly,* July 1948.

•*Midway, the Battle That Doomed Japan: The Japanese Navy's Story,* Matsuo Fuchida and Matasake Okumiya (Annapolis: U.S. Naval Institute Publication, 1955).

•*History of U.S. Naval Operations in the Pacific,* Adm. Samuel Elliott Morrison (New York: Little, Brown, 1944). Morrison wrote in vol. 4, page 185, that "Midway was a victory of intelligence bravely and wisely applied."

•"Lessons of Pearl Harbor," Samuel Elliott Morrison, *Saturday Evening Post,* 28 October 1961. Morrison concluded: "It was the setup at Washington and at Pearl, not individual stupidity, which confused what was going on. No one person knew the intelligence picture; no one person was responsible for the defense of Pearl Harbor; too many other people assumed that others were taking precautions that they failed to take."

•*Admiral Halsey's Story* (New York: McGraw-Hill, 1947).

•*Lucky Forward: The History of Patton's Third Army,* Col. Robert S. Allen, gives the only specific reference to the help that SIS gave Patton. On the other hand, the author makes biting comments about how intelligence staffs failed to use the Ultra intelligence properly.

Even Ronald Lewin's magnificent work, *Ultra Goes to War,*[19] which causes the release of many SRH documents in the National Archives, in typical British intelligence style mixes German Ultra material with the Japanese Magic material in an indiscriminate manner, and he pays scant attention to the end of the war in Europe and Japan.

Can this be linked to why Eisenhower failed to give credit to Ultra and Magic for his victories in Europe? "Absolutely," Clausen told the writer. "It was the way Ike was brought up. His behavior was indigenous to many in the Army. Of course it was absolutely priceless for Ike to know what the enemy was going to do. But it would never do for him to say so, because from his way of thinking, someone would come along later and second-guess him and ask him why he hadn't taken another course of action. If you can't find the European Magic Diplomatic Summaries files that went across Eisenhower's desk every day, it's what the intelligence people want. They wouldn't care if they destroyed priceless historical information. It would be more important to shred the material and protect their backsides in the long run."

Clausen is quick to point out that MacArthur was the complete opposite of Eisenhower when it comes to evaluating the help he received from his intelligence people. "He gave them full credit for easy operations," Clausen says. "MacArthur would avoid difficult amphibious assaults and try to strike where the attack could be carried out with the minimum loss of life. He always credited his intelligence people for getting him this information."

According to Clausen, this is one of the reasons that the intelligence people in the Pentagon, specialists such as Friedman for example, have always been upset about the lack of recognition of their contribution to winning the war in Europe. "If Eisenhower had treated his intelligence people the same way MacArthur did, Ike would have enhanced his reputation greatly. Everyone in Washington knew that Ike was being handed priceless information on a daily basis. He never acknowledged it. . . . It's sad. But that's life."[20]

---

19. New York: McGraw-Hill Book Company, 1978. This book was commissioned by the author during his thirty-five-year career as a magazine and book editor.

20. The conversations between the author and Henry C. Clausen about how Eisenhower and MacArthur differed in the way they handled intelligence and acknowledged the help they received from their intelligence staffs were conducted August 17, 18, and 19, 1992. Clausen died December 4, 1992.

✖ ✖ ✖

It is extremely important to note that while one might criticize Eisenhower for failing to acknowledge the crucial role intelligence played in his victory in Europe,[21] one cannot criticize Eisenhower for mishandling the intelligence, or for failing to wage a continuing assault on a broad front across Europe that never once bogged down, or for allowing the Germans to create a military stalemate that would have resulted in a negotiated surrender. Eisenhower's strategy in this regard is brilliant.

Nor did the Allied use of Ultra/Magic intelligence in Europe detract from the achievements of the Allied soldiers. They gave everything they had. And more. One can only praise the average infantryman. He often attacked too closely behind his own artillery barrage, knowing that it is better to lose a few men to some of his own artillery rounds than lots of men because the Germans had been given enough time to man their machine guns after the artillery stopped firing. In such terms, Eisenhower asked much of his generals and soldiers; they always delivered.

But the true significance of Magic and Ultra for the battle of Europe was, according to cryptologist Friedman, that "our commanders were able during the course of the war to place small forces in action in the right places and at the right times. But when our forces didn't have this information—and it happened, too—our troops took a beating."[22]

This was acknowledged by General Chamberlin, who was MacArthur's operations officer (G-3) throughout the war. He claimed that not only had intelligence "saved us many thousands of lives, it shortened the war by two years."

It is difficult to put a dollars-and-cents evaluation on what Magic meant to the American war effort. Friedman figured that if you used the concept of shortening the war by two years in the Pacific theater, every single dollar spent for intelligence was worth one thousand dollars spent for other military activities and materials.

As Henry Clausen put it: "The minuscule amount of money we

---

21. The story is told that Eisenhower's biographer, Stephen Ambrose, spoke to the National Security Agency. In the Q&A after the speech, Ambrose is asked whether Ultra or Magic had influenced Ike in making any of his decisions. "Never!" Ambrose is reported to have replied. The Q&A ended on this note.
22. SRH-001 (1) "Friedman Lectures on Cryptology," National Archives.

put into breaking the Japanese codes before the war was the greatest investment America ever made.''

And when you add the evaluation of Prime Minister Churchill, who said that breaking the enemy codes was worth many, many more army divisions, to that of Gen. Thomas Handy, the Deputy Chief of Staff for the U.S. Army, who claimed that it shortened the war in Europe by at least a full year (if not more), the total, worldwide return on investment in breaking the Japanese and German ciphers can never be estimated.

2

Looking back, one is staggered that, in September 1943, America has been at war for less than two years while England has been involved for four. (I speak from the American point of view, as my British wife and friends would say; the British still cannot comprehend why we stayed out of the war so long, which really is the subject of another book.) It is also interesting to note that while Pearl Harbor is America's great intelligence failure in 1941, before that time the British also suffer horrific defeats before learning how to fully exploit their own intelligence breakthroughs.

For example, in early 1939, the British chiefs of staff and the Foreign Office are often at loggerheads over matters of intelligence. Will Hitler invade Poland? If so, what will this mean to England? No one can agree.

After Germany marches unexpectedly into Prague in March 1939, the question then becomes what will happen not only to Poland, but also Romania and Russia. At the time in England, no procedure or machinery ensures the bringing together of military and political intelligence so that it can be jointly evaluated and assessed. It was not until that July that the Foreign Office and the Joint Intelligence Committee begin to cooperate. As F. H. Hinsley writes in his magnificent work, "Whitehall still had to learn how to translate principle into practice."[1]

This means the German invasion of Denmark and Norway on April 9, 1940, comes as a complete surprise to the British. There had

---

1. *British Intelligence in the Second World War,* vol. 1 (London: Her Majesty's Stationery Office, 1979), 85.

The private papers of code expert Alistair Denniston at Churchill College, Cambridge, paint a rosier picture than does Hinsley. Denniston claims the British broke the American diplomatic codes in 1922. He also claims the British Navy had one officer reading the Japanese diplomatic and naval attachés' telegrams from the twenties onward.

been many indications of an invasion, including the visual sighting of the German heavy cruiser *Bluecher* and other naval units moving toward Norway by Capt. Henry Denham, CMG. His report is ignored by the British Navy. It appears that every report slips past the various intelligence groups and interdepartmental meetings at every level.[2]

Again, the Germans achieve total surprise when they attack Belgium and Holland. They sweep around the northern flank of the Maginot Line on May 10 by driving through the Ardennes, which had long been believed to be impassable by an invasion force. (This assumption dated back to World War I, and no one had dared challenge it.) France collapses and seeks an armistice on June 16 still awaiting the German assault on the Maginot Line.

Nor has it been foreseen that the Germans—like their counterparts, the Japanese in the Pacific—would use radio messages for high-echelon operational orders. Although the British purchase of Bletchley Park in 1938, and the setting up of the famous code center promises great results, Hinsley writes with typical British understatement: "The [intelligence] staff was quite inadequate either in numbers or in its understanding of military matters. . . . Moreover, delay and confusion were imposed by the internal security arrangements which were in force for safeguarding the confidentiality of the Enigma material."[3]

But no greater failure of British naval intelligence could be imagined until the Germans announce that their pocket battleships, the *Gneisnau* and the *Scharnhorst,* have sunk the British aircraft carrier HMS *Glorious* while it was returning to England after the evacuation of Norway. As it turns out, the *Glorious* sinks so quickly that she never radios she is under attack. British radio-monitoring stations pick up four German radio broadcasts from the area, one of which is an "immediate" signal, but nothing is done with the information. An investigation proves later that the duty officer in charge at the Admiralty had not been informed of the movements of the British Navy from Norway because communications between the operational and intelligence sides of the British Navy were haphazard.

Meanwhile, the British Expeditionary Force (BEF) is backed into the sea around Dunkirk. Although the BEF has built up its intelligence

---

2. Denham was the British naval attaché to Stockholm, 1940–47. His next warning to London, on May 20, 1941, that two large warships had been sighted moving from the Baltic through the Kattegat into the outer seas, is heeded immediately by the Admiralty. This leads to the sinking of the German battleship *Bismarck*. (*Times* of London, 29 July 1993, obituary.)
3. Hinsley, *British Intelligence,* 137–38.

unit to include one major general, eighty officers and one hundred and twenty enlisted men, and during the campaign the German material intercepted reached a flood of more than a thousand messages per day, the intelligence that saved the BEF comes not from breaking Enigma codes, but from old-fashioned methods.

On May 25, the British capture the car of the liaison officer of the Commander in Chief of the German Army with Army Group B (General von Bock). Documents in the car tell the British that the Belgian Army has retired, leaving a gap between Menin and Ypres, of World War I fame, and two German corps are going to exploit the undefended opening. Lord Gort, the BEF commander, immediately orders two of his divisions, which were going to strike elsewhere, into the breach. Fortunately, they hold the line and, according to the official historian of the campaign, save the BEF from annihilation.

As one restudies these events, one cannot help but wonder what would have happened in World War II if England and America had not been forced to reorganize their intelligence staffs in order to properly utilize Ultra and Magic.

For example, the Battle of Britain opens with the Germans sending seventy aircraft on July 10, 1940, to attack the docks in South Wales. But the Royal Air Force (RAF) has the ability to husband its outnumbered forces. First, it is using the new weapon radar to locate incoming bombers. Second, use of new radio-interception techniques allows the sloppy radio security of the Luftwaffe to be penetrated for an early deduction of the target to be hit, the number of bombers in the attack, and the flight patterns of the fighter escorts. When combined with the valor and sacrifice of the men and women of an understaffed RAF, this new technological method of fighting defeats a larger foe.

What is most significant in the British effort to make Ultra work effectively is that it takes nearly two years of warfare against the Germans—and the entrenched bureaucracy within Whitehall—to make everyone work together. This means creating the machinery to break the Enigma ciphers, perfecting the decryption techniques, building the staff needed to analyze the decrypts, and creating a secure technique of getting all the information derived from Bletchley Park to the battlefield. Having accomplished this miracle, the British win the battle for Britain even though the defending force is terribly, dangerously small in number.

No wonder then that, when the British learn about how the Americans have devised a machine capable of breaking the Japanese Purple ciphers, the British look down their noses at the way the Americans are handling the operation.

They see history repeating itself.

✗ ✗ ✗

Half a world away from bomb-torn London, at Pearl Harbor, the new Fleet Intelligence Officer, Capt. Edwin T. Layton, reports for duty aboard the battleship *Pennsylvania.*[4] Layton claims he was unaware then that he is the first full-time intelligence officer for the Pacific Fleet. He also is astonished to find, when he opens the battleship's safe that contains the relevant intelligence folders, that most of the eighteen folders are empty!

In only one folder is there any information about Japan. It was Monograph #49 from the Office of Naval Intelligence (ONI) and "provided only the broadest of generalities about the imperial [Japanese] navy." As Layton comments: "It was an appalling situation."

One of Layton's first acts is to volunteer his skills to the communications intelligence unit in Pearl Harbor. The unit had been formed in 1936, but in 1940 it is overworked and understaffed. The minor Japanese code systems are not being worked on so Layton starts breaking several hundred intercepts in the WE WE (pronounced WEH WEH) cipher.

Layton quickly works his way through the intercepts and discovers that the messages he is decrypting are addressed to the Japanese forces fortifying the Marshall Islands. He charts the addressees of messages— Saipan defense force, Ponape garrison force, the submarine base on Kwajalein, and the airfield on Palau—and rushes his analysis to Adm. James O. Richardson, the Commander in Chief of the Pacific Fleet.

As Layton recalls the meeting, Richardson declared, "Now we know that the Japs are secretly violating their mandate for administering those islands. We have been trying to find out what's going on out there for twenty years, and here you've done it in twenty days."[5]

According to Layton, the tragedy of his discovery is that the Navy at Pearl Harbor *never* tells Washington what he learned about the Jap-

---

4. *And I Was There: Pearl Harbor and Midway—Breaking the Secrets* by Rear Adm. Edwin T. Layton, USN (Ret.), with Capt. Roger Pineau, USNR (Ret.), and John Costello. (New York: William Morrow & Company, 1985), 38. This book was also commissioned by the author.
5. Ibid, 52–53.

anese fortifying the Marshall Islands. Nor did Naval Intelligence (ONI) in Washington ever try to break the WE WE intercepts. The command at Pearl Harbor, and Layton, simply *assumes* that Washington is preparing the proper intelligence evaluations of how Japan was girding itself for war—but that is not the case.[6]

The U.S. Congress, when it reports in 1946 on its investigation into the disaster at Pearl Harbor, castigates the American military for *assuming* too many things. High-ranking officers testified again and again that they "assumed" their fellow officers in the other service were doing their jobs properly. If anything really upset the U.S. Congress about the debacle of Pearl Harbor, it is this by-the-book, CYA (cover your ass) behavior of the prewar officer corps in both the Army and the Navy. The Congress specifically points out: "Operational and intelligence work requires centralization of authority and clear-cut allocation of responsibility."

When Congress completes its report on Pearl Harbor, the civilian leaders of the government tell the military that they can no longer *assume* that a message sent from Washington will be properly interpreted by the commander in the field. In the future, each intelligence update should be accompanied by the best evidence of the significance of the intelligence. Of course, this is congressional hindsight in 1946, a year after World War II ends, but while hindsight it may be, in this case the judgment is accurate.

Did the findings by Congress in 1946 lead to the overwhelming micromanagement of the Vietnam War nearly thirty years later?

Going back to the Pacific in 1940: If Layton is shocked by what he finds about the preparedness of the intelligence of the Pacific Fleet when he first reports for duty at Pearl Harbor, he shouldn't have been.

In Washington, terrible feuding had been going on in the Navy Department throughout the 1930s about who would benefit most from the cryptological breakthroughs achieved by ONI, accomplished either by stealing Japanese codebooks from various embassies or breaking the Japanese codes by sheer genius. Would Naval Intelligence control the benefits from the code breaking, or would Naval Communications prevail? As it turns out, the most senior department, the War Plans Division, joins the fray and becomes the dominant force in interpreting and disseminating what is learned from radio intelligence.

The Navy's principal cryptologist, Comdr. Joseph Rochefort, believes, nine years before Pearl Harbor is attacked, that "the Cryptog-

6. Ibid, 55.

raphy Section has been and is being used by the officers concerned to further their own ends.''[7]

One must also pause to think what it must have been like to be President Roosevelt back in 1940 and 1941. Sitting in the Oval Office, Roosevelt is reading Japanese decrypts on a regular basis. They clearly prove—in the same fashion that wiretaps can prove—the aggression Japan is planning in Southeast Asia and the Pacific. They also show the linkage between Berlin and Tokyo, revealing that if Japan goes to war against America, Hitler will also declare war on America.

Also reading the same material are the Secretary of State, Cordell Hull; the Secretary of the Navy, Frank Knox; the Secretary of War, Henry L. Stimson; the Chief of Naval Operations, Admiral Stark (plus his intelligence chief); and the Chief of Staff of the Army, Gen. George C. Marshall (and his chief of intelligence). Of these men, Roosevelt is the only elected official. And he is confronted by an isolationist Congress that steadfastly refuses to listen to any argument the President might make that America must prepare for war.

What frustrations Roosevelt must have felt!

To know what the enemy is doing, but to be unable to tell his opponents in Congress the truth and convince them of the rightness of his position. Nor can Roosevelt discuss the situation with his supporters and friends. Magic is so secret, so precious, that absolute silence is the order of the day. This element of real life—knowing, but not being able to do anything about it—is ignored in all the autobiographies, the biographies and the history books.

Thus, it is almost a miracle that a draft act is enacted, and then extended by one vote in Congress. In 1940–41, America is only the sixth strongest nation in the world. Our Army numbers less than 150,000 men. This means we have fewer men in uniform than do Greece and Belgium combined. (And look what the Germans do to those armies.) Roosevelt is also successful in getting through Congress a bill to build the B-17 bomber. But only by the slimmest of margins. And the same is true of a bill to rebuild the Navy.

Meanwhile, our military is so poorly equipped that the Army's artillery is limited to four rounds per gun per day when on maneuvers. Newly drafted recruits can't draw down enough clothing to be properly outfitted. Rifle ammunition is strictly rationed. Trucks pretend to be tanks; rolled cardboard tubing is used to simulate antitank cannons.

---

7. Private papers of Capt. J. J. Rochefort, "Memorandum for Capt. Ogan re Cryptographic Section," dated 21 December 1932. And SRH-305. The National Archives.

Army intelligence is in an equally bad way. It still suffers from the five-year budget, prepared in 1937, for its Signals Intelligence Service (SIS). The plan was to increase SIS personnel from thirteen to twenty-one people by 1941. The annual budget is $54,600. As of 1940, the SIS staff has not enjoyed any administrative promotions for a number of years (President Roosevelt had directed that no promotions were to be included in the 1937 budget).

Both the Army and the Navy suffer from a lack of staff in their special signals groups. But because of the limited successes these groups have made, now five other government agencies try to horn in on signals interception and have to be fought off. (Today, in 1995, the Congress is trying to get some thirteen or fourteen disparate intelligence agencies to coordinate their efforts and cooperate with each other without much success; hopefully, the reader will suffer déjà vu.)

The struggle for recognition between the Army and the Navy becomes so bad in 1941 that it is agreed the Army will handle the decryption of the Japanese Purple messages on the even-numbered days of the month and handle the distribution of the material around Washington on the odd-numbered months. The Navy agrees to handle the decryptions on the odd-numbered days of the month and distribute the material on the even-numbered months.[8]

The system works, until the Army suddenly decides that a foreign agent is working in an office in the White House that has access to the Magic documents. Overnight the Army refuses to send any more Magic to the White House. The President finds himself partially cut off from Magic, and he relies on the Navy to supply him with the information from that time on.

It was the American recipe for disaster at Pearl Harbor.

✻ ✻ ✻

As stated earlier, only five weeks after Pearl Harbor, Secretary of War Stimson determines for himself that within the Army, and probably within the Navy, there had been a terrible failure on the part of the G-2 (intelligence) staff to properly evaluate, coordinate and disseminate the information derived from the Purple decrypts.

So Stimson calls on his old friend, Alfred McCormack of Cravath,

---

8. This means that as of 0001 hours on December 7, 1941, it is the Navy's responsibility in Washington to decrypt, translate and disseminate the Japanese diplomatic intercepts.

Swain and Moore on Wall Street, to come to Washington and take over the task of making sense out of Magic. The first so-called Magic Summaries that McCormack produces are rough. But they are far better than reading raw original texts without the benefit of expert opinion. By mid-March 1942, McCormack's new operation is churning out a daily Summary for the Chief of Staff that contains complex information written clearly in grammatical English. For the first time, these Summaries present Marshall, Stimson, and others with a detailed daily briefing of world events as seen through the eyes of Tokyo and its representatives stationed around the world. Reading them carefully gives one a sense of viewing World War II through the eyes of the Foreign Minister of Japan. It is an eerie, awesome and frightening sensation.

Each intercept set out for Marshall's attention requires the action by a specialist in that particular area.

For example, from the beginning, there is heavy emphasis by the Japanese on the importance of South America's helping Japan defeat the imperialist forces of England and America. Tokyo wants to create trading links between Japan and its new Southeast Asian Sphere of Co-Prosperity and South America. This causes Washington to spend far more time on inter-American affairs than had been expected. The Japanese linkages with Chile, Brazil and Argentina were of paramount importance to Tokyo.

In early 1939, as a result of Magic, Marshall made his first official trip to Brazil, where he proved to be a formidable diplomat, returning home with the Brazilian Chief of Staff and a party of five for a tour of America, and the important agreement that American forces could use various South American airfields to airlift cargoes from Miami across the South Atlantic to feed campaigns in Italy, Africa, Russia, Burma and China. The busiest American air base in the world in the first half of 1944 will prove to be the twin strips of Parnamirim Field at Natal, where planes land every three minutes night and day.[9]

More importantly, however, the Magic Summaries show from the *outset* of the war that Japan is concerned about Soviet plans to expand its Communist influence in the world.

One of the first such reports is sent in early 1942 by the Japanese attaché in Sofia to the foreign office in Tokyo. Russia is reported to be focusing its attentions more and more on Iran, "overpowering [the] British politically and militarily," because the British were pulling out

---

9. "Natal Journal" by James Brooke, *New York Times,* 26 April 1944, A4.

their troops for service in India and Africa. The attaché says Russian subversive activity is increasing in Iran, that "the Turks were aware of what was going on, but were not going to publicize it."[10]

The next day, a roundup of information gathered by Japanese diplomats from their German and Italian sources shows that four Indian divisions are being pulled back to India. Iran's oil wells are being guarded by only a few British troops. The Soviets have already moved two divisions into Iran and plan to send in four more. The Soviets are "using methods employed in Poland and [the] Balkans to spread propaganda" and are sending their Indian-affairs expert by the name of Agabekofu to Kabul to stir up unrest.[11]

Meanwhile the Japanese embassy in Chile reports that the newly elected president Rios has agreed with Tokyo's point of view that there is no reason to break diplomatic relations because of the inadvertent sinking of the Chilean ship *Tolten,* allegedly by a German U-boat. Moreover, Brazil, which has drafted a warning to the Axis nations, had now come to realize that to sever relations would be "tantamount to belligerency."[12]

On the following day, March 24, 1942, the President-elect of Chile is quoted as saying that he hopes "to increase Chile's friendship with Japan, and would cooperate in furthering Chile-Japan trade." Meanwhile, Argentina is preparing to send an ambassador to Tokyo, and if America opposes the move, Buenos Aires is going to ask the British to intervene in their behalf. Furthermore, should Brazil become involved in the war against the Axis, Argentina "would impose no restraints on [the] Axis powers."

In the Middle East, the Japanese diplomats in Sofia report to Tokyo that Iran has handed over control of two of its northern districts to Russia, who is actively trying to persuade the Kurds to establish a republic of Kurdistan.

According to the Japanese minister, "Russia is planning to bring the Near East and India under her control. . . . To forestall this and speed the collapse of the British Empire, there is an *urgent need to bring India under Japanese control.* A German advance into the Near

---

10. Magic Summary SRS 549, 20 March 1942, 3. War Department Assistant Chief of Staff, G-2. Referred to hereafter by Magic Summary SRS number. The SRS number is the control number given by the National Security Agency. The analysts working for Col. Alfred McCormack use the term *MS* and the date for their referring to specific documents.
11. Magic Summary SRS 550, 21 March 1942.
12. Ibid.

East is needed to supplement [the] Japanese effort."[13] The British can't let this threat to their empire in India go unchallenged. As history shows, they don't. But even more important material is soon forthcoming from Magic.

On March 31, 1942, the Magic Summary reports that three days earlier, Ambassador Oshima, Tokyo's representative to Berlin, had a face-to-face meeting with Hitler. The German Foreign Minister, von Ribbentrop, is also present. Oshima reports to Tokyo that Hitler had first congratulated Japan for the "undreamed-of rapidity" of their capture of Singapore and for bringing the war to a decisive stage. Hitler then unrolls a detailed map and gives Oshima a briefing on various battlefields around the world.

In Russia the German Army is going to avoid casualties and reduce the city of Sevastopol with unusually heavy artillery fire.

Russian forces are advancing south of Karkov and south of Lake Ilemen. But since the Russians don't know how to use airpower to support their ground forces, Hitler is confident that the Germans could split their own forces and envelop the advancing Russians. So far the Germans have lost 237,000 men killed in action, with 780,000 wounded. Of the latter, two-thirds have been treated and returned to their units.

Hitler also declares that the island of Malta is to be bombed continuously. The Germans were using new bombs that weigh 2,800 pounds and will soon introduce a heavier bomb weighing 6,550 pounds. In Africa, Hitler says the Italians are going to refit the ports of Derna and Bengasi and concentrate shipping to these ports via small, fast ships. He is very troubled that much of his air force is in Africa, supporting Rommel, when Hitler wants planes on the Eastern Front in Russia. In Europe, Hitler is also expecting a British raid, or attack, on Cherbourg or Le Havre on the Channel coast. He has sent seven mechanized divisions to France to thwart the assault.

For the strategist, this kind of information is invaluable. It doesn't have that much relevance for Washington at the moment, because American forces were not yet committed in any of these areas. But for the Russians to know that Sevastopol would not be attacked by waves of infantry, while the German plan is to envelop the Russian advance in the south, is of vital importance to Moscow.

Malta is a different question. The British Navy will concentrate on lifting the siege and breaking the new Axis shipping lines to Africa.

---

13. SRS 553.

With the news that seven mechanized divisions had been moved to Cherbourg and Le Havre, the British are pleased to know that they had drawn these divisions away from the Russian front, or the African front, while they plan an assault to be carried out at Dieppe.

And if anyone wants to know why Hitler has apparently committed military suicide by attacking Russia, Oshima's report of his conversation with the Chancellor of Germany gives a true report of Hitler's state of mind when he tells Oshima: "I knew that if I left Russia alone and continued my fight against England, [Russia] would stab us in the back when we were least able to resist. As Fuehrer, I took it upon myself to do my duty and that's why I began the war with the Soviet Union.... I knew that God, and God alone, knew whether I would win or not, but ... I could not stand and see Germany ruined. If the German people do not have the ability to win, and if they are ruined by this struggle, it will be inevitable."

From the very outset, then, it is clear to Allied military planners that Hitler is not completely rational. "I have my own reasons for continuing the fight against the Soviet," Hitler tells Oshima, "and I must say that I am thoroughly satisfied [by it]."

To be able to know within seventy-two hours what Hitler is thinking and saying to his most trusted ally is worth more than any spy group in Berlin. The trick is to disseminate this knowledge to Russia, and our own forces, without compromising the source.

✖ ✖ ✖

It is difficult to comprehend the enormity and depth of the Magic material. Produced on single-spaced, 8½-by-11-inch paper, the first month of Magic Summaries, from March 20 through April 30, 1942, when photocopied, weighed in at one and a half pounds, or about the weight of a six-hundred-page novel. Unlike a good novel, however, the dry, factual tone of the Summaries is enough to put the average reader to sleep. But for the military strategist it opens up the possibility of immediately countering enemy initiatives around the world. This means creating the proper networks within the military itself, as well as the State Department, the clandestine intelligence services, plus our British allies, so that the maximum damage can be done—without the enemy's learning the reason for unexpected defeats.

As stated previously, in early 1942, it is still too soon in the war for the Americans to make maximum use of Magic. For the present it's enough to understand the actions the Japanese are taking that will be stopped later. For example:

✖ In Tibet, the Japanese government is making "a strenuous effort" to gain direct contact with "Anti-Zen lamas" in the hopes of influencing the government. Tokyo is also trying to establish further contact via Delhi, India.

✖ In Rome, Japanese ambassador Harada is advising Tokyo that the Pope is considering appointing a delegate to the government of Chiang Kai-shek in Chungking. Tokyo is seeking to block this appointment on the grounds that most Catholics in China are already under the domination of the Japanese puppet government in Nanking.

✖ In Manchuria, the Japanese-occupied country is being swept by rumors that Japan will go to war with Russia. Tokyo wants these rumors stopped.

✖ In Turkey, the Japanese are concerned about the massing of Bulgarian troops on the Turkish border. Apparently this is being done as part of the German strategy to pressure Turkey to remain neutral. Meanwhile, the chief of Turkish intelligence is quoted as saying that Turkey would prefer the Russians in the Persian Gulf to the Japanese. The source for this information is given as conversations between the German foreign minister and Bulgarian foreign minister, Popoff, who met to discuss recent Russian moves to surround Turkey from the southeast.

✖ In Thailand, the Japanese are having problems meeting their petroleum production schedule. The engineers at the refinery at Bangkok are being replaced.

✖ In France, according to Ambassador Oshima in Berlin, the French Vichy government is negotiating about naming Pierre Laval to the Vichy government. The French want five hundred thousand French prisoners returned from Germany if Laval is to be named.

✖ In the Mediterranean, the constant bombing of Malta has kept the British fleet at bay and allowed the Axis to increase the vital flow of supplies to its troops in Africa via the port of Tripoli. The Germans also believe their forces in Africa are now superior to the British forces, because British reinforcements from the Near East have not arrived. Meanwhile, the Axis is preparing for "a push towards Suez in the spring."

During this time, the siege of Malta intensifies. The Axis flies 9,599 sorties against the island in April 1942. The situation is so desperate that the American aircraft carrier *Wasp* is sent to the region and successfully flies in forty-six Spitfire fighter planes. Also, as predicted in the Magic Summaries, Field Marshal Rommel makes his move to capture Tobruk and drive toward Alexandria, Egypt.

- In India, the Japanese embassy reports that prominent Indian citizens are "scheming" to exploit the disagreement between Sir Stafford Cripps and President Roosevelt's personal envoy to the area. The British object to what they believe is American intervention in British affairs. The Japanese want to exploit the clash between America and England.
- In Brazil, recent government actions to break relations with Japan have greatly upset Tokyo.
- In Rome, the Japanese efforts to block the Vatican from sending an emissary to Chiang Kai-shek are being rebuffed. The Pope is telling the Japanese that Rome wants only to protect Catholics in the areas controlled by Chungking.
- In Vichy, France, the Summary notes that on January 31, 1942, Adm. Jean Darlan tells the Japanese that he believes the island of New Caledonia (off the east coast of Australia) should be occupied by Japanese troops. In carrying out this mission, Darlan says that Japan should still recognize French sovereignty, that all supporters of de Gaulle should be arrested and the Japanese should govern the island via a "loyal French subject [*sic*]." Now, on March 13, Tokyo tells its ambassador to Vichy that there is a plan in the works to seize New Caledonia, "but there is no reason for it to leak out to the French."

The Americans act on this news. On March 12, American troops seize New Caledonia, prior to landing on Guadalcanal. This protects the Australian cities of Rockhampton and Brisbane from Japanese bombers. Meanwhile, the Japanese have landed troops on Dutch New Guinea, threatening northern Australia, and they have bombed the city of Darwin. Now the Americans are in a position to flank the Japanese advance.[14]

- From China, a Japanese agent reports to Tokyo that Chiang Kai-shek had rejected a "peace feeler" from Japan. The report quotes Chiang as saying: "Our economy will hold up easily for three years. A separate peace with Tokyo would mean the defeat of England and America." This message would have been reassuring to Chief of Staff Marshall; to learn from a Japanese source that Chiang is steadfast in his support of England and America means that America will support Chiang against all his enemies, internal as well as external.
- From Germany, Ambassador Oshima is reporting to Tokyo that Germany's internal transportation is suffering because 10 percent of its railroad locomotives and its river barges are servicing the Eastern Front. In the coming year, the Germans plan to build 60,000 tons of new river barges, make all the railroads in Germany double-track line, build a new rail line linking Berlin and Ukraine, build 200 locomotives, 500 passenger cars and 1,000 freight cars. New electric plants are being built in specifically named areas, including one in Norway, which will service a new aluminum plant that has just been completed. The total German aluminum production is currently 250,000 tons per year, with another 50,000 tons coming from occupied France.[15]

The examples quoted above are mere highlights of page after page of technically dry information. Nevertheless it is imperative for Chief of Staff Marshall to know precisely what his enemies are thinking. As we will see, this becomes paramount as the Americans and British advance through Europe. The most significant decrypts will be the unvarnished views of Japanese ambassador Oshima in Berlin. At the moment,

14. Admiral Darlan is still a controversial figure in French history. Some people believe he worked both sides of the street, given the evidence produced by Magic. When France surrendered to Germany, he had promised to keep the French fleet from falling into German hands. At first he failed to keep his promise and the Germans came close to seizing the fleet. Only then did Darlan order the ships scuttled. He also helped the Allies when they landed in Africa later in 1942. He was assassinated in unusual circumstances, saving the Allies "of their embarrassment at working with him," according to Winston Churchill.
15. Magic Summaries SRS 559 through SRS 580, 20 March 1942 through 23 April 1942.

Oshima replies to a question from Tokyo as to whether or not Hitler might sign a separate peace treaty with Russia, and what this would mean vis-à-vis the "national policy of the Japanese empire."

According to Oshima, Hitler has told him that when Russian foreign minister Molotov visited Berlin in November 1941, only to have negotiations halted right afterward by the Russians, that "Hitler then knew that in all probability the theater of war would expand and he might have more to cope with than he could easily face."

In April 1941, Russia and Japan agreed to a five-year neutrality pact, which will be the subject of much discussion later in this book. Germany attacks Russia on June 22, 1941. By that November 23, German troops were only thirty-three miles northwest of Moscow. With the help of "General Winter" (i.e., bitter cold and heavy snow) the Russian lines hold. The Russians launch their first major counterattack of the war on December 5, while Hitler is preparing further attacks to the south. Japan attacks Pearl Harbor that December 7. Hitler declares war on America a few days later, as the Germans had promised the Japanese they would do, and which was revealed by the Magic intercepts.

As Oshima views the current situation in March 1942, the objectives of the German army are to seize the industries of European Russia, the raw materials of Ukraine and the oil fields of the Caucasus. To Oshima this means that "the vigor of Russia will dwindle greatly, the livelihood of her people will be threatened, and an internal revolution will spontaneously occur. Then the Stalin regime will crumple of its own weight. The threat of Communist Russia will be eliminated forever. That is how [Hitler] reasons." Thus, Oshima declares, "There is no possibility of such a separate peace."

But how does the current situation affect Japan?

According to Oshima, the primary objective of Japan's thrust southward is "the overthrow of England's hegemony and *the establishment of our supremacy in the south.*"

On July 27, 1940, Tokyo issued a "Proclamation of the Greater East Asia Co-Prosperity Sphere." Germany had already defeated, or was about to defeat, the colonialist nations of France, Belgium, Holland and England. Since Japan lacked vital natural resources, she reasoned that she could incorporate into the new Japanese empire—without conflict—the Dutch East Indies (Sumatra, Borneo, Java, Celebes, New Guinea) as well as Malaya, Burma, Thailand, French Indochina, and the American-ruled Philippine Islands. The risk Japan takes, of course, is that England might not surrender to Germany, and America might join the war. Now, with America in the war and England and her colonies still fighting hard, Oshima is trying as hard as he can to push Tokyo into carrying out "Japan's great mission: *the establishment of a new order in the Far East.*"

"Are we," asks Oshima, "going to dispose of the Soviet and set up a complete and thoroughgoing sphere of coprosperity; or, stop with the destruction of Chinese, British and American hegemonies, keeping our hands off the Soviet, and let the future bring about the solution?"

What Oshima is recommending to Tokyo is that since Japan has already seized Korea and Manchuria, plus vast portions of northeast China, the Japanese must avoid war with Russia. The most important thing for Tokyo to do is establish "a thoroughgoing and comprehensive sphere of influence in the Far East."

To ensure that his plan would be considered by the most powerful departments in Tokyo, Oshima ends his message by saying that his views reflect joint studies done with the military and naval attachés in Berlin. "Please pass this information on to the Army and Naval ministers, Chief of the General Staff and the Naval Chief of Staff," Oshima asks.[16]

This is the first of many such messages intercepted in the months that follow. Washington and London now know how the Japanese are planning the future course of *their* war. Without Japan threatening to attack Russia from Manchuria, Stalin can safely call up his reserve divisions in Siberia to fight the Germans, which he does.

✵ ✵ ✵

The accuracy and significance of the Magic Diplomatic Summaries is astounding.

As Col. Alfred McCormack explains it in 1943, "practically the only good information about the relations between Japan and Russia [came] from the intercept material." There is considerable debate within the U.S. Army in 1942 about whether or not Japan will attack Russia. But, McCormack says: "When almost everyone expected Japan to attack Russia, and when MIS [the Military Intelligence Service] went on record as predicting such an attack at an early date, [my independent staff in the Secretary's office] had concluded from intercept material

---

16. SRS 565, 8 April 1942, 1–2.

that Japan had no intention of attacking Russia, [and] wanted to keep out of war with Russia at all costs.''[17]

The brilliant analyses by McCormack's staff proves the reliability of the Magic intercepts time and time and time again. It becomes almost virtually impossible for Marshall or Eisenhower to ignore the world-wide, postwar strategic implications of what the Japanese are reporting to Tokyo, or what Tokyo tells its diplomats in the field.

Magic does not lie.

To fully comprehend what McCormack is saying in 1943, one has to go back—yet again—to the beginning: Pearl Harbor. As stated earlier, Alfred McCormack was brought to Washington by Secretary of War Stimson in January 1942 after Stimson had determined that Pearl Harbor was the result of an intelligence failure.

By April 1943, the sophisticated New York lawyer has investigated and determined what the problems were. McCormack is never called to testify before Congress, but his 55-page report, written in 1943 to Colonel Clarke, which is not declassified until 1981, is dynamite even by today's standards.

What McCormack discovers is that in 1940–41 the code breaking is being done ''almost exclusively'' by the military. Much of the work is done by the Army, which is responsible for military and military/analysis traffic, including ''the large residual field that is loosely called 'diplomatic.' '' According to McCormack this means that during the war, the Army is not dependent upon the State Department for its information. On the contrary, the Army controls *all* the sources of information and unilaterally determines the order of priority in which those sources are to be exploited.

In the six-month period prior to Pearl Harbor, McCormack determines that the Army and the Navy had produced some seven thousand decrypted and translated messages, or an average of about three hundred per week. But only 1,561 of these decrypts were considered important enough for referral to higher command for consideration. The responsibility for bringing the important messages to the attention of the Secretary of War and the top officers in the Army had been vested in the Chief of the Far Eastern Section, MIS. Meanwhile, as stated earlier, the Office of Naval Intelligence (ONI) served the President, the Secretary of the Navy and the top officers of the Navy.

Alfred McCormack talked with Henry Clausen about the problems

---

17. SRH-116, ''Origin, Function and Problems of the Special Branch, MIS,'' memorandum for Col. Carter W. Clarke from Col. Alfred McCormack, 15 April 1943, 13–14.

that existed in terms of handling Magic material. McCormack found that the messages not considered important were summarily burned. Those that were important were circulated to a tiny group of people in raw, unevaluated form. Declared McCormack in his memo to Carter Clarke: "No personnel were assigned to a continuous study of the material; hence very little could be done to put any of it together in connected form."

As McCormack writes, "the Chief of the Far Eastern Section, MIS, having as such a full-time job and limited personnel, could do no more with the messages than carry important facts in his head."

A deplorable state of affairs.

After Pearl Harbor, McCormack also writes: "It became apparent that the event had been clearly foreshadowed in the Japanese traffic of 1941. The Secretary of War, and no doubt others, then concluded that this traffic had not been given sufficiently close attention, and that some agency should be set up to deal with cryptanalytic intelligence in a more thoroughgoing fashion than previously had been thought necessary. The Secretary decided that the job ought to be undertaken by a lawyer having a special type of competence and training, such as may be acquired in the handling and presentation of large cases involving complicated facts."[18]

This is why Alfred McCormack has to become a special assistant to the Secretary of War on January 19, 1942. Army intelligence dislikes what Stimson is proposing. By keeping McCormack independent and attached to his office, Stimson can protect the program he initiates. His instructions to McCormack are to study the problem and determine what needs to be done to expand cryptanalytic operations to meet the requirements of war. According to McCormack's memo, Stimson wants

---

18. The Magic intercepts demonstrated clearly to the wartime leaders of America that Japan had been involved in "a war of aggression" from the very beginning. The question of whether or not Japan was an aggressor continues today (see the *New York Times* of February 17, 1993). However, in reading the more than fourteen thousand pages of Magic Summaries for oneself, it can be seen that Japan was not forced to go to war solely because of an American embargo on oil or other vital goods. The decrypts prove that the Japanese were consumed with the idea—in their own words—of carrying out "Japan's great mission: the establishment of a new order in the Far East." The Japanese did not send businessmen to accomplish this mission. They sent soldiers.

The findings of this book are, therefore, contradictory to the writings of Prof. Richard H. Minear and former Justice William O. Douglas. In the early 1970s, after the publication of Minear's work about the validity of the Tokyo war crimes trials, the Japanese began to publicly question world opinion that they had been aggressors. This predates the declassification the Magic Summaries starting in 1978. These Summaries show the lie by the Japanese for what it is.

"all possible useful intelligence [that could be] derived from cryptanalytic material." This meant there had to be close and continuous study that pieced together intelligence in a "connected form."

From the outset, McCormack is engaged in a deadly war with the Army bureaucracy. The first battle McCormack fights—and wins—against the hidebound Army is about who are the right people to do the job, especially analyzing the decrypts. The Army believes any reserve officer, or any civilian who has graduated from college, is qualified to handle cryptanalytic material.

McCormack believes differently. Only persons with "very special qualifications" are right for the job, he argues. The most careful selection of personnel is required, and only people of "first-rate ability" should do the work.

McCormack also disagrees with the old Army practice that is to "take what looked interesting and pass it on in paraphrased form, without any attempt either to check or evaluate the information or to supplement it by collateral intelligence."

The Secretary of War and the Chief of Staff, McCormack reasons, are *"entitled"* to have every item "carefully checked, evaluated and supplemented by all possible sources of intelligence . . . their time should not be wasted in reading odd and unchecked bits of information not related to attendant circumstances and given their proper value."

It also seems to McCormack that the daily reporting of decrypts is only one part of the job. "The real job was to dig into the material," he said, "[and] study it in the light of outside information, follow up leads that it gave, and bring out of it the intelligence that did not appear on the surface."

It appears unusual, given the way the military is set up today, that back in 1942 Secretary Stimson had to call in a civilian lawyer such as McCormack and make him responsible for shaking up Army intelligence. But the Army worked by the old system back in 1941: pass the bad information along with the good up the chain of command and let someone of higher authority make the mistake. McCormack showed the Army how a lawyer is supposed to serve his client, how a subordinate should serve his superior and how the Army should coordinate its activities with other branches of the government, including the hated Navy.

For example, when the time comes for the State Department to apply pressure on Chile, and later on Argentina, forcing a cutback in coded communications from Axis diplomats operating within those countries, the Army tells the State Department exactly what kind of information the enemy is receiving from these South American sources. The Army also tells the State Department exactly how much pressure can be safely brought to bear on Argentina and Chile as justified by the facts. Lastly, if the two nations don't want to cooperate, the Army provides the State Department with "an ace in the hole" that would guarantee success if the State Department had to go that far.

As a result of McCormack's efforts, Colonel Clarke's MIS section for cryptanalytic activities is merged with McCormack's civilian staff (part of Secretary Stimson's office) to form a new Special Branch with Colonel Clarke as the chief. McCormack then makes a fatal tactical decision: he accepts the rank of colonel in the Army, which will never forgive how incompetent he proved it to be. Henry Clausen told the author that McCormack had far more authority as a civilian member of Stimson's staff. He is eclipsed when Clarke is promoted to be a general officer and McCormack is left behind. For the moment, however, Clarke is in charge of operations such as expansion of facilities; McCormack concentrates on the problems of developing technically proficient staff and getting intelligence out of the intercepts.

The most difficult part of the job, according to McCormack, is that "the most astute person, even if an expert on the Far East and possessed of a photographic memory, would derive very few connected impressions—and very little usable information—from merely reading the messages from day to day. They must be pieced together by the most painstaking and laborious process, involving collateral investigation, often of minute points."

By 1943, according to McCormack, the Army has so much information about Japanese shipping to and from Indochina and Thailand that it possesses a good picture of the ships and goods and problems that Japan is having in transporting raw material from the region and sending back the required imports. McCormack's staff has accomplished this miracle by checking and rechecking decrypts against known Japanese merchant vessels—"high class detective methods"—so the picture is clear and up-to-date. The result is that McCormack's staff establishes that the Japanese have 450,000 tons of shipping in the South Pacific.

Meanwhile, the all-powerful Joint Intelligence Committee, with the approval of ONI, is claiming that only 300,000 tons of Japanese shipping is in the area, an incredible difference.

McCormack's people bring the discrepancy to the attention of ONI. They give ONI "certain other findings on Japanese merchant shipping." Although the ONI people are polite and cooperative, they "stopped short of giving us their own secret information," says Mc-Cormack. It is only after McCormack brings the ONI to his office and shows the Navy what the Army is doing, how it is doing it and how far the Army has progressed that the Navy changes its estimates to JIC to agree with those of McCormack's staff. From then on the Navy furnishes the Army with daily reports of merchant shipping in the Far East that the Navy derives from sources other than Magic.

McCormack hopes to create "the whole picture of Japanese shipping and water-born trade." This is done in due course; American submarines and aviators succeed in sinking Japanese merchant ships beyond the wildest expectations of the Pentagon.

McCormack predicts that within a year, by 1944, his staff will have "pretty well reconstructed the economic and political aspects of the [Far Eastern picture] and be able to make increasingly accurate diagnoses of Japanese capabilities, difficulties and plans."

Meanwhile, where the Berlin diplomatic radio net could only be monitored one or two hours a day prior to 1943, a new radio intercept station is producing eight to ten hours of intercepts a day. By March 1943, McCormack's people are receiving more than twenty-two thousand intercepted messages per month, and this is but a fraction of the material available.

The potential for the future is enormous.

There are other problems. The MIS staff is too small for the amount of work that needs to be done. There were only 105 civilians processing and translating Magic traffic on December 7, 1941; as of February 1, 1943, there are 1,754 working at a signals center called Arlington Hall. (By the war's end, there will be 13,000 men and women working on a wide variety of signal intelligence, including German police signals, direction finding, map making, etc.)

The question of secrecy is paramount.

"Permanent secrecy of this operation is what we must strive for," McCormack declares, adding that the operation should be run only by the military because only the military can protect a secret. He says: "That may be too much to hope for in a democracy, but if it is possible to attain or approach it we should try to do so."[19]

Only a small fraction of the world's radio traffic can be monitored, McCormack points out. In 1943, the art of cryptography had outstripped cryptanalysis, to a point where despite the fact that modern machinery is capable of miraculous performances, "high level codes and ciphers

---

19. This is how the National Security Agency (NSA) operates today.

are no longer broken by cryptanalytic methods alone. . . . Today it is collateral intelligence which solves high-grade cryptographic systems.''

At the time, the British have a larger comparable operation than the Americans. And McCormack foresees ''problems with the British . . . as the end of the war draws near and while the terms of peace are being worked out. The divergent interests of the Allies will then come to the front . . . [and] assume major proportions in the Far East, where the approach of the British to the peace problem is likely to be very different from ours.'' We should prepare for this, McCormack says, ''and for that purpose there is no source so good as the cryptanalytic source.''[20]

✖ ✖ ✖

America has only been in the war for a year and five months, yet here is McCormack looking forward to victory and possible conflict with England concerning the different interests between the two nations when peace is achieved. How could McCormack be so sure, so early in America's war, that victory would be ours?

From his particular vantage point, McCormack is witness to what few other men are privileged to see.

In June 1942, for example, only seven months after Pearl Harbor, the American Navy repays the Japanese for Pearl Harbor. This time our naval signals specialists at Pearl Harbor predict that the Japanese will attack Midway. Adm. Chester Nimitz, who has succeeded Admiral Kimmel, arranges an ambush. In a battle that was later called the ''miracle of Midway,'' a smaller American naval force sinks four Japanese aircraft carriers, one heavy cruiser, destroys 322 planes and kills 5,000 officers and sailors. (The American losses are the carrier *Yorktown,* a destroyer, 150 aircraft and 300 men.) The battle forces the Japanese to go on the defensive for the remainder of the war.

McCormack also sees how, in August 1942, Field Marshal Bernard Montgomery takes command of the British Eighth Army in Egypt. This is after the Germans shoot down the plane carrying Lt. Gen. ''Strafer'' Gott, the British commanding general. When Montgomery suddenly appears on scene, replacing Gott, the British already know from Ultra decrypts the line of attack Rommel will make on a ridge of hills called Alam Halfa. The British also have a good idea of the date of the attack.

By now, Bletchley Park is handling the Mediterranean Ultra with

20. SRH-116, 1–55.

dispatch. So Montgomery is also aware of the status of Rommel's reserves, his lack of fuel and ammunition, the morale of his troops and his basic order of battle. Thus, Montgomery wins what historians call a "model defensive battle, by accepting the intelligence he was given."[21]

A few months later, Montgomery wins the battle of Alamein. This changes the course of the war in Africa. Montgomery has understood the significance of Ultra material from the very moment he assumed command. He uses it to win the first battles he fights, and he believes in it ever afterward.

During this time, Montgomery knows that almost every supply ship sent to bolster Rommel is being sunk, and that the Germans are blaming their Italian allies for leaking the dates and routes the ships are leaving and taking. Montgomery also knows Rommel is in ill health, that Hitler is concentrating his attention on Russia and is loathe to send reinforcements to Africa. (The British had also managed to capture Rommel's radio-intercept unit in July, which taught the British how the Germans had successfully infiltrated the British radio nets and forced the British to improve their own radio security.)

Nevertheless, the issue is in doubt as Montgomery attacks in the second battle of El Alamein in late October. British infantry strength is waning because the Germans still fight doggedly, counterattacking whenever possible. But even though he knows his own losses to be horrendous, by November 2, Montgomery knows from Ultra decrypts that Rommel is in truly desperate shape. Montgomery also knew, via Ultra decrypts, that Rommel is begging Hitler's permission to retreat. Hitler refuses, saying, "You can show your troops no other road than to victory or to death." Rommel again requests permission to retreat. Not until November 4 do Hitler and Mussolini agree. This begins the downfall of Germany in Africa.

Above all, Ultra has given Montgomery the backbone necessary to commit his forces in the face of murderous German fire. Montgomery understands from Ultra how great will be his victory if only he can prevail over his foe, about whom he knows the exact losses and capabilities.

If criticism is to be laid against Montgomery in the future, it will be that he relies too heavily upon Ultra-type information before committing his forces to action.[22]

---

21. The *Times* of London, reporting on the recollections of Montgomery's intelligence officer, Bill Williams.
22. This interpretation of Montgomery's exploits is based upon Ronald Lewin's magnificent

McCormack is also witness to, in the first weeks of November 1942, American forces landing in Africa under the leadership of Gen. Dwight D. Eisenhower. On the Atlantic coastline, U.S. forces under the command of Major General Patton land at Safi, Fedala (to swing south against Casablanca) and Port-Lyautey. Another task force hit the beaches of Oran, yet another at Algiers, sealing off the Mediterranean coast.

Now it is Eisenhower's chance to see the value of Ultra in battle.

Eisenhower knows from the outset that Rommel is begging for help from Hitler "or his force would be annihilated." British deception teams had worked hard, and successfully, with an eye cocked to the Ultra decrypts, to insure that Hitler believed that the Americans would land in other places than where they did in Africa. (The Japanese Magic messages kept mentioning Dakar as a possibility.)

However, once the Allied intentions are made plain, the Germans counter with ruthless efficiency. It is Ultra that now tells the Allies that the Germans plan to seize control of Tunisia, occupy the area of Vichy France and grab the French fleet at Toulon. (The latter move is countered by Admiral Darlan, who having failed to turn the fleet over to the British as he had promised, finally orders it scuttled in harbor, which is done.)

Next, it is a failure to exploit Ultra properly that leads to a bloody American defeat at the Kasserine Pass. According to the unpublished diaries of Eisenhower's aide Capt. Harry C. Butcher, "the explanation of the defeat, as seen by Ike, lies in a misinterpretation of radio messages we regularly intercept from the enemy. The source is known as 'Ultra' . . ."[23] As a result, the British intelligence officer assigned to Eisenhower to provide Ultra information under carefully controlled

---

work, *Ultra Goes to War,* published by McGraw-Hill Book Co. in 1978. This work was also commissioned by the author while he was an editor. In later years the author showed Lewin some of the research for this current work. Lewin said he was unaware of many of the documents he was being shown, but he believed they "were pure dynamite." Speaking about Magic at Bletchley Park in *Ultra Goes to War,* Lewin wrote: "And then there was the Japanese section. . . . The exact functions and achievements of this section have not yet been revealed." (page 134)

Another high-ranking intelligence officer, not wishing to upset his superiors, wrote the author: "I recall that Monty, somewhere in his autobiography, confessed to the press in North Africa that his modest habits required him to retire to his caravan, after a light supper, where he recites his prayers for Divine Guidance before retiring for the day. The fact is that his Divine Guidance came entirely from his Ultra briefer who flew out from Cairo each evening and crouched silently in the dusk near the unlit trailer until the pious general dismissed the press."

23. The original text of the Butcher diary can be found in the Dwight D. Eisenhower Library, Abilene, Kansas.

conditions is replaced by an old English friend, Kenneth Strong. He will remain as Eisenhower's chief intelligence officer until the end of the war. (American "Ultra" briefers are not assigned to American units until the invasion of Europe.)

The lesson Eisenhower and his unblooded American generals learn from the Kasserine Pass debacle is that when it comes to fighting, the most valuable way to use Ultra is to supplement it by local intelligence gathered the regular way: i.e., patrols, POW interrogations, local radio intercepts, aerial photos.

As we will see later on, Eisenhower learns this lesson well.

3

By 1942, the breaking of Axis military codes is providing the Allies with crucial information that allows them to win vital battles by hitting the enemy when an attack is unexpected. This happens during the crucial battle of Stalingrad.

Almost every map of this battle shows at the bottom left-hand side the Black Sea and the Crimea. The Caspian Sea is on the right-hand border. In the center of the map are arrows showing the Germans moving from west to east, from Kharkov toward Stalingrad. At the bottom of the map—and this is crucial—lie the Caucasus Mountains, and there is no indication of the geography to the south. We will see later why this overlooked area is so vital to our story.

For there are other arrows showing a German attack to the south, toward the so-called South Front and the Transcaucasus Front, which is the role assigned to the First Panzer Army under the leadership of General von Kleist. These arrows receive little attention on the map, which focuses on Stalingrad. This is an error. For if von Kleist succeeds in his drive through the Caucasus Mountains, he will arrive at the junction of the borders of Turkey, Iraq and Iran. This will create the vital linkage that Japan seeks with Germany across the Persian Gulf. And should this linkup be achieved, the ramifications for the Allies will be catastrophic.

As the German drive toward Stalingrad commences, the Magic decrypts show that Hitler wants his troops to continue attacking southward, across the Suez Canal and into Egypt—via the back door, so to speak. If this happens, Turkey most likely will have to forgo its neutrality and join forces with the Germans to save itself. A major Allied supply route for Russia, from Basra on the Persian Gulf via Tehran and then northward to Russia along the east coast of the Caspian Sea, will

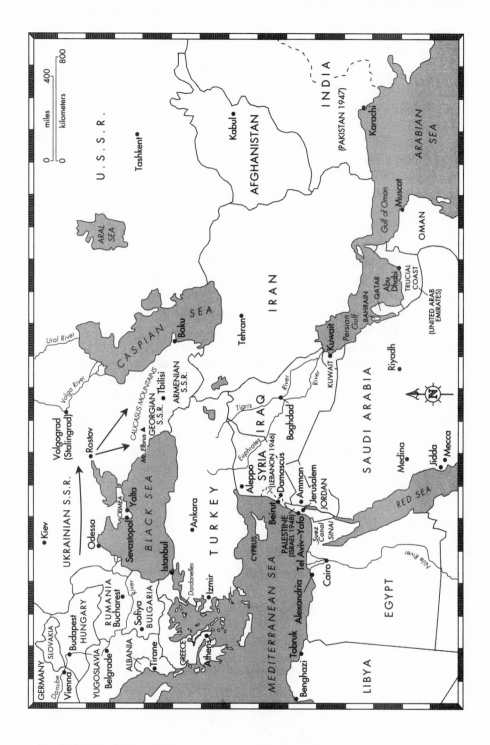

The battle for Stalingrad changes German plans to drive through the Caucasus to achieve the linkage Japan seeks with Germany across the Persian Gulf.

have been cut. The oil fields of the Middle East will be threatened by the Axis. Afghanistan and India will be isolated. Japan's goals of controlling the Indian Ocean and establishing bases in India will be easier to achieve.

Thus the battle for Stalingrad, which Churchill deems the most significant struggle of the war, is now seen as being far more important in terms of crushing the hopes and aspirations of the Axis than is generally realized. Why else would Churchill declare that ''the hinge of fate has turned'' when the Russians emerge victorious unless he had access to information that allows him to view the strategy of the battle from an almost godlike height?

It is the reading of both the Japanese and German decrypts that allows Churchill to see more clearly than most just how narrow the margin of victory had been and just how close disaster had come.

In no way does this work cast disparagement upon the brave defenders of Stalingrad, or upon those who stop the German advance through the Caucasus. Their sacrifices are truly unbelievable in terms of deprivation and loss of life. The Russian men and women who stand fast against the Nazi onslaught deserve every medal, monument and prayer that has been given them. One only hopes that in pages that follow the reader can see why these Russian men and women are asked to sacrifice everything for Stalingrad.[1]

It is at this moment in history that Germany and Japan are stopped from dividing the world and splitting the spoils of their conquest.

✳ ✳ ✳

The narrative begins on April 5, 1942, long before the British victory at Alam Halfa, when Hitler orders the German summer offensive in Russia.

On May 12, the Russians counterattack around Kharkov.

---

1. Current estimates of Soviet war dead are 25 million. The Soviet Union endured twenty times the combined losses of the British and Americans, while inflicting 75 percent of all German casualties. Historian Norman Davies points out that it can be argued that ''the Soviet Army had already broken the back of the *Wermacht* at the battles of Stalingrad and Kursk and in the offensives of 1943–1944, before the Western allies even landed [in Normandy].'' A fair statement. He also points out that, according to the magnificent research of historian Robert Conquest, it is estimated that Stalin also killed 1 million of his own people per year, and overall, his victims outnumbered those of the Nazis. The total population of the USA in 1945 was only 100 million. *The New York Review,* 9 June 1994, 20.

On May 29, the Germans crush the Russians at Kharkov, capturing 214,000 Soviet troops, plus destroying 1,200 tanks and 2,000 pieces of artillery. (In Moscow, meanwhile, Stalin still believes the main German attack will come against the Russian capital; however, this does not stop Stalin from shipping soldiers in from Siberia to fight on the western front.) On June 2, German troops under General von Manstein attack Sevastopol in the Crimea, which falls on July 3, with the loss of another 93,000 prisoners.

At this point Hitler makes his first of a series of horrible mistakes. He is so pleased by von Manstein's attack on Sevastopol that he promotes the General and sends him and his troops north to complete the siege of Leningrad. This changes the original plan for attacking the Caucasus, because von Manstein was to have crossed the narrow Kerch Strait and driven southward down the east coast of the Black Sea, protecting the western flank and avoiding the mountains farther inland.

Hitler is overconfident. He believes the war in North Africa is going well for Rommel, and because of the success of the "Desert Fox," Hitler thinks he can easily invade the Caucasus and then swing west through Iraq, attacking Egypt over the Suez Canal. But, by sending von Manstein to Leningrad, Hitler severely weakens his forces for the drive south.

Next, during the midweeks of July, Hitler issues a set of conflicting orders to the two German Army Groups that are attacking the Don River Basin and Stalingrad. Army Group A, which is under command of Field Marshal List, is told to swing southward and take over the role of seizing the coastline of the Black Sea, plus other major cities in the Caucasus, including marching on the city of Baku in the south. Meanwhile, Army Group B, for which commanders are about to be changed, is told to advance eastward on Stalingrad, seize the city and then move southward down the Volga River to take the city of Astrakhan on the Caspian Sea.

Instead of advancing on a broad front, Hitler now splits his two Army Groups so they are advancing in different directions (east and due south), leaving a large gap between them.

By August 19, Army Group B is stalled, fighting inside the city of Stalingrad. Meanwhile, Army Group A is capturing Mount Elbrus, the highest mountain in the Caucasus. This will be as far south along the Black Sea that the weakened German forces can go. Both operations are doomed because of Hitler's next decision. Seemingly on whim, he switches objectives. He becomes obsessed with the capture of Stalingrad; he forgets that he has sent his two Army Groups off on independent attacks that do not support one another. Apparently he is no longer concerned about the Caucasus, or the value of the oil fields that lie almost within Germany's reach.

By mid-September the two German attacks lose steam; Stalin now decides the time has come to counterattack. Although he still believes that a primary German thrust will be made against Moscow, he sees that the German Sixth Army, under General Paulus, and the Fourth Panzer Army, under General Hoth, are vulnerable on their flanks to both the north and the south. Why? Because these areas are not protected by German troops, but by weaker Italian and Hungarian forces.

On November 19, the Russians attack both the northern and southern flanks in a massive plan of double encirclement aimed at surrounding the German forces inside Stalingrad. Within four days, the Russians achieve their goal, linking their attacking forces on November 23, on the Don River at a city called Kalach. The entire German Sixth Army, and a portion of the Fourth Panzer Army, some twenty-two divisions totaling 330,000 men, are trapped.

Hitler then seals the fate of his men in Stalingrad when he accepts Field Marshal Goering's assessment that his Luftwaffe can supply the German forces in Stalingrad by a massive airlift. Hitler orders the Sixth Army to hold its position.

Meanwhile, British code breakers who are reading the Luftwaffe's Enigma ciphers can determine that the Germans have lost so many transport planes in trying to support Rommel in North Africa that there are not enough left to supply the Germans trapped at Stalingrad. (Almost every supply ship sent Rommel in recent months is sunk because the code breakers in Bletchley Park's Mediterranean section knew when they were sailing and their destination; in turn, this forces the Germans to send unescorted transport planes with vital supplies to Tunisia.)

The information about the lack of German transport planes electrifies London.

"Is any of this being sent to Joe [Stalin]?" Churchill asked his intelligence chief, Sir Stuart Menzies. The answer is affirmative. (The information is sent, as always, in sanitized form so that the sources and methods of obtaining this vital intelligence are not revealed or endangered.) This means that Churchill can be confident that the Germans trapped at Stalingrad are facing annihilation. Thus, even before it happens, Churchill knows his "hinge of fate" is about to turn.

✖ ✖ ✖

Let us now superimpose upon the battles of 1942 in North Africa, and at Stalingrad, the Japanese view of the war as deduced from Magic decrypts, the highlights of which have passed before the eyes of men such as McCormack, Marshall, Roosevelt and Churchill.

On April 29, 1942, shortly after Hitler orders the German summer offensive in Russia, the Japanese reports from Europe inadvertently blow the cover of Axis spies operating in America, England, Dakar, Australia and Spain. Meanwhile Baron Oshima reports from Berlin that he has had a conversation with Foreign Minister von Ribbentrop. According to Oshima: "Hitler and Mussolini are both confident what Japan, Germany and Italy can do. They are sure we can win the victory without any compromise and they determine to fight the war through to its conclusion. . . . Hitler explained the other day his plans for the Russian drive which is gradually getting under way. . . . [Saying] before winter comes, we will have given the Reds a fatal blow, severed lifelines to foreign countries, and taken over the oils of the Caucasus."[2] Thus, just as Hitler is sending off his troops toward Stalingrad, the Allies know his plans.

Around the end of April, or in early May, the Germans admonish the Japanese about their sloppy codes. Oshima tells Tokyo that he believes the Germans are reading the low-priority commercial Japanese codes, but he believes the Purple diplomatic machine code (Magic) is still entirely safe. In turn, Tokyo tells Oshima that a new commercial code is being prepared and a "total revision of Japanese codes [unspecified] has been completed, but it will be impossible to put the new codes into practice speedily because of transportation difficulties."

Meanwhile, the Japanese decrypts also tell the Americans that certain American codes are no longer secure.[3] Allied code breakers breathe a sigh of relief. The new Japanese codes can be handled. The insecure American codes can be rectified.

On June 1, American analysts decide that "the Japanese to a remarkable degree are assuming the leadership of the Axis powers in the initiation and formation of joint policies. This is particularly true in relation to Latin America. . . . The Japanese are abler men, better informed, than their German and Italian colleagues." This is particularly

---

2. SRS 585, 29 April 1942.
3. SRS 598, 12 May 1942.

true in Mexico, where Japan is trying to organize a joint response by the Axis nations to a bill being debated in the Mexican Congress that would declare a state of war with the Axis.[4]

On June 5, Baron Oshima reports to Tokyo that Germany plans to seize "the major part of European Russia by the autumn."[5] (Meanwhile the battle of Midway has taken place; there is no mention in the Magic Summaries showing that Tokyo has advised its emissaries, or its Axis allies, of the horrific defeat Japan has just endured that will change the course of the Pacific war.) In mid-June, the Berlin-Tokyo traffic reveals that Germany and Japan are concluding an agreement to supply each other with essential products under the terms of a "war-time economic agreement." The material will be transported by seven German ships, four of which are already in Japan and three of which "will reach Japan soon." In the commodities that are to be sent Germany will be 65,000 kilo tons of crude rubber, 10,000 tons of tin, 164,000 tons of oil products, manganese, quinine, opium, antimony, ferromolybdenum, molybdenum ore, asbestos, industrial diamonds, etc., for a total of 250,000 kilo tons. In return, Germany will ship Japan "patents and samples of corresponding machines [machine tools] and equipment" needed to complete Japan's military preparedness.[6]

On June 19, the German plans for the attack on the Caucasus fall into Russian hands when a German staff officer disobeys orders and carries them with him in a small plane, which is shot down. The Russians realize these plans are genuine. However, Stalin is still paranoid enough to believe that Moscow is the major focus of a German attack, and he does not plan any action in the south.

On June 24, Prime Minister Togo sends a message to his ambassador in Moscow that reveals Japan's paranoia about the way it views the war. Says Togo: "The U.S., England and the Soviet have been fighting us for many long years.... At every internal and external chance they got, either at disarmament conferences or in the League of Nations, or by use of the Chinese, as witness the Manchurian and Chinese incidents.... Finally the state was reached where outright warfare broke out in Greater East Asia. During all this time, though the appearance belied it, they have been fighting us throughout, spiritually

---

4. SRS 616, 1 June 1942.
5. SRS 620, 5 June 1942.
6. SRS 632, 18 June 1942.

and physically, it is all the same. . . . The Soviet Union . . . by their control of the communist military faction [in China] and by giving arms to the Chungking Army, are trying to get a firm grip on us. Thus they, too—nay, all of them—are fighting us.''[7]

The next day, on June 25, Togo's Foreign Office sends a circular to all the Japanese embassies, identifying the latest plan as being the product of the Japanese military. ''All British and U.S. interests in East Asia now belong to Japan,'' states the circular, ''and all British and American influence in China must be eliminated.'' The French Concession [in Southeast Asia] will not be eliminated ''immediately'' because [Vichy] France is cooperating with Japan. However, the French concession must be ''broken up'' because ''it may well become a fountainhead for activity of the Axis and various neutral countries of Europe and Asia.''[8]

At the end of June, Oshima obtains a briefing from a member of Foreign Minister von Ribbentrop's staff, identified as being ''a reliable German.'' Oshima tells Tokyo there have been ''unexpectedly great [German] victories in East [sic] Africa . . . they have been able to annihilate the British 8th Army and penetrate into Egypt.'' As for Russia, the current ''chief objectives are the capture of Sevastopol, and the battle of [name undecipherable in the Japanese text], also to take Kuyansk in the Donetz east of Kharkov, preparing the way for the attack.'' This report begins a series of strategic messages by Oshima and others, the interception and decrypting of which by the Allies will prove devastating to the German cause in Russia.

Oshima also reports (and this is not the first of such reports by Japanese ambassadors and consular officials) that he was told that when Russian foreign minister Molotov recently went to Washington, he proposed a ''comprehensive program'' for territorial readjustments. These are supposedly similar to those Molotov allegedly presented Britain's Anthony Eden when the latter visited Moscow in 1941. The earlier Japanese messages claim that Molotov told Eden that Russia would hold on to Estonia, Latvia, Lithuania and major parts of Poland after the war, which turns out to be true.

''At the time,'' Oshima tells Tokyo, ''Britain agreed to the program but the U.S. refused. It is not known whether Molotov was successful in getting the U.S. to alter its attitude [on this trip].''[9] The

---

7. SRS 638, 24 June 1942.
8. SRS 639, 25 June 1942.
9. SRS 644, 30 June 1942.

question of precisely when and how America and Great Britain learn about the Soviet plans to annex these territories is debatable. The author finds it unsettling to see the Japanese focusing on this issue as early as 1941—four years before Yalta—and apparently believing Stalin's intentions to hold on to these countries. Despite repeated denials by England and America about knowing what the Russians were going to do and when they were going to do it, the comments made by these astute Japanese diplomats bear careful weighing when it comes to creating the historical balance. All too often the Japanese estimates prove correct.

It is not until July 8 that the Magic Summaries show that the Soviets are paying much attention to the Japanese landings in the Aleutian Islands, which was a minor part of the plan to seize Midway. (The incredible American victory in this battle has still not been mentioned in the Magic Summaries, showing how desperately Tokyo wants to keep the grim details secret from its own people.) The Russian question of Japanese intentions about the Aleutians is posed to Naokichi Kitazawa, who had served as the second secretary to the Japanese embassy in Washington from 1937 to 1939. He replies that the American route to defeat Japan must be "via the Aleutians or the southern route via the Philippines. Because of Japanese military operations the southern and central route must be practically ruled out. . . . Any attempt by America to attack Japan must be by the northern route."[10]

There is a reason to include this seemingly innocuous message to Tokyo in the narrative at this time. In this case it is a question of finding out what the Japanese believe the American strategy will be in the Pacific. The planners in Washington are seeking this type of information so they can draw up strategy for future operations. One of the most difficult things for McCormack to achieve is to get the planners to coordinate their thinking with his staff so that the intelligence analysts are alert about what to look for. In this instance, for example, the Japanese message is music to the ears of American naval strategists. They are preparing to do exactly what Kitazawa says they cannot do. Thus this "innocuous" decrypt is a major indication that the Japanese are misreading American strategy in the Pacific.

To explain: After the victory at Midway, American strategists have to revise their planning with breathtaking speed. An order to seize the Solomon Islands is issued on July 2 by the U.S. Chiefs of Staff. On

10. SRS 646, 8 July 1942.

July 5, the Japanese are discovered to be building an airfield on Guadalcanal. Almost overnight the island becomes the primary target of the First Marine Division, which lands on August 7. (Another regiment of the First Marines seizes the three small islands of Tulagi, Gavutu and Tanambogo.) Once again, it is a matter of a small American force being committed without sufficient supplies and support (in this case the American Navy was soundly trounced by the Japanese in the battle of Savo Island, and the Navy, fearful for its carriers, "bugged out," withdrawing the ships carrying the Marines' artillery and other vital supplies—to say nothing of the covering force and its desperately needed firepower—leaving the First Marines on their own in desperate straits). Only by good luck and extraordinary courage do the Marines hold out. After brutal fighting, Guadalcanal falls to the Americans, despite the fact that Imperial Japanese Headquarters had decreed that the recapture of the island was top priority.

Washington now knows that it can dictate the pace of combat and how the war will be fought. It also understands the frightful cost it will have to pay in manpower to achieve victory.

✖ ✖ ✖

Another reason why the messages from Moscow are so important to Washington is that they prove, early on in the war, that our ally, Stalin, never, ever intends to allow American planes to "shuttle-bomb" Japan, i.e., allow them to depart from Alaskan soil to land on airfields in Siberia. Just as the Japanese were afraid to attack Russia, the Russians are afraid to do anything that might upset their nonaggression agreement with Tokyo. Later on, the question of shuttle bombing will become a major irritant in Soviet-American relations. Be that as it may, Roosevelt and Marshall know by reading the Magic Summaries that, from the beginning, Russia is *never* going to help us defeat Japan until it becomes expedient for her to so do. In turn, this means that the war in Europe will end in an unexpected way.

On July 12, 1942, Tokyo sends out a circular lamenting the heavy loss of Japanese merchant ships. Foreign Minister Togo is concerned that the movements of these vessels are being compromised via "radio messages sent in easily readable [commercial] codes." According to Togo, the problem is difficult to solve because the Foreign Office does not have enough personnel to handle the "infinite details" of cargoes, bills of lading, the dates the ships will leave specific harbors and the dates they will arrive at their destinations.[11] (As we know, Mc-Cormack's staff is building up this information from "commercial codes" and even greater losses are about to be inflicted on Japanese shipping.)

Meanwhile, from Moscow, Ambassador Sato reports to Tokyo about his most recent meeting with Soviet foreign minister Molotov. The first question Sato asks is the same as the one he asked earlier in April: Is Russia going to "transfer, sell, lease or lend any of its territory to the U.S. for military bases to attack Japan?"

Molotov replies, "Why, we never even discussed anything like that [with the Americans]. . . . I am telling the truth when I say we never discussed the subject." One can almost hear a Greek chorus laughing in the wings: "Ho! Ho! Ho!"

"Would I be justified in assuming that on no occasion hereafter will you ever discuss such a thing?" asks Sato.

"No," says Molotov. "Trips like this tire me too much. I don't think I will make any more of them to negotiate."

Sato concludes the meeting by saying that he hopes that "the Soviet will steadfastly maintain her present stand" of neutrality with Japan.

Molotov counters, saying, "I hope that Japan, too, will maintain her present relations with us because you know it works both ways."[12]

From Berlin on July 14, Baron Oshima tells Tokyo that Red Army resistance in southern Russia is diminishing "remarkably as compared to the past. The Germans expected it would take four weeks to capture Voronezh but it fell in eight days. The [Germans] are widening the battle into the east and the south."[13] The following day, a Japanese summary about the war in Russia reports that thirty Russian divisions were surrounded at Kharkov and "eliminated." At Korch, the Germans took thirty to forty thousand prisoners. According to the report, the Germans won a large victory, "but they also suffered a large number of casualties."

The report continues: "The war has revealed many men of Asiatic extraction among the Russian troops, men who will fight to the very end of their ammunition . . . and, at the point of capture, they will take their own lives. Many German officers have seen this and have told foreign news correspondents: 'We are fighting against Asiatics.' "[14]

---

11. SRS 650, 12 July 1942.
12. Ibid.
13. SRS 652, 14 July 1942.
14. SRS 653, 15 July 1942.

The next day, Japanese ambassador Suma reports from Madrid that he spoke with the German consul general at Casablanca, who said that Dakar is invulnerable to an Allied attack. The Germans, said Suma, do not believe the Allies can land troops "all the way from Casablanca and Tangier."[15] As it will turn out several months later, that is exactly what the Allies do, landing from Casablanca to Algiers and ignoring Dakar and Tangier.

Tokyo next asks for Baron Oshima's views about America on a number of subjects. The Baron replies, saying that America cannot understand why Japan had to attack Pearl Harbor, that Japan is going from one victory to another (apparently Oshima has either not been told, or refuses to comprehend, what occurred at Midway), and this "causes a rising suspicion that all is not well with the Allied Command. . . . The American people are not much interested in the spread of democracy throughout the earth. . . . Thus the present war has come to be a sort of racial war. In this respect the U.S. is cornered, because she herself has a racial problem. . . . The [American] government is saying that this time the U.S. will not make the mistake of retiring into her shell and will play a direct international role in establishing permanent peace throughout the world. . . . This is a point to which we should pay heed."[16]

On July 19, the Japanese ambassador to Vichy tells Tokyo that France has refused the second proposal of the U.S. concerning the French ships at Alexandria. The Americans want the ships moved to Martinique. The ambassador reports that a French official told him that "if England interferes, these ships will either resist or be sunk. We have advised the Admiralty to do so already."[17]

Meanwhile, at the Vatican, Japanese ambassador Harada talks with the Pope, who insists on meeting the envoy sent by Chiang Kai-shek. Harada is deeply upset and tells Tokyo: "How often have I been told that no organization in the world has richer sources of intelligence than the Vatican. It seems the Papacy spares no pains or troubles in schemes to get at the bottom of things throughout the world. Taking advantage of this . . . are demagogues sending the Vatican all kinds of pernicious propaganda. This is something about which we must ever be on the

15. SRS 654, 16 July 1942.
16. SRS 656, 18 July 1942.
17. SRS 657, 19 July 1942.

alert. Many of these demagogic reports would seem to concern the matter of peace in which the Vatican is much interested."[18]

The month of July ends with two startling reports about events in Siberia. In the first, Tokyo reports to its diplomats in Vladivostok that "for the second time since early this month, Soviet Far Eastern troops are being sent west on a large scale."[19] The second report comes from the Manchukuo Consulate in China, which tells Tokyo that starting on the fourteenth of July, forty military westbound trains loaded with men and "implements" passed between Irkutsk and Chita. During the last two days, nineteen empty trains have arrived and headed east (apparently to pick up more troops).

One cannot find in the Magic Summaries any indication that the Japanese passed on to their German allies the information that the Russians were pulling their troops out of Siberia and not replacing them.

✖ ✖ ✖

The month of August 1942 is pivotal in the history of World War II. During the early days, Field Marshal Rommel pounds away at the British in North Africa with great success. In Russia, the German drive toward Stalingrad and the Caucasus rolls along, seemingly unstoppable.

Reading the Magic Summaries that cross Chief of Staff Marshall's desk, however, one can see that the Japanese are deluding themselves. Furthermore, Magic is proving that the war is beginning to place intolerable strains on the Axis nations. Relationships are beginning to fray at the edges. Germany, Italy and Japan become wary of each other. The war is changing in favor of the Allies, but only a few people see it happening.

On the first of August, the Japanese in Shanghai make a formal request to the German ambassador, Stahmer, via his intelligence chief, a man named Kort. The Japanese are concerned that local Germans in Shanghai are creating dissension within the business community. The message to Tokyo is unequivocal about this, saying the "Germans are desperately doing all they can to [to get us to attack Siberia and] drag Japan into the German-Soviet war."

Meanwhile, Oshima's office in Berlin tells Tokyo that a German circular communiqué sent to all embassies and consulates, the trans-

---

18. Ibid.
19. SRS 660, 22 July 1942.

mission of which to Shanghai was intercepted by the Japanese, instructs the German diplomatic community around the world to "make [the] greatest possible propaganda use" of the alleged "free hand in Europe that the Anglo-Saxons have granted the Soviets."[20]

The following day, Japanese ambassador Tomi reports from Buenos Aires that he spoke at length with the Foreign Minister of Argentina (not named) on July 29. Tomi says that he told the Foreign Minister that "by reason of her remarkable record, Japan is now in a better position than ever for future attacks [against the Allies]," and by virtue of Germany's advance to the Caucasus, "soon she will be able to settle the war with the West." The Axis position will be impregnable. According to Tomi, the Argentine response is that the British should make peace before Germany takes Egypt and extends her influence throughout the entire Mediterranean area since, should this region fall, "the independence of India [from British rule] will be hastened."

Tomi then suggests that the Latin American nations should "get together and present a unified peace plan," sugarcoating the idea with the words that this is the "sublime mission" of Argentina. To this, the Argentine foreign minister replies that he doesn't have much hope for peace in the near future.[21]

On August 4, the critical third part of a three-part message from Tokyo, which was sent on July 27 to Baron Oshima in Berlin, is decrypted in Washington. The message clearly states and explains the decision—made at the highest levels in Japan—not to invade Siberia. The most important section says: "We believe, that ever since the beginning of the war, the policy which the Japanese government has taken has been the most favorable for completion of the Japanese-German-Italian united war, massing our reserve strength at the most strategic points. Under the present circumstances our policy is to preserve peace in the north and restrain Stalin's political influence in the East while laboring to strengthen our campaign against America and England in the Pacific and Indian Oceans.

"Therefore we hope that Germany also will fully appreciate the above is the most favorable course on the whole for the prosecution of the Japanese-German-Italian united war.

"This telegram has been discussed and approved by the Government and Imperial Headquarters."

A laconic comment added by an intelligence analyst in Washing-

---

20. SRS 670, 1 August 1942.
21. SRS 671, 2 August 1942.

ton to the Magic Summary that went to Marshall declares: "The last quoted paragraph clears up any doubt as to whether the Japanese Army is in accord with the announced policy."[22]

Also on July 27, 1942, Premier Tojo makes a speech declaring that Japan will help India gain complete independence. "Japan cannot allow an Anglo–North American presence in India," says Tojo. He also calls for the Muhammadan countries in the Near East to take advantage of the "opportunity offered them to establish free countries."[23]

The message from Tokyo to Oshima has to be forwarded from Berlin to the German southern front in the Ukraine. The German press quotes a story by the "Japanese correspondent Oshima" that contains, according to the intelligence analysts, "the familiar story of Russian prisoners who feared the political commissar as much as the Stukas and has suffered from insufficiency of food." More important to the analysts were the comments by Oshima about the decisive role played by the Luftwaffe in the battle of Rostov and the universal superiority of German weapons.

According to Oshima's report: "Continuous air attack, day and night, broke the morale of the defenders [of Rostov] and destroyed fortifications that should have withstood any bombardment. After such preparation, the German tank corps and infantry penetrated to the heart of the city. Crossing of Don [River] also made possible by support of the Luftwaffe, which completely commanded the air. Not a single Russian plane was seen by this correspondent. By July 28, [the] Germans were using the Rostov airfield, at that time only ten kilometers from [the] front. . . . German offensive weapons are ten years ahead of the technique of defense in our time. Proof of this fact provided by sight of strong fortifications in Rostov, destroyed by a single shot from a German tank gun."[24]

Another report to Tokyo of July 27, this time from Ambassador Sato, who has gone to Kuibyshev, describes conditions in Russia. According to Sato, wounded troops and refugees are pouring into Kuibyshev from Voronezh and Stalingrad, and passenger ships are being converted into hospital ships and moored to accommodate the wounded. . . . There is heavy movement of military supplies up the Volga. . . . It is rumored that the Russians have commenced prepara-

---

22. SRS 673, 4 August 1942. For the full message from Tokyo to Oshima, one must refer to SRS 674 of August 5, 1942.
23. Ibid.
24. Ibid.

tions to move their capital to Sverdlovsk [from Moscow]. . . . (The Summary then goes into direct quotes.) "The newspapers continue to emphasize the threatening crisis, and call upon the Red Army to stop the German advance. They are also attacking America and England because the 'Second Front' has failed to materialize." The Americans and British in Kuibyshev, however, recognize the difficulties of opening a second front and do not expect it at any early date. . . . There are rumors that tank and airplane factories in the Volga area are being moved to the Ural regions.[25]

On August 5, Berlin reports to Tokyo that Oshima is indeed visiting the Ukraine Command and that he has had a three-hour discussion there with Foreign Minister von Ribbentrop. According to the American intelligence analysts, the gist of the message from Tokyo, saying that Japan would not help Germany at the moment by attacking Russia in the Far East, produces only a "very mild reaction" from the Germans.[26]

Why the message from Tokyo creates only a "very mild reaction" is subject to speculation. There is no official reason.

One wonders how the course of the war might have changed had Japan struck at Siberia at this particular moment.

It is also important to note that as of this date, Stalin has not made any plans to counterattack at Stalingrad or in the Caucasus. He still believes that Moscow will be the focal point of the German assault on Russia.

All this is about to change, however. In his role as a faithful reporter of everything he sees and hears, Oshima is about to send off a series of reports that not only identify Stalingrad as the primary German attack, but also gives the Allies an invaluable report on the German order of battle for the coming fight, plus pointing out the weaknesses of the German forces as they advance, particularly on their flanks, which are protected by weak groupings of Italian, Hungarian and Austrian troops.

Stalin could not ask for more.

One must remember that Oshima is not being indiscreet. He is doing his duty. The fact that the Allies have broken the Purple codes is not his fault. The fact that Japan believes that the Purple codes unbreakable is not his responsibility. But the lesson to be learned, as American cryptological expert William Friedman will emphasize in his lectures many years later, is this: While it's important for you to

---

25. Ibid.
26. SRS 674, 5 August 1942.

be able to read the enemy's codes and ciphers, it is far more important that your own codes and ciphers remain secure—always and forever.

The vital messages from Oshima to Tokyo begin on August 6, 1942, when the Baron reports on his three-hour meeting with Ribbentrop, during which Oshima tells Ribbentrop about the message from Tokyo of July 27 about Japan's remaining neutral toward Russia. According to Oshima, Ribbentrop replies ''that naturally this is something for the Japanese government to decide for itself, and that Germany was, of course, in no position to say anything, as he had already told me. He seemed worried about the question of our joint warfare with our two allies and asked me many questions.

''[I replied] well . . . Japan is using every available way and means to bring this war to a victorious conclusion, and she is determined to do so. Please believe me when we say that, because we are absolutely sincere.''

Hitler is ''not there'' according to Oshima, but he asked Ribbentrop to ''inform him concisely'' about Tokyo's message and the Foreign Minister agreed to do so.[27]

Oshima then sends Tokyo another message, a summary report of information he has received from General Matski and ''a certain Colonel in the [German] High Command.''

''For some time it has been rumored,'' Oshima says, ''that the main German drive would be directed toward the Caucasus. . . . The German Army has now proceeded far with its breakthrough from the Southern Ukraine front, but still the Soviet Army has not shifted any particularly noteworthy forces thither. This is probably due, first, to the fact that more than half of the fifty or sixty divisions of their strategic reserves were lost in the Kharkov offensive. Second, the Soviets probably fear that in view of the way Germany attacked last year she may soon make a drive against Moscow again. . . . If the German forces capture Stalingrad, they can completely divide the Red Army. To the capture of this city the German forces attach great importance. However, what will have the greatest effect upon this is the engagement of armored units in the Stalingrad front and on the west bank of the Don [River]. . . . It is impossible to tell the strength of the Soviet forces in the Caucasus . . . it must be about forty divisions. If, on the Moscow front, the Soviet Army should discover the disposition of German forces

---

27. SRS 675, 6 August 1942.

and German plans, they might take the offensive there, but Germany is quite ready for this."[28]

✷ ✷ ✷

Meanwhile, with the American strategy to make amphibious landings in Africa in the final planning stages, it is imperative that the problem of the French fleet in Alexandria be settled. Will the fleet fight for the Axis or will it support the Allies? Are the ships even fit to fight? From Vichy, France, the Japanese ambassador reports to Tokyo that he has met personally with Adm. Jean Darlan, who says the fleet will not be moved from Alexandria. If the fleet is attacked, Darlan said, it will probably have to be scuttled since the vessels are obsolete, undermanned and have been anchored so long that their speed has been seriously reduced.

The Ambassador also quotes Darlan as saying that, prior to the fall of France, he had offered to send certain ships that were now at Alexandria to "protect" the British fleet in the eastern Mediterranean. Darlan "can never forgive the present treacherous actions and breach of faith on the part of the British."

The Ambassador concluded by saying that he believes Darlan is "strongly anti-American as well as anti-British."[29]

The Allies have their answer: the French fleet is not a viable fighting force; Darlan is not to be trusted.

In the days that follow, Tokyo reveals that the opium trade in Southeast Asia is to be divided between the two manufacturing firms Mitsubishi and Mitsui for purposes of distribution.[30] And from Bucharest, Minister Ksutsui reports to Tokyo that on the southern Russian front, the Soviets have lost twenty of their one hundred divisions. The eighty remaining divisions are suffering from a terrible loss in men and weapons, "but they have at least escaped annihilation. Nineteen divisions are retreating to Stalingrad and about thirty to the northern Caucasus, where there are in addition about twenty divisions. Their future first line of defense will be the Volga River, but they are losing the region to the west including the Maikop oil fields. . . . There was a re-

28. Ibid.
29. SRS 676, 7 August 1942.
30. SRS 677, 8 August 1942.

port that they would try to destroy the Grozny oil fields, but their retreat will be too rapid. After the fall of Stalingrad, the Red Army will retreat to Kamishin and then to Saratov. South of these places is an area settled by German emigrants, where the German Army should make good progress.''

The report continues, saying the Soviet Black Sea fleet, including one battleship and one heavy cruiser, plus four light cruisers and seventeen destroyers and other vessels, no longer have any base since the Germans captured Sevastopol. The Germans are taking over control of the Black Sea and are planning to supply part of their military operations in the Caucasus and south Russia via water.[31]

Within twenty-four hours, from Italy, Ambassador Horikiri reports to Tokyo that the Germans in Rome are pushing the idea that Stalin, upset by the fact that the Allies have been unable to fulfill their promise of a second front in Europe, may seek peace with Berlin by the autumn. The source for the information is quoted as saying that Germany "will be ready to make peace on suitable terms. As for Italy, she believes this war in Russia should be finished up summarily and this reserve of Axis troops moved south and used to turn the tide in the Near East and Middle East and in North Africa, thus deciding the fate of the present war.''[32]

The monumental news of the day, however, is the report by Baron Oshima to Tokyo about his recent trip to the Russian front. In making his estimate of "future war developments," Oshima predicts that "the German Army now expects to crush the Soviet Army before winter.''

Oshima also predicts that the German campaign in the Caucasus will be slowed because the Germans will be attacking in mountainous country with the problems of an extended supply and communications line. But, he says, "it is estimated that the Caucasus will be occupied sometime next month at the latest.''

No prediction can be made as to when Moscow will be attacked, says Oshima. But it appears that conditions will be suitable for a siege that coincides with the attack on Stalingrad. Moscow should fall before winter.

"When the Caucasus and European Russia have been occupied," claims Oshima, "a part of the German Army will be maintained there in winter quarters, facing the remnants of the Soviet Army. The main strength of the German Army will return home or be diverted to other

31. SRS 678, 11 August 1942.
32. SRS 680, 11 August 1942.

fronts. . . . It also might be that the Soviet Army will . . . launch a surprise action against the German Army. However, judging from the weakness of the Soviet's striking power, such a development is not anticipated.''

This conclusion by Oshima follows a seven-page order of battle for all the German forces in Russia. The most vital parts included the following comments:

✱ German forces in the north are to create a diversion in the whole Leningrad area.

✱ In the center, German forces are positioned to check the movement of troops southward from Moscow. Meanwhile, they are prepared to advance on Moscow in ''case of a Russian reversal in the south [Stalingrad] made it necessary [for Russian] troops to be drawn out of [Moscow].''

✱ In the south, the Sixth Army and the Fourth Armored Division were ''assigned the responsibility for capturing Stalingrad. . . . The Hungarian forces . . . were to cover the left flanks of the forces attacking Stalingrad. . . . Confronting the Russian Army in the Sea of Azov area [i.e., the right flank of the German advance on Stalingrad] is the Third Rumanian Army (consisting of two Rumanian divisions and one division of German infantry).''

According to Oshima, General Halder, his staff officers and others ''all say that Soviet military strength has declined.''[33]

But what Oshima does not realize is that he has given Stalin the key to a successful counterattack. All the Russians have to do is confirm the location of the weak Hungarian and Rumanian forces protecting the flanks of the German advance, drive through them, catch the Germans in a double envelopment and trap them inside Stalingrad.

This is exactly what Stalin orders four weeks later.

✱ ✱ ✱

In Tokyo, Foreign Minister Togo takes Oshima's report to heart, revising it in a circular sent to his diplomats around the world. Togo can see clearly the significance of the final struggle for Stalingrad.

---

33. Ibid.

As he puts it: "Stalin himself is said to have gone to the southern front and, trying to encourage resistance, ordered the Red Army to fight to the death. However, it would appear that the people are losing hope in victory. It is true that the Soviet still has quite a number of tanks but Germany has almost complete control of the air. Coupled with this, the Reich is using the principle of striking out at important objectives with carefully guarded flanks. The desperate Russians will probably concentrate their reserves around Stalingrad and in the lower reaches of the Volga, and it is here that the bloody struggle is likely to be fought out. The decisive factor in this final engagement will be the virility of these reserves."[34]

Togo also sees that the battle for North Africa is reaching a crucial stage. In rehashing the struggle for his staff, Togo points out that the Germans and Italians had attacked in late June. The Germans had found the British weaker than they had expected and by early July had reached the vicinity of El Alamein. According to Togo, the Germans outran their supply lines and now both armies are stalemated at El Alamein. But "as soon as Germany and Italy get supplies, they are doubtless determined to proceed on Cairo. England is still trying to supply Egypt with soldiers through South Africa . . . by air. . . . Germany, on the other hand, is so engrossed in the fight on the Eastern Front that she cannot keep up with the superior air forces of the enemy in North Africa. The outcome of the struggle will depend on the relative reinforcements both armies get."

Togo also believes that there is no way the Allies can open a second front in Europe at the present time. No matter how much the Soviets beg. Meanwhile, Turkey is "still sticking to her neutral policy and so long as there is no great change in the Russo-German theater of war, or at Cairo and Suez, no change in that attitude can be expected."[35]

The next day, Togo adds a further comment to his summary of the way he views the war, saying: "The French officials and people are waiting to get a clearer idea of the future of Europe and the world as a whole. . . . Spain and Portugal are still maintaining their neutrality. *In short, Germany has put her all into the mortal battle in Russia, and her success or failure will determine the attitude and relations of all the neutral countries of Europe.*"[36] (Emphasis added.)

Foreign Minister Togo is calling it correctly. The situation is cru-

34. SRS 683, 14 August 1942.
35. Ibid.
36. SRS 684, 15 August 1942.

cial for both the Axis and the Allies. General Montgomery assumes command of the British Eighth Army on August 13 and, having been warned by Ultra that Rommel plans to attack at the end of the month, tells his troops that they will stand fast and fight it out defensively at Alam Halfa. Within the next few days, the judicious use of Ultra allows the British to sink four of the six freighters carrying vital supplies to Rommel, who launches his attack on the new, untried English commander hoping that he can refuel his panzers on captured British stocks, which is no way to go into battle.

For two days Rommel tries to seize the Alam Halfa Ridge, only to suffer horrific losses inflicted by British antitank guns that are perfectly positioned thanks to Montgomery's use of Ultra.

Finally, on September 1, Rommel is forced to withdraw. The retreat signifies the end of Germany's attempts to march on Egypt and the Suez Canal.

It is not apparent to the public, but the Allies have taken a big step forward on the road to victory.

✖ ✖ ✖

The last two weeks of August are relatively tame in terms of Magic. However, events are taking place in Japan that will change Tokyo's attitude toward the war, making Japan even more belligerent than before.

As viewed through the looking glass called Magic, the world suddenly goes topsy-turvy. For the analysts in Washington, September will also bring solid proof that Japan and Germany are deliberately misleading each other. And by the end of the month, these deceptions will lead to the first indications of major disruptions in the economies and treasuries of the Axis nations.

On September 1, the German minister in Hsinking asks his Japanese counterpart whether or not Stalin is shipping troops west from Siberia to fight at Stalingrad. The Japanese ambassador reports to Tokyo that he is telling Germany that according to Japanese intelligence some fifty to sixty thousand Russian troops were shipped from the Far East to the western front. The Ambassador also tells the Germans that in the past the Russians have replaced these troops, so there probably is no great change in Soviet strength in the Far East.[37]

---

37. SRS 701, 1 September 1942.

What the Japanese have not told the Germans is that they knew that the troop trains going to Siberia were empty, although they were full on the return trip to European Russia.[38] And Oshima has already reported to Tokyo that the Germans have defeated the first Siberian troops they encountered in the Stalingrad region.

Meanwhile, the German minister talking with the Japanese ambassador in Hsinking says that since "Stalin is an intelligent person there is a possibility of overtures from Russia for an independent peace."

The Japanese reply is withering: Yes, Russia might seek peace "if Germany bore down strongly enough."[39]

And from Paris, the Japanese report that a diplomat named Achenbach, who is attached to the German embassy, has told the Japanese ambassador that "Laval's way of acting is most loyal to us Germans and it is our policy to support him as fully as possible. . . . Now Laval has informed us Germans that he wishes to cooperate with Japan, too, and we intend to make France a full-fledged member of the new European circle through [Laval]. . . . For the good of all we [Germans] would like to see Tokyo and Vichy draw closer."[40]

This is exactly what the Japanese wanted to avoid when they suggested earlier that the French holdings in Indochina should be taken over completely and the Vichy government agencies expelled.

A few days later, Tokyo communicates with Kalgan about the surplus of Mongolian opium from the latest harvest, which will produce 292 short tons. Because conditions in Central and North China are not "too flourishing," these areas can only use about 62.5 tons of the Mongolian product. Efforts will have to be redoubled to dispose of the surplus in South China. Japanese authorities and the East Asia Development Company are now proposing to ship 62.5 tons of Mongolian opium to the "southern areas" that "the Army had been planning to export to Hopei."[41]

It is at this point that the Germans begin to dissemble to the Japanese about Stalingrad and North Africa. Instead of meeting the Japanese ambassador face-to-face, Foreign Minister von Ribbentrop sends an officer from Imperial Headquarters to brief Oshima in Berlin, who reports to Tokyo as follows: "Although the Russian attack in the region of Rzhev is

---

38. Refer back to SRS 652.
39. SRS 701, 1 September 1942.
40. Ibid.
41. SRS 703, 3 September 1942.

extremely tenacious, the Germans are maintaining the defensive and constantly inflicting heavy losses. . . . The Russians are being exhausted. . . . Around Stalingrad a large number of bunkers have been captured. . . . A wedge is being driven in from the north and south and the German armies will soon join hands there—then the city will be besieged from the north, west, and south. . . . Spread out over a wide front the German Army is advancing toward the Caspian Sea and at several points have already reached the railroad which skirts the sea. . . . In the Caucasus the Seventeenth Army has already taken the important pass east of Mt. Elbrus and is advancing against Novorossiysk and Sukhumi.''

This overly optimistic evaluation is surpassed by the German interpretation of the defeat Rommel has just endured at Alam Halfa.

According to the German staff officer: ''The object of Rommel's attack, which began of the thirty-first, is to break up the extensive traffic behind the lines by decisively routing the enemy. Since this attack was made before preparations for the great offensive were finished, it follows that this is not an attempt to capture Cairo, etc. After the destruction of the enemy in El Alamein, [Rommel] plans to return to his preattack lines. However, the progress of the attack is proceeding beyond all expectations. Enemy armored corps have been wiped out and deep penetration has been made behind the enemy lines. And it appears that the results will be more than we even hoped for.''[42]

✳ ✳ ✳

It takes some time for the unexpected upheaval in the Japanese Foreign Ministry and the firing of Foreign Minister Togo to show up in a Magic Summary.

Tokyo calls it a resignation and says it occurred on September 1, but the special summary memo from Tokyo explaining events is not decrypted until September 8.

According to the summary, the militaristic Japanese cabinet has created a new department—The Greater East Asia Ministry—at the expense of the Foreign Office. The cabinet is repudiating current diplomatic procedures in the occupied countries of East Asia ''in favor of stronger methods.'' The Japanese Army and Navy are taking over running the Philippines, the East Indies and ''the southern conquered ter-

---

42. SRS 705, 3 September 1942.

ritories in general.'' This is also true in China. Liaison with Germany about India will now be handled via the military attachés in Rome and Berlin.

The old Foreign Office has lost control over foreign affairs.

The military is totally in charge of Japan.

Taking much credit in Berlin for the coup is Ambassador Oshima. He is quoted as saying: ''If you ask me whether or not the Foreign Office is taking care of foreign affairs, I tell you that aside from the South American problem it is doing nothing. Therefore I have asked Foreign Minister Togo to tender his resignation.''[43]

For Baron Oshima, the new regime in Tokyo is a welcome event. Two of the superhawks of Japanese expansionism, Oshima and Premier Tojo, are now aligned with each other. The scope of their dreaming for the future of a new Japanese world order will prove breathtaking to the civilian and military leaders of the Allies.

In Chile, meanwhile, Italy and Japan are engaged in a major campaign of political bribery. One million pesos has been deposited with the Chairman of the Upper House, identified by name as Doran. According to the Japanese, the Italians used their own funds at first, but now the Japanese are furnishing the pesos and the Italians are making the deposits. The Italians are also approaching two members of the Chilean radical party.[44]

And in Spain, Foreign Minister Serrano Suner has resigned. But this does not block Japanese minister Suma from his intelligence gathering. For example, Suma obtains from the head of the Spanish Communications Office a recently submitted report by Ambassador Cardenas in Washington made at the request of the new Spanish foreign minister, Jordana. The latter had asked his Washington staff to comment on ''the feelings of the U.S. Government and people on the current situation.''

In response, the Ambassador invites Secretary of State Cordell Hull to dine and reports that ''after dinner he [Hull] opened up, and we had quite a tête-à-tête. For your information I had someone take it down in shorthand in the next room.''[45]

Intelligence experts must have breathed a sigh of relief when they

43. SRS 708, 8 September 1942.
44. SRS 712, 12 September 1942. A special note added to this Summary by McCormack's analysts says: ''See also the Magic Summaries of July 2,5 and 11.''
45. SRS 725, 25 September 1942.

read the transcript of Hull's remarks. The canny Secretary of State obviously knew he was in enemy territory when he was asked to dinner. He reveals nothing of importance. (As we will see later, there is an unusual twist to this tale.)

On September 26, the Germans are increasing the ferocity of their attacks on Stalingrad. But the Russians are still holding on. The carnage and violence is unbelievable. Obviously, something decisive is about to occur, a watershed is being reached. Oshima recognizes the significance of the moment and reports to Premier Tojo that the Axis must "aim to win by 1944."

It is too late for Axis victory, however, but Oshima doesn't know it. The redoubtable Baron believes that Japan and Germany still have time in their favor, and Oshima tells Tojo that Japan should wage "active war in the Indian Ocean and place soldiers in part of India." He also cables Tojo a description of a talk he had with Foreign Minister von Ribbentrop concerning the general military situation and future Axis strategy.

The Magic Summary of September 26 has Oshima first analyzing for Tojo that the way the war is now going, it seems unlikely that a decisive strike can be made soon. "Consequently," says Oshima, looking to the future, "what we Japanese and Germans ought to do is break down all economic barriers and join hands between Europe and Asia. Our success in this will determine, I am sure, the outcome of the war and the fate of the Axis. In order to succeed . . . [Japan] should wage active war in the Indian Ocean and place soldiers in part of India— certainly in Chittagong and Calcutta—and make them bases for our strategy. We should do all we can to stir up hatred against England inside India. In the meantime, Germany ought to hasten her invasion of the Middle East, and together we should separate India from England. . . . Without the use of military force, it is absolutely impossible for us to control India. England and the U.S. are now gradually increasing their forces in that country, and it is no time for us to temporize. . . . Germany's achievements in Russia for this year are not yet clear. . . . But I think we may safely say she has not won a decisive victory and will, in all probability, be up against a stiff, large-scale struggle next year, too. . . . The defeat of Russia is essential to the establishment of the coprosperity sphere in Greater East Asia. Also, from the point of view of striking at the Anglo-Saxons, it is urgent that Russia be dealt with without too much delay. I suppose it is our first policy to maintain neutrality with Russia, but that cannot last. Let us maintain this neutrality for a while, settle affairs in the South Seas, all the while making ready to hit the Soviet, and when next summer comes, let us *join forces with the Germans and be in on the kill.*"[46] (Emphasis added.)

✖ ✖ ✖

Allied military planners can now appreciate the way Japanese foreign policy appears to be turning vis-à-vis Stalingrad and North Africa. If the Germans are successful at Stalingrad and in the Caucasus, it is apparent that the Japanese will consider breaking their neutrality pact with Russia, attack eastward through Siberia, and join Germany in carving up the USSR.

The Magic Summary next reveals the first portion of Oshima's incredible conversation with Ribbentrop of September 17. If this conversation was included in a spy novel, the critics would dismiss it out of hand. But since the conversation actually occurs, and Japan proposes to Germany a new way for the two conspirators to divide the world, plus demanding that Germany invade England using *poison gas,* the full text is given.

Oshima reports: "I had a talk with Ribbentrop on the seventeenth, and he explained the situation in the Soviet to me (see my [unavailable message]). Then he asked me about the military situation in East Asia, and I told him that as I had informed him not long ago, we were going to stabilize the South Seas and embark on a program of destroying as much commerce as possible in the Indian Ocean.[47] I said that aside from that I had no new reports from my government. Ribbentrop continued:

" 'Well, as for Germany, in view of the way the war is going, she feels that you Japanese should cooperate harder than ever with us and win a complete victory as soon as possible. One thing I would like to ask you is how long you think this war is going to last.'

"I replied: Naturally, I, too, think that our two nations ought to cooperate our activities more intimately than ever before. I share you opinions completely. After I get more information from my government on the military situation in the East, I will talk to you about this some

---

46. SRS 727, 26 September 1942.
47. A special note added at this point by the intelligence analysts says: "Oshima here refers to the message from Tokyo to Berlin, dated July 27, in which Tokyo stated that it intended to establish a 'solid organization in the south' and that it was 'laboring to strengthen [its] campaign against America and England in the Pacific and Indian Oceans.' " (August 4 Summary)

more; but right now, I will express a few of my own personal opinions. England and the United States are showing quite a bit of resistance in the wars in the East and in the West. But on the other hand, the Japanese and German military theaters have become more proximate. The thing that is most urgent for us now to do is to coordinate our activities in time and space. In other words, the time has come when we can fight most effectively on a cooperative basis. In this connection, the first thing we have to think about is winning a hundred-year victory. In a great war like this, naturally we hope for a swift war and a swift decision.

"Japan and Germany must not only exert their best endeavors to win a quick victory, but must, at the same time, prepare for a long war, ever keeping the trend in their favor so that the enemy cannot get the upper hand. The first thing for us to do is to try to determine just how long we can keep fighting, and, next, we must study what it is essential for us to do during that time. In my own opinion, judging from the military situation of the present day, I should say that we might aim to keep fighting until the winter of 1944, by which time we should win conclusively.

"As the first step, Japan, as I said, is determined to stabilize the South Seas area and, at the same time, invade the Indian Ocean. While we are doing that, you Germans, just as soon as you have mopped up the Caucasus, should send forces to Iran and Iraq and join hands with us Japanese across the Persian Gulf. I cannot overstress the importance of achieving this feat; and another thing, we Japanese and Germans must break down all financial barriers and open the gates to complete economic collaboration. In this way, we can establish a trend in which we will be absolutely invincible."[48]

The next day's Summary contains more of Oshima's talk with Ribbentrop, which had been intercepted but not decrypted. Oshima's final words to the Germans are stunning in their implications.

The decrypt reads: "I said to von Ribbentrop: . . . It is of pressing importance to cut off Egypt and India from England, as they are the two greatest mainstays of England and the United States. Thus a drive in this direction should be considered a matter of immediate urgency. Although Germany's war against the Soviet is progressing very favorably, the Soviet Army should be dealt a crushing blow in the next year's spring and summer drive in order to settle the military side of the Soviet problem. You should by no means fail to accomplish the several op-

---

48. SRS 727, 26 September 1942.

erations I have just mentioned during 1943. After their completion, *Germany should make absolutely failure-proof preparations for an invasion of England by the summer of 1944.* Judging from actual results, it will probably be difficult to force England to surrender by 1944 through the use of submarines and air raids alone, so that invasion is the only way open to you. Besides, this is of vital importance to us if we are going to make them accept our terms at the time of the peace conference. If Germany, from now on, prepares complete equipment for invasion, trains faithfully *and with the proper mental attitude, and uses poison gas,* I think the result will be certain. [Emphasis added.]

"Ribbentrop listened to me carefully. He said he was flying to Hitler's headquarters [in East Prussia] the next day (the eighteenth) and would tell Hitler what I had to say. [Hitler's headquarters are quite some distance away.]

"We had a talk the evening of the eighteenth after Ribbentrop returned from his visit to Hitler.

"Ribbentrop said: 'Although the Fuehrer also is considering various ways of bringing the war to favorable conclusion, he is putting special emphasis on a German-Japanese junction across the Indian Ocean. It is decided that, after occupying the Caucasus, there will certainly be an advance on the Middle East; however, the time and manner of the attack cannot yet be determined.'

"To my inquiry as to whether there were any objections to my reporting this to my own government [in Tokyo], Ribbentrop replied that there were none, but he asked that particularly strict secrecy be observed."[49]

Suddenly the upcoming battle of Stalingrad and the invasion of the Caucasus is assuming incredible proportions for the Allies.

Stalingrad must not be lost.

The Germans must not be allowed to drive through the Caucasus. The cost in lives and material be damned.

Should the Germans and Japanese connect across the Persian Gulf, as Oshima is proposing and which Hitler is reportedly considering, the new world order under Germany and Japan would create a concentration camp stretching eastward from the western shores of Ireland on the Atlantic to the eastern shores of China on the Pacific.

---

49. SRS 728, 27 September 1942.

✖ ✖ ✖

Whether or not the Japanese comprehended the defeat Rommel has suffered in North Africa, or the danger of the German undertaking at Stalingrad, is unclear from reading the Magic Summaries.

The next day, it's business as usual. Tokyo is telling its emissaries around the world that it wants to try to promote "a lively union" of all the South American nations with Argentina as its center.[50]

A day later, Oshima is reporting to Tokyo that Germany's campaign in Russia "seems to have bogged down somewhat . . . [because of the problems of] supply and reinforcements from the rear to the whole line. [But] everything is still going according to plan; no concern need be felt for future operations, and, before winter sets in, the entire Caucasus will be captured." Meanwhile, the Germans are trying to get one hundred thousand tons of French shipping to carry supplies in the Black Sea.[51]

It's a long road that has no turning, the Irish are fond of saying. But on the last day of September 1942 the Allied intelligence experts receive the first major hint that not everything is perfect between Japan and Germany.

One can almost feel the sigh of relief issued by the people of McCormack's staff as they staple this Magic Summary together. Oshima is now telling Tokyo that there is even more to his conversation with Ribbentrop of September 17, and it's about Japan's breaking the promise she made in July to supply Germany with 164,000 kilo tons of edible fats. Germany is so desperate for this material she is ready to send ten tankers to the Far East to pick up the products.

Oshima reports that Ribbentrop told him: "We Germans must have just as much cocoa oil and palm oil as you can let us have. I know that you Japanese may suffer some in the process, but at all odds we must have what we have already agreed on."[52]

Apparently the same point has also been made by German vice-minister Wiehl of Foreign Affairs, who is quoted as telling Oshima's staff: "We must have edible fats for this winter and if you Japanese don't let us have them, I do not see what we will do. . . . Our people

---

50. SRS 729, 28 September 1942.
51. SRS 730, 29 September 1942.
52. SRS 731, 30 September 1942.

will just have to go without. They will suffer in body and soul as a result. The bad effect will be extreme. . . . You promised us 164,000 tons some time ago . . . and judging from the fact that you Japanese exported a total of about 100,000 tons of coconut oil and palm oil from your occupied countries in 1937–1938, we feel justified in believing that you can accommodate us."[53]

The new Japanese Foreign Minister, Tani, replies to Oshima that, yes, there have been some supply problems, but 12,000 kilo tons of palm oil will be shipped at the end of October "as stipulated."[54]

This Magic Summary has a special intelligence note added to it, saying: "Germany has for some time looked to Japan to supply some of her edible fats. Earlier messages show that in June, 1941, Japan was purchasing such commodities on behalf of the Germans and shipping them to Germany via the Trans-Siberian Railway. . . . The statements by von Ribbentrop and Wiehl . . . are by far the most urgent pleas for these items that Germany has yet made, so far as our material discloses. They may . . . indicate some change in the situation since last April. At that time an O.S.S. survey stated that the edible fats situation was 'particularly tight,' but that Germany was thought to have a sufficient supply to fill the ration requirements from the crop year 1942–3."[55]

The German whining is obviously music to Washington's ears. If the home front is hurting to such an extent, what must the situation be for the German soldiers in Russia?

The next day's Magic Summary shows that Japan's own economy is also feeling the pinch. The German ambassador to Tokyo, Ott, reports that while the problems of edible fats appears to have been resolved for the moment, the Japanese ministries of the Interior and Finance have announced drastic changes of policy for the local prefecture budgets for the coming year. For example, the increasing lack of capital, material and labor is to be considered before every new outlay; current expenditures are to be examined to see if they can be canceled or postponed. As for new outlays, they will only be authorized if they prove necessary for air protection and other defense measures, the increase of production or "the nourishment and health of the Axis peoples." Meanwhile, local taxes will not be increased because of the increased tax demands of the central government.

The financial strains of continuing global conflict on the economies

---

53. Ibid.
54. Ibid.
55. Ibid.

of Germany and Japan now indicate a major turning point in the struggle more clearly than events on the battlefield. The memo written by McCormack to Carter Clarke proves that the Diplomatic Summaries are far more important than reported to date. Why? Because Magic gives the Allied leaders hope at the darkest hours of the war.

It also gives courage to Allied generals to fight and win when they might not have pressed their attacks, or defended their ground, more forcefully.

And, in 1943, when the all-important issue of landing troops in France appears impossible to many, Magic helps British-American strategists to begin their planning to destroy Germany and capture Berlin.

4

ow swiftly turns the tide of war when an aggressor loses the early advantages gained by surprise attacks and secrecy.

The events of 1943, a year historians have called the year of plans and planners, prove this conclusively. That January, only thirteen months after Pearl Harbor, President Roosevelt and Prime Minister Churchill meet in Casablanca, where they vow to kill the enemy by the millions and propose a toast to a previously unthinkable concept: the unconditional surrender of the Axis powers.

For those who did not know that England and America have broken the enemies' most secret codes and ciphers, the policy of unconditional surrender, declared at this time, does not appear rational. It fails to differentiate between Hitler and the German people. This leads many American soldiers, especially those who remember the bloodbath of our Civil War, to believe that a threat of unconditional surrender can only increase the willingness of the German population to fight to the bitter end. It also creates a tailor-made opportunity for Nazi propaganda minister Goebbels. He immediately begins a campaign to portray the German soldiery as being heroic knights on a holy crusade against Bolshevism. More seriously, the Roosevelt-Churchill ultimatum destroys the will of several factions inside Germany that are planning to assassinate and replace Hitler.

Nor did anyone at this moment in history appear to give deep consideration about what the term *unconditional surrender* might mean to Japan where the emperor occupies a hallowed position and can *never* be allowed to lose face. As it will turn out, the problem that arises in conjunction with this matter two and a half years later probably costs the lives of several hundred thousand Japanese.

But it can also be argued that the dreams of Germany and Japan for world conquest as revealed by the latest Magic Summaries, which patently called for the disintegration of the nations and governments of the world as they existed up to 1943, left Roosevelt and Churchill little choice. Besides the words *unconditional surrender* will sound good in the headlines. And only Roosevelt and Churchill know the "Magic" ace they are holding as a hole card.

Other major decisions are made at Casablanca: It is reaffirmed that the destruction of Hitler and Germany will be the primary order of business for the Allies. The defeat of Japan will be secondary. It is agreed that Sicily will be invaded in the coming summer (Operation HUSKY). There will also be a major invasion of Burma (Operation ANAKIM), aimed at reopening the vital Burma Road that used to carry the vital supplies necessary to keep the Nationalist Chinese forces of Chiang Kai-shek fighting against the Japanese. A round-the-clock bombing of Germany (Operation POINT BLANK) will be initiated. Lastly the Battle of the North Atlantic will be stressed. Supplies must be provided Russia, despite the fact that German U-boats sank an incredible 720,000 tons of Allied shipping in the month of November.

Meanwhile, in Russia, the German siege of Leningrad is being lifted. At Stalingrad the Russians are on the verge of annihilating the German Sixth Army.

In China, Britain and America rebuild their relationship with the Nationalist government by declaring the old treaties with China, with their extremely favorable terms to the West, null and void.

In New Guinea, the first Allied venture of American and Australian troops against the Japanese is proving successful. At Guadalcanal, the U.S. Marines, now supported by the U.S. Army, are about to secure the island and end the bloody battle.

Next, the Pacific theater becomes the subject of discussion in March 1943 during a conference in Washington. Orders are cut for General MacArthur's South-West Pacific Command to make its first so-called "stepping-stone advance" in the new Pacific war. The plan is for an attack on New Britain from New Guinea while Admiral Halsey seizes the Solomon Islands.

In May, Roosevelt is hosting Churchill in the White House at a conference known as TRIDENT. Here it is agreed that the invasion of Europe will be postponed at least a year, until May 1944. During the interim, the invasion of Sicily will be carried out as planned. Hopefully this maneuver will tie down a large number of German divisions in Italy. In fact, Italy may even be induced to quit the war, an interesting concept that antagonizes Stalin, who wants a second-front invasion of

Europe. The two Western leaders reaffirm the plan to bomb Germany by stepping up the intensity of the raids. Lastly, the Americans and the British reach agreement on making an atomic bomb.

In August, the Combined Chiefs of Staff (American and British), convene in Quebec, Canada, for the QUADRANT Conference. They agree to change the code name for the invasion of Europe to OVERLORD and set a date for it: May 1944. It is agreed that the preliminary planning for OVERLORD will be done by a British group whose leader will be known as COSSAC (Chief of Staff Supreme Allied Command) and is initially led by British lieutenant general Sir Frederick Morgan. He will also draw up plans for a simultaneous invasion of southern France somewhere on the Mediterranean coast. This will be Operation ANVIL. As we will see, this preliminary planning, done by the British, will dramatically affect the future zones of occupation in Europe after hostilities end and create extremely hard feelings between the British and the Americans.

A new South-East Asia Command (SEAC) will also be created and placed under the leadership of Adm. Lord Louis Mountbatten. The Combined Chiefs will also recognize the Committee for the National Liberation of France, under the leadership of Generals Charles de Gaulle and Giraud.

Meantime, Sicily has been successfully invaded and captured. As predicted, the Italian government of Marshal Badoglio is making contact with the British and the Americans about the possibility of an armistice.

In the Aleutian Islands, American forces are starting to reoccupy the territory lost earlier to the Japanese, while in the south, plans are being made to bypass Rabaul for a new series of attacks in the Central Pacific.

In October 1943, America agrees to the Third London Protocol and promises to furnish aid to the Russians until the end of June 1944. Ferocious German U-boat attacks against the Allied convoys on the Murmansk run cause these convoys to be suspended in March 1943 until that November. (More than 535,000 tons of Allied shipping went to the bottom that March.) So, to fulfill this promise, America will provide 2.7 million tons of aid via Soviet ports on the Pacific and 2.4 million tons via Persia. In other words, by maintaining neutrality with Russia, Japan is allowing more than 50 percent of the American aid used to defeat Germany to reach Russia via Soviet ports in the Pacific. Talk about the mysteries of the Orient . . .

In November, Churchill and Roosevelt meet again, this time in

Cairo under the code name of SEXTANT. Their discussions concern the new offensives scheduled for Burma and a future strategy for the Balkans and Italy. More important, the two men prepare for Roosevelt's first meeting with Stalin, which will be held at Tehran, Iran, at the end of the month. It will be a first for Stalin, too. He will travel outside the Soviet Union for the first time since 1917 and the Bolshevik Revolution. At the meeting, code-named EUREKA, Churchill tells Stalin about the Anglo-American plans for the invasion in the coming spring or summer. Stalin questions the Anglo-American commitment to the invasion, and Churchill tells him that, assuming the German fighter-plane forces are reduced in strength, only twelve full-strength German divisions remain in France and the Low Countries, and only fifteen other full-strength German divisions can be shifted to the invasion scene within sixty days of the landings, that "it will be our stern duty to hurl across the Channel every sinew of our strength." In other words, if the Russians slacken their efforts, the invasion will not take place.

It is also agreed at Tehran that every effort will be made to supply the partisans fighting the Germans in Yugoslavia. (The feuding between the Croats and the Serbs will later come to haunt the world fifty years after the war.)

There are also tentative agreements reached about the postwar boundaries between Russia and Poland. They will be pushed westward after the war. Also there will be a postwar partitioning of Germany. It is here that the arguments about the "sellout" of Poland begin.

Stalin also tells Roosevelt and Churchill that Russia will join the war against Japan "the moment Germany was defeated." According to British historian Martin Gilbert, Churchill orders his British Chiefs of Staff to keep the "momentous decision" absolutely secret, so secret in fact that it is "not recorded even in the secret record of the Tehran talks."[1]

After Tehran, Churchill and Roosevelt reconvene SEXTANT at Cairo in the first week of December. They agree to give the invasion (now code-named OVERLORD) and the invasion of southern France via the Mediterranean the top priority. To stabilize the Balkans, it is agreed that efforts will be made to see if Turkey can be talked into joining the Allied cause.

---

1. *The Second World War: A Complete History* by Martin Gilbert (New York: Henry Holt and Company, 1989), 478. In this brilliant work, Gilbert notes that at Tehran the Americans and British fail to tell Stalin about the latest developments concerning the atomic bomb: it can be carried by a B-29 bomber. Meanwhile, fifteen British atomic scientists are being sent to work with the Americans. In their number is the Soviet spy Klaus Fuchs.

It is here that Roosevelt lays the greatest burden of the war on General Marshall, who believed after the QUADRANT meeting in Quebec the past August that he would be given the plum of leading the Allied invasion of Europe. Now Roosevelt tells Marshall that, as the chief of staff, he is too important in his post in Washington for the President to allow him to give it up. Eisenhower will command the invasion and the attack through Europe.

It doesn't make any difference that Roosevelt's decision is the right one. The truth is that Roosevelt honestly needs Marshall; to change chiefs of staff at this point in the war could prove disastrous. The U.S. Congress has every faith in Marshall. The Congress trusts Marshall to carry out the war without engaging in partisan politics. The Congress does not trust Roosevelt in this regard. It is a tremendous compliment to the Chief of Staff. Nevertheless, Marshall's disappointment is almost heartbreaking to witness. No one needs to tell him that it was he who put Eisenhower in position, nor that should Eisenhower be victorious in Europe that he will become president and Marshall's name will be virtually forgotten.[2]

Overlooked in this year of planning, however, is a more material fact: the Americans don't yet know it, but long before D day, before the first Americans land on Normandy's beaches, they will be denied the zone of occupation in Germany their president, Roosevelt, seeks from the war. This will lead to terrible problems with England about the occupation of Berlin, and the "unconditional surrender" of Japan will be far more difficult to attain.

✖ ✖ ✖

That Roosevelt will never achieve the political goals he seeks regarding America's postwar zone of occupation in Germany is not foreseen by naive American military planners. True to their code, they are fighting to end aggression by the Axis powers. They do not view war as do the British, who believe war is a political action aimed at achieving a politically satisfactory peace. The American introduction to this philosophy begins at the Casablanca conference and the creation of SHAEF

---

2. Upon reviewing this manuscript, Robert T. Crowley wrote the author about how Eisenhower is depicted: "Central casting could not improve on the cautious, correct, obedient, dependable, disciplined fellow that Marshall put into exactly the right place." (Letter to the author, July 27, 1994.)

(Supreme Headquarters Allied Expeditionary Forces), and the naming of SHAEF's first chief of staff, Britain's Lt. Gen. Sir Frederick Morgan.

Morgan's primary assignment, as stated earlier, is to establish diversionary actions that will pin down German forces in Western Europe by threatening a cross-Channel invasion in 1943. His second assignment is to start planning for the actual invasion of Europe, Operation OVERLORD. Even more important, however, is his third job: plan for an Allied occupation of Europe in the event that Germany suddenly collapses.

This last task, code-named RANKIN, comes before the Combined Chiefs of Staff for the first time at their meeting in August 1943 at Quebec. The plan proposes specific postwar zones of occupation for Germany. Britain will occupy the northwestern zone. The Soviet will occupy the eastern zone. The Americans will occupy the southern zone. It is assumed that the zones will be the result of the culmination of a fighting advance. It is also understood by the American military that, if President Roosevelt will agree to this plan, the invasion of Europe will be easier to implement. Thus the original plan is agreed to by the U.S. military chiefs. Only later will they refer it to President Roosevelt for his approval. And that's when the fur begins to fly.

Although it is difficult to imagine that these plans for the postwar occupation of Europe were not discussed in their early stages by the Army with the civilian leadership, this is the case. In a memo dated November 10, 1943, from Maj. Gen. John H. Hildring, Chief of the Civil Affairs, to General Marshall, Hildring tells Marshall that "JCS [Joint Chiefs of Staff] has barred all civilian agencies from the early phases of civil affairs. It is unreasonable and impossible therefore in the event of a southern collapse [in Europe] to pass responsibility for relief and rehabilitation over to civilian agencies who are not present on the scene. . . . It is believed inadvisable to bother the President at this time."[3]

Despite the claims of many historians, the responsibility for the zones of occupation for postwar Germany was a British plan through and through. Conceived by Anthony Eden, polished by the Attlee Committee, promoted as the military concept of Morgan and called RANKIN A, B and C (hereafter simply called RANKIN), blessed by Churchill and

---

3. Rankin ABC 384 NW Europe (20 August 1943) Sec 1-C. This document, as were all U.S. Army papers that are cited in this work, was found by the author in the Archives in Alexandria, Virginia, back in the sixties. Since then the documents have been moved to a number of differing locations and pruned by the U.S. Army. Inquiries as to their present location should be directed to the National Archives, Washington, D.C.

the officers of his cabinet, it was pushed through the European Advisory Commission (EAC) by Sir William Strang. Later, Strang would write that he had the advantage over the Americans in these talks. They "had to telegraph for instructions to a remote and sometimes unsympathetic and uncomprehending government. . . . I had a further advantage in that the [British] Government had begun postwar planning in good time and in an orderly way."[4]

The British are running rings around the Americans. And the error committed by the U.S. Army in failing to inform the civilian authorities about potential postwar planning (or is it the error of the Roosevelt administration not to consider these issues sooner for itself?) is exposed when Roosevelt first learns about RANKIN.[5] This he does while en route to the Cairo conference aboard the battleship USS *Iowa* at 3 P.M. on November 19, 1943. The occasion is a meeting between the President and his Chiefs of Staff that is held in Admiral King's stateroom. The subject is brought up as the third topic to be discussed concerning the possibility that there might be an overall collapse of the German forces in Europe necessitating a rush forward to occupy Germany.[6]

From the outset it is obvious that Roosevelt is annoyed. One can almost feel the President's seething as he tells the Chiefs that RANKIN makes certain suppositions without saying what they really are. Of course Russia will agree to breaking up Germany after the war, the President declares. Speaking practically, he says, there should be three, and possibly five, German states after the war. Yes, America might accept the southern part of Germany as proposed by RANKIN—Baden, Wurtenburg (*sic*), Bavaria and everything south of the Rhine. On the other hand, we could take everything north and west of that area, including Hamburg, Hannover and Berlin, as a second state. A third state, that is the northeastern part, would contain Prussia, Pomerania and on south. In Roosevelt's view, these are the logical lines for splitting up Germany. There are certain factors that make this especially true. The first state is largely Roman Catholic. The second state is largely

---

4. *The Last Battle* by Cornelius Ryan (New York: Simon and Schuster, 1966), 153–54.

5. The Civil Affairs Division of the U.S. Army also committed another horrific error by failing to provide for access to Berlin by a corridor of land despite the pleas for same by the American ambassador to the EAC, John G. Winant. This resulted in the world crisis known as the Berlin Airlift.

6. ABC File 346 NW Europe (20 August 1943) Sec 1-C. Extract for minutes of meeting between President Roosevelt and the Chiefs of Staff. 19 November 1943. The paraphrase of this document is as close to the original as permitted.

Protestant. The religion of the northern state might best be called Prussianism.

Roosevelt believes that Stalin will agree to a division along these lines. The President also thinks that the Chiefs of Staff would want to make a European-wide "RANKIN" conform to such a division. Actually, he says, the British want the northwestern part of Germany and would like to see America take France and Germany south of the Moselle River. But America should not be concerned with reconstituting France, which is a British "baby." America is not popular in France at the moment.

The President continues saying that the British should occupy Luxembourg, France, Belgium, Baden, Bavaria, and Wurtenburg (*sic*). America should occupy northwest Germany where we can get our ships into such ports as Bremen and Hamburg, also Norway and Denmark. Our zone of occupation should go as far as Berlin, says the President. The Soviets can take the territory to the east. *But the U.S. should have Berlin.* (Emphasis added.)

Roosevelt is quick to spot that the British plan is for America to occupy the southern part of Germany. He is sure the British will deny America northwest Germany and Berlin. The President does not like the situation one bit.

Marshall tries to calm the discussion. The matter can be gone into again with the Combined Chiefs. He explains that the proposal before the President evolved from the concentration of American troops on the right-hand side of the axis of advance (the line of march) from England through Europe. The conceptions in RANKIN were based primarily on the military considerations of OVERLORD.

Admiral King points out that should the Germans collapse before the invasion, if the military is to follow the President's thinking, there would have to be a crossover of Allied forces. This would be particularly true if the invasion has taken place and the Allies had reached the line of the Seine River. (The planning for the invasion of Europe calls for the British to be on the left flank—the western, or English Channel, side of the advance—with the Americans on the right; King suggests that the two forces switch, or cross over, their axes of advance, which would be exceedingly difficult, if not impossible, assuming that the primary goal is to attack the Germans.)

Everything is based on the logistical reasoning for OVERLORD says Marshall. He appears to be somewhat at a loss for words as he watches the situation worsen.

King comes to Marshall's rescue. He points out there is a problem and it will have to be worked out. But the planning for OVERLORD is so far advanced at this point that it isn't practicable to accept any change in OVERLORD's deployment.

It all goes back to the ports in England says Marshall. There must be a scheme for disengaging OVERLORD at any stage of development in order to comply with the political considerations now being outlined by the President.

Roosevelt says it is his idea for our military to use as many troops as possible from America for the occupation of Germany. They can be shipped around the northern end of Scotland.

King says he believes the U.S. should have a special occupational army, under a particular command, earmarked for the occupation of Germany.

Marshall replies that the U.S. front-line troops moving on the right flank of OVERLORD should be the first ones shipped home.

Roosevelt says he thinks the divisions now in Africa, Sicily and Italy should be the first to come home. (The subject of a "points" system based on active-duty time apparently had not yet been clarified.)

The President then elaborates on the French. They are a political "headache." Their leader in exile, General de Gaulle, hopes to be only one mile behind Allied troops in taking over the French government. The President says he wants to get out of France and Italy as quickly as possible, letting the British and the French handle their problems together. As he sees it, there will definitely be a race for Berlin. He believes we may have to put our divisions into Berlin as soon as possible. He foresees a "railroad" invasion of Germany, with little or no fighting.

Marshall observes that it is most important to keep all the various commands in homogenous control. He assumes there will be no rolling stock for trains, so a RANKIN advance will have to be made by truck.

Speaking for the first time, Presidential Adviser Harry Hopkins suggests that the U.S. consider putting an airborne division into Berlin two hours after the collapse of Germany. (This idea will keep alive the idea of an airborne incursion of Berlin for the remainder of the war.)

The President then asks Admiral Leahy for his view of the occupation areas proposed by RANKIN.

From the State Department's point of view, says Leahy, we should get out of France as soon as possible. We should accept any difficulties this might entail. If we want to let de Gaulle have France, all well and good. However, whatever Allied troops there are in France when Germany surrenders will have to stay there and supervise any elections.

De Gaulle wants to start the French government right away. There may be civil war. The British should clear up this matter. Meanwhile, it would be much easier for the U.S. to handle conditions in Germany. The Germans are easier to handle than would be the French, especially under the chaotic conditions one could expect in France.

Roosevelt says that he foresees an American occupation force of about 1 million troops for Germany. He then expands on the policy of "quarantine." The big four of the United Nations could, by their police power, if necessary maintain order in Europe by the "quarantine" method. . . .

Marshall asks Roosevelt how long would it be necessary to keep one million men in Europe as an occupation force.

Says Roosevelt, at least one year, maybe two. . . . (The American forces assigned to NATO for the next fifty years will actually average around three hundred thousand.) If we take the RANKIN paper proposed by COSSAC, the British will undercut us in every move we make in the southern zone now proposed for the U.S. It is quite evident, Roosevelt declares, that British political considerations were behind the proposals in this RANKIN paper.

Again Marshall tries to argue that the occupation zones work out logically. There will be less entanglement of forces, supply lines will be shorter and more direct.

Admiral King ends the discussion saying that it's imperative to plan for the operations necessary in order to switch to the occupation area proposed by the President. The discussion is ended.

What no one has considered, however, is the reason why the British want to control northwestern Germany. It isn't so much a desire for territory as it is of fear that the Russian Army will reach the English Channel, either before the Anglo-Americans drive through France, or by attacking through the Anglo-American lines, thereby becoming a new and totally dangerous threat to England in the years to come. The British believe the American president is naive about Stalin's true motives, the American people themselves uneducated about the realities of international Communism. Once again Great Britain might have to stand alone, against a more terrifying enemy than Hitler.[7]

---

7. Confidential military sources told the author that so great was the fear that the Russians might continue attacking westward in Europe, and not stop at any proscribed line of demarcation such as a boundary of occupation, or even the Elbe River, that, in April, 1945, captured German units were being reformed and prepared by the Anglo-American forces to stop any further Soviet advance. The author has not been able to document these statements, made by officers of high rank, and can only report them as unsubstantiated comments. But given the

Roosevelt apparently does not agree with the British. It is evident from his attitude that he has no fear of Stalin or the threat of international Communism. But others in the Roosevelt administration are aware of Stalin's game plan. Even without knowing about the breaking of the Enigma and Purple codes, William C. Bullit, who had been sent by Roosevelt to be America's first ambassador to the Soviet Union in 1933, warns the President in three lengthy letters during 1943 that Stalin was not to be trusted.[8]

Reading these letters fifty years after they were written sends chills up and down one's spine. Said Bullit:

... The extraordinary valor with which the peoples of the Soviet Union have fought against the Nazis has rendered the Russians so popular in both the United States and Great Britain that all possible virtues are being attributed to the Soviet Government, and both basic Russian Nationalistic policy and the Soviet Communist policy are being overlooked. . . . The reality is that the Soviet Union, up to the present time, has been a totalitarian dictatorship in which there has been no freedom of speech, no freedom of the press, and a travesty of freedom of religion; in which there has been universal fear of the O.G.P.U. and Freedom from Want has been subordinated always to the policy of guns instead of butter.

Bullit lists Stalin's future goals: the annexation of Bessarabia, Bukonina and the Carpathians, giving Russia access to the Hungarian plain and southern Poland; the annexation of eastern Poland, plus Lithuania, Latvia, Estonia; to set up Soviet-controlled governments in Yugoslavia and Czechoslovakia; to have the French Communists dominate a de Gaulle government; to make Germany a Communist nation; to eventually reduce Poland to the status of a Soviet republic; lastly, to control the Bosporus, the Dardanelles and northern Iran.

The accuracy of Bullit's predictions is astounding. In analyzing Bullit's messages to President Roosevelt, George F. Kennan declares:

---

statements made to the Combined Chiefs by England's Sir John Dill and Air Marshal Welsh in 1944, which are quoted later on in this work, the British obviously possessed a more pessimistic view of future Soviet intentions than did Roosevelt and others in his administration.

8. *For the President: Personal and Secret—Correspondence between Franklin D. Roosevelt and William C. Bullit,* edited by Orville H. Bullit, with an introduction by George F. Kennan (Boston: Houghton Mifflin Company, 1972). This material was graciously made available to the author by Orville H. Bullit, who is the husband of the author's first cousin Laura Lee of Chestnut Hill, Pennsylvania.

"This letter, supplemented by further and shorter communications sent in May and August that year [1943], had no counterpart, so far as this writer is aware, as a warning of that date to the American President of the effective division of Europe which would ensue if the war continued to be pursued on the basis of concepts then prevailing. . . . It deserves a place among the major historical documents of the time.''[9]

As events will prove, however, Roosevelt ignores Bullit's reports. In commenting on the President's letters back to Bullit, in which Roosevelt avoids "every serious subject" that Bullit raised, Kennan says: "One . . . comes away confirmed in the suspicion that to the extent Franklin Roosevelt had qualities fitting him for the great responsibilities he bore over those years of wartime leadership, these were primarily qualities of temperament, not of intellect.''

Fortunately, if the President and certain members of his entourage are being obtuse about the future of American policy vis-à-vis Russia in Europe and the Far East, as we will see, Marshall, Stimson and Eisenhower will quickly become more realistic in terms of what has to be accomplished by American power, and just how far that power can be stretched to prevent a worldwide spread of Communism.

Perhaps that is why there appears to be some ambivalence among historians about the significance of Roosevelt's telling his Joint Chiefs that after the war he wants America to occupy northwest Germany. These historians have never worked in the White House, where a president's wish is, in reality, taken as a command. Moreover, imagine the embarrassment of the Joint Chiefs. Roosevelt has caught them being suckered by the British. The President had not been properly informed about their planning. And when he was told, he immediately said the plans should be changed. What apparently had been a logical discussion with the British was becoming a major policy fiasco. At this time the British are in charge of SHAEF'S planning, the American commander of OVERLORD has not yet been named, and suddenly the President is saying how he wants Germany to be carved up after the war. For the first time the President is giving his military chiefs their marching orders about how to end the war in Europe.

The extent of the problem can be seen in the reaction to demands Roosevelt makes. On December 2, 1943, as the Tehran conference is closing, the Assistant Secretary of War, John J. McCloy, prepares a memo for General Marshall in which McCloy says that "I have seen JCS577/3 . . . the substance of which is a recommendation that we oc-

---

9. Ibid.

cupy the northern area of Europe rather than the southern. I anticipate considerable opposition from the British to this recommendation. The British have had a long economic affiliation with this northern area and Winant [the American ambassador to London] tells me that the plan was brought out after consultation with their political and economic people. I do not know to what extent the President will adhere to the occupation of the northern areas in the face of heavy English opposition. . . . I do not know that it is worth the big fight. . . .'' (The following is added to the memo in McCloy's handwriting: ''I forgot to add that Secretary [of State Cordell] Hull has called [to say] that from a State Department point of view he had no preference as between the northern and southern areas.''[10] In other words, staffers in the office of the Secretary of War, and even the Secretary of State himself, do not comprehend the British reasoning in the matter of how best to create the new, postwar Germany.

The U.S. Chiefs of Staff next propose a revision of the spheres of occupation along the lines discussed with Roosevelt. But according to a memo from Maj. Gen. R. W. Barker for the Chief of Staff to the Supreme Commander (Designate), which is Eisenhower, and who is just getting his feet wet in his new job, ''the British Chiefs of Staff feel that, unless the reasons prompting the U.S. proposal are of overriding importance, the difficulties implementing it are such that it should no longer be proceeded with. . . . I therefore strongly recommend that the existing allotment of spheres should stand unless the circumstances described above permit replanning.''[11]

General Eisenhower, the newly appointed supreme commander, assumes command of his new posting in London on January 14, 1944. The authority previously vested in General Morgan is transferred to the American. But Eisenhower is too new on scene to prevent or influence the first formal meeting of the EAC, held the following day, at which Morgan's plan for RANKIN is presented to American ambassador Winant and the Soviet envoy, Fedor Gusev.

On February 4, 1944, at the 144th meeting of the Combined Chiefs of Staff, Admiral Leahy reopens the discussion of RANKIN, which had been listed as item six on the agenda.[12] According to King, the matter of zones of occupation is now beyond the cognizance of the U.S. Chiefs

---

10. Rankin ABC 384 NW Europe (20 August 1943) Sec 1-C.
11. ABC 38 NW Europe (30 August 1943) Sec 1-A. Memo dated 7 January 1944.
12. 384 NW Europe (20 August 1943) Sec 1-B. Extract from minutes. CCS 144th Meeting, 4 February 1944, Item 6. Subject: Operation "RANKIN" (C.C.S. 320/8, 320/9 and 320/10).

of Staff. They agreed that, from a military point of view, a changeover from the spheres of responsibility as planned by COSSAC was feasible. A decision on this matter will have to be taken at a higher level.

Ever the diplomat, England's Sir John Dill says that COSSAC's proposals had been noted at QUADRANT. A reversal had been suggested at SEXTANT. COSSAC had now reviewed matters and declared a changeover "was not possible. COSSAC had planned on what had seemed to him a logical military basis. It was the natural British desire to control the Baltic and the North Sea bases and it further seemed natural that the U.S. forces should occupy France, with which country the U.S. had been in the friendliest relations and the closest touch. . . . There were no good military grounds for reversing COSSAC's plans. . . . The British would be equipping the Dutch army, the U.S. were equipping the French armed forces."

England's Air Marshal Welsh says: "He felt it necessary to consider what was the object of the occupation of Germany. Was it merely to keep the peace for a limited period of time or to secure ourselves in the future? Plans ought to be made to push out defenses and aircraft warning systems as far to the east as possible in northwest Europe, which, indeed, was the essential line of approach to the United Kingdom. If one considered the possibilities of a future war, there seemed to be every reason why the British sphere should include northwest Europe in order to assist in making the necessary defensive preparations."

This statement by Welsh is probably the earliest official pronouncement on record saying that the British fear the possibility of a postwar attack from the east by the Soviet Union. It may also be one of the first official statements of policy considerations that will lead to the formation of NATO and the concept of containing the expansion of the Soviet Union.

Where Roosevelt had told his Joint Chiefs that he foresaw an American army of occupation in Germany for a number of years, Admiral Leahy now tells the Combined Chiefs that "he, personally, hopes that the U.S. forces in Europe would be withdrawn at the earliest possible date consistent with the stabilization of the peace . . . as early as possible after the defeat of Germany. . . . Early withdrawal would be facilitated if [the Americans] were occupying northwest Germany rather than Austria and the Balkans, in which the U.S. has no interest and where they might find themselves involved for a longer period."

One can almost hear the gentle sarcasm in Air Marshal Welsh's voice as he replies "that an early withdrawal of U.S. forces made it even more necessary for the occupation of the essential areas of north-west Europe to be undertaken by the British.''

To this Leahy says he will prepare a dispatch for the President to send to the Prime Minister dealing with the subject. Sir John Dill agrees that this is the most satisfactory solution.

There is an ''action taken'' note at the end of the discussion: ''A. Agreed that this matter was now beyond the cognizance of the Combined Chiefs of Staff and would be referred to a higher level for decision; B. Took note that Admiral Leahy would undertake to pre-pare a message for the President to send to the Prime Minister on this subject.''

Within a week, Eisenhower cables Marshall that, as the established new head of SHAEF, he is ready to reply to the President's wishes. The cable carries a special notation saying that upon decipherment the code clerk is to place the message in a double-sealed envelope and deliver it personally to the Secretary of the General Staff. In the mes-sage Eisenhower tells Marshall that he has examined all the implica-tions of the OVERLORD plan versus the various versions of the RANKIN plan in connection with the related spheres of British and American activity. While you can't separate OVERLORD from RANKIN, he believes that OVERLORD is bound to develop at least into a phase of RANKIN. If the decision is made on a higher political level to switch the British and American spheres of responsibility, Eisenhower is certain there won't be any trouble in switching the American and British forces after the situation stabilizes to allow the necessary logistical moves. The cable ends by saying that if Marshall wishes to, he can transmit Eisen-hower's feelings to the President.[13]

What Eisenhower is really saying is that anything is possible. Dur-ing an advance through Europe, the British and Americans can switch over their axes of advance, even though the British maintain that this is not feasible. But it is going to take a decision ''on a higher political level'' than Eisenhower's being commander of SHAEF for the change-over to be made. In other words, if the order isn't put in writing by the President, Eisenhower isn't going to carry the can by himself. The General is announcing himself as a true master of political games.

No matter. By the Army's failing to plan properly (and one must ask, how could the Army plan properly in the light of Roosevelt's pro-Soviet stance?), by virtue of the administration's misunderstanding of

---

13. From the personal file of Gen. W. B. Smith, SHAEF. Message No. B-142. 111215A February 1944.

the nature of the peace to come, the Americans will never recover the initiative on this issue. There will be more bitter arguments with the British about the zones of occupation. But, at this time, the deed is done. Nothing can change it. And this will affect the way the war ends in Europe and the way postwar American foreign aid is given to Europe, but restricted vis-à-vis England.

✖ ✖ ✖

Roosevelt understands the meaning of Eisenhower's cable to Marshall. Within a few days the President rallies his arguments and, on February 22, 1944, sends a memo to the Acting Secretary of State in which his first words are "I disagree with the British proposal of boundaries which would go into effect in Germany after their surrender or after fighting has stopped."[14]

The President goes on to make seven points:

"**1.** I do not want the United States to have the post-war burden of reconstituting France, Italy and the Balkans. . . . [The words are underlined in the original.]

"**2.** . . . Our principal object is . . . to take part in eliminating Germany as a possible and even probable cause of a third World War. . . .

"**3.** Various points have been raised about the difficulties of transferring [crossing over] troops . . . what is called a 'leap frog.' The objections are specious. . . .

"**4.** I have had to consider also the ease of maintaining American troops in some part of Germany. . . . The United States should use the ports of northern Germany—Hamburg and Bremen—and the ports of the Netherlands for this. . . .

"**5.** . . . I think the American policy should be to occupy northwest Germany, the British occupying the area from the Rhine south, and also being responsible for the policing of France and Italy, if this should become necessary.

"**6.** In regard to the long range security of Britain against Germany, this is not a part of the first occupation. The

---

14. ABC 384 NW Europe (20 August 1943) Sec 1-B. Memorandum for the Acting Secretary of State from the White House. 22 February 1944. WS 82.

British will have plenty of time to work that out. . . .
The Americans by that time will be only too glad to
retire all their military forces from Europe.

"**7.** If anything further is needed to justify this disagreement
with the British lines of demarcation, I can only add the
political considerations in the United States <u>makes my
decision conclusive.</u>

"You might speak to me about this if the above is not wholly
clear."

Initialed simply "F.D.R.," the memo has to be a bombshell for
the State Department. The final negotiations for the occupation zones
of Germany are being hammered out in London by Ambassador Winant. Secretary Hull's previous position as outlined by John J. McCloy
was the opposite of the President's desires, and now the President is
telling the State Department to get the agreement he wants. There is a
major misconception in Roosevelt's memo, however. The President still
doesn't understand that because Germany will be partitioned after the
war, the British are not so worried about Germany starting another war
as they are afraid of the Russians.

In another unusual twist, the President's memo is the last communication of its type that can be found in the Army's files. Perhaps
this is because Roosevelt has other things on his mind: such as winning
a fourth term of office in the upcoming 1944 elections.

According to the records of the Working Security Committee,[15]
the War Department transmits a copy of the revised American proposal
regarding zones of occupation (CCS 320/4), dated February 25, 1944,
to Ambassador Winant in London for negotiations with the European
Advisory Commission (EAC). But Winant does not present these views
to the EAC, telling the State Department he is giving his own views
to George F. Kennan, the counselor of the American delegation to the
EAC, who is returning to Washington. On April 5, these views are
transmitted to the War Department, along with the news that Kennan
had discussed the matter with the President, and "that the President
had expressed himself as being favorably inclined to an acceptance of
the western border of the Russian zone of occupation as proposed
by the British and Russian Delegations."

The War Department notes these instructions and asks the Work-

---

15. ABC 384 NW Europe (20 August 1943) Sec 1-B. WS-134. 13 April 1944. Zones of Occupation.

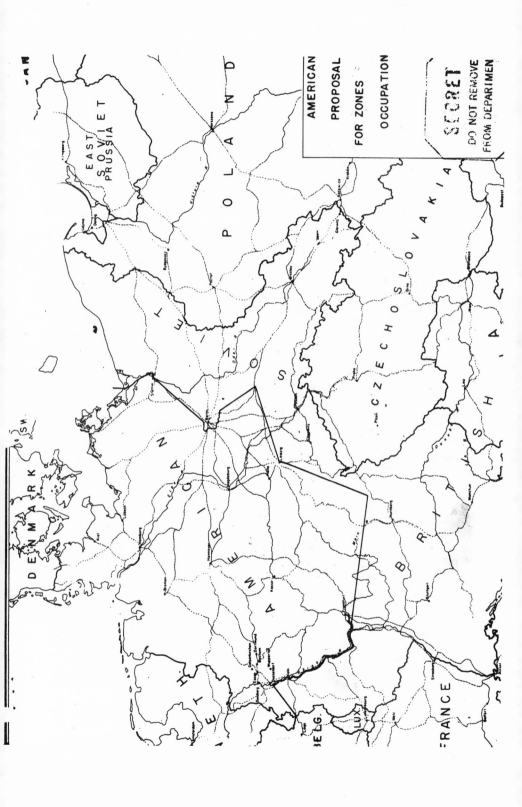

AMERICAN

PROPOSAL

FOR ZONES

OCCUPATION

SECRET

DO NOT REMOVE
FROM DEPARTMEN

ing Security Committee to prepare new instructions for Ambassador Winant. This is done. Winant is told that he may concur that the boundaries of the Soviet zone of occupation be defined as proposed by the Soviet Union. He may also concur to the boundary between the northwestern zone and the southern zone as defined by the British delegation. However, "with respect to the zones to be occupied by the U.K. and the U.S., Ambassador Winant should be instructed to adhere to the directives which were given him . . . setting forth the decision of the President that American forces should occupy the northwestern zone [which the British want for themselves]." (See the map of the proposed American zone of occupation on page 93.)

By now it is May 1944, and only a month before the invasion of Normandy. The planners are working overtime at SHAEF, defining the goals of the Supreme Commander and his choice of objectives should the invasion prove successful.[16] The most important task for the combined British-American forces is to "undertake operations aimed at the heart of Germany and the destruction of her armed forces."

The "heart of Germany" is defined, under the subheading of "choice of objective," as being "the occupation of the vitally important economic and political center of Berlin . . . is clearly our ultimate goal; but it is too far east to be the objective of a campaign in the West. A study of the economic and political factors shows that the only area in the West of vital economic importance to Germany is the Ruhr. If she were to lose the Ruhr, and consequently France and Belgium, she would lose 65 percent of her present total production of crude steel and 56 percent of the present production of coal. . . . An attack aimed at the Ruhr is likely to give us every chance of bringing to battle and destroy the Main German Armed Forces."

All well and good. But the SHAEF planners are being overly pessimistic. The maps they now prepare for the Anglo-American advance on the Ruhr show that the Allied forces will barely reach the German border near Aachen by D day plus 330 days. In reality, the war in Europe will have ended before then. Roosevelt will be dead, and the American army will, on its own initiative, establish the ground rules for halting the conflict.

---

16. Post Overlord Planning 381, vol 1. Planning Staff (SHAEF) course of action after capturing Lodgement Area (post invasion)—Main objective and axis of advance.

5

One of the questions that has worried this writer for many years was why, in November of 1943, did Roosevelt and Marshall appear to have such conflicting points of view about the British and American zones of occupation and what this might mean for postwar Europe?

The answer must have a foundation of official documentation. And so one carefully sifts through more than a million pages of documents, puts the pertinent pages in chronological order, arranges them so they can be read in approximately the same time frame as was done by the President and Marshall, and then lets the documents speak for themselves.

This historical "charting" allows one to arrive at a conclusion, perhaps not the one would expect, but a conclusion that appears logical. It is this: Roosevelt and Marshall were supposed to be reading the same Magic Summaries day in and day out, but both men read different things into, or out of, this vital intelligence. There are additional problems. Even as late as February 12, 1944, Marshall discovers that an unnamed officer on the White House staff is screening the "Brown Books," containing the Magic material, before it goes to the President. This officer marked "a very few portions for Admiral [William] Leahy's attention." And this meant that Leahy "very seldom" sent any of the material in to the President.

Marshall immediately puts an end to this chaotic structure. He immediately institutes a daily series of bound reports called the Black Book, highlighting the most important Magic material. Marshall also explains the significance of these reports to Roosevelt, who begins receiving the material every day. (Field Marshal Dill of the British Joint Staff Mission is also put on the distribution list in late June 1944.)[1]

---

1. *The Ultra-Magic Deals: And the Most Special Relationship, 1940–1946* by Bradley F. Smith,

There are other reasons why Marshall and Roosevelt view the war differently. To explain: Marshall is Army. He knows how difficult it is to create and train a huge fighting force and then get it across the Atlantic to fight an unrelenting foe—some 3,000 miles to Europe and 6,700 miles to Japan. Supply lines are difficult to maintain. One must listen carefully to one's allies and be mindful of their wishes and fears. One must also learn how the enemy thinks, understand his views of the world and what he is fighting for. Roosevelt, on the other hand, is a politician. In 1944, his greatest concerns are not about the fighting, but about electoral matters. He will need slightly more than a week in Texas and New Mexico when it comes to campaigning. And these two states are bigger than the combined land mass of France and Germany, which are the objects of the Allied invasion. According to the way the Magic Summaries read to a politician, the Allies have the war well in hand. But Marshall reads the words of a foe that is determined to fight to the death, willingly committing suicide if it will cost the lives of American soldiers and sailors.

Marshall also knows that America will need England as an ally after the war. But Roosevelt is thinking of something else. We know that Roosevelt went to Tehran hoping—nay, believing—that he alone could persuade Stalin to accept the Rooseveltian view of the world. But no one has ever put in writing Roosevelt's despair, assuming he had any, when he discovered that the murderous dictator would not convert to the President's point of view.

In early November 1942, for example, from Berlin, the Japanese ambassador, Baron Oshima, tells Tokyo for the first time the official news of the British victory at El Alamein. Oshima says that he was told by a confidential informant that "the British Army broke through a part of the German-Italian Army, which thereupon was actually compelled to retreat with a number of men being taken prisoner. . . . The present reverses are due to the numerical superiority of the English Air

---

(Novato, Calif.: Presidio Press, 1993), 186. This carefully documented work does not answer the question of why Magic material was being screened by an officer at the White House before being shown to the President, merely calling the Army's intelligence program full of "confusion and chaos." This writer questioned Robert T. Crowley on the point. Crowley said that as late as 1944, the Army believed there was an enemy agent in the White House, hence the censorship. Readers of the Clausen/Lee work, *Pearl Harbor: Final Judgement*, will recall that the Army also cut off the White House from all Magic material for several months prior to the Japanese attack for the same reason: it feared an enemy agent in the White House had access to this intelligence.

Force. . . . The German-Italian Army has not suffered a blow as claimed by the enemy propaganda.''[2]

The other important information in this particular Magic Summary deals with Japanese interference in Chilean and Argentinean affairs. Should anyone ever wish to write a novel about spying and espionage in South America, the Magic Summaries will provide startling background detail and authenticity to the proposed narrative.

Next, there is a four-day flurry of Japanese diplomatic traffic that relates to the American invasion of North Africa. On November 12, the analysts in McCormack's office report that ''it is the practice of the Japanese Foreign Minister to send out diplomatic circulars from time to time with the evident purpose of keeping the addressees posted on developments in parts of the world about which they would presumably have little information. On November 7 [it took five days to decipher this message], Foreign Minister Tani sent such a circular (from Tokyo) to Buenos Aires and various places in the Far East, containing his analysis of the 'latest situation in Europe.' ''[3]

> ''**1.** The Germans started a second attack on the Soviet, and at first it went well; but the lines spread out and supply became difficult. The Soviet forces put up such a splendid resistance that gradually the German drive lost impetus. Early in August it appeared as though Stalingrad would fall, but it still stands. Although Germany did bring down Nalchik, she has never reached the oil fields of Grozny. In the Leningrad-Moscow sector there is no change, and victory in this sector cannot be expected at least this year. Because of the snow and ice in the Caucasus, it would be utterly impossible to advance in that region this winter. Thus Germany has failed in her objective for this year in the Soviet. The fact that the Soviets show no sign of weakness and are exulting is an indication in their faith in victory has not been shattered.
>
> ''**2.** Rommel attacked the British on August 31 and ere long regained the positions from which he was driven. In the meantime, both armies have been trying to rally reinforcements and supplies, and late in October the British

---

2. SRS 770, 8 November 1942.
3. SRS 774–77, 12–15 November 1942.

made an attack, as a result of which the Germans are hard pressed.

"For several months England and the U.S. have been active in South Africa, and from the west coast of Africa they have been trying to establish a transportation route to Egypt, both by air and land. The landings of American soldiers on the coast of West Africa is something to which attention must be paid. In September, the British occupied Madagascar completely, and the spokesmen for both nations are proclaiming they will drive the Axis out of Africa and make it a point from which they can attack their enemies. This also is important when we consider India. . . .

"**3.** The neutral positions of Turkey, Spain and Portugal have not changed. . . . The fact that Germany did not come up with the expected successes on the eastern front and the losses the German forces have sustained are, it must be admitted, reflected in the neutral countries, and French cooperation with Germany may be jeopardized.

"**4.** Russia has been fighting the Germans for a year and a half. England and the U.S. have helped them scarcely at all. To be sure, they have raided Germany by air, but that is not enough to satisfy Stalin. Churchill visited him in August and explained that it would be impossible to establish a second front this year, but Stalin was unconvinced. In answer to questions from pressmen early in October, he said that a second front was a grave necessity, and that, in view of the aid Russia is giving the Allies, the least they could do would be to give more assistance in the way of a new front. Stalin was very much dissatisfied at that time. But since then the Germans have not done so well and the Stalin regime still stands. The Red Army has not been routed, nor does it appear that this will happen soon, if ever. . . . We still hear rumors of a separate peace between Berlin and Moscow. We do not believe them. . . . Winter is already at hand, and no great [German] drive can be undertaken. Hitler's reserves at home are dwindling. Even if he should try to make a separate peace with Russia, it is doubtful if the Russian people would accept it. To say that Stalin is so angry with England and the U.S. that he would make a separate peace with Germany is pure fantasy. . . .

"We believe that . . . Germany has apparently practically achieved her territorial ambitions, and that the destruction of the British Empire may not necessarily be Germany's final aim. The outbreak of the war of Greater East Asia and the participation of the U.S. therein not only made a compromise peace impossible, but, strange to say, caused the British as well as the German camp to entertain greater hopes of victory.

"There are rumors that the old Munich clique in England is gaining somewhat in popularity, but now that the U.S. is backing England, almost everyone in the [British] Empire declares that Nazi Germany must be knocked out. In short, we believe that there is not the slimmest chance that, as things now stand, the two nations will make peace."[4]

On the following day, the Magic Summary of November 13 discloses that Foreign Minister Tani has also sent out a message to Vichy, France, saying: "Extremely Urgent. Strictly Secret. The occupation of North Africa by the U.S. forces, if successful, may ultimately sway the final decision of all the neutral nations and have a decisive effect on the whole world picture. . . . Will you immediately go to Laval and with this in mind ask him what France intends to do; ask him whether or not he intends to stick to the Axis through thick and thin. Wire me back in detail what he answers. France has colonies and other interests in East Asia, and the way in which we treat her will be determined by whether or not she does the will of the Axis. If you wish, you may tell Laval so."[5]

This strong-armed threat by Japan was followed the next day with another cable from Tani to Buenos Aires in which he says: "This battle for North Africa—the way it is going—gives us no joy. Washington and London are sure to proclaim this attack as the second front and blatantly to declare that it is proceeding favorably for them. The U.S. will say that it has 'got the jump' on the Axis, and that, with a foothold in North Africa, they have strengthened the joint defense of the Americas and prevented their enemies from invading the new world. They will play this up in a big way, and this will have a terrific effect in the American states, particularly Argentina and Chile."[6]

---

4. Ibid.
5. Ibid.
6. Ibid.

Meanwhile Japanese minister Yamagata is reporting from Santiago, Chile, that because of the North African offensive, the U.S. ambassador has "greatly stimulated the activities of the anti-Nazi party," and the emergency meeting of the Chilean Congress, to discuss breaking off relations with the Axis, originally scheduled for November 17, has been moved up. Says Yamagata: "The situation can only be viewed as very dangerous."[7]

In Spain, the report to Tokyo says that the military are preparing along the Mediterranean and Atlantic coasts to meet an Allied invasion, and Spain is making preparations to capture Gibraltar and repel the Allies.[8]

The analysts on McCormack's staff in Washington discount the latter message from Spain saying that the bulletins provided by the Spanish on what is called the "TO" net in the past "have frequently proved inaccurate and at times wholly fabricated. For instance, one dated September 22 reported a lengthy after-dinner conversation between Secretary Hull and Spanish Ambassador Cardenas (September 25 Summary), but the State Department later informed us (the analysts) that Mr. Hull never dined with Cardenas, nor talked with him since he presented his credentials [in Washington]."[9]

The intelligence liaison between Spain and Tokyo throughout the war proved to be one of the most problematical in the Japanese network. Some of this was the result of disinformation sown by the Allies and swallowed by the Japanese agents in Spain. Furthermore, by its constant reports to Tokyo the Japanese embassy in Spain unwittingly blew the cover for numerous agents sent to the U.S. with credentials as diplomats or newsmen, allowing these agents to be rounded up and "turned." The Allies also used the Spanish link with Tokyo to check and see how various Allied deceptions were working.

On November 27, 1942, Japanese minister Sakamoto reports from Bern, Switzerland, to Tokyo that Renato Prunas, the Director General of the Europe-Asia Bureau of the Italian Foreign Office, has told him that the American landings in Africa have "strengthened Stalin's will to fight and, with the U.S. and England launched on their first real offensive, any talk of peace between Germany and Britain is utterly out of the question."[10]

---

7. Ibid.
8. Ibid.
9. Ibid.
10. SRS 789, 27 November 1942.

Meanwhile the Japanese have conducted a roundup of diplomatic sources to answer the question about whether or not Spain will stay neutral. (As one reads the list of names, one can see its value for Allied analysts and diplomats.) The names include:

Heyden Pynsek, Counselor to the German embassy in Spain

Mentone, Counselor of the Italian embassy in Spain

The German minister to Portugal

The Italian minister to Portugal

German foreign minister von Ribbentrop

The Chief of the Spanish Political Affairs Bureau

Portugal's Vice-Minister of Foreign Affairs

Nicolas Franco, the brother of Generalissimo Franco and Spanish ambassador to Portugal. He responds to Japan's query, saying: "Spain wants to avoid becoming embroiled in the war, but she has been attracted to the Axis camp and has territory to protect in North Africa. Therefore Spain is concentrating her attention on an attitude of nonbelligerency rather than neutrality."[11]

One cannot help but be struck by the self-interest of the many nations of Europe that have either been overrun by the Nazis or are aligned to them as "nonbelligerents." All of them have colonies at stake in other parts of the world that are threatened either by the Axis or the Allies. The fact that the home countries might be ruled at present by a German or Japanese army means less than the hope that they would be returned after the war. Self-interest never dies.

The following day, Minister Sakamoto sends another message from Bern to Tokyo about the possibility of Germany seeking a separate peace with Russia. The message is interesting, but the American analysis in Washington is more important.

Apparently Sakamoto has held a long conversation with the German undersecretary of foreign affairs, Weizaeker, who complained that "the Soviet war is an awful burden on us Germans. I am afraid we will have to give up and make some 'arrangements' pretty soon. Am I to understand that will be all right with you Japanese?"[12]

Sakamoto replies: "Well, you know our Empire has a new enemy now, the Anglo-Saxons. We rather wish you Germans would forget that Russian business and concentrate on our real foe."

To which Weizaeker says: "Well, that is all right with me, I suppose, but Chancellor Hitler says that, if German honor is to be main-

---

11. Ibid.
12. SRS 790, 28 November 1942.

tained, Russia has to be completely defeated. . . . Stalin, however has other ideas and so far has shown no sign of accommodating the Fuehrer.''

According to Colonel McCormack's analysts (hereafter simply called "the analysts"), this is the "first indication, in our [Magic] material, of any statement by a German official that Germany might consider a negotiated peace with Russia. . . . It seems quite likely that Weizaeker's remarks presage another bid for a Japanese attack on Russia. . . . If so, Weizaeker's understanding of Japanese psychology and strategy seems faulty. The Japanese government did its best to forestall the German-Russian war, has always thought it untimely and not in the interests of Japan, and the possibility of bringing about a negotiated peace has been discussed between Tokyo and Ambassador Sato in Kuibyshev [the location of the Japanese embassy in Russia]. *Sakamoto's remark about concentrating on our 'real foes' can be taken as a true description of Japanese strategy, the sole immediate objectives of which are the destruction of British and U.S. power in East Asia and the South Seas, and the wearing down of China by attrition.''* (Emphasis added.)

There doesn't appear to be much disagreement between the Japanese and Washington on the real reasons for World War II. One can only wonder what would have happened if Hitler had paid attention to the strategy proposed by Tokyo and joined hands between Europe and Asia.

Within the next week, there is a message from Ambassador Sato in Russia telling Tokyo that Soviet relations with the U.S. are improving.[13] And from Madrid, Minister Suma reports that the fall of Toulon to the Allies and the scuttling of the French fleet has made the French people antagonistic toward Germany. Premier Laval is even considering fighting against America and is quoted as saying: "Although France cannot bring herself to declare war on the U.S., if the enemy attacks us, we can defend ourselves and thus enter into a state of belligerency.''[14]

Also, for the first time, the Magic Summaries start carrying the news and results of Allied bombings on cities in the Far East such as Canton and Bangkok. These are targets that the Japanese were not prepared to defend against air attack.

13. SRS 792, 30 November 1942.
14. SRS 793, 1 December 1942.

On the first anniversary of Pearl Harbor, Tokyo sends out a summary of the war to its representatives in Russia, China, Manchuria, French Indochina, Thailand, Argentina and Chile. The analysts in Washington declare the Foreign Office message "interesting, because of its objective tone."[15]

Declares Tokyo: "Just at the time when Germany's second offensive against Russia was bogging down because of the Red Army's stubborn defense and because of the coming winter, the large-scale American and British offensive in French North Africa following well-laid plans is having a profound influence on the populace. The speedy and appropriate countermeasures which Germany and Italy have taken (reinforcing the Tunis area[16] and occupying France) appear to have somewhat saved the situation, but the enemy are continuing to send troops into North Africa and not only have they penetrated Tunis (the present German and Italian forces in Tunis are 30,000 while the British and American expeditionary force in French North Africa numbers 145,000) but Rommel's army retreating from Egypt has been pursued to the neighborhood of El Agheila by the British Eighth Army. Hence the situation in North Africa does not allow optimism.

"During the last half of November the Red Army has been launching vigorous counteroffensives in the southern and central areas around Stalingrad and the German Army seems to be falling back without pause. . . .

"While Russia retains the appearance of not recognizing the American-British invasion of North Africa as a second front, in their hearts they are well pleased, and American, British and Soviet relations are being further consolidated.

"No success can be anticipated from German and Italian schemes to win over Turkey, which will tend more and more to become pro-British. Moreover, the fact that Germany cannot seize Gibraltar at once is influencing Spain and Portugal more and more towards a policy of preserving neutrality. . . .

"Germany will probably continue to support Laval [in occupied France]. . . . The sinking of the French fleet and the dismemberment of the French Army, the last vestiges of France's sovereignty, have deeply shocked the French people . . . [their] antipathy toward Germany is be-

---

15. SRS 802, 10 December 1942.
16. Eisenhower has been criticized by British historians for not moving faster to secure this area. Author's note.

ing hardened. Accordingly it seems very doubtful whether Germany will get the cooperation from France which she expected. However, the French people have no spirit to revolt. . . .

". . . The Soviet Army is counterattacking strongly in the Rzhev and Veliki Luki areas northwest and west of Stalingrad, and one by one they are forcing the German positions, so that the German Army as a whole is being besieged. . . . The Russian counterattacks employed five times the numerical strength of the Germans. . . . In the Caucasus campaign also any further advance of the German Army will be impossible."

In making this cogent analysis of the war in North Africa and Russia, Tokyo fails to mention a single word about the war in the Pacific. Nor has there been any mention to date of the reverses of fortune to the Japanese fleet at the battle of Midway. The Japanese can be objective about the successes or failures of their ally Germany. Tokyo cannot, however, be objective about its own problems.

On December 11, Minister Sakamoto tells Tokyo that there has been considerable dissension within the ranks of the German Army leaders. According to the information gathered in Switzerland, the German generals had proposed making a major effort in Russia, but that they had also wanted to reserve enough force to meet a possible second front and strengthen Rommel to gain complete control of North Africa. Hitler, however, rejected these proposals.[17]

The German generals also wanted to capture Leningrad and Moscow in an all-out drive that would have annihilated the Russian forces. But Hitler had opposed this, too, and poured his main strength into the southern campaign. In October, von Bock had advised Imperial Headquarters against hurrying the Stalingrad campaign because of the heavy loss of troops that would result. For this he was removed from command. But his successor, Lt. Gen. Hermann Hoth, continued to give the same advice, even urging that Stalingrad "be evacuated" before the winter set in.

Meanwhile Chief of Staff Halder had been replaced by a general named Zeitzler because he "alone advocated a positive strategy."

What better news could Washington ask for. The debacle at Stalingrad is about to begin, and the Japanese are explaining in detail how the German general staff is unraveling and fighting amongst itself as disaster looms.

---

17. SRS 803, 11 December 1942.

✶ ✶ ✶

The diplomatic war for the hearts and minds of South America is continuing at an even more frantic pace.

In November 1942, the Argentinean government cracked down on the Axis diplomats, limiting the number of coded messages they could send each day. Now it is revealed that the Japanese fear that Chile will truly break relations with Japan. Minister Yamagata reports to Tokyo from Santiago that the Chilean minister of the interior, Raul Morales, has left for the U.S. carrying a "secret message from the President." Yamagata comments: "He will no doubt talk with the American authorities about getting munitions and industrial equipment. It is easy enough to see that his payment for the same will be a rupture of relations with the Axis."[18]

Next it is Chargé Kase reporting from Rome to Tokyo that the Italians "have undeniably been shaken from top to toe by the Allied landings in North Africa, the German and Italian retreat from Egypt, and the fierce bombing of northern Italian cities by British planes."[19]

The same day's Magic Summary reveals that Baron Oshima had held a four-hour meeting with Foreign Minister von Ribbentrop only forty-eight hours earlier. The analysis given Oshima by Ribbentrop is very favorable from the German point of view, and Oshima sends it to Tokyo without any critical comment.

Oshima's swallowing of Ribbentrop's falsehoods sparks a remarkable rebuttal from Tokyo within twenty-four hours. Foreign Minister Tani radios from Tokyo a strong rebuke and directly challenges "Oshima's optimism about the German military situation."[20]

Tani doesn't mince his words. One can almost sense his rage in his radiogram as he says: "As for Germany having succeeded in preparing herself for a long war by obtaining essential military materials, what about oil, as just one instance? All Germany has taken is Maikop [a small Soviet oil field]. I don't see how you can say she is so prepared.

"You say that Germany has weakened Russia. Well, what about Russia weakening Germany? . . . Russia still has plenty of soldiers and munitions plants. I think you would be very wrong if you imagined it

---

18. SRS 804, 12 December 1942.
19. SRS 808, 16 December 1942.
20. SRS 809, 17 December 1942.

impossible for the Soviets to come back with a swift blow, and that right soon. . . .

"Let the Germans take Grozny; let them take Tuapse; and let them take them this winter. Stalingrad hasn't fallen, has it? And the fact that the Germans were unable, with all their might, to take that city is an evil omen. You may say that Germany will head for the Near East after demilitarizing the Caucasus, but now that the U.S. has penetrated into North Africa, a new situation faces the Reich, and it is very doubtful if Germany can follow her preconceived plan of strategy; but even if she did, I think she would have slight chance of penetrating into the Far East. . . . However you view it, Germany cannot easily get into the Middle and Near East. . . .

"I believe Germany will put up a stiff fight for Tunis, . . . but if she doesn't [succeed], things will be bad. . . . If worst comes to worst, in order to stabilize the situation in Italy, German troops will have to take over there. . . .

"Now what we want is for Germany to get ready for a long war. We believe that we are justified in saying that gradually she is succeeding, but she is a long way from ready. She faces a much harder job than she did when the war first began, and she has a much longer road to tread than she thought she did. I hope that she will realize these things and get ready to expend her all in our common effort."

The significance of this Japanese message is that it demonstrates to military strategists that in the coming "year of Allied planning," the best thing that can be accomplished is first to drive the Axis out of North Africa, then invade Sicily, then invade Italy and pin down as many German divisions as possible. This will keep German reinforcements from being sent either to the Eastern Front or to defend the beaches of France against a cross-Channel invasion.

Japanese strategists are writing off their hopes of joining hands with the Germans in the Middle East and dividing the world. Tokyo doesn't see the Balkans, or Greece, as being important to the ultimate destruction of Germany. (This view is held only by the British.) Tokyo also sees the best way for the Allies to attack the weakest link of the Axis, Italy, and quickly knock her out of the war.

For those privileged to read the Magic Summaries, it is almost like being the coach of the New York Giants and being given the playbook of the San Francisco 49ers before a championship play-off. Yet this advantage also creates a unique problem for General Marshall. American troops are about to be committed in great numbers on the ground in Europe. Their commanders will have to be briefed about Magic and

Ultra. As will be shown later, the problem will be to get some of Marshall's top generals, not all of whom believe in intelligence or who are smart enough, in Marshall's view, to use intelligence properly.

According to Robert T. Crowley, coauthor of *The New KGB: Engine of Soviet Power* [21] and longtime expert in both military intelligence and the CIA, Marshall found his position distasteful.

"Magic posed Marshall with a terrible moral dilemma," says Crowley. "He was one of those rare men who thought people ought to tell the truth, and Magic drove him into situations where he had to obfuscate, equivocate, or leave the room. It was extraordinarily painful for him, especially with the people from the House and Senate who believed in his word."

The problem now facing Marshall says Crowley is that the Chief of Staff has a number of generals who have little experience or internal discipline regarding intelligence information. They are not tempered to intrigue as are their British counterparts. Via Colonel McCormack's staff, carefully selected young officers are assigned as special liaison officers to division, corps and army headquarters where they are taxed with the mission of persuading their respective generals to accept and act on "special intelligence," which alone the junior officer conveyed. The protection of the source of this information is vital, and in the main the liaison officers will be rewarded with the confidence of their generals. As we will see later, living in the interstices of an active unit will be awkward for the liaison officer who is compelled to disguise his true role within the unit. Later, the system will be restructured and the intelligence process accelerated to meet the increasing requirements of the senior combat commanders, who have come to understand and rely on this vital information.

One of the reasons Marshall can successfully impose this intelligence command structure upon Eisenhower and others is because the Chief of Staff is not a West Point "ring knocker." He is viewed by some as a modernist among medievalists. In sum, Marshall's integrity, intellect and fairness make him the most powerful influence in the American military.

Another of Marshall's great accomplishments is the adaptation of Henry Ford's concept of the assembly line. Marshall establishes Re-

---

21. *The New KGB: Engine of Soviet Power* by William R. Corson and Robert T. Crowley (New York: William Morrow & Co., 1985). This book was commissioned and edited by the author. The comments made by Crowley and quoted herein were made during the course of many conversations about this work. This particular conversation took place in Washington, April 16, 1993.

placement Training Centers (RTCs) throughout America. After induction and initial screening, inductees are sent to Infantry, Armor, Signal, Engineer, Air Corps, Medical, Supply, Transportation and other schools for seventeen or more weeks of training. The raw soldiers are schooled to be replacements for existing combat units and new units being formed in the continental U.S.

Meanwhile, replacement depots are also being established in Britain, North Africa and, later, in France and Italy. These "repel-depos" enable the Army to keep most combat units up to strength by the rapid replacement of casualties.

Marshall's vision also calls for the development of massive long-range logistical support systems capable of sustaining combat units with food, fuel, munitions and medical units on every front.

In the view of many, however, Marshall's greatest accomplishment is his remarkable ability to recognize the enormous value of the intercepted Japanese and German signals. To optimize this incredible intelligence advantage he selects a superior staff that can simultaneously defend and intelligently interpret the intercepts to the advantage of *all* the major American combat forces. Marshall is truly the man who makes Ultra and Magic work.[22]

There are many excellent books about the men and women involved in Ultra and Magic.[23] There is no point in wasting time covering the ground that these books have covered so well. But later in this work the reader will be given a number of examples of Ultra and Magic's use in combat situations that have not been published before. For now, however, let us concentrate on the previously unpublished Magic Summaries and show how they allowed Allied strategists to create plans that lead to one resounding success after the other.

---

22. Which is why Prime Minister Churchill blessed Marshall's name and called him "the organizer of victory." After the defeat of Germany, Churchill wrote him, saying: "It has not fallen to your lot to command great armies. You have had to create them, organize them, and inspire them. Under your guiding hand, the mighty and valiant formations which have swept across France and Germany were brought into being and perfected in an amazingly short time." *Marshall: Hero for Our Times* by Leonard Mosley (New York: Hearst Books, 1982), xvii. This work was commissioned and edited by the author.

23. See also *Ultra in the West* and *Ultra and Mediterranean Strategy* by Ralph Bennet. The author commissioned and edited the latter. Also *The Hut Six Story: Breaking the Enigma Codes* by Gordon Welchman, which the author commissioned and edited. This work created a furor in the intelligence community because Welchman was determined to expose his beliefs that both American and British signals intelligence were failing, in 1982, to heed the lessons learned the hard way at Bletchley Park during World War II.

6

As we have seen earlier, the Japanese reports from Europe to Tokyo gave the Allied planners grounds for confidence that the American invasion of Africa would be unchallenged. This proved true. By April 1943, the Japanese are confirming, almost on a daily basis, what the Allied planners next need to hear: the Axis is losing in North Africa.

From Madrid, Japanese minister Suma reports that the Spanish foreign minister, Jordana, has told him that "all news from Tunisia is bad. The Americans and British have twice as many tanks as the Axis. If things go on as they now are, an attack will be made on Italy and also on Greece, the invasion of Greece coming from the Dodecanese Islands. If the Axis is driven from Africa, we Spaniards are going to be up against some pretty hard problems."[1]

The report from Spain is confirmed the next day, April 8, when Japanese chargé Kase reports from Rome, saying: "The British Eighth Army's attack on the Mareth Line was horrible. . . . The Rommel forces are fighting a delaying action. . . . Taking into consideration the thrusts of the U.S. and French forces at Maknassy and El Ayacha, and the dread pressure from the British Eighth Army, the Axis forces are in the worst conceivable position. . . . The enemy has about twice as many men and five times as many tanks . . . [and] maintains air superiority of four to one. . . . The enemy supply situation in the entire Mediterranean is good. . . . During February 232 enemy freighters entered the western Mediterranean from the Atlantic, and during March there were 197. . . . The Germans and Italians under Rommel will have to retreat further

---

1. SRS 928, 7 April 1943. The disinformation in this message, that the Allies intend to invade Greece, is important to Washington and London because it indicates how the Axis leaders are thinking and where they will improperly commit their defensive forces.

and further northward whether they like it or not. Those Italian leaders who are best informed ... have no delusions about the calamity to come.''[2]

As another indication as to how the Axis is guessing where the next Allied invasion will take place, Japanese minister Yamaji reports from Sofia that many Axis planners believe the "Anglo-Saxons" will drive from Corfu through Greece and thence to Dalmatia. Germany is planning to prevent an Allied incursion in the Black Sea area by strongly fortifying the region running from the Turkish border to the Aegean coast. Other Axis planners discount the idea of an Allied attack in the Balkans, saying it would only benefit Russia. As an alternative they pick the Atlantic coast of Spain as the invasion area.[3]

Not all the Japanese intercepts are sober and weighty. A number contain some good gossip. For example, from Kuibyshev, where the Japanese diplomatic corps resides in Russia, Ambassador Sato tells Tokyo how a pro-Moscow Australian diplomat became disillusioned with his job. Sato reports that ''William Later, the Australian Minister, who took up his duties here last January, was formerly a labor leader in Australia and Speaker of the House. As his country's first minister to the Soviet Union, he was thoroughly convinced upon arrival that Russia was a completely idealistic socialistic state. He mingled freely with the Russians and said he was going to deepen the mutual faith of Australia and the Soviet in each other; in short, he was a real zealot. But alas! when he got down to work, he found that his theories did not fit the facts. His forthrightness was not reciprocated and he found every door barred to him. Now he tells me [Sato's neutral diplomatic source] that he does not see how it is possible for his country to deal with Russia and is very despondent. Recently he said: 'The Russian Minister in Australia is granted every liberty, but what consideration do I get? None. I cannot stay in this sort of country.' He has become so infuriated he has finally decided to leave.''[4]

The first Japanese report about the anti-Stalin activities of the former Soviet general Andrejevich Vlassov that this writer has found is dated April 27, 1943, and originated from Tokyo in a message sent by a new foreign minister, Shigemitsu, to his ambassador, Sato, in Russia. The source of the information is listed as simply a ''spy'' in Harbin. According to the message from Tokyo: ''Vlassov is now in Kiev or-

---

2. SRS 929, 8 April 1943.
3. SRS 931, 10 April 1943.
4. SRS 938, 17 April 1943.

ganizing an army. He already has a million men and the Germans are giving him tanks and airplanes taken from the Russians. Vlassov is organizing political groups, and as soon as the German forces occupy Moscow, he will quickly establish what is to be called 'a government of all the Russian people.' "[5]

The Japanese were also aware of the difficult problems facing the Allies. On April 10, Ambassador Sato reports that "the question of the Russo-Polish border, which for the past three or four weeks has been causing such a stir, is getting worse." Sato says that the negotiations on the matter now taking place in Moscow are near collapse, if not "already hopeless." Sato says the problem will cause "a very serious split in the anti-Axis camp, and will deepen England's and America's suspicions of the Soviet." Sato also points out that Moscow believes her demands about Poland are "natural and just," and criticism will only anger the Russians. "Although the trouble . . . is now hidden," says Sato, "it is boiling under the surface and sooner or later it must come out." A prescient observation.

At the end of April, the analysts in Washington report to General Marshall that "Foreign Minister Shigemitsu has sent a remarkable communication to Ambassador Oshima in Berlin, discussing the whole concept of Axis strategy during the coming year." The analysts point out that Japan and Germany "are not yet in agreement on basic strategic issues . . . and [the message] states in forthright fashion how Japan intends to prosecute the war. The opinions expressed are of particular significance because they clearly represent the views not merely of the Japanese Foreign Office but of the Japanese High Command."[6]

This vital intelligence apparently results from a series of reports sent earlier by Ambassador Oshima in Berlin to Tokyo that the Allies never intercepted. In analyzing Shigemitsu's communique, however, the analysts tell Marshall: "It appears that Hitler expounded to Oshima

---

5. SRS 948, 27 April 1943. Colonel McCormack's analysts attach their first account of Vlassov's activities to this report. They cite Vlassov's background in China as a military adviser to Chiang Kai-shek in 1938, and that, in 1942, he was named deputy commander of the Leningrad Front. Transferred later to the Volkhov Front, Vlassov was captured by the Germans in July. Nothing was heard of Vlassov until March 25, 1943, when he spoke over radio Vistula, a German propaganda station beaming programs to Russia. Vlassov renounced the Russian regime during the broadcast and said he was organizing a Russian Army of Liberation. Said McCormack's analysts: "Axis-controlled broadcasts in satellite countries have recently been playing up Vlassov's movement." Judging from the detailed amount of Magic/Ultra intercepts about Vlassov, this writer finds it difficult to believe claims by British and American officers of high rank that they were unaware of Vlassov's anti-Communist activities during the war.
6. SRS 951, 30 April 1943.

on Axis strategy for the coming year, and emphasized that Germany *intends to make another all-out drive against Russia.*" (Emphasis added.)

The analysts point out that Hitler's plan truly worries Tokyo. Thus, Shigemitsu instructs Oshima "to go straight to Hitler," taking with him the Japanese military and naval attachés, and to quickly present Japan's views. Tokyo fervently believes that "if Germany makes another all-out attack on Russia this year, leaving England and America to be finished off in 1944, Germany will only succeed in dissipating her tremendous power, meanwhile leaving America and England free to strengthen their position and finally to launch a great offensive." Japan wants Germany to fight a holding action in Russia and destroy the Allied forces in Africa and Gibraltar, thereby frustrating any Allied offensive against Europe. The most important element is to "assure the military leadership of the Axis in Europe." Meanwhile, Japan will continue its drive in the South Pacific, smashing "Anglo-Saxon offensives" in Burma and elsewhere.

In concluding his instructions to Oshima, Shigemitsu tells his envoy to emphasize to Hitler that "this is an all-out war and that we are fighting shoulder to shoulder. . . . [Furthermore] when you tell the Chancellor what we think, be careful to let him know we are not criticizing him. Tell him *that the Imperial Japanese Government has tied its fate up with his government,* and our advice to him issues from our spirit of cooperation and is very sincere." (Emphasis added.)

In less than a week's time, another major intelligence break crosses Marshall's desk. From Bucharest, Japanese minister Okubo reports that the Hungarian regent, Horthy, met Hitler on April 16 and 17 at German headquarters. It is reported that Horthy told Hitler: "We Hungarians have already lost one hundred thousand men in this bloody war, counting dead, wounded and missing. Those we have left have but few arms with which to fight. . . . We cannot help you one bit more. We are through. We are doing our best to stave off the Bolshevik menace and we won't be able to spare a single man for the Balkans."[7]

McCormack's analysts emphasize the significance of this message in a special note for Marshall and other Magic Summary readers. This note points out that, on April 22, the U.S. chargé in Helsinki reported to Washington that several Finnish journalists had just returned from Hungary, after Horthy met with Hitler, and they were impressed by how pessimistic Horthy had become. And on April 28, both the U.S.

---

7. SRS 952, 1 May 1943.

chargé in Helsinki and U.S. minister Harrison, in Bern, forwarded to the State Department reports indicating that ''general morale in Hungary is very low.''

In other words, on May 1, 1943, the Japanese told the Allies that Hungary had been knocked out of the war.

A few days later, on May 4, the Japanese military attaché in Hungary reports that while the Russians may publicly proclaim that Moscow is the key to the war in Russia, which is what they did the preceding year, ''it should be noted that the former extremely large shipments to Ryazan [a rail center southeast of Moscow] have suddenly been shifted to Kursk.''[8]

This is the first indication that the greatest battle of armored forces in history is about to take place. Another important warning is received when Japanese ambassador Sato tells Tokyo that he wants Morishima, the second-ranking diplomat in his embassy, who is temporarily in Japan, to return to Moscow. Explaining why Sato wants Morishima to return, the analysts in Washington read Sato's message: ''All things indicate that the last round of the German-Soviet fight will start any moment after the middle of May. This showdown will be extremely important because it will prove clearly how the war in Europe is to end. In other words, this is it! . . . I want you to be back here so that you can scan the situation ever so carefully with me.''[9]

The following day, in Tokyo, Foreign Minister Shigemitsu tells the Italian minister to Japan, Indelli, that Japan has adopted a new policy of conciliation with the Nanking government and that it is succeeding. Shigemitsu reports to Oshima in Berlin that he told the Italian: ''You know the U.S. is taking the attitude that she is the guardian of the European nations, especially the little ones. She says her war aim is to restore their liberty. . . . [But] the ones who really have what it takes to govern Europe are the Axis nations. It is for the Axis, and the Axis only, to say whether or not the European countries will regain their freedom.''[10]

On May 11, Ambassador Oshima reports to Berlin that Subhas Chandra Bose, an Indian pro-Axis nationalist, will soon arrive in Japan via a German submarine. According to Oshima, ''the British do not yet know that he is going to Japan.''[11] The Germans will leave it to Japan

---

8. SRS 955, 4 May 1943.
9. SRS 959, 8 May 1943.
10. SRS 960, 9 May 1943.
11. SRS 962, 11 May 1943. The British did know. The Magic Summary of February 24, 1943, had reported that Bose had sailed from Kiel harbor on February 9.

to insert Bose into situations in India and Burma whereby Bose can wreak havoc against the British Empire by leading his nationalist army and fomenting revolution. There is not enough space in this work to detail the full story of Bose's anti-British activities as revealed by the Magic Summaries during the rest of the war. It is sufficient to say, however, that Bose and his followers try to infiltrate the nationalistic movement of India, influencing the leaders thereof, but are thwarted at almost every turn by the Allied reading of Magic.[12]

A few days later, Japan's newest foreign minister, Shigemitsu, impresses the analysts in Washington with his forthright statements to Stahmer, the German ambassador to Tokyo. Shigemitsu advises Oshima of the Foreign Minister's meeting with Stahmer on May 5. The analysts in Washington declare: "The new Foreign Minister is a forceful and aggressive diplomat with a very clear idea of the program which his country and her allies should follow."[13]

According to Shigemitsu, Stahmer opened the conversation by saying: "The self-sufficiency of the Soviet is gone, and her losses are great. She hasn't many men left to call up. . . . According to our figures they have lost 11,300,000. . . .[14] This thing of winning in the summer and losing in the winter is going to stop now."

Shigemitsu reports that at this point "I held up my hand, and said: 'That will be enough. Let me have a few words. . . . The Imperial Government does not intend to criticize you for your decisions, but it so happens that we Japanese are in the same boat with you Germans. Spiritually, too, we are supposed to be, or ought to be, as one. . . . We ought to join hands and fight this war through to victory shoulder to shoulder. . . . [But] we Japanese are very much afraid of that drive you Germans are planning against the Soviet. You may use up all your expendables in men and material and repeat the same mistake you have already made twice. Then where will you be for men? Where will you

---

12. According to the analysts in Washington: Bose broke with Gandhi in May 1939 and headed a bloc pledged to extremist measures against British rule. He was arrested by the British in July 1940 and detained at Calcutta for about six months. Early in 1941 he escaped and, with the help of the Italian legation in Afghanistan, made his way to Germany. Bose lived two years in Europe, principally in Berlin, where he became the chief commentator in propaganda broadcasts used by Germany and Italy to the Far East.

13. SRS 965, 14 May 1943.

14. According to the U.S. MIS, "total permanent losses of the Red Army [at this time are] 6,000,000. The official Japanese estimate (Magic Summary 4/30/43) sets the figure at 8,800,000." It is interesting to note how carefully the analysts in Washington are following almost every inflection of the conversations reported in the Magic Summaries. As noted earlier in this work, final casualty figures for the Russian armed forces are far higher than stated at this point in the narrative. Even so, these figures are staggering.

be for supplies? . . . Our real enemies are England and the United States, and it is they whom we Japanese intend to fight. The logical thing for you Germans to do would be to fall in line with us. It would serve the interests of both of us best. If we work together, I think we can finish them off.' ''[15]

A few days later, reports to Tokyo from its diplomats in Vichy, France, and Rome prove that Premier Laval is trying to negotiate with Hitler about French territorial guarantees. The Japanese have learned that the British and the U.S. are telling General de Gaulle that the prewar French borders will be respected. Accordingly: "This gives the British and Americans a good idea of how many chips they have to bargain with. In creating a new Europe under Axis rule, Laval agreed that France would not provide military cooperation, but would supply labor, manufacture arms, and send volunteers to the Russian front."[16]

Meanwhile, from Berlin, Baron Oshima argues with Tokyo about Shigemitsu's message to Hitler. Oshima is wholly unconvinced of the soundness of his government's position and does not want to pass the message on to Chancellor Hitler. Says Oshima: "If we look back over Germany's manner of conducting the war, we can find plenty to blame her for. But . . . Germany is forced to make another campaign [in Russia] this year. . . . This is a prerequisite to the battle against the Anglo-Americans and cannot be dispensed with. . . . I can well understand why [Germany] feels she must go on. If she were merely to put up a strategic defense on a line which is two thousand kilometers long, it is even doubtful whether she could by herself hold the Russians in check for a long time. If that line were to collapse, the whole thing might be over with so far as Germany is concerned."[17]

Oshima goes on to explain that he believes the Germans can strengthen their supply lines this year and that she stands a good chance of winning her new campaign in the East. Besides, it is impossible to stop it. German troops are already being sent to the front. (A vital bit of information for Allied strategists.) And if Germany can finish off Russia, there is nothing more she could do in strategic terms for the Axis. Thus, Oshima urges Tokyo to support Germany in her coming offensive, hope that she wins, and then persuade her "to throw her main strength against England and America."[18]

---

15. SRS 965, 14 May 1943.
16. SRS 966, 15 May 1943.
17. SRS 968, 17 May 1943.
18. Ibid.

What better confirmation of Allied planning could the strategists in Washington and London ask for? With Germany fully occupied in Russia, the Allies have captured Tunis and ended the Axis threat in North Africa. Now they can plan to invade Sicily and Italy and force Germany to pull more troops out of France, thereby weakening the defensive areas where the Allies intend to invade.

On May 8, Foreign Minister Shigemitsu asked all his representatives around the world to evaluate the Allied victory at Tunis.[19] The analysts in Washington note that they express the opinion that (1) the fall of Tunisia came with unexpected suddenness; that (2) everyone predicted an Allied invasion of Sicily, Sardinia and Italy; and (3) no one believed the Allies would risk the casualties that might be caused in attacking other areas.

To this, Shigemitsu replies that "as soon as a second front appears imminent," he wants his representatives to stay in touch with each other and determine which offices should close and which should continue operations. The next day, Shigemitsu tells his people: "I know that you must be considering quite thoroughly what to do with your communications material in the case of a sudden explosion in Europe. I herewith instruct you to stand by to carry out instructions. If worst comes to worst, destroy your codes and cipher machines and take every other measure necessary for the maintenance of telegraphic security."[20]

Shades of Pearl Harbor: these instructions almost parallel those sent out by Tokyo before Japanese planes carried out their surprise attack on December 7, 1941.

Significantly, the analysts in Washington learn that the fall of Tunis shocks Hitler. According to Ambassador Oshima in Berlin, on May 12 Hitler "is undecided what to do next." But it appears that "a partial drive in the East is likely to begin this month."[21] The Magic Summaries are now showing, for the first time, that Hitler is feeling the pressure from both the West and the East. In studying the chronology of the war from this point on, one cannot help but remark that the actions on the Western and Eastern Fronts begin to have some resemblance to a good team of bridge players working a crossruff against the Germans. Just as the Germans are about to attack on one front, the Allies can mount an attack on another front, drawing German forces away from

---

19. MS (Magic Summary) 12 May 1943.
20. SRS 972, 21 May 1943.
21. SRS 977, 26 May 1943.

their initial objective and weakening both the German forces and their morale.

Intelligence experts point out that no concrete data exists regarding how Soviet military strategy reacted to strategic conditions in other theaters. But by the summer of 1944, clear ties between strategic operations in the East and the West stand out. "From this time on, the motivation underlying these linkages becomes the central question," writes Col. David M. Glantz in his provocative view of the war.[22] "The degree to which [operations] were planned has still to be proven. Yet in June [1944] major Soviet offensive activity in Belorussia followed the Allied Normandy landings by seventeen days. The second major Soviet offensive against German forces in Poland, which began on 12 July, preceded the Allied breakout from Normandy (Operation COBRA of 25 July) by thirteen days. The landing of Allied forces in southern France on 15 August and the threatened (but failed) encirclement of German forces at Falaise preceded the Soviet offensive into Rumania by five days." As intelligence officers often say, there is no such thing as a series of coincidences.

This crossruffing of strategic operations, to steal terminology from the game of bridge at which Eisenhower was expert, could only be achieved by the sharing of intelligence between Washington, London and Moscow. One wonders how this information was passed to the Russians. No one has written the full story to date. But we do know that on at least one occasion, General Marshall passed on information about German intentions to the Russians. This was at the end of the war when both sides are driving on Berlin. Marshall derived the information from Magic, from a report by Oshima about what Hitler had said he was going to do. On this occasion, however, Hitler changes his mind—without telling Oshima—and as a result the Russians suffer heavy losses when they should have had an easy time of it. Stalin vents his fury at Marshall, who tells Stalin the truth on April 10, 1945, that he had gotten the information from an intercept of Oshima's message to Tokyo. As intelligence expert Bradley F. Smith points out, "Marshall thereby revealed the Magic secret to the Soviets. . . . The Soviets therefore knew that the western secrets were the product of cryptanalysis,

---

22. *The Role of Intelligence in Soviet Military Strategy in World War II* by David M. Glantz (Novato, Calif.: Presidio Press, 1990), appendix B, 221–27. See also the chart "Correlation of Soviet and Allied Operations" on page 22 that begins 23 October 1942 and ends 16 April 1945.

whatever else they may have heard about such matters from spies such as Kim Philby, Donald MacLean and John Cairncross."[23] Smith labels this action by Marshall "simple folly."

✖ ✖ ✖

During the remainder of the month a series of intercepts are made of messages exchanged between Moscow, Tokyo and Berlin.[24] These prove conclusively that Germany is upset that Japan is allowing Lend-Lease war materials to be sent by ship to Siberia from the West Coast of America. Too, the Soviets reveal they will be adamant in refusing to allow the Americans to have airfields in Siberia that would facilitate the shuttle-bombing of Japanese cities. This means that the Americans will have to endure horrendous casualties capturing islands such as Iwo Jima and Okinawa so they can effectively hit Japanese cities with heavy bombers.

The Soviet attitude on this issue does not endear the Russians to American military planners such as Admiral King, General Marshall or Secretary of War Stimson. By May 1943, the American military is dealing with the two-faced diplomacy of Stalin. They must treat him as a faithful ally. But a careful reading of the Operations Department and SHAEF files from here on, including the inflection of sentence structure, indicates a change of attitude is taking place in the top echelons of the U.S. Army. It also indicates a severe difference in opinion is developing between the Pentagon and White House about how to view the potential expansion of Communism in the postwar era.

✖ ✖ ✖

Halfway through the year, the Magic analysts in Washington get a nasty shock. On May 18, Japanese minister Suma reports that he has spoken with Spanish ambassador Cardenas, who has just returned to Madrid. Cardenas brought up the subject of a shipment of pearls produced by

---

23. *The Ultra-Magic Deals* by Bradley F. Smith (Novato, Calif.: Presidio Press, 1993), 200. Smith writes, on page 201, that "the British continued to provide the Soviets with wrapped-up Ultra . . . well into the spring of 1945. Copies of British intelligence transmissions to the Soviets were frequently sent the U.S. Military Mission in Moscow." Details of these intelligence transmissions are unavailable.
24. SRS 975, 25 May 1943. SRS 976, 25 May 1943. SRS 980, 29 May 1943.

the Japanese firm of Mikimoto, which were supposed to be used to finance espionage activities in America, but which had disappeared while en route from Tokyo to Europe via the Spanish diplomatic pouch.[25]

According to Cardenas, the pearls were delivered to the Spanish embassy in Washington "some time ago," and the State Department has used "very unpleasant language" about the matter. Since then, Cardenas says, nearly every Spanish diplomatic pouch had been opened.

Three days later, Suma sends an "utterly secret" message to Tokyo saying: "When I was talking with Ambassador Cardenas about the pearls and other matters, twice his eyes narrowed and he said musingly, ponderingly and in a soft half-questioning voice: 'It is strange how quickly the United States finds out about matters such as these. I wonder if Japanese codes are safe.' "

On May 26, Foreign Minister Shigemitsu replies to Suma, reassuring him by saying: "I have studied the matter from a number of angles, but I cannot believe that it is the result of their having solved our codes."[26]

Despite this expression of self-delusion, a nervous quiver goes through the Pentagon, and once again, warnings go out to other agencies, such as the OSS, to halt any break-ins of Japanese diplomatic posts or attempts to steal Japanese code secrets. This was not the only time such a warning had to be sent out. On at least one other occasion, overzealous OSS agents tried to steal the codes from a Japanese diplomatic post and were nearly caught doing so. If the Americans had been caught, the damage done to the interception of Magic would have been incalculable.

This leads Maj. Gen. George V. Strong, the Acting Chief of Staff, G-2 (Intelligence), to prepare a memo for General Marshall saying that the OSS has shared with the Army the decrypt of a message dated April 13 that originated in Portugal.[27] Strong is concerned that the OSS might have stolen the document by breaking and entering or doing its own decrypting. The cipher system in which the report was transmitted was in the M/A (Military Attaché) system, which, Strong says, "is one of the most difficult enemy ciphers that have been solved. It was broken by

---

25. SRS 984, 2 June 1943.
26. Ibid.
27. SRH-113, spring 1943. "Selected Documents OSS Operations in Lisbon." Memo to General Marshall. Subject: Security Risk with OSS Operations in Lisbon. This SRH reveals similar OSS problems in Asia with units under the command of General Stilwell.

joint British-American efforts over a long period and involving some of the best cryptanalytic talent available. . . . Not only is the Japanese M/A traffic one of the most important sources of Japanese military intelligence at the present time, but it has become doubly important because of the loss of one of the two diplomatic systems [censored] . . . which was supplemented by a new system on July 1. . . . In this situation, the loss of the Japanese M/A traffic would be nothing less than a catastrophe. If the activities of the OSS in Lisbon should result in a change in the M/A system, it would be a tragic price to pay for the folly of letting loose a group of amateur spies in neutral countries. . . . As is sufficiently demonstrated by the recent report of Ambassador Hayes on OSS activities in Spain, the S.I. (Special Intelligence) Branch of that organization is full of irresponsible people, who have been turned loose in neutral countries with unlimited money to squander, operating under no proper definition of their functions and subject to no proper control. . . . It is recommended . . . that steps be taken immediately to recall from Spain and Portugal all OSS personnel, who are engaged in espionage in those countries in open violation of the directives of the Joint Chiefs of Staff, which excludes them from such activities in neutral countries."

On July 13, Brigadier Menzies of the British Joint Staff Mission, Offices of the Combined Chiefs of Staff, writes General Strong that the moral of the situation is that "no agency should attempt penetration of neutral Embassies or Legations without authority from highest quarter as any success which might ultimately be attained would if discovered alarm occupant regarding cipher security. . . . I have stringent standing orders on subject. . . . It would be advantageous to Allied cause if U.S. agencies in neutral European countries would seek advice of my local representative before becoming involved."[28]

✖ ✖ ✖

Early in June 1943, two messages from Major General Okamoto, the military attaché to Berlin, earn careful attention in Washington and London. In the first, Okamoto reminds Tokyo that the Allies are co-operating in an unprecedented fashion to share newly developed scientific secrets. The General wants Tokyo to exchange scientific advisers with Germany on the basis that "quality must always supersede considerations of quantity." Should Tokyo fail to keep up scientifically,

---

28. Ibid.

Okamoto warns, and "we are found wanting in this respect, who knows what will happen?"[29]

Three days later, another message from Major General Okamoto is intercepted as it is sent to Tokyo. The analysts in Washington note that Okamoto believes that the peculiarities of United Nations strategy prevent him from judging with "anything like precision where England and America will concentrate their activities. Will it be in the East or will it be in the West—who knows?"[30] He goes on to say: "In Europe the enemy's policy will probably be to use every possible means to keep the Russians battering the Germans. . . . Simultaneously they will be scheming to surround Germany and Italy. All the while they will be using every trick conceivable to cause Italy to desert Germany and Japan."

As time will prove, Okamoto's analysis is bang on target.

In mid-June, Washington can see that Germany is worried about a potential Allied invasion in the Balkans. From Bucharest, Japanese minister Okubo reports the Germans are more worried about an invasion in Dalmatia than they are one in Greece. This fear is driving the Germans to organize three SS divisions composed of native Bosnians. And Himmler, the head of Germany's SS forces, has been in Zagreb for that purpose.[31]

The same day's intercepts also include a message from Foreign Minister Shigemitsu to Ambassador Oshima in Berlin about the latest political developments in Moscow: the dissolution of the Comintern. Germany wants Japan to speak out on the subject. Shigemitsu says Japan should remain silent for the moment because anything Tokyo might say could be used against her, especially in view of Japan's neutrality agreement with Russia. Says Shigemitsu of Moscow's tactics: "The principle of Communism, which is world revolution, has in no wise been altered."

More important, the Magic Summary for this day reveals a shortage of rice in Korea. Japan will now have to export rice to help make up the shortfall. In the past Korea exported to Japan about 10 percent of the rice that Japan consumes. This is the first report of upcoming rice shortages in Japan.

---

29. SRS 990, 8 June 1943.
30. SRS 993, 11 June 1943.
31. SRS 996, 14 June 1943. This Japanese report was confirmed by Harrison, the U.S. minister to Bern, who reported that a new German SS division made up of Bosnian Moslem volunteers was in formation. From Istanbul, U.S. consul Berry reported two thousand Gestapo men in uniform arrived in Zagreb around May 6.

A few days later, Oshima reports to Tokyo that he relayed Shigemitsu's comments on German strategy in Russia to Foreign Minister von Ribbentrop. In reply Ribbentrop stated, as Oshima had predicted he would, that if Germany should now direct her main effort against England and America as Japan requested, she would have to withdraw a large number of her units from the Eastern Front. If, as a result of this withdrawal, the Russians should break through the German lines, the war would end in her defeat.[32]

In other words, Washington and London now know that what they had hoped would happen has indeed happened. Japan will not attack Russia in Siberia. And Germany cannot extricate itself from Russia. The German army is caught in the dangerous quicksand of a war in Russia plus war in Europe. No matter how hard Germany will fight in the future, she has already lost everything she might have hoped to gain when her troops first set out in 1939 to expand the Nazi empire.

That trouble is also brewing between Russia and Japan becomes apparent to Washington and London in the Magic messages about two Soviet ships, the *Ingul* and the *Kamenets-Podolak,* which Japan had seized and interned. The Russians had demanded that the ships be returned. Tokyo had told Ambassador Sato that he was the Japanese equivalent of a wimp when he pointed out that Moscow had valid reasons for its stance in the matter. On June 9, Sato wired Tokyo: "You certainly upbraided me about my statement that the Russians have something to say on their side. In my humble opinion this is no time for arguing and quibbling. The Soviet has already given us the choice of either following the neutrality pact according to their interpretation or fighting. . . . Our fate is in the balance, and if we tip the balance unfavorably by jeopardizing our relations with Russia, it will be too bad. You don't know how worried I am. You had better reconsider."[33]

The Japanese had been arguing they had the legal right to seize the ships because they had been transferred by the Americans to Russia after the outbreak of war. Meantime the Russians argued that they had acquired title to the vessels before Japan went to war with America. This meant the ships were owned by a neutral Russia and were being used only for Russian purposes.

It is not until June 25[34] that Washington can see just how baldly Molotov lies to Sato about the matter. "Why, we bought these ships

32. SRS 999, 17 June 1943.
33. SRS 1000, 18 June 1943.
34. SRS 1007, 25 June 1943. See also SRS 1002, 20 June 1943.

from the United States in September 1941," Molotov tells Sato, who reports the conversation verbatim to Tokyo. "It is quite clear that Article Fifty-six [of the Russo-Japanese Neutrality Pact] applies in our favor." In response, Sato tells Molotov: "Why didn't you tell me that before. This is the first time you ever told me that. . . . I will take you at your word, and now that it is understood between us that their nationality was changed before the war, the whole picture is changed."

The analysts in Washington must have chuckled as they note for General Marshall that the *Kamenets-Podolak* was transferred to Russian registry on November 20, 1942, and the *Ingul* on March 29, 1943. However, the humor of the situation pales when one considers that Molotov is also playing similar games with America.

More important is the fact that no matter how strongly Germany might state her wishes to Japan about shutting off the flow of Lend-Lease supplies from America to Vladivostok, Japan will not close down the Pacific shipping lanes. The fear of war with Russia is too great. As Sato puts it: "This question has in it the seeds that will seal our doom."

The third week of June brings welcome news to Washington and London. Reporting from Berlin, Ambassador Oshima tells Tokyo that his "regular liaison" in the German government now thinks it improbable that the Allies "will land on the Atlantic coast of France. Moreover, only a few people believe that Sicily and Sardinia will be invaded, or that landings will be made in the near future on the Italian mainland or in Southern France. Some expect that the chief attack will be made . . . in the Eastern Mediterranean with a thrust into the Black Sea."[35]

Oshima also reveals that Hitler has returned to Berchtesgaden "to make further plans for the eastern offensive," which apparently has been scaled down in anticipation of the moves England and America will make. Accordingly, a large portion of the reserve forces of the German army will be kept in Germany awaiting changes in the situation. More importantly, "at present there are not many German ground forces in Italy. . . . [But] a large number of German units are stationed in Southern France and the Balkans."

With the Allied invasion of Sicily being planned for the second week in July, Oshima's message brings considerable relief to Generals Marshall, Eisenhower and Montgomery.

There is a strange feeling to this day's Magic Summary. Reading it carefully, one notes for the first time that the Germans seem hesitant to completely reveal their future plans to the Japanese.

---

35. SRS 1005, 23 June 1943.

Two days later, Ambassador Hidaka in Rome reports to Tokyo on the strength of a conversation one of his staff held with an intelligence official in the German embassy, and a conversation between German ambassador Mackensen and Hidaka himself.[36] Apparently the Germans believe the Allies might lay siege to both Sardinia and Sicily, with the thought being that they will attack Sardinia first because it is more weakly defended. The Japanese faithfully report the German and Italian troop movements that they know about and pinpoint the location of four vital armored divisions. The Germans appear more concerned about holding the Italian mainland than they do about Sicily, which they believe will be difficult for the Allies to seize. The German ambassador acknowledges that the German military leaders do not know where the Allies will strike. He personally believes that Turkey might be in the greatest danger, nor is he sure that Spain is safe from invasion.

The next day, Oshima reports from Berlin about a meeting between the Italian ambassador to Germany and Ribbentrop.[37] The Italian says that Ribbentrop had told him that although Germany is getting ready for a big drive in the East, "she is postponing it for a while because she has to keep her eyes on England and the U.S. [The word] 'drive' does not mean the same thing as it did last year or the year before that."

When asked if the Germans are helping the Italians, Ambassador Alfieri replies that Italy's greatest need is aircraft and that Germany "is satisfying our minimum requirements." (On June 5, Ambassador Hidaka in Rome reported that the Tunisian campaign had severely weakened the Italian Air Force. Only three hundred to five hundred combat planes are left. And the total number of planes in Italy is put at fifteen hundred. Meanwhile, the German ambassador, Mackensen, complains to Hidaka that the Italians have done nothing to improve ground installations for either air force and "there is nothing we can possibly do about that.")

In other words, the Japanese are unwittingly revealing to the Allies the vital secrets that Sicily is ready for the picking, that the air defenses of Italy are weak and can easily be overwhelmed, and the mainland of Italy should be invaded sooner, rather than later.

---

36. SRS 1007, 25 June 1943. This Magic Summary is a good example of the growth of Colonel McCormack's staff in terms of producing superior intelligence. Earlier estimates of the enemy's order of battle are related to the current figures cited by Hidaka and his staff, and the Axis defense of Sicily is neatly tied into the German reserves available elsewhere.
37. SRS 1008, 26 June 1943.

✖ ✖ ✖

With the beginning of July, General Marshall learns just how effective the U.S. Navy's submarines have been in the South Pacific. A message from Saigon to Tokyo reveals that the Japanese naval authorities are now so worried about sinkings that, in the future, "no ship will be allowed to travel except in convoy."[38] This is the first report from any Japanese source indicating that the loss of ships has become a prime worry for Tokyo.

The next day, Marshall reads the pessimistic survey of the war prepared by Foreign Minister Shigemitsu that was sent as a circular to all the Japanese diplomatic posts around the world.[39] Shigemitsu points out that the German air force is growing weaker while that of England and America is "superior." According to Shigemitsu: "The people in territory occupied by Germany are unhappy, and in neutral nations the anti-Axis feeling is mounting. Italy, Rumania and Hungary are, beyond all doubt, weak in morale. . . . Those countries are unquestionably beginning to set their houses in order in anticipation of an Axis defeat."

Two days later, Minister Suma reports from Madrid that the Spanish foreign minister has told him: "Although we hear that Germany has sent twelve divisions to Italy, the latter country is still regarded as being the weakest spot."[40]

Meantime, the battle at Kursk begins. Ambassador Oshima asks about the significance of the action from his sources in Berlin. He reports to Tokyo that he was told: "The action is chiefly intended to straighten out the German line and is not the real thing."[41]

On July 9, Oshima reports that the Germans have failed in their U-boat war. The major news in this message to Tokyo is that because of new Allied techniques in defending convoys, the U-boats are ordered to end their wolf-pack attacks.[42] This is the best news Prime Minister Churchill and his staff could receive.

The English and Americans invade Sicily on July 10, 1943. On this day, the Magic Summary reports Ambassador Hidaka in Rome as saying that "there is considerable confidence with respect to the defense

---

38. SRS 1014, 2 July 1943.
39. SRS 1015, 3 July 1943.
40. SRS 1017, 6 July 1943.
41. SRS 1019, 8 July 1943.
42. SRS 1020, 9 July 1943.

of the Italian mainland. This is not true, however, in the case of Sicily and Sardinia. Sicily does not have very good lines of supply by sea, and it is expected that, if Sicily is invaded, there will be difficulty in supplying it with food and water."[43]

Meanwhile, in Russia the battle of Kursk has been raging since July 4. The scope of the battle is staggering. The German attack includes 900,000 men supported by 2,500 tanks and assault cannon. Opposing them are 1,300,000 Russian troops and 3,000 tanks. Given the even strength of the combatants, it is an attack that requires surprise if the Germans are to be successful. Thanks to Magic, all surprise was lost months earlier.

Now, faced with the invasion of Sicily on July 10, Hitler cancels his Operation CITADEL, the double envelopment of the Russian forces inside the Kursk salient. The cancellation is caused not by a lack of German success in the attack, but because the Allied landings in Sicily necessitate the shipping of German reinforcements from the Russian front to the West. Weakened by this loss of men and material, the Germans bleed and die on the Eastern Front. By mid-August, the Russians will win the greatest tank battle of the war, inflict extremely heavy casualties upon the Germans and reach the outskirts of the strategic city of Kharkov. Hitler never again launches a major attack in Russia. More significantly, from now on German forces will be completely on the defensive in the East.[44]

Only five days after the Allied landings in Sicily, from Berlin Oshima reports to Tokyo that the leadership of the Italian troops in Sicily is "weakening, and they are absolutely incapable of fighting."[45] At the moment, Berlin is undecided whether to send more German "units to that Island or to write Sicily off the books, [and] send men to Italy proper and prepare for the next American threat."

---

43. SRS 1021, 10 July 1943.
44. SRS 1023, 12 July 1943. Bern and Rio de Janeiro report that the Papal Nuncio seeks peace but wants the Allies to restore Italy's prewar colonies in North Africa.

SRS 1024, 13 July 1943. Magic analysts in Washington make their first mention of the battle of Kursk.

SRS 1025, 14 July 1943. Rome reports to Tokyo on the Allied landings in Sicily. Berlin reports to Tokyo on the battle of Kursk.

SRS 1027, 16 July 1943. Rome reports to Tokyo on the situation in Sicily. A report from Dublin links the IRA to pro-Axis activities, including a revolution in Ireland timed to begin just after the British armies invade the Continent. Consular representative Sakamoto warns Tokyo not to let the story leak out "since we do not want to interfere with the workings of the I.R.A."
45. SRS 1028, 17 July 1943.

✖ ✖ ✖

One of the great controversies of World War II is the effectiveness of the conflicting bombing campaigns conducted by the English and the Americans. The English believe in bombing by night; the Americans prefer precision bombing by daylight. None of the history books about the war mention that the Japanese determine by personal inspection that the American program is far more effective than the British one.

This comes to light as the result of a query posed by Tokyo to Oshima in Berlin in early May, asking about bomb damage to cities and, especially, factories.[46] Oshima does not reply for nearly a month and a half. Oshima then reports to Tokyo that some Italians had visited bombed cities earlier and told neutral diplomats what they had seen, "which made the Germans furious and hurt their feelings." Thus, Oshima made a formal request to visit cities that had been attacked. He and some of his staff had inspected Hamburg, Frankfurt, Mannheim, Ludwigshafen, Cologne, Kiel and Magdeburg.

According to the analysts in Washington, the principal points of Oshima's report are that Allied propaganda magnifies the damage done by bombs to factories. The nighttime bombing by the British has made no particular attempt to hit factories; instead there have been indiscriminate attacks on cities per se. The factor that is "giving headaches to the Germans" is the high-altitude precision bombing by the Americans. The source for this important information is none other than the great flier Major General Galland, now the inspector of fighter planes for the German Air Force. According to Galland, the Germans are preparing new plans of attack against the American bomber formations, and Oshima carefully lists all of them, which has to please American strategists. As a stinging rebuttal to the British, Oshima reports: "The British brag about what they did to the Blohm and Voss submarine assembly plant [in Hamburg], but with my own eyes I saw that they had scored scarcely a single hit on the machine shops."

The analysts in Washington carefully note the available British and American intelligence on the bombing of the cities that Oshima reports about. The analysts say: "In some cases Oshima's account can be reconciled with the Allied reports. In other cases, however, notably that of Cologne [where Oshima reported that only residential areas had been

---

46. SRS 1029, 18 July 1943.

hit], Oshima's account is decidedly at variance with Allied reports. But if the American bomber command needs confirmation about the success of its tactics when arguing with the British, the report from Oshima, and others that follow in the same vein, could not be more welcome.

On July 21, the Magic Summary crossing Marshall's desk includes the news from Madrid that the Italian ambassador has made a series of "very secret" statements to Japanese ambassador Suma. The Italian says: "We have come to the conclusion that Italy will be crushed; no matter how earnestly we ask Germany she will not transfer any more of her air force to Italy. . . . There is nothing for Italy to do but fight with her own strength."[47] Now is the time for the Allies to start bargaining with the Italians about their surrender.

A day later, Oshima reports to Tokyo that the German Foreign Office has told him that the German attack in Russia has been discontinued in preparation for a counterattack by Russian forces.[48]

The day after, the Magic Summary contains the entire budget recast in the coming six months for Japanese military operations in Thailand and French Indochina.[49] If the Allies are to find a weak point in the region against which to apply pressure, the information proves priceless.

✶ ✶ ✶

The first mention in the Magic Summaries about how Germany plans to defend the beaches of Europe against an Allied invasion occurs in late July 1943 in a report by the Japanese military attaché in Vichy to Tokyo. According to the attaché, he spoke with Lieutenant General Blumentritt, whom the analysts in Washington identify as being the Deputy Chief of Staff in charge of Operations at German General Headquarters.[50] Blumentritt strongly believes the Allies cannot make a successful landing in the west of Europe. "A limited number of troops might be landed initially in one area or another, but they would be wiped out before the operation is completed," he is quoted as saying. "Germany has thirty divisions stationed along the Atlantic Coast, and also has available a mobile reserve of ten to twelve armored divisions

---

47. SRS 1032, 21 July 1943.
48. SRS 1033, 22 July 1943.
49. SRS 1034, 23 July 1943.
50. SRS 1038, 27 July 1943.

which would be particularly useful if the enemy should attempt to use parachute troops on a large scale.''

This confirmation of German strength in Europe—forces so strong that Allied planners agree that an invasion at this time would be a disaster—makes the invasion of Italy a necessity. The Germans must be forced to transfer troops away from the potential beachheads in France if an invasion there is to succeed.

Meanwhile, in Berlin, Baron Oshima is finding that he is for the first time having difficulty gaining interviews with Hitler.[51] The analysts in Washington are puzzled, or worried, by this development. They note that Oshima's last face-to-face meeting with Hitler was on the weekend of April 17–18. Despite the requests from Foreign Minister Shigemitsu in Tokyo that Oshima meet further with Hitler, all of Oshima's requests have been denied for a variety of reasons. There is no explanation, however, and the analysis of events ends with the statement: ''Oshima is apparently not unaware of the extraordinary lapse of time since his first request to see Hitler. . . . The Ambassador observes that 'it seems that the Germans have a reason for not talking with me at the present time.' ''

In truth, Hitler has far more on his mind these days than meeting with the Japanese. Sicily is obviously a lost cause, and on Sunday, July 25, his partner in Italy, Benito Mussolini, is unexpectedly shorn of the power he has held as dictator since 1922. In Russia, Hitler is ordering troops from the Orel salient to the defense of Italy, and General Jodl is reported to have told the Fuehrer that ''the whole fascist movement went pop, like a soap bubble.''

The Magic Summary of July 28[52] begins a vivid insider's picture of the so-called popping. (The picture does not reveal itself in orderly fashion because of the delays in interception and decryption, but the final product is complex, detailed and precise.) From Madrid, Ambassador Suma first reports that Italian ambassador Paulucci had no prior knowledge of Mussolini's overthrow. Paulucci's personal opinion is that Mussolini had asked Hitler (in their meeting on July 19) to supply Italy with planes and tanks and to ''let Italy bring home her twenty-four divisions from the Balkans.'' Hitler refused, and when Mussolini returned home after the meeting with the bad news, the government in Rome was so upset with the Germans it kicked Mussolini out of office.

Suma chides Paulucci about what the new regime is planning to

---

51. Ibid.
52. SRS 1039, 28 July 1943.

do. The idea of continuing to fight is a farce. "Sure," says Paulucci, "I think that Italy is going to bring about a truce or make peace. All I meant to say was that I hadn't received an official message to that effect. I am sorry, old fellow, but I can't tell you anything more at all right now."

Indeed, secret contacts for an armistice have already been made with Italy. According to British historian Martin Gilbert, German intelligence has intercepted a telephone conversation between Roosevelt and Churchill about their planning for negotiating such an armistice.[53] There is a certain irony to the situation. Hitler knows what is happening, but is powerless to prevent it.

The Japanese view of events is even more pessimistic. Ambassador Suma gives Tokyo his appraisal of the situation, saying that there will be a truce "or a separate peace" between the Allies and Italy.[54] "The effect in all quarters will be terrific," says Suma. "Germany's, and particularly Hitler's, position may be jeopardized and before long we may find ourselves up against the world. We must ponder deeply the fact that the time may come when we will stand with our backs to the wall in East Asia."

This fear leads Suma to make a recommendation that represents a drastic change of position on his part. "It is becoming harder and harder for us to reach a compromise with the Soviet. In self-defense there remains to us but one alternative; that is, to overcome every obstacle, occupy the [Soviet] Maritime Provinces as quickly as possible and prepare for a long struggle."[55]

From Tokyo, Foreign Minister Shigemitsu tells his diplomats in a circular "all hands" message that he has spoken with German ambassador Stahmer and told him that "it looks as though Italy is about done for. . . . It is up to us Japanese and Germans to stick closer together. We ought to work hand in hand in the prosecution of the war from now on."[56]

From Oshima in Berlin comes the best explanation of what was said on July 19 between Mussolini and Hitler.[57] Oshima reveals that at first there was no intention of letting the news of the Hitler-Mussolini talks get out. According to Oshima: "What actually happened was that

53. *The Second World War* by Martin Gilbert (New York: Henry Holt, 1989), 448. Gilbert's view of Italy's collapse from the German point of view is brilliant.
54. SRS 1039, 28 July 1943.
55. Ibid.
56. Ibid.
57. Ibid.

Hitler explained to Mussolini that he still had to keep his main forces on the Eastern Front. Mussolini conceded this was so. They also agreed that there was a great difference between Sicily and the Italian mainland, and that, although they would endeavor to hold Sicily as long as possible with the German forces now there, they would not waste any further troops by sending them to defend the Island. However . . . if Allied forces should try to land in Italy, they would annihilate them, and Hitler promised that, if an invasion of Italy was attempted, Germany would give ample aid and send a large German force to Italy, *including some of the troops now stationed on the long coastline from France to the Balkans.* [Emphasis added.] Hitler also promised to send more airpower to Italy in the event of an invasion. . . . On the Eastern Front the Red Army is taking the initiative. Germany no longer thinks it is necessary to hold out to the death at any particular point. [She] has a highly mobile defense . . . and at present Germany has no intention of launching a general offensive.'' Oshima is also told that he cannot meet with Hitler because Foreign Minister von Ribbentrop wants to be present but that he has been ill for some time. Therefore any such meeting will have to be postponed. Nevertheless, Oshima has divined that the future of Germany has reached a watershed.

The next day, Oshima tries to find out what is really going on. He attempts to draw out the Under Secretary of the German Foreign Office, von Steengracht, by suggesting that Italy is about ''to shake hands with the Anglo-Saxons and start peace talks right off the bat.''[58]

The German's response is that even should Italy drop out of the war, Hitler is determined to fight on. As for the Italians, von Steengracht for the first time derides them to the Japanese. ''We had to keep bolstering Italy,'' he says, ''with men, arms and planes; we had to let her have too much. Take the Balkans and France; Hitler always had to be too polite to Mussolini about them. We couldn't do what we wanted to do there. Also Italy was an economic liability to us. We had to ship her large quantities of grain, coal, petroleum and metals. The Italian forces were never any good; we knew that from the start. Take last winter on the Eastern Front. Take the Balkans; the Italians caused us no end of trouble there. Let Italy drop out if she wants to, it won't hurt us any.''

As for other governments, von Steengracht says that Hungary has promised to stand by Germany. So will Rumania. And ''the Croatian Government has given us a similar assurance.''

---

58. SRS 1041, 30 July 1943.

Oshima asks if Germany won't have to take on the defense of Italy all by herself. Says von Steengracht: "Wouldn't that be frightful? . . . We are determined to maintain peace and order in Italy. . . . But even if Italy should suddenly try to rush into the arms of our foes and make a separate peace, she cannot succeed, because . . . we will . . . throw a monkey wrench into any such machinery."

In Istanbul, meanwhile, the new Italian foreign minister tells Ambassador Kurihara that Italy has only three hundred planes left in her air force and "only enough oil to last our [naval] fleet one day."[59] Says Kurihara: "When a suitable time comes, [Italy] will have to make a separate peace."

From reading the Magic Summaries and looking at them as would Generals Marshall and Eisenhower, one can see how and why the Allied negotiators are able to tell their Italian counterparts that they have only one choice: unconditional surrender. More to the point, the Allied negotiators will tell the Italians they have only ten days to accept the terms. The Italians will also be smart enough to grasp the offer within the specified time frame. An armistice between the Italians and the Allies will be signed on September 3, 1943. Now, let us examine how the Japanese give the Allies the vital information and the confidence needed to talk the Italians into surrendering.

✖ ✖ ✖

From the last day of July through the month of August, the reports Japanese diplomats provided Tokyo, and thereby the Allies, are so devastatingly accurate that Allied strategists might as well have been sitting in on the meetings these diplomats describe.

On July 31, 1943, the report from Japanese ambassador Hidaka[60] reveals that he had a final interview with Mussolini just before he was thrown out of office on July 25. The analysts in Washington note that Hidaka's report contradicts the newspaper accounts of the Italian crisis, which stated there was only one session of the Fascist Council (on Saturday, July 24, from 8 P.M. to 2 A.M., when the vote to oust Il Duce was allegedly taken). But according to Hidaka, there was a second vote by the Council on Sunday and the vote to oust Mussolini was not held until then. Say the analysts: "Hidaka's report of the conversation sug-

---

59. Ibid.
60. SRS 1042, 31 July 1943.

gests that even at that late hour Il Duce himself did not know that the jig was up.'' According to the same analysts, Il Duce spoke to Hidaka in ''a flood of words; his language was at times violent and his thoughts noticeably disconnected.''

Mussolini is quoted as saying: ''As things are going now, we cannot, without ample assistance from Germany, defend ourselves from the enemy, much less strike them. Germany should realize that Italy is very important to her.

''Always our enemies are the Anglo-Americans. Unless we defeat them, this war will never really end.

''From the very beginning, I said to the Germans, 'Fight England and America!' I tell them now that in order to do this they must, at all costs, return the Ukraine to the Soviet Union. I think if the war between Germany and Russia were to end now, Germany could fight the Anglo-Saxons without the Ukraine. Why does Germany have to take territories where no Germans live? My God! She has been able to do practically nothing since she took the areas. Look at the liability they have been to her. Look how they have harassed her. My God! I don't see why Germany can't use sense and retire to the 1939 line.

''The Soviet, too, is worn out. Beaverbrook, in a recent talk in Parliament, pointed out that she is suffering from want of food. Her supply lines are too long and her morale is not what it was. Russia is not getting along any too well with England and America. She knows they may try to grab the lion's share. On the other hand, the Anglo-Saxons are growing very suspicious of Russia. We recently heard about Stalin gathering in anti-Nazi émigrés and prisoners and organizing a free German group. *Pravda* played this up. That shows that if Hitler and the Nazis fall, Stalin will cooperate with Germany. England and the United States are horrified at the prospect.

''I knew from the beginning that nobody could strike Russia and get away with it. She is too vast. Everybody now remembers with amusement how at first Hitler boasted, 'I will defeat Russia in ten weeks.'

''I told Goering that it was asinine to fight a war in which you advanced five hundred kilometers and then had to retreat five hundred kilometers. I asked what sense was there in that. Last October several times I said the same thing to Hitler himself.

''Well, don't fool yourself, the Germans themselves are worn to a frazzle. They are sick of fighting. Not only the people, but the great majority of the military are ready to see the war done with, at least the war against Russia.

"We Italians, you see, always know when we have had enough, but those Germans don't. They go and go and go and think that, if it is necessary, there will be a time to find a way out. Let them go ahead. If they do, I can tell you there is going to be one big crack-up. . . . What a mess things are in now. Actually Hitler would like to help us if he could, but it is too late for that. All he is doing here in Italy is trying to gain time to strengthen his own fortress. Everybody feels that is the case. You know what he calls 'my fortress.' How utterly stupid it is for Hitler to retire into that shell.

"The enemy has it in for Russia. Gradually this will become apparent, but it will take time—considerable time. You Japanese go ahead and use Bose [Subhas Chandra Bose]. That is fine. But it will be next spring before you achieve anything, and that will be too late to help us.

"Can we hold out that long? As far as Italy is concerned, time has run out. Certainly, we can no longer say: 'Time is on our side.' Enemy bombers have played hell with our industries. Our synthetic petroleum plant at Livorno was bombed and it will take three or four months to get it back in shape. We have only one synthetic rubber factory—at Bologna; it is working overtime, and if they hit that, it will be a terrific military blow.[61]

"And look at the Eastern Front. Changing its tactics, the Red Army is carrying out a large-scale offensive. We hear people jokingly say that 'the big summer offensive is on and there won't be any winter.'

"Those Germans—stupid fools—don't know when they have had enough. The next time I see Hitler, I am going to say to him clearly and categorically that he must give up the fight against Russia. You Japanese please do the same thing. Tell him to quit. Maybe we can both drag Hitler away from that obsession. If we ever hope to win this war, we will have to."

Four days later the Magic Summary contains a report by Ambassador Hidaka about a conversation he had on July 27 with German ambassador von Mackensen, who said: "[The new government] Grandi and the Fascists are in a mood to compromise with the Allies. . . . The upshot of the crisis is that Fascism is dead. The Fascists are disappearing and their leaders have left no shadows behind them. . . . It is fantastic. . . . The new government looks none too good. Its statement

---

61. Mussolini's geography is wrong. The analysts in Washington note that there is a synthetic rubber plant at Ferrara, twenty-five miles northeast of Bologna. It is believed to be producing ten to twelve thousand tons per year. There is no report to date of bombers attacking the rubber plant. One can see that such an attack will soon come.

about continuing the war was very lukewarm. . . . The Italian Army favors the new setup and we will have to wait and see what its next move will be. What is happening in Sicily does not, as yet, seem to have had too bad an effect on the Army.''[62]

Hidaka's opinion of the situation is set forth in another communication to Tokyo. ''The advance of the Allies in Sicily and the lack of any appreciable German assistance have made the Italian people feel like throwing in the sponge,'' he says. ''The Italians mistrust the Germans greatly, and they feel that, once Italian cities are occupied by German troops, they will never be able to regain them. Many . . . are saying that there is no sense in fighting alongside the Germans to the common doom of both. . . . Italy can see no chance of regaining her colonies. The . . . people do not relish the idea of abandoning half their territory and retiring to the north to fight it out alongside the Germans, and they would not support a government which decided to follow that course.''[63]

The analysts in Washington note that Hidaka is saying that when Mussolini met Hitler on July 19, Il Duce must have seen that all Hitler was thinking of doing was to establish a defense line across the Appenine Mountains from Leghorn to Ancona. Thus, when the Fascist Grand Council met, Italy was faced with only two alternatives: either retire to the north and fight or get out of the war. The majority of the Council voted against withdrawing northward and continuing the war, and that decision brought about Mussolini's downfall.

Hidaka then ends his report with some prescient commentary. ''If the Germans try to take over part of Italy and defend it against the will of the Italians, the Italian troops which are maintaining order from Greece to Dalmatia and the approximately twelve Italian divisions stationed in southern France will no longer assist the Germans and . . . will welcome the enemy in. The effect on the German rear and the increased burden of the German forces will be terrible, and the Balkans and Germany's other allies will be shaken to their foundations. Unless Germany has sufficient judgment to understand the Italian crisis and to consider what is best for Italy . . . it may turn out that the battle of Italy is in fact the battle of Germany. . . . The war in Europe may become a battle for and by Germany pure and simple. This brings up very serious

62. SRS 1046, 4 August 1943.
63. Ibid.

questions as far as we Japanese are concerned, as I do not need to tell you.''[64]

The very same day, the Japanese ambassador to Turkey sends his government his views on the Italian situation. Citing the new Italian foreign minister in Istanbul as the source, the report to Tokyo says: ''[The new Italian government] hopes to establish peace very quickly on the condition that Italy remain neutral and be left out of the war. However, England and America consider it absolutely necessary to obtain Italy's unconditional surrender so that they may obtain it for military operations against Europe, and the Germans naturally have to take steps to defend northern Italy.''[65]

On the first of August, Ambassador Kurihara reports on a conversation he had seventy-two hours earlier with German ambassador Franz von Papen, who spoke with remarkable frankness about Germany's predicament.[66] ''The real problem still is the Eastern Front,'' says von Papen. ''. . . If the tide doesn't change, and the Eastern Front stays as it is today, we [Germany] will be at a loss for reserves. Then both militarily and politically our backs will be to the wall. We have to face that possibility. In order to get out of that dilemma, the only thing we can do is the thing that America and England dread most—make peace with Russia. But, as I have often explained to you, I will have to admit that I don't see how a peace with the Soviet Union can possibly be achieved.

''There seem to be quite a few Germans who want to see you Japanese attack Russia in order to bolster the German-Soviet front. But I am against it. . . . That is what Roosevelt wants. If Japan attacks Russia, American planes will smash Japan to pieces and Roosevelt will be sitting on top of the world and get himself a fourth term to boot. He is one man we do not want reelected. It would ruin us.''

Meanwhile the Japanese ambassador to Indochina expresses his concern to Tokyo about how to curtail Allied air raids that are inflicting ''serious damage upon ships, harbors, equipment and factories. [Unless we stop the raids] our plans for enterprises in Indo-China are apt to be brought to a standstill.''[67]

Four days later, the Japanese air attaché in Berlin comments on

---

64. Ibid.
65. Ibid. One wonders how the Japanese diplomat could be so accurate in assessing the Allies' bargaining position. However, we already know that German intelligence was tapping the transatlantic phone conversations between Roosevelt and Churchill.
66. SRS 1043, 1 August 1943.
67. Ibid.

an official German report advising various diplomatic offices about recent Allied bombings.[68] The raids on Hamburg are devastating: "Summing up the last three great attacks on Hamburg—about 80 percent of the heart of the city was destroyed. Only isolated blocks of houses still remain standing. Therefore, detailed report of damage impossible. Information about loss of life, which is exceptionally high, still not definite." The analysts in Washington have tried to evaluate the accuracy of similar German reports in the past. They note that military targets are rarely discussed. However, the Germans "have been quite free in describing heavy damage to dwellings and high civilian casualties; as yet, however, there has been no evidence of exaggeration in that respect."

At the moment, no one knows the death toll in Hamburg. As we will see, however, the Japanese are so worried by the "firestorm" created by mixing incendiary booms with high-explosive devices—most houses in Japan are made of wood and not the brick and stone found in German cities—that they carefully start tracking down bomb damage in Germany.

On August 8, the Japanese consul stationed in Hamburg finally makes his first report.[69] He tells Tokyo that 80 percent of the vital Blohm & Voss submarine assembly plant has been put out of commission, that various other factories and the main railroad station have been destroyed, all communications disrupted. He claims that ten thousand buildings are destroyed; three hundred thousand people made homeless. Stores and the business quarter have been burned out. He concludes: "It will be a wonder if these destroyed sections of the city can be repaired, at least during the war."

From Berlin, Ambassador Oshima reports that he sent two of his staff to Hamburg after the bombings "to give comfort to the Japanese residents there." According to his staff's report, "it has thus far been impossible to give proper attention to fire fighting and to digging people out of the ruins. The authorities have taken over the groceries. Cooked food is being distributed in the parks and public squares amidst great confusion."

---

68. SRS 1047, 5 August 1943. The German circular was dated July 31. There were three nights of raids on Hamburg. The second created the new term *firestorm*. Thirty-five thousand residences were destroyed, or about one-third of all the housing in the city. Eight square miles of the city burned on the night of July 28, and forty-two thousand German civilians were killed. This figure surpassed all the English civilians killed during the Blitz. Albert Speer tells Hitler that if more cities are bombed like Hamburg, it might be "the end of the war."
69. SRS 1050, 8 August 1943.

For the first time, the Japanese sound frightened. The fate of their homeland is becoming clear to them, and they start trying to make Tokyo understand what lies in store for the homeland.

On August 9, two reports from Ambassador Oshima confirm that he finally met with Hitler on July 29.[70] During the next two days, further comments by Oshima are translated and passed along to General Marshall and others. The principal point of the first message, according to the analysts in Washington, is that "Oshima once more told Hitler that a Japanese attack on Russia is out of the question." It is Oshima's summary of his opinions that interests the analysts most. They note that he is "considerably more pessimistic than he has been at any time since Germany's attack on Russia." Oshima believes that Germany cannot win any further victories on the Eastern Front. She will have to go on the defensive and "protect herself as much as she can." He quotes Hitler as saying that he intends to "retire into the fortress" and concentrate on rebuilding Germany's material resources. (Mussolini mentioned Hitler's retiring into a "fortress" in his conversation with the Japanese ambassador in Rome before his fall from power; now Hitler uses the term with Oshima. The concept of this "fortress" will plague American strategy at the end of the war in Europe.)

Oshima also believes that Germany is faced with a life-or-death battle with the Soviet. But the Nazi Party is still so strong politically, and Germany's military defenses so firm, that there is little cause for "undue" anxiety on Tokyo's part.

Of extreme interest to Washington is the conclusion of Oshima's message, which is given to General Marshall verbatim. "A compromise peace is out of the question," Oshima tells Tokyo. "I asked Hitler whether he intends to make peace with Russia, and he replied by stating that, unless Germany made peace with Russia and turned on America and England, no one could tell how long the war would last or how it would turn out. However, he went on to say that, if Germany is to wage a long war against America and England, the Ukraine is absolutely necessary to him and therefore he would not consider peace with the Soviet unless he got that area. And he added that as things now stand, Russia certainly has no intention of making peace with Germany by sacrificing the Ukraine."

In another fragment of Oshima's messages to Tokyo, Hitler is quoted as saying: "I am absolutely not considering making peace with

---

70. SRS 1051, 9 August 1943; SRS 1052, 10 August 1943; and SRS 1053, 11 August 1943. These reports have been combined for the sake of the narrative.

Russia. Why, don't you know that if I did that the Soviet would beyond any peradventure of doubt reach out, clasp hands with the United States and squeeze you Japanese to death between them! Japan is in a very precarious position herself, and . . .'' The message breaks off.

If anything, Oshima covers all the bases. He even talks with the head of the SS, Heinrich Himmler, about Germany's problems of pacifying Ukraine. He quotes Himmler as saying: "The trouble is there is no difference between the people in the Ukraine and those in Russia proper. They have no racial peculiarity of their own. . . . The Caucasus is quite different. . . . I must admit that Stalin is patriotic and as cunning as the devil. . . . It is only by armed conflict that we can overthrow him."[71] In this fashion Oshima is telling Tokyo that there is no hope for long-term German occupation of these areas. Tokyo's hopes for political maneuvers, or psychological warfare against Russia, are destroyed.

Oshima also talks to Himmler about the role to be played by General Vlassov. Says Himmler: "We expect some pretty good political results from him, but we are using him only as a minor figurehead. We have not the slightest intention of ever making anything of him."[72] Now the Allies know Vlassov's true value. Without a power base inside the Soviet after the war, he will be worthless to the Allies. Thus he becomes a sacrificial pawn to offer the Soviet, even though it is likely he and his followers will be executed.

Another section of Oshima's talk with Hitler is decoded, and his comments about the new leader of Italy, Badoglio, are not flattering. "When Italy joined the war in 1940," says Hitler, "as Chief of Staff [he] asked Germany to let the Italians move troops into France just after we had finished our breakthrough there. He asked us to let him attack the four French divisions guarding the Franco-Italian border. . . . We told him no. Badoglio paid not the slightest heed, and with seventeen Italian divisions, mind you, he dashed straight forward, suffering immense losses. . . . [Later] I asked Badoglio to occupy both [Crete and Cyprus]. Badoglio said he wouldn't do it. Thereafter Italy launched her attack on Greece, and the failure of that campaign is now a matter of history. As you can see . . . Badoglio is one of those know-it-alls. . . . I have already lost faith in the Italian forces. The Italian Army no longer has its will to fight." Now come the all-important words.

"The Americans and the British are unpredictable; they do not

---

fight in an outright manner the way we Germans and Japanese do. Their policy is first to get air bases and then, under protection from the air, to creep up on us. Before long, as things look now, they are going to be on the Italian mainland.

"When they land, I certainly am not going to be fool enough to fight them down at the tip of the boot. There are plenty of fine encampments north of Rome. There in natural fortifications I shall form three lines: one, over the Apennines; two, along the River Po; and three, in the Alps. Also, now that Sicily is gone . . . we Germans must strengthen our garrisons everywhere in Southern Europe. I am going to send reinforcements to the Balkans, Southern France, and Italy proper."[73]

In Washington, the analysts add a series of notes to this last statement by Hitler. They point out that Oshima "interpolates that Hitler spoke in a very determined fashion when he discussed the formation of defense lines in Italy." They also note that at least one German panzer division had recently moved into southern Italy, and there were indications that another panzer division might also move south. The so-called Eur-African Order of Battle Branch advises that the defense line of the Apennines would be Pisa-Florence-Rimini.

Hitler is drawing down his manpower from both the Eastern Front *and* the defenses of France to support the German effort in Italy. The Allies, therefore, must force Italy to surrender quickly. Allied troops must land there and Hitler must be forced to fight there, using even more divisions from France and giving the potential invasion of France a better chance of success.

But what are the realities of the German reserves that Hitler can draw upon? What manpower figures can the Allies plug into their invasion calculations?

To the rescue comes Major General Okamoto, the head of the group of Japanese "liaison men" in Europe. He sends a long report on the world situation to Tokyo.[74] He tells Tokyo that Italy's break with the Axis is already "a fait accompli"; that "fearful and frightful" Allied bombings, plus the Russian offensive, have forced Germany to go on the defensive. If Germany can partially achieve her goals in Russia, "she will be lucky."

Okamoto is known in Washington for his objective analyses of the German military machine. Particular attention is paid to his estimate

---

73. Ibid.
74. SRS 1054, 12 August 1945.

that "Germany has within her boundaries at least twenty-odd divisions of strategic reserves and can still replace them." However, Okamoto believes Germany cannot free many men for other duty unless she withdraws from the Eastern Front, and her mobilizable reserves are about to reach their limit. . . . The German Air Force, numerically speaking, is now far behind America and England. (Okamoto believes the German pilots are still superior to the Allies.) The future ability of Germany to keep on fighting and maintain her material resources "depends on what destruction the enemy wreaks by bombing." As for the matter of manpower, "if we compare Germany to Russia, Russia comes out on top. That is not a happy thing to say, but it is a fact."

Okamoto sees no hope in a split between the Allies. As for peace between Germany and Russia, he points out that Germany [the Army in particular] desires it. That with the loss of Italy, the critics of Japan in Europe will become more vocal, charging that Japan is monopolizing everything for herself in the Far East and has no plans for helping out in any effective way in Europe. He points out that many Italians believe Japan picked a quarrel with America that "is going to end in our ruin. . . . If that idea spreads throughout the world, we will have something to worry about."[75] Aside from giving the Allies a propaganda tool to use against Japan, Okamoto's report is the first of many that will over months describe how the pool of manpower available for mobilization and reinforcing the so-called West Wall on the Atlantic steadily decreases.[76]

✹ ✹ ✹

Oil.

By mid-1943, the Japanese are becoming more and more concerned about the subject. Oil is the lifeblood of the Japanese home islands. Thus, the stability of Iran is of ever-increasing concern to Tokyo. Washington is also concerned, and the Magic analysts note a special message from the Japanese ambassador in Ankara to Tokyo.[77] "The Russians are spreading a great deal of propaganda in Iran," he tells Tokyo. "They are trying to Sovietize Iranian Azerbaijan and are promising the people independence and union with Soviet Azerbaijan.

---

75. Ibid.
76. As one example, see SRS 1055, 13 August 1943.
77. SRS 1056, 14 August 1943.

They are supplying munitions to the Kurds and other minority groups and are stirring them up to revolt.'' He also points out that Russia is trying to get Communist representatives elected to the National Parliament, while England worries that Russia may extend her control to the Persian Gulf. He claims that the majority of Iranians hate both England and Russia and hope for a German victory. Followers of the former shah [Reza Pahlavi, forced to abdicate in 1941] are trying to exploit these feelings, and they meet at night with the Shah to plot the revival of pro-German sentiment.

Meanwhile, the conversation between Hitler and Baron Oshima, held nearly a month earlier, is still producing new insights for the analysts in Washington. Previously untranslatable portions of Oshima's messages to Tokyo are now deciphered and reveal that during his meeting with Hitler, the two were joined by Major General Okamoto, Marshall Keitel and Colonel General Jodl. In the presence of these men, Hitler asserted he would not press Japan to attack Russia.[78]

"In my opinion the Soviet is Japan's primary enemy,'' Oshima quotes Hitler as saying. "However, whether or not Japan is to attack her is up to Japan. . . . Far be it from us Germans to give military advice to a nation that ran such a risk and came out so victorious as Japan did at Pearl Harbor. In the fight against Russia antitank guns and tanks are extremely important. I don't know how well the Japanese forces are equipped with these weapons, but if they begin a fight in Russia and subsequently meet with disaster, all the Axis allies would be seriously hampered. No, I think we had better leave such matters up to Japan and trust her to do what she thinks is right.''

This statement is significant to Washington because it reveals that Hitler is warning his military to stop pressuring him to get the Japanese to fight Russia. (In his report to Tokyo of August 4, 1943, Okamoto stated that Germany's highest leaders "clearly understand our attitude toward Russia,'' but that the German Army does not "see quite that far.'' Okamoto warned: "We will have to watch out for these German militarists.''[79])

At this meeting Foreign Minister von Ribbentrop makes one last effort to prod Japan to attack Russia. Oshima reports that "Chancellor Hitler wheeled about and said to von Ribbentrop: 'No, it is not right to make such a request as that . . .' ''

The conversation turns to the subject of a German-Japanese

---

78. SRS 1062, 20 August 1943.
79. SRS 1054, 12 August 1943.

exchange of their "best weapons of war." Moments later, Hitler inter-rupts, saying: "That Italian situation is utterly lamentable. . . . What an ally! If we only had you Japanese in the position of Italy, we would surely have already won this fight. Ah, well, it only goes to show that the only warrior races left in this world are the Germans and the Jap-anese."

The following day produces even more conversation between Hit-ler and Oshima.[80] It becomes clear that as late as July 29, the Germans still believed they could restore Mussolini to power. Hitler was upset that "the only man who was capable of holding Italy together and my one absolutely trusted collaborator was treated like a dog." Hitler ad-vances the novel idea that the revolt had taken place because the Italian army was upset that in Sicily the Axis would court-martial officers who put up no resistance or tried to desert to the enemy.

In his summation for Tokyo, Oshima says that "although [Hitler] did not appear to be damning the Italian army . . . he has made up his mind, and, if necessary, he is ready to send German troops into Italy. If Italy tries to rush into a separate peace, he will use his troops at one of three lines to defend the European fortress."

The warning to Washington is clear: the sooner Allied troops can land in Italy, the better.

As August draws to a close, the Japanese consul in Hamburg sends a more comprehensive report on the damage caused by Allied bombs. He claims the destruction has made people throughout Germany "terror-stricken," and one can sense the consul's own fear in reading his mes-sage. "Local authorities have told me," he says, "that . . . twenty-two thousand bodies have been recovered. In addition some thirty to forty thousand bodies are still trapped in shelters. . . . In a word Germany's proud second-largest city . . . was completely destroyed. . . . Hamburg is now one great mass of ruins; I wish to make it plain that I am not exag-gerating. The restoration of the city will take fifty years even after the victorious end of the war. . . . The war has now resolved itself into one great war of attrition." The Consul concludes his report that the Japanese economic adviser in Berlin, Matsushima, visited the city and "he feels the same as I do and wishes me to tell you so."

The next day, the analysts in Washington summarize for General Marshall a series of recent messages to Tokyo about German reverses on the Eastern Front, the devastation of Allied bombing raids, the fact that Italy is out of the war, that Admiral Doenitz has admitted to Am-

---

80. SRS 1063, 21 August 1943.

bassador Oshima that the submarine campaign is not going well and Marshal Milch has also told him that the Luftwaffe "has its back to the wall."

Now, on August 21, 1943, Foreign Minister Shigemitsu sends a message to Berlin in which he asks for even more information from the German leaders.[81] What Shigemitsu wants to know in particular includes the following:

- ✱ All the German plans for carrying on the war against the British and Americans. This is aimed especially at information about the air war and the supply of aviation gasoline.

- ✱ Germany's plans for fighting Russia. Tokyo wants "very detailed information on the land and air forces which Germany intends to muster."

- ✱ Germany's industrial and food problems. This includes "munitions, transportation, the production of airplanes, fuel oil, tanks, submarines, etc. Be particularly careful to send definite figures." (General Okamoto has already reported to Tokyo that Germany will produce 15 million tons of petroleum in 1943 and he foresaw no petroleum problem "this year.") Shigemitsu doubts whether the amount of petroleum produced in 1943 will be enough, "particularly in view of our own experience. . . . Send us some very concrete information."

What more could Marshall or Roosevelt or Churchill or Eisenhower ask?

Tokyo is determined to find out the secret details of how Germany will fight the remainder of the war. The questions Tokyo wants answered are exactly what the Allies need to know if the invasion of Europe is to be successful. The Allied leaders must have breathed a sigh of relief upon reading Shigemitsu's message: the information they need so desperately will be furnished, accurately and completely, by the Japanese.

But, as we will see, the threat that this priceless information might be completely cut off, because the Americans are not properly security conscious, will hold grave consequences for the Republican nominee in the 1944 presidential election.

---

81. SRS 1068, 26 August 1943.

7

September 1943. For the first time in World War II, British-American forces are fighting on the continent of Europe, having invaded Italy on September 9: the Americans by seaborne invasion at Salerno and the British across the Strait of Messina from Sicily.

This had been preceded by negotiations in Lisbon between the Allies and the new Italian government that ended on August 20, with the Italian representative returning to Rome with the Allied demand for unconditional surrender and a ten-day deadline for acceptance. The new government lead by Badoglio accepted the Allied terms on the first of September and signed an armistice two days later. With the Allied landing force at sea, Eisenhower makes the mistake of announcing the armistice on September 8, and the Germans simply disarm the Italian ground forces. However, the Germans do not approach the Italian Navy quickly enough. The Italian ships at Taranto, Genoa and La Spezia set sail for Malta. The Luftwaffe intercepts them, sinks the flagship *Roma,* but cannot prevent the remainder of the fleet from surrendering to the Allies at Malta. The disposition of these ships will become a key element in the Magic messages since the Japanese fear these ships might be used against them in the Pacific.

The Germans, meantime, have problems of their own. They establish two defense lines: one in the north with Field Marshal Rommel in command, and another in the south under Field Marshal Kesselring. The two field marshals have presented different plans for the defense of Italy to Hitler. This means there are eight German divisions in the north and ten in the south with Hitler agreeing to the plans proposed by both his commanders. (One cannot help but wonder what would have happened at this stage of the war had the Germans fought under a unified command and not divided their forces.) By mid-September the British troops driving up from Sicily link up with the American forces that landed at Salerno. The slow, grinding attack northward commences. The horrors of Cassino and the landings at Anzio lie ahead.

During the negotiations for the Italian armistice, the Germans do their best to pacify the Japanese. The German under secretary for foreign affairs, von Steengracht, tells Oshima that "we Germans are a little suspicious of the Badoglio regime, but . . . there is little real foundation to these rumors [of a peace mission]."[1]

The more important portion of this day's Magic is an analysis of the traffic between Lisbon, Madrid and Tokyo concerning the suspicion of the Italians that "American intelligence men" have stolen the codebooks of the Japanese legation in Lisbon. As mentioned earlier, this created a furor in Washington highlighted by General Strong's memo to Marshall about the amateurs in the OSS. The Japanese side of the story begins in July, when Tokyo sends an investigator to Lisbon without telling the legation about his mission.

The investigator is Secretary Miura from the Madrid office. The Lisbon office receives him with "considerable suspicion." Returning to Madrid, he reports that he doesn't believe the codebooks have been stolen. However, he thinks the Lisbon office has been sending a large number of phony "Fuji" reports. The source for these is a former Portuguese Foreign Office employee, who allegedly provided official copies of Portuguese diplomatic wires, but which really are decoys— as Tokyo had suspected. The "Fuji" source is also suspected of working for the Allies, his purpose being to get the Japanese to transmit his reports in Japanese code, thus facilitating the decryption of the code.

When Tokyo finally tells the Lisbon office about the suspected plot, Minister Morishima loses his temper in a most undiplomatic fashion. The analysts in Washington comment that his response to Tokyo provides "an unusually enlightening illustration of characteristics which seem to be common among members of the Japanese diplomatic corps." Morishima's messages to Tokyo are given verbatim to General Marshall.

"Some time ago," Morishima complains, "Secretary Miura . . . came over here to Lisbon. I learned afterwards that he had come on a secret mission to investigate the ins and outs of my espionage net. I did not like this. . . . I go over to Madrid and lo and behold, I find that my own Foreign Office asked them to send a man to investigate me! . . . Of course none of the codebooks got out. . . . I know just how very

---

1. SRS 1075, 2 September 1943.

careful the Foreign Office is about its codes. . . . If it is a fact that the codebooks have gotten outside my office, simple resignation or *hara-kiri* would not cure what has already been done. You don't wire me anything; you have a member of another office come here and investigate me. . . . Is this a civilized way to treat a man? . . . I have never known another man to be treated as I have been treated. Now I know that codes are the very life of the Foreign Office, and now that suspicion has been cast upon me, I can never live it down. People will always be whispering behind my back. It was a sneaking, dirty trick, if you ask me. Would you please condescend to consider that I herewith resign.''[2]

The Madrid office sends messages of a similar nature supporting Morishima. Tokyo tells its diplomats to cool down. The Foreign Office wires Minister Suma that he did a good job of investigation, explaining that, "you see, the trouble was that the Military Attaché in Rome sent us some information and we simply had to act on it. Please communicate this in a suitable manner to Minister Morishima and tell him to cut out worrying and rest easy.''[3]

There were other consequences to this, however. One is that the Japanese change the codes for the military attachés—as General Strong feared they might do—and for a time the Allies lose an invaluable source of information.

Meantime, from Berlin, Oshima has been following instructions, and he reports on Germany's experience with various types of Allied incendiary bombs and also explains how the Germans are building bomb shelters for city dwellers.[4] While from Rome, Ambassador Hidaka reports that the main railway line through the city has been cut by Allied bombers both in the north and the south.[5]

The mass of information contained in the Magic Summaries now becomes so thorough and complex that the author writes the following note to himself: "From this date on, my handwritten notes will merely outline the significance of each day's Summary lest I drown in information.''

Washington has been waiting for the Japanese reaction to the Italian armistice. Apparently the surrender was accomplished without the Germans telling the Japanese about the negotiations, which seems at

---

2. Ibid.
3. Ibid.
4. SRS 1073, 31 August 1943; SRS 1080, 7 September 1943.
5. SRS 1077, 4 September 1943.

odds with the prior report that German intelligence had informed Hitler about them. Anyway, as late as September 5, Ambassador Hidaka in Rome is telling Tokyo that the Badoglio regime "was merely following an aimless day-to-day policy, relying on the Army to maintain peace and order in the country . . . and trying to appease both the Left and the Right."[6]

The next day, the report to Tokyo from Chiengnai in Southeast Asia notes that the Thai Army is bogged down by the rainy season. The Japanese are worried because the Chinese Nationalist leader, Chiang Kai-shek, is trying to get the Thai Army to revolt and join his pro-Allies Chungking army.[7]

Meantime, in Switzerland, Japanese minister Sakamoto reports on a conversation he has had with the Swiss foreign minister about the course of the war and how Japan should interpret future Allied strategy. Sakamoto quotes the Swiss as saying: "Churchill's phraseology may be considered a little bombastic, but he has the peculiar characteristic of never telling a lie."[8]

Baron Oshima's report to Tokyo about the Italian surrender is intercepted and decoded three days after the event. "Oh, how cunningly this whole thing was hidden," he tells Tokyo.[9] But what Tokyo wants to know—immediately—is where are the surrendered Italian ships located? Oshima is told to find out.

The chaos in Rome as a result of the American landings at Salerno on September 9 becomes apparent when Ambassador Hidaka reports that the German embassy staff fled the city that day, only to be halted in midjourney and told to return. Hidaka and most of his staff left Rome that same day and relocated in Venice.[10]

In mid-September, Oshima leaves Berlin to check firsthand the devastation wrought in Hamburg. His long, detailed report gives the Allies a clear picture of the destruction caused by the three raids and

---

6. SRS 1082, 9 September 1943.

7. SRS 1083, 10 September 1943. Unfortunately, for reasons of space, this work cannot go into detail about what Magic reveals about Chiang Kai-shek and his dealings with both the Japanese and Chinese Communists. Needless to say, the writer believes that much material remains to be mined by historians in this area. The first Magic Summary dealing with Chiang and the Communists is SRS 1084, 11 September 1943. One can also understand why President Truman picked General Marshall to go to China with the idea of negotiating a peace between the Nationalists and the Communists. Marshall was the only American who had the intimate background knowledge and prestige to undertake this hopeless task.

8. Ibid.

9. SRS 1084, 11 September 1943.

10. SRS 1087, 14 September 1943.

warns Tokyo of what lies ahead for Japan.[11] The next day, he files five more messages detailing the precautions being taken to reduce the damage caused by bombing.

Oshima also sends a report on the value of the Ukraine to Germany. This is important because it shows that Allied estimates of Ukrainian grain production are too low and must be revised if the Allies are to make the Germans endure a shortage of food, which, to date, they have not. The analysts in Washington note that for several years Germany has been almost self-sufficient in grains. She produces nearly 24 million metric tons yearly. The Ukraine has been supplying 500,000 metric tons says Oshima, which is more than anyone had thought. This means that on this front the German Army has been supplying itself locally, which is significant because Germany did not have to export grain to feed all her troops, nor did she have to strain her transportation system. According to Oshima, this is why Germany cannot give up the Ukraine without affecting Germany's overall food supply and national morale.[12]

It is no surprise to Washington then, that after winning the battle of Kursk in the summertime, Stalin keeps pushing his troops forward in a rolling offensive. In mid-September they are driving out of the Ukraine along the northern shores of the Black Sea. The Germans are losing their breadbasket; the Soviet has recovered it.

This leads Oshima to report to Tokyo that his usual contact in the German Foreign Office is unusually glum. "Everything is dark and gloomy on the Eastern Front," the contact tells Oshima. "Worrying will do no good. Perhaps in another week or two the Soviet summer offensive will come to an end."[13]

Stalin is no fool, however. He throws 2.5 million men into a new attack.

The Japanese in Italy also give a clear picture of the fate of British POWs in Italy. The Japanese track down how many have escaped to Switzerland, how many have been recaptured by the Germans and how many have joined the anti-German guerrilla forces.[14]

Now comes a vital report from Oshima detailing a new German effort in the U-boat war in the North Atlantic. Back in June, Tokyo had asked Oshima to report on why there had been a decline in Allied

---

11. SRS 1088, 15 September 1943.
12. SRS 1089, 16 September 1943.
13. SRS 1091, 18 September 1943.
14. SRS 1097, 24 September 1943.

shipping losses. He spoke with Admiral Doenitz and the Chief of the German Naval Strategic Section and learned that the Allies had a new direction finder and were using auxiliary aircraft carriers. This had forced the Germans to give up using wolf packs.

On September 18, Oshima learns from Under Secretary von Steengracht that Germany is going to reopen submarine warfare "with greater intensity than before." Oshima seeks another audience with Admiral Doenitz, who tells him that "I have always been confident that Britain and America can be beaten by German science." This is why Doenitz has gotten Hitler's approval to double the production of U-boats. The production schedule has been so effective that Doenitz pushed the offensive forward a month. The U-boats are also using a new method of attack. Now they will first strike the escort vessels. Torpedoes, guns and radio location apparatus have been upgraded. The U-boats can escape detection by Allied bombers in the Bay of Biscay, the main route to and from the Atlantic battlefield, because they can spot the Allied planes first.[15]

This is terrible news for the Allies. The analysts in Washington note that Doenitz has "created a research council for the constant improvement of our equipment." Furthermore, Doenitz has asked Hitler for sixteen thousand "sea cadets" to train officers for submarines and E-boats, and his request is approved. (Oshima even goes to the Chief of the German Navy Staff to confirm Doenitz's claims.)

If there is any good news in this message for the Allies, it is assurance that the new German plan of attack comes from the highest possible source. Furthermore, Doenitz admits he can no longer count on the Luftwaffe for assistance. This is the chink in the German U-boat strategy that the Allies must exploit. German aerial surveillance of the North Atlantic convoy routes must be stopped; Allied aerial supremacy over the Bay of Biscay must be established so that U-boats cannot travel on the surface by day or night.

The continuing advance of the Soviet troops on the Eastern Front is acknowledged by Baron Oshima in his report of October 1 to Tokyo.[16] He tells Tokyo without equivocation that Germany cannot advance again in Russia. The Germans have been trying to establish a final line of resistance along the Dnieper River, but, he says, they cannot hold it.

---

15. SRS 1101, 28 September 1943.
16. SRS 1104, 1 October 1943.

The accuracy of his report is upheld by the fact that Stalin opens up a new offensive to recapture Estonia, Latvia and Lithuania. In mid-October Stalin will strike again in the south on the Dnieper Bend; by the end of the month the Crimea will once again belong to Russia. The fighting is horrific, but the Germans cannot hold their defensive positions anywhere. What Oshima hopes for is the establishment of an impregnable German defense line "which the Russians will be unable to break through. If and when that time comes, Germany should in my opinion make peace with Russia, because it would be the best way to turn on America and England and win the war."[17]

The following day, from Madrid, Minister Suma makes the first pronouncement that Japan must be willing to commit national suicide, fighting the war to the death. In his opinion, this "dauntless attitude . . . will dispel the enemy's tendency to doubt the unbreakable spirit of the Japanese soldier."[18]

Declares Suma: "Lately we have gone on the defensive in the Southwest Pacific; we have evacuated Kiska; we have made friendly gestures toward Chungking. What has become of the old-time fighting spirit we showed in Korea? Why can't we develop the rich resources of our occupied territories? The enemy has the idea we are going to be a pushover. Though I am sorry to say it, their propaganda is even beginning to cause some of our own officials to doubt whether we are going to win.

"If we can thwart widespread American expectations that the war will end this year, or in the spring of 1944, not only will Roosevelt stand little chance of a fourth term, but the Americans' war fatigue will increase, their morale will be seriously affected and their home front will fall into chaos. . . .

"Since the fall of North Africa, the war has entered upon a stage equally critical for the Axis and the Allies. . . . Events of the next six months will result in a Waterloo for one side or the other, and will decide the fate of this war.

"I tell everybody that we, a nation of 100 million patriots who have not known defeat for twenty-six hundred years, will literally turn ourselves into bullets of flesh, confident in the end we will defeat the enemy; and that is the sort of spirit we must have."

---

17. Ibid.
18. SRS 1105, 2 October 1943.

✗ ✗ ✗

The idea of having to end the war by invading the home islands of Japan that are defended by 100 million suicidal human "bullets of flesh" does not appeal to Washington. The readers of the Magic Summaries know all too well the tenacity of the Japanese soldier, sailor and airman. They do not underestimate the Japanese warrior as Suma believes. What Suma does not comprehend is the concept of warfare that is being waged in Europe, which is similar to what Gen. William Tecumseh Sherman proposed to the commander of the Union forces, Gen. Ulysses S. Grant, in the American Civil War: there is little or no difference between a civilian and a soldier. The civilian who supports his nation's war effort must be made to feel the same pain and fear the soldier experiences. The war must be brought home with all its ferocity upon the civilian population. The bombing of Hamburg is a first example. Worse will have to come. The attacking Allied armies cannot be expected to fight a war of attrition after which the victor is unable to occupy the territory of the vanquished.

The Americans, Australians and New Zealanders are already painfully aware of Japanese soldiers' habit of fighting to the death. This has been evidenced in the battles on Guadalcanal, in the attacks on New Georgia, Bougainville, New Britain and New Guinea. It will become even more pronounced in the fighting for the tiny atoll of Tarawa, where American Marines suffer 3,500 casualties to inflict 5,000 on the defending Japanese. Next will come Kwajalein atoll, where the Japanese endure 8,000 casualties to 1,800 for the Americans. After that will come the battle for Eniwetok, where the Japanese fight to the last, losing 3,500 men to 1,200 Americans. General Marshall and Admiral King know that even worse casualty figures are yet to come as American forces close in and have to land on Iwo Jima and Okinawa.

The truth is this: When it comes time to invade the Japanese home islands, America will not be capable of enduring casualty figures of two to one, or even five to one. Even if Washington discounts Ambassador Suma's figuring of "100 million . . . bullets of flesh" and lowers his figure by half, or even 75 percent, the projections for American casualties in an invasion of Japan are mind-boggling.[19] At a five-to-one

---

19. During the author's thirty-year career in publishing, I was never able to commission a novel, or a combat autobiography, that spanned the entire Pacific war. The reason: American units

casualty ratio, it may well take 1 million American casualties to invade Japan.

As we will see, Ambassador Suma's call for national sacrifice will be sounded again and again throughout the war; indeed, until the very end of it.

How then can the Allies invade Japan without losing more men than the invasion is worth?

The question raised in October 1943, two years before the war's end, demonstrates clearly America's urgent need to complete construction of the first atomic bomb.

✴ ✴ ✴

On October 4, Washington decodes a message sent on September 20, by Japanese ambassador Hidaka from Venice. By now everyone knows that the Italian fleet has surrendered to the Allies at Malta. But Hidaka's sense of failure is so acute the analysts in Washington believe General Marshall should read Hidaka's words for himself. "It seems that much of Italy's naval power has fallen into the hands of the enemy," Hidaka tells Tokyo.[20] "When I think of what harm that may do to our own war effort, I am overcome with dread. . . . I had no idea he [Badoglio] would do anything like this. The treachery of Badoglio, Guriglia and their gang also caught the Germans in Rome by surprise. I feel that I did my poor best to forestall this calamity, but because I did not suspect such treason, I was unable to take suitable measures. Indeed I have no excuse. Therefore, prostrating myself, I await whatever word you may have for me."

A few days later, Oshima reports from Berlin after a two-day trip to Hitler's headquarters in East Prussia. The analysts in Washington note that he conferred with Ribbentrop and that Oshima proposed to the Foreign Minister the idea that Germany should consider making peace with Russia. According to the Washington analysts, Oshima's "account . . . is chiefly remarkable for Ribbentrop's confession that the

---

suffered such heavy casualties that no "fighting characters" survived multiple invasion landings. This publishing phenomenon was confirmed for me over the years by the agents Don Congden of the Harold Matson agency (Don was a Marine in the Pacific) and Jane Cushman of JCA Literary Agency. We all wanted such books.
20. SRS 1107, 4 October 1943.

question of peace with Russia is 'a serious one,' and that he was 'going to think about it.' "[21]

Oshima had broached the subject after Ribbentrop claimed that events in the Mediterranean had forced the Germans to withdraw twelve divisions from the Eastern Front. (This is significant proof to Washington that its strategy is stretching German military capabilities to the breaking point; twelve divisions withdrawn from the Eastern Front ensures the success of the current Soviet attacks.) The Japanese ambassador takes great pains to point out that the idea of making peace with Russia is his own idea and not that of Tokyo, which "has even forbidden discussion of such a delicate matter."

To this, Ribbentrop replies: "The Fuehrer has not changed in the slightest his opinion that this war must, and can be, decided by force."

Oshima counters, saying: ". . . When the war with Russia first began, you told me Germany's object was to inflict a terrific defeat on the Red Army and break Russia into small nations. However, in my opinion, it is now impossible for Germany to do anything like that. If the original objective cannot be achieved, why not modify your terms in dealing with Russia and emphasize knocking out the Anglo-Americans? Depending on how Russia reacts, don't you think you should reconsider the matter?"

With Ribbentrop replying, "Well, this is a serious matter, and I, too, am going to think about it," Washington begins a daily watch for the possibility that Germany and Russia might make a surprise peace, the aftermath of which could be disastrous for the Allies. Later on, as we will see, Oshima's maneuvering to create a Russo-German peace in 1943 will play a major part in Japan's diplomatic wriggling to avoid unconditional surrender in 1945. Because, to survive and maintain the territory she has conquered and still holds at the end of the war, Japan will have to find a world-power partner. For Washington, the question is, how and when will Japan try to find such a partner? In turn, this maneuvering by Tokyo will have tremendous impact on how the Pacific war ends.

For the citizens of London, this day's Magic Summary contains bad news. German propaganda for many months has been threatening retaliation against England for the heavy bombing of Germany. The best-educated guesses around the various European capitals is that the Luftwaffe will be given new planes and a new, superpowerful bomb.

---

21. SRS 1110, 7 October 1943.

Now Oshima reports that a terror weapon will be unleashed: long-range rocket guns. The date for the new weapon's use: mid-December. According to Oshima, the effect of the new weapons as a "means of military retaliation will be equaled only by the political reverberations."[22]

✱ ✱ ✱

It is amazing the tricks played by time. Fifty years ago, Allied strategists were planning where it would be safest to land an invasion force in France. As I write this book half a century later, a writer bylined only as A. Alverez proposes that for a "weekend of serious eating, sensible Londoners cross the [English] Channel." Arriving by ferryboat in Calais, the writer describes driving past "wide bays and headlands—Cap Blanc-Nez, Cap Gris-Nez—past lighthouses and the great concrete fortifications built by the Germans against an Allied invasion that never arrived in these parts."[23]

For those interested in food, the house special is a fish stew, which the chef tells Alverez is called *la gainee* and for which he learned the recipe for from his fisherman grandfather; the place to go for this gourmet's delight is the Hôtellerie de la Rivière in the small seaside town of Pont-duBriques. However, fifty years earlier, for the Allied planners of OVERLORD, the best menu to read is the Magic Summaries. And as strange as it may sound, the Japanese played a major role in how the Allies picked the best place to invade France, also in gauging ahead of time how the German defenders would react defensively.

On the front page of the Magic Summary of October 8, 1943, placed there obviously to catch Chief of Staff Marshall's eye, is a long report that has just become available in which the Japanese military attaché describes a trip he made in August with Major General Okamoto to inspect the German fortifications in France and the Low Countries. The analysts pick out the following salient points for General Marshall's attention:[24]

"The whole coastline from Holland to the Pyrenees is strongly fortified with tens of thousands of strong-point fortifications which are linked together by comparatively simple earthworks. While the defenses

---

22. Ibid.
23. The Sunday *New York Times,* 9 May 1993, Travel Section.
24. SRS 1111, 8 October 1943.

naturally vary in strength, depending upon the importance—and also upon the difficulty—of defending a given point, the Germans can reinforce them with excellent mobile reserve units.

"The strong points have been constructed for 360-degree defense. Any one of these fortifications can be defended against attacks from the rear.

"Five hundred thousand tons of concrete are being used each month in constructing fortifications and roads. Of this amount, only one hundred thousand tons are being imported from Germany.

"If Britain and America discover the state of the German defenses, they will not attempt a large-scale landing on the Atlantic coast. A sudden attack might break through the shoreline defenses, which are strong only at likely points of attack, but any landing force will eventually be pulverized by the German reserves."

In reports that follow, the Japanese will detail specifically how various landing spots are protected. For the moment, however, the key element for the Allies to know is that the Germans are adopting a defense that relies on mobile, hard-hitting reserve forces; the German plan is *not* to stop the invasion at the high-tide mark on the beaches.

The next day, Baron Oshima further describes his recent trip to Hitler's headquarters in East Prussia where he also talked at considerable length to Hitler himself. The analysts in Washington note that this is the first time since July 29 that Oshima has seen Hitler, and the conversation between the two men touches "on most of the significant developments that have occurred since then."[25] It is also noted that Oshima finds the Fuehrer "in excellent form both mentally and physically," and especially when "he started on Badoglio's betrayal or when he was launching vituperations against the Americans and the British, he slapped the top of his desk with his hand and spoke in his frank old style with boundless enthusiasm."

As is his usual fashion, Oshima reports Hitler's remarks verbatim, which makes them more interesting to read because one can see for one's self the emphasis that Hitler places on specific matters. According to Oshima, Hitler says: "I foresaw the danger that Italy would fall into her present fix, but I did not dream it would happen as it did. Really, never in the history of the world was such an act of infidelity perpetrated. If Badoglio had only opened up and told me things had reached the point where Italy could not fight any longer, why, then we Germans would certainly have made some concessions to Italy's demands and

25. SRS 1112, 9 October 1943.

would have taken measures. But instead Badoglio schemed to cut off and massacre the German forces in south Italy by assisting the landing of American and British forces in the neighborhood of Naples. At the same time he planned to seize the Alpine passes and to destroy the railway bridges and tunnels in northern Italy, thus cutting off the German forces. What utter treachery!''

Hitler then makes misleading statements about how he and Mussolini had agreed to defend Sicily. The Fuehrer also offers a backhanded apology to the Japanese for allowing a large amount of the Italian Navy to fall into Allied hands. However, it is Hitler's current plan for the defense of Italy that interests Washington. Oshima quotes him on this as saying: ''[The Allies] have two courses: either they will go north in Italy or they will try to land in the Balkans. I am inclined to believe they will take the latter course. I am going to concentrate German troops between Naples and Rome for the time being, and if the Allies go into the Balkans, I will immediately take the initiative.

''On the Italian mainland, we will have to use about eighteen German divisions at the front line, in addition to troops needed to maintain peace and order in the rear. In the Balkans our forces amount to twenty divisions. We are now laying siege to the islands along the Dalmatian coast. I feel fairly certain that we can make Dalmatia ours.''

As for the war on the Eastern Front, Hitler says: ''Because of the Italian catastrophe, I had to send a *total of 24 divisions* [emphasis added] to the Mediterranean area, which required me to take first-line soldiers from the Eastern Front and also other troops who could have been sent to the East. Also, I now have to look out for the future and keep powerful forces in reserve.'' Hitler then tells Oshima that his fighting retreat in Russia has cost the Russians 3.5 million casualties. (That is not true according to the analysts in Washington, who point out that what he tells the Japanese almost doubles all previous German estimates.) Hitler next tells Oshima that he is establishing a new defensive line in Russia ''running from Melitopol to Zaporozhye, then along the Dnieper and Sozh Rivers to Gomel, Orsha, Lake Ilmen and Leningrad. We have prepared considerable fortifications all along the line between Melitopol and the Sozh River, and we intend to hold on to them.

''In the south,'' says Hitler, ''we are in the process of evacuating the Kuban area, and in the next three or four days we will finish completely our withdrawal to Kerch. In the central sector, we are making our stand on the Sozh, but depending on whether or not the Soviet forces resume the offensive, we may fall back to the line which we have prepared on the Dnieper. In the north, if worse comes to worst, we can retire to a second defensive line, which we have prepared across a narrow strip of land adjoining Lake Peipus. By straightening out all these lines we will be able to shorten our front by about thirty percent. . . . The front for which a division will be responsible will be reduced from about twenty-five to about eighteen kilometers.''

As for Hitler's long-range strategy in Russia, Oshima reports that Hitler said: ''Since the collapse of Italy, what I have been most anxious to do is take the offensive in both the south and the east, but it has become clear that this is impossible because of a lack of planes, parts and ammunition. Therefore, I have finally *had to adopt a defensive strategy, although this is the very first time since the war began that we Germans have had to do so.* [Emphasis added.] Nevertheless, I am arranging to organize and equip forty new divisions that I can use in the East by next spring and am also preparing airplanes and other material. At that time, in conjunction with action in the south, I intend to take the offensive again against the Soviet armies.

''We are going to have many difficulties in getting out of our present straits. Meanwhile, I think it the best policy first to slap at the American and British forces as soon as we get a chance, and then to turn again on the Soviet. I want you to know that I am not worried at all about the way the war is going.

''We Germans never doubt for a moment that you Japanese will fight like hell. Now it is up to us both to work in closer unison and turn our faces toward final victory.''[26]

Hitler's final bombastic statement, the analysts in Washington laconically note, is made in reply to Oshima's assurance that, ''although we are still going to meet some stormy moments, Japan is determined to fight to the end.''

How much more could the Allied planners ask for? Oshima has done them the favor of exposing Hitler's strategy for the coming months. It only remains now for the order-of-battle experts to pick apart the information relating to the divisions and locations of defense lines that Hitler has given, apply the information to the appropriate front and get the news to the local commanders for action to be taken. It allows the Allies to play ''mind games'' with the Germans by pressuring them in opposition to German intentions, forcing the Germans to shift reserves away from German goals, and setting up the ''crossruff'' of

---

26. Ibid.

Allied attacks in unexpected places at the least convenient time for the German defenses.

The next report from Oshima to Tokyo contains the worrying note that German "spy reports" say that all the Russian troops being withdrawn from Siberia are showing up on the Eastern Front, fighting against Germany. Oshima says he "very casually asked who Ribbentrop thought it was that entertained these suspicions." Oshima then says: "From the way Ribbentrop answered, I could very clearly see that it was the German military. The German Army seems to harbor a good deal of suspicion. . . . I reminded Ribbentrop of what I had told him and Hitler before—that if we Japanese took on anything in the north it would only dilute our strength and cause an unfavorable development in the overall military picture. . . . I made it clear to him that we Japanese positively would not dream of consummating a supplementary understanding to the neutrality pact or of doing anything else which would facilitate Russia's fight against Germany."[27]

In concluding his message, Oshima advises Tokyo that relations with the German military are touchy because the "Germans have been getting hell from the Russians." He urges Tokyo to give Berlin, "particularly their military, the sort of explanations which will disabuse them of their misconceptions. I wish you would tell Ambassador Stahmer in Tokyo that we are not tying in with the Russians and have no supplementary understanding with them."

With the Tehran conference looming in the immediate future, Colonel McCormack's analysts begin untangling the spiderweb of rumors about Russian-German peace negotiations. For weeks they have been the subject of rumors in every capital around the world. According to the analysts: "There is no evidence that the rumors have any basis in fact, and there is good evidence to the contrary. . . . Ambassador Oshima was convinced that, even though Ribbentrop may be ready to settle with the Soviet, nevertheless the Fuehrer is still in control of Germany's relations with Russia and has no intention of making a peace."[28] The analysts also say, "The official German propaganda line is to stress the solidarity of Russia and England and America and to deny all reports of a Russian-German peace." Who is responsible for the rumors? According to the analysts: "German officials, as well as some other observers, profess to believe that the Russians have been manufacturing the peace rumors in order to exert pressure on the En-

---

27. SRS 1113, 10 October 1943.
28. SRS 1119, 16 October 1943.

glish and Americans to provide a second front and to yield to the Soviet's postwar demands.''

This now becomes the official American line: there will be no peace between Germany and Russia. Of course, it won't hurt to keep an eye open in the future. Unofficially, of course, the Americans start worrying about a different problem: the possibility of a peace agreement between Russia and Japan.

In the first days of November 1943 there comes a ten-day lapse in the Magic Summaries. Almost every page for these ten days is still censored fifty years after the fact. These Summaries were distributed over the signature of Colonel McCormack. Their time frame appears to cover the end of the Foreign Ministers' Conference in Moscow, on October 31, until November 12, when Churchill leaves Britain aboard the battle cruiser *Renown* for the Cairo conference (SEXTANT). The reader will recall Hitler's boast to Oshima on October 9: that he was taking Dalmatia under siege to thwart the British attack in the Dodecanese Islands. It turns out that while Churchill is at sea, he learns of the German assault in which the British garrison is routed and the islands seized by the Germans. According to British historians, Churchill's ambitions in the Balkans take a heavy blow from this news and he is forced to go ashore in Malta for two days, because of illness.

The paucity of information about the German attack leads one to speculate about this British defeat. Were the British defenders warned about an impending German attack? Was the garrison reinforced? Or was the garrison left as a sacrificial pawn in the bloody game of war?[29]

Our narrative returns to its track on November 12, as Churchill leaves England. Baron Oshima reports on a ten-day inspection tour of the German defenses on the Atlantic coast of France. The first report[30] merely outlines his itinerary, which makes the Allied order-of-battle specialists salivate as they read his movements, which are:

---

29. The question is asked because, on November 25, 1943, General Marshall asked Maj. Frank T. Hurley to deliver to President Roosevelt a series of Magic Reports for "the information of the President and Admiral Leahy." One report, dated November 23, from Sexton (52) for McCarthy, says the following: "The Germans are contemplating a series of operations to be undertaken against several island groups on the Dalmatian coast in the vicinity of Iara. These include islands of Uljan, Pasman, *RAB*, PAG, *VIR*, Solta, Brac and Hvar. The island of Ikaria in the Aegean has been taken by the Germans. The Italian forces have surrendered, but a weak guerrilla force commanded by a British captain is still operating." (Source: SRH-111 "Magic Reports for the Attention of the President," 1943–44.)

30. SRS 1850, 12 November 1943. The last SRS number for October 1943 is 1134. The first SRS number for November 1943 is 1839. The author cannot explain this gap in what should be consecutive numbering.

"24 October—Departed from Berlin for Brest, by way of Paris.

"26 October—Arrived at Brest, inspected the defenses in that region and spent the night at Le Bourg d'Ire. The party was joined in Brest by General Fahrmbacher, in charge of the defenses for that area.

"27 October—Inspected the defenses in the region of Lorient and spent the night at La Baule, where the party witnessed night maneuvers [on the Côte d'Amour].

"28 October—Visited St. Nazaire and spent the night at Nantes.

"29 October—Returned to Paris, where the party was entertained by Marshal Rundstedt.

"30 October—Traveled to Bordeaux and inspected the coastal defenses and two blockade-runners. The party was entertained at dinner by General Blaskowitz.

"31 October—Left Bordeaux and went to La Rochelle, where the party was joined by General Gallenkamp, in charge of defenses in that area."

In other words, Oshima is about to give the Allies a detailed report on the German defenses on the major potential landing sites in France on the Atlantic coast, running from Brest southward to Spain.

So important is this information that later, on December 11, Churchill wants the original copies of Oshima's messages shown to Roosevelt. (The cover letter of transmittal, which says "the Prime Minister represents the attachment of considerable importance," and eleven pages of Oshima's original messages, can be found in the appendix.)[31] The truly significant information in these messages is the following:

1. The Germans consider the beaches of Normandy to be only a *secondary* target for the invasion, which means they will keep their primary defensive forces elsewhere and the Allies will have to employ a number of subterfuges to keep the Germans thinking the way they do.
2. The Germans are planning for their mobile reserves to break up an invasion, which means secure methods must be found to keep these mobile forces pinned down.
3. Oshima gives a comprehensive picture of the German command structure as it is designed to defeat an invasion, which means that ways must be found to neutralize the effectiveness of specific commanders and their commands.
4. Not all the German troops are under the command of

31. SRH-111 "Magic Reports for the Attention of the President," 1943–44, pp. 1–17.

Field Marshal Rundstedt, which is a horrible mistake. At least twelve independent tank battalions (Tigers and Panthers), plus ten depot divisions that are training troops and several other "field divisions," will be under "the control of General 'HUROMU' in Germany." In reality, this means that Hitler controls von Rundstedt's reserves. If the invasion planners can create enough confusion in the communications between the beaches of Normandy and Berlin, Hitler will not be able to make a rational decision about when, where and how to commit his reserves. In turn this means von Rundstedt will be forced to fight without knowing where his reserves are, or when he can count on their arrival.

At the best, Oshima's reports give the Allies an excellent program for exploiting the weaknesses of the German defenses. At the worst, his reports give hope to the planners of OVERLORD when so many in the Allied forces realistically doubt the possibility of their being able to land on, let alone fight their way inland, off the beaches of Normandy.

8

hile the strategic planners are preparing in 1943 for the upcoming invasion of Europe and a massive commitment of American troops to combat on the Continent, the small group of code breakers operating in England and America is faced with a mammoth problem. How will the invasion armies be served with Ultra/Magic material?

The British have already come to grips with their problem of getting Ultra to the battlefield. The Americans have learned some good lessons from the British in Africa and Italy about the value of intelligence derived from breaking the codes that protect the enemy's communications network. But now, with the invasion forthcoming, a new American intelligence system will have to be created to disseminate Ultra/Magic for the many new American units that will be going into battle.

To pave the way for the creation of an American unit capable of responsibly handling Ultra intelligence in the European theater, on May 17, 1943, the British Government's Code and Cipher School (GC&CS) signs an agreement with the War Department in Washington providing for the complete cooperation between the signatories (note the term *signatories,* which designates the controlling office in each nation) in all matters pertaining to Special Intelligence derived from Ultra and Magic.[1] A new American unit operating in England is to be called Military Intelligence Service (MIS), WD, London. Note the American choice of initials similar to those of a British intelligence organization,

---

1. SRH-110 "Operations of the Military Intelligence Service." This file also contains a document called "An Account of the Origins and Development of 3-US." Much has been written about this operation, some of it inaccurate. Unless otherwise noted, all the information contained in this section is based on this primary source. Secondary sources will be noted so the reader can identify same.

which is intended to confuse the enemy, as well as any casual history reader.

Thus, MIS WD London will have three primary functions. First, U.S. liaison officers working with British personnel at GC&CS will examine incoming enemy decrypts, select those that should be sent to recipients in the various zones of combat and draft the signals necessary for disseminating the information. Second, American liaison officers at GC&CS will examine messages and summaries, picking out the most important for transmittal to Washington and G-2 (Intelligence) in the War Department (Army). Last, a special group of U.S. liaison officers will be properly trained at GC&CS and then attached to field commands "where an American officer is Commander-in-Chief." The function of these liaison officers will be to advise the commander on Ultra matters and "overcome difficulties that might arise in regard to difference in language." This is a polite way of saying that when the American Ultra liaison officer finds that his old-fashioned commander is unable to comprehend the significance of the Ultra secret intelligence he is receiving from a young whippersnapper without combat, or even much Army, experience, the liaison officer is supposed to find some other way of getting his message across so it can be used effectively against the enemy.

Eventually, MIS WD London will simply be called 3-US, after the number 3 of the operations "hut" in which the Americans will work at Bletchley Park.

All of this had been set in motion by a visit to England on April 25 by three Americans: Colonel McCormack, the former lawyer brought to Washington by Secretary of War Stimson and now representing G-2 (War Department), William F. Friedman, the American code genius serving as technical assistant and representative of Arlington Hall (the Army's primary code-breaking center), and Lt. Col. Telford Taylor, who will head up 3-US. The three come to England because negotiations between Arlington Hall and GC&CS about the production and exploitation of CX/MSS and similar material have run into a brick wall. For security and other reasons, the British want to maintain their monopoly and prevent Arlington Hall from setting up a separate establishment to produce and exploit CX/MSS in Washington, presumably as a part of G-2. What the three Americans first need to do is find out if Washington really needs its own CX/MSS center, or whether more satisfactory results can be obtained from having the Americans work with the British in Bletchley Park.

The fact these three can see the value of working with the British in Bletchley Park, which is five if not six hours closer to the battlefields of Europe than Washington, proves to the British that the Americans are indeed sincere about achieving the best ways to use Ultra/Magic in combat situations. The official history of Special Branch notes that "the British had developed security principals and methods well beyond the point that had been reached by the U.S. Army." The bitter negotiations between the two countries cease almost overnight. In Washington, Col. Carter Clarke and Commander Travis of Great Britain sign the agreement to share Ultra and Magic intelligence.

The official report, *Operations of the Military Intelligence Service,* also points out that many of the problems these men solve are the result of circumstances over which the Americans have no control. The U.S. entered the war some two and one-half years after the British established Bletchley Park. Another year and a half elapsed before the U.S. Army's G-2 and the GC&CS would agree to share the products of Ultra. This would have made it impracticable for anyone to have tried earlier to set up the systems that will finally be devised. The Americans have to build their organization from nothing, personnel must be trained and facilities developed. "As one examines the early records," says the *Operations* report, "the picture that emerges is of G-2 and British authorities walking around and eyeing each other like two mongrels who have just met."

In early June, McCormack and Friedman return to Washington. Colonel Taylor remains in England as chief of 3-US at GC&CS. Through June and July, Taylor confines himself almost exclusively to the Japanese diplomatic traffic, devoting little or no time to Hut 3 and its products. This is because the U.S. is assuming, as its main responsibility, the reading of Japanese material, while the British are in charge of German and Italian military and air codes and ciphers.

In late July, Taylor moves his activities to Bletchley Park. For a month he undergoes training in the mysteries of the Park's operations in general, focusing on the operations of Hut 3 where the Americans will become involved. Meanwhile, he continues working on the diplomatic traffic, transmitting by cable to Washington some of the more important items in the ISK, ISOS and related series. After a month of this intermittent service to Washington, he believes he is ready to start regular service to the War Department. Taylor has already been joined by a Major Calfee, who represents 3-US where counterintelligence is concerned. On August 23, a Major McKee comes on board. He will skillfully build up the unit, ensure that it functions smoothly and organize the all-important Field Intelligence Unit (FIU). On August 27,

3-US sends its first CX/MSS signal to Washington announcing that Army Group B, under the command of Field Marshal Rommel, is taking over command of the German forces in northern Italy.

Trouble arises immediately. The agreement signed in May suddenly unravels.

The original wording of the agreement stated that "decodes giving information regarding Order of Battle will be handled as at present, i.e., through U.S. liaison officers in [the London] War Office and Air Ministry, respectively." The War Office and Air Ministry correctly and vigorously protest Taylor's direct role in Ultra. But the reasoning for the British protest is suspect. The truth is that Taylor has discovered that the British, with good reason as we will see later, do not trust the Americans to keep the Ultra material secret. Of greater importance is the fact that, in the past, the two British ministries have transmitted only a "little order of battle intelligence derived from Source, and that in a form quite inadequate for the needs of the German Order of Battle Section in G-2." Worse, with a new phase of the war about to begin, neither British ministry is making arrangements to handle the large volume of traffic that Washington will require, and this is creating serious delays in transmittal and "perceptible irritation on both sides."

What the British are finally facing up to is the fact that the European war is about to become American-run. There will be far more American troops, airmen and airplanes, ships and landing craft involved than there will be British. It means the new war in Europe will have to be fought by American rules. No wonder the British ministries are upset.

The issue then becomes clouded by the arrival of the American assistant chief of staff and head of G-2, General Strong, on a visit to England and Bletchley Park. In September, General Menzies, General Strong, Commander Travis, Mr. De Gray, Group Captain Jones and Colonel Taylor meet. They agree that Taylor will continue selecting and transmitting CX/MSS material to Washington. However, the selection should be conservative and not include "low order" order-of-battle information. Also, the appropriate ministry must be informed of every item Taylor sends. This agreement is short-lived, however. The chief of British intelligence, Menzies, and Strong next hold a private conference; Menzies persuades Strong to end Taylor's operation at Bletchley Park.

It is safe to say that Strong, despite his rank and background, like many other generals in the American Army, did not have much appreciation about how Ultra/Magic could be used on the battlefield. While numerous discussions continue in England about the effect of Menzies's victory over the muddleheaded American chief of intelligence, Strong returns to Washington and runs into a buzz saw named Col. Carter Clarke. In one of the few confrontations in which a mere colonel takes on a powerful assistant chief of staff, in this instance Strong decides he has made a grave error. On September 15, Strong admits he is wrong. He directs Colonel Taylor to try to reinstate the previous arrangements.

It is to Taylor's credit that he is able to persuade the British on the validity of two points. The first is that intelligence of more than momentary significance, which is important enough to send out to various commands abroad, is also important enough to be sent to responsible staff officers in Washington. Information considered important enough for British ministries in terms of long-range planning is equally important for the intelligence people (MIS, WD) in Washington. Second, and this is most important, the selection of material to be passed on to Washington must not be done by British officers in British ministries, but at Bletchley Park by Americans who are familiar with the requirements of the American G-2.

It takes more than a week of parlays, but finally a conference between General Menzies, General Davidson, Group Captain Jones and Colonel Taylor reaches an agreement on September 25: Taylor will be responsible for selecting what is to be passed on to Washington and will keep the War Office/Air Ministry informed of the items passed. The new service is started up on September 27, and it is acknowledged as the birth date of 3-US.

From September through December 1943, the volume of traffic sent by 3-US is low. The British still wish Taylor to be conservative. He plays the game. Only two Americans are at Bletchley Park, while in Washington more personnel are being gathered and trained to handle the material, and a series of operational problems have to be solved.

One of the most important matters is who will be the men chosen to handle the Ultra/Magic information in the field? This is where Colonel McCormack's genius shows.[2] Rather than allow the Army to assign

---

2. *The American Magic: Codes, Ciphers and the Defeat of Japan* by Ronald Lewin (New York: Farrar Straus Giroux, 1982). Also, *Ultra Goes to War* by Ronald Lewin (New York: McGraw-Hill, 1978). Lewin does what the official records do not: he identifies the Americans sent to Bletchley for intelligence purposes. More important is the fact that the men picked by McCormack, because of their access to the incredible knowledge provided by Magic/Ultra, and because they are exceptionally intelligent and capable people, will become members of the American civilian power elite after the war.

any reserve officer or college graduate who happens to be available for the job, McCormack deems the work can "be done effectively only by imaginative persons of absolutely first-class ability and suitable training." His MIS operation reports only to General Marshall and the Secretary of War. This makes MIS vulnerable to roadblocks thrown up by civil service experts and delays posed by Army personnel officers who are angry that the unit is secret and they cannot control what is going on. And so Colonel McCormack turns to the field from which he comes, the law, and picks men of exceptional brilliance. For example, Telford Taylor will become the future prosecutor of the Nuremberg War Crimes Trials and professor of law at Columbia University. There is Inzer Wyatt, who will become a federal judge. William Bundy will become a postwar assistant secretary of state and editor of *Foreign Affairs.* Alfred Friendly will become managing editor of the *Washington Post.* Langdon van Norden will become an international businessman and chairman of the Metropolitan Opera. Curt Zimansky will be a famous philologist. York Allen will advise the Rockefeller Brothers Fund. Edmund Kellog will have a distinguished career in the American Foreign Service. Landis Gore will become a world-famous architect. Lewis Powell will become an associate justice of the U.S. Supreme Court. At the moment, however, these men are Army officers of low rank. Yet Marshall is about to give them an awesome responsibility and authority.

On March 15, 1944, Marshall will write a letter to Eisenhower spelling out in exact detail what the role of these American intelligence men *shall* be. Perhaps this is why Eisenhower never gives intelligence any credit for his success in Europe. It wasn't his idea, his baby. It belonged to Marshall, and Marshall will tell Eisenhower that, as chief of staff, he will brook no interference with this operation. Marshall orders Eisenhower to cooperate, or else. The success of OVERLORD will depend on many senior American officers, who have never before commanded large forces in battle, accepting the information provided by youthful Ultra intelligence representatives.

"Their primary responsibility will be," writes Marshall, "to evaluate Ultra intelligence, present it in useable form to the Commanding officer and to such of his senior staff officers as are authorized Ultra recipients, assist in fusing Ultra with intelligence derived from other sources, and give advice in connection with making operational use of Ultra in such fashion that the security of the source is not endangered."

In other words, the commander in the field is being ordered to deal with the Ultra representative, who, by himself, will represent the most authoritative and secret intelligence source available. As we will see, it will take considerable time before the American commanders comprehend Ultra, let alone use it properly. Too many American Ultra officers in the field, who are supposed to have secure vans and trailers, equipped with safes and guards, will find themselves in drafty, rain-wet tents without any relief, support or security. If the British had been aware that this would be the way the Americans will treat the security of Ultra, they would quite rightly have tried to close down the American involvement in the war's greatest secret. It is only by the grace of God that no German commando-type attack ever reached an American Army headquarters and the Ultra tent during the course of the war.

Speaking of British security, one of the worst lapses in keeping Ultra safe occurred in September 1944, when Brig. Tommy Hadden, CBE, was captured by the Germans during the battle of Arnhem. He had previously been secretary to the Joint Intelligence Committee, was privy to Ultra and was the duty officer who telephoned Churchill with the news that the Japanese had attacked Pearl Harbor. He spent the remainder of the war as a German prisoner without the enemy's dis-covering his secret.[3] It was a dreadful lapse of security by the British to allow Hadden to be operational in airborne landings.

At its peak, 3-US will comprise only sixty-eight personnel. Of this number, nineteen will serve in the field as SLUs (special liaison units), another twenty-four will serve as "specialists" at various commands, three will serve in London and twelve as advisers in Hut 3 at Bletchley Park. That leaves ten who actually make up the section known as 3-US. Anyone with a calculator can figure the percentage of personnel in 3-US as opposed to the 5 million Americans who will be under arms by the end of the war, and they can see how Magic/Ultra created a new elite group with special knowledge.

The postwar critique of MIS operations will say that experience proved that these men "had to have imagination coupled with analyt-ical, judicial, and unbiased minds. Intellectual ability was more prereq-uisite than any experience, military or otherwise."[4] This most likely is the reason that none of these special people stayed on in the military after the war.

According to the history of 3-US, on the whole Colonel Taylor spends "most of his time in problems outside the scope of the section. The person in charge was his deputy." Four officers service Washing-

---

3. *Times* (London), 1 May 1993, obituary, 17.
4. SRH-005 "Use of CX/MSS Ultra" by the United States War Department (1943–45), National Archives.

ton, two on military matters, two on air. (The Army critique of 3-US, produced after the war, notes officially that one of the failures of 3-US is to cope with naval matters; fortunately, as we know, Colonel Mc-Cormack will remedy that in Washington.) Two other officers will handle all of the Japanese diplomatic traffic, with two civilians serving in secretarial capacity.

By January 1944, the first of the inexperienced Americans will be groping their way "down the dark corridors of Hut 3" for their indoc-trination into the "Watch" as air or military advisers. The official his-tory notes: "Seldom have so many absorbed so much in so little time."

The staff feeding G-2 (Washington) will quickly grow from three to seven, but only five will be operational since Colonels Taylor and McKee will be devoting their full time to establishing liaison with the potential customers of 3-US information in the field. This means that G-2 Washington is now being fed even more information with items about the German Luftwaffe, local police reports and Abwehr (German Army) operations reports.

Taylor's time is spent with the American Theater Commander, who at the time is General Devers (not Eisenhower), and his chief intelligence officer, General Sibert. It will not be until mid-January 1944 that Taylor will take part in discussions about servicing COSSAC and its subordinate commands. Out of this will grow Taylor's decision to service FUSAG, which will later become General Bradley's Twelfth Army Group, as "soon as they are ready to take."

By late January, the First U.S. Army Group (FUSAG) will once a day receive a summary of Ultra messages relating to France and the Low Countries. Meanwhile, 3-US will be researching information for FUSAG's intelligence section, which has *not* yet become operational.

By now, 3-US has been recognized by the British as a fully op-erational unit and is even listed by its 3-US designation on British routing slips. Moreover, thanks to Taylor, 3-US is represented on the Western Front Committee, as well as the Black Sea and Aegean Study Groups. A 3-US member also attends the weekly SHAEF meetings prior to the June 1944 invasion.

After the invasion, Taylor will undertake servicing the American Army commands in the field with military information derived from the Japanese diplomatic traffic (Magic), which is "reaching the field only sporadically and belatedly." By virtue of Arlington Hall's contri-bution of analysis to the Magic material, these diplomatic messages will become exceptionally important to Eisenhower, not only allowing him to see the war in Europe in a different manner (i.e., through Japanese eyes), but also in understanding the between-the-lines meanings of Marshall's instructions to SHAEF, and lastly, in making his own, independent decisions at the end of the war.

It is this new service, which will be called the Bay series, that proves how 3-US has matured and become a vital intelligence operation of true stature.

It is important to remember that the primary function of 3-US is to select military and air items from CX/MSS for transmittal to Washington. Little or no guidance in what to select is given by Washington, which wants to receive "all desired intelligence." The principles of selection are never formalized or reduced to paper. From the outset a green staff at 3-US selects material for a green staff in Washington. That it all succeeds is thanks to "the unbelievable patience and interest and wisdom of key [British] people in Hut [3]."

Naturally, Washington's interest is on strategic, rather than tactical, intelligence. Thus, 3-US will send major order-of-battle items, all messages throwing light on future operations by the Axis partners, on manpower, politics and policy. And from the start 3-US sends "Flivo reports" from the front lines and significant tactical items, including police, Abwehr, diplomatic, low-grade military and air force items deemed to be of military significance. By the spring of 1944, when the primary concern of Washington and London is OVERLORD, every item relating to the Western Front is cabled to Washington, while the secondary information is sent by pouch (first by ship, later by air three times a week).

By the summer of 1944, Washington will be able to cope with all the product produced by 3-US, and G-2 is put on a par with the ministries in London. At last, Washington is getting a copy of every teleprint and report circulated in Britain. (This practice ends the heavy burden on 3-US for telling the British ministries which items are being sent to America, since G-2 is now getting everything.) It is interesting to note that it is not until America has been in the war for two and a half years that Washington is reading all the same material that the British have been reading. No wonder the British believe their intelligence and knowledge to be superior to the Americans'.

Even so, the "C" series of messages receives special attention until the end of the war. Every item sent to Washington will have to be cleared by Group Captain Jones, and many items are not forwarded. Those that are sent, marked *Eyes Only,* go only to Marshall, the G-2 (Strong, who is replaced by Bissell) and the Special Security Officer, (former colonel) now Brigadier General Clarke. Later on, the C series will be called the MCC series; Colonel McCormack will be added to the distribution list, and he will prepare this extraordinarily sensitive information for the three recipients.

The speed of the operation is also vital. If marked *immediate,* a cable sent from Bletchley Park in the morning, London time, will reach Washington the same morning (Washington time). If marked priority *important,* the cable reaches Washington the same day. If there is no priority, the cable reaches Washington the next day.

Messages sent are separated into groups arranged according to subject matter and chronology. Frequently the intercepted signal is deemed enough for Washington. But messages with a source such as Hitler or Rommel or Kesselring or Ribbentrop are sent, as we know, verbatim. The 3-US operation rarely, if ever, writes comments on the Magic Summaries. These comments are produced in Washington.

For the historian, the Army's penchant for compartmentalizing everything is frustrating. Mentioned earlier is the "Bay" system that 3-US concocted. Originally, the Bays derived from three main sources, BJs, SJAs and JMAs. The BJ series included all diplomatic traffic and those of the military attachés; the series averages about fifty messages a day, only one of which "would prove Bayworthy." The SJAs consisted of messages sent by the Japanese naval attachés in Berlin and Venice, plus messages other officials send via that link. It produces about five messages a day, from which four or five signals a week are prepared and sent G-2. According to the official operations report, "Allied intelligence benefited considerably by the fact that both the Japanese Naval Attachés who served in Berlin during this period were men of exceptional competence." They produce comprehensible and accurate descriptions of technical equipment, and "their occasional ventures into German strategy and defense were of a considerably higher order than ordinarily encountered in the attaché field."

The JMAs are messages from other Japanese military attachés around the world. Fifty or sixty of these messages are broken every day. The primary value of these messages is the material on the Allied order of battle, which proves most helpful to Allied countermeasures. It was from this source that the Allies receive the report of the military attaché in France after he accompanies his ambassador on a tour of coastal defenses.

Other Bay sources are still censored today in the official record.

Much of the early and detailed information on the German jet and rocket plane program will come from the naval attaché reports out of Berlin. And then there is the only clear statement that indicates there might be a German attack in the Ardennes, the Battle of the Bulge, which will be sent to Tokyo from Berlin by Ambassador Oshima following his last talk with Hitler in August 1944. Unfortunately, Hitler says the offensive will start in November, and his warning will not be taken too seriously. (This intelligence failure by SHAEF will be discussed later on, in its proper chronological setting. Needless to say, the British interpretation of the intelligence failures relating to the Battle of the Bulge will be much harsher about the American complacency at SHAEF than will the American critiques.)

With the focus of Washington zooming in on the impending invasion of Europe, the caliber of the daily Magic Summary that goes to Marshall's desk each morning shows another marked improvement. This is made possible by a further priority given by the War Department to the needs of McCormack's special branch, which has been drained of personnel by their departure to England.[5] McCormack is allowed an influx of new writers and editors who possess open and inquisitive minds. The primary function of McCormack's Section C is still the production of the daily Magic Summary. But now it provides an Ultra disposition map for the oral and visual morning presentation briefing for the head of G-2. This map shows "German dispositions, command and impending changes on the Italian front, the only European battlezone in which U.S. troops are [currently] engaged."

What happens next is logical. The Magic Summary readers in Washington demand more up-to-the-minute order-of-battle information, which they haven't needed before. They also ask for long-range studies based on intelligence items saying that the Germans plan to expand their parachute army, or about the collaboration with the Germans by Cetnik troops in Yugoslavia. By reading between the lines in the official report about the handling of CX/MSS, one understands the Army's method of taking over McCormack's operation as its own, which is similar to that of any large corporation. The first thing is to complain that Section C is not serving the Army properly, which is done in this official report, which says Section C "had not, however, done much with the information which might more properly have been its province. . . . It was not giving adequate training to those going overseas. . . . Nor did it yet influence the appreciations issued by the chiefs of theater branches of MIS."

This implied criticism of McCormack is outrageous. When one considers McCormack's original brief from Secretary Stimson that an

---

5. War Department, SRH-005.

outsider, a *civilian,* is to correct the Army's intelligence deficiencies that caused Pearl Harbor and get the Army's signals intelligence on the proper track, to say nothing about how the Army bureaucracy fought McCormack while he is achieving the goals demanded by Stimson and Marshall, the former Wall Street lawyer should be receiving plaudits instead of criticism. This is what was meant earlier in the book, when McCormack is faulted for giving up his civilian status: by accepting military rank there is no way he can win if he gets in a dispute with the military bureaucrats.

Now the Army reaps the fruit of McCormack's intelligence product for itself. It achieves this on June 5, 1944, the day before the invasion of Normandy, by turning the duties of McCormack's MIS Section C over to the German Military Reports Branch (GMRB). Thus, the daily publication of the Military and Naval Supplement to the Magic Summary, which also goes to Marshall, will be renamed on July 1, 1944, as the "Magic European Summary." The GMRB has a wonderful legacy from McCormack on which to base its operations that includes:

* Two complete sets of the Daily European Summary with an elaborate card index.
* Two complete sets of the Ultra signals received from GC&CS (a single set is retained by the European Order of Battle Section.)
* Temporary working maps showing various kinds of information—very detailed ground and air order of battle for a particular sector or area; divisional, corps, army and army-group boundaries; rail and road nets; airfield service ability; jet aircraft bases under construction; V-weapon sites; serviceable bridges over rivers; etc.
* Detailed running lists of information on units of particular and temporary importance (e.g., divisions of the Sixth Panzer Army in the winter of 1944–45, German Air Force jet units, etc.).[6]

Now watch how the Army bureaucrats try to play down the importance of the intelligence provided by Magic/Ultra. The official report says: "The range of subjects covered in the European Summary was limited only by the range of topics discussed in the Ultra messages, which was very wide indeed. The bulk always dealt with activities of

6. Ibid.

the German armed forces but the derivations were often many and varied.'' So detailed and so good are the Tabs (appendixes) that are being written for the daily Summary, it becomes more than thirty pages in length. Now General Clarke has to restrict these long, specialized studies to only those who requested that a particular study be made. Furthermore, in describing the work of the European Order of Battle Section of the Military Branch, which is part of the Research Unit of MIS after the 1944 reorganization, it is acknowledged that ''35 percent of the items presented were taken from Ultra traffic.''[7]

One then has to extrapolate: If 35 percent of the information furnished the European order-of-battle projections comes from Ultra/ Magic sources, this information must exert a lot of influence on the decisions made by generals such as Marshall and Eisenhower. But exactly how much influence did this Ultra information have? According to the Army's official records: ''The remoteness of the War Department and its secondary intelligence duties concerning the European war meant that the primary use of CX/MSS Ultra lays in its influence in the minds of high-ranking representatives in strategic councils.''[8] This statement is untrue considering the fact that the War Department was never ''remote'' from the European war. Eisenhower might claim he was independent, but anyone reading the daily cables of the Operations Department soon sees that no matter what Eisenhower might claim, he still answered to Marshall. Nevertheless, the Army defends its ''doublespeak'' about intelligence by saying, ''What influence [Ultra] did have could only be stated by the officials concerned, and even they would probably have some difficulty in stating today that any one decision depended on any one piece of evidence.''[9] Since we know that no one of high rank was ever allowed to speak publicly on this subject, and since later on this book will show how and why highly successful tactical decisions on the battlefield are made *solely* on the basis of Ultra/ Magic intelligence, the unbiased observer concludes that Ultra/Magic played a vast, incredibly significant role in the strategy of World War II. The failure of the American Army to be more open about it is a terrible disservice to history. It falsely enhances the reputations of various generals under the mistaken guise of helping the image of the service as a whole.

Copies of the daily European Order of Battle are difficult to find,

7. Ibid.
8. Ibid.
9. Ibid.

even fifty years after the fact. (Indeed, the author was told by a specialist in the military archives that these documents had all been destroyed.) The one copy of the European Order of Battle Summary that is released for publication is incorporated in SRH-005 and is eighty-six pages long. It is dated April 11, 1945, which is the day before American troops reach the Elbe River with orders to cross and be prepared to advance on Berlin.[10] According to the official report: "The copy shows the heading with its security warning to all readers, and the distribution list which then consisted of eleven people within the War Department above the working intelligence level, and four recipients outside the War Department, [the next two lines are censored]."[11]

The original of this report is twenty-five pages long, of which sixteen deal with developments on the Western Front and the drive across Europe to Berlin; there are three pages on developments on the Eastern Front and six pages of news from the Italian front. The bulk of this Italian information is acknowledged to be a condensed version of a G-2, AFHQ appreciation based on Ultra information, issued only two days earlier. Also attached is a sanitized study about what MIS knows in November 1944 about the newly developed German jet aircraft. (It is important to note that this information, which is first developed from Ultra sources and then confirmed by non-Sigint [signals intelligence] sources, gives the Allies an excellent understanding of the abilities, numbers and characteristics of the German jets that suddenly appear in battle and terrorize Allied bombers at the end of the war.)[12]

How anyone can read this day's Order of Battle material, with its emphasis on Ultra (Sigint) material, and then claim such material can

---

10. One of the more interesting statements in this day's Order of Battle report is found in a note saying: "Orders for [German] Western Front operations are showing an increasing emphasis on the doctrine of flank attacks . . . and on a concurrent dictum that only relatively weak forces *are to be disposed for frontal blocking against Allied thrusts.*" (Emphasis added.) In other words, let the Americans and the British advance . . . hit them on the flanks. But the Allies know what the Germans do not know: where the Allied troops are and where they are going, while the German reserves are too disorganized to be effective in "frontal blocking" or to mount successful counterattacks.

11. Ibid.

12. The first German jet aircraft shot down was on October 6, 1944, when planes in the Royal Canadian Air Force spotted a jet cruising below them and destroyed it. On December 24, 1944, sixteen German jets made the first jet-bomber attack against Liège, then attacked railway yards in the Ardennes during the Battle of the Bulge. By March 1945 jet aircraft show up regularly in all German flights.

have only little or no bearing on the strategy and tactics of SHAEF's operations in Europe, is somewhat puzzling.

But let us return to the Magic intelligence that crosses General Marshall's desk in November 1943.

✖ ✖ ✖

On November 13, in Magic Summary No. 597,[13] Ambassador Oshima describes in detail his ten-day inspection of the German defenses on the Atlantic coast of France. (As noted earlier, this report and the one of the day before about Oshima's itinerary are the ones Churchill especially wanted Roosevelt to read.) The Washington analysts comment to Marshall: "The Ambassador found the defenses imposing and the morale high, and he came away convinced that any Allied invasion attempt is doomed to failure."

But far more important to Marshall—and the planners at COS-SAC/SHAEF—is the fact that the Germans still believe the beaches of Normandy are *not* the primary landing sites for an Allied invasion when, in truth, that is where the Allies intend to attack. With this assurance, Allied planners can concentrate on continuing the series of superb intelligence deceptions that have fooled the Germans to date and will do so in the future. (So much has been written about these deceptions they will not be described here.) But how comforting it is to know that the wool one is pulling over the enemy's eyes is truly blinding him.

For the next two weeks, the Magic Summaries are dull reading. On November 26, a report from Berlin (from a still-censored source) says that "the British reports are exaggerated" regarding recent RAF raids on Berlin.[14] This source claims most of the damage is done in the outlying suburbs. But the official German report is that the old Reich Chancellery, the Foreign Office and several other government ministries have been badly damaged. Also heavily hit is the diplomatic quarter, with the exception of the Japanese and Italian embassies, plus the railway yards.

Tokyo is interested in how extensive the damage might be to Berlin and asks Oshima to answer specific questions. The U.S. analysts note Oshima says that gas and electricity have not yet been officially

---

13. SRS 1851, 13 November 1943.
14. SRS 1864, 26 November 1943.

rationed in Berlin for private homes. Hotels and rooming houses, however, have been limited by government order.

A few days later,[15] the Manchurian minister to Berlin reports that his legation is destroyed. Furthermore, he lost his documents and codebooks. Baron Oshima also reports that his residence and offices are "damaged so badly that they cannot be used." One can almost hear the analysts in Washington breathing a sign of relief upon learning their best intelligence source is still alive and kicking.

The following day, another report by Oshima[16] says that the Japanese embassy staff will move half the personnel to Boitzenburg [approximately sixty miles north of the capital]. Oshima and a part of the administrative staff will stay behind. More interesting is the rumor that a "decision has been made to evacuate the whole German Foreign Office except for certain executives and section chiefs." This is the first indication that Berlin may be losing its so-called "military importance."

The following day, from Bucharest, the Japanese military attaché reports that "as late as 11 November, the Germans had not given up hope of repairing the extensive breaches in [the Dnieper River–Zaporozhye–Melitopol defense] line."[17] The analysts note that the German counteroffensive west of Kiev began on November 18, one week after the military attaché's message. The attaché also says that if the Germans fail to hold the line, they plan to retreat to Pskov from Leningrad. (This confirms what Hitler had acknowledged earlier to Oshima: a withdrawal is possible.) On January 14, the Russians will attack the German forces that have besieged Leningrad since 1941 and drive them back.

To start December, the Japanese minister to Switzerland informs Tokyo that he has been told that the Allies will land in France, but "I am inclined to doubt it."[18] He says the Italian front is "lifeless, and British troops have had to retire from the Aegean." He also says there are some indications the Allies have decided to "invade the Balkans."

On the anniversary of Pearl Harbor, Oshima tells Tokyo just how close the Japanese embassy in Berlin came to being blown up by English bombs.[19] He says that "at least one 3,200-lb. bomb and four 1,100-lb. bombs which fell on or near the grounds of the Japanese

---

15. SRS 1867, 29 November 1943.
16. SRS 1868, 30 November 1943.
17. SRS 1146, 12 December 1943. Again, for no apparent reason, the SRS numbers for November, 1943, are higher than those for December.
18. SRS 1135, 1 December 1943.
19. SRS 1141, 7 December 1943.

Embassy failed to explode." (The numerals in this Magic Report are very faint and have been interpreted with a twelve-power magnifying glass, but one can assume that Oshima probably would have been killed if the bombs had exploded.) Despite the damage done to the city—2,500 civilians killed and some 600,000 made homeless—all the factories in the city are still functioning, and the Defense Coordinator for Berlin, General Haase, has told Oshima that the city's populace showed "remarkable calmness and a cooperative attitude. . . . We need not worry about Berlin from now on, no matter how violent the raids become."

The Japanese military attaché is also reporting to Tokyo that the Luftwaffe is developing a new fighter plane, the Messerschmitt 309. (The first hint about this plane's conception was given eleven months earlier, in the Magic Summary of January 24, 1943.) Although the plans have not yet been perfected, the attaché now recommends that experimental models be purchased by the Japanese Air Force. Tokyo replies by ordering the plans to be purchased and sent via submarine to meet the "present pressing need for a new fighter plane."

The next day, Foreign Minister Shigemitsu comments on Japan's production problems. Apparently Oshima has made some comment in a previous message that wasn't intercepted, but it provoked this reply: "We realize how vitally important it is to increase our shipping. We are haunted by the number of ships we have lost." He then reassures Oshima, saying: ". . . So far as ships and planes are concerned, we can wage successful war this year and next."[20]

On December 10, the Magic specialists decode a nine-page section of Oshima's report of November 10 in which he describes in considerable detail the organization of the German defenses in France and the Low Countries. The analysts in Washington point out that Oshima's data on the disposition of troops, the responsibilities of commanders and the systems of fortifications is reliable. They say: "In general, the Ambassador's information confirms intelligence obtained from other sources."[21] Nothing could be more welcome than having reports from the field confirmed at such a high level.

Three days later, the Magic Summary reveals the details of a conversation held between Oshima and Foreign Minister von Ribbentrop on November 25, the first such talk in more than a month.[22] Ribbentrop

---

20. SRS 1143, 9 December 1943.
21. SRS 1144, 10 December 1943.
22. SRS 1147, 13 December 1943.

says that originally the Germans had thought the Allies would invade the Balkans, but now they doubt such a move. As for an invasion of France, Ribbentrop says: "We see numerous signs that they will actually try it. I don't know where, but probably Belgium and the English Channel coast are our greatest danger."

Oshima replies: "The Anglo-Americans are pretty persistent, but personally I don't think they will start their invasion across the Straits of Dover. After my recent inspection of the coastal defenses in France—and incidentally I want to thank you for letting me make that trip—I am inclined to think that the enemy would prefer to establish a bridgehead in Normandy or on the Brittany Peninsula. If they did that, they could say that they were fulfilling their promise to Russia. And then, if they succeeded, they could attempt a full-fledged expedition across the Channel. What do you think about that?"

"Yes, that is certainly one possibility," replies Ribbentrop. He goes on to say that since the Germans have thrown the British out of the Dodecanese, the Turks will reject all the proposals made by the Allies and remain neutral. He also wants to know what the chances are of Japan's playing upon the dissatisfaction of Chungking about the Moscow Conference and getting Chungking to join with Japan's Nanking regime.

There doesn't appear to be much hope for that, says Oshima. "The pact which we concluded not so long ago with Nanking is a step in the right direction. However, Chungking is now under the spell of Anglo-American propaganda . . . what you suggest looks pretty hard to me."

In summing up the war situation, Ribbentrop says that it looks as though the Russians are "very exhausted . . . and we intend to keep fighting until we permanently cripple the Soviet. We are not going to compromise now. We are not even considering it." He discounts an Allied invasion and says that "we are going to start air raids against the British Isles, and beginning with the city of London, we will completely destroy the British mainland."

The same summary contains a report from Ambassador Kurihara in Ankara reporting that Franz von Papen saw Turkish foreign minister Menemencioglu on December 9 and asked what had occurred on his trip to Cairo. According to von Papen, the Turks were invited to Cairo by the three allies, and once there, they were again asked to join in the war. The Turks replied that their "entrance into the war would not necessarily benefit the Allies, and told them that they were going to remain neutral."

More important, according to the Turkish foreign minister, "President Roosevelt seemed very happy about the Tehran conference, and my impression was that Stalin had probably given his word that he will attack Japan once the war in Europe is over.''

The truth is that Stalin did promise Ambassador Averell Harriman that the Soviet would attack Japan ninety days after the end of the war in Europe. And, as we will see, this statement by the Turkish foreign minister sets off alarm bells in Tokyo.

The following day, Washington learns that the air raids on Berlin have had greater impact on the German government than expected.[23] Germany's diplomatic representatives abroad must limit their reports to Berlin to matters of immediate importance. Berlin also requests that no report should refer back to messages more than a week old since ''most of the Foreign Office records have been taken out of Berlin for safe-keeping.''

On December 17, the Magic Summary contains even more revelations about the German defenses of the West Wall.[24] The analysts in Washington refer Marshall back to the reports filed by Ambassador Oshima on his inspection trip. Now, they say, there's a report dated November 9 that was prepared by Lieutenant Colonel Nishi, an assistant military attaché in Berlin who accompanied Oshima on the inspection tour. Almost half of Nishi's message to Tokyo is still missing. The analysts will try to unearth it. Meanwhile they note that Nishi's report is based partly on his observations, partly on information given him by the Germans and part on data provided by another Japanese officer who worked in German Headquarters in France from September 24 through October 25. The analysts point out to Marshall where Nishi says: ''Construction of Atlantic coastal fortifications has progressed a great deal since our previous inspection in February.''

The proof that Allied deception schemes are working and confusing the enemy comes the next day with a report from Madrid.[25] Apparently the Spanish foreign minister, Jordana, has told Minister Suma that among the decisions made at Tehran, ''(1) British and American troops will launch an attack on Germany from Soviet territory, (2) the Soviet Army will send units to the Italian front, and (3) the most important landing points in France will be Biarritz, Saint-Jean-de-Luz and Marseille.''

---

23. SRS 1148, 14 December 1943.
24. SRS 1151, 17 December 1943.
25. SRS 1152, 18 December 1943.

Four days later, the Magic analysts in Washington produce for the War Department a comprehensive report that has been pieced together from fragmentary intercepts and correlated with other available data. The significance of the report is that it provides "general information about Japanese thinking on the rice problem (as seen earlier) . . . [and contains] direct and reliable evidence concerning a part of the picture which would otherwise have to be filled in largely by guesswork, namely, the question of how much rice Japan has been importing from foreign countries in recent years."[26]

A sanitized version of this report disguising the source for this information has also been prepared for release to other U.S. governmental departments. The bottom line is that in 1943, Japan will have a surplus of some 3,785,000 metric tons of rice. This means that if Japan has a poor growing year and no imports at all, she can carry on with this surplus for one year. With "normal domestic crops and no imports at all, she could keep going for about two years. With normal domestic crops and normal imports from Formosa (but with no other imports at all), Japan could continue for more than three years."

It is obvious that Japan cannot be allowed the luxury of fighting on through 1946 with ample supplies of rice. Even without imports she can fight and maintain her civilian population through 1945. American submarines must further intensify their efforts to destroy the Japanese merchant fleet.

Fortunately, Tokyo relays an earlier message the next day. Shigemitsu clarifies his earlier statement to Oshima about the status of Japanese shipping and how effective the American submarine campaign has been. The welcome news for Washington is contained in the words: "Unfortunately, present ship losses offset production, but we are firmly confident that by next March, at the latest, we can overcome this crisis and that ship construction will then begin to exceed ship losses."

With this welcome news in hand, McCormack's band of analysts prepare for the New Year of 1944.

---

26. SRS 1156, 22 December 1943.

I n the last week of 1943 and in early 1944, fighting intensifies around the world. In the Pacific, the First Marine Division lands on Cape Gloucester in New Britain while the U.S. Army's Thirty-second Division lands in New Guinea. Preparations are being made for an assault on the Marshall Islands with bloody fighting to come on Kwajalein and Eniwetok Atolls.

As a result of the Tehran conference in December, the Allies agree to give OVERLORD and ANVIL (the latter being the invasion of southern France) precedence over operations in Italy. Eisenhower turns over his role as Supreme Allied Commander, Mediterranean, to British field marshal Maitland Wilson on January 8. Eisenhower goes to England to take overall charge of military planning from General Morgan, arriving on the fourteenth. At the same time, Montgomery is given "operational charge" of OVERLORD and he also returns to England. On January 15, Sir William Strang presents the British plan for the occupation zones of postwar Europe as based on COSSAC's (Morgan's) plan called RANKIN C.

The landings at Anzio are still scheduled to take place later this month. It is hoped that this invasion will permit the Allies to outflank the Gustav Line, which runs across Italy, allowing the Germans to inflict heavy casualties and bleed the American, Canadian, British, New Zealand, Indian, Polish and French forces that must make frontal attacks against fixed positions on high ground. It will take five months— including the assaults on Monte Cassino—of dreadful fighting, until May, for the Allied forces to break out of the Anzio beachheads, break through the Gustav Line, and finally close on Rome.

Meanwhile, in Russia, Stalin's troops attack first in the south, across the Dnieper River, then in the north, liberating Leningrad, then in the middle, toward the River Styr into prewar Poland, and then again in the north, toward Estonia and Latvia.

Everywhere the fighting is bloody and relentless.

Meanwhile, from Berlin in January 1944, Oshima reports to Tokyo that the German Foreign Office building has been destroyed by Allied bombers. Its operations will be moved 155 miles southeast of Berlin, to Krummheubel in Silesia, and the diplomatic community is being asked to leave Berlin to accompany it. The Japanese have reserved a castle and two hotels at Brueckenberg—a twenty-minute walk from Krummheubel—as offices and residences for their staff. The Japanese offices in Berlin have also been repaired on an emergency basis, but to play safe, a four-man staff with codebooks and a cipher machine have also been placed in Boitzenburg, near Berlin.[1]

To the Americans, it appears that Berlin is already so badly battered that it may well be losing its military importance. Especially if various branches of the German government are forced to locate elsewhere around Germany. Thus Oshima's message is the forerunner for a mythical concept that Hitler and his most fanatical followers will, as a final resort, withdraw into the mountains of Bavaria, to a so-called National Redoubt, where they will fight to the last man. This myth will have an incredible impact on how Eisenhower and Marshall will conduct the final days of the European conflict.

A few days later, from Tokyo, Foreign Minister Shigemitsu sends a circular to various Japanese establishments in the Far East. The analysts note that on the whole, Shigemitsu's commentary on military developments in the past year is "fairly objective." The past summer destroyed Japan's "preconceived notion" that the Red Army was at its best in winter, and he concedes that the Germans may not be able "to stand firm at the Soviet-German prewar borders." On the other hand, Shigemitsu repeats overly optimistic statements relayed to him by his representatives in Europe claiming, for example, that "the reserve power of the Red Army is steadily diminishing."[2]

The most interesting part of the circular is the final section, which briefly surveys current Soviet relations with Japan. Shigemitsu says that Japanese Soviet relations "are based on the need for maintaining neutrality. It has generally been possible to maintain fairly harmonious relations. The signing of the Provisional Fishing Agreement last March was proof of the fact." Tokyo notes that Russians are still refusing to

---

1. SRS 1169, 3 January 1944.
2. SRS 1172, 6 January 1944.

give the Americans access to airfields in Siberia from which they can bomb Japan. This means "the cautious Russians will, at least for the moment, devote themselves to the war against Germany and . . . avoid getting involved in Far Eastern problems."

Meanwhile, Ambassador Oshima is worried about the safety of various portraits now in his custody of the Japanese emperor. He tells Tokyo: "We are now caring for the portraits formerly enshrined at Sofia, Bucharest, Budapest, Prague, The Hague, Antwerp and Hamburg." These Imperial items are currently stored in Oshima's air-raid shelter. A staff member guards them at all times. However, the shelter cannot withstand a direct hit, and Oshima wants permission to send all but one of the portraits to Switzerland for safekeeping.

This indication of how the Japanese government venerates the Emperor is a perfect example of the problems that will be caused by the Allies' determination that Japan must accept "unconditional surrender" at the war's end. Westerners wouldn't think twice about "enshrining" President Roosevelt's diplomatic portrait or that of the King of England. But if the Japanese are willing to worship a portrait of the Emperor, how vehemently will they defend the prerogatives of their ruling monarch when the time comes to negotiate a peace treaty? To an American politician, this question is pointless; to the American military, it represents the history of Japan's militaristic government and its policies of military aggression. In the end this will cost Japan dearly.

On January 11, the Magic Summary takes a detour from the war in general to the political turmoil in South America.[3] As late as last July, German agents were reporting that a new Argentine government was trying to create an anti-U.S. bloc of South American countries, consisting of Chile, Bolivia, Paraguay, Uruguay and Peru. If these countries did not fall in line with Argentine thinking, the Argentinean government would then supplant the recalcitrant governments with "more cooperative regimes." Indeed, German agents participated in planning to overthrow the Bolivian government during the past summer and fall.[4]

In late August 1943, according to German agents in South America, there was considerable talk about "specific plans for a revolution in Chile." They also reported that negotiations with groups in Chile

---

3. SRS 1177, 11 January 1944.
4. SRS 1177 refers the reader to the Magic Summaries of October 29, November 19, and December 19, 1943. These Summaries are still censored, however.

were going well, and Chilean military circles had "prepared everything in order to follow Argentina's example."

The German Foreign Office asked its chargé in Buenos Aires whether there was any truth in these reports. The chargé was skeptical. But in early December, the chargé advised Berlin that several groups were still plotting a Chilean revolution: (1) a military clique headed by General Berguno [a Chilean Army officer; reportedly pro-German] and Admiral Gerken [Commander in Chief of the Chilean Navy]; (2) a group of Nazis; (3) a long list of individuals. By late December, the revolutionary movement will be fashioned on the Argentine revolution and supported by five thousand trained and armed "Nacistas" adherents.

Of great interest is the news that an Argentine colonel named Perón has won governmental approval to promise the Chilean rebels financial backing amounting to 1 million American dollars. The revolution is scheduled to take place sometime after February 15, and the German chargé in Buenos Aires notes that the Bolivian revolution took place "earlier than originally intended and strengthens the present tendency to a similar proceeding in Chile, and perhaps also in Peru and Uruguay."[5]

The analysts in Washington note that the Chilean government announced in late December that it was aware of subversive activity within its military and that it is prepared "to punish immediately the individuals responsible" and to expel "unworthy" aliens from the country.

It is activities such as these that had caused Roosevelt, in August of 1940, long before the OSS came to life, to send a small undercover group headed by Nelson Rockefeller to sabotage similar Nazi endeavors.[6]

The following day, the analysts in Washington note "a rather extraordinary circular, which was sent out by the German High Command to all Arms Attachés at the end of the past year."[7] Claiming to be "an objective account of military developments during 1943," the paper is nothing but a self-serving apologia for German reverses. It also proves to Washington that the Germans have lost the ability to examine their

---

5. There is handwritten reference to the Magic Summary of January 7, 1944, but that Summary is still censored.
6. Paul Kramer, "Nelson Rockefeller and British Security Coordination," *Journal of Contemporary History* 16, no. 1 (January 1981).
7. SRS 1178, 12 January 1944.

defeats to see if there might be some unexpected cause for them. Furthermore, by laying so much blame on their former Italian allies, the Germans are demonstrating an unexpected psychological weakness. The section titled "Consequences of Italy's Weakness and Treachery" is a perfect example of muddled German thinking. According to the German High Command: "The collapse of Italy did not come suddenly or as a surprise, but was a result of a latent weakness in which the deficiency of the Italians, both in ability and in desire to fight, became ever more apparent." The sabotage of the Axis by the Italians was highlighted by three examples in which the *Wehrmacht* found itself in dire straits because of "Italian weakness." These were:

"1. The decisive November 1942 breakthrough of the Russians in the East, which brought on our defeat, occurred in a non-German sector of the front. After the initial breach, the Italian Army, which had been committed to screen the Stalingrad and Caucasus fronts, completely disintegrated and enabled the enemy to drive such a wedge into our front that it could not be removed by counterattacks. Consequently, a withdrawal along the entire southern part of the front became necessary. In the last analysis, the Italian failure caused the sacrifice of the [German] Sixth Army.

"2. In the decisive phase of the African campaign there was a complete breakdown of the Italian units, primarily because their armament, equipment and training were absolutely inadequate for modern warfare. The responsibility for that shortcoming rested largely on the clique around Badoglio, a group which was secretly fighting Fascism. It has been established beyond a doubt that German deliveries of material and raw materials for Italy's war economy were quite sufficient, but instead of being put to use, they were hoarded for the day of treachery. After German forces occupied the country, numerous warehouses were discovered containing stocks of scarcity goods of all kinds.

"3. Finally there was the conduct—bordering on open treason— of irresponsible [Italian] troop contingents: their unjustifiable capitulation and their complete lack of readiness to defend the soil of their mother country enabled the invading enemy to break through Sicily into southern Italy."

The German High Command went on to accuse the Italian Navy of treachery and cowardice. Similar accusations were made about Italian troops operating in the Balkans, Sicily, Sardinia and Corsica. "The above details present a shattering picture of monstrous treachery," says the German report. "The conspirators in the Italian nobility, in the armed forces, and in business and government circles betrayed their

German allies, who had done everything possible to assist the Italian Empire that had voluntarily joined the German side.''

The venomous report must have been pleasant reading for the recipients of Magic.

Only three pages of the Magic Summary of January 15, 1944, have been released to date.[8] But a special note on page 11 indicates that security problems have arisen regarding the Diplomatic Summaries. The note says: ''The word 'Magic' is now fairly widely used to designate intelligence obtained from radio intercept sources. It does not provide more security than other descriptive words such as 'intercept,' 'cryptanalysis' and 'code.' Accordingly, it is requested that all persons concerned be instructed to refrain from using the word 'Magic' in telephone conversations or other conversations or communications in which such other descriptive words would not be used.''

It is obvious that as more and more Americans are being involved in operations based on Magic and Ultra information, the gossiping among the military—which is overheard by civilians—threatens the Allies' greatest secret.[9] As we will see, this will become a major issue in the coming presidential election.

Meanwhile, early in January 1944, Hitler is trying to influence President Roosevelt's unprecedented bid for a fourth term in office. On the tenth of the month, the Chief of the Political Affairs Bureau of the German Foreign Office sends a long message to the German chargé in Buenos Aires, with instructions that it is to be destroyed immediately after reading.[10] Berlin announces that the German propaganda office will carry on a ''careful and energetic campaign'' to thwart Roosevelt's reelection. Berlin asks Buenos Aires for ''exact information'' on the effect of the German campaign. Foreign Minister von Ribbentrop also

---

8. SRS 1181.
9. This lack of security extended even to radio communications sent to U.S. submarines operating in Japanese waters. Lewin was so incensed by this violation of procedure he made one such message the ironic cover of his book, *The American Magic*. The message begins:

FROM: COMSUBPAC
TO: ALL SUBS GUARDING
    NPM FOX . . .
ANOTHER HOT <u>ULTRA</u> COMSUBPAC SERIAL 27 X LARGEST AND NEWEST NIP CARRIER WITH 2 DESTROYERS DEPARTS YOKUSUKA AT 5 HOURS GCT 10 JUNE AND CRUISES AT 22 KNOTS ON COURSE 155 DEGREES . . . SALMON AND TRIGGER INTERCEPT IF POSSIBLE AND WATCH OUT FOR EACH OTHER. . . . [Emphasis added.]

As Lewin explained to the author, the use of the word <u>ULTRA</u> in a British message would have resulted in extreme disciplinary measures.
10. SRS 1185, 19 January 1944.

wants to know "confidential or little-known details concerning the election prospects and the mood of the American people," plus any evaluations by the press about the success or failure of German propaganda. If the chargé in Buenos Aires cannot obtain the information from prominent people returning to Argentina from the U.S., Berlin claims that they have the means "for sending a confidential agent to the States."

The analysts note for Marshall that Franz von Papen told the Japanese ambassador to Turkey that Roosevelt is the one man the Germans don't want to see reelected, because "it would ruin us."[11] Later, on October 23, U.S. minister Harrison in Bern reports that sources close to the German legation in Switzerland claim "Hitler has ordered all possible efforts to be made to prevent Roosevelt's reelection." Meanwhile Ribbentrop is organizing a special group to launch abusive personal attacks against Roosevelt in the neutral countries, which, hopefully, would be relayed and repeated by the press in America. This is just a preliminary step.

On another subject, three days later, a fifty-plus-page report crosses Marshall's desk revealing that Japanese merchant shipping losses are so bad that Japan is trying to build small blast furnaces throughout China so that Tokyo can receive more pig iron from the territories she occupies.[12]

On January 27, from Ankara, Japanese ambassador Kurihara reports that Rumania is preparing for its coming occupation by Russian troops.[13]

On January 29, the format of the Magic Summary is changed slightly, just enough to point out to insiders that the daily reporting is now under the control of the Army, which has been noted earlier. The title "Special Branch, M.I.D." is added beneath the line saying "Assistant Chief of Staff, G-2," and the dateline is moved to another part of the page.

The next day, Oshima reports on his latest meeting with Hitler of a week earlier.[14] Oshima's message consists of six parts, of which two are missing. The four parts that have been decrypted are vitally important.

"Unfortunately, during the past year I have had to surrender the initiative on the Eastern Front because of a number of totally unex-

---

11. Referenced to MS (Magic Summary) 1 August 1943.
12. SRS 1188, 22 January 1944.
13. SRS 1193, 27 January 1944.
14. SRS 1196, 30 January 1944.

pected developments,'' Hitler tells Oshima. "First and foremost was the treachery of the Italians. If the Italian forces in North Africa had remained loyal, we could have held the Tunisian bridgehead, as we did our level best to do. Even though we did not have complete control of the sea, we could have held out. That is demonstrated by the way in which we were able to evacuate our force from Corsica. Nevertheless, as a result of Italian sabotage, Tunisia fell; then Sicily was thrown open to an invasion, and finally the Italian debacle occurred.

"At first I decided to defend a line in the northern Apennines. But the Anglo-American strategy was so utterly foolish that I got a chance to hold a line in southern Italy, a line which we had originally formed with the idea of only holding temporarily.

"On the other hand, as a result of the loss of Italy, I must admit that I have had to send thirty-five divisions to Italy and the Balkans." The analysts in Washington point out for Marshall's benefit that while "collateral evidence indicates that as many as thirty-five divisions may have been sent to Italy and the Balkans . . . a number of other divisions have been withdrawn from those areas for use on other fronts."

Hitler continues, saying: "I had to take those men from the Eastern Front, and you can well understand what a drastic step that was. Moreover, we have had to prepare on an even vaster scale for an immediate invasion in the West.

"So you can see that I have had no choice but to go completely on the defensive on the Eastern Front. First, we had planned to hold the Dnieper Line, but the Red Army stormed it in such force that we would have had to move in a great many more reserves in order to hold on there. I could not spare those reserves, for our principle is that, even though it means losing a great deal of territory in the East, we can run no risks in the West. That will be the principle upon which we conduct our war on the Eastern Front.

"Depending on what the enemy does, we may have to retire from [*sic*] a line running south from Lake Peipus in the north, and from the Dnieper bend in the south, but we will hold the Crimea. I think the Red Army's drive has been blunted, and I am confident that we will run into no military crisis in the East. Moreover, I want you to know that I do not intend to stay on the defensive there forever. Once I get a chance, I am going to attack the Red Army again.

"Now as for the question of the second front, no matter when it comes, or at what point, I have made adequate preparations to meet it. In Finland we have seven divisions; in Norway, twelve; in Denmark, six; in France and the Low Countries, sixty-two." Once again, the analysts break into Hitler's words pointing out that the Fuehrer's figures for Finland, Denmark and Norway "are in accord with collateral evidence." However, the analysts question Hitler's figures for France and the Low Countries. They believe his figures include occupational troops, not purely front-line troops. If this is true, then Hitler's figures tally "substantially with other estimates."

As if knowing that someone would be checking his assertations, Hitler next tells Oshima: "All of those divisions are not, I must admit, of the finest caliber, but I have emphasized the fact that there must be complete mobility. I have gotten together as many armored divisions as possible, including four SS divisions and the Herman Goering Division." Once again, the analysts in Washington break the narrative, commenting that there are four SS divisions in France and the Low Countries. They point out, however, that on the day Hitler spoke with Oshima he was not ready to admit that the Herman Goering Division was going to have to stay on the Italian front.

Going back to the second front, Hitler says: "But how vast is that seacoast! It would be impossible for me to prevent some other sort of landing somewhere or other. [Oshima interpolates that at this point Hitler alluded to the Allied landings below Rome at Anzio on January 22.] But all the enemy can do is establish a bridgehead. I will stop, absolutely, any real second front." At this point a part of the message is missing.

The next section starts with Oshima asking Hitler if Germany might settle the Eastern problem by political measures. To this Hitler replies: "No, I know that the only way is to paralyze Russia by force of arms. Although it is not clear how much reserve strength remains in Russia today, they have been up against it awfully hard. [Sentences are missing here, too.] Let me repeat that, so far as Russia is concerned, you can count on my striking back at her once more."

Oshima points out to Hitler that if he is going to make another attack in Russia, the Germans will have to have thirty or forty more divisions. He asks: "If the British and Americans keep up this awful howling of theirs and continue to postpone the Atlantic invasion, aren't you afraid you won't ever get a chance to send that number of divisions to the East?"

To this, Hitler says: "I do not know whether they will attack on a large or small scale, or at what point. But the Anglo-Saxons positively cannot go on without an invasion, and I, for one, think we may get a chance to give them an awful blow.

"Besides, don't forget our coming retaliation against England. We are going to do it principally with rocket guns. Everything is now ready, and practice shows that they are extremely effective. Now take this line running to the Birmingham area; that is a good place to start. [Oshima interpolates that Hitler specified a line on a map.] I cannot tell you just when we will begin, but we are really going to do something to the British Isles. We also have ready two thousand *schnell* [fast] bombers, and last night we carried out our first real bombing of London. With all these various [word missing], I believe we can gradually regain the initiative and, seizing our opportunities, turn once again against Russia.

"Let me tell you what I think of the partisans in the Balkans. Tito's followers have received lots of help from England, America and Russia and are now a rather powerful force. We are trying to quell them, and we have sent relatively superior troops to that area, but the geography is so bad that we can only get at them when we find some of them massed in a favorable spot. I imagine that the Japanese forces in China run up against this very sort of thing.[15]

"Now you want to know about the submarine war. Well, the plane detectors [radar on antisubmarine aircraft] of the enemy are so superior that we have had to absorb a lot of punishment from them, but we are now working on the following measures: (a) the use of magnetic mines; (b) increasing the speed of submarines; (c) improving our antiaircraft weapons; and (d) methods of disrupting the enemy's detectors. We are not ready yet. But by early summer we will have solved the matter, and then we will reopen the submarine war."

The remainder of the message is missing. But what a gold mine of information Hitler gives the Allies via Oshima! The historian might read Hitler's monologue differently, placing emphasis on portions that might differ from the military's thinking of the time. What is interesting to note is exactly what the analysts believed the most important portions of Hitler's words to be. In order of analytical importance they are:

1. The subject of retaliation against England. The total bomber strength of the German Air Force is only 1,980 planes, of which only 1,542 are operational. Hitler's figures are wrong. Therefore he is attaching great importance to his new "rocket guns."

2. Hitler's continuing plan "to paralyze Russia by force of arms." There will be no "political measures."

---

15. Reading Hitler's words fifty years after he says them and comparing them with the statements made by NATO military leaders in 1993–94, explaining why Western troops cannot enforce the peace in the old Yugoslavia, one experiences a profound sense of déjà vu.

3. On the subject of Germany's inability to send enough reserves to the Eastern Front to hold the Dnieper Line, the analysts point out that Hitler is willing to sacrifice this and other parts of Russia because "we can run no risks in the West."

4. On the second front: Hitler believes the Allies will land, and that they will establish a bridgehead. But that will be all they can accomplish, because "I will stop, absolutely, any real second front."

Army records do not specify exactly how this information is used by Marshall or Eisenhower, or how it is passed on to Russia. (Judging from future Soviet strategy, it seems certain that the information is passed via different channels.) But by proceeding on a chronological basis, placing one document after another in its proper niche, we can see that for the planners of OVERLORD, and those concerned about the combined strategies of the Eastern versus Western Fronts, the Oshima-Hitler conversation is a jewel beyond price.

✖ ✖ ✖

Within the next sixty-some days, especially between March 2 and April 4, 1944, seven more Magic Summaries will deal with the German defenses against invasion, ranging from Norway to the Mediterranean.[16] Often the analysts will note that the information in the Magic Summaries corroborates information gathered from other sources. But think about the meaning of the word *corroborate,* which Webster's defines as "1. to strengthen. 2. to make more certain; confirm; support." In other words, with these Magic reports in hand, the Allied planners are dealing with specific knowledge and not unsupported estimates from the order-of-battle specialists. Magic closes the circle, either before or after the "estimate" is made. With Magic in hand, the Allied plans for OVERLORD and the advance through Europe should be impeccable. This will prove to be true.

For example, on March 2, the code breakers did more work on

---

16. SRS 1228, 2 March 1944; SRS 1234, 8 March 1944; SRS 1237, 11 March 1944; SRS 1243, 17 March 1944; SRS 1244, 18 March 1944; SRS 1260, 3 April 1944; SRS 1261, 4 April 1944. These Summaries in chronological order contain the references to earlier intercepts. The quotes taken from these Summaries continue through page 197.

the messages sent to Tokyo by Lieutenant Colonel Nishi, an assistant military attaché at the embassy in Berlin. He first reported in November after Ambassador Oshima inspected Germany's Atlantic defenses. Parts of Nishi's report were carried in the Magic Summary of December 17; now the balance has come to hand. The analysts in Washington highlight three aspects of Nishi's report: (1) the organizations responsible for the planning and the construction of the defenses, (2) the methods employed and (3) the quantities of material and labor used.

On March 8, another extremely important intercept is decoded from a message sent a week earlier by Japan's military attaché in France. He tells Tokyo that the Germans now are changing their plan for defending against invasion. He points out that in December the Germans were going to rely on large-scale attacks on the invader "after he had landed" (underscoring in the original). "However," he says, "as a result of studying the problem, and because of recommendations which have been made by Marshal Rommel, the Germans have now decided that the coastal lines must be held at all cost and that the enemy must not be permitted to set foot on the Continent. . . . The changes in defense plans are the result of the German experience in Sicily, Salerno and Nettuno. In Rommel's opinion it was bad strategy to allow the enemy to land because (1) after the British and American forces had obtained a bridgehead, the Germans did not quickly move into action against them, and (2) with superiority in the air, the enemy makes it a rule to pound the rear of the defending forces and that makes impossible a defense in which small units hold the front lines and a large reserve in the rear is used for counterattacks. . . . It is also considered that it would be very unwise, from a political point of view, to allow the enemy to set foot on the Continent."

So important is this information that it is placed on the first page of the March 8 Magic Summary for Marshall's attention. The vital question is, who was the source for the Japanese attaché? The answer is not known until March 11, when the analysts deliver a new Summary to Marshall with these words on the front page: "There has now come to hand a 17 February report from the same man which seems to indicate the source of his information. The earlier message quotes Marshal Rundstedt's Chief of Staff [what an incredible source!] as follows: 'The essence of the German plan of defense for Holland, Belgium and France can be summed up in these words—*hold on to the beaches*. The strategy now is to destroy the enemy landing forces before they ever reach the beaches, or if they do manage to land, to destroy them in areas as close to the coast as possible.' No longer is the strategy to entice the enemy on the Continent a certain distance and then destroy him.... Consequently, places like the Maginot Line are of no direct importance as European fortresses; they are being used now as storage depots for arms and ammunition.''

The analysts also refer Marshall to another report by the same attaché dated February 18, in which he says: ''The German Army has recently begun the construction of obstacles in the water in order to strengthen the defenses of the coast. The obstacles consist of (a) contact mines attached to the ends of rods driven into the sea bottom, and (b) underwater barriers made by setting sharp-pointed iron poles into concrete blocks and planting the latter on the sea bottom.

''Large numbers of both types of obstacles are installed in the critical areas, extending for a distance of one hundred to two hundred meters offshore. Landing craft are either destroyed by the mines or sunk because of the holes torn in their hulls.''

On March 17, another report by the Japanese military attaché in Germany is decrypted and put on the first page of the day's Magic Summary. It is based on a December 20, 1943, conversation between the attaché and German vice admiral Buerkner (believed by the analysts to be a high official in the Abwehr). The attaché tells Tokyo that be believes Buerkner's conclusions are those of the German High Command, and he quotes the Admiral in part as follows: ''There are no indications that the enemy will attempt to land in the Balkans. Landings in Norway or in the Iberian Peninsula would be politically important for the enemy, but would be of very small value from a military point of view. The terrain of the Belgian and Dutch coast not only makes landings difficult, but does not permit the use of a large number of troops.

''Therefore, it is probable that the enemy will land in France in the Channel area and in Brittany. The landings are expected to take place either during the period from the end of February through March or in the period from May to July.... The enemy fears the reaction which a failure would cause and, therefore, will not rashly attempt to carry out landing operations. Although the enemy's large-scale plans for invasion are considered impossible of achievement, it is feared that a limited objective, such as cutting off our communications with Norway, might be attained, and efforts are being made to strengthen defenses in that region.''

The next day, March 18, Ambassador Oshima's conversation with Under Secretary von Steengracht about recent military and political developments makes page one of the Magic Summary. Under the heading "Political" on page five is a long report from Ambassador Sato in Moscow about a new Russo-Japanese agreement providing for the transfer to Russia of Japan's coal and oil concessions in North Sakhalin Island. As a result of executing this agreement, the two countries also expect to sign a Five-Year Fishery Convention in the immediate future. Reading all the correspondence between Ambassador Sato in Moscow and Foreign Minister Shigemitsu, the analysts in Washington note that Shigemitsu entered the deal with great misgivings. He warns that Sato's compromise that clinched the deal would arouse serious opposition in Japan if it became known, and the Foreign Minister demanded that the preliminary documents of transfer should be worded in a special format so that they would not have to be presented to Japan's Privy Council for approval.

On April 3, Japan's ambassador to France, Takanobu Mitani, reports on his inspection trip of the Mediterranean coastal defenses. He made the trip on March 28, accompanied by his military attaché, and his report, sent on April 1, includes the following information:

"*Mediterranean Coast East of the Rhone [River]*. It is possible that along the coast east of the Rhone the enemy will confine their attempts to commando landings————[several words missing]. However, if the enemy should occupy Marseille and Toulon, they would gain a marked political advantage. In view of the possibility that the Allies may try to land at the mouth of the Rhone and capture Marseille, the Germans are now making every effort to strengthen defenses in that area. In both Marseille and Toulon, they are rushing work to strengthen installations built by the French army, and at Marseille a submarine base is being constructed.

"In addition, fortifications and other defense installations have been built wherever necessary along the entire coast from Menton to Marseille. Tank barriers of reinforced concrete have been constructed throughout that area, and at such points as Nice, St.-Raphaël and Antibes, where the enemy is expected to attempt landings, strong defense works have been constructed. Preparations are also being made for an extensive defense in depth, utilizing topography and natural positions. At all important communications points antiaircraft emplacements are being located."

This is followed by a study of the Mediterranean coast to the west of the Rhone. In conclusion, the Ambassador says "the whole southern French coast is being transformed into a fortified defense area. Countless land and sea mines have been sown throughout the area—the total is believed to be about fifty thousand. While the preparations might seem quite paltry compared with the defenses along the Atlantic coast, they have nevertheless made astounding progress since September last year.''

For the Allied planners, this report is another pot of gold. The projected invasion of southern France, Operation ANVIL, is scheduled for 1944 with the invasion site being between the cities of Marseille and Nice. The more attention the Germans pay to southern France the better, Allied planners figure, because it takes men and materials away from the OVERLORD invasion beaches of Normandy.

In the same day's Magic Summary is a report by the Japanese military attaché to Stockholm, who has inspected the German defenses along the Norwegian coast between Bergen and Kristiansand. His most important finding is that the Germans do not have enough men to defend the coast adequately. ''In some cases a division has to protect a front of 125 miles.'' His lengthy report is a model of concise military observations.

On April 4, the Magic Summary contains more information from Ambassador Mitani. Newly decrypted portions of his message now say: ''In the opinion of the German military authorities in the Mediterranean area, the chances are that the enemy will attempt to land in the vicinity of Narbonne[17] and in the estuary of the Rhone. A landing at Narbonne would be followed by an advance westward along the Canal du Midi [which runs westward from the Mediterranean coast at Agde and connects with the Garonne River near Toulouse] in an effort to make contact with units landed in the Bay of Biscay. The forces at the mouth of the Rhone would attempt to advance northward in the Rhone basin.''

What this means to the analysts is that it appears all the Allied deception plans—Operation WADHAM, a fake plan for the invasion of Brittany in 1943; the deception plan for FORTITUDE SOUTH (an invasion in the Pas-de-Calais region by the fictitious First Army Group); the deception plan FORTIFIED NORTH (the invasion of Norway by the fictitious "Skye Force" of the Fourth Army)—all seem to have had the desired effect on the enemy. The Germans are still confused as to exactly where OVERLORD will take place, and they are committing masses of men and material in the wrong places.

These thirty days of Magic Summaries also contain other major items of note, including a plea from Ambassador Oshima that Tokyo

---

17. The analysts note that Mitani said the previous day that "the possibility of landing in the vicinity of Sète and Agde [coastal towns northeast of Narbonne] is considered especially great and the Germans are rapidly strengthening defenses in that area."

prepare itself for bombing. On March 3, Oshima tells Tokyo: "The air raids on Berlin continue, and by now 40 percent of the buildings have been completely destroyed, either by demolition bombs or by fire. Despite an all-out effort, the German Air Force has been unable to cope with the enemy's attacks. I, therefore, earnestly beg you to work in close collaboration with the military and naval authorities, in order that we can make our own preparations with the same degree of thoroughness as we exhibited at the time of our attack on Hawaii."[18]

On March 26, German under secretary von Steengracht explains Germany's decision to occupy Hungary to Ambassador Oshima.[19] The German story sounds very much like the one Hitler used against Italy. Oshima reports that he was told: "When Horthy, accompanied by his minister of war and chief of staff, came and talked with us, we Germans frankly expressed our anxiety concerning Hungary and demanded that he cooperate with us carrying out joint warfare. Somewhat to our surprise, Horthy and his military men—the latter two particularly— seemed anxious to have German forces occupy the country, and in fact asked us to do so. Consequently . . . the occupation will be completed without friction. We Germans did this because things have recently taken a bad turn for us on the southern sector of the Eastern Front. We are having to make some new strategic plans, and we may even have to retire to a line along the Dniester [River]. . . . We are now going to call back the German Minister in Hungary and send a man to Budapest with full authority to lay plans for the joint prosecution of the war. Nothing about this has as yet been published, but as soon as something has been decided, a very brief announcement will be made."

On March 28, the Japanese military attaché in Berlin reports to Japan's vice minister of war and to the Chief of the Army Air Force Headquarters that the Germans are developing the first operational jet-fighter plane.[20] The analysts note that for the past two years the Japanese have been buying prototypes and blueprints of German planes. Now, says the attaché, "we have good reason to believe that by the end of 1944 or in 1945, we shall see the appearance of a practical jet-propelled fighter. I have this from someone in the Messerschmitt Company—this source is particularly secret—that such a plane is now undergoing tests by both the Messerschmitt and Arado companies and that the one at the Messerschmitt Company is practically com-

---

18. SRS 1229, 3 March 1944.
19. SRS 1252, 26 March 1944.
20. SRS 1254, 28 March 1944.

pleted. . . . Japan should dispatch technicians at once and begin the study of this plane while it is still in the experimental stage.'' The report goes on to detail the attempted purchases of the Me-309 fighter [MS 24 January 1943; 29 April 1943; 7 December 1943] and says that Japan ''would do well to purchase the manufacturing rights for the Me-209 fighter.''

The report ends with a prophetic note: ''Germany's experiments with, and perfection of, fighter planes are very important if Japan is to secure future mastery of the air. The Germans have tentatively agreed to send one designer to Japan.''

Fortunately for America, Japan is never able to exploit these German technological breakthroughs. This will allow American B-29s to accurately firebomb Japanese cities from low altitudes. Oshima's fears about the destruction of Tokyo and other Japanese cities will be realized.

✖ ✖ ✖

After pondering the Magic Summaries for April 1944, one notices a subtle but definite change of emphasis in the contents. It is almost as though Chief of Staff Marshall has decided that the invasion in Europe will proceed successfully, the defeat of Germany is assured and now the time has come to ask the analysts to pay more attention to Japan.

Two examples of this are found in mid-April and mid-May,[21] when the analysts start producing in-depth studies of the economics of Japan. The first report is a sixty-one-page study of Japan's aluminum production capacity, especially as it affects shipping and aircraft production. The second is a thirty-five-page analysis of the Russo-Japanese agreements on fishing rights.

On April 20, 1944, the most important section of the Summary is a careful analysis of current diplomatic maneuvers between Moscow and Tokyo, but the first references go back to August of the previous year.[22] At that time, Foreign Minister Shigemitsu suggested that Tokyo send a ''special envoy'' to Moscow, who would subsequently go on to the ''countries of Western Europe.'' In due course the Russians replied: No thanks. The Soviet answer treated the Japanese suggestion as an

---

21. SRS 1272, 15 April 1944; SRS 1307, 19 May 1944.
22. SRS 1277, 20 April 1944.

opening move for a German-Russian peace negotiated by Japan. Hence the rejection and the dropping of the matter.

The subject is reopened by Shigemitsu on April 2, 1944, when he asks Ambassador Sato in Moscow to seek a meeting with Soviet foreign minister Molotov and relay Shigemitsu's personal thanks for the recent signing of the protocols regarding the Sakhalin Islands and fishing rights. Sato is instructed to give a long, flowery verbal message to Molotov concerning the "advancement of friendly relations between the two nations."

It is difficult to understand exactly what response Shigemitsu expects from Molotov. The language of the Japanese message is too flowery. But in a separate communication to Sato on the same day, Shigemitsu says that he wants Sato to keep trying to improve Japanese-Russian relations, "taking maximum care, of course, that we do not give the impression that we are weak." He then asks Sato for answers on the following questions:

1. "Can we make some private arrangement prior to the expiration of the Russo-Japanese Neutrality Pact [in 1946] which will extend the period of its validity?" This question has great bearing on how America will conduct the final stages of its campaign against Japan.
2. "With reference to my suggestion of last year concerning the sending of important personalities to Russia, is it at all possible that we can take up conversations in line with that proposal?"
3. "Is there not some way by which an understanding could be reached between Japan and Russia with regard to China?" This last question is the truly explosive one. It has to shock men like Marshall, Stimson and King. Apparently Japan is trying to set up a new Far Eastern policy that uses China as the pawn between Russia and Japan. If successful, this could change the balance of power in the Far East. It cannot be allowed. As we will see, it will become a primary—but largely unknown—reason for America's use of nuclear weapons against Japan.

While Washington ponders these developments, Sato arranges a meeting with Molotov for April 8 that lasts for more than an hour. During the meeting, and after delivering Shigemitsu's lengthy message to Molotov, Sato proposes that the long-standing problems of boundaries between Japan and Russia might now be resolved. He also suggests the exchange of commodities between the two countries "on a small scale. The exchange of a large amount of goods would be difficult, since both countries maintain friendly relations with those that would be involved."

Molotov says that Russia will ponder these questions. Then he asks: "I wonder if you have any further information to give me? If you are prepared to give me such information, I will listen to it attentively."

After some diplomatic flummery, Sato says: "I am afraid that what I have just said about the Foreign Minister's having in mind not only relations between Japan and the USSR but also world peace is in fact an exaggeration. I should correct that statement by saying that he had in mind peace between Germany and the USSR."

Molotov reminds Sato that the Russians had turned down the idea the previous year.

Sato says that his statement is basically his own observation, and he tells Molotov: "Now the Russian Government has been winning great victories one after another and has more than aroused the wonder of the world. . . . According to what I have read about the Soviet Government's position and military aims, the Red Army's war objective is the restoration of former frontiers and nothing more. If that is the case, it is only natural to think that when these frontiers have been reached, a new situation will arise. That statement may be so naive as to make Your Excellency smile, but I believe that such a development is possible."

In summing up his impressions of the meeting with Molotov for Shigemitsu, Sato reports: "In order to leave behind me a strong impression about the Soviet-German peace question, I purposely stated at the end of the interview that I was speaking about a peace with honor, not a complete surrender by the Germans. Furthermore, I was careful to alter my first remarks about Foreign Minister Shigemitsu's ideas as to world peace by saying that he was thinking about peace between Germany and Russia. Perhaps it was not necessary to make that correction, but I wanted to avoid giving the impression that Japan desires to drag the Russians in and make use of them in connection with peace between Japan and the United States." (The Magic Summary bears a strong black line in the margin highlighting this sentence; it was apparently made by some authorized reader of the original document.)

That Sato could talk about the peace question to Molotov is for him "a step forward." But he fails to ask Molotov the question that is really on Shigemitsu's mind: Can Japan and Russia form a partnership that neutralizes China and creates a new order in the Far East under the control of Russia and Japan?

This ploy will be uncovered later by Magic intercepts. For the moment, one wonders whether Sato's failure to press the issue at this time is the result of his not understanding what Shigemitsu wants, or because he believes that peace can be maintained between Russia and Japan, or because his diplomatic instincts tell him that the issue should not be broached with Molotov at this time.

Washington does not know the complete plan that Shigemitsu has in mind. The fact that a program like this is being hatched, however, is enough to spread ripples of concern through the corridors of power. The so-called "end game" that closes out the war is going to be a close run and bloody fight.

✖ ✖ ✖

Once again the focus of the Magic Summaries shifts.

During most of May, the seven most interesting items all come from Berlin. It is either Ambassador Oshima reporting on the bombing of Berlin, or speculation about where and when the Allies will land in Europe, or on the defensive theories proposed by Marshal Rommel. In late May, even Ambassador Sato makes comments from Moscow about the possibilities of a second front. And at the end of May, Shigemitsu asks Sato for more information about how to get Russia to settle the so-called "China problem."

Oshima's portrait of events in Berlin just prior to the invasion makes interesting reading.[23] He claims that the nighttime bombing has destroyed 40–50 percent of greater Berlin. In daytime, the bombers have not hit the center of the city, but the outskirts, and people "remain in the streets to watch the battle going on high in the sky, and there is scarcely any sign of cringing in their faces. However, daylight bombing has concentrated with success on particular targets, primarily industrial establishments, and it cannot be denied that communication facilities in suburban factory areas, notably Erkner, have been severely damaged."

Oshima makes a point about how the Germans maintain "excellent" civilian morale, obviously hoping that Tokyo will learn from this lesson. "After every heavy attack," he reports, "the German officials are on hand with the food and supplies for which people clamor,

---

23. SRS 1296, 8 May 1944; SRS 1300, 12 May 1944.

thereby inspiring a feeling of quiet security among the people and giving them the hope, slight though it might be, that they will be spared in the next attacks. Such measures also serve to instill in the populace the idea that the Government has ample reserves for whatever vicissitudes may come. . . . Now it is quite clear that the people's will to resist has been so intensified that they feel they have no alternative but to fight it out to the last ditch.''

As for the official reaction to the bombings, Oshima tells Tokyo that a Colonel Hermann, the commanding officer of the night fighter units of Berlin, has told him: "Day and night, night and day, the enemy is bombing us, giving us no rest from our strenuous efforts. Unless we Germans are able to move our production machinery underground, I do not see how we can hold out. The way things are going now, if our supplies are cut off [because of a failure of production], the worst may happen. You Japanese should also get busy and put your production facilities underground lest you face the same situation.''

Oshima points out to Tokyo that Hermann was speaking while under great stress: "The rate of German plane losses, coupled with the damage to the factories, makes the future look black to him. On the other hand, despite the fact that the airplane factory at Gotha suffered heavy damage, I understand it was back in operation again after only six weeks.''

The analysts in Washington insert at this point the simple comment: "The Gotha Carriage Works aircraft factory was bombed by U.S. planes on 20 and 24 February.'' It will obviously be on another target list within days.

Oshima concludes by saying: "The second front is awaited with overwhelming confidence; the theory that continuous air attacks can paralyze German defenses against it is not taken seriously.''

A few days later,[24] Oshima reports that at an informal dinner he chatted with Admiral Doenitz, who said: "My own belief is that the domestic and international position of both [England and the United States] is such that they cannot avoid attempting an invasion. However, if a second front is not attempted, Germany plans to transfer powerful forces to the Eastern Front, relying on the strength of the West Wall and striking back at the enemy by other means.'' Oshima interpolates that Doenitz is referring to "retaliatory weapons.''

The Admiral continues, saying: "Recently I received a report from Marshal Rommel regarding his inspection of various areas, including

---

24. SRS 1302, 14 May 1944.

the fortifications along the Atlantic coast. Rommel is confident that Germany will be able to repulse the enemy no matter when or where they attempt to land. As a matter of fact, we Germans hope that the attempt will begin as soon as possible. Since England and the U.S. possess very superior Air Forces, the German Army naturally expects them to carry out 'carpet-bombing' attacks, but is confident that the German defense organization can easily weather such a bombardment.''

As for the Eastern Front, Doenitz says: ''A number of German commanders in that area still want reinforcements, and even in head-quarters a large group sides with that view. However, Hitler is opposed to it, believing that the soldiers on hand for operations in the West should not be decreased. After the second front has been smashed the German Army will again turn toward the East and resume the offensive.'' But when Oshima asked Doenitz what plan Germany would follow when she resumed the offensive on the Eastern Front so as to avoid a repetition of her failure to achieve a decisive victory in 1941, the Admiral replied that this was ''a very difficult problem.''

On May 21,[25] Oshima reports again to Tokyo, saying this time that his usual contact man believes that the Allied attack (all along the line) in Italy is designed to relieve the existing deadlock.'' Further, ''the invasion of Western Europe has apparently been postponed and probably will not take place during May. The troops, which recent reconnaissance has shown to be concentrated in the south of England, are still insufficient for the task of invasion, and the troops stationed in Scotland appear to be held in readiness for a diversionary attack on Norway.''

The Germans are wrong about Allied troop strength in England, but correct in their estimate of what's happening in Italy. After extremely bloody fighting, the Polish Corps had captured Monte Cassino on May 17–18, while two days later the U.S. II Corps breaks through the left flank of Gustav Line to capture Gaeta and Itri. By now the right flank of the German Tenth Army is reeling. The Canadians and British are about to attack next. The capture of Rome will be completed within three weeks' time. Fortunately, a month before the invasion of Normandy, the Germans still seem to be confused about where and when the assault will occur.

The next day's Magic Summary[26] indicates that German confusion about the invasion of France is working in the Allies' behalf. Oshima

---

25. SRS 1309, 21 May 1944.
26. SRS 1310, 22 May 1944.

reports that Adolf von Steengracht has told him that in Italy "the enemy are using everything they have in material; the attack has been terrible. If the German Army pours in reinforcements, it might be possible to maintain the present line. But that would fit in with the enemy strategy of attracting German forces to the Italian area in anticipation of establishing a second front elsewhere. Therefore, we have retreated in certain sections. Our military are of the opinion that the time for launching the second front is not far off, since the enemy have completed military preparations for it step by step. However, as to the place of landing, the reports are conflicting."

This is the time that the Allied forces, apparently trapped at Anzio, are about to attack, breach the German lines and join the drive on Rome.

Meanwhile, from Moscow, on May 20, Ambassador Sato makes his own particularly cogent observations about the situation.[27] He says that everyone, "both friend and foe," is concerned chiefly with the invasion, and that he has become "filled with foreboding." He explains his feelings: "The lull on the Russo-German front has continued for some weeks. My Military Attaché has advised me, however, that the Russians are moving hordes of men from the north to the Carpathian area, and he is convinced that these troops will be thrown into the fight at the start of the Anglo-American invasion. From now on changes in the military and diplomatic kaleidoscope will depend on the success of the second front. In view of the enormous preparations of the Anglo-Americans, I do not believe that the Germans will be able to destroy their forces at the water's edge—there is no longer any hope of that. We must realize that they will get a foothold at many places on the Continent, and that from then on there will be a war to the death. . . . There is no hope of patching up Russo-German relations until the second front fails to materialize or at least until a truce has been concluded."

The Japanese military attaché in Moscow is calling the future course of war in Russia quite well. Stalin had planned to launch a major offensive to coincide with OVERLORD, but he was forced to postpone it when he learned in early April that OVERLORD itself was being held back for another month. What Stalin now plans are deceptions in the north and the south with the real attack to occur in the center, the mission being to throw the Germans out of Russia and "liberate" Poland. Stalin also works out with the Allies an elaborate deception plan

27. SRS 1312, 24 May 1944.

to make the Germans believe the next Russian attack will be in the south (the Russians capture Sevastopol in early May), while the Allies invade Norway.

The success of all this planning is about to bear remarkable fruit.

The Magic Summary of May 27, 1944,[28] reveals Japan's concern that Switzerland, the European banking center for the Tokyo government, believes her neutrality may be compromised. Minister Sakamoto reports to Japan that "the second front is now the gravest concern in this country. Recently the government in a very inconspicuous manner has called more men to the colors and assigned them to defensive positions along the frontiers." What the Swiss are worried about is a retreating German Army coming out of Italy. How will the Germans pass through Switzerland? Or will they try to fight from the Swiss Alps?

"If Kesselring's troops are forced to withdraw," says Sakamoto, "there seems today to be no confidence that Switzerland will be able to maintain her neutrality."

From Venice, a month-old report is decrypted. Translated for the May 30 Magic Summary,[29] Japanese ambassador Hidaka is quoted on his meeting with Mussolini just before the dictator was thrown out of office. According to Hidaka, Mussolini had a meeting with Hitler in late April during which the German leader remarked: "If the enemy should be victorious, both of us would be dragged around the world and put on display like circus freaks."

At the end of May, Foreign Minister Shigemitsu shows that he has not given up on his original idea about reaching "an understanding with Russia in regard to China."[30] In late April, Ambassador Sato had advised Tokyo that he was opposed to efforts in that direction because (1) he didn't believe Russia would assist Japan in settling the China problem, and (2) Russian cooperation might have disastrous consequences for Japan, because Russia would seize the opportunity to further the spread of Communism throughout Japanese territory.

Now Shigemitsu asks Sato for his "considered opinion" about the fact that Russia will obviously play some part in international affairs in eastern Asia. Shigemitsu thinks it would be "a great thing if we could induce the Russians to cooperate with us. What do you think of this idea and what method should we adopt in carrying it out?"

Explaining his reasoning on the matter, Shigemitsu says: "Amer-

---

28. SRS 1315, 27 May 1944.
29. SRS 1318, 30 May 1944.
30. SRS 1319, 31 May 1944.

ica and England support Chungking, while Russia favors the Chinese Communist Army. However, all three countries are bound together by a common policy—an anti-Axis policy—and there is always the danger that it might be extended to eastern Asia. Furthermore, Russia is using the anti-Chungking sentiment in America and England in an attempt to effect a compromise between the Kuomintang and the Communist Army. What then should we do in order to cope with this situation? . . . In view of the possibility of a compromise between Chungking and the Communist Army, what is your opinion as to the possibility of our using Russia as a means to bringing our war in China to a conclusion?''

Obviously Shigemitsu had not appreciated Sato's sending him an article from *Pravda* that appeared earlier in the month that was highly critical of the Chungking government. Sato said the article made him ''suspect that Russia may be about to try to weave Communist and other Leftist elements into the Chungking Government, as she so cunningly did in the case of the Free French and Badoglio regimes.''

Five days before the invasion of Europe on June 6, 1944, the Magic Summary[31] gives the Allied planners one of the greatest gifts of the war: Hitler tells Ambassador Oshima how and where and when he believes the invasion will take place, and he is 100 percent wrong! The supreme leader of Germany has swallowed hook, line and sinker every deception plan the Allies have concocted about where and when the invasion will occur. Furthermore, he tells Oshima that he is willing to surrender more territory in Italy rather than weaken his forces on the Atlantic coastline of France.

The conversation takes place on May 27 at Berchtesgaden, and its real flavor is lost in the official analysis. Thus, Ambassador Oshima's careful account is worth studying. He quotes Hitler as starting out by saying: ''It is on the Italian front that the fighting is now most acute; England and America have thrown against us an infinitude of weapons and materials. In my opinion, the main object of this new drive is to lure German military strength to that theater, and we are therefore not making too great an effort to prevent the loss of territory. Instead we are gradually retiring . . . and inflicting huge losses on the enemy.''

Hitler also announces that he is not sending any more planes to help defend Italy. It has also been decided to establish a defense ''line running from the Alban Hills on the West Coast to a point south of the Gran Sasso Mountains and finally to a point north of Pescara on the

---

31. SRS 1320, 1 June 1944.

East Coast. Therefore, while inflicting as much damage as possible on the enemy, we will retire to that line, which we will call Position C.''

Essentially, Hitler is telling Oshima that he is allowing German troops to give up Rome to establish the strong Gothic Line from which the Germans will bleed their attackers heavily. For example, the American Fifth Army will endure more than fifteen thousand casualties from late September to late October 1944, and these losses will be so great they cannot be replaced and the American drive in Italy comes to a halt.

In Russia, as Hitler sees the situation: ''The lull on the Russian front continues, but I believe that the Soviet will attack before long. For the time being, Germany has taken the steps necessary to stave off such a drive. The Hungarian Army has already sent seventeen divisions to the front, and Rumania practically the same number.[32] . . . We Germans have known all along that the Axis should have defended along the Don, but Hungary and Rumania never could grasp that fact. Now, however, the flames are close to their own borders, and the Hungarian and Rumanian forces are more aware of the peril. So far they have stood up rather well.''

Oshima asks Hitler in which direction will the Russians strike. His answer: ''I think that [the Soviet attack] will be two-pronged; in my opinion they will head northwest from the Lvov area and penetrate into central Poland, and they will also invade Rumania. I think that the drive from Lvov will come first, and the attempted invasion of Rumania afterwards.'' Again Hitler's estimate will be wrong. The attack will not start out from Lvov, but in the center, on the Belorussian Front, on June 23 and will be aimed first at Lithuania and Latvia.

It is when Oshima asks Hitler about the second front that Washington and London get the break they have been hoping for. Says Hitler: ''I believe that sooner or later an invasion of Europe will be attempted. I understand that the enemy has already assembled about eighty divisions in the British Isles. Of that force, a mere eight divisions are composed of first-class fighting men with experience in actual warfare.''

Hitler also says he believes the Allies are fully ready to invade. It is then Oshima asks him how the invasion will be carried out. Hitler says: ''Well, judging from relatively clear portents, I think diversionary

---

32. Collateral information gathered by the Washington analysts indicates that Hitler's figures regarding the Rumanian divisions "is substantially correct, but the total Hungarian strength on the southeastern front is probably no more than eleven divisions."

actions will take place in a number of places—against Norway, Denmark, the southern part of western France and the French Mediterranean coast. After that—when they have established bridgeheads in Normandy and Brittany and have sized up their prospects—they will then come forward with an all-out second front across the Straits of Dover. We ourselves would like nothing better than to strike one great blow as soon as possible. But that will not be feasible if the enemy does what I anticipate; their men will be dispersed. In that event, we intend to finish off the enemy's troops at the several bridgeheads. The number of German troops in the West still amounts to about sixty divisions."[33]

Oshima then reminds Hitler that in their last meeting, the Chancellor had told the Japanese that if there was no invasion, "you thought you might blast southern England with rocket guns and then find an opportunity to take the initiative again on the Eastern Front. Well, since then, the Anglo-Americans have been bombing the Channel area more heavily than ever; I wonder if those weapons you were going to use against England have not been destroyed."

"No," says Hitler. "Those guns are in an arsenal made of impermeable concrete. They are in no danger."

"If the Anglo-Americans do not stage an invasion," Oshima asks, "don't you think it would be a little dangerous to return your troops to the Eastern Front?"

"Well, I have no intention of waiting forever for them to come," Hitler replies. "I will give them two or three more months; if they don't come then, Germany will take the offensive. By that time, we will have finished organizing and equipping additional forces and will have between sixty and seventy [new] divisions, including forty-five armored divisions [Oshima interpolates that he is not sure his memory is correct on the figure forty-five]; we will then be in a position to attack. I have already exceeded my goal for SS divisions; twenty-five of them are now practically organized and equipped."[34]

The conversation between Oshima and Hitler continues for another four pages in the Magic Summary. Full of facts and figures about air-

---

33. The analysts in Washington note that "Hitler's figure is in substantial accord with other estimates."
34. The analysts in Washington note that Hitler's figures for the new SS divisions "tallies approximately with collateral evidence." The number of men in a German division is, however, far smaller than in an American division. Thus a matchup of forces on a division-versus-division basis will create an improper estimate of the forces involved. In the American first and second Heavy Divisions, for example, the total manpower for each division is three times the usual number of men contained in a single division.

plane production, the performance of German versus Russian tanks, the effectiveness of Soviet artillery, the submarine war, the most important information for Marshall and Eisenhower is still the revelation that Hitler, at this late date, is confused about Allied intentions about invading France. This has to be one of the greatest "mind games" ever played in the history of warfare. And with Marshall and Eisenhower knowing what they know, it is imperative that the Allies strike as quickly as possible with Operation OVERLORD so that they can take full advantage of having seen all of Hitler's cards before the invasion hand is played.

✖ ✖ ✖

For some unexplained reason—coincidence? fate?—the seventy pages of declassified Magic Summaries from June second through the seventh contain not a single word worth mentioning in this account about the forthcoming invasion, which occurs on June 6, 1944.

The first Magic Report comes on June 8, from Vichy, France.[35] Based on a report made June 6 that Ambassador Mitani forwarded to Tokyo, Magic discloses what he learned that morning from a member of the German embassy staff:

"a. It seems that the enemy is planning to occupy the Cherbourg Peninsula.

"b. A squadron of four battleships and twenty cruisers is cruising off Le Havre.

"c. Amphibious operations on a small scale, but employing large numbers of landing craft, have been carried out between Trouville and Dives [eleven miles WSW of Trouville].

"d. A division of British troops has been dropped by parachute, but the greater part of them have been wiped out.

"e. Parachute troops have been dropped on small airfields in the area between Le Havre and Boulogne.

"f. At present there do not seem to have been any landings at Calais, but a large-scale air bombardment is under way.

"g. At 4 A.M. the railway line between Vichy and Clermont-Ferrand was cut at Randan, thirteen kilometers from here. Emergency precautions are being taken.

---

35. SRS 1327, 8 June 1944.

"h. Upon receiving information of these operations, [Premier] La-val said that it was not bad news.

"i. Paris is calm."

The next day, both Vichy and Berlin report on the invasion to Tokyo.[36] The actual intercepts are of messages sent on June 7, and because they are intercepted in England, they reach the SHAEF planners at least six hours before they cross Marshall's desk. The significant element of these reports is they show continued confusion on the part of the German defenders. They have not comprehended the situation. For example, from Vichy, Ambassador Mitani tells Tokyo that the Germans say that "since yesterday the shelling in the Calais-Dunkirk area has been so intensive that it is believed the Anglo-Americans are planning to land here." (The Allies have no such plans.) Next, Mitani tells Tokyo: "The enemy appears to have assigned American forces to the Cherbourg area and British forces to the Le Havre area. However, that demarcation does not appear to be too rigid, since the troops dropped at Caen included both American and British soldiers." (Actually, three airborne divisions, one British and two American, had been dropped but were scattered by high winds. Nevertheless they were successful in their operations, seizing vital bridges, knocking out coastal artillery, and preventing German reinforcements from attacking the American troops landing on Utah Beach.) Mitani also tells Tokyo: "On the first day, four groups of airborne troops—two British and two American—and at least three bridgeheads between Trouville and Dives were wiped out by the Germans." (Not true.) Mitani continues: "Last night more airborne troops landed west of Cherbourg, and fighting is now going on at various points on the Cotentin Peninsula as well as Bayeux. The Luftwaffe spotted thirty enemy ships in flames just off Le Havre, but whether they were warships or merchant ships could not be determined." (These are the ships attached to deception plan TRACTABLE, which works to perfection, as does deception plan GLIMMER in the region of Boulogne and Calais.) Mitani concludes, saying: "Quiet reigns in Paris, Marseille and throughout France; however, the Maquis [the French resistance] are keeping up their work."

Word of the invasion does not reach Ambassador Oshima until the morning of June 7, twenty-four hours after the invasion started. That afternoon, Oshima is briefed by his "usual contact man," and he tells Tokyo that "although the German High Command realizes that landing operations were likely to be carried out this week because of

36. SRS 1328, 9 June 1944.

the favorable meteorological conditions, on the sixth the weather was unfavorable and it is not clear why such a day was chosen.'' Oshima's report is more accurate than Mitani's. Oshima tells Tokyo that the Allies have ''managed to establish a bridgehead on a coastal strip about twenty-five kilometers wide. However, the Germans still have nests of resistance in those areas and are continuing to fight. Both Bayeux and Caen are still in German hands.''

On the other hand, Oshima is also the victim of German confusion. He tells Tokyo that the Germans are bringing up reserves from the rear when, in reality, they are having difficulty moving because of Allied air superiority. Oshima also says that Berlin (for this one must interpolate Hitler) is unsure whether or not large-scale landings will be carried out elsewhere, especially around Le Havre and Dunkirk. German submarines are being sent to the Normandy coast. So are night fighter planes. Meanwhile, in the Mediterranean, Allied forces have been concentrating near Corsica, and the Germans are unsure whether they will land on the southern coast of France or in the Leghorn area.

One of the most important elements of the invasion, keeping Hitler and his generals guessing, is being accomplished. (Before dawn on June 6, von Rundstedt believes that a landing will take place in Normandy, and he asks Hitler for permission to move two panzer divisions forward to defend the beaches. Hitler tells von Rundstedt to wait until daylight when the situation will be clearer. This proves to be a crucial delay.) The Magic Summaries will show that German confusion continues. This is vital for the success of the Allied cause because, on the first day of the invasion, the fight for the beaches of Normandy is not as successful as the British and the Americans had planned. Indeed, at the end of D day they are far short of their target lines of advance. On the positive side, however, some 150,000 troops are ashore and digging in. Every hour they stay in place, or slowly work forward, means it will be that much more difficult for the Germans to dislodge them.

''One cannot overstate the importance of the fact that the commander of the invading forces knew that Hitler was not committing his reserves,'' says Robert T. Crowley. ''The significance of this priceless information gave Eisenhower and his staff a sense of confidence that rubbed off on everyone. It helped make the troops believe they would succeed. And the credit for creating all the deceptions, fooling the Germans and getting inside Hitler's brain belongs to the British. They were, in 1944, a generation ahead of everyone in this regard. I don't know anyone better in terms of psychological warfare than the British. They were the masters of the game.''

In the coming days the struggle by the Allies to consolidate and break out of their beachheads, and the attempts by the Germans to prevent them from doing so, mark the key to the Allied victory in Europe. The Germans cannot compete against the Allied air superiority. Nor can they defy the weight of Allied naval gunfire from the battleships and cruisers patrolling as close to the beaches as they dare. Thus, even when they are committed, German reserves cannot be sent directly to battle in a way that allows them to use their strength to the fullest. More important is the fact that Hitler still believes the major Allied thrust will be made east of the River Seine and Le Havre. This region is being defended by the German Fifteenth Army. And Magic reveals that Hitler will not allow the transfer of elements from the Fifteenth Army to Normandy to crush the invaders.

Meanwhile, the fighting is desperate. American, British and Canadian forces attack again and again. The Canadians are faced by the Twelfth SS Panzer Division (Hitler Youth), which employs a fanatical series of counterattacks. The British valiantly try to drive to the east, but are stopped cold by determined German defenders. Meanwhile, it takes twelve days for the Americans to drive westward off Utah Beach and seal off the Cotentin Peninsula with its all-important deep-water port at Cherbourg.

Supplies for the Allies become a crucial factor. The Allies have created artificial "Mulberry" harbors at two beachheads, Omaha and Gold. But, on June nineteenth through the twenty-second, a violent Channel storm tears up these supply havens.[37] Fortunately, the Allies have landed twenty divisions of troops and are now fighting the Germans on a more-or-less even basis. It will take some weeks to repair the Mulberries, however, and when Cherbourg is finally captured by the Americans at the end of June, the Germans will have done such a thorough job of destroying the docks and port facilities that it will take considerable time for the port to become fully functional.

Despite the brilliant performance of Magic prior to and during the invasion, the issue still boils down to the courage and endurance of individual Allied soldiers. They don't know what's on Hitler's mind. Their job is to close with and destroy the enemy, fight their way off the beachheads and drive through the hedgerows of Normandy. These

---

37. Another amazing Allied venture was a number of temporary pipelines that ran under the English Channel to the invasion site. These petroleum lines were called Pluto. One of them ran from the Shanklin Chine on the Isle of Wight, which is owned by the author's sister-in-law, Mrs. Anne Macpherson Springman. The site is now an official D-day museum.

men—infantry, airborne, tankers, artillerymen, fliers, sailors, Marines and coast guard—are the real heroes of OVERLORD. Nor should the luster of their achievements be dimmed when one asks, What would have happened if the Allies were not able to read the German and Japanese codes? Would the outcome of the invasion have changed if the Allies did not know Hitler's innermost thoughts, the defensive plans of his generals, before the first Allied troops waded ashore?

One reads how, on the first morning of the invasion, stubborn German defenders almost caused General Bradley to give up sending in the follow-up waves of landing craft at Omaha Beach.[38] In turn this would have prevented Bradley from committing reinforcements to Utah Beach. If Omaha Beach cannot be secured, the Americans will then be separated from the British by more than twenty miles of land. This would have been an open invitation to the Germans to drive a wedge between the Americans and the British invasion sites. Had this happened, a situation would have developed that the military dryly calls a separation of forces that leads to "defeat in detail."

Given the close-run nature of the struggle, it is safe to say that Magic gives the Allied leaders a sense of security, a sureness of their actions, a belief that God really is on their side. In the future these leaders say that their doubts nearly overwhelmed them. But the fact remains that Magic gives them the ultimate in psychological support. Magic helps them face the darkest moments of battle and permits them to keep committing troops when more prudent commanders might not.

This being true, it seems only fair to say then that, without Magic, the invasion of Normandy might well have failed.

✖ ✖ ✖

The invasion of Europe brings the Allied use of Magic to a vital junction: a tactical application of intercepted enemy messages for operational use versus the strategic application of intercepted enemy messages for planning on a grander scale. One surmises that the success ratios of Allied endeavors when Magic/Ultra was properly used was so

---

38. *Eisenhower: At War, 1943–1945* by David Eisenhower (New York: Vintage Books edition, October 1987). This vivid account of the invasion, written by Eisenhower's grandson, clearly shows how both the British and the Americans were nearly hurled back into the sea. Yet nowhere in this account is there any mention of Magic or Ultra. The author says only that the Allied deception plans were so successful that "the specter of landings at Calais probably reinforced the German inclination to procrastinate." (p. 272)

devastating that Allied intelligence still wishes to keep historians guessing about particular specific engagements by withholding this information. One only has to read what has been released to date to understand, when Ultra/Magic is properly used, just how badly the Allies mauled the German forces by hitting them unexpectedly and continuously in every way possible. Conversely, as noted earlier by William Friedman, when Ultra/Magic did not provide advance warning, at times Allied forces were hard hit.

Perhaps that is why, in the last pages of Field Marshal Montgomery's autograph book, Prime Minister Winston Churchill writes about Montgomery as the "Commander who marched from Egypt through Tripoli, Tunis, Sicily & Southern Italy, & through France, Belgium, Holland & Germany to the Baltic & the Elbe *without losing a battle or even a serious action.*" (Emphasis added.)[39]

Churchill is quite right to point out the greatness of Montgomery's generalship, plus the valor and competence of his British troops. But to achieve the victories that Montgomery records, while denying the role that Magic/Ultra played in them, makes the Field Marshal look better than he really is.

In one sixty-eight-page report by U.S. Army Ultra representatives, one of these intelligence specialists, Lt. Col. Adolph G. Rosengarten Jr., attached to the First U.S. Army, writes: "Intelligence is unimportant when you are winning and even though we were reading the enemy's mind, it mattered not for he did not have the means to carry out his intentions."[40]

An Ultra officer for the U.S. Third Army, Capt. George C. Church, laconically states: "Ultra continued to be of great value in foreshadowing or confirming the identifications made by actual contact and in providing an insight into the intentions and operations of the German commanders."[41] The examples of operational successes created by Ultra that Church produces, which made Patton's armored forces seem invincible, are enough to make a German panzer general gnash his teeth with anger.

In the Sixth U.S. Army Group, Ultra officer Maj. Warner M. Gard-

---

39. *Ten Chapters* (London: Hutchinson & Co., Ltd., no date). This excerpt is taken from the small autograph book kept by Montgomery from the time he took command of the Eighth Army in the western desert of Egypt on August 13, 1942. Prime Minister Churchill, at various stages of the war, would record his impressions in the book.
40. SRH-023 "Reports by U.S. Army Ultra Representatives With Army Field Commands in the European Theater of Operations 1945," 4.
41. Ibid.

ner lists a series of operational successes directly attributable to Ultra information that at times kept "the Seventh Army largely intact," a subtle way of explaining other amazing tasks of offense and defense.[42]

There are hundreds of pages of these SRH-type reports that give pinpoint details about how Ultra is employed to destroy advancing German forces unexpectedly, or to bomb German airfields just as new squadrons are to fly in, or allowing the Allies to attack where the Germans are weakest. The focus of this work, however, is on the strategic picture. So let us examine in more detail what the Allied planners knew about the German reaction to the Normandy invasion and what this means to the Allied planning staff.

From D day onward, almost every Magic report contains new information indicating that Berlin (i.e., Hitler) is still confused about developments in Normandy. (The reports also continue to grind out extensive analyses about the supplies of petroleum products for Japanese-occupied China, and the creation of small blast furnaces throughout China to provide Japan with more iron and steel.) Among the first invasion reports are accounts of how elements of the Maquis have seized a series of towns in south-central France.[43] The same Magic Summary reveals to Marshall that on June 8, Ambassador Oshima is telling Tokyo that "the German Army has been concentrating its reserves and is beginning to attack. . . . The [Allied] strength in the principal beachhead area is estimated to be about four infantry divisions, one tank division and two airborne divisions [these figures are way off]. . . . It is uncertain whether the enemy will try to land in the Calais-Dunkirk area; however, an enemy squadron which had been operating off that coast has now been withdrawn. So far there are no signs of any landings on the Brittany peninsula."[44]

On June 8, Ambassador Mitani reports that a German diplomat in Vichy tells him that "German authorities believe that there may well be landings in the immediate future at Genoa, at Sète on the south coast of France, and possibly at other points."[45] (The Germans are still being fooled by Allied deception plans.)

On June 9, Ambassador Oshima talks with the German Foreign Office and reports that "at first the Allied attack was resisted by local German reserves, but on 8 June reserve divisions were brought into

---

42. Ibid.
43. SRS-1331, 12 June 1944.
44. Ibid.
45. Ibid.

action. It is considered that the best plan is to assemble a heavy concentration of fire and to deliver a concerted attack on the enemy; accordingly, assault guns, etc., are now being brought up. When they arrive, an attack will be launched, but it takes time. It is estimated that the enemy's strength is six infantry divisions, two tank divisions, four airborne divisions, and parts of two other airborne divisions. The enemy is sending in strong reinforcements. . . . Special precautions are being taken in the Calais and St.-Malo areas, but at present there are no indications of landings there. . . . At the moment it is impossible to deal with the enemy's warships. . . . The enemy is very effective in bombing German reinforcements en route to the front, but they cannot prevent them from being brought up. In spite of difficulties, the whole German line is being reinforced.''[46]

On June 10, from Vichy, Ambassador Mitani tells Tokyo that the "Censor of Military Information" (there is no indication if the source is German or French) has told him: "The Germans estimate up until yesterday the enemy had committed seventeen divisions, including— nine infantry divisions (three British, two Canadian, four American), one British armored division, two British tank divisions, and one British and two American parachute divisions (the makeup of the other two divisions is not known). In view of the statements of prisoners that the enemy intended to use about fifteen divisions to occupy the Cotentin Peninsula, it would appear they found the German defenses stronger than anticipated and had to throw in more strength than planned. The Germans estimate that the number of troops now on the British mainland available for use to Montgomery amount to some eighteen divisions, and they do not think that Eisenhower will allow Montgomery any more than that. . . . Yesterday [the Ninth] British units advanced southward from Bayeux and Isigny. . . . Later in the day an American force consisting of one tank division and four infantry divisions attacked north [*sic*] and west from Carentan. At the same time, the British dropped new parachute units behind the German rear. Although many German units were forced to retreat, the American advance was stopped.''[47]

Meantime, in Moscow, Ambassador Sato is telling Tokyo that he is aware of a recent Reuters dispatch saying that one object of American vice president Henry Wallace's trip to Chungking is to arrange for the transfer to China of some of Russia's Lend-Lease war supplies as the

---

46. Ibid.
47. Ibid.

war in Europe draws to a close. "I must tell you that we have to view this matter realistically and with great concern," Sato tells Tokyo. "Russia is really neutral as between Japan and America, but as between Japan and China, she can be called not unneutral. . . . This matter concerns the fate of the Russo-Japanese Neutrality Pact and bids fair to present us with a great dilemma in the future."[48]

Only four days after the invasion, on June 10, Oshima receives a thorough briefing from von Steengracht. On June 11, Oshima reports to Tokyo. On June 13, Marshall is reading the text.[49] The German point of view is fascinating. Oshima quotes von Steengracht as saying: "Although Troarn has been captured by the enemy, Caen is still in German hands, and the attack of enemy tank forces, which headed west and southwest near Bayeux, was stopped at a point several kilometers from that town. The glider units near Coutances were practically wiped out; in addition, enemy attempts to land (1) with a group of more than forty transports at Barfleur and (2) near Trouville were repelled.

"A review of the battle so far indicates that the enemy chose as their chief objective Le Havre, Cherbourg and the intervening Caen area. They seem particularly interested in Le Havre, as is shown by the fact that they have made several attempts to land at Trouville. Although the Cherbourg zone was defended by only a relatively small number of local defense troops, the enemy invasion there was beaten off fairly thoroughly and any airborne troops that landed were finished off in short order. . . . So far, the Allies have failed to capture a good port, which makes it difficult to bring in supplies. Furthermore, only the eastern part of the Cherbourg peninsula is controlled by the enemy; the western side is free of them. Therefore, although we are still uneasy about the fate of Cherbourg—as I stated, there were only a few local defense forces there—nevertheless, we do not believe its situation is critical.

"Because the Allies at first failed to achieve their primary objectives, the German military feared that they might abandon their initial campaign and attack another area. However, they subsequently expanded and consolidated their forces so that it would not now be easy for them to abandon the present action. Although we have no news at all about any attempted landings elsewhere, such a development is still a real possibility and we Germans are on a strict lookout.

"After the enemy's real plans [on the Normandy peninsula] be-

---

48. Ibid.
49. SRS 1332, 13 June 1944.

come evident and after we Germans have let as many of them as will come ashore, we intend to drive them off with one blow. . . . To be honest with you, the enemy air forces are bombing points in the rear, such as Flers and Laval, so intensely that it is impossible for us to transport and concentrate German troops in that vicinity. It is for that reason, I think, that we have not yet counterattacked.

"Germany is most concerned about the superiority of the enemy air forces and the fire from naval guns. As for the quality of the soldiers, the British appear to be better than the Americans.

"The enemy, generally speaking, make the Vire River the dividing line between their two forces, with the British on the east side and the Americans on the west. Their invasion forces are continually increasing and consolidating, and we consider the report that they are now employing seventeen divisions to be quite accurate." (This figure is the same as given Ambassador Mitani the day before.)

On the following day, June 14, the invasion news is only the third item of military importance marked for Marshall's attention.[50] The first item is still censored today. The second item is a lengthy report from Minister Tsutsui in Bucharest. Conditions in Rumania are becoming desperate, he says. "The Germans and the Rumanians seem resigned to the idea that they will not be able to do anything but retreat when the Soviets launch their large-scale offensive. The idea has depressed the Rumanian people to such an extent that they are wholly bent on working for their personal advantage without exerting themselves over the war."

The only fresh news about the invasion is from Vichy. Ambassador Mitani confirms that German strategic reserves are still sitting in the rear, "but it is expected they soon will be [brought up]." The cover story given by Mitani is that the Germans in Paris are saying "it is their policy to permit the enemy to land a great number of men and then wipe them out."

As long as Hitler dithers and keeps the reserves from driving the Allies back into the sea, the invaders have every hope of succeeding. The question now becomes, can the Allies break out of the beachheads before the reserves come up?

On June 15, Marshall reads Mitani's report of June 12 about the massive disruptions by the French resistance, the Maquis, throughout southern France.[51] Guerrilla activities in the regions of Cantal, Corrèze,

---

50. SRS 1333, 14 June 1944.
51. SRS 1334, 15 June 1944.

Creuse, Dordogne, Haute-Loire and Puy-de-Dôme have forced the Germans to divert precious troops to maintain order. Another nine regions in south-central and west-central France are also in turmoil; the Germans may have to assume full executive power there, too. The success of the Maquis brings relief to Allied planners.

Another report from Mitani[52] includes the welcome news that the Germans believe the Allies have committed eighteen divisions of troops "experienced and of good quality" on the beachheads. Their numbers are estimated between 350,000 and 400,000. Meanwhile, Mitani reports, "the enemy has assembled about fifty divisions in the Hull area and in Scotland, and the Germans anticipate that landing operations will be attempted in the Dunkirk and Ostend area." Furthermore, the recent bombings of German airfields in northern France makes "the Germans think that those [attacks] were in preparation for a landing in the Calais area."

This report is sent Tokyo on June 13, meaning that for a full seven days Hitler has allowed the Allies to build up their strength while guessing that they will attack in other places.

It is this indecision that costs Hitler the battle of Europe.

✖ ✖ ✖

The German failure to act decisively is reinforced the next day. Again Mitani reports from Vichy[53] that "the Germans guess that the enemy plans another large landing and have not yet ventured a decisive counterattack. . . . There has been talk that the Germans will disband the French government, but the Germans, I think, have to use the Vichy government to the utmost, and they seem to be trying to prevent Pétain from losing prestige. So long as the German Army can keep going, the Vichy government will continue to exist."

Meanwhile, from Tokyo, Foreign Minister Shigemitsu tells Ambassador Sato that he agrees with the Ambassador's concerns about Vice President Wallace's trip to Moscow.[54] Shigemitsu agrees that any diversion of Lend-Lease arms by Russia to China "might well have a real and very terrible effect on the prosecution of our war in China."

The analysts in Washington point out that Shigemitsu worries that

---

52. Ibid.
53. SRS 1335, 16 June 1944.
54. Ibid.

"lately America's concern over China has been on the increase."
He believes that Wallace was sent to China principally to encourage
and unite all elements, so that Chungking could continue the fight
against Japan.

"It is clear that Wallace is also planning to shape and solidify an
American-Soviet-Chinese bloc, and for that reason his itinerary passes
through Russia," Shigemitsu tells Sato. "Somewhere along the line he
will have a talk with Molotov himself. . . . The Russians will go a long
way in complying with his ideas. We must keep an eye on Wallace's
moves."

The following day, Oshima tells Tokyo that on June 15 he spoke
again with Under Secretary von Steengracht.[55] The Germans were reportedly exercising special vigilance "along the northern coast of
France, particularly between Dieppe and Boulogne, in anticipation of
further enemy landings."

Oshima then reports that he chided von Steengracht about his earlier statements that the Germans were going to counterattack the bridgeheads. Oshima says he was told that the Germans did attack on
midnight of the twelfth, but "in order to maintain absolute secrecy,
Marshal Rundstedt has issued strict orders that no announcement concerning the attack be made."

This counterattack is too late. By the twelfth of June the Americans had linked Omaha and Utah Beaches, captured the vital town of
Carentan and are ready to dash to the west coast of the Cotentin Peninsula to seal off the port of Cherbourg. Meanwhile, Hitler still refuses
to commit reserves from the Fifteenth Army. (In actuality, the Allies
will not make another landing until August 15, some two months later;
then Operation DRAGOON, which was formerly ANVIL, will send Allied
forces ashore in southern France, all along the coast near Cannes.)

With the battle for the beachheads still raging in Normandy, Tokyo
suddenly rethinks its Indochina policy. On June 15, Foreign Minister
Shigemitsu sends two "extremely secret" messages to Ambassador Mitani in Vichy informing him of Tokyo's new program.[56] In view of the
invasion, Shigemitsu tells Mitani, and "in case France should lose her
position as a pro-Axis independent nation, we will split Indochina off
from her mother country."

The analysts in Washington note for Marshall's attention that Japanese Minister Tashiro in Hanoi has told Tokyo that he foresees having

---

55. SRS 1336, 17 June 1944.
56. SRS 1337, 18 June 1944.

to keep some of the present French administration in Indochina no matter what. He points out that doing so might present problems for the Japanese control of Indochina and for Japanese prestige throughout the Co-Prosperity Sphere. But these are the operational facts. From these signals, Washington concludes that Japan is "reluctant" to take over Indochina completely, because "they are hampered by a shortage of available trained Japanese administrative personnel."

Nevertheless, with the invasion of Normandy, a new and secret race between America, England and Russia to create the postwar world is off and running. Sooner or later, politics must take precedence to battlefield objectives. Difficult choices will have to be made.

10

Foreseeing a collapse of Vichy France, in mid-June 1944 Japan creates her new foreign policy for Indochina. The idea is to split Indochina from France and place the former French colony directly under Tokyo's control. One might call the process "annexation." Washington learns of this when Shigemitsu tells Mitani in Vichy that "we will presently decide on the time and manner of this action. If the situation makes it impossible to do otherwise, we must expect to use armed force and make ready in every way to do so."[1] The key to everything will be whether or not the Germans set up a "phantom regime" should the Vichy government be overthrown. "We might start off by letting French Indochina maintain a formal link with her mother country," says Shigemitsu. "But step by step we will strengthen our grasp until Indochina is completely under [our] military control. In any event, we must be very careful, because this decision makes no provision for French Indochina to become an independent nation [i.e., presumably under nominal Anamese rule] anytime soon."

The same Magic Summary also reveals to Washington that Japan is unhappy with its current puppet government in Burma. In a report sent Tokyo earlier in March, Japanese ambassador Sawada said: "There are very few men in the [Burmese] ministries who have skill in political administration, and they often do not follow [Premier] Ba Maw's policies." Sawada suggested creating "a planning board of capable Japanese counselors and, under them, competent Burmese, who would formulate various policies and see that they were carried out." Washington does not know, however, whether Sawada's proposal has been adopted.

---

1. SRS 1339, 20 June 1944.

A few days later, Tokyo's attention turns to Russia's role in the Far East.[2] Summarizing the situation for Marshall, the analysts in Washington remind him that, a month earlier, Foreign Minister Shigemitsu had asked Ambassador Sato if, in his "considered opinion," Russia might be induced to aid Japan (a) in bringing the war in China to a close and (b) in preventing an effective reconciliation between the Kuomintang and the Chinese Communist Army.

Sato's lengthy reply is carried in two messages of June 3 and 10, and it's negative. According to Sato, Russia currently has little influence in China and is engrossed in fighting Germany. When the European war is over, Russia will presumably try to extend her influence throughout Eastern Europe and the Middle East before becoming interested in the Far East. Sato warns that Japan should not draw Soviet attention to the Far East. Any participation by Russia in the affairs of that area would be to Japan's disadvantage. The fact that Japan and Russia recently concluded a Fisheries and North Sakhalin Agreements (which is how the Japanese now refer to the agreements) does not offer any hope that Russia will cooperate with Japan against the interests of England and America. Last, Sato warns, there is a real danger of some type of reconciliation between the Kuomintang and the Chinese Communist Party, especially in view of American efforts in that direction. Russia might also urge the Communists to cooperate with Chiang Kai-shek, which would prevent any peace agreement effected solely by America. It would also keep the U.S. from gaining a preponderant position in China, while giving the Communists the opportunity to strengthen their position at the expense of the Kuomintang.

Speaking with considerable foresight, Sato tells Tokyo: "As for the Kuomintang itself, in a certain sense its greatest fear is not of Japan, but of the Chinese Communist Party, since the latter may someday become the leading party in China. As a result, the Kuomintang is inclined to leave the defeat of Japan up to America and is devoting its entire energies to the preservation of its position."

The next day, the primary item of the Magic Summary[3] is a conversation in Berlin between Under Secretary von Steengracht and Baron Oshima. The talk is held on June 19, nearly two weeks after the invasion. Now the real reason for Hitler's indecision in sending reinforcements from the Fifteenth Army to Normandy is clearly stated: Hitler is

---

2. SRS 1340, 21 June 1944.
3. SRS 1341, 22 June 1944.

convinced that General Patton and his troops have still not come ashore; Hitler believes they will land elsewhere on the Continent.

Unknown to Hitler, Patton has been in Normandy since June 6, and the Allied correspondents have agreed to keep his presence there a secret. When the time is ripe, plans call for Patton to take over the Third Army, and his tanks will sweep around the German flank to the east. Incredible as it may seem, the Allies will continue to fool Hitler and the German High Command about the location of Patton and his troopers for another three weeks. In football terms, this has to be one of the better hidden ball tricks in the history of the game.

Anyway, the full flavor of Hitler's thinking is revealed in von Steengracht's words as reported by Oshima: "The offensive planned by the German Army against the Normandy beachhead has been limited so far to small-scale counterattacks by the infantry, since enemy air superiority has made it very difficult to assemble tanks and artillery. The enemy has now sealed off the Cherbourg peninsula; since Cherbourg itself is defended by a relatively small number of German troops, we are afraid that it may soon fall."

Von Steengracht continues: "Information obtained from prisoners, captured documents, etc., indicates that twenty-three divisions commanded by General Patton are being held in readiness to make new landings. This threat is one reason why Germany has avoided pouring in a great number of men into the Normandy area. . . . The forces under Patton's command are in addition to the total of thirty-six divisions assigned to Montgomery. [Ambassador Mitani had reported from Vichy on June 9 that the Allies were attacking with seventy divisions and thirty of them were assigned Montgomery.] As originally planned [by the Allies], Montgomery was to capture both Cherbourg and Le Havre with seventeen of those divisions and then advance with his main forces southeast along the Seine River; simultaneously, Patton's force was to land in the area east of Dieppe. However, Montgomery has already employed twenty-five divisions—of which two have been annihilated and others have suffered considerable losses—and is still fighting his way forward west of Caen. Nevertheless, we still consider Patton's forces will probably land between Dieppe and Boulogne, and preparations have been made accordingly.[4] . . . [Meanwhile] Russia, in the

---

4. There were ten deception plans for phony invasions, ranging from Norway and Sweden to France, Spain, Italy, Greece, Turkey and Rumania. The best was the creation of the First U.S. Army Group (FUSAG) whose commander, General Patton, was supposed to invade the French coast between Calais and Boulogne. There was also a fictitious British Twelfth Army. The fact that Hitler believed these deception plans were real two weeks after the Normandy invasion

opinion of the German High Command, will launch an offensive either
(a) immediately after the landing by Patton's forces or (b) when the
Anglo-American drive in the West makes it necessary to summon
German forces from the Eastern Front. The present onslaught of the
Russian Army against the Karelian Isthmus is extremely violent, and it
is impossible to predict whether the Russians can be held at the Viipuri
Line, as we hope." (Viipuri's fall was announced by the Soviet mid-
night communiqué of June 20.)

Von Steengracht goes on to talk about the success of the latest
German secret weapon, the V-1 rocket or "buzz bomb," which is now
being used against England. As the first rocket "terror" weapon, the
buzz bombs are causing considerable concern among the British civilian
population.[5]

To digress for a moment: Magic and Ultra give the Allies priceless
information throughout the war. But at times even the best signals intelligence cannot compete with having a good agent on the ground.
Two examples prove this. One is the story of Col. Michel Hollard,
DSO, a Frenchman and secret agent, who first warned England about
the threat posed by V-1 cruise-type missiles. He created a network of
more than a hundred agents throughout France (both the occupied and
unoccupied parts), many of whom were in key positions for observing
German operations. Hollard first heard about strange construction sites
in northern France in the summer of 1943, and upon visiting the sites,
he not only stole their construction plans, he saw that their takeoff strips
all pointed toward London. This information completed the package
being put together by Allied intelligence on the secret weapon. The
authorities in London then asked Hollard to provide accurate measure-
ments of a flying bomb. He found one in the railway station at Auffay
and, posing as a rail employee, measured its various components. As
one result, Hollard was called by Sir Brian Horrocks, a corps commander for Montgomery, "the man who literally saved London."[6]

---

caused him—and him alone—from sending massive reserves against the beachheads, saving
them from potential annihilation.
5. The Germans launched 10,500 V-1 rockets at England. Only 20 percent penetrated British
defenses, but these destroyed 1.1 million homes and killed ten thousand people. One shudders
at what might have happened had the rockets been more accurate (25 percent flew off course
because of a navigational malfunction). In 1994, the British press announced the discovery of
an unpublished manuscript by the novelist H. E. Bates that had been censored for fifty years
because "Bates insisted on telling the truth about the extent of civilian casualties." Bates's
casualty figures were lower than the final figures cited above. (See *The Times* (London), 17
January 1994.)
6. *The Times* (London), 23 July 1993. Obituary: Col. Michel Hollard, DSO, engineer and former

Another example involves the exploits of Standish Masterman, OBE, a research chemist in rocket development. In the summer of 1944, when word reached London that the Germans might be developing a true rocket weapon, the V-2, to replace the V-1, Masterman went to Poland, via Tehran and Moscow, to study a rocket-firing installation abandoned by the Germans while retreating from a Russian attack. At the time, skeptics did not believe the Germans could launch a long-range rocket, even though portions of such a missile had been recovered in Sweden and Poland after misfires. The team of experts—British, American and Russian—assigned to the case were baffled when they first arrived at the captured launch site. The records of V-2 firings were missing. These would have provided the amounts of fuel, range and payload. A careful search of the site finally turned up the crucial missing documents. But these had "already been used as lavatory paper by German troops who had found themselves in short supply of that commodity in their precipitate retreat in the face of the Russian offensive. Nevertheless the task of decipherment had to be faced, and a painstaking but necessarily grisly restoration process finally confirmed that the rocket could reach London." Unexpectedly, the Russians proved to be "the most squeamish participants in this dirty work of reconstruction. The British members of the delegation took a wry 'the things we do for England' view of the unsavory but vital job. The conclusive results of this research—that the V-2 was a genuine ballistic missile . . . were somberly proved to be accurate when at 6:43 P.M. on September 8, 1944, the first V-2 landed on Chiswick, west London. It was followed only seconds later by a missile strike against Epping. These were the precursors of 1,190 V-2s that killed 2,724 people and wounded more than 6,000 before the launch sites were overrun by the invading Allied armies."[7]

✖ ✖ ✖

To go back to the invasion: On June 27, 1944, three weeks to the day after the landings in Normandy, Ambassador Oshima discusses Germany's military situation with von Steengracht of the Foreign Minis-

---

intelligence officer, died on July 18 aged ninety-five. He was born in northern France in 1898. See also Hollard's biography, *Agent Extraordinary,* by George Martelli, published in 1960.
7. *The Times* (London), 23 July 1944, 17. Obituary: Standish Masterman, OBE, died on June 16, 1994, aged eighty-one.

try.[8] According to Oshima, von Steengracht said: "The fall of Cherbourg is going to have a bad effect from a psychological and political point of view, rather than a military one. . . . Up to now, Germany's losses have been surprisingly few.

"According to high German leaders, the forces under Patton are still assembled east of Southampton and are preparing a fleet of more than three hundred and fifty [sic] vessels of various sizes in order to stage another invasion in the near future. It is impossible to be certain where such a landing will occur, but indications point to the area east of the present bridgehead and including Le Havre. Germany hopes to surprise this invasion force and, after destroying it, to proceed to make short work of the Anglo-American forces in Normandy; at the present moment we are sending additional troops to the west from our center."

The subject now switches to the Eastern Front. Again von Steengracht drops some vital strategic intelligence. "The Soviet drive in the East is very powerful," he tells Oshima, "and has resulted in the recapture of Vitebsk. However, in view of the German strategy to reach a showdown in the West, we are prepared to abandon considerable territory in the East; in the central sector we may have to give up Orsha and Mogilev [recaptured on June 27 and 28, respectively, according to Russian communiqués] and retire to the west of the Berezina River. Whatever the cost may be, the Fuehrer will contrive to destroy the Anglo-American forces in northern France, and once he succeeds in that, I believe the tables will be turned."

Von Steengracht also lets slip that because the Finnish Social Democratic Party, the most important in Finland, has been negotiating for peace with Russia, Foreign Minister von Ribbentrop has flown to Helsinki to plead with the Finnish leaders. Accordingly, Finland will continue to fight the Soviet, and Germany is going to send armored units to help. A new Finnish cabinet will be formed "and the makeup . . . will probably be similar to that of the present one."

On July 1, 1944, the title of the Magic Summary becomes " 'Magic'—Diplomatic Summary," indicating the changes taking place within the U.S. Army intelligence mentioned earlier.[9] The first item for Marshall's attention this day is Oshima's personal estimate of Germany's military situation, which he sent to Tokyo on June 24.

---

8. SRS 1349, 30 June 1944.
9. SRS 1350, 1 July 1944. This day's Summary carries the note: "For reference to issues prior to 1 July 1944, the designation MS, with the appropriate date, will be used; for those for 1 July and after, the designation DS, with the appropriate date, will be used. The numbering of the issues will continue in the same series."

Oshima says that Germany's confidence in Hitler has increased because he predicted the Allied invasion and built the fortifications to halt the invasion. But Oshima also says he does not agree with the German interpretation of events. "In my opinion," he says, "the German Army may actually have tried to seize the opportunity for an immediate counterattack, but the movement of troops for such an offensive was seriously interfered with by enemy air attacks. In addition, Germany suffered particularly large losses in tanks and guns, and the Anglo-Americans, because of their naval and air superiority, were able to land additional troops and to bring up supplies more rapidly than was expected. Finally, the fact that strong forces under Patton are still in England and are expected to make new landings has prevented Germany from pouring a major force into Normandy. At present the Germans are waiting for Patton to attempt a landing at some point in northern France before they launch a general offensive with a disposition of troops that will be most favorable from a tactical standpoint."

Oshima also says it appears that the Germans are concentrating troops in the West, taking some from the reserves within Germany. As for the attack by Patton, he says: "The expected landing may come (1) relatively soon and in conjunction with the operations in Normandy— the Germans consider this very likely—or (2) only after the enemy has taken Cherbourg, brought up reserves and heavy equipment, and extended their bridgehead to include Le Havre. In the latter event, Germany may have to attack the present bridgehead with all available force without waiting for a new landing."

Oshima concludes: "A final decision in France cannot be expected for some time, and meanwhile we must be prepared for developments unfavorable to Germany in the East and in Italy. The Germans will not pour any large number of troops into the Eastern Front, even at the risk of losing territory; on the Italian front they hope to stop the enemy at the Apennine Line, but if the situation deteriorates further, they may retreat to the mountainous districts in the north, offering resistance step by step. It is estimated that such a strategy will give Germany sufficient time for a decisive battle in the West. I believe that Germany will have many difficulties during the next few months, but the Anglo-American landing forces will also face trying times. Although no one is able to prophesy what course the war will take, it is worthy of note that in Germany military leaders, official circles and the general public are all perfectly calm and confident of victory."

The slowness of the Allied advance off the beachheads in Normandy is noted in America. The military correspondent for the *New*

York Times, Hanson Baldwin, reports that the speed of the Allied advance in Normandy as compared to the Soviet achievements is becoming "a grim jest." He writes: "It is said that we will soon have to adjust our artillery fire to avoid laying down a barrage on the Russians advancing from the east."

On July 5, Marshall is presented with the latest conversation between Ambassador Mitani and the German ambassador to Vichy, France, Otto Abetz.[10] The two meet in Paris. Abetz tells Mitani: "The naval and air strength of the enemy in the Normandy offensive is great; the present ratio between German and enemy air forces is such that it is best not to talk about it. While the German Army has fought well, it has not been able to achieve much, having been unable to strike a really heavy blow. Such tank units as have been sent to the battle area have not yet been put into action since they are waiting for more fighter support." Abetz goes on to confirm almost everything Oshima has already reported to Tokyo about the overall German military situation.

When Marshall has finished reading Mitani's report to Tokyo about Germany's situation, he next turns to a lengthy report his analysts have prepared about the economic value of Indochina to Japan.

The analysts refer back to November 1940, when a Col. Kenryo Sato, who was then in Indochina handling negotiations with the French, sent a message to Tokyo arguing vigorously for the strategy that Japan later adopted: i.e., the occupation of Indochina, followed by measures to neutralize the U.S. fleet, and finally an invasion of the whole South Seas area.[11] Back in 1940, Sato predicted that "our [Japan's] food question, to say the least, would be settled, and we would get plenty of timber, rubber, tin and all kinds of minerals."

By studying all the intelligence traffic and related material, the analysts in Washington now tell Marshall that "the Japanese have never succeeded in exploiting Indochina to the extent Sato envisaged, nor to the extent which has been generally supposed." Exports from Indochina will be lower in the future because of Allied air attacks on industrial areas and the seaports, plus the submarine attacks on shipping. But "the impending drop in exports should not bring about an immediate decisive change in Japan's overall economic position." The report covers exports of rice, maize, rubber, coal, zinc ingots, scrap iron, iron ore, manganese, hides, silica sand, lacquer, resins and salt. The upshot:

10. SRS 1354, 5 July 1944.
11. Ibid. Sato later became a major general and, at this time in the narrative, is Chief of the Military Affairs Bureau of the War Ministry.

the naval activities aimed at cutting off Japan from *all* sources of commodities must be strengthened if her economy is to be strangled.

The period of July 6–9 marks the end of the Allied deception plans for a second invasion across the Channel allegedly to be led by Patton. The Germans are aware that tide and lunar conditions preclude any such invasion in northern France. Unable to blame himself for failing to drive the Allies back into the Channel, Hitler fires von Rundstedt, replacing him with von Kluge, who has earned his spurs against the Russians. Reinforcements are freed up from the Fifteenth German Army, and Hitler orders a large-scale attack against the British at Caen. Fortunately, operational Ultra intercepts give the invasion force the new German orders in time to prepare a defense. The Allies repulse the determined counterattack, which suffers from having too little logistical support and comes too late.

Meanwhile, in Tokyo, Premier Tojo has met with German Ambassador Stahmer on June 28, and Foreign Minister Shigemitsu sends Oshima on July 6 an account of Tojo's statements.[12] The analysts in Washington pick out eight points for Marshall's attention, ranging from Tojo's interpretation of Allied strategy in the Pacific, and his belief that the enemy has "merely been scratching at the outer wall" of Japan's defenses. But it is by reading Tojo's words as a whole that one comes to a differing view of the message's significance. First Tojo believes that a long war will benefit Japan. The Allies will wear themselves down and be forced to negotiate an end to the war. Last, Tojo is sure that the Allies will not be able to dictate unconditional surrender to Japan.

"The ultimate strength of Japan lies in her national structure," declares Tojo. "The Japanese people are firmly united by the spiritual concept of one people and one family grouped around the Imperial household, and they will literally fight to the very end, no matter whether they are on the front line or on the home front. The honorable way in which our soldiers are dying on the various Pacific Islands is a manifestation of that spirit. Because of the imminent crisis facing them, the Japanese people will manifest their power to a greater degree from now on."

While Tojo is saying that there might well be an invasion of the main islands of Japan, he is also declaring that any such attack will

---

12. SRS 1360, 11 July 1944.

result in a god-awful bloodbath. For a soldier such as Marshall, who recognizes the finite strength of the globally displaced American military, this type of battle must be avoided at all costs.

✖ ✖ ✖

The invasion of Normandy pushes aside what would otherwise be momentous news: on June 5 the U.S. Fifth Army enters Rome. So far the Allied forces have suffered forty thousand casualties in their drive north from Sicily. Meanwhile, the Germans lost only twenty-five thousand men.

In the weeks that follow, the Allies drive steadily northward in Italy, gaining the ground that Oshima has told Tokyo the Germans will give up easily. Even so, Field Marshal Kesselring retreats so skillfully that the Allies cannot at any time outflank him. By mid-July of 1944 he is successfully entrenched behind the Gothic Line, which stretches from La Spezia on the west coast to Rimini on the east coast. This ends the current Allied advance in Italy, especially since a large number of men from these forces are transferred for the upcoming invasion of southern France.

In the Pacific, the Second and Fourth U.S. Marine Divisions land on Saipan on June 15; two days later they are joined by the Army's Twenty-seventh Division. Fighting is fierce. The Battle of the Philippine Sea takes place June 19–20. Three Japanese aircraft carriers are sunk. American pilots shoot down 284 Japanese planes in what is called the "Great Marianas Turkey Shoot," which breaks the back of Japanese naval airpower.

Saipan falls on July 9, but at a terrible cost. The officers commanding the Japanese defenses, Admiral Nagumo and General Saito, commit suicide rather than surrender. They also order their men to make a final suicide attack. The Japanese lose 26,000 men out of a garrison of 32,000. The Americans endure 16,500 casualties from dead, wounded and fever. This casualty ratio of 1.5 Japanese to 1 American sends shivers through the planners who are preparing for the day that U.S. troops will have to invade the beaches of Japan.

The pressures facing the Axis leaders mount. On July 18, General Tojo is forced to resign as prime minister. His conduct of the war is openly criticized and his replacement will be Gen. Junaki Koiso. On July 20, high-ranking officers in the German military fail to kill Hitler in the famous bomb plot at the Fuehrer's headquarters in East Prussia.

The conspirators are all arrested. Those who are not shot on the spot will be subjected to show trials and hanging. Even Field Marshal Rommel is implicated and will be forced to commit suicide. The outcome of the failed assassination increases Hitler's distrust of his generals and seriously weakens the German war effort.

On July 13, Ambassador Oshima had met with Under Secretary von Steengracht of the German Foreign Office. Oshima's six-page report to Tokyo[13] contains some interesting items, not the least of which is Hitler's belief that, as of July 13, Patton is still going to lead a second invasion force.

"According to intelligence in our possession, it appears that virtually all the forces assigned to Montgomery are already in the Normandy area," Oshima quotes von Steengracht as saying. "But no part of Patton's army has yet been landed. We believe that Patton's forces will land in the neighborhood of Dieppe, in view of the fact that the enemy has made daily large-scale air attacks on coastal positions in that area. This seems to indicate that the enemy is going to use the very same technique he employed in bombing the Normandy area before the landings there. We have not changed our plan of making a surprise attack upon the newly landed forces and then launching a general counteroffensive upon the enemy forces in Normandy. . . . We are quite satisfied with the war situation in the West. Of the reserve forces under Rommel, the greater part of the Tiger and the Panther tanks are still being held back for a possible counteroffensive against the Anglo-American forces within the present beachhead. However, the superiority of the enemy air forces is so great that, if German forces penetrate deeply into Normandy, they might be cut off. We are at present trying to increase our air forces in the West, and from the beginning of August on, a greater degree of progress may be expected.

"In Normandy the enemy has recently been carrying out violent attacks, using material to an extent that has seldom been seen in the past. However, we Germans have just about completely repulsed the American attack on St.-Lô and have turned back the British Army every time it has tried to make any advance from the positions it captured in the suburbs of Caen."

Although Oshima's report details more German retreats in Russia and Italy, the doughty Baron concludes that the German leaders are confident that "gradually the situation will take a turn for the better."

The truth of the matter is different, however. One wonders how

---

13. SRS 1366, 17 July 1944.

badly von Steengracht is fooling Oshima, or whether it is Oshima who wants to be fooled. Apparently, Oshima wants to swallow von Steengracht's misrepresentations, so he does. What Oshima does not know is that on June 29, Hitler met with Rommel and von Rundstedt at Berchtesgaden with the Fuehrer demanding the containment and annihilation of the Allied beachhead. Von Rundstedt declared that he lacked infantry, so he could not organize his tanks for a full-scale attack. The two generals propose the evacuation of Normandy, which Hitler refuses. Von Rundstedt resigns on July 2 and is replaced by von Kluge.

Aware that the Germans are massing forces against the beachhead area, and fearful that they might fulfill their promise to bring up more air support, the Allies agree that the British will make an all-out attack east of Caen. It is hoped that the Germans will react to the threat of this breakout by massing their forces opposite the British. If this occurs, then the Americans will attack westward, through St.-Lô, Coutances, Avranches and toward open country. If they can achieve this goal, the Americans will then advance both east and west, clearing Brittany and preparing the drive for Paris. Rommel is gravely wounded by strafing RAF fighters and is invalided home. By the end of the month, the combined British and American attacks have succeeded. The Americans break out. The German forces in Normandy are about to be overwhelmed.

The first available diplomatic report from Germany confirming the attempt to kill Hitler is in a message sent July 20 by Ambassador Oshima.[14] "At 8 P.M. today," Oshima tells Tokyo, "Under Secretary for Foreign Affairs von Steengracht told me that he had been in direct telephone communication with Foreign Minister von Ribbentrop at High Command Headquarters, and that Ribbentrop had requested him to advise me that Hitler is absolutely all right and was not hurt at all."

Twenty-eight pages of this day's Magic Diplomatic Summary concern Japan's aluminum production. Faced with the possibility of running out of bauxite because of a lack of shipping, Japan has been revising her aluminum production program. Washington notes that any Allied action that cuts off, or materially reduces, Japan's bauxite imports will have an immediate effect on her aluminum production. In turn this will lower her aircraft production within six months. In the past, Japan has been building sixteen thousand planes per year. Since Japan has no stockpile of bauxite, the analysts note that she can import

---

14. SRS 1371, 22 July 1944.

this vital mineral "only by forgoing imports of other high-priority items." The Japanese war industry is about to be strangled: American submarines are doing what the Germans nearly accomplished with Great Britain.

At this time, Ambassador Oshima's rosy view of German military strength is challenged by the Japanese military attaché in Bucharest.[15] "The showdown for Germany in Europe is here," declares the military attaché. "And for Germany to save the situation at home or on the front is next to impossible. We Japanese must give up all idea of expecting anything from Germany. Japan, unaided, must now stand or fall on her own."

He continues: "The German Army has lost most of its mobility, and the quality of its troops has declined. Front-line troops are numerically inferior to the enemy; they have fallen into a defensive frame of mind, and they think only of saving their lives. Too many defensive operations and especially too many retreats have lowered the morale of the Army disastrously. In every sector, the situation is deteriorating hour by hour."

The analysts in Washington note for Marshall's attention that "so far as is known, Japan's civilian diplomats in Europe have filed no such unqualifiedly pessimistic reports."

During the next two days, Oshima gives Tokyo, and the Allies, a wealth of details about the attempt on Hitler's life.[16] Oshima confirms the attacker's identity, gives the names of other members of the rebels in the officer corps and says who has been arrested.

The next most important item is a report on the German military situation. Oshima is briefed about activities on both fronts, Russian and Normandy. Von Steengracht is becoming pessimistic for the first time about Normandy, saying: "We may have to be satisfied [there] with defensive operations for some time. The next month or so will doubtless be the most painful period for Germany."

What really interests the analysts, however, is a comment that von Steengracht makes about how best to defend large areas of territory. He says: "Some members of the German High Command appear to hold the view that, on a front extending over two thousand kilometers, purely defensive action is ineffective and that accordingly it is neces-

---

15. SRS 1437, 26 September 1944. Although the message is dated July 22, it apparently was not available until September 26. It is attached to another gloomy message sent by the Japanese military attaché in northern Italy and dated August 17, which the analysts in Washington note as being "just one week before Japan started pushing for a German-Russian peace."
16. SRS 1372, 23 July 1944; SRS 1373, 24 July 1944.

sary for us to carry out some sort of a mobile defense, possibly consisting of limited attacks in certain sections of the front, depending on the disposition of the enemy forces.''

This information is of great significance. Arguments are brewing between the British and the Americans, who hold the view that on a military drive through France into Germany, the Allies will achieve the most success by advancing on a broad front and keeping the German reserves stretched thin. The British, on the other hand, will argue for quick, deep penetrations of enemy territory. The problem with this strategy, as Montgomery will find out later at the Battle of Arnhem, is that the attackers tend to find themselves being counterattacked on the flanks, cut off from support from the rear and wiped out.

Knowing that the Germans do not like defending a wide front, and understanding that Magic/Ultra will give him the most accurate information as to which points are weakest in the overall enemy defensive line (to say nothing of following the precepts of Gen. Ulysses S. Grant in the American Civil War), Eisenhower will choose the strategy of attacking on a wide front. By constantly pressing forward, first in one area and then another, by using intelligence to learn where the enemy is weak, Eisenhower can negate the German philosophy of the ''mobile defense.'' It will also allow the employment of the great superiority the Allies have over the Germans in artillery.[17]

This means little to the average front-line soldier. The fact that Magic/Ultra may shorten the war and make his job easier is not known to him, so it can do little for his morale. All he knows is that some idiot back at division or Army headquarters has put him and his buddies in a place where there is heavy German fire.

✖ ✖ ✖

The Allies are about to drive on Paris in mid-July 1944, but the questions about the zones of occupation for the British and the Americans, and the seizure of Berlin, are still unsettled. Eisenhower finds himself in the unusual predicament of attacking the heart of Germany without

---

17. Ronald Lewin, author of such significant books as *Ultra Goes to War*, once told the author that in his opinion it was the way the British and the Americans used their artillery that was the real key to this Allied superiority. Lewin fought in Egypt as a forward observer, and later as an artillery battalion adjutant from Normandy to the Elbe.

knowing what his American political masters wish him to achieve. It is a difficult situation.

In Washington, the problem is concisely summed up for Marshall's Chief of Staff, General Handy, in a detailed memo prepared by General Lincoln.[18] The latter reports that "in the Combined Chiefs of Staff the British have refused to agree to the American proposal [made earlier by President Roosevelt] concerning RANKIN case C [and the American occupation of northwest Germany] and the matter has been left to higher authorities. On 12 July [44] the U.S. Chiefs asked for an agreement on their proposal for planning purposes. The British have taken no action. . . .

"It is understood the President has asked the Prime Minister (a) to agree to the U.S. proposal; (b) to issue a directive to General Eisenhower to prepare plans on the basis of the U.S. proposal. No knowledge of any action on the part of the Prime Minister.

"On the European Advisory Council the British and the United States have reached an agreement on boundary lines between zones and that Russia will occupy the Eastern Zone. No agreement in the European Advisory Council on zones to be occupied by the United States and the United Kingdom. As to Austria, the President has agreed to a tripartite occupation, but as stated, the United States will send only a token force. The Combined Chiefs of Staff were so informed on 12 July.

"At Quebec on 23 August 1943 the Combined Chiefs approved in principle the digest of the RANKIN plan prepared by the COSSAC staff. It is known that this plan was based on a study prepared by the posthostilities planning subcommittee of the [British] War Cabinet. It allocated southern Germany, France and Belgium to the United States and Holland, Denmark, Norway and northwest Germany to the British.

"COSSAC was directed to prepare detailed plans. On 8 November [1943] the U.S. Chiefs of Staff informed the Combined Chiefs of Staff that they were not giving approval to COSSAC's plan because of far-reaching political and economic implications. On 4 December the U.S. Chiefs at Cairo asked that *the zones as set forth in COSSAC's plan be switched.* There followed an exchange of memoranda between the United States and the British which did not result in an agreement, and

---

18. ABC 38 NW Europe (30 August 1943) Sec 1-A. Memo, 22 July 1944. Fr: Gen. Lincoln; To: Gen. Handy. This memo, and others following, are quoted directly and, where necessary, in full because the author has learned from experience that many officials and historians find it difficult to accept his account of the arguments between the Americans and the British about zones of postwar occupation without comprehensive documentation.

Combined Chiefs agreed the matter would have to be handled between the Heads of State. [Emphasis added.]

"SCAEF's staff and subordinate headquarters concerned have prepared voluminous and detailed plans for RANKIN 'C' with zones according to the British proposal. It is understood these are being constantly revised and kept up-to-date to account for changes caused by operations.

"There has been no planning undertaken on the basis of the American proposal. It must be noted that the deployment of troops, the supply and facilities required, and a general administration would be the same regardless of the forces employed. A great portion of the plans could probably be converted to the U.S. model merely by writing the British terms, units of measure, etc., into the American equivalents, vice versa.

"Gen. Somervell has stated that the American proposal is logistically feasible in light of the tactical plan for Overlord.

"How do we stand if we have to go into Rankin in a hurry? On the United States side there are six divisions, two armored, two infantry, two airborne, in the United Kingdom. Logistical troops and air forces in the United Kingdom should be more than adequate. Available cargo shipping, personnel and amphibious support should be more than adequate.

"The British probably have about the same number available, some of which are limited in employment.

"Our figures indicate the sixteen U.S. divisions ashore or going ashore, and the fourteen British divisions ashore, should have complete complement of equipment and supporting troops and should reasonably be able to make a rapid march towards Germany, if all resistance ceased without extensive demolition. The large airborne lift in Europe, plus the two American and two British airborne divisions in the United Kingdom, should facilitate matters."

The State Department is also concerned. On August 4, Washington sends instructions to Ambassador Harriman in Moscow telling him: "The Russian representatives on the European Advisory Commission have stated that they are unable to proceed further with development of plans for military occupation of Germany until a decision is reached between the British and ourselves as to our representative zones of occupation in the Anglo-American area."[19] Washington tells Harriman

---

19. ASW 370.8 Germany Zones. 4 August 1944. Cable AMEBASSY, LONDON, marked NO DISTRIBUTION.

that the question cannot be solved at the present time, saying that "in view of the agreement already made that the Soviets may police all that part of Germany in which they have expressed a desire to exercise control, we are unable to understand why they are concerned with the necessity of deciding this question before proceeding to any others. . . . Please press upon [Foreign Minister] Molotov the necessity for the Soviet representative on the European Advisory Committee to continue discussion of general occupation questions pending settlement between British and ourselves of our respective zones of occupation."

To put it another way, at this time the Russians know what they intend to get out of winning the war. The British also know what they want. The Americans do not. By stalling the negotiations in London, the Russians are hoping to gain even more land or other advantages.

By mid-August 1944, the Allies have successfully completed their invasion of the south of France (Operation ANVIL became Operation DRAGOON). The Germans suffer a major defeat in the Falaise Pocket, losing ten thousand dead on the field of battle plus fifty thousand captured, to say nothing of incredible amounts of material. To the south, Patton's tanks are advancing by leaps and bounds. On August 25, French and American troops enter Paris.

With considerable foresight, on August 17 Eisenhower sends a message to the Combined Chiefs in which he declares that the Allies may be faced with the occupation of Germany sooner than had been expected and that SHAEF is preparing plans to meet the situation.[20]

"All we can do now is approach the problem on a purely military basis," says Eisenhower. He explains that SHAEF planning will concentrate on defeating the enemy on the basis of the "present deployment of our armies." This means that the British Twenty-first Army Group will be to the north, the American Twelfth Army Group will be in the center and the American Southern Army Group will advance from the Mediterranean. "Unless we receive instructions to the contrary, we assume this solution is acceptable. As a matter of fact, this is the only basis of planning available to us, considering our present deployment, the situation which may confront us, and the absence of certain basic decisions as to the zones of occupation."

It no longer matters what zone of occupation President Roosevelt wants. His desires have been overtaken by events. And Eisenhower has covered his political flanks neatly by employing the phrase "unless we

---

20. Records, Chief of Staff, SHAEF, Eclipse 381, Case 1, vol. 1. Cable—Fr: Eisenhower; To: AGWAR for Combined Chiefs. No. FWD 12936 *SCAF 65*. 17 August 44.

receive instructions to the contrary." As of this date, the zones of occupation for postwar Europe become a fait accompli.

The following day, Eisenhower's plan is partially approved. The Chiefs of Staff notify Eisenhower that AMSSO is in complete agreement with the "solution" suggested in Eisenhower's SCAF 65.[21]

However, a problem remains in Washington. President Roosevelt still doesn't want to accept the southern zone. A lengthy memorandum is prepared for Under Secretary of War John J. McCloy on the matter. Another approach to the President by the Joint Chiefs of Staff has been ruled out. The alternative is the one suggested by McCloy some weeks ago: i.e., "requesting authority [from Roosevelt] to negotiate with the British on the assumption that we would take the southern zone but that our lines of communication would not go through France. General Roberts believes that we must pin our hope on getting this problem resolved on the second method, and asked if you [McCloy] would ascertain from Mr. [Harry] Hopkins how the matter now stood and undertake to push it to some conclusion."[22]

With the capture of Paris, Field Marshal Montgomery is quick to present his personal views concerning future operations in Europe. He sends a nine-paragraph message to Eisenhower on September 4 in which he says: "We have now reached a stage where one really powerful and full-blooded thrust toward Berlin is likely to get there and thus end the German war."[23] Montgomery believes the Allies don't have the logistical ability to maintain two attacks. The attack on Berlin should have all the support possible with other operations doing the best they can on what supplies are left. The only other possible thrusts would be one via "the Ruhr and the other via Metz and the Saar." Time is vital says Montgomery. The selected attack must be made immediately. Any attempt to compromise the situation can only prolong the war. He says: "I consider the problem viewed as above as very simple and clear-cut. The matter is of such vital importance that I feel sure you will agree that a decision on the above lines is required at once."

Montgomery ends by saying that if Ike should come and visit the

---

21. CofS Records, SHAEF, Eclipse 381, Case 1, vol. 1. Fr: AMSSO; To: JSM, Washington; passed to: SHAEF for info. No. OZ 4532. 18 August 44. TOO 181355Z August 1944. TOR 201420B August 1944.

22. ASW 370.8 Germany. x-Gerhart. 19 August 44. Memorandum for Mr. McCloy. Initialed H.A.G.

23. Personal file of Gen. W. B. Smith, SHAEF. No. M-160. Fr: Montgomery; To: Eisenhower. 0402056 September 1944.

British Twenty-first Army, Monty would like to give him lunch so the two can discuss the matter. He adds, however: "Do not feel I can leave this battle just at present."

It takes a week for Eisenhower to reply. He does so in a low-key letter sent to his three top commanders in the field: Montgomery, Gen. Omar Bradley, commanding the American Twelfth Army Group, and Gen. Jacob Devers, commanding the Sixth Army Group, consisting of the Seventh U.S. Army and First French Army in the South.[24]

Writes Eisenhower: "We shall soon, I hope, have achieved the objectives set forth in my last directive (FWD-13765) and shall then be in possession of the Ruhr, the Saar and the Frankfurt area. I have been considering our next move.

"As I see it, the Germans will have stood in defense of the Ruhr and Frankfurt and will have had a sharp defeat inflicted on them. Their dwindling forces, reinforced perhaps by material hastily scratched together or dragged from other theaters, will probably try to check our advance on the remaining important objectives in Germany. By attacking such objectives we shall create opportunities of dealing effectively with the last remnants of the German Forces in the West. . . . Clearly Berlin is the main prize, and the prize in defense of which the enemy is likely to concentrate the bulk of his forces. There is no doubt whatsoever, in my mind, that we should concentrate all our energies and resources on a rapid thrust to Berlin.

"Our strategy, however, will have to be coordinated with that of the Russians, so we must also consider alternative objectives.

"There is the area of the northern ports, Kiel-Luebeck-Hamburg-Bremen. Its occupation would not only give us control of the German Navy and the North Sea bases, of the Kiel Canal and of a large industrial area, but would enable us to form a barrier against the withdrawal of German Forces from Norway and Denmark. Further, this area, or a part of it, might have to be occupied as a flank protection to our thrust to Berlin.

"There are the areas of Hanover-Brunswick and Leipzig-Dresden. They are important industrial and administrative areas and centers of communications, on the direct routes from the Ruhr and Frankfurt to

---

24. Post Overlord Planning 381, vol. 1. Letter from Eisenhower to Montgomery, Bradley and Devers. 15 September 1944. The letter was approved by Gen. W. B. Smith in draft form on 14 September and returned to G-3, which submitted the letter for approval on 11 September. The second-to-last paragraph, about Berlin, was inserted in black printing in pencil, in what appears to be Eisenhower's handwriting. A photocopy of the actual letter (GCT 370-31/Plans) that was sent to Bradley is in the author's possession but is too faint to be reproduced.

Berlin, so the Germans will probably hold them as intermediate positions covering Berlin.

"There are the Nuremberg-Regensburg and the Augsburg-Munich areas. Apart from their economical and administrative importance, there is the transcending political importance of Munich. Moreover, there may be an impelling demand to occupy these areas and cut off enemy forces withdrawing from Italy and the Balkans.

"Clearly, therefore, our objective cannot be precisely determined until nearer the time, so we must be prepared for one or more of the following:

"A. To direct forces of both army groups on Berlin astride the axes Ruhr-Hanover-Berlin *or* Frankfurt-Leipzig-Berlin *or* both.

"B. Should the Russians beat us to Berlin, the northern group of armies will seize the Hanover area and the Hamburg group of ports. The central group of armies will seize part, or the whole, of the area Leipzig-Dresden, depending upon the progress of the Russian advance.

"C. In any event, the southern group of armies would seize Augsburg-Munich. The area Nuremberg-Regensburg would be seized by central or southern group of armies, depending upon the situation at the time.

"Simply stated, it is my desire to move on Berlin by the most direct and expeditious route, with combined U.S.-British forces supported by other available forces moving through key centers and occupying strategic areas on the flanks, all in one coordinated, concerted operation.

"It is not possible at this stage to indicate the timing of these thrusts or their strength, but I shall be glad to have your views on the general questions raised in this letter."

Almost instantly, Bradley places his plans for the seizure of Berlin on Ike's desk. For the first time, the strategy that will create the postwar Europe is being projected for consideration. This includes the shocking news for the British that Eisenhower intends to cooperate with the Russians and much of his planning will be based on what the Russians will or will not do. Soviet troops are already much closer to Berlin than are the Allies. It is logical to assume that the Russians may seize Berlin. Should this happen, then the key will be for the British forces to seal off the Danish peninsula, and protect the North Sea, by seizing the northwestern areas of Germany, especially the ports of Kiel, Luebeck, Hamburg and Bremen. Again, depending on what the Russians do, the Americans will try to seal off a Soviet advance into Italy by attacking as far to the east and south as possible (around the northern border of

Switzerland). The key language is Eisenhower's reference to cutting off German withdrawals from specific areas such as Italy.

Needless to say, this concept does not sit well with Montgomery or Prime Minister Churchill. They want to seize Berlin because of its political significance. Another major question will be liaison with the Russians. How will it be affected? Who will run it? The questions are studied at SHAEF. On September 17 the first paper is produced.[25] The memo has two objectives: to examine what happens when Allied forces near the radius of action of the Russian armies, and to examine what action Eisenhower should take to meet the situation.

The memo states: "Should the Germans continue to hold up the Russians in Eastern Germany, we may have the opportunity to cross the boundary [of the Russian zone of occupation that has already been agreed to] and advance on Berlin. We should not fail to make the most of this opportunity in order to further the defeat of Germany, and any withdrawal of AEF forces from West of the agreed boundary which subsequently becomes necessary can be easily effected. Such an advance would be fraught with the possibility of clashes between the two armies. . . . The existing channels with Moscow, through the Combined Chiefs of Staff, is considered too slow for effective coordination of such matters."

The best and most obvious conclusion is that Eisenhower and SHAEF should be allowed to communicate directly with the Soviet High Command in Moscow.

This suggestion will not sit well with the British. They believe that control of the politics of war will slip from their grasp.

Meanwhile, the British-American problems regarding the postwar zones of occupation are well-known in Moscow. One source of Moscow's information is Harry Dexter White in the Treasury Department. His role as a Soviet agent will not be discovered until after the end of the war. An unsuspecting John J. McCloy sends him on September 20 the information about the zones of occupation that were decided upon at the Quebec Conference.[26]

---

25. SHAEF File #322.01-1/GPA Liaison with Russians. Memo by SHAEF planning staff on liaison with Russians (first draft). This memo signed by J. Wilson Jr. for W. G. Mackenzie, Maj., CAC Section, Planning Staff. Copies to Brig. Gen. K. G. McLean (G-3 FWD). See also: final draft 17 October 1944, McLean memo 10 October 1944, Marshall cable 20 October 1944.
26. ASW 370.8 Germany. Zones of occupa. a-White, Harry x-Treasury (White, Harry). 20 September 1944. WDOAS:JJMcC:NZW. The memo reads:
    Dear Harry:
        Here are the zones that were decided on at Quebec. You will note that
    in addition to the main zone we have full control of Bremen and Bremerhaven.

In Europe, Eisenhower sends a "Dear Monty" message to the British commander, hoping it will mollify him.[27] Eisenhower thanks Montgomery for his recent messages, saying that before receiving them Ike had assumed that Montgomery was basing his suggestions on the concept that Allied operations had reached a point where they could make a single thrust all the way to Berlin, with all the other troops practically immobile on the rest of the Western Front. Ike says he didn't agree with that idea, but he does agree wholeheartedly with Montgomery in attaining the immediate objective of the Ruhr.

Ike says there will be a battle-plan conference that afternoon after which the full details will be sent Montgomery. "No one is more anxious to get to the Ruhr quickly," declares Eisenhower. "It is for the campaign from there onward deep into the heart of Germany for which I insist all other troops must be in position to support the main drive. The main drive must logically go by the north. It is because I am anxious to organize the final drive quickly upon the capture of the Ruhr that I insist upon the importance of Antwerp. As I have told you, I am prepared to give you everything for the capture of the approaches to Antwerp, including all the air forces and anything else that you can support." The message ends with: "Warm regard, Ike."

✖ ✖ ✖

The end of September 1944 marks a turning point in American presidential politics. Roosevelt is running for an unprecedented fourth term. He is opposed by the former Republican governor of New York State, Thomas E. Dewey. The Republicans running the Dewey campaign claim that Magic is being openly discussed by the military in the Pacific theater of operations. They intend to use this knowledge in the forthcoming election to discredit Roosevelt and show that he must have known beforehand about the Japanese attack on Pearl Harbor.

We also have rights through other ports.

Sincerely,
(Signed) JOHN J. McCLOY

This evidence of the type of information White was able to pass on to Moscow has not been made public before. It certainly would have given the Russians an edge at the EAC bargaining table in London, allowing them to exploit the split between America and Britain. It may also be surmised that this type of information caused White to help prepare the controversial Morgenthau plan for a postwar "pastoral Germany," which created great dissension among American leaders as the war drew to a close.

27. Personal file of Gen. W. B. Smith, SHAEF. No. FWD 15407. 22 September 1944.

A large portion of the sixth and final lecture by William Friedman on the history of cryptology (as mentioned earlier) deals with this vital moment in American politics.[28] According to Friedman, Marshall writes two letters to Dewey, who rejects the first without reading it completely. On September 27, 1944, General Marshall writes again. This, too, is hand-carried by Col. Carter W. Clarke. In the letter Marshall "begged the Governor to say nothing during the campaign" about the fact that U.S. government authorities had been reading Japanese codes and ciphers *before* the attack on Pearl Harbor. Not only was the information true, Marshall tells Dewey, "but much more important were the facts that (1) the war was still in progress; (2) the Japanese were still using certain of the pre–Pearl Harbor cryptosystems; and (3) the U.S. government was still reading highly secret Japanese messages in those systems, as well as highly secret messages of other enemy governments. Therefore, it was absolutely vital that Governor Dewey not use the top-secret information as political ammunition in his campaign."

In writing to Dewey, Marshall promises him that only nine other people know about the letter. One of them is Admiral King, the Chief of Naval Operations, who concurs with what Marshall is doing. The others who know are seven key officers responsible for the security of military communications and Marshall's personal secretary. The President is not being told about the letter. Neither is Marshall's boss, Henry L. Stimson, the Secretary of War.

Marshall's action is without precedent in the annals of American politics. And why is Marshall doing this? He writes: "I am persisting in the matter because the military hazards involved are so serious that I feel some action is necessary to protect the interests of our armed forces."

Marshall goes on to explain that America possessed a wealth of information regarding Japanese moves in the Pacific in 1941, and this information was given the State Department by the military. This material "unfortunately made no reference whatever to intentions toward Hawaii until the last message before December 7, which did not reach our hands until the following day, Dec. 8."

Marshall also explains that the Allies are breaking both German and Japanese codes. Then he points out: *"Our main basis of information regarding Hitler's intentions in Europe is obtained from Baron Oshima's message reporting his interviews with Hitler and other officials to the Japanese government."* (Emphasis added so the reader

---

28. SRH-004 "The Friedman Lectures on Cryptology," 131–82.

can ascertain how important Marshall believed these Magic messages to be.)

As for other areas of the war, Marshall spells it out for Dewey.

* Magic won the battle of the Coral Sea.
* Magic won the battle of Midway.
* Magic told us in advance that the Japanese were going to land troops in Attu and Kiska off the Alaskan coast.
* We are sinking the Japanese merchant shipping because Magic gives us the sailing dates and routes of their convoys. Says Marshall: ''Operations in the Pacific are largely guided by the information we obtain of Japanese deployments. We know their strength in various garrisons, the rations and other stores continuing available to them and what is of vast importance, we check their fleet movements. . . . The current raids by Admiral Halsey's carrier forces on Japanese shipping in Manila Bay and elsewhere were largely based in timing on the known movements of Japanese convoys. . . . You will understand from the foregoing the utter tragic consequences if the present political debates regarding Pearl Harbor disclose to the enemy, German or Jap, any suspicion of the vital sources of information we now possess.''

Thus, Tom Dewey becomes the first person outside of Roosevelt and the high command to know the full story behind Magic and what it means to the war both in Europe and the Pacific. From his experience as a prosecuting district attorney, he knows all too well the value of secret wiretaps. He also knows the furor that is caused when a ''leak'' of secret wiretaps causes a major investigation to collapse. In this case, and against the advice of top supporters, he determines that Marshall is truthful, and the Republicans cannot take the risk of losing American lives, or prolonging the war, by revealing the Magic secret. He returns the letter to Marshall's emissary, Colonel Clarke, and goes back to his campaign, never mentioning the subject. Many Republicans in Congress come to believe that this is what cost him the election. They cannot comprehend what Dewey understood in an instant, and when the war ends, they determine to seek revenge.

As a result, as Henry Clausen explained to me, just before congressional Pearl Harbor hearings open in November 1945, the Republicans on the committee blithely release the news that before and during the war the British and the Americans had broken both the German and

Japanese codes. This breach of national security is done after Marshall begs the committee to keep the secret. The committee refuses, publishing Marshall's correspondence with Dewey. Thus, our Congress gives our former enemies the first knowledge that their codes had been broken, to say nothing about breaching America's diplomatic confidence with the British. The latter are livid with rage about the disclosures. And rightly so.[29]

The anger of the U.S. Army with Congress at this time also nears the boiling point. Again, Henry Clausen explained why to the author. Taking a page from the British, who, after the war, are selling captured German Enigma code machines and low-grade ciphers to third-world nations, supposedly giving them secure communications, the U.S. Army allows the Japanese to believe that we had never broken their Purple diplomatic codes. Consequently the Japanese keep using the same codes after the war's end. The revelations by Congress cost the Army its ability to monitor diplomatic traffic, which would ensure the Japanese are living up to the terms of the surrender and adhering to the directives of the postwar government installed under General MacArthur.

President Roosevelt went to his grave never knowing about Marshall's letter to Dewey.

---

29. The only saving grace in this debacle is that the press does not follow up on the news that the Allies had also broken the German Enigma codes.

11

A careful reading of Marshall's letter to Dewey indicates that Marshall told Dewey everything. Not so. When dealing with intercepts, and intelligence people, frequently what is not said can be more important than what is said.

It is a problem endemic to the interpretation of signals intelligence, which is the cornerstone of Roberta Wohlstetter's highly acclaimed study of Pearl Harbor.[1] Unfortunately, to illuminate her message she borrows from the U.S. Navy a term from communications theory called *noise*. This "noise" is the "confusing buzz" created by competing information that prevents the most important message from being heard clearly and distinctly. Thus Wohlstetter accepts at face value the statement of the Navy's Commander Kramer, who was the chief translator and responsible for distributing Magic in Washington before Pearl Harbor, who claimed that the significance of the most vital Japanese intercepts was not clear-cut or "materially different" from a mass of other information that was being intercepted.

Other intelligence experts disagree with the Navy's theory as espoused by Wohlstetter.

"If you want to hear noise, you will hear noise," these experts say in rebuttal. "Noise is the excuse you give when you've screwed up in your evaluation of Sigint [signals intelligence]." And, as Henry Clausen told the author, "the Navy uses the argument about 'noise' to seduce writers like Wohlstetter into supporting the Navy's side of the argument about Pearl Harbor. She never spoke to me. I could have straightened her out quickly. After all, she lives only a few miles from me."

---

1. *Pearl Harbor: Warning and Decision* (Stanford, Calif.: Stanford University Press, 1962).

What the experts point out is that in 1941 the Navy was listening for the wrong information. Warnings sent by London to Washington were turned into two different messages by the Navy Department and sent to Admiral Kimmel at Pearl Harbor on December 3, 1941. These messages were explicit. One said that "highly reliable information" said that urgent instructions had been sent to Japanese diplomatic and consular posts around the world to destroy most of their codes and ciphers. The second message sent Kimmel on December 3 could be considered a breach in security. This message referred to "Circular Twenty Four Forty Four from Tokyo [on] one December," indicating clearly that either Washington or London was breaking the Japanese codes. The message also said that Tokyo was ordering its embassies and consulates in various capitals around the world to immediately destroy their codes *and more importantly* their Purple code machines. Kimmel was also told that British Admiralty in London reported that the Japanese embassy in London had already complied with Tokyo's request to *destroy its Purple machine.* (It was this vital information that Kimmel failed to pass on to Gen. Walter Short, who bore the joint responsibility for defending Pearl Harbor.)[2]

Today's intelligence experts, as confirmed by Henry Clausen, ruefully acknowledge that the phony "noise" the Navy claimed it heard was due partially to the widely held, racist belief that the Japanese were inferior to the Americans, and the American military's deep-seated premise Japan could not, and would never, attack Pearl Harbor, even though an air attack had been proven possible during war games. Despite the fact that a surprise air attack was proven feasible, and both

---

2. *Pearl Harbor: Final Judgement* by Henry C. Clausen and Bruce Lee (New York: Crown, 1992), 234–35, 442–43. See also Pearl Harbor Committee Exhibit 37, pp. 40–41, PHA Report, p. 100. Kimmel and his fleet intelligence officer, Capt. Edwin T. Layton, also failed to pass on to the Army at Pearl Harbor another warning from the British in Asia on December 3 that America was about to be attacked. During his investigation into what caused the disaster at Pearl Harbor, Henry Clausen gathered another two hundred intelligence messages the British in Asia sent the Navy at Pearl Harbor. These were not forwarded to Washington prior to the Japanese attack. Clausen collected them for his report to Secretary of War Stimson. The Republicans on the Pearl Harbor Committee tried to keep Clausen's report to Stimson under wraps. When Clausen finally testified before the committee, his statements sent shock waves through the hearings and changed the course of the committee's findings. It determined that both the commanders of the Army and the Navy failed in their mutually dependent duties to defend Pearl Harbor. More importantly, the committee found great fault with Army and Navy intelligence. It also accepted the Clausen hypothesis that the entire *system* for the collection, coordination and evaluation of intelligence was flawed. Clausen was the first to testify publicly about the need for a centralized cryptologic structure, and his report to Stimson, critical of the cryptological process as it existed in 1941, helped lead to the creation of a certified cryptologic structure (i.e., the NSA) after the war.

the Army and the Navy Departments in Washington had warned the respective commands at Pearl Harbor that the dangers envisaged in order of their importance and probability were (1) air bombing attack and (2) air torpedo attack, such an attack was generally believed to be beyond Japanese capabilities.

The Navy also was pinning its hopes on intercepting a so-called Winds Code message that would give the timing for the start of any conflict. This Winds Code was to be broadcast by Tokyo in the emergency event that *regular commercial radio and teletype channels* suddenly went out of service. The broadcast would say which country, or countries, Japan would be going to war against. The ironic fact is, however, that up until the moment war broke out, the regular Japanese commercial and teletype channels never stopped. There was no communications emergency or need for Tokyo to broadcast a Winds Code message. The Purple diplomatic messages from Tokyo, ordering the destruction of ciphers and code machines, were, in actuality, the equivalent of the Winds Code being put into effect. But because of fallacious "noise" no one—either in Army or Navy intelligence—interpreted these messages properly.[3]

Anyway, what Marshall is not telling Dewey is this: by late September 1944, the Japanese are sure that Germany is going to be defeated. To try to save the overall situation, Japan is seeking to negotiate a peace agreement between Germany and Russia. And to protect themselves, it appears that *the Japanese are going to try to strike a deal with Russia about jointly running the Far East after the war.*

Marshall also knows that Stalin intends to export Soviet Communism throughout the postwar world. The question is how and when will this expansion begin. If Baron Oshima is for the Allies the main source of Hitler's intentions in Europe, as Marshall told Dewey, then the link between Ambassador Sato in Moscow and Tokyo will be the primary source of Soviet and Japanese intentions for the postwar Far East. The end game is beginning.

---

3. The author wishes to point out that the Army must bear an equal share of the blame for the disaster at Pearl Harbor. Not only did General Short fail to coordinate plans for defending the fleet while it was in the anchorage, which he was ordered to do with the Navy, it appears that Short was unfit for a potential combat command. The responsibility for appointing Short can be attributed to Marshall. Other errors can also be traced to Marshall's desk. But Marshall did warn Short in writing on several occasions to be alert against a surprise enemy air attack. Short failed to follow these, and other, orders. As stated earlier in this work, the author concurs with the concept that the entire *system* of intelligence failed in 1941, and this was the primary cause of Pearl Harbor.

✖ ✖ ✖

In late July 1944, Oshima is feeding Tokyo with more juicy items about the abortive assassination of Hitler.[4] There is also a great deal of speculation on the diplomatic wires about who will be in the new Japanese cabinet now that Tojo has been forced aside in favor of the relatively unknown Koiso. The analysts in Washington are kept busy footnoting and identifying each new name in the cabinet.

For example, Oshima has a three-hour conversation with Foreign Minister von Ribbentrop at Hitler's headquarters in East Prussia.[5] According to Oshima, Ribbentrop describes the attack on Hitler in detail and confirms that General von Beck was the ringleader of the revolt. For the analysts, the high point of the conversation comes near the end, when Ribbentrop admits that the Germans are giving some thought to peace. But he insists that neither he or Hitler will make any move at the present, saying that to do so could only cause Germany harm. It is from Oshima's accurate quoting of Ribbentrop that one gets the full flavor of the moment.

Answering Oshima's question about what lay behind the attack on Hitler, Ribbentrop says: "Although no definite answer can be given until our investigation progresses further, I think that there was a plan to seek a compromise with England and the United States after the plotters had seized real power for themselves. However, while there is some suspicion that the bomb which Colonel Stauffenberg used was British, we have not yet obtained any proof that Beck was in touch with England and the U.S."

After talking about the latest events in France (Hitler still believes Patton is going to make a separate invasion), Oshima and Ribbentrop run through the other battle and diplomatic fronts: the Eastern Front, the Italian front, Finland, Hungary, Rumania, Bulgaria, Spain and Portugal, Turkey and Italy. It is here that Ribbentrop talks about the possibility of a German peace with Russia: "We have found our way out of the deadlock caused by the defection of Italy. Nevertheless, the fact that forty million Italians went over to the enemy was without doubt the severest blow that Germany could have suffered.[6] . . .

---

4. SRS 1377, 28 July 1944.
5. SRS 1378, 29 July 1944. The conversation took place July 23.
6. The analysts in Washington note for Marshall that "last month both Mussolini and Marshal

Both Chancellor Hitler and I are fully aware that Germany now has a desperate fight on her hands. As a method of getting out of this crisis, some thought is being given to the possibility that peace might be established between England and Germany or between Germany and some other country, but for either Chancellor Hitler or me to undertake such a thing under present circumstances would, in reality, be the same as carrying on negotiations for a surrender. To embark on such a serious business merely as a political move without a mailed fist to back it up is not the road to complete success, and would only do us harm. There-fore, Germany's foreign policy will be, one, to strengthen her union with friendly countries; two, to guide the neutral countries into an at-titude favorable to her; and three, to devote her entire strength to push-ing the enemy into an awkward diplomatic position.''

The conversation ends with Oshima reassuring Ribbentrop about the new Japanese cabinet. ''[It] was set up in order that our national strength might be increased and in order that Japan might devote herself more completely to the prosecution of the war,'' Oshima tells the Ger-mans. ''There is no change in our foreign policy, and our cooperation with Germany is going to be stronger than ever.'' As for Tokyo's policy toward Russia, Oshima says: ''Naturally, there will be no change. Therefore, please set your mind at ease.''

In a separate message to Tokyo summing up his opinion of the meeting with Ribbentrop, Oshima advises Tokyo that while Hitler will successfully purge the Army of ''the faction which is causing the trou-ble . . . it will almost inevitably have unpleasant domestic and foreign repercussions.'' As for the current military situation, he says: ''It must be recognized that the Germans' strategy of first routing the invading army in the West and then turning to the East has failed. The offensive of the Russian Army in the East is making exceptionally rapid progress and its pressure is increasing daily. While there has been no change in Germany's basic strategy of waging a decisive battle on the Western Front, at present it is vitally necessary to stabilize the Eastern Front, a task to which every effort is being devoted. The success of [Germany's] intended offensive there will depend on the Russian's strength.'' As for the peace proposal suggested by Ribbentrop, Oshima doesn't believe that Hitler has ''any such intention.''

The question has been raised, nevertheless. Sooner or later, either Berlin or Tokyo will do something about it. Meantime, it is obvious to

---

Graziani complained bitterly to Japanese ambassador Hidaka that the Germans had refused to provide the Italian forces with arms (DS 12 July 1944).''

Washington that Operation COBRA, and breaking out of the Normandy beachheads, will help thwart Germany's attempt to stabilize the Eastern Front.

A few days later, Washington's attention is drawn to Indochina. Japanese ambassador Yoshizawa in Saigon reports to Tokyo that one of his staff has talked with the Frenchman heading the Diplomatic Bureau of the government, named Boissanger, and with Governor General Decoux.[7] The Vichy French have told the Japanese that if France is overrun, the current Vichy government "will liquidate itself. In anticipation of that event, arrangements have already been made to confer on the Governor General plenary powers over Indochina." Should he assume these powers, "the Governor General will continue his policy of cooperation with Japan in order to preserve the status quo of Indochina. . . . An Anglo-American victory would lead to aggression and pressure on the French Colonies. That would be distasteful to French Indochina because of the threat to France's rights and interests, and everything would no doubt be done to cooperate with Japan."

With information such as this flooding in from the Japanese side, and with the demands being made by de Gaulle about France's regaining her former colonies after the war, Washington soon finds itself losing patience with its ally.

On August 11, 1944, Washington learns that the seeds sown two weeks earlier by Ribbentrop in his conversation with Oshima are bearing fruit. From Tokyo, Foreign Minister Shigemitsu instructs Sato in Moscow to find out if Russia is willing to assist in bringing about a negotiated peace in the Far East. This is the first time the Japanese have been willing to make the suggestion openly.[8]

The analysts note that Shigemitsu's instructions are cautiously worded, but they "clearly imply that he has in mind a move by Russia to initiate peace discussions between Japan and the Anglo-Americans, and a similar move by Japan to bring about peace between Russia and Germany."

The flavor of Shigemitsu's message is significant. "In Europe, the war has now taken an extremely disadvantageous turn for Germany, on both the Eastern and Western Fronts," he tells Sato. "It is also inevitable that this time of national crisis will witness a rebirth of the tensions which have existed since the establishment of the Nazi regime

---

7. SRS 1386, 6 August 1944.
8. SRS 1391, 11 August 1944.

(witness, for example, the attempt against Chancellor Hitler) and it will be difficult to alter the situation in the future.

"In the Pacific, the American offensive is becoming violent. The enemy has already broken into our territorial waters and by means of absolute superiority on the sea and in the air is steadily drawing nearer to our homeland itself with the intention of severing our sea communications and destroying our shore installations. This situation will become increasingly serious as Germany's military strength diminishes. . . . With the war situation developing to their advantage, England, America and Russia—along with China—are now planning to hold discussions in the U.S. regarding the organization of the postwar world. In this connection, differences will inevitably develop between them, but it is clear that no actual rift will occur until after the end of the war. Nevertheless, this point is the sole enemy weakness of which we can take advantage. . . . Japan and Russia . . . are neutral toward each other. . . . In the postwar world one cannot foresee any clash on interests between these two countries either in Asia or in Europe."

It is at this juncture that Shigemitsu is making a grave error. As we know, Stalin has already promised the Allies that he will attack Japan after the war in Europe ends. He has also told Ambassador Harriman that he will attack exactly ninety days after hostilities cease. There is no record of what Marshall or others may have thought about Shigemitsu's false assumption as they watch events unfold.

"In the light of this situation," continues Shigemitsu, "I wonder whether Russia would not consider it being to her advantage, both from the internal and external points of view, to advocate peace at the present time. Accordingly, we should find out at the Kremlin whether Russia would take the initiative in such a peace movement, or whether this will have to be left to the United States and England. (Theoretically speaking, Russia and Japan, being neutral countries, could jointly take the initiative for peace.) I should like you to sound out Russia's views on these points, preferably during an interview with Foreign Commissar Molotov. I would also appreciate your own observations on this question.

"Please be careful how you handle this wire," concludes Shigemitsu.

It takes five days before Washington receives the decrypted version of Sato's reply to Shigemitsu. In Sato's opinion the approach Tokyo suggests is inappropriate.[9] In his view Russia "will continue to

---

9. SRS 1396, 16 August 1944.

insist on the complete destruction of Nazidom so that Germany will no longer be a menace to the maintenance of peace in Europe.'' To make a move such as Tokyo suggests might cost Russia her voice in the management of postwar affairs in Europe. Nor will England and America grant Japan a peace more favorable than what Germany will receive after her defeat. Sato says: ''It seems clear that Japan is in a far worse position than Russia to undertake any initiative for peace. . . . I think it would be unwise to have any exchange of views with Russia on the subject. That could lead to no beneficial result and would, I fear, give the impression that our fighting spirit has already begun to decline. The problem is essentially one of comparative strength, and our first task by all odds is to check America's plans. In view of the fact that the Greater East Asia war was begun in the first place without regard for the international situation, I think there is nothing to do but try *to reach a decision by force of arms;* and that we must resign ourselves to the fact that the time has not yet come for the intervention of diplomacy.'' (Emphasis added.)

In making his statement, Sato is pointing out to Tokyo that he was in retirement when Pearl Harbor was bombed, and on several previous occasions, he has hinted to Tokyo that he believed going to war against the Allies to be a terrible blunder. His words will sting when read in Tokyo.

✖ ✖ ✖

As described earlier, when Marshall wrote to Dewey, the Chief of Staff points out just how difficult it is to keep the secret of Magic. He tells Dewey how the OSS tried to steal codes from the Japanese consulate in Lisbon. (The background of this event was discussed earlier.) As a result, the military attachés changed their codes, blocking off a fabulous source for the Allies.

In one example of just how valuable these military-attaché messages are, consider the information contained in a report filed to Tokyo on August 17 by Major General Shimizu, the Japanese military attaché in northern Italy.[10] The analysts note for Marshall that Shimizu ''is probably the most pessimistic of Japanese observers in Europe.'' Also that he advocated a Russo-German peace a year ago (MS 24 April

10. SRS 1435, 24 September 1944. It took more than a month for the code breakers to read this message, sent on August 17.

1944). "It is of some interest," say the analysts, "that one week after the above report was sent to Tokyo, Ambassador Oshima was instructed to inform the German leaders of Japan's view that Germany should make peace with Russia."

According to Shimizu, the situation in Europe is very bad indeed. The depths of his despondency can be understood only by reading his actual words, which include the following: "We must recognize the fact that the Anglo-Americans and the Russians are not likely to commit any serious errors in the prosecution of the war and that Germany has slight hope of victory. . . .

"Despite the unfavorable turn of the war and the incessant bombing, Hitler still maintains his resolute will to fight, and the morale of the [German] people remains good. However, the German Army—in view of the deterioration of its Air Force, the clumsy direction of its strategy, and its own dwindling strength—no longer has the might and confidence it once possessed. Not even changes of strategy on the Russian Front, nor the appearance of new secret weapons, nor a display of vigor in the defense of Germany can effect any great changes in the situation. If the Germans continue to fight on three fronts against such powerful enemies, they must inevitably go down to defeat on all those fronts. We must boldly face the possibility of Germany's collapse, and in addition we must refrain from indulging in wishful thinking and in optimistic estimates of our own strength. . . .

"It is very probable that the Germans, by shortening their lines and by taking up natural defensive positions along the Vistula and in the Carpathians, will be able to stave off a Russian invasion of Germany. However, in view of the present state of morale in the Army and the friction between the Army and the Party, it is hard to guarantee that the Germans will fight as hard in the East as they have up to now.

"On the Italian front the natural barriers of the Apennines will enable the German and Italian armies to hold out for a long time; however, I believe that the enemy will take the logical step of carrying out landings in the rear and flanking attacks from France. After putting up a stout resistance on the Po River line, the Germans and Italians will have no alternative but to effect a gradual withdrawal to the mountains on the German-Italian border and to hold out there. . . .

"The enemy may very well be planning to avoid the cost of breaking through natural defenses by invading the Balkans with a strong force and threatening Germany from the rear. However, the ability of the enemy to assemble sufficient strength for such an operation will depend on the outcome of the fighting in France."

General Shimizu has a good grasp of SHAEF's strategy. One wonders if Eisenhower ever appreciated the irony of the situation.

The next day, August 18, Oshima reports to Tokyo on military developments in Europe.[11] As usual his source is Under Secretary von Steengracht, who tells him on August 16 that the Americans have moved unexpectedly around "our left flank [in Brittany] so as to encircle the main strength of the German Seventh Army. At present fierce attacks are being made to close the gap between Argentan in the south and Falaise in the north. The enemy's overwhelmingly superior airpower hinders the moving up of reinforcements." The German plan is to get the Seventh Army out of the trap and establish a new battle line. They will try to anchor the right wing at Le Havre "and retreat to a line stretching southeast along the Seine as far as Paris."

Von Steengracht admits that "the situation for Germany is indeed very bad and is not going according to plan; the chief reason for this is the inferiority of our air force." He also acknowledges the Allied invasion of southern France, but tries to dismiss the event.

He says, "The enemy troops which have landed between Cannes and Toulon amount so far to about one division." He believes the landing points will be expanded to form a "bridgehead," but the area is "scarcely suited to large-scale operations, since the available roads are only along the coast."

He also claims that Hitler is planning a large-scale attack in the East. But he has to admit that the initiative is now in the hands of the Russians, and he cannot say when the German counterattack will take place.

A few days later, Oshima tells Tokyo[12] that he has been told the Germans may concentrate their troops south of the Loire River and they will launch a counterattack from there. On the other hand, the Germans may withdraw to the east-central part of France. Oshima says he was told: "Such a withdrawal would cause Germany to lose her Atlantic submarine bases and would be a drastic measure; however, Germany's most important aim now is to maintain control of the launching sites for the V-1 and also for the V-2. The V-2 is expected to be used shortly. Although details about it are not known, it is said that its effectiveness is about ten times that of the V-1 and that sufficient supplies have already been accumulated to make continuous firing possible."

---

11. SRS 1398, 18 August 1944.
12. SRS 1402, 22 August 1944.

For the Allies, this news about the V-2 rocket could not be worse. British defenses have been mobilized to defend against the V-1, which can be shot down by antiaircraft guns or fighters. The V-2 appears to be a true ballistic missile, however, and there is no conventional defense against a rocket that falls without warning from a great height. Now one can appreciate how the work of British rocket expert Standish Masterman, as described earlier, rounded out the picture for Allied intelligence. (The British accounts of Masterman's exploits do not mention the role played by the Diplomatic Summaries in alerting Allied intelligence about the V-2.)

The only way the nerves of British civilians can be calmed will be by the capture of the V-2 launching sites. It will be some time before this is accomplished.

At the end of August, Tokyo suddenly becomes aggressive about seeking peace between Germany and Russia. Accordingly, Foreign Minister Shigemitsu tells Oshima that the Japanese Supreme Council for the Conduct of the War, which had been formed on August 5, has "resolved to strive for the conclusion of peace at once" between the two warring nations.[13] The message instructs Oshima to "go at once to High Command Headquarters, [and] inform Foreign Minister von Ribbentrop that it is the view of the Japanese Government that a German-Russian peace should be speedily concluded."

The reason for this being, "the Japanese Government has for some time desired that Germany should make it possible to concentrate her entire strength in the West by concluding a peace with Russia. . . . In case the German authorities do not show any immediate inclination to agree, you should continue to do your utmost in order that our wishes may be realized."

The analysts in Washington note "the blunt language used by Shigemitsu is without precedent."

The same day's Magic carries a "Special Supplement" about German intelligence in Berlin sending "agents, radio equipment and other material" on a German ship from Europe to Argentina. The plan had been uncovered the previous February when a number of German agents in Argentina were arrested.

Early this past May, however, the ship made landfall on the Argentine coast near Mar del Plata, some 250 miles south of Buenos Aires, where two agents and their equipment were put ashore. Another such voyage is being scheduled for the end of August. This marks the

---

13. SRS 1405, 25 August 1944.

beginning of the Allied watch on the flight of German officials and Nazi gold to Argentina as the defeat of Germany becomes more and more apparent.

Replying almost immediately to Shigemitsu's request that he seek a meeting with Ribbentrop about peace between Russia and Germany, Oshima tells Tokyo he has duly requested the required audience.[14] He then asks five detailed questions that he expects the Germans to raise. It is apparent that Oshima does not share Shigemitsu's views on the matter. And by Oshima's asking if Japan ever sounded out Russia before about this, it appears that he was unaware that Tokyo had ever proposed sending Moscow a "special envoy." The Russians had rejected the move at the time, only to have Japan repeat the idea this past April with the Russians again saying no to the idea.

Oshima's questions to Tokyo are dubbed "troublesome" by the American analysts. This proves to be the case. A few days later, Foreign Minister Shigemitsu instructs Oshima to "carry out immediately my instructions, without waiting for a complete answer to the questions you have raised."[15] Shigemitsu acknowledges that Tokyo's reasoning "may be at variance with the aims of the German leaders." But he also says that "Japan does not know the aims of the Anglo-Americans, nor those of Russia.... If the German government cannot seek peace with Russia at this time, or if there is some reason for Germany's not desiring to seek it, I should like to receive a frank report on the subject—as detailed as possible."

The following day, it becomes apparent that Tokyo's latest message to Oshima has crossed in the mail with Oshima's latest message to Tokyo. Oshima had not yet received Shigemitsu's latest instructions when, on August 29, he told Tokyo that he had already tried to meet with Ribbentrop.[16] Because of the Rumanian crisis the meeting had to be postponed.

However, Oshima has forwarded the thrust of what is to be discussed via Ribbentrop's subordinates.

Oshima also says that "in view of the present situation, I, too, believe that it is reasonable for the Japanese government to hope for a German-Russian peace." The Japanese diplomatic moves will continue.

Meanwhile, the repercussions from the abortive assassination attempt on Hitler spread. A decrypt of Oshima's message of August 17

---

14. SRS 1406, 26 August 1944.
15. SRS 1410, 30 August 1944.
16. SRS 1411, 31 August 1944.

to Tokyo is the second item to be brought to Marshall's attention as September begins.[17]

Oshima has been advised by his usual "contact man" that the public trials after the bomb plot gave the enemy too much propaganda. Now the trials are being conducted in secret. Oshima quotes his source as saying: "The only well-known military figures whose status is still in doubt are Genobst. Halder [retired] and Genobst. Fromm [replaced by Himmler as commander of the Home Army]. Genmaj. von Tresckow, chief of staff of an army in Army Group Center on the Eastern Front, appears to have been one of the ringleaders."

The analysts point out that, back in early August, Oshima reported that Halder was under suspicion because of his relations with von Beck. Fromm's position was "not clear." He was supposed to have concurred in orders issued by Olbricht, a leader of the plot, but after learning that Hitler was alive, Fromm ordered Olbricht's execution.

Oshima reveals that two more members of the Foreign Office are listed as collaborators. One is named von Haeften (deputy head of the Division for Cultural Propaganda), who "knew what was going on but failed to report the matter." The other, Adam von Trott, has been "engaged in intelligence activity, particularly in regard to India. [He] is said to have attempted to establish direct contact with the Russians in Stockholm and to have possessed a list of Foreign Office personnel who were to be liquidated."

Oshima says he now believes that since some of the plotters were caught trying to escape to Russia, "I myself believe that ideological leanings of the conspirators made them willing to conclude peace with Russia."

This latter conclusion differs from Oshima's earlier ideas in that he first thought the plotters were going to try to make peace with England and America.

Meanwhile the analysts in Washington note that von Trott had been identified by Oshima in the past as the official in charge of Indian Affairs. He has been dealing with espionage and propaganda there. And according to the OSS, in 1942 von Trott made several trips to Switzerland bearing proposals for a negotiated peace, that he had been "anti-Nazi since 1939 and has belonged to an 'undercover organization' in Germany."

As revealed by the Magic Summaries, the depth of the Allied

---

17. SRS 1412, 1 September 1944.

knowledge about the inner workings of the German government is astounding.

On September 2, the Magic Summary is quoting Foreign Minister Shigemitsu as suggesting to Oshima that the Germans should consider using the current negotiations with Finland as the cover for Russo-German talks about peace.[18] Meanwhile, Oshima and Tokyo compare their respective estimates of Germany's production of war materials the past year.

Oddly enough, the Japanese estimates agree with American estimates except for the production of tanks. The Japanese believe the Germans built at least 1,300 while the American figure is much lower, only 300–350 tanks. In a war of attrition in terms of production capabilities, it is ever clearer that the Allies will dominate.

In early September, there come the first plainly spoken words by Japanese diplomats admitting they fear an attack on Japan by Russia.[19]

Ambassador Sato is the first to speak of the matter. He tells Tokyo that "while Russia's penetration of the Balkans will necessarily lead to rivalry between the Anglo-Americans and herself, it will not cause any actual rupture in their relations, at least for the duration of the war against Germany." Sato deplores the fact that Japan cannot exploit the split between the Allies. He foresees being attacked by all three. He says: "The situation plainly demands that we strengthen our determination to continue our dashing fight to the very end and to pursue a course of action which will not bring shame upon the leading power in Asia."

In Madrid, Ambassador Suma is of the same opinion. He warns Tokyo about Germany's "grave situation."

"It would only be wishful thinking," he says, "to believe that such a man as Stalin would hold fast to friendly ties with Japan at the risk of being outstripped by England and America [presumably in the Far East]. If we are to gain the ultimate victory, we must abandon vain hopes and plan to meet difficulties boldly. We must recognize that Russia is likely to come into the enemy's camp."

Their note of defiance, their desire to fight to the death, will be noted by Marshall.

In the same Summary, Oshima's usual "contact man" is being quoted about German reverses. In Rumania, three or four German divisions "are being encircled by Soviet forces, but there is still hope

---

18. SRS 1413, 2 September 1944.
19. SRS 1414, 3 September 1944.

they may be extricated. A retreat in that area to the Carpathians cannot be avoided. . . . We have no choice but to evacuate our forces from Bulgaria, and the disposal of German units in Greece and Yugoslavia is becoming a problem. . . . As for Italy, one hears the opinion expressed that it would be best to forget about prestige and withdraw to the Alps. . . . On the Western Front, the enemy now have sixty-two divisions in northern France and about twenty in southern France. Germany will try at least to avoid losing the V-1 bases, but with the war's increasing momentum, one cannot say positively what line we will be able to hold.''

In painting this pessimistic picture, Oshima says he has also been told that Marshal Kluge died suddenly of heart failure and has been replaced by Marshal Model.

More important for the Allies is the news that 2–2.5 million Germans are being mobilized into the Army. The problem, according to Oshima's informant, "will be one largely of organization and equipment.''

✵ ✵ ✵

Meanwhile, Japan is focusing again on China.

On August 30, 1944, Foreign Minister Shigemitsu tells Ambassador Tani in Nanking that "at a recent meeting of the Supreme Council for the Direction of the War, it was decided as a matter of fundamental policy . . . to undertake certain political activities vis-à-vis Chungking with the idea of bringing to a conclusion the China problem. . . . The Premier shall keep in touch with the Foreign Minister and carry on these political activities through the National [Nanking] Government of China. No other type of approach shall be undertaken. Progress shall be reported to the Supreme Command of the Army and the Navy.''[20]

At this point in the Magic Diplomatic Summary, the analysts provide Marshall with a brief résumé of the history of Japan's attempts to solve the so-called "China problem." Remembering the McCarthy years, the reader might be interested in seeing exactly how, in the real time of World War II, the intelligence experts in Washington viewed the relations between Japan and China.

According to the analysts, the Japanese made several attempts to negotiate peace with Chungking during 1940 and 1941. These efforts

20. SRS 1415, 4 September 1944.

failed, largely because the Japanese were unwilling to give a definite commitment about withdrawing their troops from China. In January 1942, the Japanese cabinet decided not to deal directly with Chiang Kai-shek, "fearing that he would only seize on any Japanese [initiatives] as a sign of weakness." Nevertheless, Japanese Army officers in China continued for some time to initiate more than a score of peace feelers, and the Foreign Office clearly hoped that a peace could be arranged. In May 1944, Shigemitsu asked Ambassador Sato in Moscow whether there was any chance of Japan's "using Russia as a means of bringing our war in China to a conclusion (MS 31 May 1944)."

In September 1944, Japan still finds herself mired in a war with China—a nation too large for her to conquer, occupy or pacify. The Japanese Supreme Council for the Direction of the War understands that the war is not going in Japan's favor. So the question now will be how can Japan keep China under control in the postwar years so that China does not threaten Japan. At the same time, the Diplomatic Summaries prove that Japan will want the Americans and British blocked from gaining any greater influence in postwar East Asia.

On September 5, Shigemitsu tells Sato in Moscow that Tokyo wishes to send a "special envoy" to the Russians for "a complete exchange of views with the Russian Government."[21]

Tokyo is thinking of sending former premier Koki Hirota (1936–37), who also had been ambassador to Russia and foreign minister. This is Tokyo's response to Sato's comments in August urging Tokyo to postpone trying to find out if Russia would be willing to assist in bringing about a negotiated peace both in Europe *and* Asia. (Sato told Tokyo that he didn't believe Russia would be willing to make peace with Germany, and that Japan was in no position to take the initiative for peace so far as her own war was concerned.)[22]

The analysts in Washington note that Shigemitsu had not pressed Sato on the subject. Instead, on August 24, Shigemitsu tells Oshima in Berlin to inform the Germans about Japan's belief that Germany should seek peace with Russia.

The Axis radio news broadcasts announce that on September 4, Ambassador Oshima confers with Hitler and Ribbentrop at High Command Headquarters.[23] The next day, Oshima tells Tokyo that both Hitler and Ribbentrop said that "there was no possibility of a

---

21. SRS 1417, 6 September 1944.
22. Ibid. This message refers the reader to DS 11 August 1944 and DS 16 August 1944.
23. SRS 1418, 7 September 1944.

German-Russian peace at present.'' So long as the Russian military position is favorable to Moscow, Stalin would reject any peace overture. Ribbentrop said, in Hitler's presence, that Japan should not attempt to sound out Soviet opinions on the matter because the Russians would think that the overture had been requested by the Germans. Ribbentrop also said there was no truth to the rumors that Germany was already sounding out Russia through contacts in Stockholm.

Hitler also tells Oshima that he will have to attack once more on the Eastern Front. And because Ribbentrop occasionally supports Oshima's remarks, the Japanese ambassador concludes that Japan should continue to find out Russia's views on the matter by some other method that will not embarrass Germany, and should make another strenuous effort to persuade Germany to make peace.

The analysts note for Marshall that while Oshima's report is sent on September 5, it did not reach Shigemitsu's desk on the morning of the sixth. This explains why he has now sent an impatient message to Oshima asking for at the least the gist of the conversations, ''since we have some matters here which we have to decide very quickly.''

The following day, Oshima expands on his conversation with Hitler.[24] The talks covered the military situation in Europe, the aftermath of the failed assassination attempt, plus political developments in the Balkans, Slovakia, Finland and France. One of the more interesting comments made by Ribbentrop is that the German problems on the Eastern Front are due largely to one of the ringleaders of the July 20 plot, Major General von Tresckow, who, without permission, ordered a retreat. The General was then reported to have been so conscience-stricken that he went to the front lines and committed suicide.

For Marshall and Eisenhower, the comments by Hitler have particular relevance.

''In an area such as France, where there are good roads,'' says Hitler, ''once the German lines have been breached by a large task force, it was necessary to fall back to new positions. Accordingly it was determined to withdraw most of the forces to the West Wall, even from the Antwerp area, leaving behind garrison troops in the most important coastal fortifications, such as Bordeaux, Le Havre and the Brittany ports. . . .

''From the beginning we have realized that in order to stabilize our lines it would be necessary to launch a German counterattack. Ac-

---

24. SRS 1419, 8 September 1944.

cordingly, troops are now being massed southeast of Nancy with the intention of striking from the flank at the American forces on the southeast wing, which have been pursuing us in five or six columns, each composed of three to four divisions. . . .

"In that attack it is planned to employ Army Group ["G"] commanded by Genobst. Blaskowitz and also troops moved up from Germany itself. Except for small security detachments operating on the banks of the Loire and rearguard units in the area of the Rhone River, the main strength of Blaskowitz's Army Group is falling back to a planned line without suffering serious losses. . . .

"The offensive which I have just mentioned will be only for the purpose of stabilizing the present front. However, when the current replenishment of the air forces is completed and when the new army of more than a million men, which is now being organized, is ready, I intend to combine the new units with units to be withdrawn from all possible areas and to open a large-scale offensive in the West."

Oshima reports that at this point he asks when this major offensive will be launched.

"At the beginning of November," replies Hitler. "We will be aided in holding off the enemy during September and October by the comparatively rainy weather, which will restrict the enemy's employment of their superior airpower."

Oshima says he worries that Germany might not be able to hold her battle lines in the West until she's in a position to launch a real offensive. He is also concerned about a delay in the offensive caused by organizing and equipping the new troops.

"I have complete confidence in the West Wall," says Hitler. "Furthermore, even though [word or words missing] . . . line may require some withdrawal, I expect that for the most part we shall be able to maintain it. As for our ability to organize and equip new troops, I do not believe there will be any difficulty, in view of the efforts of [Albert] Speer [Minister for Armaments and War Production]." Later in the conversation he claims that Germany has enough raw materials stockpiled that even if she is encircled by the Allies, she can fight on for another two years.

What does Hitler mean about withdrawing German troops from every area to launch a large-scale offensive in the West, Oshima asks. "What areas do you have in mind?"

Says Hitler: "My plan is to withdraw the maximum number of troops wherever possible. I am thinking of evacuating Greece and the Balkans and defending either a line stretching southwest from the southern Carpathians in Transylvania to Yugoslavia, or a line stretching west from the old Hungarian border.''

The conversation continues and Oshima sums up his impression for Tokyo saying that "Hitler's decision to conduct a general mobilization and then to launch a great offensive on the Western Front with troops drawn from all possible areas is, in my opinion, the correct step for Germany to take in the present situation. Furthermore, if Japan can bring about a German-Russian peace before the time set for such an offensive, Germany would without a doubt be able to achieve a decisive and imposing victory on the Western Front.''

Oshima then begins to cover the flanks of his conclusions saying that "the German leaders are not at present prepared to seek such a peace.'' As for the big attack, "such an offensive will not be an easy matter at all.'' Because Hitler seemed apprehensive on a number of points, Oshima ends his message to Tokyo by saying: "It is difficult to form an exact estimate of the probable success or failure of such an offensive.''

As it will turn out, the upcoming German offensive that Oshima is reporting to Tokyo will be postponed from November to December. It will be called the Battle of the Bulge. And because Oshima discounts Germany's ability to wage such an offensive, the warning in his message to Tokyo about a major offensive per se will be forgotten, or considered outdated, by the generals at SHAEF when December rolls around.

After one places an overlay made up of the Magic Summaries upon the chronology of events, one then reads the correspondence between Montgomery and Eisenhower about their "broad versus narrow front'' controversy in a completely different light. Given the realities of the situation, and the German strategy as revealed by Hitler to Oshima, one questions how Montgomery can believe that Germany is ripe for the picking via a swordlike thrust through northwest Europe.

The reality facing Eisenhower is that on September 3, 1944, the front in Europe stretches from Switzerland to Brussels and Antwerp. Montgomery has failed as yet to liberate the vital ports of Le Havre, Calais, Ostend and Dunkirk. For the moment the Allied forces are reliant on supplies shipped into Cherbourg, way back on the Normandy peninsula. These are sent to the front by truck convoys called the Red Ball Express. The problem is there aren't enough trucks and drivers to deliver the fuel, ammunition and other supplies needed to keep mechanized armies moving forward.

While Montgomery wants to attack and force his way across the

Rhine, forgetting about the supplies needed by any other allied forces except his own, Eisenhower is reading the warnings in Oshima's account of his meeting with Hitler. For Oshima is talking about *two* attacks. The first is a counterattack by Army Group G under Gen. Blaskowitz that is aimed at stopping and destroying the tankers in Patton's Third Army and the combined forces in Devers's Sixth Army Group. Without fuel and ammunition, which will have to be diverted to Montgomery, Blaskowitz's attack will succeed. And if Montgomery fails in his attack—and he will fail, leaving his flanks exposed—then Eisenhower can foresee German Army Group G wheeling north and west to trap vast amounts of Allied soldiers and supplies.

Eisenhower's decision to fight on a broad front might antagonize Montgomery. But given the intelligence he possesses about German intentions, Eisenhower's strategy will prove prudent and correct.

✳ ✳ ✳

The more one compares the information contained in the Magic Diplomatic Reports with the day-to-day strategy followed by Eisenhower, the more one becomes convinced just how important the Magic material proves to be for SHAEF's planning staff. Also, one can understand the depth of anger William Friedman felt when he complains that Eisenhower never gave the slightest credit to the incredible intelligence that was provided him hour by hour, day by day.

Those who believe in Eisenhower's greatness offhandedly dismiss the notion that the Magic Summaries had anything to do with his success. But if one compares the SHAEF planning proposals versus the orders Eisenhower issues, and then one overlays the information received via Magic upon both sets of documents, Ike's battlefield strategy suddenly appears as a deadly game of bridge. For this German move there is a trump; for another German move there is a finesse. Because he can read the enemy's hand tactically and strategically, Eisenhower dominates the battlefields of Europe.

For example, Allied troops enter Paris on August 25, 1944. On September 1, Eisenhower assumes control of the Allied ground units in northwest Europe. (That same day Montgomery is promoted to the rank of field marshal.) According to most historians, the consensus at this moment is the German Army appears ready to collapse. Patton's Third Army has liberated Verdun and is closing on the Moselle River and the fortress city of Metz. In the south, the American/French Sixth

Army Group is taking Dijon and moving toward Epinal. The U.S. First Army is moving toward Cambrai and St.-Quentin while the British Second Army enters Arras. On the Channel Coast the Canadians are preparing to take Le Havre and Dieppe. And by September 11, Allied troops—Troop B of the Eighty-fifth Cavalry Reconnaissance Squadron, Fifth Armored Division—cross the River Our and are the first to invade Germany.

But this does not take into consideration the problems facing the Supreme Commander. First, there are the logistical problems mentioned earlier. The Allied forces have outrun their supply lines. Second, Field Marshal Montgomery picks this time to say he can see the imminent collapse of Germany and he demands to be allowed to make a thrust for Berlin at the expense of all the other Allied units. Third, Magic informs Eisenhower that Hitler has just told Ambassador Oshima that he intends to counterattack in the south with Army Group G. Fourth. With supplies at a desperately low ebb, can the Allies support a thrust by Montgomery and defend against an attack by Army Group G? Fifth, the Magic Summaries clearly show that Germany will not at this time seek a peace with Russia. Lastly, the Magic Summaries indicate that both the Germans and the Japanese are preparing to fight to the bitter end. There will not be a negotiated surrender. Nazism will be destroyed only by force of arms. Unconditional surrender will only be enforced providing the last German guerrilla unit is wiped out.

✖ ✖ ✖

On September 9, Oshima reports to Tokyo that Hitler appears to be having second thoughts about Japan's proposal for a German-Russian peace.[25] Oshima spoke with von Steengracht two days earlier, and the Under Secretary had taken pains to assure Oshima that Hitler and Ribbentrop were worried that they might have given the impression that they completely disapproved of the Japanese proposal. This was not the case. The matter was under consideration. But how much consideration von Steengracht could not say.

The same day's Summary also includes the gist of Oshima's conversation with Ribbentrop of September 4 in which Oshima com-

---

25. SRS 1420, 9 September 1944.

ments that there seems to be increasing discord between Russia and the Anglo-Americans and this presents a "golden opportunity for Germany to negotiate peace with Russia."

"Your statements are abstract and theoretical; I have to deal with realpolitik," replies Ribbentrop. ". . . In our opinion Stalin will never accede to a negotiated peace as long as Russia is not in a position of extreme weakness since he aims to Bolshevize Europe and the support he is now getting from England and America gives him a golden opportunity to do so."

Hitler confirms this for Oshima later on.

"I have made it a point to study carefully the policy and plans of my enemy Stalin," Hitler tells Oshima. "He, like myself, is a leader of a dictatorial state, and therefore I believe that I fully comprehend his way of thinking. It is my opinion that, as long as Russia retains her strength, Stalin will not accept any peace offer."

Oshima reminds Hitler that "according to what you told me in the fall of 1935 [the analysts note for Marshall that Oshima was military attaché to Berlin from 1934 to 1938], it was Germany's intention to split up the Soviet Union into several small states, and it is my understanding that was still Germany's objective at the outbreak of the Russo-German war. However, at present don't you think that such a scheme is utterly impossible?"

"Such a goal seemed possible during 1941 and 1942," says Hitler, "when the German Army was advancing on a line from Moscow to Stalingrad. However, as was not unnatural, we suffered some setbacks on the Eastern Front." Hitler continues, hinting that his aims in Russia are not what they used to be. But still, he and Ribbentrop ask that Japan avoid sounding out Russian opinion on the question of peace.

A few days later, the split between Germany and Italy becomes wider. Ambassador Hidaka reports that on August 28 and 29 he conferred with Premier Mussolini at Lake Garda.[26] The analysts state that the Ambassador's report of the meeting "reveals a crestfallen, disillusioned Duce, who at one point protested: 'I simply cannot bear being called a mere puppet of the Germans and the misfortune of the Italian people. . . . If I should end up as a laughingstock, it would be of no help to the Germans in their present plight. Do you suppose Hitler has ever thought of that?' "

Mussolini tells Hidaka that the Germans are confiscating Italian

---

26. SRS 1424, 13 September 1944.

equipment and supplies on a wholesale basis throughout northern Italy. Recently, the Germans surrounded a number of Italian airfields, cut off communications, and demanded that the Italians choose between joining the German Air Force and swearing allegiance to Hitler, or serving in antiaircraft units. Mussolini also says he is receiving reports that the Allies are dealing more skillfully with the Italians than the Germans. He also thinks the northern Italians might "actually welcome the coming of the Anglo-Americans."

Meanwhile, in Tokyo, Foreign Minister Shigemitsu broaches the idea with Ambassador Stahmer that Germany should make peace with Russia.[27] Even Japanese premier Koiso speaks with Stahmer on the subject. Stahmer is quoted as saying that if the Anglo-Americans and Russians "decide they cannot carry out their present objective of destroying Germany," only then will a chance for diplomatic intervention be possible.

The conversation between the German ambassador and the Premier ends with Koiso saying: "If we are able to check the virus of Bolshevism now, we shall be able to destroy it for the sake of everlasting world peace, and I am grateful to Chancellor Hitler for his determination to stamp out Bolshevism. However, I fear that Americanism also is aiming to destroy the 'morale' [he uses the English word] of the human race and the principles by which all the peoples of the world can win a place for themselves. Therefore, the spread of Americanism must be absolutely checked. . . . Now I should like to know whether the German people have any thought of joining the Anglo-American camp and making Russia a common enemy."

To this Stahmer replies: "Neither the German people nor the German government has any such thought. . . . I am certain that Germany will not consider any peace which compromises her honor or threatens her existence."

By the middle of September, the situation in Hungary becomes one of panic. According to the Diplomatic Summary,[28] American minister Harrison in Bern reported on September 8 that he had received a request from the Hungarian government for an armistice of certain stated terms. Harrison replied that "all efforts to bargain before a surrender are in vain." He also said that the Allies wouldn't make any deal without "the concurrence of the Soviet Union."

---

27. SRS 1425, 14 September 1944.
28. SRS 1426, 15 September 1944.

On September 11, the Japanese chargé in Budapest tells Tokyo that after a conference lasting from midnight to morning, the Hungarian government decided to ask for peace terms with the Soviet Union "and so notified Germany."

He also tells Tokyo that the Hungarian government would have preferred negotiating with the Anglo-Americans. But "it appears that at Tehran Hungary was allotted to the Soviet sphere of influence with the result that the Anglo-Americans have refused to enter into negotiations with Hungary."

A few days later, the German government officially notifies Tokyo that Hitler will not seek peace with Stalin.[29] German ambassador Stahmer meets with Foreign Minister Shigemitsu on September 14 and tells him: "My government has informed me that Chancellor Hitler made the following points during his recent conference with Japanese ambassador Oshima. At the present moment Russia does not have the slightest intention of making peace with Germany. Until Russia comes to realize that she cannot succeed in her war against Germany, she will not consider any peace offer. Although the German Government thanks the Japanese Government for its suggestions, Germany does not wish that any steps at all be taken vis-à-vis Russia."

This ends Japan's far-fetched hopes for negotiating a peace between Russia and Germany that would allow Germany to concentrate her forces to fight solely against the British and the Americans.

The next day, Foreign Commissar Molotov rejects Tokyo's offer to send a special envoy to Moscow.[30] A prime reason for the negative response is that Molotov does not want to give the Americans and the British the wrong idea about "an attempt to bring about a Russo-German peace."

More important, Molotov starts playing "mind games" with Sato. As it will turn out, Molotov lies outrageously to Sato. He fools the Japanese ambassador into believing that since nothing has changed between Russia and Japan in months past, nothing will happen in the future that can't "be dealt with through the usual diplomatic channels." Molotov never gives the slightest hint that Stalin has told the Americans and the British that Russia will attack Japan ninety days after the end of hostilities in Europe.

Sato happily concludes his message to Tokyo, saying: "I was un-

---

29. SRS 1429, 18 September 1944.
30. SRS 1431, September 20 1944.

able to notice anything in Molotov's attitude to indicate that Russia will take advantage of Japan's present plight and apply pressure on her in concert with England and America.''

There is only one mention of Operation MARKET GARDEN in the Magic Summaries. On September 18, Oshima informs Tokyo that von Steengracht has told him that Allied airborne troops have been dropped in Holland.[31] According to the German under secretary, ''the landings took place chiefly in the Arnhem area. We are endeavoring to wipe out the airborne forces with our troops in that area, but I am unable to say anything at all as to future prospects.''

Indeed, the Germans wipe out the Allied force. This mistaken thrust into Germany by Montgomery, who hoped to capture a bridge over the Rhine River, costs the Allies eight thousand out of ten thousand men. The operation is noted for the brilliant fighting of the elite airborne forces. However, the operation proves Montgomery's strategy wrong, and Eisenhower's right.[32]

At the end of September, Oshima files a pessimistic but accurate report to Tokyo about the internal situation in Germany.[33] The analysts in Washington break out and focus on items from the message relating to the possibilities of peace overtures to Russia. But the broad-brushed picture painted by Oshima is one of Germany preparing herself for a fight to the death.

''Despite the unexpected failure of her defensive tactics on the Western Front,'' says Oshima, not realizing how much he has helped the Allied cause, ''Germany is increasing her military preparations and still intends to conduct the war on the theory that the decision will be reached by force of arms.'' This is said in regard to the possibility of Germany's seeking peace with Russia as Tokyo wants.

As for the overall scene, Oshima says: ''Germany's reverses have dealt a great and desperate blow both to the Government and to the people in general, and there is no room for doubt that even today the spirit of the people is heavily weighted down. . . . The fact that the various small

---

31. SRS 1432, 21 September 1944.
32. See *Eisenhower at War, 1943–1945* by David Eisenhower (New York: Random House, 1986), 441–85. According to David Eisenhower, General Bradley ''suspected that the point in initiating the maneuver [MARKET GARDEN] was not to end the war but 'to force Eisenhower's hand on the [control of] the U.S. First Army.' '' (p. 442) But ''if Eisenhower refused MARKET GARDEN and its promise of Berlin, history might never forgive him.'' Thus Eisenhower approved ''an operation that probably neither man wanted, [which] was very likely to go forward at the risk of annihilating the airborne units and postponing necessary projects elsewhere.'' (p. 458)
33. SRS 1441, 30 September 1944.

countries that have fallen by the wayside so far are being dealt with just as Russia wants, without any support whatsoever from England or the United States, has strengthened Germany's determination that only force of arms will decide the war. At present Germany's greatest need is not to hold territory but to gain sufficient time to complete a general mobilization and to equip those thus mobilized. . . .

"Germany is not only confronted by a war on two fronts but also she is faced with the fact that the war strength of Soviet Russia is incomparably greater than that of Russia in the last war. . . . Conditions during the next few months will undoubtedly be the most critical ever for Germany. Yet the German Government and people are resigned to the worst and are determined to continue the fight to the very end. . . .

"I believe it unlikely that Germany will collapse suddenly."

With this overview of the war provided by the Magic Summaries, it is only logical that the planning staff at SHAEF carefully reevaluates the upcoming advance into Germany.[34] Their conclusions are logical, simple, yet difficult to achieve. The direction for Eisenhower is clear. "Our main object must be the early capture of Berlin, the most important objective in Germany," declares the planning staff. "Speed in our advance to Berlin is essential, if the enemy is not to be given breathing space to build up his forces by withdrawal from other countries, to carry out demolitions and to prepare defenses."

This report is approved. A few hours later it is put into action by a 5¼-page-long mimeographed document.[35]

"The object of our further advance will be to destroy all power of resistance in Germany," the report says in paragraph eleven. "This will entail the seizure of the most profitable objectives in Germany and the destruction of the remaining enemy forces which will presumably stand in defense of these objectives. . . . In addition to the above factors consideration must be given to the political importance of Berlin and to a lesser extent of Munich. Furthermore, strategically it is important to occupy Hamburg-Kiel and Nürnberg-Munich areas, to divide such enemy forces as remain in Scandinavia and in Italy and the Balkans from those in Western Germany."

---

34. Post Overlord Planning 381, vol 1. Memo by SHAEF Planning Staff concerning the advance into Germany after the occupation of the Ruhr. 24 September 1944. This report is signed by W. G. MacKenzie, Maj., GAC, Sect. Planning Staff.
35. Post Overlord Planning 381, vol 1. Report by SHAEF FWD G-3/Appreciation . . . No. GCT/370-31/Plans PS-Shaef (44) 38 Final (Revise). 24 September 1944.

In ending, the report states: "It is concluded that Berlin is the single most important objective."

But Eisenhower has not yet received any political direction from President Roosevelt about capturing Berlin. Furthermore, he doesn't believe that the invasion of Germany will be a walkover.

Ike makes all this plain in a memo to Chief of Staff Marshall.[36]

"Recently General Anderson came back from Washington giving me two of the major decisions of the Quebec Conference, namely, that Strategic Air Forces were no longer under my command, and that future occupation of Germany would be on strictly nationalistic lines with Allied headquarters abolished," Eisenhower writes.

"The first of these decisions I already knew about, since it was placed into effect immediately the decision was taken. . . .

"With respect to the decision to divide Germany on nationalistic lines, I had known for a long time the way political thought was leaning and I was not astonished. Naturally, I always knew that decisions between governments would have to be taken on a tripartite basis, and the suggestions I advanced had no implication of making Great Britain and the United States political partners vis-à-vis the third member of the triumvirate. My thoughts were restricted to the military problem; that is the use of armed forces for carrying out the decisions of the government. I felt that on the western boundary of the Russian area we should use the same system in the control of military forces that brought about victory. All this had been presented many times to my superiors, and since they have decided otherwise, this is the last time my own ideas on the subject will be expressed. I assume that at an appropriate time he will communicate to me something of your ideas as to the forces and commanders for which you will have immediate need in the Japanese War after we have finished this job. I will be prepared to give you, whenever you may desire, my opinions as to the qualifications of the senior officers that will be available and for which you have needs as division, corps, army and even group commanders. This will likewise apply to the air side.

"I must confess that post-armistice matters do not occupy any great share of my thoughts. We still have a long ways to go here because the intention of the enemy, which I think is becoming obvious, to continue the most bitter kind of resistance up to the point of practical extermination of the last of his armed forces. Thereafter, we may be faced with some kind of guerilla problem."

---

36. Source: Imp Memos for C/S. Letter from Eisenhower to Marshall. 25 September 1944.

The way the war in Europe will end is, in Eisenhower's mind, pretty well carved in stone. Hitler will fight to the end. He will sacrifice the German Army, and the Navy and the Air Force. After that, the Allies may have to cope with guerrilla forces. And this leads to the acceptance of one of the greatest myths of the war: Berlin might fall, but Hitler will fight on from an Alpine Redoubt.

12

The defeat inflicted by the Germans upon Operation MARKET GARDEN, plus the lack of supplies, which is exacerbated by Montgomery's failure to seize the port of Antwerp and its surrounding approaches (thereby insuring the port's being operational), dooms the Allies from rushing forward in Western Europe during the fall. It will take another seven months of fighting before the Allies reach the Elbe River and the gateway to Berlin. During this time, the British and Americans will argue vehemently about how best to attack Germany, about zones of occupation, and about how to coordinate their advance on Berlin with that of the Russians.

Fifty years after the fact, many American battlefield commanders still believe they had orders to take Berlin, and that Eisenhower should have let them do so. These commanders also believe they were capable of taking the German capital. But the cables between Eisenhower and Marshall show clearly that for both men Berlin lost its luster as a military prize by late March 1945—before the final drive on the Elbe begins.

Why would Berlin lose its significance as a military target? As we will see, the Magic Summaries lead the Americans to believe that "Fortress Berlin" is not worth the effort. Eisenhower will even base his final argument with the British about not capturing Berlin on the Diplomatic Summaries.

The final months of the war are also influenced by a multitude of unexpected intelligence: how the Japanese interpret events as they watch the Americans and British rush toward Berlin from the west and the Russians from the east; how the Japanese reports influence Eisenhower's planning; how the British misunderstood Eisenhower's intentions; lastly, there is the myth of the so-called National Redoubt.

The Diplomatic Summaries provide the key about why the Russians were allowed to seize Berlin. Using these documents as an overlay on the dates orders are given and events unfold, we can see how the Diplomatic Summaries influence the plans that SHAEF draws up. We also see how Eisenhower turns these plans into orders. In turn, we can comprehend the turmoil these orders create among the British. Last, we can comprehend the confusion of the battlefield commander who doesn't know the Magic story.

As for the logistics in the fall of 1944, the supply problems for the Allies will not be solved until a deep-water port near the front lines can be captured and restored to operation. Since the British are responsible for the western and northern flanks of the Allied advance, Montgomery is ordered to do what he should have done earlier: clear the Scheldt waterway and open the port of Antwerp. He gives this task to the Canadian First Army. It involves bitter fighting. The Canadians suffer heavy casualties and succeed in their mission. But because large and complex minefields must be cleared, and the fighting is so bitter, it is not until November 26 that the first Allied merchant vessels can unload in Antwerp.

Keep in mind, too, that the intelligence revealed by Magic is influencing the war in both Europe and the Pacific. A cleavage in thought appears to be developing among various Japanese political groups about seeking a negotiated peace in the Pacific. One report, from the military attaché in Turkey, Major General Tateishi, contains some exceptionally violent comments about the alleged appeasers.[1] Tateishi first refers to an article, apparently written for an unnamed English publication, predicting that once key points of the Japanese mainland are successfully occupied by the Allies, a "spirit of defeatism" will spread in Japan.

According to Tateishi: "Before the beginning of the war there were pro-English Japanese diplomats. . . . There may now be certain retired high-ranking diplomats . . . who are plotting for peace through neutral countries. The Greater East Asia war will be tremendously difficult in the future, and I believe that our sole policy must be to prosecute this holy war with the feeling that we are 100 million brothers all preferring death to dishonor. . . . If the nucleus of such a peace party exists [in Japan], it must be wiped out at once."

In closing, Tateishi says that there should be a systematic reorganization of overseas operations; the code communications of the Foreign Ministry should be taken over by Imperial Headquarters. This

---

1. SRS 1453, 12 October 1944.

statement must have sent a flicker of alarm among the code analysts in London and Washington. Fortunately, Tokyo takes no such action.

However, a second message in the same day's Summary comes from Shozo Sato, the Berlin representative of Japan's Ministry of Home Affairs. In a carefully worded inquiry he asks Tokyo, in the event of Germany's collapse, is there any chance "of taking advantage of that opportunity to stage a diplomatic coup?"

Washington notes that no reply to Sato's inquiry has been received.

Again, Tokyo's attention focuses on China. Foreign Minister Shigemitsu sends out a lengthy review of recent developments.[2] In August, Shigemitsu had said "it does not seem that any of the issues of the dispute [between the Kuomintang and the Chinese Communists] were settled by the visit of [American] Vice President [Henry] Wallace to Chungking, and all negotiations now seem to be at a standstill." (DS 1 August 1944)

Now, says Shigemitsu, Chungking has made a series of concessions to the Communists. Relations are not as strained as they have been in the past. "However," he says, "as a result of the favorable turn which public opinion both at home and abroad (particularly in the U.S.) has taken toward the Communists, they now feel their strength and are stubbornly refusing to compromise on domestic issues. They are maintaining their local political and military autonomy and at the same time are planning to participate in the Chungking government."

He also notes that the two Communist delegates in Chungking are returning to Yenan, and the Communists are sending a mission there. "The results ... of the Kuomintang's attempt to reach a rapprochement with the Soviets," he predicts, "are bound to have tremendous effect on the political situation both in China and throughout the world."

In mid-October, Oshima reports from Berlin that the Germans are benefiting from the slowdown of the Allied advance in the West.[3] He also reports on the recent uprising in Warsaw and the aftermath of the July 20 "incident." "It is thought that the next three or four weeks will be extremely critical ones for Germany," Oshima says his usual contact man told him. "If we are able to extricate ourselves from the present situation and tide things over until winter, we are not without hope of being able to make great plans—both military and political— for the future."

---

2. SRS 1455, 14 October 1944.
3. SRS 1456, 15 October 1944.

Once again the German use of the Russian general Vlassov comes to the fore. Himmler meets with Vlassov on September 29 in what Oshima calls an encounter "of great significance; it demonstrates that Germany has no territorial aspirations in the East. It also shows Germany's intention to make greater use of Russian military units, which up to now have achieved excellent results." But the Germans are also telling Oshima that Hitler had never agreed to set up an opposition Russian government under Vlassov, because "any such move would have to depend on future unpredictable developments."

To put it bluntly: Hitler is casting Vlassov adrift. Branded as mercenaries and without a country, Vlassov and his men will be doomed when the war ends.

According to Oshima, the July 20 "incident" (the failed assassination attempt on Hitler) has been brought to a conclusion with the execution of a number of civilians, many of whom were from the old land-owning families. "To date about one hundred persons have been executed," Oshima was told, and "it is thought that everyone directly involved has been discovered."

The following day, Shigemitsu sends out a lengthy circular to his diplomats around the globe about how he views the world situation. He says that Japanese shipping has been the major objective of air attacks on Manila.[4] "The Anglo-Americans are attempting to blockade our sphere of power by combined land, sea, and air operations," he says. "They are planning to use all the warships of their allies in order to safeguard their sea communications."

As for the war in China, the way it's going "is causing the Allies great concern, and criticism of Chinese incompetency has arisen. Efforts are being made to force a political compromise between Chungking and Yenan so as to combine their military forces and enlist the sympathy of Russia. . . . [The] project for the economic development of China must be watched very closely. We desire reports from every quarter on Soviet plans vis-à-vis China and the extent of Allied economic assistance."

In Europe, Shigemitsu believes the Western Front has been stabilized. If this continues, "various political changes may be expected. Nevertheless, we must recognize that the very worst may happen to Germany. If it does, our information is that there will be no suit for peace and that the people will resist to the very end by means of guerrilla warfare."

---

4. SRS 1457, 16 October 1944.

Thus, in mid-October 1944, Tokyo produces the first intelligence that there might be guerrilla warfare in Germany after a surrender is negotiated. It is also the second indication that the Germans might gather for a final stand in the so-called National Redoubt.

As October progresses, the Magic Summaries contain more and more material about Asian affairs—Burma, India, French Indochina, Formosa, China—than in the past. One can almost sense the focus of the analysts in Washington sliding away from Europe toward the Far East. The shift is so gradual, so smoothly accomplished, just like the great telescope on Mt. Palomar silently swinging toward another galaxy. Still, the amount of information coming out of Europe is astounding.

For example, the Germans apparently are happy with their current strategy, which they call the "Atlantic fortress." Quoting the Chief of the German Intelligence Office, Western Section, the Japanese military attaché to Berlin, Major General Komatsu, reports that when the Germans were withdrawing from France, they had to make a difficult choice.[5] Should they give up the harbors along the coast? Or should they "sacrifice some forces and keep the enemy from using the ports for a certain length of time. The latter course was chosen, and although our manpower losses have been considerable, we have effectively checked the enemy's strategy."

That is why, in the third week of September, Eisenhower decides that priority had to be given to opening up the Scheldt waterway and the port of Antwerp.

Meanwhile, the planning directives are being prepared for whoever will be the district commander of Berlin. So far he is unnamed. A meeting is held at 1635 hours on September 26 in the G-3 Division Conference Room (#93) in the Hotel Trianon to discuss the various drafts.[6]

It appears that Anglo-American forces might enter Berlin in two ways: either "as the culmination of a fighting advance" or "after surrender." In the first instance it is assumed American and British troops will reach Berlin before the Russians. The plan acknowledges that Berlin falls within the Russian zone of occupation. Thus, a simultaneous

---

5. SRS 1458, 17 October 1944.
6. Memo by SHAEF FWD Planning Staff, 387.4-20 "GPS Policy Regarding the Occupation of Berlin." In another memo, January 23, 1945, the SHAEF planners showed their anxiety that the Russians might be first to reach Berlin. The SHAEF planners asked various groups under SHAEF command how many of their people would be ready to jump into planes and leave for Berlin within seventy-two hours of the city's collapse.

occupation of Berlin after a sudden surrender would find the three Allies moving only into their respective sectors.

On October 27, 1944, the minutes of Eisenhower's meeting on September 22 with his commanders is released.[7] The overall concept of the SHAEF operations is announced with the caveat that everyone concerned differentiates "clearly between the logistical requirements for attaining objectives covered by present directives, including seizing the Ruhr and reaching the Siegfried Line, and the requirements for the final drive on Berlin." It is generally accepted that "the possession of an additional major, deep-water port on our north flank was an indispensable prerequisite for the final drive deep into Germany."

The envelopment of the Ruhr from the north by the British Twenty-first Army Group is "the main effort of the present phase of operations." The American Twelfth Army Group is to continue its thrust "so far as its current resources permit towards Cologne and Bonn." They should be ready to seize any favorable opportunity of crossing the Rhine and attacking the Ruhr from the south when the maintenance situation permits. The remainder of the Twelfth Army Group (i.e., Patton's Third Army) is to take no more aggressive action than is permitted by the "maintenance situation after the full requirements of the main effort have been met." The Sixth Army Group is to continue operations with the capture of Mülhausen and Strasbourg. This should contain enemy forces and so assist the northern thrust.

Most important, the "Twenty-first Army Group is to open the Port of Antwerp as a matter of urgency and to develop operations culminating in a strong attack on the Ruhr from the north."

The problem will be that the port of Antwerp will not be captured and opened for operation until the last week of November.

Back in Washington, John J. McCloy in the Pentagon finds another worrisome problem.[8] It is becoming apparent that various papers on the allocations of zones of occupation merely define their boundaries. The papers do not acknowledge the right of postwar U.S. occupation forces "to make use of other ports and lines of transportation and supply than those through Bremen and Bremerhaven." It had been contemplated that the Americans would also be able to use the full port facilities of Rotterdam and Antwerp. But nothing has come of this.

---

7. Post Overlord Planning 381, vol. 1. Memo for C/S from CLB concerning the Supreme Commander's Conference. 27 September 1944.
8. Memo for the Chief of Staff from John J. McCloy. JCS 577/20 "Allocation of Zones of Occupation in Germany." 24 October 1944.

What McCloy wants is a guarantee, not yet given by the British, that American occupation forces can receive adequate supplies in a timely fashion. What is surprising is that Washington is suddenly starting to worry about future British cooperation.

✖ ✖ ✖

Back in the Far East, Japanese ambassador Tani summarizes for Tokyo the recent peace talks between China and Japan. He expresses his gloom for the future of Japan, saying one of his informants from Chungking has told him: "The United States has insisted, in the name of democracy, that Chungking negotiate with the Chinese Communists, and this has deepened the skepticism of Chungking toward the Americans. There is absolutely no possibility of mutual collaboration between the Kuomintang and the Chinese Communists."[9]

Meanwhile, a conference between Churchill and Stalin has been held in Moscow from October 9 through the nineteenth. At issue are the nations that will be under Russian and British control after the war. The really sticky ones are negotiations about Poland, especially the new Soviet-Polish border, which Stalin wants based on the boundary of 1939 and gives the city of Lvov to Russia. Churchill agrees with the plan, saying he will placate the Polish contingent in London. The Poles will not be placated, however. A festering diplomatic problem will develop.

From Berlin, Ambassador Oshima reports about the conference to Tokyo on October 24, three days before Prime Minister Churchill makes his report to the House of Commons.[10] According to Oshima, von Steengracht told him: "The Polish problem involves a question of face and Churchill therefore took a very firm attitude at Moscow. As a result, the conversations ended without any agreement between Stalin and himself on that question.

"The points on which agreements were reached in Moscow are as follows: Finland, Norway, Rumania, Hungary and Yugoslavia are to be

---

9. SRS 1466, 25 October 1944. The failure of American intervention will be noted again. SRS 1487, 15 November 1944, will define that relations between America and Chungking "have almost reached the breaking point as a result of successive interference of the Americans in matters military, political and economic." At one point in the latter message the Japanese seem to be chortling that the Americans are trying to persuade Chiang Kai-shek to provide arms to the Communists.
10. SRS 1470, 29 October 1944.

in Russia's sphere of influence. The foreign relations of Greece are to be directed by Great Britain so that the British may preserve prestige.''

Oshima goes on to say that Albania will be ''included in the British sphere of influence, but the decision as to her boundaries is to be delayed until after the war.'' As for Iran, England ''has agreed to an expansion of Russia's sphere of influence,'' and England will pressure the Iranians to grant oil concessions to Russia. Problems about the Dardanelles are postponed until after the war. And Stalin firmly refuses to grant Siberian air bases to England and America.

Oshima also says there is dissension within the British delegation to Moscow. In England the Conservative Party is upset because British demands were not agreed to by Stalin. There is much criticism of ''Eden's handling of his discussions with Molotov.'' Last, ''the Allies have come to no agreement on what should be done with Germany after the war, because Russia's attitude has not yet been determined.''

Oshima asks von Steengracht for the source of this information. His reply: ''It is received in a certain way from the Polish and Norwegian governments in London—intelligence which past experience has shown to be quite reliable; its source is kept secret even in our Foreign Office.''

It appears that some disinformation is being fed the Germans and, in turn, the Japanese. What the Germans don't know is that on October 18, the principal Allied diplomats, Molotov, Eden and Cordell Hull, agree that none of them will consider any separate peace negotiations with Germany. Furthermore, 5 million tons of supplies will be sent Russia by America in the coming months. Norway will not be in the Russian sphere. But Rumania and Bulgaria will be. Hungary is supposed to be under equal Soviet and Western controls. Most important: Stalin confirms to Churchill that Russia will declare war on Japan after Germany is defeated.

Meanwhile, the analysts in Washington track down what they call ''the travels of a rumor.''[11] The delicate language in which this report is phrased for Marshall indicates a serious breach of security has occurred and its source located. According to the analysts: ''Early in October, the Japanese heard that, in President Roosevelt's view, Russia would launch an offensive against Manchukuo within a month if Germany were to collapse. According to the report received, President Roosevelt had so told 'a certain Senator close to him'; the Senator relayed the information to Finnish Minister Procope before he left the United

---

11. SRS 1475, 3 November 1944.

States; Procope got word to the Finnish Minister in Sofia; the minister gave the story to a correspondent of the Japanese newspaper *Asahi;* the correspondent duly informed the Japanese Military Attaché in Sofia, and the Attaché reported the matter."

The next day, the Magic Summary reveals that the Germans have acquired samples of the American miracle drug penicillin from Spain.[12] This past May, the Japanese military attaché in Berlin advised Tokyo that German laboratories were "unable to achieve the excellent results announced by American scientists (MS 19 May 1944)." The acquiring of the wonder drug is accomplished by J. F. Bernhardt, the head of a German-controlled firm operating in Spain called Sofindus. The analysts in Washington note they have found out that Bernhardt has long been smuggling wolfram and other vital supplies from Spain to Germany. He also has excellent relations with important Spanish officials.

Since July, American manufacturers have been allowed to make regular air shipments of penicillin to Spanish consignees approved by the Combined Blockade Committee in London. The analysts note that according to the Foreign Economic Administration the only Spanish consignees to receive a shipment of penicillin to date are a Dr. Remigra Romero and the Federico Bonet Co.

On November 7, 1944, Pres. Franklin D. Roosevelt is elected to an unprecedented fourth term in office. He is extremely ill, however. The secret is kept from the American people. His failing health will have grave consequences on the way the war will end.

The same day, from Moscow, Ambassador Sato tells Tokyo that Stalin has made a speech in which for the first time he speaks "of Japan as an 'aggressive nation' and our capture of Hong Kong, Singapore, etc., as 'unpleasant facts.' He characterized our early victories as notable examples of aggression comparable to Germany's invasion of White Russia and the Ukraine, and stated that it would be necessary in the future to prevent aggression of this sort."[13]

Sato analyzes the speech as being "the pledge of a firm union between England, America and Russia in the pursuit of their war against Germany." However, he fails to comprehend the real significance of the message: Stalin is publicly signaling that he will soon turn against Japan.

---

12. SRS 1476, 4 November 1944.
13. SRS 1481, 9 November 1944.

✖ ✖ ✖

From mid-November through mid-December 1944, the information
from Europe in the Magic Summaries mainly concerns Japan's continuing efforts to create a peace between Germany and Russia.[14] As we
will see, these Summaries also carry clear warnings that Germans are
about to go on the offensive on the Western Front. It will not be until
1981 that the U.S. Army will release a critique damning SHAEF'S
pre-attack analysis of what is called the Battle of the Bulge.[15] This
forty-four-page report clearly demonstrates what went wrong, saying:
"There were several factors which tended to downplay intelligence in-
dicators, creating a mind-set among senior U.S. commanders which
lessened their concern for a German counteroffensive. They . . . are
summarized here—

> ✖ "U.S. emphasis on offensive rather than defensive oper-
> ations;
>
> ✖ "U.S. conclusion that the enemy was geared to stopping
> an Allied attack against the Ruhr/Cologne complex and
> that the Germans were most likely to attack when the
> Allies crossed the Roer River;
>
> ✖ "U.S. belief that von Rundstedt rather than Hitler was
> controlling German strategy in the West;
>
> ✖ "U.S. view that Germany's lack of fuel would cause an
> enemy offensive to fail, and;
>
> ✖ "U.S. conviction that any attack the enemy might be ca-
> pable of mounting would only lead to quicker German
> defeat."

---

14. SRS 1491, 19 November 1944: Oshima meets with Goebbels. SRS 1492, 20 November
1944: Oshima meets with Ribbentrop; Molotov meets with Sato in Moscow. SRS 1495, 23
November 1944: More Oshima and Ribbentrop, plus a warning of forthcoming German offensive in the West. Also SRS 1496, 24 November 1944: More about the forthcoming German
offensive. SRS 1499, 27 November 1944: Another Japanese peace move with excellent analysis
by Washington. SRS 1503, 1 December 1944: More Oshima and Ribbentrop, who says "Stalin
promotes Roosevelt." SRS 1508, 6 December 1944: Oshima is angry at Shigemitsu. SRS 1520,
18 December 1944: Tokyo tells Sato to see about both peace with Germany and a general
world peace.
15. SRH-112 "Post Mortem Writings on Indications of Ardennes Offensive December 1944,"
including USAWC Study Paper, Classified Annex to USAWC Study Paper, and Project No. 1352-
A Reports.

The report acknowledges that Allied aerial reconnaissance during November "constructed an imposing picture of the German buildup in the north," including large night movements and daytime enemy columns on the roads. And while the front facing the American VIII Corps was quiet, units of the 4th, 28th, and 106th Divisions reported in the last days before the offensive "increased vehicular activity, the fact that a woman escapee claimed that the woods were jammed with equipment,[16] and four prisoners of war in U.S. hands reported that fresh troops were arriving for a big attack around 16 or 17 December, certainly before Christmas. However, only one piece of this information, that about increased vehicular traffic, reached Twelfth Army Group Headquarters in time."

According to Gen. Omar Bradley, "during the middle of November, G-2 reported that the Sixth SS Panzer Army had been moved . . . to an area near Cologne. Another Panzer Army, the Fifth, was reported to have massed its tanks a little farther north. So conspicuous were these telltale signs of von Rundstedt's apparent attempt to nab us astride the Roer that we should probably have sifted them for evidence of deception. But if anyone on the Western Front sniffed in those preparations an intent to mislead us on a German offensive elsewhere, he certainly did not share his suspicions with me."[17]

One of the problems at this point in the war is that the Allies have enjoyed for several years, as Mr. Winterbotham puts it, having "the enemy's intentions handed to them on a plate, [and they] had come to rely on Ultra [Magic] to such an extent that when it gave no positive indication of the coming counterattack, all other indications were not taken seriously enough."[18] Winterbotham points out that there was a lack of high-grade Ultra before the attack. However, he also claims there was "logistical Ultra" that was not properly analyzed.

But what none of these reports or books show is what was available to Marshall and Eisenhower via the Magic Summaries.

Looking at the mass of information that was available, and granted this is fifty years after the fact, it seems incredible that no one examined more carefully the warnings provided first in September,[19] and later in November, by Baron Oshima. But let us grant that people read various

---

16. In 1983, Charles B. MacDonald, Deputy Chief Historian, U.S. Army, located and interviewed this woman, Elise Dele. She became a major character in MacDonald's best-selling *A Time for Trumpets* (New York: William Morrow, 1985), which the author commissioned and edited.
17. *A Soldier's Story,* by Gen. Omar Bradley (New York: Henry Holt, 1951), 439.
18. *The Ultra Secret* by Frederick Winterbotham (New York: Harper and Row, 1974), 254.
19. SRS 1419, 8 September 1944.

intelligence reports in different ways. This makes it easier to understand the mind-set of SHAEF in November 1944.

For example, SHAEF ignores the vital indications of a German counterattack contained in Baron Oshima's report of his November 15 interview with Ribbentrop in Sonnenburg, some sixty miles east of Berlin.[20] The two men meet for lunch. It lasts about three hours.

Ribbentrop reveals for the first time that Hitler's eardrum was injured in the abortive assassination attempt of July 20. Because he neglected to treat it, he is suffering from headaches. (Five days earlier, Oshima reported that Hitler had been confined to bed for ten days.) Now Hitler is "in perfect health" and is busily engaged in operational planning and rebuilding the German Air Force.

The analysts in Washington summarize the report for Marshall: Hitler is reported as believing that Germany cannot win by defense alone. He is also opposed to a war of attrition. There has been no change in his intention to undertake a large-scale offensive as soon as possible. No definite time or "method" has been decided on; the offensive will probably be in the West, but Germany may be forced to concentrate large forces in the East.

The analysts also note that Ribbentrop claims Germany's oil position is improved. Sufficient oil for large-scale operations is assured. All this information should have sounded a large warning bell at SHAEF.

The full text of Oshima's message, with its verbatim quotations of Ribbentrop, is not decrypted until November 23.[21] It reports the German foreign minister as saying: "Both the Eastern and Western Fronts are now stabilized. . . . Russia is talking about resuming her attack on East Prussia, and indeed there are signs of such an attack; however, Germany has made adequate plans for that contingency. A considerable number of German troops are being used to combat the Allied offensive in the Lorraine area, but we do not claim any particular successes in our operations there."

Oshima asks Ribbentrop about the comments Hitler made back on September 4 when he told Oshima: "I intend . . . to open a large-scale offensive in the West." Has there been any change in that intention?

"No," says Ribbentrop. ". . . At the moment I can unfortunately tell you nothing. . . . *I believe that Germany's plans, as in the past, are based primarily on an offensive in the West, although the time, method,*

---

20. SRS 1492, 20 November 1944.
21. SRS 1495, 23 November 1944.

etc., cannot now be precisely determined. However, depending on the enemy's intentions, a situation may be created where we Germans, who are operating on interior lines, may have to concentrate large forces in the East.'' (Emphasis added.)

Oshima recalls that, back in 1918, Germany's last offensive ''actually hastened Germany's defeat.'' He says ''the enemy assault within Germany is now being calmly repulsed by defensive methods; therefore, don't you think it would be a wiser plan for Germany to fight a war of attrition?''

''Absolutely not!'' declares Ribbentrop. ''The Chancellor believes we cannot win this war by defense alone and has reiterated his intention of taking the offensive right to the bitter end. However, I repeat that I myself can say nothing definite at this time.''

As is his usual custom, the next day Oshima follows up the verbatim account of his meeting with Ribbentrop with his personal analysis for Tokyo of what the Foreign Minister actually meant.[22] Oshima points out that Germany may lose territory on all fronts, but there is no danger of an early collapse. The question will be whether Germany ''can build up her strength to return to the offensive. Considering Ribbentrop's statement in light of my 4 September conference with Chancellor Hitler, I think we may accept at face value the Foreign Minister's assertions that the German leaders definitely intend to resume the offensive. However, largely because I do not have accurate information on the enemy's strength, I cannot draw any conclusions as to when Germany will be able to undertake an offensive, or on what scale, or with what success. Even the Germans would be hard put to answer these questions.''

Oshima then adds up the problems facing Germany, then the elements favoring the Germans. They are: ''(a) The crack German divisions used in the West this summer are now resting and refitting in the rear; (b) the Volksgrenadier divisions are expected to receive further equipment while the Volkssturm will be trained and equipped; (c) some of the new planes can be used to support ground operations; and (d) Germany is expected to begin more intensive submarine warfare which may interfere with enemy supply lines.

''In the long run, Germany's leaders, confronted with the fact that the battle lines have contracted virtually to the prewar boundaries of Germany (with the exception of Norway), will have no choice but to open a road of blood in one direction or the other. The chance may

---

22. SRS 1496, 24 November 1944.

come after the enemy's overhasty [current] offensive has been repulsed.''

Looking at Oshima's comments coldly and calmly fifty years after
they were made, one can see how his caveats about German capabilities
to go on the offensive could, and probably did, negate the significance
of the vital information he receives from Ribbentrop. In turn, this could
lead the intelligence staff at SHAEF to believe that Oshima will alert
SHAEF beforehand about when the German offensive against the West
will begin.

As mentioned earlier, this is the same error American intelligence
made before Pearl Harbor. In 1941, Washington believed it would receive via the Winds Code and the Purple intercepts the information
about when the Japanese would attack. Just as we expected Japan would
attack *somewhere* around December 7, 1941, we also knew in late 1944
that Hitler would go on the offensive *somewhere*. Yet on both occasions
we were badly surprised.

Unlike Pearl Harbor, however, the Allies turn the Battle of the
Bulge into a great victory. The Germans inflict more than fifty thousand
Allied casualties in killed, wounded and missing. However, the Germans suffer seventy thousand casualties of a similar nature. They also
lose another fifty thousand troops as prisoners of war. In terms of material, the Germans lose six hundred tanks, sixteen hundred airplanes,
and countless vehicles. According to a top commander in the German
Air Force, the ''Luftwaffe'' received its death blow in the Ardennes.
. . . It was decimated while in transfer, on the ground, in large air battles, especially during Christmas, and was finally destroyed.''[23]

But it is the Russians who truly reap the benefits. In his attack
Hitler committed too much of his mobile reserves in order to achieve
a breakthrough and reach Antwerp. (It is interesting to note how both
Eisenhower and Hitler recognized the need to possess Antwerp.) No
sooner had the German attack been broken in the West, then, on January 12, 1945, five Russian army groups crush the unsupported German
lines in the East and begin a massive advance toward the Oder River
and Berlin.[24]

✖ ✖ ✖

---

23. *The First and the Last* by Galland, 321.
24. SRH-112 "Post Mortem Writings."

Even while the Battle of the Bulge is raging, the day-to-day chores of conducting the war continue.

On Christmas, 1944, Marshall advises Eisenhower that President Roosevelt has sent a message to Stalin asking the Russian leader to receive one of Eisenhower's staff officers so the war effort between the two Allies might be better coordinated. The same cable also advises that Stalin has suggested to Churchill that the Allies might outflank the German West Wall by passing through Switzerland. Stalin has also mentioned the same to American ambassador Harriman, saying that some Allied troops could be transferred from Italy and they could join hands with the Russians in Vienna.[25]

The next day, the Combined Chiefs inform Eisenhower that Stalin has accepted the proposal put forward by Roosevelt and Churchill. They instruct Eisenhower to send a "qualified staff officer at once" to discuss the Western Front with Stalin and ask that Eisenhower acknowledge the message with the name of the staff officer at once.[26]

As the New Year starts, in Washington John J. McCloy prepares a cable for Ambassador Winant in London saying that the Americans have no choice now but to let the British occupy the northwest zone of occupied Europe. The deal will be that the Americans will be allowed to completely control the Bremen and Bremerhaven enclave, including military government, although it will be considered a subdistrict of the larger, British-controlled area.[27]

The Americans will also enjoy free transit of goods and material on the basis "the British interest in possible movement through the American zone to Austria" is so evident that the interests of both nations in these matters are mutually recognized. McCloy tells Winant that the American Joint Chiefs are unhappy that the British have put them in this bind. But "there is no halfway point of control that can be worked out certainly not at high level. In view of our predominant and important interest as well as the fact that we relinquished control of the northwest zone on this condition, real [U.S.] control is essential."

Winant is asked to get the London War Department to agree. If they do so, a "sharp issue" will have been put to rest. But the hard

---

25. Personal File Gen. W. B. Smith, SHAEF. No. WX-82070. Fr Marshall to Eisenhower. TOO 251602z, December 1944.
26. Personal File of Gen. W. B. Smith, SHAEF. No. WX-82144 *FACS 118.* Fr AGWAR to Eisenhower. TOR 262115A, December 1944.
27. ASW 370.8 Germany, 5 January 1945. Memo for General Hildring. Proposed draft cable to Winant re control of German zones. From the Office of the Assistant Secretary.

feelings caused by the British negotiations over this matter will fester in the minds of many Americans.

The Battle of the Bulge is also worrying Eisenhower about his abilities to achieve "definite and accurate conclusions" in future operations. He cables Marshall on January 7, asking for additional troops. He suggests that the Army's limit on manpower be raised by deducting the number of medical patients from the total allowance, or by pulling some divisions from the Italian front. "Maybe the Marines would like to turn over a hundred thousand to us," he suggests. Most important, he wants to know when the Russians will begin "a sustained major offensive" that will force the Germans to send reinforcements to the Eastern Front.[28]

Marshall replies the next day. Every effort is being made in the U.S. to supply Eisenhower with enough troops to meet his requirements. Bull and Tedder have been sent to Moscow to find out what action the Russians are taking. Marshall believes that unseasonable thawing has halted the Russians. If no answer is forthcoming, Marshall promises he will press the matter at the upcoming meeting with Stalin at Yalta. Meanwhile, the major American effort will be on the Western Front.

Marshall also says: "It may be, however, that we face a situation requiring major decisions in order to prevent this war dragging on for some time. Your personal estimates are the best guidance. . . . Can you sometime in the next week sit down and send to me for my personal use in discussions with the other Chiefs of Staff your broad personal estimate of the resources required and the steps which need to be taken to bring this war in Europe to a quick conclusion?"[29]

The heat is on. Marshall is asking Eisenhower to move quickly. This is real pressure. Far more pressure than the British arguing for a single thrust on Berlin. What Marshall is saying between the lines is that the war in Europe must be ended quickly because the timetable for ending the war with Japan is being interfered with.

It takes Eisenhower several days to gather his thoughts. He replies on January 10 in two lengthy cables, with several more yet to come. The first is something of a personal message to Marshall.[30]

---

28. Personal File of Gen. W. B. Smith, SHAEF. No. S-74003. Fr Eisenhower to Marshall. 7 January 1945.
29. Personal File of Gen. W. B. Smith. No. W-88482. Fr Marshall to Eisenhower. TOO 081502Z January 8 January 1945.
30. Personal File of Gen. W. B. Smith, SHAEF No. S-74437. Fr Eisenhower to Marshall. 10 January 1945.

Here the Supreme Commander says he believes that "the issues at stake are so great, and the consequences of victory or defeat so vital to our cause, that there should be achieved the greatest possible degree of conviction among all responsible parties" regarding the lines of action to be followed.

Eisenhower also says he is puzzled by "continuous insistence upon particular points in the arguments" that have been presented to him. His own conviction of long standing about the attack north of the Ruhr is that it should be "as strong as it possibly could be built up." It should also be under a single commander, presumably Montgomery. Eisenhower refers to his insistence that the invasion through the Twenty-first Army territory must support thirty-five divisions, not the twenty-five divisions the Twenty-first Army calls for. "All concerned," says Eisenhower, "know that I have constantly struggled toward the conditions and the time that particular invasion could be undertaken on the strongest possible basis."

The Ruhr cannot be attacked frontally, Eisenhower argues. This huge industrial area is, therefore, a definite "dividing line between practicable channels of approach" into Germany and a logical division of "battle command responsibility." He is upset that "the CIGS and Montgomery consider that it is perfectly logical to make an attack into Germany on the front from Bonn northward and with the rest of the line south of Bonn remaining substantially as at present." As Ike sees it, it will be impossible to defend such a British-inspired maneuver from counterattacks.

The next question is from which point on the Rhine the *supporting* attack for the main operation should come. The Bonn-Cologne area provides the attacker with difficult terrain. This area "would be farther from the junction with the main attack, east of the Ruhr, than would one launched from Frankfurt." All of this would be academic, he says, if only the Allies attained "our first and vitally important winter task, which is the closing of the Rhine from Bonn northward."

The idea behind any supporting attack is to make the enemy "disperse his strength and permit us the use of all possible crossings" so the Allies can put enough force in western Germany "to complete the conquest."

The Supreme Commander emphasizes that in all his conversations with CIGS and others, he has always shown his intent as being: "(1) to concentrate [his forces] north of the Ruhr and (2) to launch a supporting attack with troops that were available after the complete satisfaction of the requirements of the main attack from such locality as study and continuous examination would indicate to be best.'' Various conditions, such as the Germans flooding the ground west of the Roer dams (which they will later do), the strength of enemy forces, will influence the latter point.

Speaking as a faithful servant, Eisenhower then says that should the Combined Chiefs of Staff decide the location for the main attack on Germany, he can ''accept such a decision loyally and as always do my utmost to carry it out.'' He stresses again that only a firmly situated flank on an easily defended line will prevent more Allied troops being immobilized than can be afforded.

He concludes by stressing once again that ''the Ruhr is the logical dividing line,'' a belief that he has arrived at by reducing ''my own nationalistic tendencies'' and ignoring ''the personal ambitions of any individuals.''

This clever and politically correct analysis will turn Marshall more than ever into Eisenhower's advocate when the Combined Chiefs of Staff meet to discuss the invasion of Germany. Not only is the mood in the Pentagon somewhat anti-British at the moment, because of the way Britain haggled over the zones of occupation, but it is becoming apparent to the Americans that while they are supplying the majority of the troops, guns, trucks, ships, aircraft, needed to win the war, the British political agenda for postwar Europe, the Balkans, Greece, India and the Far East differs from that of the Americans. The dislike of British foreign policy is particularly evident in the U.S. Army and the Navy. So when it comes to playing king of the mountain among the Combined Chiefs, Marshall is not going to be denied. Eisenhower will be given a free hand.

The second message is Eisenhower's long, personal review of the campaign in Europe to date, plus an outline for future plans.[31] He begins by emphasizing that all of the planners, British and American, have agreed that when the invasion of Germany becomes possible, it should be by the north flank based on studies of the terrain, ''our own lines of communications and location of important geographical objectives.''

This general operation was ''outlined by my staff and approved by me'' long before D day and was confirmed by all as the ''principles before the invasion.'' Plans were upset, however, by the initial rush through France. The speed of the advance prevented all the troops that were then north of the Paris–Bonn line of advance from being thrust

---

31. Personal File of Gen. W. B. Smith, SHAEF. Fr Eisenhower to Marshall. No. S-74461. 10 January 1945.

into the attack. Several difficulties had to be faced. Maintenance of armored vehicles was one.

The drive against a demoralized enemy gave Montgomery some hope of gaining a bridgehead over the Rhine and the Siegfried Line above Arnhem before the enemy could reorganize and recover. But this proved impossible to achieve. The enemy succeeded "in getting troops into Holland that were capable of making a desperate stand in the Arnhem region."

Eisenhower says that even placing the Airborne Army at the disposal of the British Twenty-first Army Group could not overcome the enemy. Thus, "the hope of a quick breaching of his final defenses was defeated." Even the immobilization of three divisions then in Normandy to provide motor transport for hauling supplies to Montgomery failed to provide adequate strength, although five hundred tons of supplies per day were being unloaded at Brussels.

"We had to revert to our original pre–Dog Day [D day] plan of opening Antwerp before we could deploy in adequate strength in the North," says Eisenhower.

Another problem that arose subsequent to the breakthrough beyond Paris was the establishment of a firm front in southern and southwest France to prevent a large number of enemy troops from concentrating and harassing operations against the Allied right flank. The cheapest protection was to join Devers's left flank as it came out of the Rhone Valley, reducing German strength "by the amount that we could capture behind the two forces." However, "although joining hands with Devers was obviously the most desirable thing to do, the need for all maintenance resources on the northern flank in exploitation immobilized for a considerable period the bulk of Patton's forces. Throughout that period all priorities in supplies went to 21st Army Group and the northern flank of Bradley's forces."

Eisenhower says the next stage will be to have Devers move along the Vosges Mountains to the south, Bradley's Twelfth Army will face the Siegfried Line in the center, and Montgomery's Twenty-first Army Group, having secured Antwerp, will move its forward units along the Maas River.

Says Eisenhower: *"It was my one conviction, and it still is, that in order to concentrate north of the Ruhr all the forces needed for a successful invasion of Germany, we must have throughout the rest of the front a very firm defensive line which can be held by minimum forces"* (Eisenhower's emphasis). This line "is preferably the Rhine," held "substantially throughout" so that we do not "have always to face up to the proposition that the enemy, protected by his very strong Siegfried fortifications, can concentrate swiftly for counterthrusts against our lines of communications.'' The Rhine would give us the opportunity to threaten the enemy and force him to disperse defending forces, making a northward invasion of the Ruhr much easier.

In late October and early November Eisenhower recalls, Bradley made his principal effort toward Bonn-Cologne as an axis of advance, with a secondary advance into the Saar Valley to draw off enemy forces. Because of the terrain in the north, Bradley could use only limited divisions at a time. With the aid of Devers's threatening advance in the Saar Valley, Bradley's own advance proved effective. All of this effort, says Eisenhower, was *"to permit the greatest possible eventual concentration in the north"* (his emphasis).

Eisenhower also says that as early as November 1 ''the possibility of a hostile counteroffensive'' by the enemy through the Ardennes began to be considered. Eisenhower says he discussed this with Bradley, who thought ''it would be an unprofitable region for the enemy to use, and if he made such an attack, it would subsequently lead to our advantage. At worst it was a reasonable sector in which to take a risk, and risks have to be taken somewhere.''

Eisenhower also says that everyone he spoke with besides Bradley at the time felt as follows: ''We did not believe that the hastily trained Volkssturm divisions could be used effectively in an offensive. We did not consider that in wintertime the enemy could supply a major thrust permanently through the Ardennes.'' It was also thought that the enemy could not capture any ''really vital targets'' and ''the Ardennes attack would be a strategic mistake for him.''

Although it was important to ''throw back or destroy the enemy in the south,'' the constant buildup was in the north. There the First and Ninth Armies had priority in ammunition, replacements and new units. ''Moreover, Bradley definitely limited the time available to Patton for making one more effort to achieve a victory in the Saar Valley.'' Patton's final attack was fixed for December 19, after which, regardless of results, divisions were to be transferred north. The Twenty-first Army Group was meanwhile limited to the defensive along the whole northern flank. The terrain and flooding (caused by the Germans opening the floodgates of the Roer dams) prevented offensive actions, except one in January/February between the Meuse and the Rhine as a preparation for crossing.

The ultimate plans as outlined by Eisenhower are ''to cross the Rhine north of the Ruhr in great force. From this we have never varied and the only difference in concepts of which I am aware involve the preliminary tasks that must be accomplished and the possible location of supporting attacks.'' The plan Eisenhower outlines is divided into three phases: ''(1) to defeat the enemy west of the Rhine and close the Rhine north of the Moselle; (2) to force the passage of the Rhine; (3) to advance east of the Rhine.''

As currently planned, operations will bring us ''on to the Rhine at the essential crossing places between Nijmegen and Wesel.''

Several other factors are to be considered in carrying out these proposals. Crossing the Rhine on the narrow front of Nijmegen–Wesel is risky. The river and areas on both sides are flooded during the spring. Then there is the extent that subsidiary attacks by Allied forces ''can be relied upon to divert enemy forces from the sector of our main attack.'' Because of these variants, Eisenhower makes it obvious that no plan can be crystallized at this time ''but must await the development of the situation in Europe as a whole and on this front in particular.''

Eisenhower also says his plan ''is predicated on deploying thirty-five divisions north of the Ruhr.'' He emphasizes ''there will not be *two* main attacks,'' and the locations for subsidiary supports ''is under constant study.''

In conclusion, Eisenhower declares there ''is no difference among any of us about the necessity for having a concentrated force in the north when crossing the Rhine is attempted. My plans call for the availability of all the forces that can possibly be sustained. The point we must consider is what must be our own general situation when we are ready to undertake this great operation *without fear of our flanks and without expending for purely defensive purposes more strength than we can afford.*'' (Emphasis added.)

To Eisenhower, this means the entire front will be divided into three areas of operation. The first will be in the north where ''hostile forces are to be defeated west of the Rhine and preparations made for a crossing north of the Ruhr.'' The second will be in the center where heavy forces will drive on an axis of advance of Prüm–Bonn in preparation of crossing the Rhine ''in support of the northern thrust.'' The third area will be south of the Moselle where the ''whole task is defensive unless opportunities (which now seem rather remote) later should open the Frankfurt area.'' If this occurs, then Devers's forces would also be able to advance across the Rhine.

By repeating himself ad nauseam in these messages, Eisenhower is saying plainly to Marshall that he is tired of British insistence that

Montgomery's forces are the most important part of the Allied command. He points out that he has done everything he could during the attack through France to support Montgomery, including the immobilization of Patton's troopers plus many other American forces. Needless to say this favoritism of Montgomery infuriated many American commanders. And despite this support, Montgomery has failed to deliver.

Now Montgomery wants to be stroked further. He wants to be assured that his forces will be the strongest and the first to strike into the heart of Germany. Eisenhower has promised this. But the Supreme Commander also points out that the fortunes of war must be taken into consideration. Unexpected things might happen. And happen they do. Totally unexpectedly, the Americans will seize an intact bridge across the Rhine at Remagen on March 7. Its location is well to the *south* and *east* of the Ruhr. The Americans will then move troops across the river and secure the bridgehead. This means that the American forces in the center suddenly become more capable of advancing into Germany and flanking the Ruhr from the south than can Montgomery from the north. As fate decrees, it will take another three weeks before Montgomery's forces can cross the Rhine in the north. And in the next forty-eight hours after Montgomery crosses, the Americans will also have crossed the Rhine in two more places to the south. Then, in another five days, the Free French Army will cross the Rhine farther east, near its headwaters.

So instead of Montgomery enjoying the glory of being first across the Rhine, with the chance to be the first to drive deep into the heart of Germany, lady luck denies him his opportunity. No one could have guessed that the Rhine will no longer be a barrier to the Allied advance. Or that by late March the entire German nation will be ripe for invasion.

To demonstrate how improbable such a scenario seems at the time—from early January through February 6, 1945—the maps that accompanied all the planning at SHAEF at this time estimated by May 1, 1945, Allied forces could only advance *as far as the Rhine.*

✖ ✖ ✖

To explain SHAEF's estimates, we must go back to January 15, when Eisenhower addresses Marshall's question about forcing a quick decision in Europe.

The worst thing that could happen in Eisenhower's view would be a "weak and ineffectual Russian offensive. I do not even mention a lack of a Russian offensive, for without this a quick decision cannot be obtained."[32] If the Germans pull troops from Italy or Norway, Eisenhower estimates they can maintain one hundred divisions. Otherwise they will have only eighty understrength divisions. (A Russian offensive would pull some of these divisions away from the West to the Eastern Front.)

At the moment, SHAEF's division strength numbers seventy-one "with many of the U.S. divisions seriously understrength in infantry." The French divisions are "except for one, of low combat value." If the Allies can close along the Rhine from north to south, Eisenhower will need only twenty-five divisions. If the line remains as it is currently, but with the Colmar pocket destroyed, he will need thirty-five divisions. If the line remains as it is without destroying the Colmar pocket, Eisenhower will need forty-five divisions. (The Colmar pocket is a salient on the west bank of the Rhine between Strasbourg and Mulhouse held by the German Nineteenth Army of eight divisions.) The truly important point is this: "If a markedly successful Russian offensive is maintained and if the Rhine can be substantially closed, our planned strength *should* be sufficient." If more strength is needed, it will take longer to invade Germany and end the war quickly.

Eisenhower ends the cable asking Marshall to read this lengthy memo in conjunction with the ones "I have sent you recently on related subjects."

At the time Eisenhower sends his analysis to Marshall about ending the war quickly, a meeting is held in the Kremlin between Marshal Stalin and a number of high-ranking Allied officers.[33] Eisenhower will be given what he so desperately desires.

After greeting everyone, Stalin makes a surprise statement: "The Red Army is now engaged in a large-scale offensive. This offensive has been prepared for over a month and was then held in abeyance waiting for weather conditions which would favor the employment of the Soviet artillery and air forces." (This confirms Marshall's analysis in his cable to Eisenhower of January 8.)

Stalin says he was aware of the German attack in the Ardennes. He acknowledges receiving a communication from President Roosevelt

32. Personal File Gen. W. B. Smith, SHAEF. Fr Eisenhower to Marshall. No. S-75090. 15 January 1945.
33. Records of CofS. Memo of conference between Air Marshal Tedder and Marshal Stalin on 15 January 1945. No. 380.01/1. Those present: Air Chief Marshal Sir Arthur Tedder; Maj. Gen. H. R. Bull; Maj. Gen. John R. Deane; Adm. E. R. Archer; Brig. Gen. T. J. Betts; Mr. Arthur Birse (interpreter) and Marshal Stalin; Army General Antonev; Mr. Pavolov (interpreter).

asking Stalin to meet with Eisenhower's representative. He had also received from Churchill a telegram in which the Prime Minister asked, not whether the Russians were going on the offensive, but merely if the Russians had planned for an offensive. Stalin says he understood the situation at once and, in view of the Allied need, decided to launch the operation that had been prepared regardless of the weather. From 150 to 160 Russian divisions are involved; they will be attacking for two and a half months, depending on the condition of the ground.

Stalin details the various tasks assigned to the commanders on each front, giving precisely the objectives of each of the four offensives begun around January 12, and he concludes by saying that the ultimate objective is to establish a line on the River Oder. He then adds that he doesn't know whether or not this all will be possible.

Now the Allies comprehend that the Russian offensive is aimed at reaching the Oder, only about thirty-five miles from Berlin. Meanwhile, the Americans and British have not yet crossed the Rhine.

Marshal Stalin then speaks of the problems the Russians have had with enemy agents. He says that the Germans, after they are driven out of occupied territory, always leave behind agents, who are Latvians, Lithuanians, Poles, Rumanians and Ukrainians. No Russians are enlisted as agents. They use Russianized Germans, but no Germans from Germany. The agents are surprisingly well trained and organized, well equipped with radios. The situation cannot be tolerated. The Russians always institute a painstaking cleanup, and he suggests that the Allies will find the same conditions in France and Belgium, particularly in the areas that are Germanized. He says that the cleaning up of enemy espionage in the rear areas is just as important as building up the supplies needed for an offensive.

Then Stalin inquires whether or not Eisenhower believes the claims made by the Germans that they had frustrated the Allied offensives for a maximum of six months to a minimum of two months. His sarcasm is easy to spot.

Air Marshal Tedder replies with a list of contemplated Allied operations.

Midway through the presentation, Stalin interrupts to ask if the port of Antwerp is working. He is told that it is working, and working very well.

Tedder returns to the Allied plans and talks of the problems of crossing the Rhine. According to the engineers, the optimum time for this is between early March and mid-April. He describes the plans for strategic Allied bombing: communications, oil, railroads and waterways. The next strategic consideration facing the Russians and the Allies, he says, is the question of timing operations in the spring when thawing conditions will presumably prevent Russian forces from moving forward, but at the same time would allow the Allies to cross the Rhine.

Stalin interrupts. Is Tedder implying, he asks, that the Allies might have to wait until summer before attacking and crossing the Rhine?

Tedder assures him that the Allies have no intention of letting up. Stalin then reverts to the Ruhr, saying: "Yes, it is obvious. It is obvious to us. It is also obvious to the Germans. Difficult country is not so obvious."

Now Tedder explains SHAEF's plan for a secondary thrust through Frankfurt.

Next, Stalin asks for the Allied estimates of Germany's strategic reserves. On hearing them, Stalin comments on the value of operations around Budapest, which have attracted fifteen German divisions to defend the area. The Germans have twelve divisions south of Budapest, which is very stupid of them because, in his opinion, they now have no trained reserves whatsoever and they cannot move these kids back to the central battlefront.

Tedder says that it appears that the Germans will be hard put to provide mobile reserves in view of the character of the new Volksgrenadier divisions. He then asks the Russians about German ammunition supplies.

Stalin comments that the German concentration of artillery is weak. The largest concentration of guns ranges from fifty to eighty per kilometer. In World War I, he says, German artillery was very good. But in this war they neglected artillery in favor of tanks. Now some deterioration is evident even from their normal artillery standards. The Germans are habitually digging in their tanks. This shows German deterioration and also provides a sign that the Germans cannot think offensively anymore.

Stalin also wants to know if the Allies have faced any new German tanks. He is told, yes, the Tiger. Stalin says the Russians have found them on the Eastern Front, too.

Stalin asks Tedder's opinion of the deterioration of German Air Force personnel. The two conclude that the Luftwaffe is suffering from a lack of training, perhaps induced by a lack of petroleum. Considerable numbers of German pilots are still willing to fight hard, but those who know how to do it are relatively few.

Tedder reverts to the timing of operations and asks Stalin if it would be possible to keep the Hun anxious from mid-March to late May, when weather conditions on the Eastern Front usually preclude large-scale operations. Stalin replies that it will be possible to keep the Germans anxious until the end of May, when the weather will again favor large-scale operations. Stalin says: "I cannot guarantee a large-scale offensive in this period, but we have organized units and provided methods for keeping the Germans stirred up at our strength on the Eastern Front."

According to Stalin, it is a question of dealing short, sharp blows with two or three infantry regiments backed up by heavy artillery support. Stalin also points out that the German communications system permits the rapid movement of German troops between fronts, but he is sure that *nothing* would move from east to west during the spring thaw.

In his opinion, Stalin says that the war will not end before summer. Furthermore, there is no one inside Germany around whom opposition to Hitler can coalesce. Stalin believes the final break in Germany will be caused by famine. The grain-growing regions of Germany's satellites are no longer under German control. The current Soviet offensive will be conducted in the heart of Germany's own granary. Of course the Germans can produce a lot of potatoes, he adds, but he believes they will require grain, which will not be available, to fight a prolonged war. Don't forget, he says, the Germans are frugal and enduring. They have more stubbornness than brains. They should not have undertaken the Ardennes offensive. It was very stupid of them.

Even now, says Stalin, the Germans must be moving troops from the West to the East. If they don't do this, they cannot resist in the East. The weight of the current Red Army offensive is such there is no possible local shuttle of reserves in the East. When fair weather arrives and the German Air Force of two thousand planes is confronted by ten thousand Soviet planes, their situation will become even more unsatisfactory.

He then alludes to the German "prestige garrison" in Latvia. Here, too, matters are working to Soviet advantage. Thirty German divisions are locked up in Latvia. If the Germans attempt to evacuate them, the Russians are in a position to destroy them at sea. Even if they do evacuate, this will release an additional fifty Russian divisions, which can be moved more rapidly than can the Germans for use in the decisive areas of operations.

Stalin next asks about Allied policy regarding strategic reserves.

Tedder explains the situation. He also says that the Allies' hold on Alsace has been weakened to provide reserves and forces for the counteroffensive. In consequence, the Allied hold on Strasbourg might become precarious.

Stalin remarks that this proves everything in this war is important. Strasbourg might not be of great military value. But if the Germans recapture it, the victory would give them great political and psychological capital. In his opinion, the Allies would be wise to maintain at least ten divisions in their strategic reserve. He then reverts to the problem of enemy agents and urges the Allies to be particularly careful in those areas that have had pro-German leanings—especially Alsace and Malmédy.

Stalin is then asked how Russia proposes to exercise military control of occupied territory.

Stalin replies that this is a special task. It needs special forces. Standard Army divisions are not suitably organized or trained for this work. The Russians have solved the problem using special troops (Cheka) organized into divisions. These divisions have no artillery. But they are strong in automatic weapons, armored cars and light armored vehicles. They also have well-developed investigation and interrogation facilities.

The Russians are already using them to deal with all unreliable elements encountered in occupied territories. Stalin considers these troops to be indispensable. He goes on to say that these troops are not organic to armies. Each army is responsible for the security of the area it occupies. It is behind the Army's rear artillery batteries where these Cheka divisions are deployed.

Tedder then asks, on the basis of this current visit, whether Stalin would be receptive to a visit at a later date by General Eisenhower. To this Stalin says he would not presume to invite Eisenhower to come because he did not think it possible for Eisenhower to detach himself from his headquarters for such a visit. Perhaps if a pause in operations occurs, it might be feasible. Of course, any visit such as the one now being made by Tedder's group is always profitable.

Now Stalin inquires about the use of Allied tanks and how they are equipped. After telling him, the delegation asks the same question about Soviet tanks. Stalin replies that his tanks now carry 80-, 85- or 102-mm cannons. The self-propelled guns are 85-, 122- and 152-mm weapons. The heaviest Soviet tanks weigh about forty-five to forty-six tons, and he says he is particularly pleased with the performance of the new 100-mm guns.

Now Stalin says, in effect: "We have no treaty, but we are comrades. It is proper and also sound selfish policy that we should help each other in times of difficulty. It would be foolish for me to stand aside and let the Germans annihilate you. They would only turn back on me when you were disposed of. Similarly it is to your interests to do everything possible to keep the Germans from annihilating me.''

The meeting ends. When Tedder expresses his gratitude for Stalin's reception of this delegation, Stalin replies: ''I am embarrassed by your expression of gratitude.''

This meeting is reported in full because of its extraordinary significance. First Stalin is promising the British and the Americans, although they have no formal agreement with Moscow, that he will keep the Germans busy until mid-May. This gives Eisenhower the chance to recover from the effects of the Ardennes offensive, rebuild his forces, and continue his assault on the Siegfried Line without fear of a major German counterattack. Stalin also knows that Eisenhower now is in his debt.

The size of the Russian Air Force, the armament of the Soviet tanks, the use of Cheka security forces, the overall ruthlessness of Stalin's demeanor, send warning shivers down the Allies' spines. The differing perceptions of how much of a threat Stalin is to the future peace of postwar Europe will cause much friction between the British and the Americans.

Nevertheless, at the moment Eisenhower has much to be grateful for. He cables Marshall to thank Stalin for his help and to congratulate him on his successes. Marshall replies, saying: ''In the future I suggest you approach them in simple main street Abilene style. They are rather cynically disposed towards the diplomatic phrasing of our compliments and seem almost to appreciate downright rough talk.''[34]

And just how do the Americans and British view the war in Europe at this time?

On January 16, 1945, the Joint Intelligence Committee for SHAEF offers a surprising analysis. The battle for France has cost the Germans a million casualties. Once the Germans were able to stabilize the front along the frontiers of Germany, Hitler called for a supreme effort to be made. All available manpower was mobilized to rebuild the Western armies. Still the battle for the Roer and Alsace-Lorraine has cost them another 360,000 casualties. The German Air Force has been totally reorganized. All the long-range bomber units have been disbanded.

---

34. Personal File of Gen. W. B. Smith. No. W-22163. Fr Marshall to Eisenhower. 17 January 1945.

Bomber pilots are being reconstituted as fighter pilots or fighter-bomber pilots or moved into jet aircraft, which are coming into service. The Germans still have a force of eighteen hundred single-engine fighter pilots in the West, which can be used for the defense of the Reich against Allied bombers, or in ground support of German troops.[35]

In other words, SHAEF intelligence doesn't think the Germans are going to roll over and play dead.

A few days after the SHAEF intelligence committee makes its report, the Combined Intelligence Committee makes its report to the Combined Chiefs of Staff.[36] It is interesting to see how the Combined Intelligence Committee adapts itself to the ideas and attitudes of the SHAEF Intelligence Committee.

The conclusion is that while Germany's "functional situation is relatively weak and deteriorating in comparison with the basic military and economic resources of her enemies," Germany still can, at times, "achieve a local and temporary superiority of immediate available strength."

In other words, the Germans can rely on the Siegfried Line as a strong defensive asset. As long as they can sally forth in counterattacks from these positions, they can keep the fighting on the Western Front west of the Rhine. The Germans have more divisions now than they had a year ago, although they are not of the same caliber. The Air Force is numerically the same as it was the previous year. And if the Germans can keep the Allies stopped west of the Rhine, prevent supplies from being brought forward to Allied troops, keep the U-boat war going at full speed and continue the rocket attacks on Antwerp and England, Hitler hopes to wear out his enemies before his own resources are exhausted. This will gain time so that the anticipated dissensions between the Allies can be fully developed. In turn this will negate the Allied goal of an unconditional surrender and Germany can negotiate an acceptable peace.

The Siegfried Line and the Rhine present the two biggest obstacles to the British and American forces. In the east, the Red Army "is sweeping across western Poland. The vital industrial area of upper Silesia is directly threatened. . . . No strong barrier to the Soviet advance exists between the Vistula and the Oder River." This means the Rus-

---

35. SHAEF Joint Intelligence Report for Combined Intelligence Committee. ABC 381 Germany (29 January 1943) Sec 2-B, tab CIC 41/14. 16 January 1945.
36. Report by Combined Intelligence Committee to CCS. ABC 381 Germany (29 January 1943) Sec 2-B, tab CIC 47/14. 24 January 1945.

sians will be in position to launch a decisive attack on Berlin by May or early June.

The report vindicates Eisenhower's analysis that he must close on the Rhine along its entire length before he can drive a stake through the Ruhr, the industrial heart of Germany. It also demonstrates that the Americans and the British must keep their bickering to a minimum and not become distracted from the goal of achieving unconditional surrender.

In retrospect it is surprising just how conservative—and wrong— the Joint Committee's estimates are about how the battle against the Siegfried Line will proceed. The Committee evaluates battlefield conditions on January 16, February 1 and February 6, 1945. The best the Allies will do, the Committee believes, is to advance only as far as the Rhine by the first of May.

t is easy, fifty years after the fact, to criticize the SHAEF Intelligence Committee estimates for early 1945 as being too conservative. At the time, the Germans are fighting savagely on the northern flank against the Canadians and the British. Hitler is desperate to hold on to the areas west of the Rhine River, which, because of its value as a supply route and a defensive line, means holding at the Siegfried Line and the Roer and Maas Rivers, too. The Roer dams will be opened by the Germans to flood the northern areas across which the Allies plan to attack. The scenario is grim. It is impossible to predict the events that will overtake current SHAEF planning.

Needless to say, the SHAEF Intelligence Committee estimates and Eisenhower's proposed broad-front strategy do not please the British. They apparently have not learned from the disaster at Arnhem that the Germans still can control a localized battle. Nor have they comprehended the defeat Hitler endured by striking foolishly in the Battle of the Bulge. They will present their case at a final series of meetings between Allied leaders, which are in the works. First there will be a British-American meeting from January 30 through February 2, 1945, at Malta. Next a meeting from February 4 through 11 between Churchill, Roosevelt and Stalin at Yalta.

In a preliminary conference at Malta, the British military chiefs drive home the point that they do not wish Eisenhower to wait until Allied forces have closed on the west bank of the Rhine for its entire length before attempting to cross the river. In fact they are so worried that they tell Eisenhower's Chief of Staff, Walter Bedell Smith, that they are afraid that Ike won't even attempt to cross the Rhine—even in the north—until all the areas west of the river have been cleared.

Smith cables Eisenhower that he is telling the British that while Ike intends to close the whole length of the line, SHAEF is not going to hold up operations until this has been accomplished and that Eisenhower intends to seize a bridgehead wherever possible. The British want this in writing. Chief of Staff Marshall suggests that Ike amend his plan, called SCAF 180, to satisfy the British.[1]

The following day Eisenhower cables Smith that he agrees with the rewording expressed in Smith's message. Eisenhower tells Smith to assure the Combined Chiefs that he will seize crossings over the Rhine in the north as soon as feasible and without waiting to close the Rhine throughout its length. Eisenhower also pledges to advance across the Rhine in the north with maximum strength and ''complete determination immediately the situation in the south allows me to collect necessary forces and do this without incurring unnecessary risks.''[2]

Only now will the British accept the overall concept of a broad-front advance. Fate, however, will render the British negotiations meaningless.

At almost the same time the British are haggling about crossing the Rhine, the first elements of Marshal Georgi K. Zhukov's army of more than a million men are suddenly arriving on the banks of the Oder River. The Americans and British haven't yet reached the Rhine and the Russians are already within only thirty or forty miles of Berlin. Thus, when arriving at Yalta on February 4, President Roosevelt laughingly tells Marshal Stalin that the President has made bets with various officers aboard the cruiser on which he traveled about whether the Russians will capture Berlin before the Americans retake Manila in the Philippines.[3]

Stalin wryly remarks that he is sure the Americans will seize Manila before the Russians take Berlin. He knows that hard fighting is taking place on the Oder River line. (Manila falls on March 3; Roosevelt loses.)

Stalin has other, more weighty, matters on his mind. He must clear his northern flank in Pomerania along the Baltic coast. He also knows of the German attack coming in Ukraine. It will be a last-ditch stab by the Germans to retain the vital oil fields of Lake Balaton. By beating

---

1. Personal File of Gen. W. B. Smith. No. Cricket 18. Fr Smith at Malta to Eisenhower. 30 January 1945.
2. Personal File Gen. W. B. Smith. Fr Eisenhower to Smith (attending Cricket conference at Malta). 31 January 1945.
3. In their 186th meeting, the Combined Chiefs of Staff agree to accept the following dates for ending the war with Germany: (a) earliest date: 1 July 1945; (b) date beyond which war is unlikely to continue: 31 December 1945. (ABC Europe 5 August 1943) Sec 1-D. Memo for the record. 6 February 1945.

the Germans to the punch, rearranging his forces and going on the offensive, Stalin's forces on the Third Ukranian Front will overwhelm the Germans, forcing them to retreat in great disorder, which infuriates Hitler. Suddenly, in a massive reversal of fortune, by early April, Russian troops will also be in the outskirts of Vienna.

It is at Yalta that Roosevelt swallows the bitterest pill. The war has progressed so far that the Allies must now formally agree to military zones of occupation in postwar Germany.

In a letter from the Acting Secretary of State to the Secretary of War written shortly before Yalta, Ambassador Winant in London reported that the Soviet government had approved the EAC agreements on control machinery for Germany and the protocol on zones of occupation in Germany. Winant had been authorized on January 25 to give formal notification of the American government's approval of the control machinery for Germany. However, the U.S. has held off officially approving the EAC agreement on zones of occupation.[4] At Yalta, Roosevelt must face reality: the British and Russians still demand the zones they proposed earlier.

Roosevelt has no choice but to acquiesce and accept the zone of occupation he doesn't want.

But no agreement is made about who will capture Berlin.[5]

✼ ✼ ✼

With the Russians so close to the German capital, back at SHAEF various elements of the planning staff have started rearranging their operational schedules. For example, the commanding general of the Fifteenth Army, which is supposed to occupy Berlin under early RANKIN (but now called ECLIPSE) conditions, is now told to draw up new

---

4. ABC Europe (20 August 1943) Sec 1-F. Memo for the record signed with initials LHS. 12 February 1945.

5. The U.S. Navy's analysis of the Magic Diplomatic intercepts, prepared by OP-20-3-G50 for the Chief of Naval Operations, says bluntly: "The Ambassador to Portugal interpreted Roosevelt's willingness to make certain concessions to Stalin on the Polish Question as indication that America intended to follow Russian lead in European matters. In return the Soviet may have planned to enter the war against Japan. All agreed that Stalin had been the 'big shot' of the conference and that it had been his victory. . . . [Otherwise] the Japanese [foresee] the collapse of Germany with a strongly dominated Russian postwar Europe." The only optimistic sign was that "America and Britain have gained the first steps toward a five-power alliance which is many times more valuable." Notes on the Crimea (Yalta) Conference (PSIS 400-5) SRH-070.

plans on the assumption that the Russians will enter Berlin ahead of the Allies.[6]

The SHAEF Joint Intelligence Committee has determined that the Russians have achieved such overwhelming success that the Eastern Front has become the overriding concern of the German High Command. At least eight German divisions, including the whole of the Sixth SS Panzer Army and some six hundred to seven hundred aircraft, have left the West for the East. It is believed that this will bring the Russian advances to a halt east of Berlin.[7]

Some two weeks later, the SHAEF Joint Intelligence Committee releases a remarkable report. It concerns "the strategy of the Nazi Party and the ability to resist of such forces who will continue to obey the Party, on the assumption that, in the east, Berlin has been captured and the Russians are ready to continue their advance."[8] The report says there is some "slight evidence of a determination to hold an inner fortress in the Austrian Alpine provinces of Vorarlberg, Tirol, and Salzburg" should northern Germany fall to advancing Allied forces.

"The capture of Berlin in itself would *not* lead to a general collapse of the Nazi regime within a short space of time," the report continues. ". . . The loss of the Ruhr might well have more serious repercussions on the [German] will to resist, both military and civilian, than the capture of Berlin. . . . There are a number of recent reports which suggest that Hitler and the Nazi leaders intend to establish their headquarters in the Salzburg and Berchtesgaden area. . . . To sum up, we consider that the possibility of the Nazi leaders attempting to hold the southern defense zone and the kind described above should be taken into account in planning and that Allied operations to clear it will probably be necessary in the event of either Hitler or Himmler remaining a free agent. . . . The greatest danger . . . is that the Nazi leaders, by continuing to hold out, will help to identify the Party as the focus of national resistance and thus perhaps ultimately preserve the Nazi tradition as the focus of national resurgence." (Emphasis added.)

This extraordinary document refutes Churchill's vehemently stated

---

6. The original code name RANKIN had been changed to TALISMAN. But the name TALISMAN had then been compromised by a breach of security. The final term for the speedy invasion of Germany should there be a general collapse of the government has become ECLIPSE.

7. ABC 381 Germany (29 January 1943) Sec 2-B, tab CIC M/Info #40. Report by SHAEF Joint Intelligence Committee (signed by K. W. D. Strong, J. H. Lewes, C. M. Grierson, R. Collins). 1 February 1945.

8. ABC 381 Germany (29 January 1943) Sec 2-B. Report by British members of the Joint Intelligence Committee. JIC Memo 32. 18 February 1945.

reasons for capturing Berlin that will be the eye of the storm among the British and the Americans in the months to come. It also sets the tone for the upcoming debate within SHAEF as to how Eisenhower can best aim his forces to achieve the stated strategic goal of destroying Germany's ability to wage war, and the unstated goal of blocking Russian movement westward.

Back in Washington, staffers in Counter Intelligence have enjoyed a field day. At long last their operation will have a major impact on the war, as the purple prose in their internal memos proves. In one report, Col. D. G. White opens the floodgates. "Not enough weight is given to the many reports of the probable Nazi last stand in the Bavarian Alps," he asserts. "The Nazi myth, which is important when you are dealing with men like Hitler, requires a *Götterdämmerung* at least of all the present public figures in the Party, SS and extreme Wehrmacht elements. It may be significant that Berchtesgaden itself, which would be the headquarters of such a stand, is built on the site of the tomb of Barberosa, who is believed in German mythology to be likely to return from the dead."[9]

White goes on to say that if the Bavarian redoubt could maintain itself for six months to a year, in that time it could direct and nourish underground resistance among the German youth. He also points out that the Germans have had lots of experience with underground movements in countries they have occupied, so they should be effective in organizing a resistance-type operation in occupied Germany. He also says that he is looking forward to discussing the matter at length with British intelligence specialist Furnival Jones the following day.

At SHAEF, Eisenhower spells out his thoughts to Bradley. The letter is written on heavy vellum paper and typed single-space. It starts simply: "Dear Brad: I am sending this letter to you personally in view of its secrecy . . ."[10] The Supreme Commander spells out, step by step, his latest plans for crossing the Rhine and capturing the industrial might of the Ruhr. He advises Bradley that a similar letter has gone to Montgomery in the north and Devers in the south. The letter will get Eisenhower in trouble with Montgomery later on. Eisenhower previously promised to give Montgomery all the support he can—according to the agreement reached at Malta via the Cricket messages—and later, Mont-

---

9. Memo from Col. D. G. White, GS, G-2(CI) to Colonel Sheen (head CI) and Lieutenant Colonel Macleod (civil security). GBI/CI/CS091.4-1 (Germany). Underground movement in Germany. 12 February 1945.

10. 12 Army Group Record File #371.3, Military Objectives, vol. 6. Letter from Eisenhower to Bradley. 20 February 1945.

gomery will try to hold Eisenhower to his word when events are forcing Eisenhower quite rightly to revise his thinking.

The following day, in Washington, a memo from an Allied source in Switzerland (identified to only a few as being the Swedish military attaché in Bern, allegedly based on reports from his colleague in Berlin) states: "The Nazis are undoubtedly preparing a bitter fight from the mountain redoubt." Defending troops will be in units of one thousand to four thousand men at first. Later they will be joined by "some of the toughest Waffen SS and other crack SS divisions when the regular organized resistance ceases. Hitler himself stands at the head of the redoubt army, with Himmler as Chief of Staff. . . . Some of the fanatics believe they can hold out for at least two years when the war-weary Allies will agree to an armistice, allowing the nucleus of the Nazi regime, strengthened by the myth of moral victory, to survive and organize a new totalitarian regime and a new war."[11]

This report is so detailed, and sounds so much like Stalin lecturing the Allies in Moscow a few weeks earlier, that one wonders whether or not the report is disinformation spread by the Russians. The original warning about the Alpine Redoubt comes from Magic, however, and the Japanese reports from Berlin will constantly harp on the theme. There will be reports about moving major departments of the German government to other cities because Berlin is no longer functioning as the capital of Germany. Before long, as we will see, the concept of Hitler's last stand will take on a life of its own. Furthermore, in the coming forty-five days, only one week longer than it took the British and American invasion forces to subdue the island of Sicily, an area of Germany twenty times larger than Sicily will be overrun, and the entirety of the Nazi forces remaining beyond the Rhine will be dismembered and destroyed.

✖ ✖ ✖

Meanwhile, from behind the scenes, Magic has been playing a major role in what the Allies are accomplishing.

Back on December 19, Ambassador Oshima revealed that the German counterattack through the Ardennes—the Battle of the Bulge— is "strategically an adjustment and only tactically an offensive. As originally conceived," he tells Tokyo, "its aim was to deal a fatal blow

---

11. GBI/CI/CS/091.4-1 (Germany) Underground Movement in Germany. 21 February 1945.

to the American First Army or, failing that, at least throw the enemy's operations into confusion. The Germans would be fully satisfied if they could drive back of the Maas [River] the American forces which have penetrated into Germany itself."[12]

The Magic Summary of the following day also contains reassuring news for the Allies.[13] On December 23, Oshima sends a report to Tokyo in which he synthesizes comments made to him by his "usual contact" (on the 22) and Gottfriedsen of the Foreign Office (on the 21). The Germans are telling Oshima that they are trying to keep everything secret, because the Allies are underestimating the strength of the German attack.

"Thus far the offensive has been toward the west," Oshima tells Tokyo. ". . . I gathered . . . that the British and American forces in the Aachen area and to the north have been picked as the general objective. As I have already reported [on December 18, Oshima reported that the Germans would turn their offensive to the northwest, which they did], the Germans may be planning an attack not only on the American First and Ninth Armies, but also the British and Canadian forces as well. Both men said that the acquisition of territory was not an objective and there would be no deep penetration into France . . . they confined themselves to saying that possibly the attack might turn in the direction of Antwerp."

The Germans had been surprised to capture many American soldiers "before they could put their shoes on." Also surprising was the American front lines were "the entire enemy strength" and there were no reserves. The Germans were being cautious about the future; they fear a counterattack by superior motorized forces. Also, they estimate that the Russians will launch a large-scale offensive in the East "at any time."

These Magic intercepts explain why, at the very highest levels of command, the British and Americans view the battle differently. In Washington, neither Marshall or Stimson believe that Antwerp is in any danger. As veterans of World War I, both men remember well the Ludendorf offensive of March 1918. Then the German attack was forced to retreat, and eventually the Germans had to sue for peace. The worst that can happen now, they believe, is that the city of Liege might fall to the Germans, and the U.S. First Army might be shattered, which would cause the fighting in Europe to last longer.

The Battle of the Bulge is fluid. Army historian Forrest Pogue re-

12. SRS 1527, 25 December 1944.
13. SRS 1528, December 26 1944.

calls that Marshall believes the best way to help Eisenhower is not to bother him. When members of his staff ask how Eisenhower can best be helped, the Chief of Staff orders that no messages be sent to SHAEF by the Pentagon unless he approves them. This appears to be the right decision, because Eisenhower has more than enough on his plate at the moment. He doesn't need to be micromanaged by the Pentagon, which is half a working day behind him in real-time terminology.[14]

In the next series of Magic reports, Oshima tells Tokyo that the Germans will not advance beyond the Meuse. Especially when they are facing the loss of Budapest to the Russians.[15] Meanwhile the Japanese reveal their most recent plans for taking over French Indochina, and the French governor Decoux is promising continued cooperation.[16]

On January 8, Oshima reports to Tokyo about another conversation with von Steengracht about the continuing battle for Bastogne.[17] The Germans are attempting a second time to sever the corridor into the besieged town, "but the operation is costly and may not be successful. . . . We Germans should be entirely satisfied by the heavy losses inflicted on the enemy. . . . [Their] weakness [on the Western Front] lies in the fact that, since they had no reserve forces in the rear, they have been pulling out troops from various points along the entire front and have also been bringing up forces which had been besieging the German garrisons in the coastal ports. Taking advantage of that situation, we Germans, as you know, are regaining ground in all sectors from the Saar on south. Furthermore, since we apparently still possess reserve forces, other attacks will also be possible."

From the German point of view then, as expressed by Magic, one can understand the logic of Eisenhower's thinking. Without adequate reserves, Eisenhower must keep his broad front moving forward, using mobility to prevent the Germans from massing for counterattacks. One

---

14. In the book *Eisenhower: At War 1943–1945* by David Eisenhower, one gets the impression that Eisenhower thinks that Marshall abandons him at this time, which is not the case. Eisenhower never cables Marshall about the Ardennes or asks advice, especially about transferring American troops from Bradley to Montgomery's command. Since both men are reading the Ultra and Magic reports—Eisenhower receives his information at least five hours before Marshall—the two could not consult in real-time language. Marshall's patience in the matter is proper. However, tension between the two men is rising. The issue will be a speedy end of the war in Europe, which Marshall wants, versus Eisenhower's cautious approach of the moment.
15. SRS 1535, 2 January 1945. It is reported that at a conference on the morning the battle for Bastogne begins, Patton remarked that the Germans should be allowed to advance as far as Paris so the Allies can "chew them to pieces." To this Eisenhower replied that the Germans should not be allowed to reach the Meuse.
16. SRS 1538, 5 January 1945.
17. SRS 1544, 11 January 1945.

can also see just how relieved Eisenhower had to feel with the news from Moscow that Stalin understands how perilous the situation is on the Western Front and how necessary the Russian attack from the Vistula to the Oder is becoming.

Now Oshima drops important strategic news. He reports that "Chancellor Hitler believes that at present the Western battlefront should be emphasized. . . . He wants to avoid the error of conducting operations on two fronts. Therefore . . . a determined campaign to retake Budapest will not take place. [Hitler is giving Budapest to the Russians and, by January 27, they will be only twelve miles from the city.] "However," Oshima continues, "the Chancellor hopes to be able to bring about a fundamental change in the Budapest area as well."

This warning of an impending German attack near Budapest, and the oil fields in the Lake Balaton area, allows Stalin to set a trap. All he has to do is follow the travels of the Sixth SS Panzer Army from west to east to know where the spearhead of the German assault will come from.

Despite the near panic caused at the time by the German counter-offensive in the Ardennes in the Anglo-American press, half a century later historians view the battle as being a mere temporary setback for the SHAEF forces. This is precisely the view Baron Oshima expresses to Tokyo on January 11, 1945, following his conversation with Ribbentrop four days earlier.[18] According to the German foreign minister, once again Oshima reports that the German attack was not designed to be a decisive one and its results will be limited. But at least it has checked Eisenhower's plans for the invasion of Germany and has stabilized the Western Front, which is true. What is false is Ribbentrop's assertion to Oshima that the operation will have a beneficial effect for "the great German offensive to be undertaken in the future." As has been pointed out earlier, in the Ardennes Hitler weakened his strategic reserves beyond recovery.

What Ribbentrop foresees are the splits in the enemy camp coming out into the open. He tells Oshima: "If Japan and Germany stick together, fight hard, and prepare to meet any change in the situation, an opportunity [apparently for a peace move, the analysts in Washington insert] will surely come which can be used to advantage." Meanwhile, the chances for a negotiated peace between Germany and Russia have not improved. According to Ribbentrop, Hitler is being particularly cautious, and he urges Japan to "exercise the utmost care

---

18. SRS 1548, 15 January 1945.

in her handling of the matter, [because] a wrong move might destroy the German people's will to fight.''

The next day, Oshima gives Tokyo more intimate details on the results within Germany after the abortive attack on Hitler's life of July 20, plus a detailed lineup of the new German commanders in the field as a result of Hitler's latest reorganization of the German Army.[19]

In Moscow, Ambassador Sato is telling Tokyo that he is rather pessimistic about extending the current Russo-Japanese neutrality pact.[20] This is followed by another report from Oshima that Germany is facing a dire crisis on the Eastern Front.[21] According to Oshima's "usual contact man" the new German defense line from Silesia southward is given precisely along with the expected fallback positions. The Germans are crediting the Soviet success to the number and quality of Soviet tanks and also the Russian superiority in aircraft and artillery. Perhaps more important is that "Russian advance units [have started to] carry their own fuel, ammunition, food, etc., so that large tank units can advance in all directions after breaking through the German lines, and this has resulted in the developments of new tactics.'' The speed of the Russian advance is also preventing the Germans from mounting local counterattacks.

On January 27, 1945, the analysts in Washington bring to Marshall's attention an extremely gloomy forecast for the war from Japan's point of view. It is signed by the Vice Chief of the Army General Staff, Lt. Gen. Hikosaburo Hata.[22] The report is aimed at a time span covering the first six months of 1945 and is sent as a "personal" circular to all the Japanese military attachés around the world. According to the analysts in Washington, the forecast "displays an unrelieved pessimism on all aspects of the war which is entirely without precedent in available traffic out of Tokyo.''

Among the reports predictions are:

1. The Americans will probably attempt to invade Japan proper "about the middle of the year and the possibility of an even earlier landing must not be discounted.''
2. The Allies will land on the Malay peninsula during the spring or summer.

---

19. SRS 1549, 16 January 1945.
20. SRS 1554, 21 January 1945.
21. SRS 1559, 26 January 1945.
22. SRS 1562, 29 January 1945.

3. As China increases her war strength, she will begin counteroffensives against the Japanese.
4. The developments of the war and Allied "political maneuvers" will engender in all the countries of Greater East Asia, except Manchukuo, an increasingly uncooperative attitude toward Japan.
5. [On or before April 25] Russia will abrogate her neutrality pact with Japan. She may, for a while, remain neutral. But "if developments in the Greater East Asia war make it favorable for her to do so . . . Russia is very likely to commence armed warfare against Japan in the latter half of this year."
6. As for the fate of Germany: "We cannot but forecast that by this summer or autumn the worst will have come to Germany."

The gloomy nature and the high rank of its originator starts a discussion in Washington between those who believe the military in Japan is about to collapse and those—such as Stimson and Marshall—who believe the Japanese will fight to the end. The analysts note for the record that Japanese diplomats are not nearly as pessimistic as Hata. Yet, by virtue of Hata's military experience (he was military attaché to Moscow in 1934–35, Assistant Chief of Staff of the Kwantung Army and now is Vice Chief of the General Staff), he is in the best possible position to evaluate Japan's military future.

It is the last paragraph of Hata's forecast that truly reflects the beliefs of the Japanese Army. This Marshall knows. And it must worry him. For Hata says: "The war is about to enter upon that phase in which we shall face the enemy in a life-and-death struggle. The Empire, beset with difficulties which will henceforth grow increasingly grave, preserves unaltered her conviction of inevitable victory and devotes to this decisive struggle her every grain of strength, that she may emerge victorious."

The old soldiers in the Pentagon understand that the blunt directness of Hata's language promises that the invasion of Japan will cost the Americans dearly. The estimates of American casualties in the event of an assault on the home islands start rising higher and higher.

The month of February 1945 is remarkable in that the Magic Summaries demonstrate a growing divergence of opinion between the Japanese military and its diplomats. The diplomats seem to be unable to retain their objectivity. They report the horrors of the war, but they do not seem to comprehend the reality of what they witness. The military attachés, on the other hand, comprehend that the war is lost and they are preparing for the final battle.

The Magic Summary of February 1 has Ambassador Oshima reporting that the Soviet Army is throwing 260 divisions into its attack.[23] However, according to German estimates, Oshima says the Russians will not be able to reach Berlin in a single thrust. (The MIS reports to Marshall that they estimate the Russians are using 300 divisions in the attack, but they make no comment about whether or not the Soviets will reach Berlin.)

Twice more Oshima warns about the German attack on the Eastern Front.[24] He also explains to Tokyo the risks associated with the plan, saying: "The success or failure of the operations planned for the Eastern Front will be the key to the course of the entire European war." He also points out that the weakening of the German Army in the West invites another risk: that of an Anglo-American offensive. For the moment he isn't concerned about the Western Front. The Allies have not yet crossed the Rhine. Nevertheless, on his own authority he tells Tokyo that he is taking certain prearranged security measures, including the burning of some of his cryptographic materials, in the event of the fall of Berlin.

The following day, Oshima tells Tokyo that Berlin is having problems handling the refugees from eastern Germany, that coal is being severely rationed, so is gas and electricity, plus there's a spreading curtailment of transportation facilities. Also, preparations are being made for the defense of the city.[25] Oshima acknowledges that the German people are depressed, but he says they are "maintaining extraordinary composure" and that there are no signs that a "state of political disorder exists or that the Germans have lost their fighting spirit."

By mid-February 1945, Oshima is telling Tokyo that the Allied attack in the West on the Nijmegen area cannot be considered a full-fledged offensive.[26] "It is clear that Germany is taking a 'risk,' " says Oshima, using the English word, "on the Western Front in order to fight a decisive battle in the East." As a result of the Battle of the Bulge, which stopped the Anglo-American assault, he continues, "it is

---

23. SRS 1565, 1 February 1945.
24. SRS 1566, 2 February 1945, and SRS 1570, 6 February 1945.
25. SRS 1571, 7 February 1945.
26. SRS 1577, 13 February 1945.

thought that there is not one chance in ten thousand that the German lines on the Western Front will collapse as a result of the expected [Allied] offensive.''

Now one can comprehend the shock that will pierce every German's heart when the news is released in about two weeks' time that the Allies have captured a railway bridge across the Rhine at Remagen.

Toward the end of the month, the Magic Summaries reveal that Foreign Minister Ribbentrop is launching an appeal to England and America to make peace with Germany.[27] The appeal is made on February 16 to the German minister in Dublin, Hempel. He is instructed to get the message across to ''important English and American personalities.'' Ribbentrop makes no specific reference to terms, but stresses the point that Germany may soon be forced to make a choice between East and West. If America and England are not willing to make terms, Germany will be forced to negotiate with Russia.

The analysts in Washington believe Ribbentrop also sent the same message to chiefs of the German missions in Madrid, Lisbon and to the Vatican.[28] But on February 20, for no given reason, Ribbentrop chokes off Minister Hempel from acting by saying, ''I request that you wait for further instructions from here.''

At the month's end, in Moscow, Foreign Minister Molotov completely fools Ambassador Sato.[29] The two men meet on the twenty-fourth, and Sato suddenly tells Tokyo that ''Molotov as usual was amiable and smiling and I was conscious of the warmth of his personality throughout the entire interview.'' Thus, Sato goes on to reassure Tokyo that all is well with the Russo-Japanese Neutrality Treaty, even though the Anglo-Americans at Yalta and elsewhere ''have vigorously pushed their schemes to drag Russia into the war against Japan. I believe, however, that the Russians rejected those demands and still adhere to the position that Russo-Japanese relations concern only those two countries and are not subject to outside interference. . . . I do not expect any change in Russia's attitude.''

Sato believes that it will be possible to negotiate the renewal of the treaty between the two nations, and he tells Shigemitsu what he believes Japan should be willing to concede to Moscow, point by point. One reads the Magic Summaries and can imagine Molotov playing Sato, one the angler and the other the trout. When Sato finally com-

---

27. SRS 1587, 23 February 1945.
28. SRS 1590, 26 February 1945.
29. SRS 1591, 27 February 1945.

prehends how he has been duped by the canny Russian, his humiliation will be total, and tragic.

Meantime Japan is planning the complete takeover of French Indochina.[30] The Japanese Supreme Council for the Direction of the War finally acts, and on March 1, it decides to seize control of the territory unless the French governor general agrees to specific Japanese demands. If the French accept the Japanese demands, the administrative machinery of the French Government General will continue to operate, but some French troops will be disarmed. If Japanese demands are rejected, the French administration will be set aside, all French forces disarmed, resisting elements will be jailed and all French citizens will be placed under "restrictions." As the analysts in Washington view the news, the latest policy represents a substantial victory for the Japanese Army in terms of who controls the government in Tokyo.

Meanwhile, on February 19, Vice Admiral Abe, Japan's representative to the Tripartite Pact Commission in Berlin, and Naval Attaché Kojima, have sent Tokyo a long report on Germany's "overall situation."[31] The analysts pull specific excerpts out of the long text for Marshall's attention: "It appears that the German Army is planning in the near future to stake everything on a large-scale counterattack [in the East], based on the Prenzlau area (60 miles NNE of Berlin) and the Cottbus area (62 miles SE of Berlin) . . . the chances of success are poor."

The report continues, saying that if the attack fails, Germany's "ability to conduct the war will be lost" and there will be danger of a "complete collapse, except for a certain amount of guerilla warfare." Should the Russians approach Berlin, "Hitler and the government officials would remain in the capital to the end and fight on with determination. . . . It is not known whether Hitler plans to commit suicide when he has lost all hope of a German recovery; if he should, German strength in the East would collapse rapidly. For the present, however, there is every evidence that the troops have the situation under control. . . . Now, more than ever, no country would seriously consider political entanglements with the present Nazi regime. . . . The principal German idea is that Germany will probably soon be forced into total surrender, without [any possibility of] a choice between Russia and the Anglo-Americans." (This report casts doubt on the concept of an Alpine Redoubt, but it receives little attention.)

As of the first of March 1945, Marshall and Eisenhower are pre-

---

30. SRS 1593, 1 March 1945, and SRS 1597, 5 March 1945.
31. SRS 1596, 4 March 1945.

sented with some serious choices to make. It appears that Berlin will fall to the Russians. Will Hitler commit suicide in a last-ditch battle in Berlin, or will he transfer his command post and his remaining forces to an Alpine Redoubt? There is no doubt in either man's mind about Stalin's intention to seize as much of Europe as he can while also spreading the message of Communism throughout the world. So, if the Soviets are to take Berlin, how should the Allies maneuver in the coming months to keep the Russian army from overrunning Europe? Last, what is the limit of American power in the European war when so many American troops will have to be put on ships and sent to the Pacific for the invasion of Japan? Stalin already knows that there are no strategic reserves behind the Allied front lines. How will he play the game?

It is easy to predict that both Germany and Japan are teetering on the brink of collapse. Yes, there is a schedule for the invasion of Japan. But first Germany has to surrender unconditionally. Given that British and American forces are still bogged down west of the Rhine, one of the greatest natural barriers in Europe, who can guess the future with any accuracy? Will the Americans even be able to reach their zone of occupation before the Russians?

The intangibles facing Marshall and Eisenhower pose one of the most formidable problems of the entire war.

14

ooking at strategic planning for the final drive across the Rhine and into Germany from the point of view of Chief of Staff Marshall in March 1945, suddenly the war in the Pacific presents unexpected problems. Always it has been the agreed policy amongst the British and the Americans that the war in Europe will have precedence over operations against Japan. Events in the Pacific, however, are progressing to a point where this agreement about Europe is about to be stretched to the breaking point.

Even more important, President Roosevelt has returned from Yalta, weary, sick to near death, his condition hidden from the public by a press that refuses to report what it is witness to. One of the most poignant accounts about Roosevelt's health at this crucial time is found in Ambassador Bullit's book, *For the President*,[1] in which he quotes the recollections of Mr. Offie, who says: "I saw Mr. Roosevelt the last time personally on board the S.S. *Quincy* in Algiers Harbor. He received me flanked by his daughter, Anna. He looked ghastly, sort of dead and dug up. The same reaction was had by Doug MacArthur, who had come down from Paris with his chief at that time, Mr. Caffery, as well as by Kirk, our Ambassador in Rome, who knew Mr. Roosevelt well from college days. Harry Hopkins was carried off the S.S. *Quincy* on a stretcher and, accompanied by Chip Bohlen, was flown to Marrakech to get strength enough to be flown to the U.S. Pa Watson, who died en route to the U.S., was under an oxygen tent, and another principal aide was in the sick bay with a bad case of influenza. As Kirk said [to me], 'C.O., this is really a ship of death and everyone respon-

---

1. Edited by Orville H. Bullit (Boston: Houghton Mifflin, 1972).

sible for encouraging that man [FDR] to go to Yalta has done a disservice to the United States and ought to be shot.' "

Thus, a small band of men—Stimson, Marshall, King, Leahy, Eisenhower (none of whom are elected officials)—must assume the burden of prosecuting the war. (Vice President Truman never receives a briefing on the war until he assumes the presidency.[2]) This means that the war in Europe must be ended as quickly as possible, and with a minimum loss of American lives. It also means that instructions will have to be sent Eisenhower about how best to end the war quickly and link up with the Russians.

Historians with an oversimplistic view still claim that Eisenhower made all his own decisions about the fate of the war in Europe. The best way to demonstrate that this is not the case is to present what is called, when I worked for *Newsweek,* a "tick-tock," or a chronology of events that details day-to-day, hour-by-hour events. The author believes that, in the pages that follow, by creating this chronology of official, but hitherto unreported documents, the general public can, for the first time, see the effect of Marshall's planning on the outcome of the war in Europe.

At the moment, however, a quick review of major events in the Pacific is in order:[3]

> ✖ January 1945. Adm. William F. Halsey flies to Pearl Harbor to meet Gen. Douglas MacArthur and to solicit comment from MacArthur about the invasion of Japan. The conferees decide tentatively that two invasions of the Japanese home islands will be necessary to bring about the unconditional surrender of Japan.
>
> The overall invasion plan of Japan is called DOWN-FALL (in the same manner that the overall invasion of Europe was denominated OVERLORD). The DOWNFALL plans call for two separate operations, four months apart, that will entail a truly massive use of ground, sea and air power: *twice* as large as the landings in Normandy. The first invasion is called OLYMPIC and is designed to secure an eight-thousand-square-mile foothold on the southern

---

2. The author's father, Col. E. Brooke Lee, former Speaker of the Maryland House of Delegates and a leader of the state's delegation to the Democratic convention of 1944, played a behind-the-scenes role to help Truman win the vice-presidential nomination.

3. The author is indebted to Robert T. Crowley for his help in locating people who were involved with Pacific Planning for the U.S. Joints Chiefs and who verified the facts reported herewith.

coast of the island of Kyushu. OLYMPIC will be launched on November 1, 1945.

Four months later, on March 1, 1946, a second invasion, called CORONET, will be launched. This will be the final, all-out attack, centered on Honshu, the most heavily populated of the Japanese home islands.

✱ February 1945. At a meeting of Stalin, Roosevelt and Churchill at Yalta, Stalin agrees publicly to intervene against Japan within ninety days of the German surrender. As demonstrated by the Magic Summaries, the Japanese have reason to fear an attack by Russia. Over decades the Soviets have endured the results of the surprise attack by the Japanese on Port Arthur, the destruction of the Imperial Russian fleet in the Tsushima Straits, the Japanese annexation of Korea, the Japanese occupation of Manchuria, plus the bloody battle of Nomonhan. Marshall knows that Stalin's promise is not an idle one. The intervention of the Soviets against Japan could threaten the balance of power in postwar Asia.

✱ February 19, 1945. U.S. Marines land on the heavily defended island of Iwo Jima. They secure the island on March 16, but only after suffering horrific casualties.

✱ March 3, 1945. Manila is occupied by American forces.

✱ March 9–10, Tokyo. Low-level, incendiary bombing of Japan's capital destroys one-quarter of the city's buildings. More fearsome is the number of dead: eighty thousand. Another 1 million are made homeless overnight.

Knowing that American troops will attack Okinawa on April 1—about the same day Eisenhower will unleash his final assault on Germany—Chief of Staff Marshall must also face the gloomy predictions about the cost of invading Japan. The first attack, OLYMPIC, will be made by 776,700 assault troops, or all the combined forces of the U.S. Marines, supported by Sixth Army infantry, on dozens of small beaches extending more than 250 miles around Kyushu's southern shores. The estimate for U.S. Marine casualties in the attacking force was nearly 100 percent; one former Marine told the author that the Corps would have ceased to exist as we know it today.

Operation CORONET, which would be twice again the size of OLYMPIC, will require twenty-eight divisions and support elements (approximately 2 million men). The majority of these troops will come from the European theater. They will be American troops. No British are included.

In the year 1945, the U.S. armed services number approximately 12 million, or about 10 percent of the general population of the time (120 million). Based on the thirty percent ratio of casualties already experienced on Iwo Jima (buttressed later by the casualty figure on Okinawa), the worst projections are from 1 million to 1.5 million casualties in a ninety day invasion of Japan. The mean casualty figure is 1.25 million, or approximately 1 percent of the general American population. In terms of the manpower pool of military-aged males, more than 15 percent of all American able-bodied males alive in 1945 will be killed or wounded invading Japan.

Such casualties are unacceptable to everyone in the Pentagon. When the time is ripe, the White House will have to be consulted.

As Marshall reads the daily Diplomatic Summaries about Japan's intentions to fight to the death, a shiver has to run up and down his spine. Another problem he must face is that in the weeks following Yalta there has been no change in instruction from his commander in chief, President Roosevelt: America is engaged in a war in which "unconditional surrender" is the only acceptable ending. Thus the planning staff at the Pentagon concludes the war can only be won by the invasion of Japan. (It is important to note that the secret of the atomic bomb is so closely held, the majority of the planning staff have no knowledge of the bomb's being built.)

As explained to the author, the conventional plans for invading Japan call for the destruction of every major factory, city, railroad, seaport, "or any goddamned structure that would be the least bit useful to the Japanese," as Robert Crowley confirms it.[4]

The oldest American battleships will anchor off the invasion sites and march the fire of their heavy-caliber guns up and down, back and forth, like plowing fields. (Instead of leaving for fresh ammunition, the shells and powder will be brought to the battleships: seven-hundred-plus rounds at a time.) The newer, faster battleships will parade around the home islands bombarding as far inland as their guns can range. Meanwhile, some fifteen hundred B-29 bombers will attack cities and towns from a low level day after day, night after night.

---

4. So great is the destruction of Japan to be that American invasion forces will carry with them enough locomotives, rolling stock, steel rails and ties, to rebuild the entire Japanese railway system. This vast inventory of equipment is actually built and shipped to the Pacific in readiness of the invasion. After the war, the major part of this material, according to Robert Crowley, is dumped in the Pacific.

"It is doubtful," says Robert T. Crowley, "that any Japanese historian, who has focused on the closing days of the war, can ignore the fact that the Twentieth Air Force's firebombing campaign, which is under way at this time, and which kills hundreds of thousands of Japanese civilians, incinerates thirty-eight populous cities [with one hundred forty more cities on the target list], is far more devastating to Japan than the two atomic bombs we dropped. The Japanese have never considered that we were prepared to wipe out their entire civilization, their cities, their population down to the last man, woman and child, if it meant saving a million American casualties in an invasion. But that is the truth of the matter."

The horror of the idea—a million American casualties to invade Japan versus the choice of destroying Japan's entire civilization!—is not lost on Marshall. He looks toward Europe and recognizes that, since Yalta ended, Eisenhower has also been left swinging in the wind. He, too, has no instructions from the Commander in Chief about what to do in Europe. Should Eisenhower capture Berlin? Marshall knows that Roosevelt has expressed himself orally on this. The Commander in Chief wants America to capture Berlin. But he has never said it on paper, turning his wishes into an order. It is also apparent that he probably never will do so.

It is obvious to Marshall and others that Roosevelt is dying and that is why, at the end of March, the Chief of Staff will provide Eisenhower with detailed instructions about how to end the war in Europe.

These instructions will provoke a real change in strategy and a bitter fight with the British—for which they have always blamed Eisenhower.

✖ ✖ ✖

In the first days of March, the British strategy for Europe still demands that Montgomery will spearhead the primary attack on Germany. One has to give the British credit for trying to be the tail that wags the dog. But eventually the dog, in this case the Americans, becomes annoyed. Finally it becomes furious at a British military system that is working hand in glove with politicians who wish to restore prewar monarchies and colonial-style governments to power after World War II.

Fifty years after the fact, one might as well say it straight from the shoulder: Many American commanders in the field resent the British. As for the British, they know Europe well, but are ignorant about America and American customs. Much of the discord can be traced directly to the historical background of the American military. According to the American Constitution the American Army is made up of militia that returns home after the shooting ends. As of 1941, America never had a large standing army. The Americans naively believe that politics and soldiering are distinct and separate. In the British Army, however, the high-ranking officer is urbane, well-educated and believes in pursuing his nation's political goals through military action.

As the G-3 (operations officer) for General McLain's XIX Corps, Col. George B. Sloan explains the prevailing American view at the time: "The British always were thinking of war in political terms. Every conference we had with them had a political undertow, a secret agenda, and they wiped the floor with us. Here I am at the time, twenty-six years old, not long out of West Point, and I had never had a single course in geopolitics or European history. We were engineers, artillery, infantry. None of us were trained in politics. It was a difficult time."[5]

It may seem somewhat petty today, but other, more senior American officers are upset by American concessions over the years to an ally who appears at best to be "superior" to the men and women from "the revolting colonies." (It was not unknown for a British officer to remark to a newly arrived American: "How nice of you to join us at last.") These American concessions go back to the earliest days of the U.S. campaign in Africa. Then there is Eisenhower's granting operational command of the OVERLORD invasion forces from June until September 1944 to Montgomery. Next are the bitter negotiations for zones of occupation in postwar Europe. Other American commanders believe Eisenhower made unnecessary sacrifices in terms of American lives and material so that Montgomery could make a disastrous blunder in his MARKET GARDEN operation at Arnhem. Last, Eisenhower's transfer of American forces to Montgomery during the Battle of the Bulge infuriated a number of American commanders, most notably Bradley.

It is easy to understand why then, with the British again wanting everything—men, material, weapons, fuel—to be given Montgomery for the final drive into the heart of Germany, when American troops

---

5. Interview with the author in the Pentagon, January 1963. After the war, a group of young, up-and-coming West Point veterans like Sloan pushed for educational reform at West Point. Today's cadets are well-grounded in the background that Sloan lacked in 1945.

on the front lines now outnumber the British four to one, that the American commanders object. Put it another way: in early March 1945, the British want fifty divisions of American and French troops to sit, twiddling their thumbs, while Montgomery invades Germany using only thirty-five divisions of troops—Americans and British—all operating solely under English control.

Of course, it is Eisenhower's job to solve this kind of intramural jealousy. He has done brilliantly to date without having any formal directives to follow. But it is an almost impossible job.

There still remains the most difficult question of all: what to do with Berlin? Capture it if possible, or forfeit it to the Russians?

Eisenhower knows the Allies have formally ratified the zones of occupation at Yalta. Yet Churchill is constantly reminding Eisenhower that these zones are not binding on military operations. In other words, from the Prime Minister's point of view, if one expects to exercise control of a specific zone, one had better capture that zone. As will be shown, the implication now becomes the hidden agenda of Churchill's diplomacy: capture as much of Germany as possible, including Berlin, then try to renegotiate with the Russians. Many Americans believe that Churchill is hoping he can negate the problems created at Tehran and Yalta, rearranging the deal with Stalin over Poland, a bitter disappointment that is being used by the Polish government in exile to threaten the Prime Minister's political future.

However, Churchill's concept of war and diplomacy doesn't sit well with a small-town, Kansas-bred soldier like Eisenhower, a man who has always abided by West Point's honor code and who has served his country all his life without thought of running for political office. In the absence of instructions from *his* commander in chief, Eisenhower, like Marshall, must approach the situation as being a question of defining the proper military objectives for the Allied forces. This means extracting British political objectives from the equation. It also means the Americans are taking over the European war.

Another vital factor is the pressure from Marshall on Eisenhower to end the war quickly, with a minimum loss of American lives, in preparation for invading Japan. In all his ruminations to Eisenhower at the time, Churchill never shows any real understanding about this particular matter.

The new American strategy will frustrate Churchill. It nearly drives him frantic. To the Prime Minister, and the British, Europe means more than Japan. Again and again, Churchill will badger Eisenhower about Berlin and what Churchill believes the Allied goals in

Europe should be. The resulting friction between the two men and their governments means that the "special relationship" will be exacerbated but, fortunately, never ruptured.

✖ ✖ ✖

Reading the Magic Diplomatic Summaries in the order they cross Marshall's desk, one sees that on the day the Americans capture the railway bridge across the Rhine at Remagen, March 7, the Germans give Ambassador Oshima a particularly gloomy report on the war. However, the American seizure of the bridge—a vital wound—is mentioned not at all.[6]

According to Oshima, probably *before* Berlin is aware about Remagen, von Steengracht tells him: "For the past two or three days the war situation in both the East and the West has been extremely unfavorable for Germany. On the Western Front the Anglo-American forces have reached the Rhine on a rather broad front, while on the Eastern Front the Russian Army has succeeded in enlarging its breakthrough in the Pomerania area by means of an overwhelming number of tank detachments. Indeed, the intention of the Russian Army appears to be to destroy the German Army in that area and to advance to Stettin Bay, in order to have its right flank covered during the main offensive [against Berlin].

"In the sector east of Berlin the Russians do not yet hold an adequate bridgehead [indeed the largest, in the vicinity of Kientz (forty-eight miles ENE of Berlin) is no more than one or two miles deep, although nineteen miles long]. In order to launch an offensive from that sector, therefore, they will have to enlarge their bridgeheads. Judging from the general picture, our military authorities have concluded that the Russian preparations for their offensive will be completed after the twentieth of this month."

The analysts in Washington note for Marshall's attention that the Associated Press for this date reports that German broadcasts on this day say that Marshal Zhukov's forces are launching an all-out offensive. But German communiqués for the day mention only attacks designed "to gain positions for major operations."

---

6. SRS 1601, 9 March 1945. This is only the second-most important item of the day in the Diplomatic Summary, the first being the latest news about the proposed Japanese takeover of French Indochina.

Oshima's report continues: "On the Western Front, the German Army will take advantage of the Rhine River and will be able to obstruct its crossing for a considerable period by holding operations." (The analysts in Washington note for Marshall: "The 1st Army's crossing at Remagen was effected on the 7th.")

"Thus," Oshima continues, quoting von Steengracht, "conforming to this pattern of a two-front war, the best plan is to make use of the [word missing] of time thus gained and reach a decision with the Russian Army, using as many troops as possible. The German command, while recognizing the difficulties caused by the lack of weapons and the inferiority of the Air Force (the aid given the Russian Army by the Anglo-American air forces must be taken into account), will probably carry out shortly a decisive action with vigorous resolution, since this is the last opportunity. However, in view of the situation, I do not know whether the German Army will go forth and challenge the enemy to a decisive battle, or wait for the enemy to sally forth and then destroy him."

The third most important item of the day for Marshall's eyes is the first prediction that the Germans will abandon Berlin. This is made in a message of March 5, but not translated until March 9, by Shozo Sato, the Berlin representative of the Japanese Home Ministry. According to Sato, Japanese nationals other than diplomatic staff have been evacuated "to a place one hundred kilometers southwest of Berlin." He also comments: "It is believed that the abandonment of Berlin will take place after another month."

The following day, another earlier report by Oshima is given primary ranking for Marshall's attention.[7] On the fifth, the Ambassador and his military attaché, Lieutenant General Komatsu, plus a number of other Japanese officials, attend a luncheon given by the Military Attaché Section of the German Army. Among the Germans is an unidentified general described only as the "head of the Far Eastern Section of the German High Command," and Colonel von Tippelskirch, the head of the Attaché Section.

According to Oshima, the German plan for a counterattack to relieve Russian pressure on Berlin is being shifted to the area southeast of Berlin. The Germans believe that Soviet preparations for a direct assault on Berlin "will be completed in one or three weeks [and] the Germans apparently have to forestall this by taking to the offensive themselves." (The analysts note for Marshall that this conforms to what

---

7. SRS 1602, 10 March 1945.

Oshima has been told by the Germans and reported to Tokyo in the past.)

Oshima also reports that German munitions production is being hurt by a lack of liquid fuel, transportation problems and the coal shortage. However, fuel for German tanks and trucks at the front is "being guaranteed."

As far as reserve forces go, Oshima claims "there is still no shortage of reserves. Since the young officers and men now being called up have received a thorough Hitler Youth training since the outbreak of the war, they are fully trained as military reserves and their morale and quality is good."

The Germans estimate that the Russians are using ten thousand to eleven thousand tanks on the front line. And they estimate the total number of tanks the Russians have at present is thirteen thousand. (At this point in the text, the analysts in Washington note that "if the figures on Russia's tank strength include self-propelled artillery, they are in general agreement with [our] MIS [Military Intelligence Service] estimates.")

As for the strength of Russian infantry, Oshima reports that on the Eastern Front there are some 450 divisions with an average strength of six thousand men, although some crack divisions have nine thousand men. (Again the analysts in Washington remind Marshall that MIS estimates there are some 430–460 Russian infantry divisions on the Eastern Front with an average strength of approximately seventy-five hundred men.)

From this stunning intelligence, for the first time one can comprehend what worries the American planners. The Russians have nearly 3 million infantry, plus nearly thirteen thousand tanks (including mechanized artillery) on the Eastern Front. Will this vast horde of Russian troops, which outnumbers the SHAEF forces by about more than two to one, stop at some agreed-upon line of demarcation? Or will the Russians sweep on, breaking through the thin British-American front lines, and drive westward to the English Channel? Churchill might want to seize Berlin, advance eastward and then try to renegotiate with Stalin. But does it make sense to antagonize such a formidable foe?[8]

---

8. In *Eisenhower at War* by David Eisenhower (New York: Random House, 1986), on page 485, the author says there are 2.7 million Americans in Europe. Of this number 437,000 are Air Force and 740,000 are attached to Comm-Z. Of the remaining 1.233 million (*sic*), slightly more than 50 percent are combat soldiers. Later, on page 525, David Eisenhower says that after the Battle of the Bulge, the typical American division was operating only on 70 percent combat strength. This author believes that if these figures are correct, they indicate that the Magic/

Before an answer to these questions can be found, the Vice Chief of the Japanese Army General Staff sends from Tokyo, on March 8, a circular reviewing Japan's overall situation to the military attachés stationed around the world.[9] The analysts in Washington pick out the most significant items for Marshall's study. A large part of the circular, they note, consists of affirmations "that Japan is making full preparations for the 'decisive phase of the war' and is taking all the necessary 'countermeasures' to meet her growing difficulties." Two major factors influencing Japan's actions come to light. First because of shipping losses, transportation is now Japan's greatest problem. Second, the Japanese now recognize that the southern areas of Asia that they occupied earlier "are as good as lost to them and [they] are making every effort to build up a self-sufficient war economy in Japan, Manchukuo, and China."

There are two statements in the circular that indicate the Japanese Army is worried that some elements of the population are not entirely willing to carry on the war. The circular speaks of "an element of unrest." In another instance, it mentions that "throughout the homeland there are elements which we will have to watch carefully lest they endanger the conduct of the war."

In Washington these statements will be given far greater weight than they deserve by those who believe a peace with Japan can be negotiated either before the Americans invade or before the atomic bomb is dropped. As we know from the Diplomatic Summaries, however, the Army and Navy are in complete control of the Japanese population. If there are any elements of the citizenry that might wish to negotiate a peace, the military already knows who they are and preparations have been made to contain their activities.

The truly significant part of the circular—that the military is preparing for the "decisive phase of the war"—is another warning to Washington that the Japanese Army will fight to the end.

Meanwhile, the sixth SS Panzer Army shows up spearheading a German counterattack named Spring Awakening around the northern end of Lake Balaton. Historians have noted that the Russians were warned late in February or early March that a German counterattack is coming. By March 15, the thirty-five German divisions involved are in

---

Ultra intercepts proved more valuable than anyone has ever dared acknowledge, and one can understand Friedman's statement about the Americans committing smaller forces yet winning major battles.
9. SRS 1607, 15 March 1945.

headlong flight—without Hitler's permission. The Fuehrer is so angry about matters that he orders Dietrich's Waffen-SS troops to remove their distinctive and highly valued divisional insignia.

On March 15, Ambassador Oshima confirms rumors in the press that Field Marshal von Rundstedt has been relieved of his command on the Western Front.[10] Oshima reports that the change of command was "on account of illness." (There is no mention of the real reason: Hitler's displeasure that the Americans captured the bridge at Remagen.) Oshima also confirms that Field Marshal Kesselring will most likely be the replacement.

Another question arises at this time. Was a decision made by the German High Command to hold fast on the Eastern Front and allow the Allies to seize Berlin, join hands with the Germans and save them from surrendering to Moscow? Despite the claims made by some American officers interviewed by the author that they believe this was the case, no documentary proof has been found that substantiates the claim. The author has reviewed all the orders issued by the Army High Command on the Western Front (OKW) for this period. There is not the slightest hint that the Germans intended to allow the Americans or the British to seize Berlin in a walkover.[11]

But let us return to Ambassador Oshima's message to Tokyo of March 15 in which he says: "Although it is difficult to discover information about the time, the plan, and the scale of the decisive battle which the German Army is planning to fight on the Eastern Front, I am summarizing for your information the impressions which we have received from recent conversations with the Germans.

"So far as the date of the German counterattack is concerned, it appears that considerable time will be needed for preparation, and there are some who say that they have been led to believe that it will take place about the middle of April. Although it is realized that the danger to Berlin will thereby be increased, *it is being said that Berlin is making preparations to defend itself to the death* and that, if the Russian forces cross the Oder and advance on the capital, Germany will take advantage of that situation and *attempt to annihilate the Russian Army.* A considerable number of people are saying this might not necessarily be impossible for Germany to achieve." (Emphasis added.)

Let us pause for a moment and consider the significance of

---

10. SRS 1609, 17 March 1945.
11. Copies of these translated orders are still in the author's possession. They can be reviewed by qualified interested parties upon written application.

Oshima's words. Following the capture of the bridge at Remagen, Eisenhower and Bradley can now visualize the Americans spearheading the attack on Berlin. And when the Americans reach the River Elbe in early April, Eisenhower and Bradley will then discuss the cost of storming Berlin, which Oshima says is a city preparing to "defend itself to the death." The two American commanders will guess the cost of capturing the German capital to be around one hundred thousand casualties.[12] They will also be aware that their troops are already deep into the Soviet zone. If the Americans abide by the terms of the zones of postwar occupation, they will have to turn over to the Russians every foot of ground they have conquered. To waste more American lives on soil that will be occupied by the Soviet Union seems senseless.

There is another consideration. Should the Russians be allowed to attack Berlin and reap vengeance for what the Germans have done to Russia? Some historians have claimed that Eisenhower wanted the Germans to be punished, but there is no evidence to support the argument.

What does appear to have passed through the minds of many American—and certainly some British—commanders is this: The Allies need time to prepare themselves to repel a possible Soviet attack through the Allied lines toward the English Channel. With Berlin being an obvious Soviet target, why not let the Russians and the Germans fight it out on the streets of the city? House-to-house fighting invariably produces dreadful casualties. Hopefully the Russians will suffer such heavy losses they will be unable to attack us, too.

A goodly number of American commanders, whose troops were on the Elbe by mid-April 1945, expressed this concern to the author. These commanders were convinced at the time that the Russians would try to move westward by force. Their stories of how they impressed the folly of such an attempt upon the Russians are fascinating.

Let us return again to Oshima's report to Tokyo of March 15, in which he continues: "Everyone is unanimously agreed that German operations on the Eastern Front should take the form of a crushing battle. However, the original plan to launch a counterattack from the Pomeranian area has been frustrated, and as a result the offensive is

---

12. Bradley told Cornelius Ryan that he gave Eisenhower this estimate immediately after seizing a bridgehead across the river Elbe on April 12, 1945. "Certainly I did not expect to suffer one hundred thousand casualties driving from there [the Elbe] to Berlin," said Bradley. "But I was convinced that the Germans would fight hard for their capital. It was in Berlin, as I saw it, that we would have suffered the greatest losses." Bradley first revealed this figure in his memoir, *A Soldier's Story*, but he never said *when* he gave this estimate to Eisenhower until speaking with Ryan. See *The Last Battle* (New York: Simon & Schuster, 1966), page 321.

now scheduled to be launched from the south only. The thought now seems to prevail that Germany may attack from Upper and Lower Silesia and endeavor to encircle the Russian forces on a large scale." (This apparently is how Marshall's warning to Stalin shortly after Yalta went awry; events moved faster than Oshima could report them.)

Oshima continues his report saying that Germany is suffering because of the inferiority of her air force and tanks and because of the damage to her transportation system by continuous enemy air attacks. "Although these difficulties are recognized," he says, "there is still quite a strong feeling of unwillingness to admit defeat, and there are some who say the advance of the Russian Army deep into German territory provides a golden opportunity for a battle of annihilation, so the fighting spirit is still high.

"As to the situation on the Western Front," concludes Oshima, "it is considered regrettable that a crossing on the east bank of the Rhine [at Remagen] should have been permitted, even if only in one sector. While such a crossing is not to be taken lightly, both because of its military and political significance, it is still considered that Germany's most urgent need is to fight a decisive battle on the Eastern Front. Accordingly, the Germans say that it is inevitable that various sacrifices should have to be made on the Western Front, but no one is pessimistic because of the war situation there."

For the first time, then, we can see how Marshall formulates the strategy he will propose to Eisenhower. Oshima is giving Marshall the solution by revealing that the Germans are going to send their best troops to defend Berlin along the Oder River line. The Germans are prepared to sacrifice territory in the West if necessary. For Eisenhower the primary task will be exploiting the bridgehead at Remagen and moving Allied forces rapidly eastward toward the Elbe.

A few days later, Oshima reports again to Tokyo.[13] He says that on March 17, he gave an "informal dinner" for the Military Attaché Section of the OKH, the Army High Command, and that Genobst. Guderian, the OKH chief of staff, attended. (On January 5, the analysts in Washington note, Oshima was told that Guderian had command of the entire Eastern Front in addition to his duties as OKH chief of staff.) It is Guderian whose armored techniques brought about the collapse of France in 1940 in only twenty-seven days, and he nearly accomplished the same in Russia. Oshima's summary of Guderian's "very frank" remarks carries great weight in Washington and at SHAEF.

---

13. SRS 1613, 21 March 1945.

According to Guderian, Oshima reports that the Russians will launch their next offensive either toward Berlin or Bohemia and Moravia. Since Russian tank forces have been pulled back from the front lines, and the Germans don't know where they are, it's difficult to predict exactly what will happen. Most likely the first attack will be aimed at Bohemia and Moravia. Then Berlin. The quality of Soviet infantry has declined. But so has the quality of the German soldier. What has been bad is that the Germans have been retreating for two years and the front-line troops have had to depend on Germany's building new weapons instead of repairing those damaged on the battlefield. (The Germans had found in the past that they could repair 75 percent of the tanks damaged in an attack.) The truth is the Germans are running short of tanks and cannons. The Air Force lacks not only planes but fuel.

Oshima quotes Guderian as saying: "The Panzerfaust is very effective and is responsible for one-third of the [enemy] tanks destroyed. Since this weapon [a shoulder-fired weapon] demands soldiers who are brave enough to draw close to the tanks, it would surely be effective in the hands of the Japanese Army and I recommend its use."

Apparently Washington has been worrying that the Japanese would acquire this weapon. The analysts note that Hitler had given the Japanese the plans and manufacturing rights for the Panzerfaust the previous fall. But they determine "it is probable that no models or plans have reached Japan."

Meanwhile, from Tokyo, Foreign Minister Shigemitsu discusses at length with Japanese ambassador Tani in Nanking the possibility of having Chiang Kai-shek use his good offices to create a peace between Japan and the United States.[14] Previously Tani had thought that they could affect a peace between China and Japan. Then Tokyo could persuade the Chinese to declare war on England and America to protect East Asia from "Anglo-American aggression." Now, Tani believes, even if Chungking (the Nationalists) could somehow be persuaded to join with Japan against England and America, the latter would still win. Thus, the way to protect East Asia is to arrange a general peace. Nothing will come of this diplomatic claptrap, however. (How Tani could delude himself into believing what he is telling Tokyo is beyond the writer's comprehension.)

At the end of March, for the first time in a recorded conversation with a Japanese official, a prominent German gives way to what the

---

14. SRS 1615, 23 March 1945.

analysts in Washington call "complete despair."[15] The German is Vice President Puhl of the Reichsbank, who meets with Kojiro Kitamura of the Yokohama Specie Bank on March 22 to discuss "quite delicate matters." Puhl is quoted as telling the Japanese: "The fate of Germany is really hanging in the balance. . . . The German people are very weary . . . they have abandoned themselves to despair. . . . The chances are the end of the war will come all too quickly."

Kitamura says, "Puhl explained how insignificant and meaningless the Volkssturm is, and lamented that we Germans are a Hell people [*Hoellenmensch*]. . . . The personnel capable of building a new Germany is totally lacking, and judging from those facts, we may say that the advent of a 'new Soviet Germany' is almost certain. I do not believe that the siege of the Nazi Berchtesgaden will last very long."

Puhl refers to reports that Hitler might get into a plane loaded with bombs and blow himself up over the Baltic. In which case, he says: "Among the German people there are a million persons who still worship the Chancellor, and if he should destroy himself in that way, they would make him a hero and a god."

It is then Puhl reveals a great secret. The Reichsbank has constructed a secret vault at Weimar (137 miles southwest of Berlin) and has already moved its gold bullion and documents there. The town of Weimar suddenly becomes an important target for the Americans. They want the gold and the records.

During the first days of April, Oshima reveals to Tokyo that Hitler personally put an end to Ribbentrop's peace feelers to the West.[16] Just a month earlier, Ribbentrop had instructed German minister Hempel in Dublin to pass on to "important British and American personalities" a lengthy argument that England and America should make peace with Germany to forestall a German-Soviet peace. On March 22, the *London Daily Telegraph* published a report that Irish prime minister De Valera had transmitted a German peace proposal to U.S. minister Gray, who promptly denied the matter.

According to Oshima, Ribbentrop's latest proposal is based on the premise that America and England might turn on Russia after defeating Germany. Thus, Stalin might be willing to consider an alliance with Japan and Germany in order to oppose America and England. Ribben-

---

15. SRS 1623, 31 March 1945. This Summary contains approximately one hundred pages on the railroads of North China–Mêngchiang, which the Japanese consider to be a vital part of their economic and military machinery.
16. SRS 1624, 1 April 1945; SRS 1626, 3 April 1945.

trop proposed on March 19 that the Japanese float this balloon in Stockholm with the Russians. But when Oshima meets Ribbentrop again on March 27, the Foreign Minister says that Hitler is still convinced that Germany must "rely on military results till the bitter end." Oshima asks if he can present the arguments in behalf of such an alliance in person to Hitler. Ribbentrop concurs.

The following day, however, Ribbentrop tells Oshima that he has seen Hitler again and that, as a result, he is obliged to ask Oshima to do nothing more. He says that Hitler is completely opposed to the idea of approaching Russia, especially when no peace with Russia appears possible. Oshima asks Ribbentrop if Hitler still opposes peace with England and America. The answer is that the Chancellor "categorically refuses such a thing."

Thus Marshall and Eisenhower know the current state of Hitler's thinking. It is virtually certain that the Germans will fight to the end.

Two more important events occur in the Magic Summaries. Early in the afternoon of April 5, Ambassador Sato sends word to Tokyo that at 1 P.M. Foreign Minister Molotov had asked the Japanese ambassador to see him at three o'clock.[17] Later in the day, Sato sends a paraphrase of the stunning document he is handed at the meeting—the Soviet government's formal notice of abrogation of the Neutrality Pact—plus an account of the conversation. The analysts in Washington note that Japan had no advance warning of Russia's move, and that the fall of the Koiso cabinet in Japan, which was announced about two hours before Sato saw Molotov, is not related to the meeting. They also point out to Marshall that at first Molotov, whether deliberately or otherwise, makes Sato think that Russia regards the pact as no longer being in effect. Later, Molotov agrees that the pact would not expire for another year. When Sato expresses hope that neutrality can be maintained between the two countries, Molotov replies that (1) "while the pact remained valid Russia's attitude would have to be set accordingly," (2) as to the period beyond, Russia would listen to anything Japan might have to say.

The following day, Sato sends Tokyo his notice of resignation.[18] "For the past three years," Sato tells the Foreign Office, "I have been serving without interruption in Russia. It is true during that time I was able to keep Russia faithful to the Neutrality Pact, but now I have received notice of its abrogation. Nothing more regrettable could have

---

17. SRS 1629, 6 April 1945.
18. SRS 1630, 7 April 1945.

taken place. May God grant peace to the heart of the Emperor. I certainly have disappointed the hopes of our people, and have no excuse to offer to the Government. It must have been a lack of effort on my part that has brought things to such a pass, alas, just when the war situation is so critical. I feel very deeply that I cannot avoid responsibility for this development, and I therefore humbly tender my resignation.''

One can empathize with Sato in this matter. He has been thoroughly fooled. Even so, Tokyo will keep him in his post.

The Magic Summary of April 6 also reveals that in Japan the military is ordering the evacuation of thousands of houses in parts of southern Kyushu in preparation of invasion. At least twenty-two cities and towns are affected. The significance of all this is not lost on Marshall. The Russians have served notice that they will attack Japan sooner rather than later. What will happen to the industrial areas of Manchuria and Korea? Meanwhile, the Japanese are preparing to defend the beaches suitable for invasion.

Time is running out.

The war in Europe must be ended soon.

✖ ✖ ✖

Given the vital Magic intelligence that we now know to be in the possession of Marshall and Eisenhower, one must compare the information derived from Magic against the official records of the time. Doing so gives one a new understanding of previously confusing events.

For example the actual dates of ratification for the zones of occupation by the Allies are spelled out only in a letter from Joseph C. Grew, the Acting Secretary of State, to Secretary of War Stimson.[19] Grew's letter is unusual in that it starts out by saying: "Thus far the members of the European Advisory Commission [EAC] have recommended to their governments only three documents." The three papers have now been approved by all the Allies, and Grew lists the dates on which formal notification of the three governments was received.

The first document is the unconditional surrender of the Axis powers. Next there is the protocol between the U.S., U.K. and the USSR

---

19. ABC Europe (20 August 1943) Sec 1-F. Letter from Joseph C. Grew, Act. Sect. State Dept. to Henry L. Stimson. 28 February 1945.

on the occupation of Germany and the administration of "greater Berlin" as amended on November 14, 1944. According to Grew's letter: "This protocol was signed by the members of the European Advisory Commission (EAC) on 12 September 1944. . . . Notification of the President's approval of the protocol as amended was received by the Department of State on December 4, 1944. Pending the conclusions of conversations between British and American Military authorities with regard to the zones, however, it was not until February 1, 1945, in a telegram sent from Malta by the Secretary of State that Ambassador Winant [in London] was authorized to inform the EAC of this government's approval of the amended protocol. The official protocol of the British Government was announced on December 5, 1944, and the Soviet Government made known its approval February 6, 1945."

Thus we can understand Marshall's and Eisenhower's concern about the politics of ending the war in Europe. It is not until February 1945—four months before the war actually ends—that they know positively what part of Germany the American forces are supposed to occupy after the war's end.

Then there is the question of what the Russians are planning. On the first of March, as SHAEF forces approach the Rhine from the west, Eisenhower cables his representatives Deane and Archer in Moscow.[20] "In view of the great progress of the Soviet offensive," Ike writes, ". . . with Oder bridgeheads established and German road nets now available . . . [will there be] a lull in [Russian] operations mid-March to mid-May?" Ike also wants to know "whether there is likely to be any change in the extent to which the Soviet action will hold German divisions on the Eastern Front?"

A few days later, from Washington, Gen. John E. Hull, the Chief of Staff for Operations–Pentagon, sends a cable to Deane in Moscow asking a vital question that was forgotten in the negotiations of the EAC.[21] Now that Yalta has proven to be an unhappy experience for the British and the Americans, someone has realized that Berlin will be inside the Soviet zone of occupation. The city will be garrisoned by the three Allies after the war, but there is no guarantee of access for the American and British troops who will be stationed there. Now Hull wants Deane to "present the agreement regarding freedom of transit

---

20. 312.3-1 Corresp & Communication with the Russians. Cable from Eisenhower to Deane and Archer (Moscow). No. FWD 17471. TOO 011910A. 1 March 1945.
21. ABC Europe (20 August 1945) Sec 1-F. Memo: Fr General Hull to Deane in Moscow. 3 March 1945. (Concurred to by the British on 9 March 1945.)

across zones of occupation to the Soviet General Staff.'' Says Hull: ''United States Forces in zones of triparted zones of occupation will require regular access by air, road and rail to the main U.S. zones.''

It had been difficult negotiating a similar deal with the English. With the Russians it turns into an international crisis called the Berlin Airlift.

On March 6, the day before Bradley's forces seize the railway bridge at Remagen, Eisenhower receives a reply to his questions about Soviet intentions. Archer and Deane have seen General Antonov, Chief of Staff of the Red Army. He asks that the following response be passed on to Eisenhower: ''Soviet troops will continue the present advance as long as weather permits. If the weather gets very bad, the Soviet troops will continue operations of a local nature for the purposes of tying down the German forces in action on our front.''[22]

Now Eisenhower has confirmation that the intelligence in the Magic Summaries is correct. German forces are moving to the Eastern Front. The Russians say they will keep the Germans occupied there. Eisenhower could not ask for better cooperation from Antonov. The chances for a successful drive by the British and American forces through the Ruhr is assured.

Two days later, Eisenhower cables Marshall in Washington to announce one of the most significant actions of the European war: ''Last night, First Army captured railway bridge intact at Remagen. Bradley is rushing troops to secure adequate bridgehead with the idea that this will contribute greatest possible threat as [a] supporting effort for [the] main attack.''[23]

The significance of this message lies in the idea expressed: that— at this time—Eisenhower is not yet thinking of using Remagen as the major jumping off point for Bradley's thrust across Germany. Eisenhower says the main attack will still be made by Montgomery's forces in the north. A problem will develop, however. The U.S. Ninth Army, which is under Montgomery's command, has also closed up to the Rhine as of March 6. But, as said earlier, the remainder of the British Twenty-first Army Group will not reach the west bank of the Rhine until March 10. Worse, Montgomery's forces in the north will not be

---

22. 312.3-1 Corresp & Communications with the Russians. Cable from Archer and Deane (Moscow) to Eisenhower. No. MX-23082. TOO 062335A TOR 070731A.
23. 381 Post Overlord Planning, vol. 3, (January–March 1945). Cable from Eisenhower to Marshall. No. FWD 17645 (SCAF 223). TOO 081234A.

ready to cross the Rhine until the night of March 23/24, some two and a half weeks later.

Meanwhile, much of Montgomery's thunder is being stolen. Patton's U.S. Third Army catches the German defenders asleep at Oppenheim and crosses the Rhine on March 22, the night before Montgomery does. Then, immediately after Montgomery crosses the Rhine in the north, the U.S. Third Army makes two more crossings at Boppard and St. Goar on March 24/25. Next, the U.S. Seventh Army also crosses the Rhine near Worms on March 26; the French First Army crosses the Rhine near Germersheim on March 31. Thus, instead of having only Montgomery's Twenty-first Army Group across the largest natural barrier in Germany as originally planned, Eisenhower suddenly finds all his forces are across and ready to advance. This development demands a new strategy.

✖ ✖ ✖

To go back to the seizure of the bridge at Remagen on March 7: Two days after the event, H. R. Bull makes notes of his phone conversation with General Bradley at 7:30 P.M. following ''our discussion of plans with General Eisenhower and informed [Bradley] as follows: [Eisenhower] wants the Remagen bridgehead firmly held and developed to secure it with a view to an early advance to the southeast. He authorizes the employment of five divisions for this purpose immediately. We will give you further details later concerning the plan to be developed and timing. General Bradley stated that this message fits into just what he is now planning and what he has done to date. He indicates he may eventually need one more division. He stated that he plans to push the bridgehead out ten kilometers from the bridge, to include a section of the Autobahn.[24]

Meanwhile, the SHAEF Intelligence Staff is reviewing its options in the light of recent developments.[25] The first pages of the current Weekly Intelligence Summary focus on the successes of the Soviet Army on the Eastern Front. The Germans are losing all along the Baltic coast. Pomerania is falling to the Russians. All along the Eastern Front, from north to south, the Russians are steadily forcing the Germans to

---

24. 381 Post Overlord Planning, vol. 3 (January–March 1945). Memo for the record by H. R. Bull concerning his phone conversation with General Bradley. 9 March 1945.
25. SHAEF Intelligence Weekly Intelligence Summary (for week ending 11 March 1945).

pull back. Meanwhile, "the mystery of the assault on Berlin continues unclarified," says the report. "Moscow has not yet given any official notice of the great operation, but the Russian radio has hinted, and German sources have placed Zhukov's spearheads over the river at Seelow, twenty-eight miles from Berlin."

The Intelligence Summary says that on the Western Front, Allied success has been such that the enemy's overall strength "again sank during the week from 5–10 percent." At least twenty-four German divisions have been reduced to "skeletons, and in some cases to mere staffs or to nothing at all."

As for current developments in Berlin, the Summary claims that ground sources in Berlin have been reporting the preparations for the defense of the city. Citizens, refugees, everyone, are being drafted into labor gangs working on an outer perimeter, a second in the suburbs and the third within the heart of the city. "Berlin is well suited for defense purposes," says the report. "Sources agree that the outer defenses are based on the natural barriers of the chain of lakes and small rivers, at a radius of thirty to fifty kilometers from the center of town. . . . In the heart of Berlin, preparations for street fighting are well under way. Ground sources report the construction of innumerable bunkers, pillboxes, and underground shelters, and the mining of all important buildings. Air cover shows concrete antitank walls, probably with firing positions, at all bridges, street crossings, and other strategic locations. . . . It is evident that the German High Command has no intention of relinquishing Berlin without a bitter struggle, and that every effort is being made to convert the Capital into a formidable fortress."

Next comes the analysis of the so-called Alpine Redoubt. "Theoretically," declares the SHAEF Intelligence Staff, "the last stronghold of Germany consists of the Alpine blocks. . . . Defended both by nature and by the most efficient secret weapons yet invented, the powers that hitherto guided Germany will survive to organize her resurrection. . . . In fact, the main trend of German defense policy does seem to be directed primarily at the safeguarding of the Alpine zone. . . . Air cover shows at least twenty sites of recent underground activity . . . for stores and personnel. . . . The evidence indicates that considerable numbers of SS and specially chosen units are being systematically withdrawn to Austria. . . . It seems reasonably certain that some of the most important ministries and personalities of the Nazi regime are already established in the redoubt area. The Party Organization are reported to be in the Vorarlberg region, the Ministry for Propaganda and the Diplomatic Corps in the Garmisch-Partenkirchen area, the Reich Chancellery at

Berchtesgaden, while Goering, Himmler, Hitler and other notables are said to be in the process of withdrawing to their respective personal mountain strongholds.''

It is obvious from this report that SHAEF Intelligence believes that the Alpine Redoubt will be a more important target than Berlin. One also notes that the SHAEF Intelligence Staff uses the term "ground sources" to identify specific items of intelligence. There is no indication as to how reliable these sources might be. Since the Alpine Redoubt will turn out to be a hoax, one wonders why, at this particular time, the best minds at SHAEF are thinking this way.

On March 11, the Russians send a message via the American Military Mission in Moscow to the War Department in Washington asking the Americans to bomb the "Citadel."[26] Located about 5½ kilometers southeast of Zossen and 1 to 1½ kilometers east of the wide superhighway (Reichsstrasse 96) running from Berlin to Dresden, the Citadel had been built underground in 1939. About six kilometers square in size, it was the German army's equivalent of the Pentagon in Washington. Yet until the Russians ask the Americans to hit it with heavy bombers, the Allies do not know of its existence. The Soviet request ends with the words: "The German General Staff, if still located there, will receive damage and losses which will stop its normal work.''

Four days later, Allied bombers hit the target, on March 15. Unfortunately, the raid accomplishes only superficial damage. But Allied intelligence people are deeply impressed by the Soviet knowledge of the area.

Meantime, some British staff at SHAEF are trying to gear up for the possibility of a German collapse. This would create ECLIPSE conditions leading to a pell-mell Allied rush to secure their zones in Germany. Thus H. W. Faulkner in the Office of the Allied Naval Commander in Chief asks Lt. Gen. Sir F. E. Morgan if SHAEF can give an approximate date when ECLIPSE might become operational.[27] Says Faulkner, an error on the early side would at least jolt the slowpokes into getting on with the job. "Incidentally," he adds, "I hear that the Twenty-first Army Group are planning for ECLIPSE on 1st May.''

26. OPD Cable File. Fr Military Mission, Moscow, to War Department (copy to Eisenhower). No. MX 23173 (CM-IN 11902). 11 March 1945.
27. File CofS, SHAEF, 381 Eclipse, Case 1, vol. 1. Letter. To: Lt. Gen. Sir F. E. Morgan, KCB, SHAEF FWD. Fr H. W. Faulkner, Office of the Allied Naval Commander in Chief, Expeditionary Force. 14 March 1945.

Faulkner adds that the British Navy is trying to base its plans (for clearing minefields and opening deep-water ports, etc.) on the assumption there will be six weeks notice before the declaration of "A" day. By working backward, the Navy had reached this six-week figure, which is why they need warning as to when A day might occur. (When Eisenhower finally sends out a notice that A day is fast approaching, the British reply that it will be impossible for them to have their naval forces ready on April 15 and that only a few would be ready by the end of April. The American naval forces are prepared for ECLIPSE operations by the second of April.) In any event, Morgan bucks the naval request upward the following day in a brief note saying: "Can you tell me what is the form, if any, on naming the happy day?"[28]

On March 20, the OSS produces a report, taken up by the Joint Intelligence Committee, dealing with potential German resistance after the assumed loss "of the Ruhr, the Saar, and the great industrial cities of North Germany."[29] Once again the Alpine Redoubt is considered a possible retreat for die-hard Nazis.

It is also obvious that if Eisenhower is going to send his ground forces racing across Germany, they will need tactical air support. The Air Plans Section reports that by using existing bases, such air support cannot be guaranteed beyond the radius of the Giessen-Frankfurt area.[30] When airfields can be moved forward to the Frankfurt area, tactical air support could be extended another hundred miles. "And once those airfields in the same grouping which are east of the Rhine are available, then a further extension of fifty miles or so should be possible. This would bring our spearheads up to the Magdeburg region."

This is vital information for Eisenhower. Tactical air support can be provided for a rapid advance in the center sector across the Rhine into Germany. Note also that the tactical air people have not been asked whether or not air coverage can be extended to Berlin. Apparently, by the third week in March, the concept of capturing the German capital has already been discarded by Eisenhower. Also, it is becoming more and more obvious that Montgomery's Twenty-first Army Group will not be leading the attack through Germany. It will be done by American

---

28. Records of CofS, SHAEF, 381 Eclipse, Case 1, vol. 1. Letter. Fr Lt. Gen. F. E. Morgan to AsstCofS, SHAEF G-3. 15 March 1945.

29. ABC Germany (29 January 1943) Sec 2-B. OSS Report—general summary. Appendix B, JIC 264.

30. SHAEF 18015/Plans, GCT 370-47. Appreciation of Future Operations, Air Plans Section. This document, headed "Loose Minute," is signed by T. P. Gleave, Head of Air Plans Section. 21 March 1945.

forces moving into central, southern and eastern Germany where the going is easier and tactical air support can be provided.

On March 21, the British naval forces receive an answer to their query about A day.[31] Major General Bull tells the Deputy Chief of Staff that he thinks the "best guess that can be made that ECLIPSE might well occur is when we have developed a really strong effort over the Rhine." This would be about April 15. Once the Allies isolate the Ruhr, the "cessation of organized enemy resistance will become more and more probable."

Bull then says he believes it "very rash" that the Navy expects six weeks warning prior to A day. But since they want an optimistic estimate, Bull says to tell them to plan on April 15. Following Bull's instructions, Morgan writes Faulkner the same day, giving the fifteenth as the estimate for A day.

The significance of the tactical air evaluation prepared for Eisenhower on March 21 becomes apparent with the comparison of two evaluations of the same date that are prepared in Washington. They are called *German capabilities after Allied breakthrough east of Rhine*.[32] The Pentagon strategists, in the first paragraph of the evaluation, say: "Due to the rapid deterioration of German capability to resist on the Western Front, it is estimated that at any time after *April 1* [emphasis added] the Allied Forces will be in a position to erupt from bridgeheads on the east bank of the Rhine into Germany."

In its conclusion, the evaluation says: "Once the Allied Armies have broken out of the Rhine bridgeheads, a rapid and bold advance along the general lines indicated below would be the most effective means of causing a German collapse on the Eastern Front and of preventing the possibility of organized resistance in the so-called 'southern redoubt.' " The lines of advance are specifically laid out. There are six of them:

---

31. CofS File, SHAEF, 381 Eclipse, Case 1, vol. 1. Memo GCT/370-27/Plans. Fr Maj. Gen. H. R. Bull to Deputy CofS. 21 March 1945.
32. OPD 381 TS Sect IV (cases 81 thru 99) (21 March 1945). Memo from Marshall to General Hull. 18 March 1945. This memo carries a handwritten note: "Gen Hull: Note recommendations at end. sgd/ GCM" Also attached is a handwritten note saying: "Col Treacy—Gen Lincoln has seen—Dispt msg, attached was dispatched as WAR-59315 27 March 1945." sgd/illegible. A second evaluation with the same case file source, but dated 23 March 1945, from Maj. Gen. Clayton Bissell to Major General Hull, bears a cover memo saying: "These two papers [dated 18 March and 22 March] concern the matter about which we were talking this morning." The two memos are identical with the exception of the key dates in paragraph one: April 10 in the first version versus April 1 in the second version.

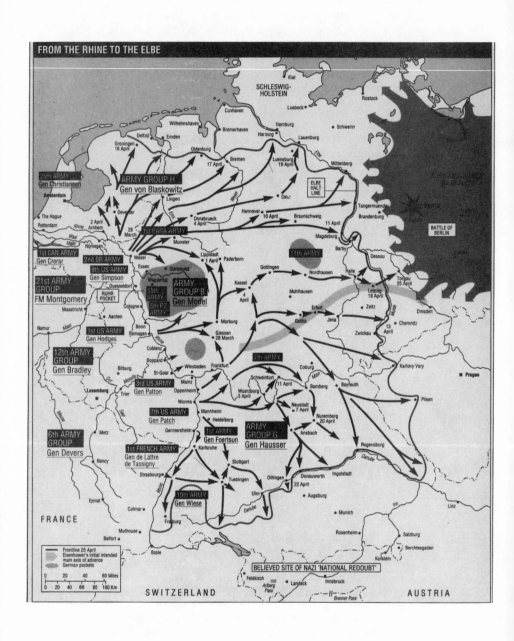

FROM THE RHINE TO THE ELBE

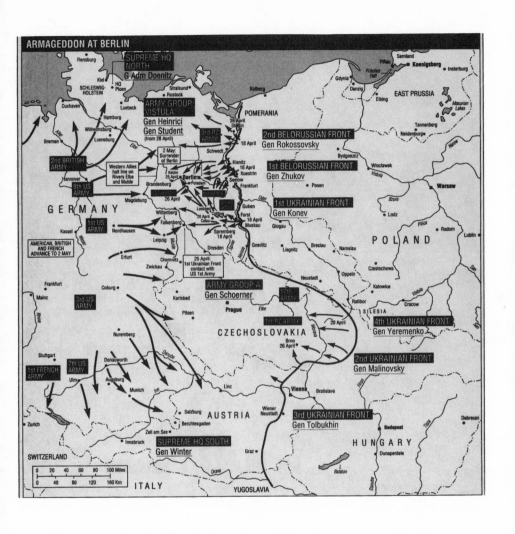

ARMAGEDDON AT BERLIN

SUPREME HQ NORTH
G Adm Doenitz

Flensburg
Kiel
SCHLESWIG-HOLSTEIN
HQ Ploen
Cuxhaven
Stralsund
Rostock
Luebeck
Hamburg
Wilhelmsburg
Lueneburg
Bremen

ARMY GROUP VISTULA
Gen Heinrici
Gen Student
(from 28 April)

3rd Pz ARMY

2 May: Surrender of Berlin
Western Allies halt line on Rivers Elbe and Mulde

2nd BRITISH ARMY
9th US ARMY
Hannover
GERMANY
Magdeburg
1st US ARMY
Kassel
Nordhausen

AMERICAN, BRITISH AND FRENCH ADVANCE TO 2 MAY

Frankfurt
Mainz
Rhine

3rd US ARMY
Coburg
Karlsbad
Pilsen

1st FRENCH ARMY
Stuttgart
7th US ARMY
Nuremberg
Donauworth
Ulm
Augsburg
Munich
Zurich
SWITZERLAND

SUPREME HQ SOUTH
Gen Winter

Berchtesgaden
Zell am See
Innsbruck

ITALY

Kolberg
POMERANIA
Schwedt
Stettin 25 April
18 April
Kienitz 16 April
Kuestrin
Seelow
Frankfurt
Brandenburg
Potsdam
Berlin 25 April
20 April
26 April
Wittenberg
Falkenberg
Leipzig
Erfurt
Zwickau
Chemnitz
Dresden
Guben
Forst 16 April
Muskau
Spremberg 18 April
Cottbus
Calau
Spree
Goerlitz

25 April: 1st Ukrainian Front contact with US 1st Army

2nd BELORUSSIAN FRONT
Gen Rokossovsky

1st BELORUSSIAN FRONT
Gen Zhukov

1st UKRAINIAN FRONT
Gen Konev

Glogau
Liegnitz
Breslau
Namslau
Oppeln
Ratibor

SILESIA
Katowice
Cracow

ARMY GROUP A
Gen Schoerner

17th ARMY
1st Pz ARMY 20 April
Prague
CZECHOSLOVAKIA
Morava
Brno 26 April
Linz
Vienna
Bratislava
Wiener Neustadt
AUSTRIA
Salzburg
Graz

Drava
Balaton

SUPREME HQ SOUTH
Gen Winter

YUGOSLAVIA

Pillau
Samland
Koenigsberg
Insterburg
Frisches Haff
Gdynia
Danzig
Elbing
EAST PRUSSIA
Masurian Lakes
Tannenberg
Neidenburg
Bydgoszcz
Wloclawek
Vistula
Warsaw
Posen
Lodz
POLAND
Radom
Lublin
Czestochowa
Vistula

4th UKRAINIAN FRONT
Gen Yeremenko

2nd UKRAINIAN FRONT
Gen Malinovsky

3rd UKRAINIAN FRONT
Gen Tolbukhin
Budapest
HUNGARY
Dunapentele
Debrecen
Danube

0 20 40 60 80 100 Miles
0   40   80   120 160 Km

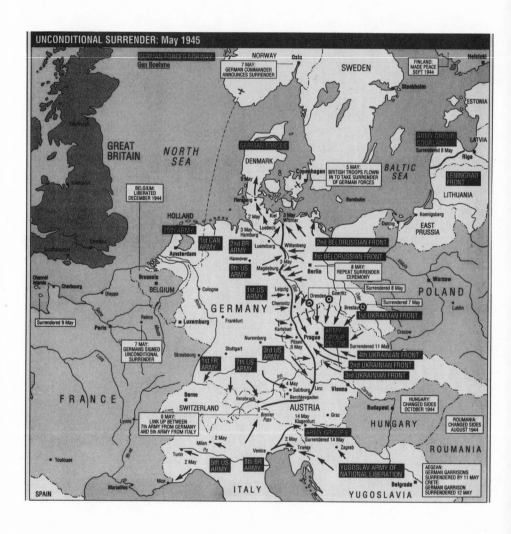

UNCONDITIONAL SURRENDER: May 1945

GERMAN FORCES NORWAY
Gen Boehme

NORWAY
Oslo

7 MAY:
GERMAN COMMANDER
ANNOUNCES SURRENDER

SWEDEN

FINLAND:
MADE PEACE
SEPT 1944

Helsinki

Stockholm

ESTONIA

GREAT
BRITAIN

NORTH
SEA

Edinburgh

Liverpool

ARMY GROUP
COURLAND
Surrendered 8 May

Riga

LATVIA

LENINGRAD
FRONT

LITHUANIA

BALTIC
SEA

5 MAY:
BRITISH TROOPS FLOWN
IN TO TAKE SURRENDER
OF GERMAN FORCES

GERMAN FORCES

DENMARK

Copenhagen

Bornholm

Koenigsberg

EAST
PRUSSIA

Danzig

BELGIUM:
LIBERATED
DECEMBER 1944

HOLLAND

Amsterdam

25th ARMY

1st CAN
ARMY

2nd BR
ARMY

9th US
ARMY

5 May

Flensberg

2 May Kiel

3 May Wismar

3 May
Hamburg

Luebeck

Lueneburg Wittenberg

Hannover

Magdeburg

3 May

Berlin

2nd BELORUSSIAN FRONT

1st BELORUSSIAN FRONT

8 MAY:
REPEAT SURRENDER
CEREMONY

Warsaw

POLAND

Surrendered 8 May

Lublin

Channel
Islands

Cherbourg

Dieppe

Brussels

BELGIUM

Cologne

GERMANY

Leipzig

1st US
ARMY

Chemnitz

Dresden

Goerlitz

Elbe

Breslau

Oder

Surrendered 7 May

1st UKRAINIAN FRONT

Cracow

London

Southampton

Seine

Paris

Reims

Surrendered 9 May

7 MAY:
GERMANS SIGNED
UNCONDITIONAL
SURRENDER

Luxemburg

Frankfurt

Karlsbad

Nuremberg

Prague

6 May

ARMY
GROUP
CENTRE

Surrendered 11 May

4th UKRAINIAN FRONT

Strasbourg

Stuttgart

Pilsen

3rd US
ARMY

2nd UKRAINIAN FRONT

3rd UKRAINIAN FRONT

Loire

FRANCE

1st FR
ARMY

7th US
ARMY

Berne

SWITZERLAND

Innsbruck

Inn

4 May

Salzburg Linz

Vienna

Danube

Lyons

6 MAY:
LINK UP BETWEEN
7th ARMY FROM GERMANY
AND 5th ARMY FROM ITALY

Brenner
Pass

AUSTRIA

Klagenfurt

Graz

Budapest

HUNGARY:
CHANGED SIDES
OCTOBER 1944

14 May

HUNGARY

ROUMANIA:
CHANGED SIDES
AUGUST 1944

Rhône

2 May

Milan

Po

ARMY GROUP E
Surrendered 14 May

2 May

Toulouse

Turin

2 May

5th US
ARMY

Venice

Trieste

Zagreb

ROUMANIA

SPAIN

Marseilles

Nice

8th BR
ARMY

ITALY

YUGOSLAV ARMY OF
NATIONAL LIBERATION

Belgrade

YUGOSLAVIA

AEGEAN:
GERMAN GARRISONS
SURRENDERED BY 11 MAY
CRETE:
GERMAN GARRISON
SURRENDERED 12 MAY

    a. Münster-Bremen-Hamburg (Eisenhower extends this line to Luebeck)
    b. Hamm-Bielefeld-Braunschweig-Magdeburg (on the Elbe)
    c. Mainz-Erfurt-Jena-Halle-Leipzig
    d. Frankfurt-Würzburg-Nürnberg-Regensburg-Linz
    e. Karlsruhe-Ulm-Munich-Innsbruck
    f. Karlsruhe-Black Forest-Friedrichshafen.

As we can see, every one of the six lines of advance proposed by Marshall on March 27 will be followed scrupulously by Eisenhower. The maps on pages 346-48 illustrate the final advance and ultimate positions of the American, British and Russian armies at the time of Germany's surrender in May.

Attached to this Pentagon evaluation of March 27 is a study called the *Line of Demarcation Between Anglo-American and Soviet Operations (22 March 1945)*. The study says it appears the Germans will use all their forces to hold out against the Russians in the East. This could lead to a situation in which American and British forces, which are operating deep inside Germany (and are deep within the Soviet zone of occupation), will be faced suddenly by German troops fleeing from the East in disorganized fashion.

The Pentagon planners refer to a similar situation that occurred in 1939 in eastern Poland when German troops attacking east clashed with Russian troops moving west, because there was no prearranged line of demarcation between the two armies. To avoid a similar clash between the Allies and the Russians, the Pentagon suggests that "steps be taken immediately to establish a line of demarcation between operations of the Anglo-American forces entering Germany and Austria from the west and those of the Soviet forces entering from the east."

Next the Pentagon study gives a "tentative line of demarcation." It is "from Wismar south along the lakes and canals to Ludwigslust inclusive, thence along the Elde River to the Elbe River, thence along the Elbe River to the Saale River, thence along the Saale River to Zell exclusive, thence along the Nab River from its headwaters at Brand to the Danube River, thence along the Danube River to its junction with the Enns River to Radstadt, thence along the Radstadt-Villach Highway to Arnoldstein, thence south along the Italian-Yugolslav frontier to Fiume inclusive."

Unofficial word about the Pentagon's evaluation circulates at SHAEF before the official word is sent. The concept is approved by Marshall, and he notifies SCAEF of these recommendations on March

27, 1945, only a few days before Eisenhower sends his armies off on their final drive across Europe.

Given the specifics of the six primary lines of advance Marshall wants Eisenhower to follow, plus the crystal-clear line of demarcation that is suggested the Supreme Commander should negotiate with the Russians, it is obvious that Eisenhower is finally receiving firm instructions about how to invade Germany and meet up with the Soviet Army. He is not forbidden to take Berlin. Nor is he told to take the city. What he is told to do is set up a line of demarcation on the west bank of the Elbe River, which precludes an advance into Berlin.

Judging by the way Eisenhower accepts these "suggestions" made by Marshall—following the recommended lines of advance, halting his attack on the banks of the river Elbe, just short of Berlin, then spreading out his forces north and south along the proposed line of demarcation—one can say that, at the final stage of the war in Europe, Chief of Staff Marshall, in his usual courteous, gentlemanly fashion, gives Eisenhower his marching orders. And Eisenhower follows them.

Eisenhower will take the credit later on for conquering Germany. But the strategy of Eisenhower's campaign is created in early March by Marshall and others in the Pentagon.[33]

According to SHAEF records, Eisenhower visits Bradley on March 23 at Ninth Army headquarters. From SHAEF, Lt. Gen. Sir Frederick E. Morgan sends a telex to Eisenhower suggesting that Ike, assuming he approves, should send a cable to the Combined Chiefs of Staff along the following lines:[34] Concluding operations west of the Rhine, SHAEF has reviewed the plan of future operations as outlined in SCAF 180 and amended by SCAF 194. In doing this the original directive from the Combined Chiefs has been kept in mind—namely that the object is to "undertake operations aimed at the heart

---

33. Civilian supporters of Eisenhower's being the sole architect of victory in Europe say that at no time is Eisenhower "ordered" to do anything by Marshall. For example: "On all this, Eisenhower had no specific guidance. He relied on his personal judgment, reinforced by months of consultations and recent CCS silence," writes David Eisenhower in *Eisenhower at War* (p. 729). This argument begs the question. When an all-powerful chief of staff such as was Marshall "suggests" a strategy, the subordinate carries it out or proposes a viable alternative. Eisenhower never presents an alternative. He does what is recommended. In this situation the subordinate, Eisenhower, reaps the rewards of success. If the strategy had failed, Eisenhower could say that he had followed "suggestions" made by the Pentagon. He could not then be faulted for violating guidelines. It is what corporate strategists call a "win-win" situation for Eisenhower. The situation also illustrates why the men who occupy the position of chief of staff are forgotten by the public soon after the fighting stops.

34. Personal File, Gen. W. B. Smith, SHAEF. Fr General Morgan to Eisenhower (c/o Ninth Army). 231930A March 1945.

of Germany and the destruction of her armed forces." Furthermore, SHAEF has always been aware of the importance the Combined Chiefs have placed in a northern line of approach into Germany as opposed to the southern route.

Since SCAF 180 was sent (before the Malta conference began at the end of January) continues Morgan, the situation has improved and we have reached the Rhine throughout its length before launching operations east of the river. This means there will be a marked economy in forces needed to maintain the rear areas and thereby makes more forces available for continued advances than was considered possible. Morgan suggests that Ike should take the position that he is of the belief that the Ruhr must first be isolated. Operations north of the Ruhr have only limited possibilities because of restricted routes. The maximum force that can be deployed in that area—until railroads have been run across the Rhine—amounts to some thirty-five divisions. Therefore, there will be some forty other divisions available for the offensive that cannot be deployed in the north for at least two months after Montgomery's crossing the Rhine.

According to Morgan, Eisenhower will be able to widen the base of his operation to exploit the plan to isolate the Ruhr by his new ability to advance in force from the south. This will greatly increase the speed of deployment of offensive forces since it will allow them to use two bridgeheads and operate on a wider front.

These northern and southern attacks would be instructed to link up in the Lippstadt-Arolsen area to the east of the Ruhr. They would then clean up the area enclosed within their pincer movement. It would be necessary to complete this operation before moving further with attacks into Germany. On the other hand, Germany's strength to resist might be so weakened at this point that further advances could be made concurrently. Therefore Eisenhower will allocate initially three armies of thirty to thirty-five divisions to thrust north of the Ruhr, three armies of thirty to thirty-five divisions to thrust from the Saar, employ two armies in a defensive role along the upper and middle Rhine respectively, and retain six divisions in SHAEF reserve (not including the airborne divisions), with the idea of exploiting either of these thrusts as may be expedient.

This strategy, prepared for Eisenhower by his trusted British aide, Sir Frederick Morgan, acknowledges that Montgomery can no longer be the main attack into Germany. That the British drive will have no railway support for several months, and that only thirty to thirty-five divisions can operate in the area, forces Morgan to agree to using the

Remagen bridgehead as a starting point for a second, so-called "supporting" drive into Germany.

All is well and good between the British and Americans at this point.

It's the recommendations from Marshall in Washington that will create the bitter debate. The planners in the Pentagon, plus Eisenhower and Bradley and other American commanders in Europe, can now visualize a much grander assault than does Morgan. The time has come to make full use of the southern-German terrain the British assigned the Americans when COSSAC was planning the invasion. The Americans want to let their tanks run the German fox to ground as quickly as possible, as far east and south as possible.

Thus, on March 24, Eisenhower cables Marshall, saying that the recent victories west of the Rhine have resulted in the planned destruction of large elements of the available enemy forces on the Western Front.[35] Without appearing overly optimistic, he believes that the Allies face opportunities today toward which they have struggled and which must be boldly seized.

Eisenhower also says that the American Third and First Armies have won two cheap bridgeheads. They can be consolidated and expanded rapidly into a major drive that will make our northern operations much more effective. He is prepared for tough resistance, but he believes the "enemy strength on the Western Front is becoming so stretched that penetrations and advances will soon be limited *only by our own maintenance.* [Emphasis added.] Already we have employed to the north all the forces that we can maintain effectively east of the Rhine for the coming few weeks and I am directing the most vigorous action on all fronts. I intend to reinforce every success with utmost speed."

Two days later, on March 26, Marshall sends a cable (originated by General Hull) for Eisenhower's "eyes only."[36] According to Marshall the British Chiefs are worrying seriously about SHAEF's concentrating every bit of strength on the Western Front. (Eisenhower had asked that a division be transferred from another theater to support Montgomery on the Western Front.) Marshall says the British now propose moving a division from Italy so it could be operational on the

---

35. OPD Cable File. Fr Eisenhower to War Department No. FWD 18141 (SCAF 244) CM-IN 25925. 24 March 1945. The cable is sent the CCS for action. Copies are also sent in Washington to Admiral Leahy at the White House, General Arnold, General Hull, General Bissell, Admiral King, CNO, CofS.

36. OPD Cable File. Fr Marshall to Eisenhower—eyes only. No. WARX 58795. 26 March 1945.

Western Front by early May rather than moving the Forty-sixth Division, which couldn't be ready for action until June.

Marshall points out that Eisenhower's message of the twenty-fourth, saying that German strength on the Western Front is so limited that SHAEF's success can only be halted by logistic capabilities, when combined with other comments, brings into question the need for shifting any troops to the Western Front. Says Marshall: "You should not weaken the forces in Italy unless you have urgent needs for this particular division."

On March 27, Eisenhower cables Montgomery that he is emphatic in his belief that SHAEF should not take a division from Italy if it makes that front "passive."[37] Eisenhower had first proposed that Montgomery look into a troop shift when contemplating an airborne operation in Kassel, which is no longer feasible. Because of the changing situation, Eisenhower will be using the majority of his transport aircraft for supplying the armored columns as they advance. Therefore, the British division should not be transferred.

On March 27, the same day that Marshall's instructions for Eisenhower arrive at SHAEF, Montgomery issues his orders for a drive on the Elbe, with the Second and Ninth Armies acting as spearheads.[38] The right of the U.S. Ninth Army will be aimed at Magdeburg and the left of the Second Army at Hamburg. The left flank of the Ninth Army will be the line Münster-Hanover-Wittenberg. The left flank of the Second Army will be Hengelo-Lingen-Haselünne-Bremen-Hamburg.

In telling Eisenhower what he has done, Montgomery says, "I have ordered Ninth and Second Armies to move their mobile and armored forces forward at once and to get on through to the Elbe with the utmost speed and drive. . . . Thereafter the axis on which my tactical headquarters will move will be Wesel-Münster-Wiedenbrück-Herford-Hannover-thence via the autobahn to Berlin. I hope."

This precipitous action by Montgomery, attacking without orders from SHAEF, precipitously naming Berlin as his eventual goal, apparently defying the recommendations made by Marshall (assuming Montgomery knew of them; it is believed he did), creates a major problem for Eisenhower. We will see it grow in the days to come.

The second major problem of the day for Eisenhower is the cable

---

37. Personal File, Gen. W. B. Smith, SHAEF. Fr Eisenhower to Montgomery. No FWD 18212. 27 March 1945.

38. Personal File Gen. W. B. Smith. Fr Montgomery to Eisenhower, No. M-562. TOO 271810A Mar TOR 272025A Mar. 27 March 1945.

from Marshall.[39] Based on the memo and "suggestions" of March 18 and 23 mentioned earlier, Marshall says that from reading the current operations reports it looks as though the German defense system in the West may break up. This would permit Eisenhower to move a "considerable number of your divisions eastward on a broad front." Marshall then asks Eisenhower what his views would be toward the "possibility and soundness" of pushing U.S. forces "rapidly forward on, say, the Nürnburg-Linz or Karlsruhe-Munich axes?"

Marshall explains, saying the idea behind this is that in a situation where Germany is breaking up, rapid action might prevent the formation of any organized resistance areas. "The mountainous country in the south is considered a possibility for one of these."

Marshall also goes on to say that he believes that one of the problems arising out of a rapidly disintegrating Germany will be that of meeting the Russians. "What are your ideas," he asks, "on control and coordination to prevent unfortunate instances and to sort out the two advancing forces? One possibility is an agreed-upon line of demarcation. The arrangements we now have with the Russians appear to be quite inadequate for the situation you may face and it seems steps ought to be initiated without delay to provide for the communication and liaison you will need with them during the period when your forces may be mopping up in close proximity or in contact with the Russian forces."

This cable changes the strategy for ending the war in Europe.

First, Marshall makes operative the "suggestions" made by the Pentagon planners in their memos of March 18 and March 23 (which are noted to have been transmitted on March 27 to SHAEF). Second, Marshall is recommending that Eisenhower swing the First French, the Seventh U.S. Army and, more important, Patton's Third U.S. Army southward into Austria and Czechoslovakia. Third, Marshall establishes the Alpine Redoubt as a strategic military target. Fourth, by stressing the establishment of a line of demarcation, and "suggesting" that "steps ought to be initiated without delay," Marshall is telling Eisenhower to open an independent line of communication with Stalin. As for the line of demarcation, Eisenhower is to prepare to hold on the River Elbe: i.e., not take Berlin.

All of this ties in with previous planning done by SHAEF. The

39. OPD Cable File. Fr Marshall to Eisenhower. No. WAR 59315. 27 March 1945. (See footnote 32.) The author is unable to determine which problem arrived on Eisenhower's desk first: Montgomery's order to attack, or Marshall's so-called marching orders.

question had already been raised by General Bull about informing Stalin of SHAEF's operational planning and asking his views on timing.[40] According to McLean there is no harm now in telling Stalin about operations PLUNDER and VARSITY. On the other hand, Stalin is only likely to tell SHAEF the possible date for the thaw on the Eastern Front, and SHAEF has already asked for this. McLean suggests that SHAEF await the result of Operation THUNDER, and Eisenhower's decision about Frankfurt-Kassel, plus the "paper now on the stacks regarding our future advance after isolating the Ruhr. I should then spill all the works and ask how this will tie in with his [Stalin's] strategy."

Thus, March 27 and 28, 1945, become two of the pivotal dates of strategic planning for the European war. Acting on Marshall's cable of the twenty-seventh, Eisenhower sends on the twenty-eighth his reply to Washington.[41] He tells Marshall that he sent today a message to Marshal Stalin via Deane and Archer in Moscow asking where the Americans and British should meet with Stalin's forces. Says Eisenhower about Marshall's suggestions: "My views agree closely with your own, although I think the route of Leipzig-Dresden to be the primary one." It provides the shortest route to the Russian positions and it divides Germany roughly in half. (This is the only change that Eisenhower makes as a result of the recommendations made by Marshall.) Eisenhower also says he would also seize the sole remaining German industrial area to which the German High Command Headquarters and governmental ministries are reported to be going. (Here Eisenhower acknowledges that he will be following the Magic Diplomatic Summaries to determine how he will locate specific new targets.)

Eisenhower also says he agrees with the importance of forestalling the chance that the enemy might form areas of organized resistance. He will attack toward Munich and Linz as soon as it is feasible.

Eisenhower points out that his earlier messages to Marshall explained his views about control and coordination between the Allied and Russian forces. "I am still attempting to do everything possible to perfect that liaison between our forces," says Eisenhower. "I know the present failings in this respect and I'd appreciate any help you might be able to give me. I don't think we can hold ourselves to a specific line. However, I've asked Deane to approach the Russians with the

---

40. SHAEF Files #322.01-1/GPS Liaison With Russians. Memo dictated by K. G. McLean, G-3 Div (FWD), to DAC of S, G-3 Div (though Chief Ops Sect). 23 March 1945.
41. OPD Cable File. Fr SHAEF FWD (Eisenhower) to War Department (Marshall—eyes only). No. FWD 18272 (CM-IN 29847). TOO 281905A TOR 280125A. 28 March 1945.

thought that when our forces meet, either one will withdraw to its occupation zone at the request of the opposite side.''

Following another of Marshall's recommendations, the message
Eisenhower sends to Deane and Archer in Moscow is explicit.[42] Eisenhower says that operations in Europe have reached a point where it
is "essential" that "I know the Russian plans" in order to achieve
the most rapid success. He asks the Military Mission to give the following "personal" message to Stalin and do everything possible to obtain
a reply.

First says Eisenhower, my immediate intentions are to encircle and
destroy the enemy forces in the Ruhr and thereby isolate this area from
the rest of Germany.

Second, Eisenhower believes this operation will last until the end
of April, or possibly earlier, and his next task will be to join hands
with Soviet forces.

Third, the best route for the Allied armies would be Erfurt-Leipzig-
Dresden for establishing a linkup with the Russians. This is the area to
which the main offices of the German government are being moved.
When the situation permits, says Eisenhower, he will make a secondary
effort to establish a junction with the Soviets in the Regensburg area
and thereby prevent the consolidation of German defenses in a redoubt
in southern Germany.

Before deciding firmly on his plans, says Eisenhower, he wants to
coordinate them as closely as possible with those of the Russian armies
in both direction and timing. Therefore, he asks: "Can you tell me
what are your intentions and let me know how far my proposed operations coincide with your plan of action?"

Eisenhower also offers to send officers to help in this liaison, to
complete the destruction of the German forces in the immediate future.

Also on March 28, Eisenhower alerts all his forces that ECLIPSE
conditions—the collapse of the German government that would lead to
a general advance through Germany—might become operative as early
as April 15.[43] Therefore, all the Allied services are advised that they
should be ready to assume their administrative responsibilities for running a defeated Germany should this occur.

---

42. OPD Cable File. Fr SHAEF FWD (Eisenhower) to War Department No. FWD 18264 (SCAF
252). CM-IN 29759. Received 1935z via Red Tube in Washington. 28 March 1945. To be
relayed to Military Mission in Moscow with copies to CCS, British Chiefs of Staff, SHAEF Main.
43. OPD Cable File. Fr SHAEF FWD (Eisenhower) to War Department—CCS. No. FWD 18281
(SCAF 253). 28 March 1945.

By now the situation paper on which Montgomery bases his order of March 27 to attack Berlin arrives at SHAEF.[44] Says Montgomery:

"**1.** We have won the battle of the Rhine.

"**2.** During March the average number of prisoners taken every day by the Allies on the Western Front is ten thousand: making a total of over a quarter of a million. The enemy divisions were all very weak when the battles for the Rhine began; they are getting no replacement and now are mere skeletons; there are no fresh and complete divisions in the rear and all the enemy will be able to do is to block roads and approaches with personnel from schools, bath units, pigeon lofts, and so on.

"**3.** The time has now arrived for quick and determined exploitation by armored and mobile units of the Twenty-first Army Group."

The "INTENTION" portion of Montgomery's plan is "to exploit the present situation rapidly, and to drive hard for the line of the river Elbe so as to gain quick possession of the plains of northern Germany."

The last paragraphs carry the Field Marshal's exhortation: "This is the time to take risks and go 'flat out' for the Elbe. If we reach the Elbe quickly, we win the war."

No one can say that Montgomery hasn't analyzed the strategic situation correctly. But the problem is one of command. Who is running SHAEF? Montgomery or Eisenhower? Who is supposed to give the order for SHAEF forces to advance east of the Rhine? It's the Supreme Commander, who happens to be Eisenhower, not Montgomery.

There are two versions of Eisenhower's response to Montgomery. The more impressive document is the original draft.[45] The Supreme Commander says he agrees with Montgomery's plans "up to the point of gaining contact with Bradley east of the Ruhr. However, thereafter, my present plans now being coordinated with Stalin are as outlined in the following paragraphs."

At this juncture Eisenhower tells Montgomery that as Supreme

---

44. 12 Army Gp, AG Records File, #371.3 Military Objectives, vol. 6. General Situation Papers and Orders 21 Army Gp. Signed Montgomery. No. M-563.

45. SHAEF 18015/Plans. Subject: Outline of Army Group Plans. File no. GCT 370-46/Plans. Fr SHAEF FWD Eisenhower to TAC HQ 21 Army Group for Field Marshal Montgomery's eyes only. The cable for the record, often referred to by historians, is found in Personal File of Gen. W. B. Smith, SHAEF. Fr Eisenhower to Montgomery. No. FWD 18272.

Commander he is altering Montgomery's proposed attack. Eisenhower instructs that the U.S. Ninth Army will revert to the command of General Bradley and his Twelfth Army Group as soon as Montgomery joins hands with Bradley in the Kassel-Paderborn area east of the Ruhr. As Eisenhower sees it: "Bradley will be responsible for mopping up and occupying the Ruhr and with the minimum delay will deliver his main thrust [in the draft the original wording "our main thrust" is crossed out and changed to "his main thrust"] on the axis Erfurt-Leipzig-Dresden to join hands with the Russians."

Eisenhower tells Montgomery: "When your forces reach the Elbe it may again be desirable for Ninth Army to revert to your operational control to facilitate the crossing of that obstacle." Then, added in pencil are the words: "If so necessary orders will then be issued."

The message continues: "Devers will protect Bradley's right flank and be prepared later when the situation permits to advance to join hands with the Russians in the Danube valley."

The message concludes with the casual note: "As you say, the situation looks good."

Given Montgomery's behavior, some historians consider Eisenhower's response to be measured and thoughtful. Others consider Eisenhower's words to be rude. Whatever their intention, they infuriate Montgomery and Churchill.

Eisenhower is telling Montgomery that east of the Ruhr his attack will be stripped of a major striking force, the American Ninth Army, at the moment Montgomery will try to race to the Elbe. (One should keep in mind that Montgomery's own plans called for having the Ninth Army to mop up the Ruhr.) Furthermore, Eisenhower is telling Montgomery once and for all time that Eisenhower will be the one who will contact the Russians, negotiate with the Russians and Montgomery will kindly stick to doing what he is told to do.

Suddenly, the British plan to attack Berlin, as outlined by Montgomery's planning map of March 27, is no longer operational.[46] Any bridgeheads across the Elbe, which Montgomery had envisaged as being won by *his* troops between Wittenberg and Magdeburg, and which represent the key to the road net to Berlin, will instead be made by American troops under American control.

The next day, Eisenhower tells Bradley and Devers about the latest

---

46. SHAEF 18015/Plans. File no. SHAEF Map No. 65 AB.

developments.[47] He says his plans are now being coordinated with Marshal Stalin. As soon as Bradley and Montgomery join hands near Kassel, the Ninth Army will revert to Bradley's command. Bradley will be responsible for occupying the Ruhr and, with a minimum of delay, will then make his main thrust on the route Leipzig-Dresden to meet the Russians. The Twenty-first Army, i.e., Montgomery, will protect Bradley's flank on the boundary Münster-Hanover and thence to Wittenberg or Stendal as to be decided later.

When Montgomery reaches the Elbe, the Ninth Army may revert again to Montgomery's control to "facilitate the crossing of that obstacle." If this is necessary, the orders will be issued then. Devers will still protect Bradley's right flank and will be ready to move forward to meet the Russians on the route Regensburg-Linz. Eisenhower also tells his two commanders that Montgomery knows all about the plan.

This same day, the twenty-ninth, the British Chiefs of Staff release a lengthy report in which they review the planning date for the end of the war against Germany.[48] The report shows a considerable difference in opinion on the part of the British Chiefs in that they are more pessimistic about the war's ending than are Eisenhower and Marshall. Eisenhower has just declared that ECLIPSE conditions may occur around April 15. "We do not consider, however," say the British Chiefs of Staff, "that there is sufficient likelihood of this timing being realized to justify for planning purposes, [April 15] as the earliest date for the defeat of Germany." The British Chiefs believe the "reasonably favorable case" would be "the end of organized German resistance by the end of June." They say this is "the earliest date on which the war is likely to end. . . . The date beyond which the war is unlikely to continue is November 1, 1945."

It is apparent that the British Chiefs of Staff are marching out of step compared with Eisenhower, Marshall and the Pentagon. The British Chiefs apparently have no sense of urgency about ending the war in Europe as quickly as possible. Not for them is there any worry about an invasion of Japan, which is scheduled for November 1, 1945. If the Americans operate via the schedule proposed by the British Chiefs, the invasion of Japan might have to be delayed until the spring of 1946, a situation for the Americans that is completely unacceptable.

---

47. Personal File of Gen. W. B. Smith, SHAEF. Fr Eisenhower to Bradley (12th Army) & Devers (6th Army). No. FWD 18302. 29 March 1945.
48. ABC Europe (5 August 1944) Sec 1-D. Memo fr British Chiefs of Staff to Combined Chiefs of Staff. 29 March 1945.

Meanwhile, Montgomery is wiring Eisenhower that he has received the Supreme Commander's message FWD 18272.[49] Montgomery understands Ike is changing the command setup, saying: "If you feel this is necessary, I pray you do not do so until we reach the Elbe as such action would not help the great movement which is now beginning to develop." The hidden meaning of Montgomery's message is this: If you take the Ninth U.S. Army away from my command, do not expect me to put a full effort into driving into Germany. Indeed, this is what will occur. Montgomery will fall behind and Eisenhower will have to expedite the closure on the Baltic at Luebeck to keep the Danish peninsula from the Russians.

From Moscow comes word from Archer and Deane that they, the British and the American ambassadors, have asked Stalin for a conference on March 30, saying they had important information for Stalin from Eisenhower.[50] Since Stalin is expected to ask additional questions, "we all here agree . . . and . . . urgently recommend that you furnish us as quickly as possible with as much of that information as you consider advisable."

Now comes the official British storm of fury about American strategy.

Marshall cables Eisenhower saying that he (Marshall) has just been handed a memo by Field Marshal Wilson in Washington.[51] Says Marshall, the British Chiefs of Staff are concerned with the contents of Eisenhower's SCAF 252, both "as regards the procedure which has been adopted by General Eisenhower and, what is more important, the change in plan which is implicit in his message to Marshal Stalin. . . . They feel strongly that the existing strategy, i.e., that the main thrust should be made across the open plains of northwest Germany, with the object of *capturing Berlin,* should be adhered to." (Emphasis added.)

The British say that current strategy will allow them to open German ports in the west and the north and sever all German communications with Holland. It would also "annul the U-boat war." Last, "we should be free to move into Denmark, open a line of communication with Sweden and liberate for our use nearly 2 million

---

49. Personal File Gen. W. B. Smith, SHAEF. Fr Montgomery to Eisenhower. No. M562/1. TOO 291955A March 1945. TOR 292106A March 1945.

50. SHAEF Sigs File 373.5, vol. 1. Cable from Deane (Moscow) to Eisenhower. No. M-23519 (FS-IN 3805). TOO 291545Z TOR 291713A TOR (FWD) 291727A. 29 March 1945.

51. SHAEF Sigs File 373.5, vol. 1. Cable from Marshall to Eisenhower. No. W-60507 (FS-IN 3855) TOO 29211131Z TOR 30004A. 29 March 1945.

tons of Swedish and Norwegian shipping now lying idle in Swedish ports. We should also be able to assist Norway.''

The cable goes on to say: "Prior to your dispatch of SCAF 252 have the naval aspects listed by the British been considered? Your comments are considered a matter of urgency.'' The British have told Marshall, who tells Eisenhower, they will give the Americans a full exposition of their views on the coming day. What really must have irritated Eisenhower is Marshall's apparent forgetfulness that, only forty-eight hours earlier, he ordered Eisenhower to (1) create the new SHAEF strategy for ending the war in Europe, and (2) contact Stalin and set up a feasible line of demarcation.

Meanwhile, Eisenhower has already approved launching the American attack east of the Rhine. At 4 A.M. on the morning of March 29, an order is cut at the headquarters of the U.S. Second Armored Division (Heavy) that sends adrenaline rushing through the men who read it (see appendix). Basically, the order refers commanders to the current G-2 (Intelligence) report of March 28. It also tells them they are to attack the next day, March 30, passing through the XVIII Corps, secure crossings over the Dortmund-Ems Canal, continue to attack and cut communications east of Hamm, and "be prepared to immediately continue [attack] to [east] on BERLIN."[52]

Furthermore, the order states: "Where necessary, bypass resistance. . . . Roads and bridges must be kept clear and traffic kept moving. . . . Unit [commanders] and all officers will take every means to prevent jams or traffic blocks. All [elements] will push aggressively and rapidly taking every opportunity to exploit any success. . . . Columns will continue [advance] day and night." Early the next day, March 30, as American troops start moving eastward, Eisenhower sends a brief cable to Marshall saying that he's preparing an immediate reply to Marshall's message (W-60507) of the previous day.[53] It should reach Marshall in a few hours. Eisenhower is quite blunt: the British charge that he has changed plans has "no possible basis in fact. The principal effort north of the Ruhr was always adhered to with the object of isolating that valuable area."

Eisenhower says he is sticking to his old plan of launching one attack from the Ruhr, conceived to accomplish "in conjunction with

---

52. 602-3.2 G-3 Jnl & File. 2nd Armd Div Part II March 1945. AUTH: CG 2 Ad. F323341 290400A March 1945. Sgnd: Johnson G-3. White Cmndg.
53. Personal File Gen. W. B. Smith, SHAEF. Fr Eisenhower to Marshall. No. FWD 18331. 30 March 1945.

the Russians'' the destruction of Germany's forces. He maintains that if he is to disperse his forces along the northern coast before his objective is accomplished, he will be left with forces too weak to accomplish a drive through the center. He concludes, saying: "My plan will get the ports and all the other things on the north coast more speedily and decisively than will the dispersion now urged upon me by Wilson's message to you."

A few hours later, the full response from SCAEF is on its way to Marshall.[54] Eisenhower tells Marshall that he has received the same protest about "procedure" in a scrambled telephone conversation with Prime Minister Churchill the past night.

"I'm completely in the dark as to what the protest concerning 'procedure' involved," says Eisenhower. "I have been instructed to deal directly with the Russians concerning military coordination. [This puts the monkey on Marshall's back, where it properly belongs: Author.] In the first place there is no change in basic strategy. The British Chiefs of Staff last summer always protested against my determination to open up the Frankfurt route because they said it would be futile and would draw away strength from a northern attack. I have always insisted that the northern attack would be the principal effort of that phase of our operation that involved the isolation of the Ruhr, but from the very beginning, extending back before D-Day, my plan, explained by my senior officers, has been to link up the primary and secondary efforts in this Kassel area and then make one great thrust eastward."

Even a quick examination of the decisive direction for this thrust, says Eisenhower, after the linkup in the Kassel area has been completed, shows the principal effort under existing circumstances should be toward Leipzig. This is where the majority of the remaining, functioning German industry is concentrated. It is where the German ministries are believed to be moving. Eisenhower also points out that his plan does not force Montgomery to move his forces southward.

"You will note that his right flank will push forward along the general line Hanover-Wittenberg," says Eisenhower. "Merely following the principles that Field Marshal Brooke has always shouted at me, I am determined to concentrate on one major thrust, and all that my plan does is place the Ninth U.S. Army back under Bradley for that phase of the operations involving the advance of the center from Kassel

---

54. SHAEF Sigs 373.5, vol. 1. Cable from Eisenhower to Marshall. No. FWD-18345 (FS-OUT 1184) TOO 301342A. 30 March 1945.

to the Leipzig region, unless, of course, the Russian forces should meet us on this side of that area.''

Theoretically, there has been no change in strategy in terms of driving eastward. But there most certainly has been a change in who will get the glory, for being the first to cross the Elbe or the first to meet the Russians. The American commanders also read the words ''be prepared to attack Berlin'' or ''advance on Berlin,'' and they begin hoarding ammunition and fuel for what they believe will be the greatest attack in American history.

Again, Eisenhower tells Montgomery that once the goal of driving eastward to the Elbe has been completed, the British can have the U.S. Ninth Army back under their command again if necessary to assist them in clearing up the whole coastline to the north at Luebeck. Then, ''after strength for this operation has been provided, it is considered that we can launch a movement to the southeastward to prevent Nazi occupation of a mountain citadel.''

The Supreme Commander says he has carefully considered the naval aspects of the situation. He clearly understands the advantage of gaining the northern coastline at an early date. That is the next item on the agenda after the primary thrust places the Allied armies in a decisive position. Opening the harbors of Bremen, Hamburg and Kiel involve operations against the Frisian Islands and Helgoland, plus extensive minesweeping. This, plus operations into Norway and Denmark, are a later phase of operations.

It is Eisenhower's firm belief that a concerted drive by the Twelfth Army Group in the center, protected to the north by the British and to the south by the Sixth Army Group, is the surest way to quickly paralyze the German war effort.

''May I point out that *Berlin itself is no longer a particularly important objective*,'' says Eisenhower. (Emphasis added.) ''It's usefulness to the Germans has been largely destroyed and even his government is preparing to move to another area. What is now important is to gather up our forces for a single drive and this will more quickly bring about the fall of Berlin, the relief of Norway and the acquisition of the shipping in Swedish ports than will the scattering around of our effort.''

As for the British argument about the quality of the northern terrain, Eisenhower says: ''I should like to point out that the so-called 'good ground' in northern Germany is not really good at this time of year. That region is not only badly cut up with waterways but the ground during this time of year is very wet and not so favorable for rapid movement as is the higher plateau which I am preparing to launch the main effort. Moreover, if, as we expect, the Germans continue the widespread destruction of bridges, experience has shown that it is better to advance across the headwaters than to be faced by the main streams.''

Now some of Eisenhower's anger spills over. ''The Prime Minister and his Chief of Staff opposed [operation] Anvil,'' he says. ''And they opposed my idea that the Germans should be destroyed west of the Rhine before we made our major effort across that river; and they insisted that the route leading northeastward from Frankfurt would involve us merely in slow, rough country fighting. Now they apparently want me to turn aside on operations in which would be involved many thousands of troops before the German forces are defeated. I submit that these things are studied daily and hourly by me and my advisors and that we are animated by one single thought which is the early winning of this war.''

Eisenhower then lists the main points that he plans to follow in his operations. His last comment deals with a matter about which he is obsessed: flexibility. According to Eisenhower, maximum flexibility of operations will result from a concentration of maximum force in the center.

Events will prove him correct.

Meanwhile, Eisenhower dispatches a cable to Churchill, saying basically what he has told Marshall.[55] But there is an interesting little twist in it about crossing the Elbe. Eisenhower tells the Prime Minister that as soon as the Ruhr has been encircled, ''I propose to drive eastward to join hands with the Russians or to attain the general line of the Elbe. Subject to Russian intentions, the axis Kassel-Leipzig is the best for this drive, as it will insure the overrunning of that important industrial area, into which the German ministries are believed to be moving; it will cut the German forces approximately in half and it *will not involve us in a crossing of the Elbe* [emphasis added]. It is designed to divide and destroy the major parts of the enemy remaining forces in the west.''

While this will be the main thrust, Eisenhower also says once its success is assured he will take action to clear the northern ports. As far as Kiel is concerned, this will mean a crossing of the Elbe, and Montgomery will be responsible for this. If necessary to help Montgomery

---

55. SHAEF Sigs File 373.5, vol. 1. Cable from Eisenhower to AMSSO (personal for Churchill). No. FWD-18334 TOO 301135A (FS-Out 3914). 30 March 1945.

to achieve this goal, Eisenhower will reinforce the British forces. In addition, Devers will be prepared, when the above requirements have been met, to drive to the south to prevent any German consolidation there and to join with the Russian forces in the Danube.

Eisenhower concludes, saying: "I trust this added information will make clear my present plans. Naturally they are flexible and subject to change to meet unexpected situations." This last statement is conciliatory. But Eisenhower has made it clear to Churchill that he does not plan on crossing the Elbe to take Berlin. The golden goal Churchill seeks is being denied him.

One major question the strategic planners still have not agreed on is the validity of the existence of the Alpine National Redoubt. A major report, prepared by the Research and Analysis Branch of the OSS in London, released earlier as document RAL148, is updated and released a second time.[56] The thirty-three-page report is inconclusive as to whether or not the Redoubt truly exists. It says the initial reports about the possibility of a redoubt's being built began to trickle in during September 1944, when the German armies collapsed in France. The analysts say: "The volume of intelligence increased considerably during October and November and has continued to flow in at a fairly steady rate ever since." The report does not name specific sources for this intelligence, however.

More worrying is the fact that there is virtually no recent aerial intelligence (photo reconnaissance) of the areas in question. The report also acknowledges that when asked about redoubt plans, the questioned prisoners of war have so far given opinions rather than facts, and the opinions were generally to the effect that no such thing was possible— certainly not on a large scale. Some sources were suspected as being so close in their stories that "collusion must be suspected."

In conclusion, the report says: "The available evidence does not indicate the preparation of a coherent defense system over a wide area of the Alps nor does it tally with reports purporting to describe the outline of the redoubt. . . . It is suggested that reconnaissance be flown."

At this time, it is apparent that one major reason given for turning the American attack southward is somewhat deceptive. (The account of the German banker contained in Magic about the Reichsbank's hiding

---

56. OSS (Research and Analysis Branch). An interim survey of available intelligence (summer 1944 to mid-February 1945). R&A No. 3005. 30 March 1945.

of its gold reserves in southern Germany is a much better reason, but, for obvious reasons, it cannot be used.)

Suddenly the White House inserts itself into the situation. General Hull, Chief of Staff for Operations–Pentagon, originates a cable for Marshall to send to Eisenhower.[57] The White House press secretary, Daniels, has told the Pentagon that President Roosevelt believes a message from Eisenhower to Roosevelt, concerning the possibility of guerrilla warfare after VE (Victory in Europe) day, should be released to the public in order to prepare them for this possibility.

This is the only communication the author found in the Army's records showing presidential interest in the way the war will end in Europe. Thus one must look upon this cable with a jaundiced eye. Would it be possible that the Pentagon wanted support for the National Redoubt theory and that someone, possibly General Hull, planted the seed in Secretary Daniels's mind, thereby concocting a "presidential cover" for Eisenhower's actions? The author posed this question to General Hull, who smiled and congratulated the author on having done his homework, but refused to comment.

At the same time, the Washington representatives of the British Chiefs of Staff deliver to Marshall their "full exposition" about matters developing at SHAEF. They are disturbed by the content of Eisenhower's telegram to Stalin. To them it seems to be a change of plans. The telegram also contains insufficient information as to Eisenhower's intentions. More important, they have gained the impression that the northern part of Germany is not receiving the attention that "the consideration of wider issues outside the purview of General Eisenhower demands."

The British review again all that has been said before—the north German ports, the shipping in Swedish ports, the liberation of Norway. They say: "The saving of thousands of Dutchmen from early starvation is of high political importance."

Most worrying of all, "the emphasis placed by General Eisenhower on the main thrust to an axis Kassel-Leipzig-Dresden causes the British Chiefs of Staff much concern. They do not suggest that the Combined Chiefs of Staff should butter [sic] the hand of the Supreme Commander in the field. Nevertheless, they do feel that the Combined Chiefs of Staff *cannot divest themselves of the responsibility for directing the major strategy to be adopted in any theater* [emphasis

---

57. OPD Cable File. Fr War Department (Marshall) to SHAEF FWD, Rheims (Eisenhower). No. WAR 61319. CM-OUT 61319. 30 March 1945.

added]. They therefore feel strongly that, before any further action is taken with Marshal Stalin, the Combined Chiefs of Staff should have an opportunity of reviewing General Eisenhower's plan as a whole.''

The British then ask for an expression of the views of the U.S. Chiefs of Staff. The British also ask that the U.S. Chiefs agree to tell Eisenhower to delay submission of further details for Stalin, as requested by General Deane, until the Combined Chiefs of Staff confer and tell Eisenhower how to proceed. The British even draft a telegram to this effect.

A short time later, the Combined Chiefs of Staff cable Eisenhower asking for amplification of his original message to Stalin (SCAF 252 of March 28).[58]

Meanwhile, General Hull in the Pentagon cables Deane in Moscow.[59] Hull tells Deane that the British Chiefs of Staff gave the Combined Chiefs of Staff a message from his British associate, Archer, in Moscow revealing the substance of the message Deane had sent to Eisenhower asking for more information for Stalin. Hull says that the Pentagon assumes Deane gave Stalin the contents of Eisenhower's message as soon as he received it. Hull also requests that copies of Deane's communications to Eisenhower be sent to the War Department, which Deane failed to do, thereby allowing Marshall to be blindsided by the British when first they came to his office to complain.

Having gotten the facts before him, Marshall now sets to work to support Eisenhower in this time of crisis. General Hull drafts a memo for Admirals Leahy and King, and the Secretaries of the Joint Chiefs of Staff.[60] There are three different drafts of this memo, each of which is almost entirely rewritten by Marshall's bold handwriting. Using a nib pen, Marshall inserts and then deletes the following from the second draft: "The U.S. Chiefs of Staff do not recall that Berlin has ever been given to General Eisenhower as a directed objective. As to other points raised by the British Chiefs of Staff . . ." Obviously Marshall is furious with the British.

Included with the draft memos are two draft cables, handwritten

---

58. FACS (2-27-45) thru 261 (7-13-45). Cable. Fr CCS to Eisenhower. No. WARX 61296 *FACS 170.* 30 March 1945.

59. OPD 381 TS Sect IV (cases 81 thru 99) (21 March 1945). Cable from General Hull, Asst CofS, OPD to Deane (Moscow) with copy to Eisenhower. No. 61011. 30 March 1945.

60. OPD 381 TS Sect IV (cases 81 thru 99) (21 March 1945). Memo from General Hull to Leahy, King, Secretaries JCS. 30 March 1945. It is believed that the background of this memo and the memo itself have not been published before.

by Marshall, which also are never dispatched. The draft cables say that Eisenhower was correct in communicating with the Commander in Chief of the Soviet Army. The two unsent drafts are then boiled down and their sentiments expressed in the message quoted at the end of the final, official memo.

The final version, which Marshall signs before delivering it to the British, starts out saying: "The Chiefs of Staff asked me to send for your consideration the enclosed proposal as a reply to the British Chiefs of Staff's memoranda. . . . The U.S. Chiefs of Staff are not in agreement with the views of the British Chiefs of Staff. . . . As to the procedure of General Eisenhower's communicating with the Russians for the purpose of coordinating the junction between his advancing armies and those of the Soviets, this appears to have been an operational necessity in view of the rapidity of the advances in Germany.

"The U.S. Chiefs of Staff are not in accord with the proposal of the British Chiefs of Staff to send a directive to the Chiefs of our Missions in Moscow in reference to General Eisenhower's message to Marshall Stalin. To discredit in effect, certainly to lower the prestige of a highly successful Commander in the Field does not appear to be the proper procedure. If a modification of the SCAF 252 is to be made, it should be communicated by General Eisenhower and not by the Combined Chiefs of Staff over his head."

The memo continues, demolishing the British arguments point by point. The wording is almost the same as that used by Eisenhower in presenting his case to Marshall. After saying that the U.S. Chiefs believe Eisenhower's course of action will secure the northern ports "and everything mentioned [by the British] more quickly and much more decisively than the course of action urged by the British Chiefs of Staff," Marshall fires a devastating broadside.

"The battle of Germany is now at a point where the Commander in the Field is the best judge of the measures which offer the greatest prospect of destroying the German armies where there's power to resist. . . . General Eisenhower now has the enemy off balance and disorganized and should strike relentlessly with the single objective of quick and complete victory.

"While the U.S. Chiefs recognize that there are important factors which are not the direct concern and responsibility of General Eisenhower, they consider his strategic conception is sound from the overall viewpoints of crushing Germany as expeditiously as possible and should receive full support.

"There is also the view of the U.S. Chiefs of Staff that Eisenhower should be free to communicate with the Commander in Chief of the Soviet Army.

"The U.S. Chiefs of Staff propose the following message be dispatched to General Eisenhower: 'The Combined Chiefs of Staff request you furnish them with an amplification of the views expressed in your SCAF 252. They further request that you delay in furnishing further details regarding SCAF 252 in response to message of inquiry to you from General Deane until you hear further from the Combined Chiefs of Staff.' "[61]

Marshall concludes his memo to the British by saying: "The U.S. Chiefs of Staff are now of the opinion that in all probability the amplification of SCAF 252 will not cause a revision of their views as expressed in this paper."

This statement by Marshall is of great significance. He firmly tells the British that the mission of the American army in Europe is not to take Berlin, but to insure the destruction of the German armed forces as quickly as possible. Marshall also hands over to Eisenhower the power to bring the war in Europe to its conclusion under the terms Marshall previously recommended to the Supreme Commander.

Unless something totally unexpected occurs, Berlin will be allowed to fall to the Russians. No matter how Churchill and the British may argue, no matter what they do, Marshall has complete confidence that Eisenhower will carry out his marching orders.

✖ ✖ ✖

At this time many American front-line commanders become confused about their role vis à vis capturing Berlin. All their orders—battalions, divisions, corps—will make reference to being prepared to advance on Berlin. What only the Supreme Commander knows is that Marshall wants the demarcation line set up at the Elbe, short of Berlin.

Late this day, Washington time, Marshall sends a "personal" message to Eisenhower describing his memo to the British Chiefs of Staff.[62] Marshall explains that the British claim they don't want to tie the hands of the Supreme Commander in the field, but they believed that Eisen-

---

61. This message was sent as drafted. FACS (2-27-45) thru 261 (7-13-45). Cable fr CCS to Eisenhower. No. WARX 61296. FACS 170. 30 March 1945.
62. OPD Cable File. Fr Marshall to Eisenhower—personal. No. WAR 61337 (CM-OUT 61337). TOO 2125. Originator: General Hull. 30 March 1945.

hower's message to Stalin was concerned with much wider issues that were outside the Supreme Commander's duties. This portion of the message appears to be in Marshall's own handwriting: "The issues outside the purview of SCAEF are—the U-boat war, Swedish shipping, the political importance of saving thousands of Dutchman from starvation, and the importance of a move into Denmark and liberating Norway. Therefore the British request a delay of further details to Deane in Moscow until you hear more from the CCS."

The real meat of Marshall's message is that the U.S. Chiefs have replied to the British saying they are not in agreement with the views of the British Chiefs. Eisenhower's procedure in communicating with Stalin seems to have been of operational necessity. Any modification of this should be done by Eisenhower and not the Combined Chiefs. Furthermore the course of action outlined by Eisenhower to Stalin appears to be "in accord with agreed strategy and SCAEF's directive, particularly in the light of recent developments."

The U.S. Chiefs agree that Eisenhower has deployed the maximum number of troops possible across the Rhine to the north. The secondary effort to the South is creating splendid results and is being exploited to the limit of logistics. Therefore, this should make it possible for the northern effort by Montgomery "to accelerate its drive eastward into Germany." Lastly, the U.S. Chiefs believe that SCAEF's plan will win the northern ports and other items mentioned by the British faster than could be done by the course of action recommended by the British.

Now Marshall passes the torch of command to Eisenhower. He tells Eisenhower the battle for Germany has reached the point where the field commander should make the judgments about what should be done. It does not appear sound to turn away from the weakness of the enemy. Says Marshall: "The single objective should be the quick and complete victory."

While the U.S. Chiefs recognize there are factors that don't directly concern SCAEF, they consider his plan to be sound and will give it full support. SCAEF should also communicate freely with the commander of the Soviet Army.

Although the U.S. Chiefs have asked SCAEF for further amplification of his message to Stalin, and that SCAEF not send any more information to Stalin until hearing more from the Combined Chiefs, the U.S. Chiefs do not believe that the amplification of SCAF 252 will cause them to revise their planning or the views they've expressed. In concluding, Marshall suggests that Eisenhower amplify his views on ending the war for the understanding of the Combined Chiefs.

Any further amplification will be superfluous. The deed is done. Just as the British feared, the Americans are taking over the running of the war. Viewed in the hindsight of fifty years of peace in Europe, Marshall and Eisenhower made the right decisions.

Knowing that his SHAEF representatives in Moscow are scheduled to meet Stalin on the night of March 31, that same morning Eisenhower sends a cable to Deane asking him to withhold the detailed information that Eisenhower sent amplifying his SCAF 252.[63] Then, following Marshall's suggestion of the day before, Eisenhower sends a cable to the War Department for the Combined Chiefs (with an informational copy for the British Chiefs of Staff), giving greater detail about his plan.[64] He tells the War Department that he has sent the details Deane requested to Moscow, but after receiving Marshall's last cable, he has instructed Deane not to give these details to Stalin.

Eisenhower then expounds on his strategy. The first element is to drive eastward after the offensives on the northern and central fronts have joined hands. The main object is to split and annihilate the German forces. After this is accomplished the rest will occur. Obviously it would be a help if we could link our forces with the Russians. The place where we will be able to meet the Russians depends in some ways on what their plans may be. From our viewpoint three strategic areas are of principal importance. To the north there is Hamburg and Kiel. In the center, the area of Leipzig. In the south, the area of Nürnburg-Regensburg-Munich. As to the capital of Germany, Eisenhower says: "Berlin as a strategic area is discounted as it is now largely destroyed and we have information that the ministries are moving to the Erfurt-Leipzig region. Moreover, it is so near the Russian front, once they start moving again they will reach it in a matter of days." In explaining his reasons for discounting Berlin as a "strategic area," it is interesting to note that, while not saying so, Eisenhower is relying on the Magic intercepts to support his argument for chasing down the still-operating departments of the German government.

Next, Eisenhower reminds the British that the terrain is easier in the center—across the plateau of Germany—than in the north. And if we continue on the Leipzig route, it is doubtful that we would have to "cross the Elbe at all before joining with the Russians." Also to be

---

63. Files of CofS (SHAEF/18015/2). Cable from Eisenhower to Deane and Archer (Moscow). No. FWD 18372. 31 March 1945.
64. ABC 384 Europe (5 August 1943) 1-D. To War Department (Combined Chiefs) fr Eisenhower. Info: British Chiefs. No. FWD 18403 (SCAF 260) CM-IN 33260. 31 March 1945.

considered are the northern and southern areas. For the moment the Allies must select one attack on which to concentrate our main efforts, even if it means neglecting the others. By placing our main attack in the center, besides attaining the advantages listed before and joining hands with the Russians, the Allies can retain flexibility of operations and reinforce, if necessary, for the northern drive and second, the southern thrust, according to how the fluid situation develops.

To mollify the British, Eisenhower promises that after joining with the Russians, or "even sooner if we can, the northern armies can be reinforced and the [U.S.] Ninth Army can come to the aid of the British and Canadian forces in their efforts to clear the entire coastline west of Luebeck." He also says, "Of course my plans will remain flexible and I must be allowed freedom of action to cope with the fluid situation. Maximum flexibility will result from a concentration initially of maximum force in the center."

Though sound and logical in strategic terms, Eisenhower's plan still does not mollify Prime Minister Churchill. With Roosevelt being so ill, however, there is no political leader in America who can listen to the Prime Minister's arguments and act on them.

Also on March 31, Eisenhower sends the requested message to President Roosevelt saying that the "further along we get in this campaign the more likely it becomes that the German forces on the Western Front will never effect a clean-cut military surrender."[65] Most likely a proclamation of VE day will occur only if the Allies make the proclamation rather than by the collapse of German resistance. Looking further, all areas containing fragments of the German armies—paratroopers, panzer and SS forces—will have to be taken by use of force or threat of force. This could lead to guerrilla warfare that would require large numbers of troops to suppress. Among the major items Eisenhower will attend to is the prevention of an Alpine Redoubt. This cable now gives Eisenhower a political reason, besides a strategic rational, for diverting American troops away from Berlin toward southern Germany.

Eisenhower also cables Marshall that his amplification of information sent to Deane does not go beyond what Eisenhower has told Marshall. He also assures Marshall that in the future, he will make sure

---

65. OPD Cable File. Fr SHAEF FWD, Rheims (Eisenhower), to War Department (Marshall—personal). No. FWD 18380 CM-IN 32997. 31 March 1945.

that copies sent from SHAEF to the Moscow mission are repeated to the Combined Chiefs and the British Chiefs.[66]

The issue of whether or not a National Redoubt truly exists will not easily be settled, however. The latest OSS report for the end of March concludes: "There is still no sign of a coherent line of defenses being built all around the Alpine bastion; though such line can be discerned even along the northern approaches to the Alps."[67] Despite this discouraging news, Eisenhower now has enough cover—via intelligence from the Magic Summaries, plus the "interest" of the White House—to justify his southern strategy.

Next, Eisenhower sets out to mollify Montgomery. He sends a long message to the Field Marshal explaining in detail his plans for attacking the center of Germany. Eisenhower summarizes all the items he has presented Marshall and the Combined Chiefs. He also explains that since Bradley's forces will be the ones straining to break away to Leipzig (the Fifteenth Army will now do the mopping up in the Ruhr), Eisenhower says he believes it imperative that Bradley be allowed to make the decision about when to make the final attack eastward. However, Eisenhower promises that he will warn Montgomery at least twenty-four hours in advance of the removal of the Ninth Army from his command and in selecting the moment since the primary concern is maintaining Montgomery's advance to the north. Furthermore, Eisenhower reassures Montgomery that an American formation would again be under his control for later operations beyond the Elbe.

"You will note that in none of this do I mention Berlin," says Eisenhower. "That place has become, so far as I am concerned, nothing but a geographical location, and I have never been interested in these. My purpose is to destroy the enemy's forces and his powers to resist. Manifestly, when the time comes, we must do everything possible to push across the Elbe without delay, drive to the coast at Luebeck and seal off the Danish peninsula."

March ends with two messages from Deane in Moscow. In the first, Deane explains how the mixup about SCAF 252 escalated into a major flap.[68] He acknowledges that he made an error in not sending copies of his cable to Eisenhower to the CCS and the British Chiefs.

---

66. Personal File of Gen. W. B. Smith, CofS, SHAEF. Fr Eisenhower to Marshall. No. FWD 18393. 31 March 1945.
67. OSS Detachment (Main). No. RAL 148.3. National Redoubt—Survey of Available Intelligence to the End of March 1945: Excerpts from—.
68. Personal File, General W. B. Smith, SHAEF. Fr SHAEF Mission, Moscow (Deane), to AGWAR (Marshall) SHAEF FWD (Eisenhower). No. MX 23558. 31 March 1945.

He ends saying: "Shall not make that mistake again." (Deane also suggests setting up a radio-Teletype for direct communications with SHAEF since the equipment is in Moscow.)

The second message from Moscow dated March 31 confirms that the strategy Marshall proposed earlier to Eisenhower will be acceptable to the Russians.

A meeting was held tonight in the Kremlin, Archer and Deane inform Eisenhower.[69] Stalin and Molotov are present. The Americans give Stalin a copy of Eisenhower's message, SCAF 252, in both the English and Russian text. First Stalin reads the message. Then the Americans point out the operations described on a map. Stalin's immediate reaction is that the plan is good. But he refrains from committing himself until he can consult with his staff, saying that he will give his answer the next day. According to Deane and Archer, Stalin is apparently impressed with the direction of the attack in central Germany. Also with the secondary attack taking place in the south. The Americans urge Stalin to give them his views so the plans of the Soviet and American armies can be successfully coordinated. They also point out that Eisenhower hopes to establish a liaison team arrangement with an exchange of officers to be based both at SHAEF and Moscow.

The Americans also ask Stalin to give his estimate of the current situation. He replies that he can't do that immediately, but would do so the next day. He then counters by asking if the Americans are prepared to give Eisenhower's estimate at that moment. The Americans rise to the occasion, giving highlights of how SCAEF views the current situation. Stalin next asks if Eisenhower has any knowledge of Germany's prepared positions toward the center of Germany. The Americans said he does not. What about the withdrawal of German troops from Norway? asks Stalin. The Americans reply that Eisenhower had given them no indication that he possessed such knowledge.

Stalin's next question is whether the advance for the secondary attack in the south of Germany would originate from Italy or the Western Front. The Americans explain that the impetus for the drive will come from the Western Front. When Stalin says he is interested, the Americans then review the German order of battle on the Western Front. Stalin next wants to know if the Americans can verify Soviet intelligence. Are there sixty German divisions on the Western Front?

---

69. OPD Cable File. Fr Military Mission, Moscow (Archer & Deane), to War Department No. MX 23572 (CM-IN 173). (1 copy to WD; 1 copy Eisenhower—eyes only; 1 copy to AGWAR for Combined Chiefs of Staff; 1 copy for British Chiefs of Staff).

The Americans say they have identified sixty-one German divisions so far and give Stalin the latest changes in the order of battle. Stalin also wants to know if the Germans have any additional reserves on the Western Front. The Americans say that to the best of their knowledge no such reinforcements exist. Stalin is greatly impressed with the number of German prisoners the Allies had taken recently. He comments that such numbers would certainly help finish the war soon.

American ambassador Harriman then asks about the weather on the Eastern Front. Stalin says that conditions have improved considerably. Harriman asks whether or not Stalin's prediction that his operations would be bogged down by the end of March might still be true. Stalin replies that the situation is much better than what he had anticipated. The floods came early this year, he says, and the roads are now drying. Stalin gives the Americans the impression that his Russian armies are not hampered by weather. The Germans are resisting fiercely in Czechoslovakia, but this resistance will be overcome. He also says that the Germans had concentrated ten divisions northeast of Lake Balaton, but his armies had defeated them.

The Germans, Stalin explains, are concentrating their resistance in the Bratislava Gap, but he is confident they will be overcome. There are still sixteen German divisions in Latvia. But he thinks they can only rescue three divisions, with their artillery, and this will take them a month. Clark Kerr of the American embassy says that the Soviets have made a valuable contribution by capturing Gdynia and Danzig. Stalin says it took a week to reduce Danzig. Stalin says that only about one-third of the Germans there wanted to fight. As the Red Army approached, the SS troops shot down those who wished to surrender.

Throughout the entire discussion, Stalin has apparently been considering Eisenhower's plan. He suddenly switches the conversation back to it and says he thought the plan is a good one. It accomplishes the most important thing of all—dividing Germany in half. Then he says he believes that the last stand of the Germans would be made in the mountains of western Czechoslovakia and Bavaria. On this note the meeting ends. Stalin promises that he will reply the next day to Eisenhower's message and his plan of operations.

As it turns out, no further reply is really necessary. There is no treaty with Stalin, nor a handshake deal. But the Americans and the Russians have a realistic understanding about how, in military terms, the war in Europe will end.

15

Shortly before Deane and Archer meet with Stalin on March 31, back in Germany, at the headquarters of the Second Armored Division, Col. Briard P. Johnson, G-3, carefully signs an overlay map he has just prepared. It is to be sent by courier to corps headquarters. The map spells out the route of attack proposed by Maj. Gen. Isaac Davis White, Commanding, that his division will take in attacking Berlin.

There are two sections of the map. The second begins with the city of Magdeburg, on the west bank of the River Elbe. From here the division will hook up two of its combat commands—A and B—for a final drive on the German capital. The assault will follow the most direct route into Berlin. Day-by-day lines of advance are cautiously drawn in, showing a ten-mile gain each day for seven days. Each advance line has a code name. From west to east they read: SILVER, SILK, SATIN, DAISY, PANSY, JUG and GOAL.

The last line of advance, GOAL, runs through the city of Berlin, which is delineated on the map by a large blue swastika. (See map on opposite page.)

At this point in the war, the Second Armored Division is the most powerful division ever formed. Designated as a ''heavy division,'' it is, in actuality, three divisions in strength, and its division artillery is the equivalent of that of a full Army corps. On the road, with its tanks and artillery strung out in route order, the division is seventy-two miles long. It is an awesome striking force.

What White hopes for is that his troops won't have to stop for the proposed advance lines. If everything goes smoothly, White believes, and it appears from intelligence that it will, the Second Armored should be in Berlin forty-eight hours after it crosses the River Elbe.

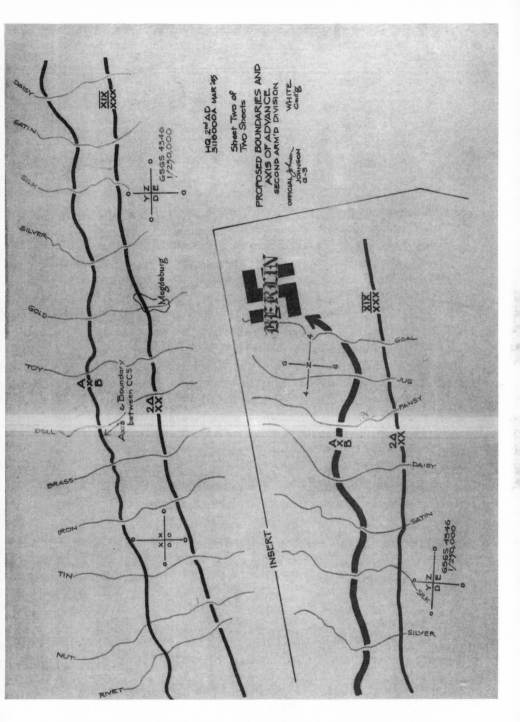

Second Armored Division's assault plan from Magdeburg to Berlin, March 31, 1945.

✖ ✖ ✖

I. D. White's planning is timely. The U.S. First and Ninth Armies meet at Lippstadt the following day, April 1, and the encirclement of the Ruhr is completed, trapping German Army Group B inside the net. This sets the stage for White's troops to start rumbling toward the Elbe.

It is also Easter Sunday.

Prime Minister Churchill, already upset by Eisenhower's direct communications with Stalin, is even more upset by the reactions of the British Chiefs of Staff. He considers their arguments as presented to Marshall to be very weak. Thus, he decides to become involved.

He dispatches a cable to Roosevelt, saying at first he believes there has been a misunderstanding on both sides, which he is anxious to "disperse without more ado."[1] He is concerned that it might be thought that "we wish in the slightest degree to discredit or lower the prestige of General Eisenhower in his increasingly important relations with Russian commanders in the field. All we sought was a little more time to consider the far-reaching changes desired by General Eisenhower in the plans that had been concerted by the Combined Chiefs of Staff at Malta and had received your and my joint approval. The British Chiefs of Staff were naturally concerned by a procedure which apparently left the fortunes of the British Army, which though only a third of yours still amounts to over a million men, to be settled without the slightest reference to any British authority."

Churchill is laying out the basic thrust of his argument all the while praising Eisenhower. He also agrees with the procedure proposed by the U.S. Chiefs for contacting the Russians and says he's sorry the British hadn't thought of it themselves. But then he gets down to brass tacks: He is upset by implications in the recent correspondence in that they "did not do justice to our [British] efforts or contributions. Both at Caen in the Normandy battle and lately on the front north of Wesel, we have the task of forming the hinge to the main American swing. ... Therefore, it could not be expected that in discharging this duty very spectacular results could attend our indispensable action. In the Rhine battle we had to fight onwards alone in the northern hinge for thirteen days longer than was arranged on account of the opening of the [Roer] dams by the Germans which inevitably delayed the coming

---

1. ABC Europe (5 August 1943) Sec 1-D. Cable fr Churchill to Roosevelt. No. 931. 1 April 1945.

into action of the Ninth U.S. Army. . . . From February 9th when we began, down to March 29th (the latest date for which I have figures) the twelve or thirteen divisions of His Majesty's Forces which were engaged suffered a loss of over twenty thousand casualties. I do not think any American Armies to the southward suffered more, and some of them, thank God, suffered very much less. Therefore I feel sure that you will not feel discontented with our efforts. . . . Having dealt with and I trust disposed of these misunderstandings between the truest friends and comrades that ever fought side by side as Allies, I venture to put to you a few considerations. . . . The Allied Armies of the north and center should now march at the highest speed towards the Elbe. Hitherto this axis has been upon Berlin. General Eisenhower on the estimate of the enemy's resistance, to which I attach the greatest importance, now wishes to shift the axis somewhat to the southward and strike through Leipzig, even perhaps as far south as Dresden. He withdraws the Ninth U.S. Army from the northern group of armies and in consequence stretches its front southward. I should be sorry if the resistance of the enemy was such as to destroy the weight and momentum of the advance of the British Twenty-first Army Group and to leave them in an almost static condition along the Elbe when and if they reach it. I say quite frankly that *Berlin remains of high strategic importance* [emphasis added]. Nothing will exert a psychological effect of despair on all German forces of resistance equal to that of the fall of Berlin. It will be the supreme signal of defeat to the German people. On the other hand, if left to itself to maintain a siege by the Russians among its ruins and as long as the German flag flies there, it will animate the resistance of all Germans under arms.

"There is moreover another aspect which it is proper for you and me to consider. The Russian Armies will no doubt overrun all Austria and enter Vienna. If they also take Berlin, will not their impression that they have been the overwhelming contributor to our common victory be unduly imprinted in their minds, and may this not lead them into such a mood which will raise grave and formidable difficulties in the future? I therefore consider that from a political standpoint we should march as far east into Germany as possible and that should Berlin be in our grasp we should certainly take it. This also appears sound on military grounds."

In summation, Churchill says that the differences that exist between the two Allies "would seem to be the following, viz, whether the emphasis should be put on an axis directed on Berlin or on one directed on Leipzig and Dresden. This is surely a matter upon which a reasonable latitude of discussion should be allowed our two Chiefs of Staff's Committee before any final commitment involving the Russians is entered into.'' The Prime Minister ends by saying that he is quite willing that this personal message, which is not a staff communication, should be shown to Marshall.

There is a certain shrewdness to the last statement. Churchill knows that Roosevelt is ill and is resting in Warm Springs, Georgia. Thus he suspects that any reply will come, not from Roosevelt, but Marshall. A reply will be sent over Roosevelt's signature. As we will see, this message creates something of a mystery. (The message was not made available to the author, who suspects that Marshall dispatched it without Roosevelt's ever having seen it.)

The weakness of Churchill's argument is apparent, however. He cannot prove to Marshall that Berlin has either strategic or military importance. Churchill's contentions are based on politics and political appearances. He does not answer American fears—which have not been expressed openly—that Montgomery, even if he still commands the U.S. Ninth Army, will move too cautiously toward the Elbe. (Many American commanders believe that Montgomery will not move forward until conditions are to his liking.) Churchill also fails to take into consideration the American concern with ending the war in Japan. He is at odds, too, with Marshall's orders to Eisenhower to cooperate with the Russians. Thus, his argument will not be acceptable to the U.S. Chiefs of Staff.

Churchill also addresses a cable to Eisenhower.[2] The message is similar in thought to the one he sends Roosevelt, but now Churchill places even more stress on the necessity for seizing Berlin. He writes: ''I do not know why it would be an advantage not to cross the Elbe. If the enemy's resistance should weaken, as you evidently expect, and which may well be accorded, why should we not cross the Elbe and advance as far eastward as possible? This has an important political bearing, as the Russian army in the south seems certain to enter Vienna and overrun Austria. If we deliberately leave Berlin to them, even if it should be within our grasp, the double event may strengthen their conviction, already apparent, that they have done everything.

''Further, I do not consider myself that Berlin has yet lost its military and certainly not its political significance. The fall of Berlin

---

2. OPD Cable File. Fr AMSSO to SHAEF FWD (Eisenhower). No. 2072. Later, in his message No. 2096, Churchill will try to worm his way out of the situation by claiming he misunderstood the role Eisenhower assigned Montgomery because of a "clerical error."

would have profound psychological effect on German resistance in every part of the Reich. While Berlin holds out, great masses of Germans will feel it their duty to go down fighting. The idea that the capture of Dresden and junction there with the Russians would be a superior gain does not commend itself to me. The parts of the German government departments which have moved south can very quickly move southward again. But whilst Berlin remains under the German flag, it cannot in my opinion fail to be the most decisive point in Germany.

"Therefore I should greatly prefer persistence in the plan on which we crossed the Rhine, namely that the Ninth U.S. Army should march with the Twenty-first Army Group to the Elbe and *beyond to Berlin* [emphasis added]. This would not be in any way inconsistent with the great central thrust which you are so rightly developing as the result of your brilliant operation of your armies south of the Ruhr. It only shifts the weight of one army to the northernmost flank and this avoids the relegation of His Majesty's forces to an unexpected restricted sphere."

Churchill ends the message saying that he views these cables between him and Eisenhower just as if they were unofficial talks. Churchill says he might use some of his arguments in other quarters, but not in reference to anything that might have passed between the two themselves. Churchill's message must worry Eisenhower. He answers promptly, disputing Churchill's charge that he had changed his strategy in any way, and that Churchill still misunderstood what Eisenhower intends to do.[3]

The Supreme Commander writes: "I have not changed any plans." But he has made certain regroupings to cross the Rhine and continue the main thrust in the north, to isolate the Ruhr and "disrupt, surround or destroy" the Germans defending that area. "This is as far as strategic objectives of this force have ever been definitely approved by me because obviously such a victory over the German forces in the west and such a blow to his industrial capacity would necessarily create new situations requiring study and analysis before the next broad pattern of effort could be adequately sketched."

This reply is somewhat disingenuous considering the instructions Marshall has given Eisenhower about driving to the Elbe and linking

---

3. Personal file of Gen. W. B. Smith, SHAEF. Fr Eisenhower to Churchill. No. FWD 18428. 1 April 1945.

up there with the Russians. The Supreme Commander maintains that the current situation is one that he has presented to his staff for "more than a year" as the one "toward which we should strive." The Allied forces should cross the Rhine and form a great triangle around the Ruhr with the apex resting in the Kassel area. The next step is to determine the blow that will be the most destructive to the Germans. "I have never lost sight of the great importance of the drive to the northern coast," says Eisenhower, "although your telegram did introduce a new idea respecting the political importance of the early attainment of particular objectives. I clearly see your point in this matter."

But, says Eisenhower, he believes the main difference between what he proposes and what Churchill wants is *timing*. "Even this might be relegated to a matter of relative unimportance depending upon the degree of resistance met," he says. First he will concentrate his efforts in the center to gain the position he needs. Then as the situation develops, the next move will be to have Montgomery cross the Elbe, "reinforced, if necessary, with American troops, and reach at least a line including Luebeck on the coast." If resistance should crumble, there will be little "difference in time between gaining the central position and crossing the Elbe." But, should resistance be harder, it would be necessary to concentrate the Allied efforts one at a time so as not to allow the forces to be dispersed by trying to do all these things at the same time.

Eisenhower says he is hurt by Churchill's charge that he was planning to assign British forces to an "unexpected restricted sphere." There is nothing in the past record that would indicate such an idea. It didn't seem to make much difference whether or not the U.S. Ninth Army was commanded by Bradley "until I can be assured that our rear areas are substantially cleaned out and the thrust to Leipzig is successful." The maximum delay on Montgomery's plans would be that he might have to postpone his power thrust across the Elbe; this must be put off until the rear is in satisfactory shape. In conclusion, Eisenhower tells Churchill about plans to be carried out under Operation ECLIPSE. Should ECLIPSE conditions occur, Eisenhower assures Churchill that Berlin and Luebeck will be the primary targets of a swift Allied advance.

In essence, Eisenhower gives Churchill the slight hope of seizing Berlin only if ECLIPSE conditions occur (upon the sudden collapse of the German armies in the West, or a decision made by the Supreme Commander that German forces are so weak his troops will advance as quickly as possible on certain strategic targets). But Churchill is greatly reassured by the promise that Eisenhower will seal off the Danish peninsula at Luebeck, thereby protecting the Scandinavian countries and the English Channel coast from further penetration by the Soviet armies.[4]

✖ ✖ ✖

Still the most important person for Eisenhower to hear from is Stalin. And while Churchill is burning up the cable wires with his correspondence to Roosevelt and the Supreme Commander, Stalin asks the Military Mission in Moscow to deliver a "personal and most secret telegram" to Eisenhower. The message is brief. Only seven short paragraphs. For Eisenhower's future planning it is vital.[5] Stalin first acknowledges receiving Eisenhower's telegram of March 28. Then he says:

1. Your plan to cut the German armies in two by joining forces with the Soviet armies entirely coincides with Soviet plans.

2. I agree with you that the proper meeting place should be in the areas Erfurt, Leipzig and Dresden. The Soviet High Command believes that the main blows of the Soviet armies should be made in that direction.

3. Berlin has lost its importance as a strategic target. We will allot our secondary forces in the direction of Berlin.

4. The Soviet High Command also approves your plan of a

---

4. In reporting this correspondence between Churchill, Roosevelt and Eisenhower, most historians fail to include Churchill's complete statements regarding his beliefs about the military and political importance of the Allies capturing Berlin. Neither do their accounts include Eisenhower's statements that he has never changed his plans, even though Churchill's telegrams make the charge.

It's not that Eisenhower tells a lie. He never did change his plans. He simply doesn't reveal what Marshall ordered him to do regarding the Elbe, Berlin and the Russians.

Compare, for example, the text of Eisenhower's message as reported above, concerning the advance by Allied forces based on the possibility of there being ECLIPSE conditions, versus the U.S. Army's position for the past fifty years. As paraphrased by Army historian Forrest Pogue in his chapter called "The Decision to Halt on the Elbe," in the official history *Command Decisions,* the Supreme Commander's words suddenly become: "As for the drive to Berlin, [Eisenhower] made no promises. If it could be brought into Allied orbit, he declared, honors would be equally shared between the British and U.S. forces."

5. OPD Cable File. Fr Military Mission, Moscow (Archer & Deane), to War Department No. MX 23588 (CM-IN 983). Copy sent SHAEF FWD for Eisenhower, AGWAR for Combined Chiefs of Staff, British Chiefs of Staff. The message is relayed via the War Department Code Center for action CC/S; info: Leahy, Arnold, Hull, Bissell, King, CofS.

second ring comprised by a meeting of our forces in the area of Vienna, Linz, Regensburg.

5. The beginning of the main Soviet blow in the north will be the second half of May. The thrust toward Vienna is already under way. This plan, however, may be altered by changing circumstances, i.e., a rapid retreat of German forces. The weather will also play a large role.

6. The General Staff is studying the problem of communications, and their decision will be communicated at a later date.

7. The number of German troops on the Eastern Front is gradually being stepped up. The Sixth SS Tank Army has moved to the East along with three divisions from northern Italy plus two divisions from Norway.

Stalin is not telling the whole truth. Eisenhower knows that the Soviets are going to allot more than "secondary forces" to attack Berlin. He also knows that Soviet troops have already nearly destroyed the Sixth Panzer Army north of Lake Balaton (the remnants of the German Sixth Army and the Sixth SS Panzer Army have been combined). The Russians are only about 50 miles from Vienna (the Allies about 450). It is obvious that the Russians will seize Vienna before the British-American forces can reach the Elbe. But Eisenhower is pleased. He has what he needs, the Russian agreement that they accept the Elbe as a line of demarcation.

On this April Fools' Day, however, if Eisenhower is planning to stop at the Elbe, his field commanders are still ignorant of his intentions.

At the headquarters of the American XIX Corps, Col. George Sloan, at twenty-seven the youngest corps G-3 in the Army, is busy preparing letter of instruction No. 134. This order will send Maj. Gen. Raymond S. McLain's troops, a force larger than the entire Union Army at the battle of Gettysburg, to Berlin. The order changes only slightly the plan Gen. I. D. White proposed a day earlier. Now the boundaries between the Second Armored Division and the Eighth Armored Division are established as running through Brandenburg, on the outskirts of the German capital. Still, the Second Armored is ordered to "continue advance on Berlin in zone." The plan also calls for the Eighty-third Infantry Division "when relieved by 95 Inf Div [to] follow closely 8 Armd Div in zone; prepared to pass through 8 Armd Div; continue advance on BERLIN."

To make his intentions doubly clear, McLain prepares a special memo explaining his plans to General White. "We will probably get a zone of action slightly wider than that portion of the corps zone now north of our combat command boundary. General McLain desires that the Second Armored Division push on as rapidly as possible in the new zone. Secure crossings over the Weser [River] and the Elbe [River] and be prepared to send strong combat patrols into Berlin."

The idea of being the first Allied troops into Berlin galvanizes the men of the Second Armored.

April 2, 1945

A cable from Prime Minister Churchill is among the first to reach Eisenhower's desk this morning.[6] In it Churchill thanks Eisenhower for his message of the previous day, saying: "It would be a grief to me if anything in my last disturbs or still more pains you. I only meant that the effect of the Twenty-first Army Group arriving on the Elbe so spread out that it would be condemned to a static role would be a good deal less than we hoped for, namely, to enter Berlin side by side with our American comrades."

As mentioned earlier, Churchill says he was given this impression by a misprint in Eisenhower's message (FWD-18334, paragraph 4), which apparently reached Churchill in garbled form as follows: "Montgomery will be responsible on patrol task and I propose to increase his forces, etc." Churchill now reads the message as saying: Montgomery will be responsible "for these tasks"—i.e., the clearing of the northern ports and crossing the Elbe. Churchill says the "clerical" error caused him to believe the British would be employed only in a static role, and that the error "will surely explain my phrasing to you." Then Churchill says: "Returning to my main theme, I am however all the more impressed with the importance of entering Berlin, which may well be open to us by reply from Moscow to which you, in paragraph 3, say 'Berlin has lost its former strategic importance.' This should be read in light of what I mentioned of political aspects. I deem it highly important that we should shake hands with the Russians as far to the east as possible."

Churchill goes on to say that he has communicated with Roosevelt concerning British confidence in Eisenhower. Furthermore, the arrival

---

6. Personal File of Gen. W. B. Smith, CofS, SHAEF. Fr Prime Minister to Eisenhower. No. 2096. 2 April 1945.

of Eisenhower's SCAF 260 has "largely allayed" the fears of the British Chiefs. The issue is smoothing itself out. Churchill hopes that Eisenhower understands British concern to his first message since they had no knowledge of what was taking place until they saw Eisenhower's telegram to Stalin. Says Churchill: "Again my congratulations on the great developments. Much may happen in the West before the date of Stalin's main offensive."[7]

Since Stalin has said that the Russian attack on Berlin is scheduled for mid-May, Churchill is trying to get Eisenhower to commit himself to saying that if he can take Berlin on the cheap, he will do so. (The Prime Minister is still unaware that the plan for stopping at the Elbe came from Marshall.)

Now another blow to Churchill's hopes is delivered in Washington, and perhaps the mystery of the message sent to Churchill allegedly by Roosevelt is solved. Adm. William D. Leahy, the President's military adviser, in a memo dated April 2, 1945, writes on White House stationery to General Marshall about Churchill's cable to the President of the previous day.[8] Titled "Memorandum for General Marshall," Leahy's comments scuttle Churchill's hopes in two brief sentences.

"The attached message No. 931 from the Prime Minister is forwarded requesting the preparation of a draft reply," writes Leahy. "It seems to me that Eisenhower's SCAF 260 covers the question at issue and should have our full support."

Given the fact that Roosevelt went by train to Hyde Park, New York, on March 24, returned to Washington by train on March 28, left Washington by train on the afternoon of March 29 and arrived in Warm Springs, Georgia, on the morning of March 30, it is entirely possible that Roosevelt never sees Churchill's cable of April 1. Leahy's response in behalf of the White House to Marshall's query about drafting a reply to the Prime Minister appears to have given Marshall the freedom to reply as he wants.

Meanwhile, Marshall is preparing a seven-and-a-half page, single-spaced memorandum for the President explaining his view about how the war in Europe will end.[9] According to the Chief of Staff, by about

---

7. FWD 18428, 1 April 1945, originated Eisenhower. FWD 18334, FS-Out 1188, 30 March 1945, originated G-3 (General Bull). SCAF 260, FWD 18403, FS-OUT 1244, 31 March 1945, originated G-3 (General Bull).
8. ABC Europe (5 August 1943) Sec 1-D. Memo/letter on White House stationery. Fr Leahy to Marshall. 2 April 1945.
9. OPD 381 TS Sect IV (cases 81 thru 99) (21 March 1945). Memo from Marshall to President Roosevelt dated 2 April 1945. Carbon copies: Leahy, Sect. of War, Sect. of State, OPD.

the end of April, military operations on the continent of Europe will probably have reached the final stage—mopping up. By April 20, Allied forces should reach the Elbe River between Magdeburg and Halle. To the north, the British advance is likely to be slower and shallower. In south Germany, Nuremberg and Stuttgart will probably be in Allied hands by April 20 and Munich by May 1.

The Russians, Marshall believes, should be able to begin their general offensive by April 10 and by about May 1 should be in contact with American forces along the Elbe south of Berlin. (This actually occurs on April 25.) Most of Saxony and Czechoslovakia will probably have been overrun. German troops will probably still be resisting within a large north-German pocket, including the provinces of Berlin, Mecklenburg, Schleswig-Holstein, as well as the peninsula of Jutland and the Danish islands.

In Austria, the Russians by May 1 will probably have cleared Hungary, captured Vienna and should be moving toward a junction with American forces near Linz.

The real problem is this: "On 1 May, neither a cohesive west nor east front will probably exist," writes Marshall. "It is more likely that there will be a series of western and eastern pockets in which encircled fragments of the once-formidable German Armies will be fighting on with dogged fanaticism—so long as Hitler leads them. . . . It is of importance to recognize now, where on 1 May, such pockets of resistance will probably be located. However, it is impossible to go further at this time than to suggest the likelihood of resistance in certain areas. Chance will play a leading role."

One pocket Marshall foresees developing is in northern Germany with twenty to thirty German divisions making a last stand. As for the National Redoubt, he protects his flanks by declaring that "the many rumors as to German preparations for the defense of the 'Alpine Redoubt' are believed to lack substance." It will all depend on whether or not "Hitler and his subordinate Nazi leaders, or the German High Command, will have transferred their headquarters into the 'redoubt' area. If Hitler does so, a fairly formidable military task requiring a considerable number of divisions may still confront the Allies." A third potential pocket is "fortress Holland." A fourth may be in the Black Forest. A fifth in Thuringia. "Leadership, or lack of leadership, will prove a determining factor to how long the fighting will continue," says Marshall. Where Hitler goes the strongest resistance will be encountered."

By May 1, he also predicts, the economic structure of Germany will not be good. There is the possibility of drastic starvation conditions in much of West Germany by September. There is little hope that either civilian or military elements will overthrow the Nazi government in the final stages of the war. Says Marshall: "Hitler has the creation of his myth of the future ever uppermost in his mind, and he knows full well that his future with the German people, and his place in the history of the world, depends on the dignity of his exit. Any cowardice, faltering, or negotiating with the Allies in this last hour would destroy the great tragic myth he is seeking to create. If Hitler is true to the character he has shown in past crises, he will make his exit bravely and dramatically and thus remain a psychological force for his enemies to reckon with for decades."

In this fashion Marshall presents to the President an entirely different concept of the way to end the war in Europe than does Prime Minister Churchill. No seizing of Berlin with the possibility of then moving eastward for Marshall. No "political goals" for Marshall. Compared to Churchill, Marshall's analysis of what will happen within Germany appears more realistic. He also does not say that it is his plan for Eisenhower to wait for the Russians on the river Elbe. He does point out that fighting can continue anywhere in Germany after May 1, but that it largely depends on where Hitler is to be found, which may or may not be in Berlin. Last, he knows that if Roosevelt ever reads his memo, Admiral Leahy will add the final bit of argument: We must get our boys out of Europe so we can invade Japan.

Back at Supreme Headquarters in Europe, Eisenhower is preparing an order for his top ten field commands that gives no indication that he is planning to stop on the Elbe.[10] The Supreme Commander announces that since the Ruhr has been isolated, he hopes to begin an attack on the axis (route) Kassel-Leipzig to make contact with the Russians. On the fourth of April, the U.S. Ninth Army will revert to Bradley's command in the Twelfth Army Group. The northern armies (i.e., Montgomery) will continue to advance on the axis Hannover-Bremen. Afterward they will launch a thrust to the Elbe in conjunction with protecting the left flank of the central force. They will be prepared to seize a bridgehead over the Elbe and conduct operations to the east. The central group of armies will mop up the Ruhr. Then it will launch

---

10. SCAF 151 (20 December 1944) thru 275 (12 April 1945). Fr Eisenhower to War Department and ten related field commands (including Montgomery). No. FWD 18475. SCAF 261. (This message is to have limited distribution and is to be delivered only to the addressees or their appointed representatives.) 2 April 1945.

its main attack on the Kassel-Leipzig axis. It will take advantage of any opportunity to capture a bridgehead across the Elbe and move on toward the east. The southern armies will protect the flank of the central armies and will be prepared to launch an attack on the axis Nuremberg-Regensburg-Linz, to prevent the consolidation of German resistance to the south.

In checking what this order means to a battlefield commander, those interviewed by the author agreed that by directing his central armies to seize any opportunity to capture a bridgehead over the Elbe and to be prepared to "continue the advance to the East on Berlin," Eisenhower means he is preparing a final drive on Berlin. Thus, these generals made immediate preparations to invest Berlin.

From Eisenhower's point of view, however, he wants this order to spur his generals onward. It is almost like a football coach offering a fabulous reward to his players before the championship game. In this instance the coach's technique is successful. Nothing makes a general advance faster than the chance for immortal fame—and the capture of Berlin will guarantee this.

April 3, 1945

On this date, the relations between America and Great Britain vis-à-vis the Russians reach a new low. To the western Allies it appears that the Russians are intent on breaking every agreement made at Yalta. Furthermore, Stalin is angrily charging that England and America are trying to negotiate a separate peace with the Germans in Italy, which he believes will be extended to the Western Front where the British and American forces would advance unopposed by any German troops.[11]

As the reader will recall, the negotiations Stalin refers to were first mentioned by the Japanese in the Diplomatic Summary of March 15. Given that Stalin also learns so quickly about the most secret negotiations between Allen Dulles of the OSS and the Germans, the author wondered whether there was a leak in the OSS office in Bern, Switzerland. The author posed this question to Robert Crowley, also asking if the Dulles operation had been as good as Dulles supporters claim it to have been. To the author's surprise Crowley replied in writing, say-

---

11. The author recommends that the reader check Churchill's *Triumph and Tragedy*, Feis's *Churchill, Roosevelt and Stalin*, Wilmot's *The Struggle for Europe*, and David Eisenhower's *Eisenhower at War, 1943–1945*.

ing: "Previous activities of Allen Dulles had threatened the intercept community. On one occasion, he sent nearly current, verbatim German Order of Battle data without realizing that such information required *special* handling. The Allied signal community was stunned by the prospect that the German monitors might immediately recognize the message content, abruptly alter their military ciphers and launch an intensive investigation to find the source of the betrayal. Fortunately, no such investigation was detected.

"On the second occasion, information relating to Dulles' surrender negotiations with representatives of German military forces in northern Italy came to the immediate attention of Moscow by *intercept and penetration of Dulles' communications.* The Soviets made a violent protest charging that the unilateral negotiations were proof that the U.S. and Great Britain were attempting to accept the surviving German military forces for later use against the USSR. [Emphasis added.]

"My source [for this information] was George Bowden, a close friend of my father's and a law partner of my older brother. Bowden, like Donovan, had undertaken foreign intelligence missions for President Roosevelt in the thirties and acted, in effect, as the counterintelligence chief of the embryonic OSS. Bowden's health was fragile and he proposed that he be replaced by the young lawyer, James Murphy, who headed his law office in Washington. Murphy assumed the post as the first chief of X-2, the OSS' Counterintelligence and Counter Espionage branch and came to be very highly respected by officers who served with him during the war.

"On the two occasions cited above, Bowden was asked, by FDR via Donovan, to travel to the Swiss station to subdue Dulles and stop his feckless, unilateral mischief. It is regrettable that we do not have the records (and devastating) comment of David K. E. Bruce and General Donovan on this subject.

"Shortly after General Smith left the Agency (CIA) to become the Under Secretary of State, I was invited to an informal meeting with Allen Dulles, who succeeded Smith. At the time, I asked Dulles about James Murphy. Dulles said he knew Murphy, but had lost contact with him. I then asked him about the role of George Bowden in the OSS. Dulles' demeanor dropped to 10 degrees below zero and, after a long pause, he replied tersely, 'I don't know.' The interview ended on that note."[12]

---

12. Letter from Robert T. Crowley to the author of August 27, 1994.

✖ ✖ ✖

In Washington, on the morning of April 3, 1945, the planners at the Pentagon are deeply concerned about the chasm developing between Moscow, London and Washington. Thus, Chief of Staff Marshall prepares a record memo about the latest problems with the Russians.[13] Marshall notes that various recommendations have been made, by people such as General Deane in Moscow, General Key of the Allied Control Commission (Hungary), and Ambassador Harriman, to counter the latest incidents of poor Soviet behavior. Among the many problems with the Soviets is the failure by Deane and Harriman (including two messages from President Roosevelt to Marshal Stalin) to obtain Soviet authority for the use of American personnel and the facilities of Poland, behind the Russian armies, to aid in locating and assisting liberated American prisoners of war.[14]

Says Marshall: "Above instance of arbitrary Soviet actions seem indicative of increasing uncooperative attitude on part of Soviet government. On the other hand, they may possibly be the results of unrelated causes. Soviet action in the military field may be a reflection of difficulties in diplomatic fields or matters of interest to U.S., British and Soviet governments. It is even conceivable that the Soviet actions may be provocative and intended to invite retaliations which should be used as an excuse by the Soviets to abrogate commitments. Action recommended by Deane, Harriman, and Kaye is retaliatory in nature and might provoke adverse Soviet reaction. On the other hand, action of this nature might bring to a stop undesirable trend which has developed. The strong feeling of Deane and Harriman should be given due weight."

Marshall believes the problems are serious enough to be considered by the Joint Chiefs, whose recommendations should be coordi-

---

13. ABC 384 United Nations (14 July 1944) Sec 1-B. Memo by Army Chief of Staff Concerning Difficulties with the Russians.

14. The author located one such American prisoner, who was captured in Africa and liberated by the Russians in Poland. He was offered the choice of being shot along with other Russian prisoners in the camp, or fighting his way into Berlin with the Red Army. He chose Berlin, shooting his way through the city. He alleges he and his Russian platoon massacred more than two hundred civilians. When the fighting stopped, he was congratulated for his competence in killing Germans by his Russian battalion commander, given a special pass, a small sack of potatoes and was told to walk west to the Elbe where the Americans were encamped.

nated with the State, Navy and War Departments and then submitted to the President for "his decision."

It appears that the first discussions relating to the Cold War are beginning in the Pentagon. The records indicate that the Army is preparing to bury any traces of Marshall's message of March 27 giving Eisenhower his instructions about contacting Stalin and setting up a line of demarcation on the Elbe. A memo for the record is prepared that has only limited circulation.[15] Its subject: "The actions taken by Generals Hull and Lincoln direct with Chief of Staff Marshall." The text as follows is verbatim with comments that identify special designations presented in brackets:

"**1.** CM-OUT 59315, 27 March, Chief of Staff suggested to SCAEF certain developments of strategy and necessity for closer liaison with Russians in order to prevent unfortunate incidents when forces meet. [This refers to Marshall's instructions to Eisenhower of March 27.]

"**2.** Subject message CM-OUT 59315. Refers to SCAF 252, in which SCAEF communicated with Stalin through Military Mission, Moscow. SCAF 252 also outlined SCAEF's plans for completing defeat of Germany and joining hands with Russians.

"**3.** Subsequent to receipt of subject message [SCAF 252], various other messages arose out of SCAF 252. Action on these other messages, accomplished by Generals Hull and Lincoln direct with the Chief of Staff, also took care of subject message.

"**4.** No further action on CM-IN 29847 is necessary. [CM-IN 29847 is Eisenhower's message for the eyes only of General Marshall numbered FWD 18272 of March 28 in which Eisenhower acknowledges receipt of Marshall's instructions, says that he agrees with them, and that he has sent off a message to Archer and Deane in Moscow.]"

Thus the Chief of Staff and his two compatriots, Hull and Lincoln, acknowledge their roles in stopping the Allies on the Elbe, close the books on the matter and consign their actions to files that historians are unlikely to see.

---

15. OPD 381 TS Sect IV (cases 81–99) (21 March 1945). Memo for the record (signed by initials PWT). Distribution of this message is limited to AC/S, OPD and Chief S&P (Strategy & Planning). Subject: Action taken by General Hull and Lincoln direct with CofS. 3 April 1945.

Meanwhile, at SHAEF, General Bull prepares a cable for Moscow that would establish a common policy to be adopted when Allied and Russian forces meet. What Bull seeks is a way to obtain mutual agreement by "the force commanders in contact, but not below Army Group level, that either side will withdraw behind the interzonal boundary on the request of the other." Because relations with the Russians are deteriorating, the cable is not sent. For the first time, one suspects that SHAEF's policy might change. Allied troops might not withdraw immediately from ground they have taken and that is designated as part of the Soviet zone of occupation.

April 4, 1945

At SHAEF headquarters, Maj. Gen. K. W. D. Strong, the Acting Chief of Staff of Intelligence, estimates German losses on the Western Front between October 1944 and the end of March 1945.[16] According to SHAEF's figures, prior to February 8, approximately 30 percent of the German Army's potential strength had been destroyed by the Allies. Then the Russian offensive in the East drew five infantry and seven panzer-type divisions from the Western Front, weakening German forces in the West even further. Next, from February 8 to March 31, the Germans suffered one hundred thousand dead and long-term wounded, plus another four hundred thousand prisoners. This represents 50 percent of the German forces in the West.

In five months time, the British/American forces have inflicted more than 1 million casualties on the German armies.

Now that 325,000 men of German Army Group B are trapped inside the Ruhr, it becomes apparent that the Allied columns racing for the Elbe should not expect any serious resistance. Using SHAEF's own figures, one can figure that only 175,000 German troops are left to protect the heart of Germany from the American and British troops driving toward the Elbe and Berlin. Since Stalin has access to these intelligence estimates, one can understand why he might believe reports from his own intelligence operations that the Americans and British have made a deal with the Germans to take Berlin.

Meanwhile, Gen. Omar Bradley releases his Letter of Instruction

---

16. Personal file of Gen. W. B. Smith, SHAEF. A compilation of enemy losses west of the Rhine prepared by Maj. Gen. K. W. D. Strong, ACoSS, G-2. 4 April 1945. This report challenges Eisenhower's estimates. On January 15, 1945, Eisenhower estimated Allied forces would be opposed by one hundred German divisions. But as of December 16, 1944, only seventy German divisions were on the Western Front.

Number Twenty to his generals commanding the First, Third, Ninth and Fifteenth Armies.[17] The Twenty-first Army Group under Montgomery to the north will move eastward on "a thrust to the river Elbe in conjunction with and protecting the left (north) flank of Twelfth Army Group." The assignment for the Twelfth Army Group comes in two phases. In the first phase it will mop up the Ruhr pocket and then regroup for strong offensive action to the east. In the second phase it will "attack on order along the axis KASSEL-LEIPZIG to gain contact with the Soviet forces. It will exploit any opportunity for seizing a bridgehead over the ELBE River and be prepared to continue the advance to the east thereof."

The assignments in the second phase vary for the different armies. For example, the First Army will drive to the east on the Kassel-Leipzig axis, exploit any chance for seizing a bridgehead over the Elbe and be prepared to advance to the east. The Third Army under Patton "will advance on order to the east in zone, maintaining contact with Sixth Army Group troops to the right as far as Bayreuth. Be prepared to advance to the east or southeast." As for the Ninth Army, it will "advance on order to the east in zone, maintaining contact with Twenty-first Army Group on the left. Exploit any opportunity for seizing a bridgehead over the ELBE River and be prepared to continue the advance *to the east on BERLIN* or to the northeast." (Emphasis added.) The Fifteenth Army will "occupy, organize and govern" all the German territory west of the Rhine and be prepared to do the same east of the Rhine. The orders are received by SHAEF and time-stamped at 5:30 P.M., April 4, 1945.

Bradley is following Eisenhower's lead. The Ninth Army is being told to be prepared to advance on Berlin. Patton's Third Army is being told to prepare to swing its drive away from Berlin and toward the southeast. The situation is fluid. Ambiguity is the order of the day.

Suddenly the question "Does the National Redoubt really exist?" becomes the focal point of arguments in both SHAEF headquarters and the Pentagon in Washington. The reader recalls that on March 25, Col. William W. Quinn, the Intelligence Chief of the Seventh Army, sent SHAEF a strongly worded estimate saying there would definitely be a Redoubt ("the Nazis will defend with eighty crack units from one thousand to four thousand men"). The report had been turned in to SHAEF G-3 (Operations) and not G-2 (Intelligence). The Deputy Assistant

---

17. 381 Post Overlord Planning, vol. 6. 1 April 1945 to 30 April 1945. 4 April 1945. Letter of Instructions Number Twenty. Auth: CG, 12 AG.

Chief of Staff, G-3, Whitely now sends the report to General Bull suggesting that Eisenhower might want to be acquainted with the latest information on the Redoubt and asking: "Do you agree substantially with the conclusions of G-2 Seventh Army?"

The reply from the head of SHAEF intelligence, General Strong, is frosty.[18] He tells Whitely in G-3 that G-2 is producing a JIC paper, plus "a complete consolidated, detailed intelligence report, the material for which has already been put out in various publications and it is on this that this [Quinn's] paper was based." According to Strong, SHAEF intelligence has kept Eisenhower currently informed. Furthermore, "we do not entirely agree with the conclusions. Paper returned."

Apparently Quinn is trying to justify the continuation of the Seventh Army's assignment to crack the National Redoubt. The sudden shift of other American forces to the south and southeast apparently worries the command staff of the Seventh Army that they might lose the glory of taking Hitler's last stronghold.

Back in Washington, others agree with General Strong's analysis that there is little chance of there being a National Redoubt. The Military Intelligence Service, which has supplied so much information for the Magic Summaries, and the OSS are convinced the Redoubt doesn't exist. The two organizations submit as Enclosure B a sixty-one-page mimeographed study on the Redoubt.[19] In brief, this study disputes the theory that the Germans could hold out in the Redoubt area located in the mountainous area bordered by south Germany, Austria, Czechoslovakia and north Italy. It ticks off the strategic necessities for a successful defense: oil, coal, steel, food, fabricating facilities, transportation, aircraft production, defense. The area lacks all these essential elements. Moreover, "the known fortifications are generally inadequate to give the defenders much advantage."

At least one other G-2 is sure that the Redoubt does not exist. Colonel Oscar W. Koch, G-2 for Patton's Third Army, is credited as being the only senior intelligence officer to predict the Battle of Bulge. In early April, Koch says he and his staff "reached our conclusions that the Redoubt was mythical. I had a map showing that nothing had been moved into the area of any military consequence, or indicating any buildup there in the last months of the war. We wrote it off, but

---

18. 370-32 (OPS A) German National Redoubt. Subj: Memo concerning National Redoubt. 4 April 1945.
19. ABC 381 Germany (29 January 1945) Sec 2-B. Report by the JIC on German Capabilities for Continued Resistance in the South.

it kept bobbing up. To convince everybody, including ourselves, we worked it out again. The Redoubt didn't exist. General Patton told people about our findings. He was told we were the only ones who thought that way."[20]

At this point, the British Chiefs of Staff ask for a meeting with the U.S. Chiefs regarding Eisenhower's strategy in Europe.[21] It is obvious that Churchill has taken them to task for they now echo his thoughts almost exactly. The British Chiefs say that Eisenhower's recent telegrams explaining his strategy have done much to allay their anxieties. However, they say, "sufficient emphasis does not appear to have been placed on the desirability of maintaining the momentum of the drive in the north, particularly toward Berlin."

The British Chiefs point out that Stalin has told Eisenhower that his drive on Dresden and Leipzig, to meet SHAEF forces, will not begin until mid-May. And in Stalin's telegram to Eisenhower of April 1, he gives no indication of the date on which he intends to launch his "secondary forces" in the direction of Berlin. These two factors, coupled with the obvious psychological and political advantages in reaching Berlin as soon as possible, seem to the British Chiefs of Staff to point to the desirability of Anglo-American forces capturing Berlin as soon as it is possible. "All these thoughts may well be in General Eisenhower's mind, but they do not appear to be reflected in the messages we have seen," say the British. They believe "it would be appropriate for the Combined Chiefs of Staff to give General Eisenhower guidance on the matter."

The second point is the question of procedure regarding the handling of matters of strategic policy with the Russians. In the past both the Americans and the British have strongly believed that in correspondence with the Russians the correct levels should be maintained. That is to say, heads of state should communicate with heads of state, the high command with the high command and the commanders in the field with commanders in the field. The British Chiefs of Staff note that the U.S. Chiefs of Staff believe that, in view of the rapid advance in Germany, Eisenhower had no alternative but to communicate directly with the Russians on this plan. The British Chiefs, however, are not convinced of this. They believe that in the future there should always be sufficient time for the proper channels to be used. For example, the

---

20. Author interview with Oscar Koch 16 December 1962.
21. ABC Europe (5 August 1943) Sec 1-D. Memo. Fr Reps of British Chiefs of Staff to CCS. 4 April 1945.

fact that the Russians are not proposing to start their drive until the middle of May places Eisenhower in a very favorable position to discuss with the Combined Chiefs of Staff any further major points that might arise. In the coming weeks there will almost certainly be other matters of high strategic importance requiring discussion with the Russians, and the British Chiefs believe it is important that an agreement be reached on the procedure to be used.

In closing, the British say: "If the United States Chiefs of Staff agree with the above, we would ask them to suggest a manner in which this guidance should be given to General Eisenhower."

Night falls in Washington. The question as to how to reply to the British is unresolved.

April 5, 1945

Early this morning, Montgomery announces the linkage with the Twelfth Army Group behind the Ruhr in the Paderborn area and the surrounding of an estimated 150,000 Germans inside the Allied net.[22] What changes Montgomery might have made in his plans, or in the British argument for racing to Berlin, had he known that more than double that number of German troops were out of the way, one can only speculate. But then no one really knows what the total bag of German troops in the Ruhr will be.

Montgomery also announces that the U.S. Ninth Army has reverted to the command of the Twelfth Army Group. Says Montgomery: "This new plan has definite repercussions on the operations of Twenty-first Army Group, and certain modifications are now necessary in the orders contained in M-563 dated 28 March 1945." Thus Montgomery alerts his troops that they may not attack Berlin.

Meanwhile, at SHAEF, approval is given for a special flying squad of war correspondents, which would be highly mobile and have its own radio communications, to cover important events under ECLIPSE conditions.[23] This readying of the press indicates that Eisenhower is preparing for the collapse of the German armed forces.

Next, Eisenhower cables the War Department saying that unless Washington thinks it is "unadvisable," he will communicate with the Military Mission in Moscow about identifying air and ground units to

22. 12 Army Gp. AG Records File, #371.3 Military Objectives, vol. 6. General situation paper and orders to 21 Army Group signed Montgomery. No. M-567. 5 April 1945.
23. War Diary, SHAEF CofS, General Smith. 5 April 1945.

avoid unnecessary contacts that might result in tragic incidents. (One can see that the problem of "friendly fire" is as true for Eisenhower in 1945 as it will be for Operation Desert Storm and its aftermath some fifty years later.)

Then Eisenhower says: "It doesn't appear wise to restrict our operations to a specific line established in advance. Both fronts should be free to advance until contact is imminent. Thereafter the following arrangements can be made: (A) Depending on operational necessity, forces of either army will be withdrawn behind the boundaries established in the EAC PROTOCOL by mutual arrangement. (B) These requests will not be made or considered below the level of Army Group." Eisenhower says he is ready to send a representative to Moscow to discuss the situation, and he ends his message saying: "Please try to obtain agreement to this policy and advise of any counterproposals."

In this fashion Eisenhower bucks the discussion at SHAEF back to Marshall.

In Washington, a memo is prepared for Marshall to circulate for discussion about the issue raised by the British Chiefs of Staff.[24] The hypothesis is that the issues raised by the British have, at least for the present, been overtaken by Eisenhower's latest messages and Marshal Stalin's reply to Eisenhower and the rapid development of events in the field.

For the Americans, the key to Eisenhower's plan is found in SCAEF's statement: "Until it is clear that the enemy is so reduced in strength the simultaneous drives against the (several) strategic areas are possible, one must be selected on which our efforts will be concentrated, if necessary at the expense of the others." Eisenhower has selected what he believes to be the principal strategic objective. It will result in the maximum destruction of enemy military power. And he is energetically directing the maximum available strength to that end. "The U.S. Chiefs of Staff continues to regard this plan as sound."

The U.S. Chiefs also believe that such psychological and political advantages as would result from the capture of Berlin ahead of the Russians should not override the imperative military consideration, which in the opinion of the U.S. Chiefs is the destruction and dismembering of the German armed forces. As a matter of fact, Berlin lies

---

24. ABC Europe (5 August 1943) Sec 1-D. Memo fr General Marshall courtesy General Hull to Leahy, King, Giles, for their consideration. 5 April 1945.

within the center of impact of the main thrust. The present boundaries indicate that it would probably be within the right-hand axis of advance of the Ninth Army Sector or the left of the Fifteenth Army.

The British Chiefs have raised a question of procedure. But the U.S. Chiefs believe that no further guidance is required by nor should be given to Eisenhower, at least pending receipt of Marshal Stalin's views concerning communication. While Marshal Stalin is the head of the Russian state, Eisenhower's dealings with him have been in his capacity as Commander in Chief of the Forces on the Eastern Front. There does not appear to be any other military head in Russia. It might be desired that Eisenhower should communicate with General Antonov, the Chief of Staff. Experience, however, has shown that attempts to secure information or decisions on any lower level than Stalin results in an interminable and unacceptable delay.

The speed with which our armies are driving into Germany so far outstrips the best possible speed of action by the agencies of the Combined Chiefs of Staff as to prohibit thought of review of operational matters by this or any other form of committee action. As an example, the current series of CCS805 papers began on March 29; it is now April 5 and we are still discussing the matter. The present situation in Europe will not permit any such administrative delay or discussion. As the situation stands today, the center is a pocket, the right is rapidly moving and the left is making marked progress. Overnight, the situation may change. Even now, our air forces are overlapping in their offensive against the enemy. "Only Eisenhower is in a position to know how to fight this battle."

In view of the above, the U.S. Chiefs of Staff believe there is "no present necessity for giving guidance to SCAEF as suggested . . . and he should be released from the restriction" contained in the British message about communicating with the Soviets. The U.S. Chiefs propose a draft cable allowing SCAEF to communicate with Soviet Military authorities as necessary to coordinate Allied operations with Soviet operations.

There is irrefutable logic behind the American argument. Since they first crossed the Rhine a few weeks earlier, the Allied forces have regrouped and their armies of the center have isolated the Ruhr pocket, which is seventy miles long and fifty-five miles wide. The central armies have also driven another thirty miles deeper into Germany. In fact, as of this date, April 5, some elements of the U.S. XIX Corps, i.e., the Second Armored Division, have charged one hundred and thirty miles inside Germany. And`to the north, the British Eleventh Armored

400 ≡≡≡≡≡≡≡≡≡≡≡≡≡≡≡≡≡≡≡≡≡≡ Bruce Lee

Division of Montgomery's Twenty-first Army Group has advanced a few miles farther east than the Americans.

What had long been considered impossible is about to occur. Only a few miles ahead of the Allied forces lies the boundary marking the Soviet zone of occupation. From now on, the British and Americans will be faced with the problem of sacrificing Allied troops for ground that they will have to turn back to the Russians.

April 6, 1945

Three significant messages originate from Chief of Staff Marshall on this date. All three are sent to Eisenhower from Washington between afternoon and evening.

The first cable brings up a prickly subject: What should the Allies do with postwar Germany.[25]

Marshall reports there has been a discussion between Army G-2 and Secretary of War Stimson about what effect the total destruction of industry in the Ruhr will have on the economic future of Europe. Marshall also says that Leahy, King, Handy and Hull all oppose "asking you this question."

The Chief of Staff reports that besides the many considerations involved in the campaign to destroy German military strength, there are two schools of thought circulating in the government in Washington. One would prefer a "postwar pastoral" Germany, i.e., the plan proposed by Secretary of the Treasury Morgenthau that would basically turn Germany into a big farm. The other plan is concerned with leaving some industry in order to aid the rest of Europe that doesn't have the same industrial capabilities as can be found in the Ruhr.

"Don't compromise yourself," says Marshall, "or limit your intentions, but, for no one else's eyes but Stimson's, my own, Hull's and Handy's, could you supply us with your present intentions towards the Ruhr pocket and your view to the need or possibility by which the Ruhr might be sealed off. I believe your forces are already hard at work on operations against the pocket. This cable mustn't embarrass you or limit your view or intentions. I have no views as yet on the matter, except that I think the fat is probably now in the fire and whatever the political conclusions it is too late, too impractical to take any action for any reason."

---

25. OPD Cable File. Fr AGWAR (Marshall) to SHAEF FWD (Eisenhower—eyes only). No. W-64236. TOO 061935Z April. TOR 062315B April.

In the second cable, Marshall reports that Churchill has given in to the American arguments.[26] The Prime Minister has sent a message to the President saying that Eisenhower's main plans have turned out to be smaller changes than what the British had first thought and that his personal relations with you are most cordial. "Further that he regards the matter as closed and to prove his sincerity uses one of his very few Latin quotations, 'amantium irae amoris integratio est,' which I understand means, 'lovers' quarrels are a part of love.' "

Marshall continues, saying that Churchill believes it regrettable that Eisenhower's telegram to Stalin was sent without anything being disclosed "to our Chiefs or our Deputy, Air Marshal Tedder, or to Montgomery. Can you tell us if Tedder was informed or consulted concerning the matter?"

The last sentence of the draft of this message as penned in Marshall's own hand actually reads: "It did not seem to me necessary that Montgomery be informed. Was Tedder informed on the matter?" Marshall then rewords the cable the way it is sent.

The third cable reports the results of the latest discussion between the U.S. Chiefs and the British Chiefs of Staff.[27] Marshall repeats for Eisenhower the essence of the arguments in his memo of the previous day. As for communicating with the Russians, Marshall says: "The Combined Chiefs of Staff consider you should proceed with communications with the Soviet military authorities required to effect coordination between your operation and theirs."

Eisenhower is now free to act as he sees fit. But he must not forget his earlier instructions from Marshall to halt on the banks of the Elbe River.

April 7, 1945

One of Eisenhower's first actions this day is to answer Marshall's questions posed the day before about the fate of German industrial areas inside the Ruhr pocket.[28]

The elimination of German forces in the Ruhr is a necessity, says Eisenhower. At the least they can be pushed into a small area where they can be contained by a small number of Allied troops. Then the

---

26. OPD Cable File. Fr AGWAR (Marshall) to SHAEF FWD (Eisenhower—eyes only). No. W-64244. TOO 062002Z April. TOR 062335B April.
27. SHAEF Sigs 373.5, vol. 1. Cable from Marshall to Eisenhower. No. W-64349 (FS-IN 5055) TOO 062208Z TOR 070630B. 6 April 1945.
28. Personal file Gen. W. B. Smith. Fr Eisenhower to Marshall No. FWD 18697. 7 April 1945.

Germans can starve themselves into surrender. This policy is necessary because Allied troops are needed for the advance and securing the rear areas behind the advance.

In reducing the Ruhr pocket, Eisenhower says the Allies have no intention of inflicting useless damage. "There will be certain assets remaining and I realize that they should be preserved so far as possible so that the political heads of the United Nations may later dispose of them as they see fit." However, says Eisenhower, he can't afford to allow the Germans to remain in the Ruhr pocket, occupying the huge area that they control, so his attacks will continue until a point has been reached where it is cheaper to contain the enemy than destroy him. Meanwhile, the air force has stopped attacking targets in the pocket unless they are purely military.

Upon reviewing this message in Washington, Gen. John E. Hull, the Chief of Staff for Operations, sends it with a memo to General Marshall recommending that Marshall hand this message personally to Secretary of War Stimson.[29] Hull also writes: "There is no strong reason for not showing this message to Admiral Leahy, Admiral King and General Giles, [but] I think it is inadvisable to do so. As far as I know, this question has not been raised officially by anybody outside the War Department. If the question is raised, we have the answer to it. On the other hand, if too much circulation is given to this message, it may get an argument started."

What we are witnessing is the birth pangs of the concept that after the war America will have to play a major role in rebuilding Europe, even Germany. The Army will oppose the Morgenthau plan. The Marshall Plan will be the impetus that rebuilds Western Europe and begins fifty years of peace.

Eisenhower's second message to Marshall this morning answers the questions posed by the Chief of Staff regarding Eisenhower's communicating with Stalin. The Supreme Commander also addresses the question of whether or not Air Marshal Tedder was informed of Eisenhower's first message to Stalin.

The first message Eisenhower sent to Stalin was, he says, "only a military move taken in accordance with ample authorizations and instructions previously issued by the Combined Chiefs of Staff." The thought that he should have conferred with the CCS never crosses his mind, because he believes that since he is the head of the Allied military

---

29. OPD TS Sect IV (cases 81–99) (21 March 1945). Memo from JEH to Colonel McCarthy. 7 April 1945.

forces in the West that it is natural to ask the head of the Russian forces about the direction and timing of their next offensive, and to outline his own intentions.

Currently Eisenhower is holding up his latest communication with the Russians about mutual identification of ground and air units that should be established by the Military Mission in Moscow. Eisenhower wants speedy action because time is important. The tactical air forces of both sides will soon meet each other daily in combat conditions.

Eisenhower praises the abilities of the British members of SHAEF. He says that Air Marshal Tedder has been freely consulted on the outline of the major plan of operations and on the necessity of making efforts to coordinate activities with the Russians. However, Tedder was not present at SHAEF when the first message was sent to Stalin and he did not see the message. But, says Eisenhower, "he completely agreed in principle with the action taken."

Eisenhower then ends saying that he concurs with the message Marshall delivered to the British Chiefs about not limiting Eisenhower's freedom to act.

In Washington, General Hull reviews this cable, too, and writes a memo to Marshall that the last paragraph should be deleted and the rest of the text should be passed to Field Marshal Wilson for distribution among the British.[30]

The third message Eisenhower sends to Marshall on this date is sent "eyes only" for the Chief of Staff.[31] The cable contains Eisenhower's personal reasons for his reluctance to consider Berlin as a "major objective." First, says Eisenhower, Berlin has lost a great deal of its former military importance because of heavy bombings and the transfer of parts of the governmental offices to other locations. (One can see that Ambassador Oshima's reports on conditions in Berlin have deeply impressed the Supreme Commander.) Second, to insure the division of the German forces on the Western Front, he points out that his major thrust should be made toward Leipzig. He says: "You will note that in Stalin's reply to my message he agreed that the best place for us to meet was in the Dresden-Leipzig area, which is deep into that part of Germany that the Russians are eventually to occupy." (It is

---

30. OPD 381 TS Sect IV (cases 81–99) (21 March 1945). Memo from JEH to Marshall. 7 April 1945.
31. Personal file of Gen. W. B. Smith, CofS, SHAEF. From Eisenhower to Marshall—eyes only. No. FWD 18710. 7 April 1945.

obvious that Eisenhower believes an agreement has been struck with the Russians on this.)

Once the thrust to Leipzig has been successful, Eisenhower points out that the Allied left flank should be firmly anchored on the coast near Luebeck, the boundary of the British occupation zone. This will prevent the Russians from occupying any part of the Danish peninsula, and it will keep them away from the sea-lanes that are all-important to the British. "To this extent," says Eisenhower, "I thoroughly agree that the northern thrust is the most important one." (Eisenhower obviously believes that this option is more important for the British than taking Berlin.) And then Eisenhower tells Marshall: "Another move that seems most important is a thrust through the southern mountainous areas, as suggested in one of your telegrams." (This is a significant statement about the way Eisenhower reacted to Marshall's so-called suggestions of March 27/28; the Supreme Commander is telling Marshall that he has followed orders, and if Marshall wants him to do something different, he had better advise him quickly about same.)

Eisenhower points out that if the Allies are successful, a quick glance at the map will show what huge areas will be in their possession and, as a result, how many units of the Allied forces will be engaged in maintaining law and order in the rear, to say nothing of how badly the Allied supply lines will be stretched. "Our front will then be a bit thin," he remarks dryly.

The movement toward Leipzig is the proper one in terms of direction, says Eisenhower, warming to his favorite theme, because it gives him flexibility to maneuver after having divided the German armies.

"At any time that we should seize Berlin at little cost we should, of course, do so," claims Eisenhower. "But I regard it militarily unsound at this stage of the proceedings to make Berlin a major objective, particularly in view of the fact that it is within thirty-five miles of the Russian lines. I am the first to admit that war is waged in pursuit of political aims, and if the Combined Chiefs of Staff should decide that an Allied effort to take Berlin outweighs purely military considerations in the theater, I would cheerfully readjust my plans and thinking so as to carry out such an operation. I urgently believe, however, that the capture of Berlin should be left as something we would do if feasible and practicable as we proceed on the general plan of (A) dividing the German forces by a major thrust in the middle, (B) anchoring our left flank firmly in the Luebeck area, and (C) attempting to disrupt any German effort to establish a fortress in the southern mountains."

On another front, on this date, SHAEF gives the OSS approval to send missions to Denmark and Norway. The struggle to wrest the Scandinavian countries from the hands of the Germans, and to keep them out of Stalin's clutches, is beginning.[32]

Something out of the ordinary now happens in the Pentagon. It appears that Eisenhower's reminder to Marshall about who conceived the sending of U.S. forces southward to the so-called Redoubt area makes somebody rethink the bidding for this maneuver. To date, there is no evidence that the Redoubt exists. But, suddenly, a report by the Combined Intelligence Committee is circulated with the following memo: "Note by the Secretaries: The enclosed report prepared by the Joint Intelligence Committee on its own initiative is circulated for information."[33] The report starts out saying: "We adhere to the view that the Nazi leaders are most unlikely to surrender and that they will attempt to prolong resistance . . . in the south with such forces as are there and can be withdrawn further from the debacle in the north." The report notes the "economic resources for the region are insufficient to support a prolonged organized defense." But then it concludes, saying: "Guerrilla resistance, however, may well be continued in the mountainous areas of the south for a considerable time after organized resistance has ceased."

Why circulate this report now? It is the same report, drawing the same conclusion, as the report circulated on April 4 that was prepared by Combined Intelligence Staff, also on its own initiative. . . .[34] The use of the term "prepared . . . on its own initiative" is what triggers an alarm bell. The combined secretariats are not supposed to submit material on their own initiative unless something extraordinary is in the air. Both reports refer to previous submissions (CCS 660/3 and CIC 47/14), and both of these referrals were submitted for consideration back on January 24, 1945, when Allied strategic planners thought it unlikely that our forces will be across the Rhine.

In other words, the material is hopelessly out of date.

Thus Eisenhower's message to Marshall causes the Pentagon to begin a feverish review of the case for and against the Redoubt. Is this the best way for Marshall to justify the strategy that he suggested to

---

32. War Diary, SHAEF CofS, General Smith. No. 314.81/3. 7 April 1945.
33. ABC 381 Germany (29 January 1943), Sec 2-B. Report by Combined Intelligence Committee. Tab No. CCS 660/3. The introductory memo is signed by A. J. McFarland and A. T. Cornwall Jones.
34. ABC 381 Germany (29 January 1943), Sec 2-B. Report by Combined Intelligence Committee on German Capabilities for Continued Resistance in the South. Signed by James S. Lay Jr. and J. A. Davison.

Eisenhower? Most likely. Otherwise, if American troops are not needed to smash a stronghold that does not exist, there would be ample forces available to smash Berlin before the Russians can cross the Oder River.

When the author interviewed General Hull on the matter, the General refused to comment. He suggested that the author return to his office (at that time in the *Reader's Digest*'s Washington bureau just south of DuPont Circle) and wait for a phone call. The phone call that came, within a matter of hours, was an invitation to visit Gettysburg and interview Eisenhower.

At this interview, Eisenhower refused to comment for the record about how or why he had come to believe that Berlin was no longer a military target. (Unfortunately, at that time the author did not know about the Magic Diplomatic Summaries and could not ask any questions related to intelligence matters.) Despite this roadblock, as Cornelius Ryan remarked to the author after the meeting, "Ike sure gave us everything else we need for the book."[35]

It is the author's belief, however, that because the OSS and MIS had submitted their sixty-one-page report on April 4, which thoroughly challenged, if not completely disproved, the existence of the National Redoubt, Marshall's staff begins taking unusual steps and submits outdated intelligence reports to prove their argument with the British that Berlin is no longer a viable military target as compared to the Redoubt.

Marshall supporters may challenge this, of course. But it is extremely difficult to challenge documents that prove something out of the ordinary occurred.

April 8, 1945

On this date, Mobile Field Interrogation Unit #5 of the U.S. Seventh Army interrogates Mag. Gen. Ralph George Edgar Joachim Graf von Orila, who, until he is captured, is the Commanding General of the German Thirteenth Corps.[36] According to the report, the General discloses that "source neither has any knowledge of, nor does he be-

---

35. *The Last Battle* by Cornelius Ryan (New York: Simon & Schuster, 1966). In an informal comment, Eisenhower acknowledged to Ryan and this writer that he could have taken Berlin. Eisenhower also said that he had no intention of taking Berlin, even if he had a four-lane highway into the city and a brass band waiting there for him, because the agreement concerning the zones of occupation would have forced him to give the territory he had taken back to the Russians. (Letter from this writer to James Monahan, Senior Editor, *The Reader's Digest,* 22 July 1963.)

36. PW Intelligence Bulletin, Mobile Field Interrogation Unit #5, 7th Army. 8 April 1945.

lieve in, the establishment of a national redoubt. He admits, however, that some Nazi leaders in conjunction with fanatical SS troops might attempt a last stand in order to die like heroes.''

Orila was captured on March 30 when the German 719th Infantry Division, which had been detailed to hold the Saar-Lateurn-Rodern sector of the Seigfried Line, was destroyed by the Allied offensive.

Also captured is Brig. Gen. Heinrich Gaede, the Commanding General of the 719th Infantry, plus his chief of staff, Herman Miltzow, and two orderlies. They were trying to make their way back to the Rhine, but were spotted by a detail of civilian workers while hiding in a bunker near Bergsabern.

According to the interrogation report, General Gaede also claims ''to have no knowledge of any measures being taken to transform the German and Austrian Alps into a fortress. Gaede does not consider guerrilla warfare likely, because, in his opinion, it is unsuited to the mentality of the German people. He believes that the primary concern of the Germans living in rural districts will be the sowing of fields and the cultivation of crops to prevent starvation in the coming winter.''

It is interesting to note that these field interrogations are made by staff of the Seventh Army, whose intelligence chief, as reported earlier, steadfastly maintained that the Redoubt existed.

Back at SHAEF, the Joint Intelligence Committee points out that the Germans will continue withdrawing troops from Norway.[37] However, they say in their latest study, ''when organized resistance in Germany crumbles, there may still be some eight divisions, below strength and with low morale, in Norway. These might be prepared to surrender to a token Allied force, but we cannot count on this. In our view, therefore, it is necessary to plan for an assault on Norway in order to reduce the enemy garrison.''

Another reason, apparently valid, for not taking Berlin.

At the moment, Norway is more important to the British than to the Americans. Later, it will become a cornerstone of NATO and the northern flank for the West's containment of the Soviet Union.

Meanwhile, Eisenhower finds himself composing another strong message to Field Marshal Montgomery, who has just requested ten American divisions for an attack on Luebeck and Berlin.

Eisenhower writes: ''As regards Berlin, I am quite ready to admit that it has political and psychological significance, but of far greater

---

37. ABC 381 Germany (29 January 1943) Sec 2-B. Report by SHAEF Joint Intelligence Committee (Strong, Betts, Lewes, Grierson). Tab No. CIC M/Info #58.

importance will be the location of the remaining German forces in relation to Berlin. It is on them that I am going to concentrate my attention. Naturally, if I can get a chance to take Berlin cheaply, I shall take it."[38]

Back in Washington, Marshall writes three memos.

The first goes to President Roosevelt. Short, only four paragraphs long, it outlines Marshall's recent activities concerning the dispute about Eisenhower's communicating with the Soviet High Command.[39] One wonders why the memo is so spare in detail or commentary. The conclusion is that either Marshall wanted the memo to be confusing to someone in the White House, or else Marshall wanted to ensure that the White House could not leak anything to the press.

The second memo Marshall prepares is for Admiral Leahy, the President's military adviser.[40] Says Marshall: "I quoted to General Eisenhower a part of the Prime Minister's message to the President stating 'It was a pity that Eisenhower's telegram was sent to Stalin without anything being said to our Chiefs of Staff or to Tedder or Montgomery.' Attached is a copy of Eisenhower's reply, *for your eyes only*." [Emphasis added.]

Marshall's third memo goes to Field Marshal Wilson.[41] "I am enclosing a personal message which I have received from Eisenhower," Marshall writes. "The matter of 'arrangement for mutual identification of air and ground troops' is of pressing concern. We have had several recent incidents involving clashes between U.S. Army Air Forces and the Russians. It does not seem we can justify delay in getting to Eisenhower freedom of action."

---

38. The author was not permitted to review the original text of this message. The quotation comes from Dr. Forrest Pogue's chapter "The Decision to Halt at the Elbe" in the U.S. Army's official history *Command Decisions*. In view of the fact that Dr. Pogue's paraphrasing appears to be shaded to follow the U.S. Army's policy of not upsetting the British, as demonstrated earlier, one wonders as to the accuracy of this statement he attributes to Eisenhower in which he uses the word "shall." This denotes an entirely different attitude on Eisenhower's part from what he has written recently to Marshall. The author believes the Supreme Commander's statement to Marshall more accurately reflects his true intentions: He will not take Berlin unless ordered to do so.

39. OPD 381 TS Sect IV (cases 81–99) (21 March 1945). Memo from Marshall to FDR. Attached to this memo are cables FWD 6246 (CM-IN 18707) and WAR 64349.

40. OPD 381 TS Sect IV (cases 81–99) (21 March 1945). Memo from Marshall to Leahy. The memo refers to message CM-IN 6246 (FWD 18707). 8 April 1945.

41. OPD 381 TS Sect IV (cases 81–99) (21 March 1945). Memo from Marshall to Field Marshal Wilson. Attached to this memo is a copy of CM-IN 6246 (FWD 18707).

April 9, 1945

Eisenhower meets with the commander of the Strategic Air Force, Gen. Carl Spaatz, General Bradley and other air-ground commanders.

The consensus is that the Ruhr pocket will be eliminated in ten days' time, by April 19. (It will actually surrender on April 18.) The Allied armies will be able to move forward within ten days' time. Delays, if any, are not expected to offer the enemy any real chance to prepare his defenses. Expectations are that the Allies should close on the Elbe before May 15, and current estimates of enemy strength put their forces at approximately ten to twelve divisions. Meanwhile targets for strategic bombing are becoming more and more limited.[42]

Basically, the strategic bombing war in Europe is ended. At best it appears there are only 120,000 German troops standing between the Allied soldiers on the Western Front and Berlin. The estimate that the ground forces will reach the Elbe only by mid-May is incredibly conservative. What's going on?

Montgomery might be asking himself the same question. He replies to Eisenhower's message of the previous day saying only: "Have your letter of April 8. I will operate along the northern flank 100 percent and will make every effort to draw the enemy away from the main thrust being made by Bradley's forces."[43]

Nowhere does Montgomery mention taking Berlin, even if it can be done cheaply. Nor is there any reference to British and American troops sharing the glory of marching side by side into the German capital, which is most unlike Montgomery. Has Montgomery given up on the idea? Again, one must ask, what's going on?

First, it is apparent that Washington is going to halt the bombing of German cities. Gen. Hap Arnold, Commanding General of the U.S. Army Air Force, cables General Spaatz that Washington believes the situation is changing so rapidly in Germany that it is now advisable to examine the continuation of strikes against German cities.[44] "We've decided that no great advantage can be gained by continuing such attacks since results won't become apparent until hostilities cease," Arnold says. "Furthermore we don't want to destroy any housing or other

---

42. OPD Cable File. Fr CG, U.S. Strategic AF, St.-Germain, France, to War Department No. UA 67210. 9 April 1945.
43. OPD Cable File. Fr 21 Ar Gp (Montgomery) to SHAEF FWD (Eisenhower—eyes only). No. M 1070. TOO 090925B April. 9 April 1945.
44. OPD Cable File. Fr General Arnold to CG, U.S. Strategic AF, Europe (Spaatz). No. WAR 65558 (CM-OUT 65558). 9 April 1945.

facilities that will be needed for occupation troops.'' However, it might still be necessary to attack targets directly behind the front lines. ''I trust you will agree to the above . . . ,'' says Arnold in signing off.

The next significant message from Washington announces that the Combined Chiefs of Staff have bought the concept of moving into southern Germany as well as preparing to invade Norway.[45] The Combined Chiefs tell Eisenhower that they believe ''resistance may continue in German garrisons now located in inactive theaters after German forces in Germany have collapsed.'' The CCS estimates that from six to ten German divisions may be left in Norway, and they may have enough supplies to keep the Allies from landing in various Norwegian ports. These troops are likely to be of low caliber and may, or may not, offer determined resistance. It all depends on the determination of their commanders.

The CCS also believes that Swedish bases may be needed for direct entry into Norway. There have been indications that the Allies might receive Swedish assistance in taking Norway, but it's still too early to say if this help will really be forthcoming. At the moment two Swedish divisions are operational and six more can be mobilized in less than two weeks. The CCS says: ''It might be reasonable therefore to plan on receiving help from at least four Swedish divisions along with help from 650 aircraft.''

Therefore Eisenhower is requested to draw up a plan, based on the assumption that there will be organized resistance in Norway, and that Swedish bases and military forces will be available for an Allied push to regain Norway. The plan is to be prepared immediately so that it can be positively presented to the Swedish government.

April 10, 1945

On this date Bradley reports to Eisenhower about his latest conference with Montgomery at Second British Army Headquarters.[46] Two major points have been discussed and agreed on. First, the Twenty-first Army Group is not in a position to advance to the northeast and at the same time carry out its mission assigned by Eisenhower, i.e., protect the left flank of the Twelfth Army Group. Montgomery estimates that

---

45. OPD Cable File. Fr CCS to Eisenhower, FYI British Chiefs as FACS 173 from CCS. No. WARX 65684 (CM-OUT 65684). Info: Leahy, King, Arnold, Hull, Bissell, CofS. 9 April 1945.
46. 12 Army Group, AG Records File #371.3 Military Objectives, vol. 6. Letter fr Bradley to Eisenhower. 10 April 1945.

before he can protect Bradley's flank his troops will have to clean out the vicinity of Bremen, and that would take until April 14. "In view of the fact that resistance is light at the present time," says Bradley, "we desire to continue our advance to the east. I, therefore, told Marshal Montgomery that I was prepared to accept responsibility for protecting our own flank and relieve him of that mission for the time being."

The second major point demonstrates that Eisenhower and Bradley were correct in figuring that if Montgomery couldn't lead the dancing, he would be a reluctant partner in the victory ball. According to Bradley, Montgomery "asked me to deliver the message to you that in considering the amount of help necessary for him to carry out his mission beyond the Elbe, he recommended a change in the boundary between the Twelfth and Twenty-first Army Group as follows: Celle-Welzen-Neu-Danchau, all inclusive to Twenty-first Army Group. It is to be noted particularly that this change of boundary takes place after we have established ourselves on the Elbe River. Marshal Montgomery stated that if we could take over this additional stretch of the Elbe River, he would have sufficient British forces to carry out his mission beyond the Elbe."

At this point, it appears that Montgomery is giving up all hope of moving his troops into Berlin. By asking the Americans to take over a longer section of the Elbe River from east to west, the British forces will be on the Elbe too far to the west ever to have a chance of reaching Berlin.

Meanwhile Capt. R. E. Berger writes up and submits his interrogation of SS-Standartenfuehrer Franz Schreiber along with an interesting introduction.[47] "Because of recent indications of activity within the area . . . the concept of the National Redoubt has become a very real thing in the minds of the Allies. However, it is interesting . . . that *none* of the high-ranking Wehrmacht or SS officers who have passed through 6824DIC (MIS) in recent weeks—and several general officers, General Staff officers, and many officers of field grade are included—have ever heard of the 'National Redoubt' prior to capture. When the subject was discussed with them, there was almost universal agreement that such a 'last-ditch defense' was, from the military point of view, ridiculous and impractical, but that Hitler and his Party satellites might very well attempt such an undertaking. . . .

---

47. 6824 (DIC) MIS. Summary interrogation report of SS-Standartenfuehrer Franz Schreiber by R. E. Berger, Capt. Inf. 10 April 1945.

"The prisoner, Schreiber, is a forty-one-year-old professional soldier from Dresden. He enlisted at age sixteen, became a captain in the Wehrmacht, then transferred to the SS in 1937, because of greater opportunity for promotion. In 1941, he and his troops went north where they fought with, and then against, the Finns for three and a half years. In December 1944, Schreiber and his division (the Sixth SS Mountain Division) is moved to the Western Front and Schreiber has a somewhat independent command called Kampfgruppe Schreiber. He believes himself [to be] a professional soldier who has lived with his troops for four years, cut off completely from Party control and interference. According to Schreiber, a withdrawal of troops to a National Redoubt would cause widespread hatred against the Nazis in Germany, because of the unnecessary lengthening of the war. But he also believes the idea is consistent with Hitler's policy and that it is feasible for a period up to a year. However, he never heard of the idea until after he is captured." The report continues: "The prisoner states that mountain troops can best fight defensively during the winter months. If the inner ring of the National Redoubt is not reached [by the Allies] before November, even a small force could hold out until after May of the next year."

At this point in the report, someone unknown underlines the sentence and writes: "Make this separate sheet for the enemy redoubt."

Despite the fact that none of the prisoners interrogated had ever heard about a National Redoubt prior to their capture, when the idea is put in their minds, they all say it is possible. And even though an experienced SS Mountain trooper such as Schreiber says that Allied mountain troops could wipe out the Germans, unit by unit, during the summer, he tells his interrogation officer what he believes his interrogator wants to hear. In retrospect, a good attorney could say that the prosecution led these witnesses to create projections that are unrealistic. And this proves to be the case fifty years after the fact.

But back in April 1945, SHAEF and Washington want to, nay, have to, believe in a National Redoubt to justify their strategy. Also to be remembered is Eisenhower's comment to Marshall about the amount of territory that the Allies will occupy. (When unconditional surrender finally arrives on May 7, the Allies have moved so far south into Germany, and north from Italy, that they seal off the Russians from using the Brenner pass into Italy, plus protecting the northeastern border of Switzerland.

In all truth, the British and Americans could not have done more to protect Europe against further Soviet advances to the west than they do. Marshall and Eisenhower understand that power is finite. Military occupation of territory is more important than political considerations. More importantly, by the time of unconditional surrender, the Allies have stretched their supply lines to the limit. They are beyond the capabilities of tactical air support. They have no railroad support. The soldiers have done their job, and done it well.

Thus from numerous interrogations such as Schreiber's, the SHAEF Joint Intelligence Committee submits on this date its latest report concerning the National Redoubt.[48] Declares the Committee at the outset: "There have been many reports that the enemy is preparing a fortified area in western Austria from which he will continue resistance to the last.... There appears to be little chance of a national surrender.... The objects of a final stand in a redoubt would be (a) to involve the Allies in a difficult winter campaign, thus dragging on the war; (b) to occupy an area from which trained and fanatic saboteurs and guerrillas could infiltrate into Germany, and from which directions could be issued to Germany and to the Wehrwolf and other subversive organizations; (c) to create a legend that Nazism, the symbol of Germany, never surrendered and thus keep alive the tradition of German militarism."

So concerned is the SHAEF JIC that it says at the end of its four-page report that "the full details should be passed to the Russians of existing intelligence on the Redoubt."

Given the fact that Stalin's comment to Tedder and Deane apparently set off the alarm bells within SHAEF about the Redoubt theory in the first place, one wonders today, who was fooling whom? And for what reasons?

Meanwhile, in Washington, the Joint Intelligence Committee of the Air Force has its latest report circulated within the Combined Intelligence Committee.[49] The six-page report concludes that the continued maintenance of strong German forces on the southeastern and southern front "appears designed to assure the deep protection of the southeastern and southern flanks of the Alpine redoubt and to furnish eventual manpower for any final stand that may materialize...." Until Germany collapses, "it is believed that the enemy will continue to fight ... especially if some form of a last stand materializes in the area

---

48. JIC SHAEF (45) Papers. SHAEF JIC report concerning the National Redoubt. This report was signed by K. W. D. Strong, T. J. Betts, C. M. Grierson, E. K. Thompson. 10 April 1945.
49. ABC 381 Germany (29 January 1943) Sec 2-B. Report by Joint Intelligence Committee (Air Force) signed by T. S. Airey, F. Wooley, T. C. Wynne. Once again, the combined secretariat of James S. Lay Jr. and J. A. Davison circulates a report "for the information of the Combined Intelligence Committee." 10 April 1945.

of the 'National Redoubt.' '' On the file copy read by the author, this latter statement is marked in the right-hand margin by bold, black, vertical pencil lines.

Some Allied commanders are still focusing their efforts toward the east. Lieutenant General Patton issues orders for his Third Army with the estimate: "The enemy continues his efforts to defend and delay, utilizing hastily formed miscellaneous units."[50] Patton then tells his tankers that they will "resume the advance 11 April 1945; main effort on the left (north); seizes a bridgehead over ELBE RIVER in zone; prepared to continue advance east or southeast on orders from Twelfth Army Group."

Even now, Patton is hoping for a chance to swing north and west into Berlin.

April 11, 1945

Truth is stranger than fiction. On this day, the legal experts at SHAEF waste hours debating whether or not Eisenhower is authorized to communicate with Marshal Stalin through the Military Mission in Moscow without previously securing the approval of the communications by the Combined Chiefs of Staff.[51] The in-house confusion is heightened by the fact that Eisenhower does not show anyone the cabled instructions he received from Marshall dated March 27. Why? Because it is apparent to Eisenhower that Marshall may have superseded his authority by telling Eisenhower to contact Stalin. It is this that is upsetting the British so much: Who's running the war?

For example, paragraph 2.B. of the Nevis memo reads: "The U.S. Chiefs of Staff reply to the British Chiefs of Staff relative to this point stated 'SCAEF's procedure in communicating with the Russians appears to have been an operational necessity.' In this connection also FWD-18345, General Eisenhower states 'I have been instructed to deal directly with the Russians concerning military coordination.' '' (A handwritten note in the margin of this memo says: ''What authority.'')

Since Marshall's authority is never quoted, all the references in this document related to the argument at hand are improperly based on

---

50. Headquarters, Third United States Army. AG 370.2 GNMCC. Register No. TUSA 2012. 10 April 1945. Harry H. Anderson, a good friend of the author's, fought under Patton and recalls the General saying: "I don't care who you sleep with, but there will be no fraternization with the Germans."

51. 312.3-1 Corresp & Communication with the Russians. Memo from A.S. Nevis, Brig. Gen., GSC, Chief Ops Section, to DAC of S, G-3. 11 April 1945.

other communications. The best the Eisenhower people can do is rely on Marshall's statement (in W-64349) that "Eisenhower's dealings with Marshal Stalin have been directed to him in his capacity as Commander in Chief of Forces on the Eastern Front and not that as Chief of State."

Also there is the recommendation made by Marshall, but not yet fully confirmed, that Eisenhower "should proceed with the communications with the Soviet military authorities required to effect coordination between your operations and theirs."

It is apparent that the cables between Marshall and Eisenhower of March 27/28 are being kept from the staff at Supreme Headquarters. Eisenhower protects his bosses' flanks.

Meanwhile, Eisenhower is cabling the War Department that he is preparing a new general estimate of the war situation—especially regarding the scope of future operations—and will submit it soon.[52]

Late in the day, Eisenhower cables Washington again, this time about five encounters between Russian and American aircraft on April 2.[53] "In all of these encounters the American aircraft were fired upon," says Eisenhower, "and in one or two cases the fire was returned." The Supreme Commander says that he has withheld action as requested by the British Chiefs of Staff on April 6, but unless something is done quickly to correct the situation, "it is inevitable that some serious incident will occur with regrettable results."

Eisenhower's strong feelings on the matter have apparently been prompted by two events. The first is a cable from the British Chiefs of Staff, undoubtedly initiated by Churchill.[54] The message says that the sender has spoken with Air Marshal Tedder about the way Eisenhower should seek an understanding with the Russians. Tedder has obviously been given his own new set of marching orders. For in the next two sentences, the British declare: "The senders believe that as long as hostilities continue, when SHAEF and Russian Forces meet they should establish a boundary between them by mutual agreement. The sender is thoroughly opposed, for both political and military reasons, for any mention to be made of the interzonal occupation boundaries as sug-

---

52. SCAF 151 (20 December 1944) thru 275 (12 April 1945). Fr Eisenhower to War Department/CCS. No. FWD 18932 (SCAF 273).
53. 312.3-1 Corresp & Communication with the Russians. Fr Eisenhower to AGWAR (CCS). No. FWD 18966 (SCAF 272). TOO 111945. 11 April 1945.
54. SHAEF File 322.01-1/GPS Liaison with Russians. Cable from AMSSO (Chiefs of Staff) to JSM Mission Washington—for info to SHAEF. No. 2282 TOO 111100Z TOR 115500B April. 11 April 1945.

gesting a line of demarcation between the advancing Allied and Soviet Forces."

If the British should learn now that Marshall wants Eisenhower to stop at the Elbe, the fragile bonds that hold England and America together might rupture. The delicacy of the situation is reflected in the paper submitted by the British Chiefs of Staff to the Combined Chiefs of Staff in Washington.[55] No document delineates more clearly than this one the differences between how the Americans seek to end the war in Europe and the way the British do. One can see the potential for immediate trouble with the Russians should the British attitude prevail.

After the usual bits of introductory flannel, the British get down to cases in paragraph 3 by saying: "The British Chiefs of Staff feel that after the initial contact [with the Russians] and so long as the continuation of operations by forces under the Supreme Commander, Allied Expeditionary Force (SCAEF), and by Russian forces adjacent to them is in prospect, boundaries will have to be fixed by mutual agreement between local commanders (with references if necessary to higher authority) in accordance with the operational and administrative needs of the situation. The British Chiefs of Staff are strongly opposed, however, both for military and political reasons, to any mention being made of the international occupational boundaries for the purpose of defining areas during the continuance of hostilities and they suggest that paragraph 3 of SCAF 264 might be altered to read:

" '3. All hostilities continue. It does not seem practicable to restrict our operations or areas by a demarcation line prepared in advance. Both fronts should be free to advance until contact is imminent. Thereafter the provision of responsibility should be defined by boundary lines to be agreed upon by groups of armies. On cessation of operations our respective armies will stand fast until they receive orders from their governments.' "

The British paper ends by recommending "the dispatch of the draft paragraph to the Supreme Commander. . . ."

The British do have a way with words. "On the cessation of operations our respective armies will stand fast until they receive orders from their governments" sends shivers up and down the spines of the Americans. This would negate Marshall's orders to Eisenhower, completely hog-tie Eisenhower from freedom of action by sending his

---

55. ABC 384 Europe (5 August 1943) Sec 1-E. Memo. British Reps of British Chiefs of Staff to Combined Chiefs. 11 April 1945.

forces eastward into Berlin and who knows where else, and then have him maintain his position until he is told to withdraw by his government. And what happens if the British refuse to withdraw? Do the Americans withdraw and leave the British to fight the Russians alone? And what about the proposed invasion of Japan? Questions come so hard and fast the mind boggles. Meanwhile, Russian suspicions are already aroused because the Americans are advancing deep inside the so-called Russian zone of occupation.

The State Department believes that this invidious sentence proposed by the British is inspired by the Foreign Office, or most likely Churchill, in a desire to capitalize on a bargaining position that would be achieved by having Allied troops located inside the proposed Soviet zone of occupation. The British might want to negotiate a number of points—the existing problems regarding Poland, or completing the formation of the Allied Control Commission (ACC) machinery, merely being the starters.

Never will the Americans agree with the British proposal.

Finally a compromise is reached and the Combined Chiefs agree on what to tell Eisenhower.[56] They inform him that his proposed plan, as outlined in his SCAF 264, should be changed to read: As long as the war continues, it doesn't seem "practical" to restrict our operations to a specific line of demarcation that's been previously established. Both fronts should have the freedom to advance until contact with the Russians is imminent. From that point on, the responsibility for the division (between forces) should be agreed by the armies themselves.

Now the operative word becomes "practical." Eisenhower has already ordered his troops forward based on the strategy proposed by Marshall. It is doubtful that it will be "practical" to change it. But it explains why Eisenhower will ask Bradley a few days later how many troops will it cost to take Berlin.

Meanwhile, events taking place on the battlefield are overwhelming the negotiations between London and Washington.

For example, on this morning, Bradley reviews his current operations order for his First, Third and Ninth Armies.[57] The order is brief, concise and reflects none of the commotion going on at SHAEF or in Washington and London. It reads:

---

56. OPD Cable File. Fr CCS to Eisenhower. No. WARX 66731 (CM-OUT 66731). Info: Le? King, Arnold, Hull, Bissell, CofS. 11 April 1945.
57. Reg. No. G-6092. 370 (CG). Current Operations. AGTSCG File 371.3. Copy No. 6 (copies. 11 April 1945.

"**1.** The purposes of present operations are, first, to reduce the Ruhr pocket and, second, to advance to the general line WITTENBERG - MAGDEBURG - DESSAU-LEIPZIG - ALTENBURG - PLAUEN - BAYREUTH and to seize bridgeheads across the Elbe River from MAGDEBURG to DESSAU, both inclusive.

"**2.** This position will then permit us to operate either toward BERLIN, directly to the east, if such move is necessary to gain contact with the Russians, or launch an attack to the southeast. If the advance to this general line is made rapidly, we will have about reached the limit of our supply until such time as the railroads can be brought into operation. Any advances in force beyond this general line will be limited to those necessary to take advantage of proper obstacles such as the MULDE River."

Yes, Bradley is telling his forces that they may attack Berlin, but he now adds the caveat that they will advance only "if such move is necessary to gain contact with the Russians."

What Bradley doesn't know, of course, is that on this day the Second Armored Division is busy making its single greatest advance for the entire war. The Second Armored is also about to render his latest operations order meaningless by achieving the desired goals the order set forth while it is being sent forward to the combat commands. Second Armored tankers are crashing through fifty-seven miles of crumbling German defenses. The Division is living up to its nickname of Hell on Wheels. It seems appropriate that on this day its code name is Powerhouse.

By noon, April 11, Combat Command B of the Second Armored reaches the little town of Anderluck, where it runs into a column of German infantry. The Germans barely have time to raise their hands as the fast-moving tankers roar past them, waving the dispirited Germans back toward the American rear. The column sweeps onward to Klein-Oschersleben, where it pauses two hours for refueling.

The tankers drive east again during the afternoon. The biggest problem they face is the mass of displaced persons clogging the road seeking safety in Allied care. As evening starts to fall, the column pours through Bad Salzelman and into the town of Schoenebeck. Here the River Elbe sweeps in from a big bend to the southeast and heads northwest—a broad stretch of river seven miles long—toward the town of Magdeburg.

Official records slide over the fight made this evening for the all-important bridge that crosses the Elbe at Schoenebeck and controls the road to Berlin. However, the author interviewed Maj. James F. Hollingsworth, who led a desperate attempt to capture the bridge.

Catching a German column retreating northward, Hollingsworth orders his tanks forward and cuts the line of German armor fleeing across the bridge over the Elbe. Hollingsworth orders roadblocks set up facing south. Then he hitches his own tank, plus others, to the newly formed rear of the Germans moving to the bridge. He shoots his way forward through Schoenebeck and comes within forty yards of entrance to the bridge, where he is badly wounded. He stays on to lead the fight, but at midnight he collapses and is sent to the rear. His tankers withdraw to the outskirts of town and coil up for the remainder of the night.

When they advance the next morning, April 12, the Germans blow up the bridge.

The incredible advance by Hollingsworth and his troopers of the Second Armored throws the well-laid plans of SHAEF into the wastebasket.

But, as so often happens in war, even more fateful and unexpected events are to occur.

16

O n this eventful day, from SHAEF, Eisenhower sends a
cable to the Military Mission in Moscow stressing the
importance of creating positive identification signals for
U.S./Russian air and ground forces to prevent incidents
that are likely to occur in the "heat of battle."[1] Eisenhower also reit-
erates his latest instructions: "While hostilities continue, it does not
seem practicable to restrict our operations to areas by a demarcation
line prepared in advance. Both fronts should be free to advance until
contact is imminent. Thereafter, the division of responsibility should be
defined by boundary lines agreed between groups of armies."

If there are problems about setting up means of identification and
other signals, Eisenhower says he is ready to send Air Marshal Tedder,
or some other qualified staff officer, to Moscow to confer on the subject. It is politic, of course, for Eisenhower to accept the wording
imposed upon him by the Combined Chiefs of Staff. Deep in his heart,
however, he knows full well what Marshall wants him to do. And, as
we will see, he does it.

Meanwhile the question of Eisenhower's authority to communicate
with the Russians is closed, at least as far as SHAEF is concerned.
General Nevins has written a cover to his memo of the day before for
the Deputy Acting Chief of Staff, G-3, in which he says: "I have
consulted with the Secretary General's Staff, who states that he believes
the authority for [Eisenhower's action] to be contained in FACS-118
copy of which is attached." Then there is a handwritten note referring
to FACS-118 that says: "Eyes only—no copy." An agile way of doing

---

1. SCAF 151 (20 December 1944) thru 275 (12 April 1945). Cable: Eisenhower to War Department and Military Mission, Moscow. No. FWD 19003 (SCAF 275). 12 April 1945.

business. In effect, Nevins is telling G-3: believe what I say, what you can't read doesn't concern you.

The cover memo is returned this morning with the handwritten comment: "Ops— Many thanks. We can breathe again!" The signature is illegible.

Up forward, at headquarters of the Twelfth Army Group the planners are considering a one-page draft of a plan based on what will happen if Eisenhower declares "ECLIPSE conditions exist" or if there is a sudden German surrender or collapse. Section 3, part e., states: "First Allied Airborne Army is planning, contingent on the situation and availability of troops, airborne operations to seize BERLIN and KIEL."[2]

At 2 P.M. Bradley sends a message to Devers advising him of what the Twelfth Army Group is doing. Says Bradley: "Twelfth Army Group is now advancing on the line Wittenberg-Magdeburg-Dessau-Leipzig-Altenburg-Plauen-Bayreuth and to seize bridgeheads across the Elbe River from Magdeburg to Dessau both inclusive. Advance in force beyond this line is not contemplated for the present except as may be necessary to take advantage of a proper obstacle such as the Mulde River."[3] In other words, as of two in the afternoon of April 12, with his troops of the Second Armored Division already on the banks of the river Elbe, Bradley does not at this time contemplate moving farther toward Berlin. Only if ECLIPSE conditions occur will Eisenhower move to take the German capital. On the front lines, however, no one is aware of Bradley's reticence.

In early evening, Brig. Gen. Sidney R. Hinds, commander of the Second Armored Division's Combat Command B (there are three combat commands in the division, A, B and R, with each combat command having the strength in men and material of a full combat division), watches his troops pile into Dukws (amphibious two-and-a-half-ton trucks) and plow across the Elbe's cold, swift current. As Hinds recalls the operation in speaking with the author, the river is almost flooded and it's about five hundred yards from bank to bank. The first troops over are solely infantry, with light weapons. Their task is to clear a small bridgehead and hold it while the engineers prepare a pontoon bridge. If successful, Hinds will next send tanks and artillery to expand the bridgehead and advance.

Evening in Europe, depending on the times used (daylight savings

---

2. Headquarters Twelfth Army Group. Operations Plan ECLIPSE, third draft, Brief. 12 April 1945.

3. 12 Army Group Record File #371.3 Military Objectives, vol. 6. No. QX-31587. TOO 1214000. 12 April 1945.

or European summer time) is either five or six hours ahead of New York City time, where it is only early afternoon. The news of the Second Armored's crossing the last water barrier to Berlin flashes across the Atlantic. In its second night edition, the *New York World Telegram* carries a "screamer" headline in seventy-two-point type: "NINTH SMASHES ACROSS ELBE, TEARS INTO LAST 50-MILE LAP OF RACE FOR BERLIN." A subhead reads: "Patton spurts 46 miles; now only 90 from Reds; tanks sighted at Halle."

Beneath the headlines runs a breathless and understandably inaccurate story by Boyd D. Lewis, United Press war correspondent, that reads:

"American Ninth Army tanks smashed across the Elbe River today, striking into the last 50 miles before Berlin.

"To the South, Lt. Gen. George S. Patton's Third Army splintered the Germans' east front supply line with a 46-mile dash for Halle and Leipzig, less than 90 miles from the Red Army.

"The crossing of the Elbe, last river barrier before Berlin, was made by the Ninth Army's Second (Hell on Wheels) Armored Division at an unspecified point near the fortress city of Magdeburg, 60 miles west of Berlin and 115 miles from the Russian lines.

"First reports indicated the Americans may have captured intact one of the six Elbe bridges in the Magdeburg area, opening the way for a full-scale armored drive into the doomed German capital.

"The Ninth Army troops spurted 55 miles through the weakest enemy opposition to reach the Elbe yesterday. This pace, if it were continued, would threaten to carry their battle flags into Berlin by nightfall. The slashing drive raised the imminent threat of disaster for perhaps one million Germans facing the Red Army along the Oder River line 117 miles to the east.

"Four more Ninth Army divisions were crowding on the heels of the Second Armored, ready to swing across the Elbe and break into the rear of the Germans' Oder River defenses."

A later edition of the *World Telegram,* the 7th Sports Final, changes the headline to read: "NINTH LEAPS ELBE, SPEEDS ON." The new subhead reads: "49 Miles From Berlin in Sweep to Join Reds." Boyd Lewis rewrites his earlier story. His new lead proclaims: "American 9th Army Mobile Forces broke across the Elbe River at Magdeburg today and raced for Berlin and a juncture with the Red Army.

"Unofficial reports put the rampaging 2nd (Hell on Wheels) Armored Division within 49 miles of the German capital and about 100 miles from the Russian lines. (The frequently unreliable Paris radio said that Allied troops have dropped by parachute 16 miles from Berlin. Earlier unconfirmed reports said that the chutists were dropped at Brandenburg, 20 miles west of Berlin.)''

To dramatize the news, *Telegram* editors run a boxed paragraph with the story that says: ''The distance between the point of the farthest American advance and Berlin—49 miles—is about equal to that between Manhattan Island and Newburgh, NY.''

The papers sell like hotcakes. Within less than an hour the newsstands are bare. Suddenly another edition arrives and the newsboys begin an urgent cry: *''Extra! Extra!''* Their high-pitched yelps stop people in their tracks. Now they spot a truly shocking new headline: ''ROOSEVELT DIES SUDDENLY.''

The drive on Berlin is forgotten.[4]

April 13, 1945

Roosevelt's dying the previous afternoon in Warm Springs seems to paralyze the military and political leaders in Washington, London and SHAEF.

A number of excellent books deal with the events of this day.[5] But a careful study of the cable logs on this day for both the Operations Department in Washington and at SHAEF headquarters reveals nothing in the way of messages concerning the President's death. The files are unbelievably thin.

The major message for the date is a cable from the Combined Chiefs to Eisenhower about the procedure for announcing Victory in Europe (VE) day.[6] The Combined Chiefs believe that VE day can be declared before all the centers of resistance are mopped up. Therefore, the Combined Chiefs want Eisenhower's recommendations as to what conditions will be necessary for the announcement of VE day. The Combined Chiefs believe that a suitable procedure might be for recommendations ''to be made by SCAEF and, if indicated, by SCMED

---

4. In a conversation with the author, Gen. A. C. Gillem Jr., the commanding general of XIII Corps, said that just before he died, Roosevelt read a copy of the *Atlanta Constitution* that ran a front-page map showing where the Ninth Army had crossed the Elbe at Magdeburg. At the time of this interview, a copy of the paper hung on the wall in Roosevelt's bedroom in Warm Springs, Georgia.

5. David McCullough's magnificent biography *Truman* is superb on events in Washington on this day. One should also read Churchill's description of events, plus Herbert Feis's Pulitzer Prize–winning work, *Churchill, Roosevelt, Stalin*.

6. OPD Cable File. Fr Combined Chiefs of Staff to SHAEF FWD (Eisenhower). No. WARX 67669. Copies to: CG, AFH, Caserta, Italy (Alexander); British Joint Staff Mission, Washington. 13 April 1945.

to the Combined Chiefs. Result: Russian, British, U.S. heads of state will make simultaneous announcements. Appreciate your comments workability of this plan.''

More important, however, for the Americans is the question: Who's running the war?

It turns out that the new President, Harry S. Truman, has never been given a single, top-secret briefing on the war until the day after he takes the oath of office in his new role as Commander in Chief.

On Friday, April 13, Truman meets with Secretary of War Stimson, General Marshall, Admirals Leahy and King, and the new Secretary of the Navy, James V. Forrestal. According to the diary of Secretary Stimson, the elder statesman present, Truman ''made the impression of a man who is willing and able to learn and to do his best, but who was laboring with the terrific handicap of coming into such an office where the threads of information were so multitudinous that only long previous familiarity could allow him to control them. On the whole my impression was favorable although, as General Marshall said in the car coming back with me, 'We shall not know what he is really like until the pressure begins to be felt.' ''[7]

According to Pulitzer Prize–winning historian Herbert Feis, who was deeply involved with the events of the time, and who discussed with the author on a number of occasions the events of this day, Truman is smart enough to know that Roosevelt has complete faith in Stimson and Marshall. Truman is also a combat veteran of World War I. He understands that the best thing to do is to keep the winning team intact and keep them following the course of action initiated under Roosevelt. The most important thing is to follow the recommendations of the men who have served Roosevelt so well and have already won the war for America. And this Truman does until he's learned enough to make his own decisions.

In other words, with Roosevelt dead, there isn't the slightest chance that Churchill can persuade Marshall that the Allies should take Berlin, either for political reasons or to force the Russians into a new round of negotiations. On matters such as this, President Truman will defer to his Chief of Staff.

But if there exists a certain state of paralysis in Washington this day, it doesn't extend to the battlefield. In the Pacific, the battle for Okinawa is unbelievably bloody. The Japanese launch massive kamikaze attacks on ships in the invasion fleet; twenty-eight are hit, and three sunk, by the

---

7. Henry L. Stimson, *Diary*, 13 April 1945.

suicide planes. President Truman will learn that Okinawa cost 34,000 Army battle casualties, plus another 7,700 Navy personnel, while killing or taking prisoner 81,000 Japanese. This ratio of casualties, approximately one to two, is unacceptable if America is to invade Japan. (On March 27, the Japanese commander of Iwo Jima, General Kuribayashi, committed suicide rather than surrender his 21,000-man command. Only 1,083 men of the Japanese garrison survived, and they had cost the Americans 25,000 casualties, including 7,000 dead, in the most costly American battle of the war.)

In the Southeast Asia theater, Mountbatten is about to retake Burma. Again the fighting is unbelievably ferocious.

In Italy, a new Allied offensive, which began on April 9, is in full swing and German Army Group C will be destroyed in a few weeks of fighting. This new offensive is instrumental in keeping German units from withdrawing into the Alps, which had been Field Marshal Kesselring's plan but had been rejected by Hitler.

On the Eastern Front, the Soviets are cleaning up their right flank (to the north) in East Prussia and Pomerania. The Berlin front remains a salient needing support on both the northern and southern flanks. Farther south, the Russians have penetrated Germany and are crossing the Czechoslovakian border on their way to Prague. Vienna is about to fall to the Russians, who are pushing deeper into Austria.

The map of Europe is being remade.

Now let us examine the Western Front. Starting at SHAEF, we work our way down the chain of command to the fighting.

At SHAEF the future operations of the Twelfth Army Group are placed under two headings.[8] The first one is organized: "(a) Seizing Dresden; (b) Operating as situation permits to destroy enemy east of the Elbe in conjunction with Soviets by capturing Berlin; (c) Defensive in remainder of zone." The second section is the "troop allocation for defensive, offensive, occupational and 'St.-Nazaire' objectives."

At Ninth Army Headquarters, Lt. Gen. William H. Simpson, Commanding, outlines current operations for his three corps commanders.[9] According to Simpson, "the purpose of present operations are . . . to advance to the general line WITTENBERGE-HAVELBERG—along the HAVEL River to the lake southwest of BRANDENBURG—south along the PLANE River to RADICKE—south to the Elbe in the vicinity

---

8. SHAEF G-3 DIVISION (FWD). Future Operations Western Front. GCT 370-47/Plans. 13 April 1945.
9. Headquarters Ninth U.S. Army. Office of the Commanding General. Current Operations. 13 April 1945.

of WITTENBERG. This position will be held with minimum infantry forces in order to permit the assembly of a large reserve and the immediate resting and refitting of our armored divisions preparatory to further operations either directly east toward BERLIN, if this is necessary to gain contact with the Russians, or to launch an attack to the southeast. No advance will be made beyond this line except proper reconnaissance to determine enemy dispositions. XIII Corps will be prepared to take over from SECOND BRITISH ARMY along the line of the Elbe to a point approximately thirty five miles northwest of WITTENBERG.''

Simpson is not telling his men that they will capture Berlin outright. But he does say that they should be prepared to advance across the Elbe as far as Brandenburg, on the outskirts of Berlin. But will it be necessary to do this if SHAEF's desires are ''to destroy [the] enemy east of the Elbe in conjunction with [the] Soviets by capturing Berlin''? It sounds as if SHAEF prefers the Russians destroying the Germans trapped between the Oder and Elbe Rivers even if it means the Russians will take Berlin. No matter. Simpson prepares for any eventuality.

Further down the line, the approach is more aggressive. At General McLain's headquarters at XIX Corps, Colonel Sloan prepares letter of instruction No. 143 in which he sets the proposed boundaries between XIII and XIX Corps effective on Army order.[10] The boundary as proposed runs east through Brandenburg and up to Potsdam ''with running rights to XIX Corps through POTSDAM.''

Sloan figures the next stop has to be Berlin.

According to the records of the Second Armored Division, the Thirtieth Infantry Division continues to make good progress on the left.[11] On the right, the Eighty-third Infantry Division establishes a bridgehead across the Elbe River at the town of Barby against moderate resistance. The weather is clear to overcast late in the period described; visibility two to three miles. Combat Command A reports that Task Force A seizes a bridge across the Weser-Elbe canal and enlarges its bridgehead, coming under heavy fire from antiaircraft emplacements to the west. All routes into Magdeburg are explored with patrols; strong enemy reaction is met in all instances on approaches to the city. Task Force B remains in defensive positions, maintaining roadblocks and

---

10. Headquarters XIX Corps. Letter of Instruction #143. 131030B April 1945.
11. Headquarters Second Armored Division. No. 69. From 122400B April 1945 to 132400B April 1945. Combat Invu #253 2 A Div. D625942.

sweeping the enemy from the area. Positions are intermittently under heavy fire from enemy antiaircraft installations. Task Force R remains [in the rear] maintaining order. It is prepared for early relief by the Eighth Armored Division.

Combat Command B reports that its crossing of the Elbe continues via bridging operations. At first light the bridge comes under observed fire from antiaircraft positions in the vicinity of Prester, and several sections of the bridge are destroyed. Efforts to repair the bridge are fruitless and the site is abandoned at 4 P.M. in favor of another site upstream. At the other bridgehead, infantry launches a limited-objective attack to enlarge the bridgehead. Resistance comprises heavy-caliber artillery, antiaircraft, small-arms fire. At the end of the period, the infantry of the 119th are enlarging the bridgehead to the south to cover the new bridging operation.

Combat Command R reports that it is containing the city of Magdeburg, probing the outskirts with patrols, destroying several antiaircraft guns and taking prisoners. It is also conducting route reconnaissance with the view of crossing the Elbe River in the Eighty-third Infantry Division zone.

The Eighty-second Armored Reconnaissance Battalion reports that it is continuing screening operations within the division zone. It is patrolling to the north, meeting strong resistance. It seizes the city of Neualdensleben and destroys fifty-seven antitank guns in the railroad yards.

April 14, 1945

This day brings the end of the Allied drive on Berlin.

During the last ninety-six hours, the Americans have made the greatest single-day advances in military history. And as General Hinds puts it, only a series of coincidences keep the Second Armored Division from going to the capital of Germany.

A recap of events begins with the first shooting light on the morning of April 10, when General McLain unleashes the tank columns of his XIX Corps and they set off for the Elbe. The previous night, the tanks had been coiled around the little town of Hildesheim some sixty-five miles from Magdeburg and the river Elbe. The tankers had thought they would be staying at Hildesheim for several days, supposedly regrouping. Hildesheim marks the western boundary of the agreed-to Soviet zone of occupation. The American tankers believed they would not move into the Russian zone until an agreement had been reached with the Russians authorizing such a move. This means that when the tanks of the XIX Corps move out suddenly on the morning of April 10, they leave behind all their supporting trucks, which, because of the projected halt for several days, had been sent to the rear for fresh supplies.

When General White gets the word to advance at Second Armored headquarters, he calls for Col. Paul A. Disney, commander of the Sixty-seventh Armored Regiment, the lead unit. Disney recalls coming up to White and barely having time to say hello before White says: "Take off for the east." Thinking that his men are all on stand-down, Disney asks, "What's the objective?" White barks one word: "Berlin."

The tactics for an armored advance such as the Second Armored is making is to bypass all strongpoints of enemy resistance. With a column of tanks, half-tracks, motorized infantry and artillery on the road grinding forward at a combat speed of four miles an hour, the lead vehicles must keep moving at all costs. Even a brief halt to demolish a roadblock will create a traffic jam of epic proportions in the rear. So whenever a roadblock is spotted, or if a concentration of enemy forces is expected ahead, the lead tanks swing off the road, going through fields, or using secondary roads, to bypass the obstacle.

In a situation like this, it is usual for a general officer to ride in his jeep just behind the first echelon of tanks. He keeps in radio contact with the tanks and the Piper Cub observation plane that swoops and circles directly in front of the column looking for the enemy. If the plane spots Germans ahead, it radios back to the general, who will then stand up in his vehicle and make hand signals directing his tanks to the right or left to the quickest and clearest way forward.

On this day, at Twelfth Army Headquarters there is a fifteen-foot-long map of Europe on the wall so that Bradley and his staff can glance up at the situation markers and quickly spot where their troops are. By the morning of April 11, the forward lines of advance appear as long fingers searching for the river Elbe. To the north is the spearhead of the Eighty-fourth Infantry Division. Immediately to the south, on its flank but way in the lead, is the Fifth Armored Division. Below that is the Thirtieth Infantry Division. Next to the south are the powerful combat commands of the Second Armored. Farthest to the south is the Eighty-third Infantry Division.

By the morning of April 12, the map at Twelfth Army Headquarters shows the immensity of the gains. The Second Armored had advanced its sixty-five miles to the Elbe in little more than thirty hours. That night they cross the Elbe.

On the morning of April 13, the map at Twelfth Army Headquarters shows that to the north the Fifth Armored Division has also reached the Elbe at both Wittenberge and Tangermünde, where the bridges across the river are blown up by German engineers as the Americans approach within yards of these objectives.

On the morning of April 14, the headquarters map shows that both the XIX Corps and the XIII Corps have closed on the Elbe at numerous points. Two bridgeheads across the Elbe are made. Only one is secure, however.

On the banks of the Elbe, on the morning of April 12, the morning after Major Hollingsworth charged for the bridge at Schoenebeck only to have it blown up in his face, the men of Combat Command B of the Second Armored reorganize for an assault across the river. At one in the afternoon, General Hinds issues verbal orders for a night crossing, which is an unqualified success. His infantry has little trouble setting up their perimeter on the east bank of the Elbe. Meanwhile, searchlights were turned on and pointed skyward. The reflected "artificial moonlight" allows engineers to start building a pontoon bridge.

Throughout the night, and early the next morning, sporadic artillery fire falls around the site where the bridge is being built. But the German fire is not heavy enough to keep the engineers from their work. However, around nine-thirty this morning, the Germans move a forward observer into place and he directs the artillery fire so it falls on the half-completed bridge.

As Hinds recalls it for the author, the German fire is not battery type. That is, it does not fall in salvos. It is simply one shell after another from approximately ten or twelve guns, which the Americans cannot locate. Neither can Hinds's troopers find the hiding place of the German artillery observer, even after searching Schoenebeck house by house.

It is obvious that the observer is being forced to change his location, however. The artillery fire slackens. Work on the bridge resumes. At eleven-thirty, the bridge is three-quarters completed (some previously damaged pontoons have not yet been replaced, however), and it's within seventy-five yards of reaching the eastern bank of the Elbe. Suddenly, the site is hit by heavy German fire. Three men are wounded at the eastern end of the bridge. Most of the pontoons are destroyed, including those that are assembled and at the water's edge.

One should reflect at this point about the lack of air cover. Remember that back in March, Eisenhower planned for air cover only as far as the Elbe. And that, according to the Air Force, it would have been stretching the limit of their planes' capabilities. What has happened is that the Second

Armored has advanced at far greater speed than anyone had dared anticipate. So now it is beyond the range of ground-support fighter-bombers. And while there have been numerous requests for air support from XIX Corps Headquarters, and lengthy conversations with the Tactical Air Command, as reported by Colonel Sloan to the author, no air support has been forthcoming. The Tactical Air Force has also refused to move its airfields forward to keep pace with the Allied advance. The XIX Corps, desperate for air support, even went so far as to offer to capture, clear and hold enemy fields from which fighter-bombers can safely fly. The Air Force rejected this offer. So here on the Elbe, Hinds and his men have to do without air support. (The reader will recall that the Air Force had warned planners at SHAEF that ground-support operations were not being considered east of the Elbe.)

Now, with no bridge, Hinds and I. D. White confer and decide to gamble while they still have some element of surprise. There has not yet been any serious opposition thrown against their infantry on the other side of the river. So, during the night of April 12, the night of Roosevelt's death, they order the troops on the east bank to slip southward and establish a new bridgehead.

The night maneuver is successful. The new site is secured, and on the morning of April 13, a cable is run across the river to create a ferry capable of carrying tanks and antitank guns to the east bank. The problem now is that the riverbanks slope gently away from the shore. First, the west bank has to be bulldozed so the ferry can reach the riverbank and be loaded. A ramp is built with loads of rubble dumped at the water's edge. Sporadic artillery fire begins to fall. The first cable, the all-important guide cable, is damaged and has to be repaired. By noon the work is completed and the ferry is ready to cross.

Even with the approach ramp, the ferry, when loaded with the bulldozer, sticks hard aground. It has to be pushed into deeper water by everyone present. Finally floating free, the ferry starts its first trip. However, the river's swift current holds it back, and Captain Youngblood, commanding Company D of the Seventeenth Armored Engineer Battalion, commandeers a Dukw. He speeds across the river and lashes the Dukw to the ferry and boosts its speed. Suddenly, in a million-to-one shot, a single enemy artillery shell severs the ferry's guide cable.

"Well, there it goes to hell," Hinds thinks to himself. He watches helplessly as the Dukw, the three pontoons that make up the ferry and the bulldozer are swept downstream and thrown against the east bank.

In taking stock of the situation, Hinds receives another shock. He has enough cable, but he only has one pontoon left, not enough for a ferry.

Meanwhile, on the east bank, the element of surprise has been lost. One of the last battle groups in the German Army arrives at the front, and Hinds has to watch helplessly as six or eight German tanks overrun his infantry. General White now drives to the bridgehead site to confer with Hinds. They reach a decision quickly.

While Hinds and his troops have been battling to cross the Elbe, some five or six miles to the south the Eighty-third Infantry Division, which, with all its combat experience in Europe has never spearheaded a river crossing, has successfully thrown a pontoon bridge across the Elbe at Barby.

In compiling his famous combat interviews for the U.S. Army, S.L.A. Marshall reports: "As he brought his men to the riverbank for the Infantry crossing, Col. [Edwin "Buckshot"] Crabhill had gone up and down the line exhorting his men with these words: 'Don't waste the opportunity of a lifetime. You are on your way to *Berlin!* You can get across without having a shot fired at you. But you have to move *now.* Don't wait to organize. Get going. Get over there in any shape that you can.' "[12]

"It was in this fashion that the battalion crossed the river. It had proceeded without order and with the men scrambling for the boats as fast as they could go. Crabhill said he actually booted some of his men in the pants to make them move faster."

In interviewing men of Eighty-third Division, the author verified that Crabhill is a tiny, peppery man who drives his troops hard. No one disputes the story that he kicked his men to make them move faster. As it turns out, Crabhill calls the play perfectly. The battalion crosses the river without a shot being fired.

To the north, Hinds and White quickly agree. Hinds will stay at the bridgehead area and pull his troops back from the east bank in as orderly a fashion as possible. White will go to the Eighty-third Division's bridgehead taking Combat Command R with him. White will then supervise crossing the Elbe with Combat Command R, which will split into two groups. One force will swing north and relieve the pressure on Hinds's forces on the east bank. The second group will help the Eighty-third Division maintain the bridgehead and prepare to drive on Berlin.

The conference ends. White sets off for the Eighty-third Division bridgehead at Barby.

Hinds is then approached by a war correspondent. Later, he will be unable to recall the correspondent's name.

---

12. Combat Interviews S. L. A. Marshall: 83rd Inf Div.

"General, how do you broadcast news reports to your men?"

"Usually we let them tune in the radios in their half-tracks," says Hinds.

"Are you sending any news to the other side of the river?"

"No. We don't have any time for that now. We've got a goddamned hot fight on our hands over there and we don't have time to sit around listening to the radio."

"But what are you going to tell the men about the President?"

"President? What about the President?"

"Why, didn't you know?" says the correspondent. "Roosevelt died a day and a half ago!"

Hinds is stunned. Then his professionalism takes over. The first thing to do is get his men back from the eastern bank. He turns his back on the correspondent and begins working on the problem.

The situation is serious. But Hinds isn't too worried. He believes his soldiers are the best in the American Army. They have been through three years of combat, and he knows a good percentage of them will return. A tank attack doesn't kill all the defenders. There has to be lots of infantry behind the tanks to do a thorough job, and he didn't see that many German infantry. As it works out, Hinds is right. The initial withdrawal is orderly. In the evening several hundred more of his men approach the river's edge and shout for transportation. They bring back an almost equal number of prisoners. Still he loses a total of 304 men. One battalion loses 7 officers and 146 enlisted men killed, wounded or missing.

What no one on the front lines knows is that Eisenhower and Bradley have conferred about the bridgehead at Barby. At the end of the phone conversation, Eisenhower asks Bradley what his estimate is of the cost to break through from Barby and take Berlin. Replies Bradley, "I estimate that it might cost us one hundred thousand men." There is a pause in the conversation. Then Bradley adds: "It would be a pretty stiff price to pay for a prestige objective, especially when we know that we've got to pull back and let the other fellow take over."[13] Nor does anyone know that the SHAEF planning staff has on this day produced a long set of recommendations about "how our operations should be developed after we have reached the Elbe."[14]

---

13. *The Last Battle* by Cornelius Ryan (New York: Simon & Schuster, 1966), page 321. The footnote on this page in Ryan's book correctly sets the timing for this all-important conversation. Bradley acknowledged that he failed to date this anecdote when he related it in his book, *A Soldier's Story.*

14. 381 Post Overlord Planning, vol. 6. (1 April–30 April). Memo by SHAEF G-3 FWD. Approved by SHAEF planning staff. 14 April 1945.

"With our armies on the Elbe, it is clear that the ultimate defeat of Germany is assured," the memo states. ". . . It is reasoned that our strategy should be directed to dividing and isolating the enemy's remaining forces. The isolation of the enemy in the north from the south by joining hands with the Russians in the center should first be assured. Further subdivision should then be our aim, and effort should be allocated to this as soon as possible. . . . It is concluded that in order to destroy the enemy's will to resist, our ground and air operations should be directed primarily towards thrusting towards Luebeck and Linz and secondarily towards capturing Berlin. . . . It is concluded that operations to deny the enemy the southern redoubt should be conducted with the main thrust to join hands with the Russians in the Salzburg-Linz area and a concurrent subsidiary thrust to capture the key areas of the inner fortress. . . . It is concluded that operations to deny the enemy the opportunity for a prolonged resistance in Norway should be given high priority."

This memo leads Eisenhower to cable the Combined Chiefs "my thoughts on future operations."[15]

Writes Eisenhower: "Having completed successfully my thrust in the center, my next object is to defeat the Germans as quickly as possible." Eisenhower's use of the personal pronoun in "my" thrust, and "my" next object raises a few eyebrows in Washington. The Supreme Commander says the quickest way to divide the enemy in the north is to drive toward Luebeck. To the south "we will join with the Russians on the axis of their drive up the Danube Valley." As for the German capital, it would be "most desirable to make a thrust to Berlin as the enemy may group forces around his capital and, in any event, its fall would have great effect on the morale of the enemy and our own peoples. But, as explained below, this operation must take a low priority in point of time unless operations to clear our flanks proceed with unexpected rapidity."

Eisenhower next details his planned operations for Denmark and Norway, reducing the National Redoubt, opening the port of Hamburg, reducing the fortress areas still held by the Germans in Holland or in the island areas. Again he says that because of the urgent importance of beginning operations in the north and the south, our operations toward Berlin must take "second place and await the development of the situation."

---

15. OPD Cable File. Fr SHAEF, Rheims (signed: Ike) to Combined Chiefs of Staff. No. FWD 19190 (SCAF 280). 14 April 1945.

Therefore, "I plan: (A) To hold a firm front in the central area of the Elbe. (B) To start operations towards Luebeck and Denmark. (C) To initiate a powerful thrust to meet Soviet troops in the Danube Valley and crack the Redoubt. (D) Since the thrust on Berlin must await the outcome of the first three above, I do not include it as part of my present plan.

"To summarize: I will stop on the Elbe and clean up my flanks. I will communicate this plan with Marshal Stalin if agreeable with you." From the tone of this cable, Eisenhower is letting the Combined Chiefs know that they are now dealing with *the* Supreme Commander.

In his next cable to the War Department, Eisenhower now plays a different game.[16] He warns that "present information shows that the Germans will try to prolong resistance with every means in their power. This resistance will be carried out to the bitter end in the most inaccessible areas in Europe." He then goes on to list eight "areas where resistance will most likely continue; they are also the areas for which I am likely to be responsible."

Therefore, Eisenhower declares, "it would be wise to postpone the declaration of VE day until it would appear that there are not months of fighting still ahead of our Allied troops." VE day should result from "a coordinated agreement between all the Allied governments, on a signal from SACMED and myself to the Combined Chiefs of Staff. I am also aware of the urgent necessity for the release of troops from this theater for the war against Japan. . . . Redeployment . . . should not be related to the declaring of a VE day but should be done according to the progress of our operations."

Given that Germany will surrender unconditionally in about three weeks' time, this ultracautious estimate about the possibility of there being "months of fighting still ahead" is more in keeping with Eisenhower's usual flank-protecting estimates for future operations.

April 14 ends with a late cable from Moscow.[17] Red Army chief of staff Antonov meets with Archer, Olsen and Roberts. The Russian recommends that the overall signal for a meeting between forces would have the Russians fire red rockets and the Anglo-Americans use green rockets. Tanks will carry a white stripe around their turrets plus a white cross on the top of the turrets for both the Russian and Anglo-American forces.

---

16. OPD Cable File. Fr SHAEF (signed Ike) to War Department No. FWD 19189 (CM-IN 13216) (SCAF 279). This message is a reply to FACS 180, which is W 67669. 14 April 1945.

17. 312.3-1 Corresp & Communication with the Russians. Cable from Archer and Olsen to Eisenhower. No. MX-23875 TOO 142150Z TOR 150235. 14 April 1945.

These are suggestions only, he says, and the Russians are quite willing to accept any better system of identification.

Now Antonov really gets down to brass tacks. Referring to Eisenhower's message of April 12, "Antonov raised a question . . . saying he did not understand clearly the meaning of the expression, 'The division of responsibility should be defined by boundary lines to be agreed upon between groups of armies.' He inquired if this meant any change in the zones of occupation previously agreed upon by our respective governments. He was assured that the reference was to tactical areas and that no change was implied in the zones of occupation. Antonov requested that confirmation be obtained from Eisenhower on this point. In discussing the subject, Antonov indicated that he understood that upon completion of tactical operations the Anglo-American forces would withdraw from previously agreed Soviet zones of occupation." In concluding the meeting, Antonov says there isn't any need for Eisenhower to send such a high-ranking officer as Tedder to Moscow.

There is no mistaking the seriousness of the question that Antonov raises about the Anglo-Americans withdrawing from the agreed-upon Soviet zone of occupation. The Military Mission in Moscow is correct in its interpretation of events, and in its explanation to Antonov. Chief of Staff Marshall has decided that the Americans will not play the game the way the British wish them to. Eisenhower will not take Berlin. Once the tactical situation straightens itself out, the Americans will turn over the ground they have taken that is to be part of the Soviet zone of occupation.

The only problem is that no one has told the troops.

April 15, 1945

Early Sunday morning, April 15, General Bradley calls his Ninth Army commander, General Simpson, and orders him to fly to Twelfth Army Group Headquarters at Wiesbaden. Bradley won't tell Simpson what it is he wants to discuss.

Simpson later recalled for the author that when he lands, Bradley is waiting. "We shook hands, and then and there he tells me the news. Brad said, 'You must stop on the Elbe. You are not to advance any farther in the direction of Berlin. I'm sorry, Simp, but there it is.' "

"Where in the hell did you get this?" asks Simpson.

"From Ike."

Simpson is stunned. "All I remember is that I was heartbroken. I got back in the plane in a kind of daze. All I could think of was how am I going to tell my staff, my corps commanders and my troops? Above all, how am I going to tell my troops?'' Simpson returns to his headquarters and passes the word to his corps commanders. Then he flies to the Elbe knowing that if he doesn't pass the word himself, he cannot trust the men at the point to halt their advance on Berlin. Especially when it appears ready for the picking.

Meanwhile, after assuring himself that as many men as possible have returned from the east bank of the Elbe, Hinds drives back to division headquarters. Word has come down that Simpson is present, and during the drive, Hinds worries that Simpson is going to chew him out for losing so many men on the far side of the Elbe.

''Maybe the old man didn't like the way we crossed the river,'' Hinds recalls. ''Anyway, we say hello, and he asks me how we're getting along. I say that I guess we're all right now, General. We had two good withdrawals. There was no excitement and no panic and our crossings at Barby are going good.''

''Fine,'' Simpson says. ''Keep some of your men on the east bank if you want to. But they're not going any farther.'' He looks steadily at Hinds. ''Sid, this is as far as we're going.''

Hinds is shocked. ''No, sir. That's not right. We're going to Berlin.''

Hinds can see that Simpson is struggling with his emotions. ''Sid,'' he says gravely, ''I have just come from General Bradley's headquarters. We are not going any farther. This is the end of the war for us.''

Hinds is very tired and all raw emotion. He can see that Simpson is terribly upset. There is nothing he can say. So without replying, and forgetting all courtesy—a good-bye, a handshake, a salute—Hinds turns on his heel and rushes off.

''I didn't mean to be discourteous, or anything like that,'' Hinds says later. ''But, oh, hell! What else could I do or say? Later on, Simpson told me he understood.''

Simpson next drives to Barby where Gen. I. D. White is pushing his Combat Command R across the Eighty-third Division's bridge, now appropriately signposted ''Truman Bridge.'' Once again, Simpson relays the order to halt and hold.

Meanwhile, to the north, Maj. Gen. Alvin C. Gillem Jr.'s XIII Corps (made up of the 5th Armored, the 29th, 35th, the 84th, and 102nd Infantry Divisions) are preparing to cross the Elbe and drive on Berlin. Bridging is ready, maps are prepared, battalions are fueling their assault boats, when the phone calls come from higher headquarters. Hold on the Elbe, do not cross.

How close are the Americans to taking Berlin? The three-page G-2 estimate of April 14 for the XIX Corps is originated by Col. Washington Platt, who sees the situation thusly: "The German Army in the West has been virtually destroyed. . . . While . . . in many places the enemy still resists with discipline and tenacity, his task is hopeless and his continued existence as a territorial unity in Europe is only a matter of a few weeks. Today . . . our front lines lie only 70 miles from Berlin and 120 miles from the Russian front.

"Convinced that the [enemy] units in the West can no longer stop us and that the miscellaneous elements from the various *Wehrkreis* we enter can cause little more than a brief delay, the only remaining vital question is—will the enemy shift a potent mobile force from the East Front to try to halt us?

"It does not seem probable that a strong mobile force will be shifted to combat our attack."

Colonel Sloan, the operations officer for the XIX Corps, supports Platt's view, saying there is every possibility that within forty-eight hours of resuming the advance, the lead elements of American armored troops will enter Berlin.

This belief is also expressed to the author by Maj. Gen. Alvin Gillem, commanding the XIII Corps. "We were hoarding gasoline, ammunition, every necessary item of logistical importance on our drive to the Elbe," he tells the author. "When we crossed the Elbe, my troops would have had everything they needed to take Berlin. We would have been alongside XIX Corps all the way. Forty-eight hours. That's all it would have taken."[18]

---

18. Gillem's statement is important. SHAEF believes logistics are weak at the Elbe, but much documentary evidence disputes this concept. The battle-wise field commanders know how to scrounge extra trucks and supplies. They have done so. According to front-line telephone logs, they believe there are enough supplies on the east bank of the Elbe to support the Second Armored's attack on Berlin even if the bridge at Barby is destroyed. But with orders to halt at the Elbe, the question whether an attack on Berlin without air support would be successful becomes moot.

17

A s of April 15, 1945, the American forces are halted on the Elbe. They will not advance on Berlin unless ordered. There should be no fighting between advancing American and Russian forces, unless the Russians decide to force the issue. A good deal of mopping up and bureaucratic housecleaning remains to be done, however. This involves both Europe and Washington.

At SHAEF the primary concern is how to support the British advance beyond Hamburg to Kiel and Luebeck, thence north into Denmark, plus supplying British forces advancing westward into Holland, which still involves some nasty fighting.[1] The study SHAEF produces assumes that two U.S. armies will remain relatively stationary along the Elbe, that one U.S. army advances southeast along the Nuremberg-Regensburg-Linz axis, that another U.S. army will advance on Munich, then forward into the Innsbruck area. Meanwhile, allowance is made for the French to capture the Black Forest area. The problem is logistical. Supplies are short. Only one railway bridge is in operation across the Rhine. It cannot supply everyone's needs. The SHAEF staff concludes that as of May 1, only twelve British divisions can be supported as far forward as Hamburg. "If some of these divisions are needed to reach Kiel," says the study, "Twenty-first Army Group can only be maintained by proportionally reducing the number of divisions on the Elbe." American forces can be "supported in limited operations into the Innsbruck area provided that no advance is made beyond the Elbe."

Not until May 15 will it be possible for American forces, after contacting the Russians on the Regensburg-Linz axis, to "be supported

---

1. 381 Post Overlord Planning, vol. 6 (1 April–30 April). Study by SHAEF G-4 (Mov&Tn Branch) concerning the requirements and potentialities for support of projected operations.

in extensive operations into the Redoubt area and also in an advance on Berlin. And these capabilities, the report says, "are contingent upon a second bridge across the Rhine and the completion of an additional through route to support the [U.S.] Ninth Army."

Thus, at noon, April 15, Eisenhower sends a message to all his commanders with the advisory: "Limit distribution of this message to absolute minimum. Delivery only to addressees or his appointed representative."[2] In this telex, Eisenhower instructs Montgomery to cross the Elbe, secure Hamburg and advance to Luebeck. Meanwhile, the British and Canadians are to clear western Holland and the coastal belt that threatens the approaches to Hamburg. Montgomery will also prepare to liberate Denmark.

The central group of armies will secure their present bridgeheads over the Elbe, and "offensive operations beyond the Elbe will be undertaken only on later orders." These armies will also "launch a powerful thrust to join hands with the Russians in the Danube Valley." The southern group of armies will "occupy western Austria and that part of Germany within its zone of advance."

Next, Simpson writes his orders for the three corps under his command. Essentially, "Ninth Army will not advance beyond the ELBE River. The front will be held with minimum Infantry and Cavalry forces, with substantial local reserves. All armored divisions will be held in reserve."[3] The XIII Corps will be prepared to extend its sector on the Elbe and "assist the Second British Army."

The basic strategy of the Twelfth Army Group is to "regroup without delay in order to launch a strong offensive to the southeast in conjunction with Sixth Army Group. First and Ninth Armies will defend along the current front of Twelfth Army Group with minimum forces in order to permit the concentration of a strong striking force under Third Army to the south of the present army group south boundary."[4]

These orders are confirmed by a cable Eisenhower sends to the War Department and eight other commands.[5]

---

2. 12th Army Group Record File #371.3 Military Objectives, vol. 6. Cable from Eisenhower to CG 12 AG; CG 6th AG, CG FAAA; ANCXF: C/C EXFOR; ACC-IN-C 2nd TAF, CG 9th AF, CG 1st TACAF. No. FWD 19226 (SCAF 281). TOO 151200B. 15 April 1945.
3. Headquarters Ninth U.S. Army. Future Operations. AGTS No. 2795. 15 April 1945.
4. 12th Army Group Record File #371.3 Military Objectives, vol. 7. Operational Directive from General Simpson to CG XIII Corps, CG XVI Corps, CG XIX Corps. 15 April 1945.
5. SCAF 276 (4-12-45) thru 349 (5-6-45). Fr Eisenhower to War Department and eight other commands. No. FWD 19226 (SCAF 281). 15 April 1945.

Also this afternoon, Eisenhower cables the Military Mission in Moscow in answer to Antonov's questions of the night before.[6] Eisenhower says: "My proposals were confined strictly to the tactical phases of this campaign. It is my conviction that when the Red Army and my troops make contact on any part of the front, we should adopt the simplest possible coordinating practices in order that we may devote our full energy to concerted action on other parts of the front until the enemy's organized resistance has completely dissolved. Your assurances to Antonov are confirmed." Meanwhile the proposals for marking tanks are being studied. "Definite answer will be sent to you as quickly as possible."

Another Eisenhower message goes to Marshall.[7] This is in reference to Marshall's message of April 12 (W-66921), and Eisenhower says he believes that the Supreme Command must remain responsible for operations in Europe until the mopping up has been completed, such as the Redoubt and Norway. The Supreme Commander must also remain in control until the British and American forces have moved into their respective occupational zones. Eisenhower also wants the Combined Chiefs to reach firm understandings with the Russians about moving to their respective zones of occupation, because Eisenhower believes that if the Russians ask him to move some of his forces, he will be forced to do so. As he puts it: "I do not see how I could refuse to do so without the danger of creating grave misunderstandings if not actual clashes. Military Mission Moscow's cable MX-23875 of fourteenth April is a clear indication of Soviet suspicion on this question of zones of occupation."

In Washington, meanwhile, General Lincoln remains entangled in arguments with the British about whom Eisenhower can communicate with in Moscow.[8] The British are still trying to prevent Eisenhower from communicating directly with Marshal Stalin. The British want the instructions to Eisenhower to read: "Communicate to the Soviet General Staff and not to Marshal Stalin." Lincoln says that he will not accept the latter phrase ("and not to Marshal Stalin"), which is a matter that has to cleared with Chief of Staff Marshall. Now, says Lincoln, the British have finally accepted our proposed message to Eisenhower, adding the phrase, "repeat Soviet General Staff" to the message. "This

---

6. 312.3-1 Corresp & Communication with the Russians. Cable from Eisenhower to Military Mission, Moscow. No. FWD 19274 (SCAF 282) TOO 151930B. 15 April 1945.
7. Personal File Gen. W. B. Smith. Fr Eisenhower to Marshall. No. FWD 19256. 15 April 1945.
8. ABC Europe (5 August 1943) Sec 1-E. Memo fr General Lincoln to General Hull. 15 April 1945.

was obviously their idea of emphasizing that Eisenhower should not talk to Stalin.''

Of greater significance is another memo from General Lincoln to General Hull showing just how carefully Marshall's staff in Washington looks after Eisenhower and insulates him from these unpleasant negotiations with the British. Marshall and his staff protect the Supreme Commander, advise him on strategy, allow him to act independently so that he can fulfill his instructions—handling millions of troops in the field is an incredibly difficult job in itself—while avoiding numerous political and strategic pitfalls. The fame that comes with being Supreme Commander accrues to Eisenhower. The great achievements of Marshall and his staff will be forgotten in a few years' time. But that is the essence of staff work. It always has been; it always will be.[9]

The main concern in Lincoln's memo is giving Eisenhower freedom to act vis-à-vis the Russians and the probability of their demanding that Allied troops withdraw from Soviet territory that they occupy. According to Lincoln's thinking, there are only two reasons not to give Eisenhower the freedom he requests in this matter: ''(A.) Lack of confidence in Eisenhower—i.e., fear he will give way to Russian pressure in spite of military considerations or that he will become embroiled with the Russians. Obviously this point is unsound.

''(B.) To use our presence in Russian territory as a lever to get them out of our territory in Austria, perhaps Bavaria and perhaps Denmark. Also there are other differences with the Russians which might be involved. Points against this are: (1) Eisenhower is the Commander who has to carry out the orders and is left holding the sack while we dicker with the British and the Russians. (2) All the forces involved are going to be U.S. and it will be the U.S. embroiled with the Russians, yet bound by this agreement with the British in CCS805/10 which would prevent us from getting back into our own zone.

''Acceptance of the [British] proposal in CCS805/10 is unsound because it forces us to wait while we get a British agreement. Experience has shown this could be days. The action is to leave it to Eisenhower with instructions to keep the CCS informed. *That puts the U.S. in the bargaining position where they can accept or reject a British proposal, rather than in the position of the present proposal by which the British can stalemate Eisenhower's American Forces into a row [argument] with the Russians or alternately the U.S. must issue unilateral orders to Eisenhower.*'' (Emphasis added.)

---

9. ABC Europe (5 August 1943) Sec 1-E. Memo fr General Lincoln to General Hull. 15 April 1945.

The latest British proposal, that Allied troops should hold firm in territory they have occupied, waiting for instructions from their various heads of state, ignoring meanwhile any and all Soviet requests that they pull back to their respective zones of occupation, is still on the table. It is obvious that the proposal irritates Marshall and his staff. It seems highly probable that the British hope to use the U.S. troops as sacrificial pawns by forcing the Americans and the Russians into a confrontational position with lots of shots fired and men killed. In turn, this will allow Churchill to call for a renegotiation of various agreements that he doesn't like between the three Allies, thereby prolonging the conflict in Europe and postponing the invasion of Japan by at least half a year.

Thus, Lincoln recommends that Eisenhower be instructed to avoid confrontation with the Russians. Lincoln says: "As to the adjustment of forces after cessation of hostilities in an area, your troops should be disposed in accordance with military requirements regardless of zonal boundaries. You should adhere to this principle in your dealings with the Russians and arrange for progressive readjustments designed to get U.S. and British troops in control of their zones and out of the Russian zones. You will, inasfar as is permitted by the situation, obtain the approval of the CCS prior to any adjustment except local adjustments made necessary by operational and administrative reasons."[10]

Meanwhile, Chief of Staff Marshall clears, via a telephone conversation with Admiral King, the two latest papers from Eisenhower for the plan of a final campaign in Western Europe, and on Archer and Olsen's latest message.[11] The papers are also cleared with the Air Force. The Chief of Staff requests that the papers be presented to the British at once, with the recommendation from the U.S. Chiefs of Staff that "they have examined Eisenhower's appreciation and plan according to his SCAF 280 and 'consider it sound.' " The U.S. Chiefs of Staff also recommend that Eisenhower be told of their decision. Also, Eisenhower is to be told that the Combined Chiefs are studying the manner of

---

10. The British reply to this reasoning complains that Eisenhower is being given too much authority. They say: "The withdrawal back behind interzonal boundaries is a question of high political importance which must be considered by Heads of State. Quite frankly, we think the idea behind it is that, by remaining for a time in parts of the Russian zone in Germany, we shall have something with which to bargain if the Russians are spread out over the Anglo-American zones in Austria."

ABC Europe (5 August 1943) Sec 1-E. Memo fr British reps of the British Chiefs to CCS. 17 April 1945.

11. ABC Europe (5 August 1943) Sec 1-D. Memo fr Gen. G. A. Lincoln to General MacFarland. Plan of campaign in Western Europe. 15 April 1945.

withdrawing forces to their respective zones of occupation and Eisenhower will hear shortly on this matter.

Back in Europe, German intelligence officers stationed along the Oder River, where the Russians are massing their armies, finish their interrogation of a captured Russian soldier of the Seventy-ninth Garde Rifle Division. A copy of the interrogation is flashed to headquarters, Foreign Armies East, and immediately forwarded to the intelligence center in Berlin. The report reads: "The prisoner declares the major attack [on Berlin] will start not later than April 16. Artillery will prepare the attack with three to four hundred shots per gun. Each [Russian] regiment will be prepared to attack with one hundred tanks, equipped with 180-mm guns and newly developed 180-mm mortars. The purpose of the offensive is to get to Berlin ahead of the Americans. Russian officers expect skirmishes with the Americans. One should cover the Americans 'by mistake' with artillery fire so they feel the force of Russian artillery. Soldiers were ordered to fix their uniforms, to shave and wash themselves every day so that they make a civilized impression."

Late this night, a long meeting is held in Moscow with Marshal Stalin.[12] At the end of the meeting Ambassador Harriman says to Stalin that the Germans are claiming that the Soviets are planning to immediately renew their attack on Berlin. Stalin replies that there is indeed going to be an offensive and that he doesn't know if it will be successful. However, the main blow of this attack would be aimed toward Dresden, not Berlin, as Stalin has already told Eisenhower. Meanwhile, the initial Russian attack on Berlin has begun. It is clear that the Soviets expect to be involved in combat with the Americans at some point or other.

One wonders what other intelligence is available to Chief of Staff Marshall. For during this period, the Second Armored troopers on the Elbe continue "improving defensive positions. . . . [Division Artillery] fired defensive missions for all units. Maintained air observation over Magdeburg and river."[13] The Americans are preparing for more than a welcoming barbecue for their "friends" from the East.

In the days that follow, Eisenhower prods the slow-moving Montgomery toward Luebeck. The Field Marshal complains "the plan

---

12. OPD Cable File. Fr Military Mission, Moscow (Olsen & Archer), to War Department Copy sent to SHAEF FWD, "eyes only for Eisenhower," also for CCS, and British Cs of Staff. No. MX 23897 (CM-IN 14852). 16 April 1945.
13. G-3 Periodic Report No. 72. Hq 2nd Armd Div. 162400B April 1945.

couldn't be carried out quickly because you took the Ninth Army from me on April third which left me very weak.''[14] By April 24, the Russians have fought their way through half of Berlin. Casualties on both sides are enormous. On May 2, Montgomery reaches Luebeck and seals off the Danish peninsula. The Scandinavians are protected. Two days later, on May 4, the U.S. Seventh and Fifth Armies join hands beyond the Brenner Pass, isolating the Redoubt area, and seal off northern Italy from the Russians. On May 6, the Nazi forces in the Redoubt area surrender. The general surrender of Germany follows on May 7.

The Cold War in Europe begins.

✕ ✕ ✕

Among all the complexities involved during the Allied advance across the Rhine and onward to the Elbe, one tends to forget the importance of the intelligence that pours out of Berlin in the Magic diplomatic messages to Tokyo. Reviewing it now, one can see how this intelligence impacted upon the actions of the Americans and British in the closing stages of the war in Europe.

On April 5, Ambassador Oshima reports to Tokyo that German Foreign Minister von Ribbentrop asked Oshima to call on him. During their meeting, Ribbentrop reveals that someone (unnamed) approached Hitler on this very day about peace with Russia. The Chancellor reiterated his previous decision. However, says Ribbentrop, Hitler would ''be disposed'' to seek peace with Russia if it is possible. Germany would never make peace with England and the U.S.[15]

In the same Diplomatic Summary, Oshima also tells Tokyo he was advised on April 7 that the ''occasion may arise in which we [Berlin] would move the German government temporarily to southern Germany.'' The Protocol Department of the German Foreign Ministry requests that the Japanese embassy staff be reduced to the very minimum immediately. A special train is to leave for Badgastein (about forty-seven miles south of Salzburg, near Berchtesgaden and the Redoubt area) on April 8, and the Germans want as many Japanese diplomats on the train as possible. Oshima goes on to list eleven members of his staff who will be on the train. (The analysts in Washington note for

---

14. OPD Cable File. Fr 21 Ar Gp (Montgomery) to SHAEF FWD (Eisenhower—eyes only). No. M-576. 272257B April 1945.
15. SRS 1632, 9 April 1945.

General Marshall that a large number of Japanese nationals, including Oshima's wife, have already been relocated in Badgastein.)

The same report also contains the details of a conversation Oshima held with Under Secretary von Steengracht on April 4, who says that the Russian advances in the Vienna region are forcing the Germans to give up the greater part of Croatia and fall back on a line including Zagreb. Von Steengracht says that the Germans may even be forced to fall back to their own territory. In that case, the line in Italy will also have to be pulled back to the German frontier.[16] Von Steengracht also reveals to Oshima that the Russians are withdrawing one army from East Prussia and another from the Danzig area. One of these armies has already appeared on the lower Oder River on the Berlin front.

As for the encirclement of the Ruhr, this means that "from the standpoint of ordnance production, the fact that Thuringia is in danger is more unfortunate." (This is the last bastion of German weapons production and is located in southern Germany, on the border of Bavaria.) Meanwhile the Anglo-American shattering of the Rhine line "was completely beyond German expectations." The necessity will be to stabilize the Western Front somehow, and this will "involve abandoning and retreating from the line of the Upper Rhine." (This opens up the way for the American drive into southeast Germany.)

From this single Magic Diplomatic Summary one can comprehend the reasoning behind the American decision to stop at the Elbe. There is no better way to prevent Germany from attempting to make peace with Russia than to have American forces in position on the Elbe so they can threaten to take Berlin. The paranoia of Stalin prevents him from thinking that peace with Germany might be possible and that he can march into Berlin without casualties. His primary goal is to beat the Americans into the Nazi capital. Meanwhile, the Americans need the Germans and the Russians to fight it out in Berlin so that the Russians will be too weak after the battle to try bullying their way into Western Europe. Also, the Americans are tracking via the Magic Diplomatic Summaries the movements of the German government as it breaks up and sends its departments southward. The so-called National Redoubt is used more and more as a cover story for the real objectives, revealed by Magic, that the Americans seek: the remnants of the German government, specialist personnel, munitions factories, German

---

16. The Allies rely on this information to begin their final offensive in Italy on April 9, which allows them to seize the Brenner Pass and move as far eastward as Venice and Trieste.

gold, archives, the inner workings of the officialdom that makes Germany run.

Two more extremely important Magic Summaries cross the desks of Eisenhower and Marshall just as American troops are establishing bridgeheads on the Elbe. The first is dated April 13 (SRS 1636) and is issued the morning after President Roosevelt's death. This report quotes an April 11 message from Oshima containing a vast amount of information obtained on March 29 under the heading "Organization and Defense of Berlin." Oshima notes at one point in the report that it is difficult to determine how much of this report is applicable in general terms and how much to the city of Berlin alone.

The defense of the city is now in the hands of a *Gauleiter,* Dr. Josef Goebbels. A proclamation calling for the defense of German towns "to the last," issued as a supplement to the OKW communiqué of April 12, is signed by Keitel, Chief of the OKW, plus Reichsfuehrer SS Himmler and by Martin Bormann, Chief of the Chancellery of the Nazi Party.

Oshima reports: "In accordance with Chancellor Hitler's orders, Berlin is to be made into a fortress city." The total number of Volkssturm troops in Berlin is "approximately four hundred thousand." (The analysts in Washington note that this figure agrees with that given Oshima by Goebbels back in November 1944.)

If it is true that there now are four hundred thousand properly armed Volkssturm, properly trained and deployed, when used defensively in house-to-house fighting, these troops can, and will, exact a high casualty ratio on attacking forces. With the Americans needing every able-bodied soldier that can be employed invading Japan, the idea of attacking Berlin—without air support—becomes thoroughly unpalatable.

The second vital Magic Summary (SRS 1637) is dated April 14, the day the Eighty-third Infantry Division crosses the Elbe at Barby and Eisenhower confirms to Washington he is holding fast on the Elbe as expected. Ambassador Oshima elaborates on his message of the day before. Again his source is Gerhard Schach, the deputy *Gauleiter,* and members of his staff.

At present the population of Berlin is estimated at 3–4 million.[17] Originally some 1.2 million were evacuated, but recently five hundred thousand more refugees have poured in from the east. (On March 8, Oshima reported that "permission has been granted for women and

---

17. According to the 1939 *World Almanac* the prewar population of Berlin was 4,242,501.

children under ten to leave Berlin, a move doubtless designed to ease the housing problem.'' DS 13 Mar 45) The primary problem after air attacks on the city is the restoration of transportation facilities. Next in order of importance is the restoration of the water supply, communications facilities, etc. Food is being dispersed as much as possible, preferably in underground warehouses. Claims Oshima: ''None of the attacks on Berlin so far has caused a large-scale loss of food supplies.'' In the event that Berlin is surrounded, arrangements have been made to use filtered water from the Spree River, etc., in addition to well water. (According to the analysts in Washington, 90 percent of Berlin's water supply ordinarily comes from wells.)

Thus the picture of ''fortress Berlin'' is clearly drawn for the Americans. Some 3.5 million citizens, protected by four hundred thousand Volkssturm, plus an unspecified number of regular Army troops, are in the city. They have adequate food and water supplies.

This picture contradicts the beliefs of Generals Simpson, Bolling, Gillem, Hinds and White (include Patton, too) that they can easily storm Berlin. One must remember that they are not told about the incredible intelligence both Washington and SHAEF possess—the source of which has never been acknowledged in various histories, memoirs and biographies until this book. For the men who make the decision to halt at the Elbe, the Magic Diplomatic Summaries clearly demonstrate an undeniable fact: Berlin is *not* a cheap target, or even a viable proposition for the American forces.

Today, one can now see, and say, that the decision to halt at the Elbe, first recommended by Marshall and confirmed later by Eisenhower during combat, was prudent and correct.

✖ ✖ ✖

The following day, Tokyo's actions remind Washington that the defeat of Japan is ever more imperative. Apparently replying to a request for information, the Vice Chief of the Japanese Army Staff in Tokyo sends the military attaché in Berlin an ''estimate of the situation now that Russia has served notice of her intention to abrogate the Neutrality Pact.''[18] Tokyo believes that Russia ''considers Japan just like an enemy country.'' But America ''will not necessarily demand immediate participation by Russia in the war against Japan. Russia, however, will

---

18. SRS 1638, 15 April 1945.

carefully gauge the decline in Japan's military strength and, at an appropriate stage of the American offensive, will probably seize some pretext or other to enter the war against our country. . . . Russia's projection into the Far Eastern picture would make her relations with America increasingly complicated and delicate.''

The race for postwar control of the Far East is on. Stalin has told the Americans that Russia will enter the war against Japan ninety days after the cessation of hostilities in Europe. Can America beat the Russians to the punch, defeat Japan, and create the balance of power it wants in the Far East?

✖ ✖ ✖

On April 16, the Magic Diplomatic Summary confirms that Ambassador Oshima is asked to leave Berlin at 10 P.M. on the evening of April 13.[19] Oshima tells Tokyo: "I telephoned Foreign Minister von Ribbentrop and asked him whether the German High Command and Government were also being moved, saying that I wished to maintain close contact with them to the very end.

"Ribbentrop replied that the withdrawal of the diplomatic corps had been decided upon that day by Chancellor Hitler and added, begging me keep the fact very secret: 'It is planned to transfer the German High Command and Government to the south after developments have been studied a little longer.' "

The analysts note for Marshall that Oshima, his military and naval attachés, plus thirteen other Japanese officers, are leaving Berlin at 3 P.M. on April 14. Another ten diplomats, led by Counselor Kawahara, will remain in Berlin to handle communications, guard the Imperial portraits stored in the air-raid shelter, and protect local Japanese residents. The analysts also point out that Oshima does not know exactly where "in the south" the German government will be located. However, it seems unlikely that Badgastein would have been picked for the diplomatic corps if the government wasn't planning to settle "in the same general area."

Oshima also speaks with Ribbentrop during the day of April 13, and Ribbentrop reported on his conversation with Hitler on the evening of the twelfth. According to Ribbentrop, Hitler has "still not abandoned hope that there will be a turn in the war situation. On the Eastern Front

---

19. SRS 1639, 16 April 1945.

there are strong indications that the Russian Army will launch a large-scale offensive from the Oder front in the next few days, but we expect to be able to repulse it. The penetration of the Anglo-American armies is very deep, and it is urgently necessary to stabilize that front, at the very least. Therefore, we will have to counterattack at once. While one cannot prophesy today as to the success of the attack, I think that it will be carried out soon.''

Indeed the counterattack on the Elbe is carried out on the thirteenth, and while it is not a major counterattack, it is enough to stop Hinds's infantry, which was unable to move armored support across the Elbe.

Meanwhile, the Japanese consul Korda reports from Hamburg that northwest Germany is suffering badly. ''As a result of intense air attacks and machine-gunning,'' he says, ''refugees are pouring into the streets and fields. The food situation is deteriorating and there is a serious lack of the necessities of life. The people are indeed in dire distress. Since the collapse of the Western Front, the war can hardly be called war, but is rather, I regret to say, a vast and one-sided display of destruction and bloodshed by the enemy.''

The next day's Magic Summary[20] carries a message of April 15 from Counselor Kawahara in which he relays information obtained from Paul Schmidt, Chief of the Press Section of the Foreign Office. According to Kawahara, ''the German High Command Headquarters is still in Berlin. Practically all of the Finance Ministry, the Ministry of the Interior, the Reichsbank, etc., and a large part of the Economic Ministry have left; however, the Propaganda Ministry and DNB [German News Agency] are remaining almost in their entirety. All of the Protocol Section of the Foreign Ministry is leaving. However, a skeleton staff of about eighty Foreign Office personnel, including Under Secretary von Steengracht and the various section chiefs, are remaining, although prepared to leave at any time.''

With information such as this pouring into SHAEF, the job of rounding up these personnel is becoming a game of hare and hounds, with the Japanese telling the hounds where their quarry is going.

Another report on April 16 from Kawahara reveals that the Germans are misreading events on both the Oder and the Elbe.[21] Berlin believes its defense on the Oder is very good when, in reality, it is crumbling. Berlin also believes that the major Russian assault from the

---

20. SRS 1640, 17 April 1945.
21. SRS 1642, 19 April 1945.

south will not be launched for several days. (The Russians have already made great gains in this area.) Von Steengracht also says that the Elbe River front has been "stabilized, [but] the situation in Saxony is very bad. The American forces, following the superhighway from Thuringia, are attempting to push ahead to Dresden, and their vanguard has already reached Chemnitz. Kesselring—who is now in Berlin—remains supreme commander in the West. . . . Government agencies for the most part have been moved to South Germany, but Chancellor Hitler himself—together with Goering, Goebbels, Ribbentrop and Himmler—still remains in Berlin. [Hitler] is said to have gone to inspect the Eastern Front yesterday."

If there are any regrets on the part of Marshall or Eisenhower that the men they would like most to take prisoner are still in Berlin, these feelings have never been made public. Because of Magic, however, no one can say that the Allies did not know the whereabouts of Hitler and his top henchmen during the final days of Berlin.

Meanwhile, and again thanks to Magic, American troops are rounding up Germany's hidden supply of gold. On April 12, Kojiro Kitamura, the representative of the Yokohama Specie Bank assigned to Switzerland, reports that he talked recently with Vice President Puhl of the Reichsbank. The German finance specialist is "very unhappy" about recent news articles describing the Allied seizure of gold hidden in the Merkers salt mines in Thuringia. According to Kitamura: "The amount of gold involved [reported in the press to be estimated at one hundred tons] and other aspects of the matter seem to have been rather exaggerated. I understand that in addition to the gold in question the Reichsbank has deposited gold in various places in southern Germany, especially in the vicinity of the Swiss border."

If one was truly cynical, the question might come to mind, Was it the fear of a Russian advance toward the northern-Italian border that spurred American troops to advance so quickly and seal off this vital area from the Red Army? Or was it the knowledge of hidden German gold? Another novel in the making. . . .

The following day, the Magic Summary shows just how difficult the new government of France intends to be about Indochina.[22] According to recent French intelligence reports, as the analysts in Wash-

---

22. SRS 1643, 20 April 1945. If one should complain about the Allies "reading" French messages at this point in the war, the reply is that it is obvious that General de Gaulle is concerned only with promoting the colonial policies of prewar France, plus establishing France as a major world power, at the expense of the British and the Americans.

ington note for Marshall, the French resistance forces in Indochina have made their withdrawals wherever possible into the mountainous region of extreme northwestern Laos. A command post and airfield are being prepared in that area at Namtha (just south of the Yunnan border and fifty miles east of the old Burma border). Most of the French units in northern and eastern Tonkin, cut off from retreat to Laos, have moved into China. The analysts believe that northwestern Laos will "be the area chosen for a final stand."

On April 18, the French Foreign Office advises its ambassador in Washington that, on April 7, General de Gaulle sent a message to General Sabatier, the commander of the French forces in Indochina, saying: "The [French] Government insists expressly that a portion, however small, of Indochinese territory [remain] in our hands. This territory will provide the means of establishing the authority of a representative of the Paris government and will constitute the starting point of its political action."

This message will lead up to the ultimate French disaster at Dien Bien Phu (when Eisenhower rightly refuses to come to the aid of the French who are trapped there) and, later, the American debacle in Vietnam.

✖ ✖ ✖

Two days after the Russians begin their drive on Berlin, the Germans continue to misread events on the Eastern Front.[23] Is it a need for self-delusion? Or do the Germans really believe they can hold back the Russian advance? As we will see, the similarity in thinking on the part of the Germans at this final stage of the war, as compared to that of the Japanese government just before the atomic bomb drops, in terms of believing something favorable will happen at the last moment to save the nation-state and its leadership, is something akin to national self-hypnosis.

Counselor Kawahara in Berlin reports that on April 18 he spoke with a German official (the analysts in Washington are sure it is von Steengracht), who comments: "On the Eastern Front before Berlin, the German defense continued to be very successful as of yesterday. In a four-day period, 319 out of 900 enemy tanks have been destroyed. . . . On April 16, Chancellor Hitler issued an order of the day to the German

---

23. SRS 1644, 21 April 1945.

troops on the Eastern Front which established as the prime objective the striking of a blow at the Soviet Army. The purpose of such a blow is not only to improve domestic morale, but also to bring Stalin to a frame of mind in which he would be ready to negotiate with Germany. (With Roosevelt's death, great difficulties in Anglo-American relations with the Soviet Union will probably arise, but it will be some time before that occurs. Germany places no great hopes on such a development and still puts primary emphasis on the need to gain military success.)''

German military success is an impossibility. But the Germans cannot comprehend this. They do the Allies a great favor, however. Already they have destroyed approximately half of the Soviet tanks on the Berlin front, if German reports are to be believed. As it turns out, when the Russians finally reach the Elbe and meet with the Americans, the U.S. commanders are appalled at how weak the remnants of the Red Army forces appear to be.

Almost immediately, Magic shows how the tide of war changes for Berlin. At 10 P.M. on April 21, Japanese Counselor Kawahara files a ''very urgent'' message from Berlin to Tokyo.[24] He reports that ''this morning the Under Secretary for Foreign Affairs [von Steengracht] and the head of the Political Section [Hencke] left Berlin. Although the German High Command and Foreign Minister von Ribbentrop are still here, I think they also will leave sometime today or tomorrow. The battle line is very near, and shells have already begun to fall within the city, so I have decided to destroy all my [cryptographic materials]. Hereafter I will communicate with you by means of the [prearranged] 'memory code.' ''

Berlin is about to be overrun.

Meanwhile, the same day's Magic Summary reveals that the Russians are building up their strength in the Far East. From Moscow, Ambassador Sato reports on April 14 that a Japanese courier has seen some startling sights. Sato says: ''A courier who arrived here on the eleventh reports that on his journey across Siberia he observed some 25,000 men, 540 to 550 planes, 150 tanks, and about 540 to 550 motor vehicles being transported eastward. If this process continues, it will result in considerable strengthening of the Russian military forces in the Far East. This situation needs careful watching.''

This report is one of the first that details how the Soviets are rushing troops, tanks, planes, artillery and support units to the Man-

---

24. SRS 1646, 23 April 1945.

churian border. According to Col. David Glantz, Chief of Research with the Soviet Army Studies, the Russians will capitalize on their local intelligence: that huge sections of the Grand Khingan Mountains are unprotected when just weak Japanese forces in these mountain passes could stop the Russians cold.[25] Next, the Russians use ''political finesse to dull Japanese apprehensions,'' and they lie and fool the Japanese diplomats. In reality, the Japanese will fool themselves because they are hoping against hope that the Russians won't attack. In truth, the Japanese know full well how many Russian troops are being shipped to the Manchurian border. They talk themselves into ignoring the situation.

What the Americans don't know, however, is that the Japanese Army has withdrawn nearly a million troops from Manchuria to defend the home islands of Japan and Okinawa, where the fighting is horrific. ''This was a miscalculation on our part,'' Robert T. Crowley, who was then in military intelligence and went through Korea after the Russians withdrew, explains to the author. ''The Japanese didn't use radio transmissions to send the orders transferring these men from Manchuria, and so we didn't get the news. We believed the Japanese in Manchuria would give the Russians a tremendous struggle—just as they done to us all across the Pacific. . . . Yes, this was a major intelligence failure that allowed the Russians to literally walk into Manchuria and Korea.''

Meanwhile, the Magic Summaries reveal that more high-ranking Germans are leaving, or have left, Berlin. The acting Japanese naval attaché in Berlin, Captain Taniguchi, advises Tokyo on April 15 that some of the military and naval attaché staffs left for Lake Waller (nine miles northeast of Salzburg).[26] ''The German Air Force Staff Headquarters is being gradually transferred to that area from various scattered points,'' Taniguchi reports.

While the Air Force moves south, the German naval command moves north. In the same Summary, Vice Admiral Abe, the Japanese representative on the Tripartite Pact Commission, reports on April 18 that he plans to follow Admiral Doenitz, who ''intends to stay in northern Germany.'' He adds that Admiral Raeder (Inspector of the German Navy) is also reported to have moved north, and Vice Admiral Buerckner (Chief of the OKW Foreign Department) is accompanying Abe.

---

25. *The Role of Intelligence in Soviet Military Strategy in World War II* by David M. Glantz (Novato, Calif.: Presidio Press, 1990).
26. SRS 1648, 25 April 1945.

Apparently the command of the Germany Navy is relocating in the Hamburg area from where it will control the U-boats still at sea.

The next important news from the Japanese in Germany comes on the first of May, when Ambassador Oshima reports to Tokyo from Badgastein that "according to reports, the Fuehrer has remained in Berlin."[27] Foreign Minister von Ribbentrop is also planning to leave Berlin for south Germany, while von Steengracht and most of his staff are already in the Salzburg area. The Protocol Staff and the Political Section of the Foreign Ministry are nearby, says Oshima. So is the Papal Nuncio. The Ambassador concludes, saying: "We have not been able to make contact with Berlin and are not likely to in the future, because of the incessant bombing of the city. Unfortunately, the facilities for communication and transportation here are quite primitive. Newspapers usually arrive a day or two late . . . and we rely almost exclusively on the radio to keep abreast of latest developments."

Berlin is about to be encircled.

It has become clear that the Americans are not crossing the Elbe. Hitler orders the remnants of Wenck's Twelfth Army to forget the Elbe front and move east to link up with Busse's Ninth Army and relieve the Russian pressure on the capital. But it is far too late for such relief.

The Russians encircle Berlin on April 25, trapping part of the Fourth Panzer Army and the Ninth Army inside the city's limits. Wenck's forces try to break the Soviet grip on April 26, but are stopped cold.

On April 29, the final battle for the Reichstag begins.

On April 30, Hitler commits suicide. Eisenhower agrees with the Russians on a line of demarcation of Karlsbad-Plzen in Czechoslovakia that prevents Patton from capturing Prague ahead of the Russians.

On May 1, Goebbels, his wife and six children kill themselves.

On May 2, Berlin surrenders. Montgomery's troops seal off the Danish peninsula by capturing Luebeck just before the Russians arrive.

The casualty figures for the battle of Berlin are subject to debate. At least 100,000 German civilians were killed. The number of military casualties is unknown, but the Russians captured 480,000 prisoners in two weeks of fighting. Soviet Defense authorities told Cornelius Ryan that they had "in excess of 100,000 men killed" from the Oder River to the capture of Berlin. Ryan wrote: "To me that figure seems high, but it may have been deliberately inflated to dramatize the victory." It

---

27. SRS 1654, 1 May 1945. On April 23, Hitler announced his plan to stay in Berlin and commit suicide rather than surrender to the Russians.

is this author's belief that Ryan wanted to downplay the Russian casualties because (1) he was writing for the *Reader's Digest*, which, for its own political purposes, did not want to acknowledge the true sacrifice by the Russians during the battle, and (2) Ryan didn't want to dispute Bradley's estimate of 100,000 casualties (killed, wounded and missing). Nearly fifty years after the battle for Berlin, British historian and military expert Charles Messenger writes "the Russians suffered more than 300,000 casualties."[28]

This latter figure would appear correct. A high price for a city with no military significance.

On May 7, the Germans sign an unconditional surrender at Reims.

On May 8, the Russians insist on another surrender ceremony that takes place in Berlin.

From May 9 through May 14 scattered fighting continues in Czechoslovakia, Yugoslavia and Austria.

The British arrest Admiral Doenitz and his government on May 23, after ensuring that all of Germany's U-boats have surrendered.[29] The fighting in Europe ends. The Americans turn their attentions on Tokyo. But peace in Europe does not end the problems there.

For example, on May 3, the Tripartite meeting of foreign ministers begins in San Francisco with Russian foreign minister Molotov telling the Americans that the Russians have arrested sixteen Polish negotiators after asking them to come to a conference. This causes Churchill to cable Truman to warn that the Russians now hold "the Baltic Provinces, all of Germany to the occupational line, all Czechoslovakia, a large part of Austria, the whole of Yugoslavia, Hungary, Rumania, Bulgaria . . . all the great capitals of middle Europe including Berlin, Vienna, Budapest, Belgrade, Bucharest and Sofia . . . an event in the history of Europe to which there has been no parallel, and which has not been faced by the Allies in their long and hazardous struggle."

Churchill's recital of facts doesn't cut much ice with the Americans. They can look at a map as easily as can the Prime Minister and

---

28. *The Chronological Atlas of World War II* by Charles Messenger (New York: Macmillan Publishing Company, 1989), 223. The author believes this is the best such work published on World War II. It appears Messenger had access to much intelligence information he could not publish as text in England, because of the Official Secrets Act, but his maps reveal this special knowledge.

29. During these final days, Vice Admiral Abe's reports to Tokyo provide the Allies with intimate knowledge of how Doenitz, as Hitler's successor, conducts the new German government. Abe also reveals the whereabouts of such notables as Himmler, Marshal Keitel, Albert Speer, Julius Dorpmueller and others. Abe also reveals how he redistributes Japanese naval personnel in Europe. SRS 1664, 11 May 1945.

can also point out that, originally, it was believed that British/American troops would never cross the Rhine before the end of the war. Furthermore, the Allies are darned lucky that the Russians don't hold a lot more real estate in Europe than they already do. A lot of Eastern Europe has been lost to Soviet occupation. But Western Europe is saved. Wouldn't it be more helpful if the British looked at the situation in a more positive light?

Eventually the meetings in San Francisco will see the beginning of the United Nations. But before the U.N. Charter is signed by the five Great Powers (America, Britain, China, France, USSR), grown from three to five in recent weeks, the Magic Diplomatic Summaries reveal to Marshall and his staff that some of our Allies may not be acting in such a friendly manner after all.

By the author's count, the Magic Summaries of May 1945 reveal that, at one time or another, the Americans are reading the diplomatic messages of at least twelve supposedly friendly nations. It is significant to note that many of the Latin American diplomats are of the highest caliber. Their suggestions and recommendations, their insights on world power and stability, are invaluable to the San Francisco conference and in creating the United Nations. One wishes there were time to explore all this more fully, but the subject is worthy of a separate book by someone more knowledgeable in these matters.

It is the duplicity of France that shines forth.

The Magic Summaries show France cuddling up to the Russians to create a new balance of power in Europe that is favorable to the French. The hatred of all things English and American by Premier de Gaulle is demonstrated day after day. France immediately begins meddling in the internal affairs of Lebanon and Syria. Unrest, bloodshed, and hysteria become commonplace in the region as France tries to reassert her faded authority. How much of today's problems in the Middle East (to say nothing of the Far East) can be traced to the ill-conceived actions of the French back in 1945 is difficult to say. But every historian should be familiar with the secret activities of various governments as revealed by the Magic Summaries from April through August 1945.

18

The conventional wisdom about why two atomic bombs were dropped on Japan is that the Japanese wanted to negotiate a peace with the United States, but they were not prepared to accept unconditional surrender. Furthermore, the Americans were reading Magic and they knew the Japanese wanted to negotiate, but this only made the Americans "all the more determined to force Japan to its knees."[1]

A careful study of the Magic Diplomatic Summaries that were declassified only in January 1993 produces a different rationale for the use of atomic weapons against humankind. The end of World War II marks the demise of the European nations, including Great Britain, as colonial powers. Churchill knows this, accepts it as fact and tries to work within the new framework of world order. Many others in the British establishment do not. The British universities, for example, are infiltrated by Soviet spy networks such as the one of Blunt, Philby, Burgess and MacLean. Dedicated to their belief in the superiority of Soviet Communism over American democracy, acting in the belief that they will personally profit materially when the great revolution takes place in England, at the end of the war—and throughout the Korean War—they work to promote Communist rule in Asia and elsewhere.

This creates one set of postwar problems for the United States.[2]

Another set of problems is created by the French, who want In-

---

1. *The Second World War: A Complete History* by Martin Gilbert (New York: Henry Holt and Company, 1989), 701.
2. Remember that, in 1941, the U.S. Army suspected an enemy agent might be working inside the White House and for several crucial months before Pearl Harbor unilaterally refused to submit Magic intelligence to the President. The Army then performed a background check on all recent American graduates of Cambridge and Oxford. The results of this investigation have yet to be released.

dochina restored to France. Then there are the Dutch, who want the Dutch East Indies returned to them. And there is Portugal, who wants its Far Eastern holdings returned, too. To say nothing of the British, who also want their colonies such as Hong Kong and Malaya restored to the Crown. Most worrisome of all, however, is the encroachment of the Soviet Union in Asia. Stalin demands to participate in ruling a defeated Japan. He also wants control of Manchuria and Korea. He wants Communism to take over China, ideally under the guidance of Russia. In turn, he hopes that Communism will spread southward to countries like Iran through which he can control vital oil, rubber and mineral resources. Because the white colonial Europeans have been proven fallible and, at times, powerless by the fierceness of the Japanese military during the war, Stalin believes that Communism can infiltrate many countries, particularly those resentful of British, French and other European influence or control, by using those nations' "nationalism" to serve Soviet interests. As the Magic Summaries next reveal, in the final days of the war, in a desperate attempt to save themselves, the Japanese prove they are willing to make a deal with Stalin that will allow him to achieve his goals in Asia. A thorough consideration of the Diplomatic Summaries makes the argument for using nuclear weapons more understandable.

Fifty years after the first atomic bomb is dropped, it is easy to criticize its use because of knowledge gained only after the war ends. The account presented in this work, however, is the sole factual record of what the British, who consented to use of the bomb on July 4, 1945, and the Americans *knew at the time.* It is the equivalent of court-approved wiretap, or a videotaped confession after a criminal has been advised of his rights. Here is the proof of the implacable opposition to unconditional surrender, amply documented in the most confidential and high-level communications among the men who rule Japan. They still believe that they speak to each other in private. In reality, their innermost thoughts, their hatred of America (the Japanese prove themselves just as racist as the worst of any other nationality), their belief in their self-righteousness, cross the desks of General Marshall and Secretary Stimson, and now, President Truman, every morning. The Magic Summary arrives with the regularity of the *Washington Post,* and the information in the Magic Summaries convinces the judge and jury in Washington—based on what they hear—to take extreme but necessary measures to destroy the Japanese government.

For the first time, the average reader can evaluate the evidence presented to the American leaders that forces them to make their agonizing and painful decision. The ultimate argument is twofold: First, the Americans refuse to accept the concept of the Japanese military's being allowed to inflict more than a million casualties on American troops, not to mention their own people, in an invasion of Japan. It is clearly understood that the Japanese leaders are fully prepared to sacrifice virtually their entire population. Second, it is hoped that the bomb will alert Stalin, and all those would-be tyrants in Asia and the rest of the world, that war can no longer be "politics by other means." A terrible new weapon exists that demands the cessation of territorial acquisition and the immediate return of peace.[3]

✖ ✖ ✖

Only three days after the Germans officially surrender, the first headline on the Magic Diplomatic Summary for Marshall's attention is: *"Japanese fear of an attack by Russia"*.[4] The Magic Summary reveals that on May 7, the day Germany surrendered, the Vice Chief of the Japanese Army General Staff sends the following message to his military attachés in Stockholm and Lisbon: "Russia's anti-Japanese attitude has clearly become more vigorous since her recent action with respect to the Neutrality Pact. Particularly since late February or mid-March, there has been a steady increase [at name of place missing] of Soviet troops, particularly air [force] personnel, which have been transferred from European Russia. We must view with alarm the possibility of future military activity against Japan."

The analysts in Washington note for Marshall's attention that on April 27, Foreign Minister Togo advised various Japanese diplomatic establishments in the Far East that "we are extremely interested in obtaining information with respect to Soviet armed strength, weapons and the like." Togo instructed his diplomats to send in promptly any intelligence they might glean. What the Japanese do not know is that Stalin has promised to attack Japan ninety days after hostilities in Europe cease. The countdown clock in Moscow is already ticking.

Meanwhile, the French Foreign Ministry is sending its ambassadors in Chungking and Moscow an account of a conversation of May 1

---

3. In preparing this work, the author interviewed more than two hundred American veterans of the European and Pacific theaters of war. *All* of these men applaud the decision to use nuclear weapons on Japan. Many of them say they believe the atomic bomb saved their lives. They also voted for President Truman.
4. SRS 1663, 10 May 1945.

between Foreign Commissar Molotov and Foreign Minister Georges Bidault.[5] The Russians are proposing a compromise to the current Franco-Soviet pact. Bidault recommends acceptance and comments: "The Russian Government, which has been able to find out here [at the San Francisco conference] that it is not surrounded by universal sympathy, is obsessed by the idea of an anti-Soviet coalition."

The same Summary carries reports by the Chileans, Ecuadorians, Peruvian and Venezuelans relating to regional pacts. The mutual security system proposed earlier at Mexico City is considered imperative. Some of the messages reflect a conviction that "a determination to resist Soviet Russia is growing among the American countries, including the U.S." The Venezuelan foreign minister describes a joint conference with Mr. Nelson Rockefeller thusly: "As [we] had anticipated, the American delegates are now beginning to speak of Communism as they once spoke of Nazism and are invoking continental solidarity and hemispheric defense against it." The analysts in Washington point out to Marshall that a "sizable portion of the Latin American traffic from San Francisco, including the Venezuelan message last quoted, is being transmitted by radio and may be readable by the Russians."

Stalin must know by now that he can no longer fool the Americans about his intentions. Before his death, Roosevelt had become totally disenchanted with the Soviet leader. Now Stalin is faced with a new president, Truman, who is an unknown quantity. For the moment, America is being run by hardheaded, practical military types. It is a much different situation from those years before when the White House was more optimistically inclined toward Moscow.

On May 12, 1945, the first item in the Magic Summary is a report from Japan by Portuguese minister Fernandez saying that the public's attention "is completely centered on the Okinawa struggle, which, according to the Admiral in command of the Japanese Navy, should decide the war in the Pacific."[6] The Japanese maintain that "four hundred American ships have been sunk or damaged; and the propagandists are using this to draw the conclusion that the [American] fleet has been so weakened that it is unable to invade Japan. Nevertheless, the fortification of coasts and mountains continues, giving the impression that this country, like Germany, is disposed to prosecute the war to its very end without the least probability of victory. Numerous changes are being made in the Army High Command, and a national guard is being or-

---

5. SRS 1662, 9 May 1945.
6. SRS 1665, 12 May 1945.

ganized to fight as guerrillas against the invaders. The [air] attacks on Japan's principal cities have had tremendous results, Tokyo being unrecognizable.''

The next item in the Magic Summary is a gloomy report from Moscow by Ambassador Sato sent on May 9 to Tokyo. The analysts dissect Sato's message for Marshall in their usual precise fashion, but they lose the flavor and tone of the message itself. Attached as an appendix to the daily Summary, it reads as follows: ''We must expect that world opinion will soon be mobilized by the Anglo-Americans in a campaign to crush Japan, who will be regarded as the only country disturbing international peace. Although one of the reasons given by Russia for abrogating the Neutrality Pact—i.e., that Japan has been aiding Germany—has now become meaningless in view of Germany's unconditional surrender, Japan is still at war with Russia's allies, America and England. Russia, therefore, may use this as a justification to enter the war against Japan at any time she desires; moreover world opinion would welcome such a development since it would bring the war to an earlier end. Indeed we must recognize that Russia, who generally speaking has been checkmated in her relations with Japan since the time of the [Russian] Revolution, has never been blessed with such an opportunity to settle her accounts with us. In any event, Russia is undoubtedly planning to seize the power of life and death over Japan, and whether or not she actually participates in the war, her position vis-à-vis Japan will become increasingly strong.

''In the light of the above, we Japanese are in no position to prevent Russia from participating in the war or from adopting any course she desires. . . . If Russia should decide to make use of her favorable position vis-à-vis Japan without actually resorting to war, she may seek to mediate peace in the Pacific war—the Anglo-Americans are now paying a tremendous price on Okinawa and will in the future in Central and South China. If, backed by their vast power, the Russians were to succeed in effecting such a peace for the benefit of the Anglo-Americans, they would achieve without effort an international position surpassing that of their allies, a point which will not escape the eagle-eyed Stalin. Any peace imposed under such circumstances, however, would be very close to unconditional surrender and would, of course, involve the dissolution of our Army and Navy—indeed it would be impossible to secure Anglo-American consent to any other peace. The demands of the Russians themselves, which would probably revolve around the dissolution of the Portsmouth Treaty, might be more or less as follows:

"**a.** Return [to Russia] of South Sakhalin. [The Sakhalin Islands, and other items below, still are a point of dispute fifty years after Sato writes this memo.]

"**b.** Cancellation of Japan's fishing rights [in Soviet waters].

"**c.** Opening of Tsugaru Strait [between Honshu and Hokkaido] to Russian shipping.

"**d.** Return of Manchukuo to Chinese rule.

"**e.** Transfer [to Russia] of the North Manchurian Railroad and of all other strategic railway lines in Northern Manchukuo which have been constructed by the Japanese.

"**f.** Placing of Harbin under Soviet administration.

"**g.** Transfer to Russia of Japan's lease to the Kwantung Territory.

"**h.** Incorporation of Inner Mongolia into the Soviet part [i.e., Outer Mongolia].

"**i.** In addition, the Russians are also likely to bring up the disposition of Korea and the question of China and other matters.

"The Russians would certainly be prepared to back up fully any demands they might make and we should have no other alternative but to give in or fight.

"Since her recent action with respect to the Neutrality Pact, Russia has been rapidly increasing her military strength in Eastern Siberia. It is, of course, impossible to say whether this is being done for defensive or offensive purposes, but in any event, if the suggestions that I have made above are sound, these increases in military strength must be considered as stemming from Russia's intention to bring pressure to bear upon Japan.

"On the other hand, we must not overlook the following factors which might either modify or delay Russia's plans as I have outlined them. . . . [But] we can expect that the Russians will bring pressure against us. However, even if they do not and elect to remain on the sidelines for the duration of the Pacific war, it is essential for us to increase our war strength to the utmost. Otherwise we will be forced to dance whatever tune strikes the Russian fancy." Oshima then offers a series of suggestions to shorten Japanese lines of communication, abandon Thailand and Indochina, curtail operations in South China "and devote our efforts exclusively to the strengthening of our North China defenses in preparation for a war of attrition." Then he says: ". . . I think we should act with decision and dispatch in shortening our battle lines so that we can continue our private war against the Anglo-Americans while standing on the defensive against any treacherous moves which the Russians may make.

"Even so, my greatest concern is the aerial bombardment of Japan. Although we may feel that our stubborn fighting in the Okinawa area has made the enemy realize that he is not prepared for landings on Japan, it is still impossible to devise a complete defense against enemy air raids from the Marianas. The continuation of these air attacks will necessarily weaken our military strength, and once the enemy's European air forces are transferred to the Pacific, our damages will exceed anything we can imagine, so that we may be facing the same situation that led to the downfall of Hitler Germany."

Also in the same day's Magic Summary, Takanobu Mitani, the former Japanese ambassador in Vichy, who recently fled from southern Germany to Switzerland, reports from Bern and frankly urges Tokyo to sue for peace immediately "on the most favorable terms possible." Japan should act quickly, he says, and present England and the U.S. with peace terms Japan would be willing to accept, "devising some way by which we can gain the full confidence of our adversaries." The task will be difficult, both as to timing and method, but "if we think of the great mission of our country in East Asia, and try to plan for the distant future, we will have to bend all our efforts today to this end."

A few days later, the first item in the Magic Summaries for Marshall's eyes is a "report on public opinion in Japan."[7] This is a circular sent out by the Vice Chief of the Japanese Army General Staff, and it contains the following comments on "the situation in the homeland." According to the Vice Chief: "There are signs of a somewhat optimistic trend of feeling [about the situation on Okinawa where the fighting for the southern tip of the island is incredibly ferocious]. If results do not come up to expectations, however, the effect on all ranks of people at home and abroad will be quite profound.

"It is thought [apparently by the public] that the enemy's next operations will be an attack on the homeland. In the hope that such an attack may be prevented, there is a strong tendency to put great reliance on the Okinawa operations. There are increasing signs, however, that some are resigned to the inevitability of an invasion and are urging that the homeland be readied for the decisive struggle. All sorts of opinions are prevalent as to the time of the enemy's attack, but it is worthy of

---

7. SRS 1667, 14 May 1945.

note that on 11 May President Minamis of the Japan Political Association [Japan's new political party] emphasized that the country must be in a state of complete readiness during June.

"The people regard the organization of the People's Volunteer Corps as the most important domestic problem.[8] Since they feel that the Corps will lend support to already established organizations and will be the means of assuring victory, their enthusiasm is intense. They are earnestly striving to complete the formation of the Corps all over the country by the end of May.

"Both officials and the public are eagerly awaiting details of the Volunteer Combat Corps being planned by the armed forces." (The analysts in Washington tell Marshall that no such organization has as yet been mentioned by Tokyo broadcasts.)

Meanwhile, in the same day's Summary, Japanese minister Kase forwards a long report prepared by Secretary Yosano, who had been stationed in Germany until mid-March. He attributes Germany's defeat to three things: The devastation of air attacks, which, he claims, disprove the theory that a country cannot be defeated by air attacks alone. "The German people have lost in air attacks all their material property except their land," he reports. Then there is Germany's failure to win over and retain the support of the peoples of the countries it occupied or controlled as well as the neutral countries. Lastly, the failure to negotiate a peace in good time.

Also in the same Summary is a report that the German minister in Bern advises his ally, Minister Kase, that "my final word as a friend of Japan is that she must not follow in Germany's tracks. Japan's [position] is different from [that of] Germany. She still has a great variety of occupied areas which she should give up in order to work for a political settlement. At present, even if she yielded [them] temporarily, she would not have to give up territory basic to her existence.

"Germany is burned absolutely to the ground. Even with such good luck as a war between Russia, England and America, it will, I think, require at least a hundred years for Germany to rise again. I had been advising my Government for several years to settle the situation politically, but, although there were various opportunities [to do so]

---

8. The analysts note for Marshall that "according to the Tokyo radio, the People's Volunteer Corps is to include all able-bodied civilians. Its duties will be to carry out emergency work on constructing defense installations, decentralizing industry, and improving transport and food and lumber production. Members of the Corps are also to act as firefighters, and, in times of 'more acute crisis,' as armed units."

here [in Switzerland] Germany did not take the least advantage of them.''

The Magic Summaries of May 15 and 18 contain the arguments of Ambassador Kase in Switzerland that Japan should seek a political settlement to the war.[9] One extremely interesting bit of commentary comes from Kojiro Kitamura of the Yokohama Specie Bank, who makes the following points:

1. In financial circles in Zurich, it is commonly observed that within a month or two Japan will end the war. Many among the financial group take the view that Japan will avoid Germany's tragic end, and that England and the U.S. "from the point of view of relations with Russia" will not drag Japan down to ruin as they have Germany.

2. The almost unanimous view in informed Swiss circles interested in Japan is that, once Russia joins England and America in the Pacific war, Japan will suffer an even worse fate than Germany, and that after the war the British and Americans will find that, as in Europe, they will have a great deal of trouble with Russia. Some even go so far as to say that there might be a "Soviet Asia."

Ambassador Kase has his own strong opinions. He observes that "the Anglo-Americans have finally come to realize that the only result of their victory in Europe has been to give Russia a free hand on that continent and their only remaining hope is that Russia will not extend her influence to the Far East.''

When it comes to fighting to the death, Kase offers these thoughts to Tokyo: "There are those who earnestly insist that the policy of the Empire must be to continue the fight. They reason that if we can make a second Iwo Jima of the homeland and continue steadfastly to the bitter end to inflict heavy losses on the British and Americans, trying at the same time to improve our relations with Russia, then even England and the U.S. may change their attitude and the way may be open for a basic change in the situation. The advocates of this view hold that any idea of stopping halfway—the idea of 'victory in defeat'—will forever destroy the existence of the Empire. . . .

"[But] by fighting on to the bitter end we shall be doing nothing more than following the path which Germany has taken. Furthermore,

---

9. SRS 1668, 15 May 1945; SRS 1671, 18 May 1945.

our people, unlike the Germans, prefer meeting an honorable death to surrendering, and in view of this trait of character there is a possible danger that our people may be exterminated.

"We would then become ... no longer a nation. The eternity of our Empire is truly in grave peril."

Kase then suggests that Tokyo asks Russia "to use her good offices in return for what we would be able to offer her." He also points out to Tokyo that "if we make a peace proposal, the enemy will surely demand unconditional surrender and it cannot be denied that a failure may have the most serious results both at home and abroad. But success or failure will depend upon the terms which the Empire can make up its mind to offer (even among the enemy there are differences of opinion about unconditional surrender). . . . In my opinion the great necessity is to do something at once. . . . Although all aspects must be considered, a distinction must be drawn between the Empire—which is to be eternal—and the responsibility of the present generation. To bear a temporary shame and avoid the worst—the destruction of the foundation upon which our national strength could be rebuilt—is certainly the way to respect the memory of our fallen heroes."

Such advice is pouring in for Tokyo to ponder. The financially minded Swiss are recommending that Japan cut its losses as quickly as possible. Surrender and then resurrect Japan. Many others suggest the same. But no one in the Western world comprehends the grip the Japanese military holds over the Japanese government. At a time when a sane, rational government should be seeking to end the war and save its populace, it is becoming clear that the Japanese military are preparing to sacrifice the nation's entire citizenry in an attempt to negotiate terms with the enemy. Furthermore, if Tokyo has any questions about Soviet intentions in the Far East, the Magic Summary of May 19 proves that Japan is being adequately warned about the Russian troop buildup in its backyard.[10]

The first item for Marshall's attention on this day is a roundup of Japanese reports on Russian military movements to the Far East. It begins with the reminder that a month earlier, Foreign Minister Togo instructed his diplomats to send in any data they might obtain "with respect to Soviet armed strength, weapons and the like."

As a result, on the first of May, Ambassador Yamada in Hsinking reported that a Japanese diplomatic official who just arrived from Mos-

---

10. SRS 1672, 19 May 1945.

cow observed, while traveling through Siberia, "an average of thirty eastbound trains a day carrying military supplies and troops (including [each day] about ten thousand troops and planes, guns, motorized vehicles, etc.)." Two more reports, on May 3 and 14, say that Japanese couriers have observed Russian troops and military equipment being moved to the East. The couriers reported that "the only trains traveling eastward were military trains," and most of them seemed to have come from European Russia.

One doesn't have to be a genius to figure out that Russians are moving about three hundred thousand men per month to the Far East. And since they are moving their troops by train, the Russians are sending more troops, plus the necessary logistical support, to the Far East faster than the Americans can move their troops from Europe via ships to invade Japan. The strategists in Washington can clearly see the real possibility of a struggle developing between America and Russia to control the postwar balance of power in Asia.

On this same day in Washington, another unusual document surfaces in the Magic Summary. The analysts tell Marshall that the document is "just now available," and it is based on two messages sent by the Japanese military attaché in Berlin on May 5, 1942. The material is a "Russian plan for offensive operations against the Japanese Army in Manchukuo," which the military attaché said was compiled by the German Army General Staff from "such sources as captured documents and statements of prisoners of every type, particularly Red Army staff officers who had recently been stationed in the Eastern Russian area."

The plan calls for simultaneous attacks against Manchukuo from the west, north, and east. It is accompanied by a drive on northeastern Korea from the Maritime Province. The map that accompanies this plan turns out to be similar to the attack the Russians will actually make at the start of their campaign. The difference between the old plan and the new plan is that the Russians will not stop at the Manchurian border but will sweep down into Korea.

Meanwhile, Japanese minister Nishi in Manchuria has been asking Tokyo's approval for a scheme whereby "as a first step toward the improvement of Russo-Japanese relations" Manchukuo would offer to supply Russia with soybeans and "other cereals" in exchange for "platinum, gasoline, timber, etc." Foreign Minister Togo agrees with the plan, and on May 13, Nishi offers Russia to barter five hundred thousand tons of soybeans and other cereals. (The analysts in Washington note that "this scheme represents the only current effort of the Japanese to cement their relations with Russia.")

Almost simultaneously, the Vice Chief of the Japanese Army General Staff notes the increased Soviet troop concentrations in the Far East and, on May 10, says: "We must view with alarm the possibility of future [Soviet] military activity against Japan."

✖ ✖ ✖

The Magic Summary of May 22, 1945, has as its first item of information for Marshall's attention the latest "Japanese defense measures."[11] According to the "Weekly Intelligence" circular sent out on May 19 by the Vice Chief of the Japanese Army General Staff, "a popular demand has arisen for rushing preparations against an enemy invasion of Japan."

Furthermore, "as one means of speeding up preparations, the Cabinet decided on 18 May to set up strong Regional Administrative Inspectorates General [in Japan proper] which would embrace the present Regional Administrative Councils. [These would have close relations with the local Army and Navy commanders, note the analysts in Washington.] . . . The organization of the People's Volunteer Corps is being stressed to the utmost and is being made the very foundation for civilian organization. Furthermore, the central authorities have virtually completed steps for carrying out, in case of necessity, a separate conscription law which would convert the Corps into a Volunteer Combat Corps and place it under Army command for assignment to important functions in national defense. Regional organization is proceeding enthusiastically."

Only two days later, the analysts in Washington again bring to Marshall's attention the message sent from Moscow to Tokyo on May 9 by Ambassador Sato (previously referred to in SRS 1665) saying that Russia now has an unprecedented opportunity to "settle her accounts" with Japan. Russia might well enter the war or seek to mediate a peace that "would be very close to unconditional surrender" and would involve substantial concessions—territorial and otherwise—to Russia.[12] The analysts point out that Sato is now, on May 22, advising Minister Morishima (Sato's right-hand man, who is currently in Tokyo) that the "trends" mentioned in his earlier report would, in his opinion, "demand particular attention by July or August."

---

11. SRS 1675, 22 May 1945.
12. SRS 1677, 24 May 1945.

✖ ✖ ✖

Meanwhile, in French Indochina, the situation as described to French ambassador Bonnet by Paris is that, as of April 18, General Sabatier is being forced to withdraw into China. French military operations are strictly localized in the vicinity of the Chinese frontier. Only one group has been able to maintain itself in northwestern Laos (about three hundred men as of May 18), and it is requesting equipment and munitions. The meaning of this message to Washington is clear: After cooperating with the Japanese throughout the war to save Indochina for Vichy France, the current so-called French resistance movement in the region has been thrown out of Indochina by the Japanese. The white man has been vanquished in Indochina. It is no longer "French." It should no longer be called a "colony."[13]

✖ ✖ ✖

The following day, Foreign Minister Togo sends to Ambassador Sato in Moscow the "gist" of a talk made early in May by Lieutenant Colonel Hamada, described as an intelligence officer on the Kwantung Army staff (and probably a former member of the military attaché's staff in Moscow), to a group of Japanese diplomatic officials in Manchukuo.[14] According to Hamada, it is difficult to say whether the Russian military buildup in the Far East is aimed at bringing pressure on Japan or launching an attack against Japan and Manchukuo, or because "Russia's gaze extends from Outer Mongolia and western China toward India, Tibet, Iran and the Middle East. Assuming, however, that the Russians do intend to attack Manchukuo, they will probably try to gain a quick victory by using overwhelming force—at least double the strength of ours—since a long war would tend to unsettle their social structure. . . .

"We must be on guard as soon as we notice any marked movement of trucks toward eastern Siberia. The Russians at present have

---

13. When Eisenhower became President, he understood very well that the "white colonial powers" had no place in the future of Indochina. The country did not belong to the "white man." This is why he refused to help the French at Dien Bien Phu.
14. SRS 1678, 25 May 1945.

about forty-thousand trucks in that area and will need another sixty thousand for an invasion of Manchukuo. In any event, they will need at least three months to transport the necessary troops and armaments [to eastern Siberia]." What Hamada has missed, or not said, is that Japanese couriers have already noted the movement of trucks in vast numbers to the Far East.

Meanwhile, the same Summary of May 25 notes that Matsutaro Inoue, the Japanese counselor in Lisbon, approached a "reliable" OSS agent in that city, who happened to be working for a German news agency, to find out from the American embassy how the U.S. feels about a negotiated peace, since Japan would in no event accept unconditional surrender. Prefacing his comments by saying, "Do not gain the impression that this is a peace feeler," Inoue then says, "get in touch with the Americans and ask them what they want in the Far East. The Japanese emperor cannot surrender unconditionally. We know that the U.S. bombers will hopelessly smash Japan."

The Americans know that Inoue has no authority to make such a request of the U.S. government. Furthermore, as the analysts point out, he has been making remarks such as this as far back as September 1944, when he "wistfully discoursed on the futility of war between the U.S. and Japan." Since Inoue is acting solely on his own initiative, no response is forthcoming.

✻ ✻ ✻

On this day, May 25, the U.S. Chiefs of Staff agree that Operation DOWNFALL—the first invasion of Japan—will occur on November 1.

✻ ✻ ✻

In the days that follow, Tokyo acknowledges that it has lost the opportunity to make peace with the Nationalist government in China. No matter what, the Americans will have to be brought into the picture in China, an anathema to Tokyo.

As May draws to an end, another report of Soviet military movements in the Far East crosses Marshall's desk. Ambassador Sato gives the details of what Japanese couriers witnessed while traveling the Trans-Siberian Rail Road in mid-May. From May 12 to May 16, the couriers kept watch twenty-four hours a day; on the seventeenth and eighteenth they kept an eighteen-hour watch. Altogether they observed 195 eastbound military trains (averaging 28 per day) and they carried an estimated total of 64,000 troops. These were "largely antiaircraft defense units, labor units and construction units" or "rear units from the Russo-German front." The trains also carry about 2,500 trucks, 500 fighter planes, 120 medium tanks, 320 antiaircraft guns, 600 antitank guns, 131 field guns, 300 collapsible boats and pontoons, 10 carloads of bridge girders, and 20 carloads of rails. The couriers also spot in the rail yards at Chita, Itursk, Taishet and Omsk an aggregate of about 500 tank cars carrying fuel oil or aviation gas. They also spotted another 400 tank cars moving east.

This is a tremendous amount of men and material. Given the warning made by Lieutenant Colonel Hamada, it appears the Russians are shipping more trucks to the East than he would have believed possible.

✖ ✖ ✖

On this day, May 28, Stalin meets in Moscow with Roosevelt's former adviser Harry Hopkins and tells him that Russia will go to war with Japan in mid-August. Stalin also insists that Russia will share in occupying and running a postwar Japan.

✖ ✖ ✖

The next day, from Bern, French ambassador Hoppenot sends Paris the following story, which he attributes to "Swiss sources":[15] A number of German engineers who worked for the Nazis on the V [rocket] weapons have begun working in Russian war plants. Hoppenot claims: "Various technicians are said to have reached Sweden during February and March with passports which had been turned over to them in Germany by Soviet agents. . . . In addition, other engineers, captured by the Russians during their advance, are said just to have reached Russia. It is even said that some Russian commandos have recently kidnapped various specialists in American and British zones of occupation." The analysts in Washington note that Hoppenot has "an affinity for sen-

15. SRS 1682, 29 May 1945. After the fall of Vichy France, the new French government of de Gaulle failed to introduce new codes, using instead the same ciphers the Allies read throughout the war.

sational information, [and] he concluded his report as follows: 'Of course I am conveying this startling news only in the strictest confidence.' "

As we learn later, the Americans and British are also doing the same thing as the Russians—scooping up German rocket scientists.

✻ ✻ ✻

On May 31, the first item in the Magic Summary is the news about an "extremely friendly" conference held on May 29 in Moscow between Soviet foreign minister Molotov and Japanese ambassador Sato.[16] Not all of Sato's comments are available for Marshall as yet. But it appears that Sato expressed to Molotov the "earnest hope that no important change" would take place in Russo-Japanese relations. He was advised by Molotov: "You already know Russia's answer on this point. The Soviet Union does not believe that its notification with respect to the abrogation of the Neutrality Pact has brought about any change in the existing situation." The analysts point out for Marshall that when Molotov told Sato on April 5 of Russia's decision to abrogate the pact, Molotov acknowledged that the pact still had a year to run and said: "The attitude of the Russian government will have to be set accordingly."

The complete text of Sato's meeting with Molotov is not ready until the following day, June 1, and the tone of Sato's report to Tokyo on this date differs substantially from the next day's report.[17] One dislikes saying how baldly someone lies, but in this case Molotov lies so blatantly that he actually gets the Japanese to believe him—at least for a time.

Not only does Molotov tell Sato that Russia is still observing the Russo-Japanese Neutrality Pact, he goes on to say: "Russia is not a belligerent. We have had our fill of war in Europe and our only desire is to obtain a guarantee of future peace." This makes Sato report, with what appears to be incredible wishful thinking, that he could not help feeling that Molotov's cordiality may have been due "to the fact that Russia has adopted a policy of concentrating on internal problems and of not concerning herself with Far Eastern questions."

---

16. SRS 1684, 31 May 1945.
17. SRS 1685, 1 June 1945; SRS 1685, 2 June 1945.

The analysts also note for Marshall that Sato replied, in answer to a question by Molotov about the duration of the Pacific war, that it "is a matter of life and death for Japan, and as a result of America's attitude, we have no choice but to continue the fight."

By the next day, however, Sato suddenly reverts to his earlier and more pessimistic views. Now he gives his "humble opinions" on the interview in a message he transmits in a cipher system rarely used and believed to be available, in Moscow, only to him and, in Tokyo, only to top members of the Foreign Office.

The analysts in Washington comment that Sato is still impressed with the cordial atmosphere of the interview and with Molotov's statement that Russia's abrogation of the Neutrality Pact has not changed her "neutral attitude" toward Japan. (Of course Sato does not know what Stalin has told Harry Hopkins, who is still in Moscow, about Russia's intention to attack Japan and share in running a defeated Japan.) But now Sato repeats his earlier predictions of May that, by July or August, Russia will have completed her military preparations in the Far East and will then either open hostilities against Japan or—depending on the prevailing situation—seek to mediate a peace. And contrary to what he said the day before, Sato now claims that with the defeat of Germany, Russia has come to feel an increased interest in the Far East. The most hopeful note Sato can now attach to the dialogue is that Molotov agreed to see him only a few hours after he asked for a meeting, which means that the Russians "are not taking us lightly."

So today Sato concludes that "we are facing future trouble with Russia and it is absolutely essential that we take steps to meet this situation." He urges that Japan should at the very least take "decisive action" in settling all pending controversies with the Russians. He also requests that Foreign Minister Togo to "please have the Supreme Council for the Direction of the War decide how far they are willing to go in making concessions to Russia."

This last statement sets off alarm bells in Washington.

✶ ✶ ✶

Other problems suddenly pop up in the Magic Summaries.

In recent months, the analysts note, a large volume of Greek traffic concerns the question of northern Epirus, the region of southern Albania that the Greeks have long claimed. Now the Greeks are worried that the regimes of Hoxha in Albania and Tito in Yugoslavia will success-fully oppose Greece's demands.[18] How will the issue be decided?

Meanwhile France is demanding a portion of Germany that she can occupy. And, in the Middle East, France has inserted herself in Lebanon and Syria to such an extent that King Ibn Saud is telling President Shukri Quwatly of Syria to "remain calm and seek a solution with the French—short of any infringement of [Syrian] independence."

In another message, the King tells Quwatly: "Put your trust in God, and then in the Allies, especially England. I have requested [the British to mediate], not on your side or on the side of France, but satisfying you and France. This would be best; otherwise, all action is profitless."

Elsewhere, the Russians are pressuring Turkey to renegotiate their mutual agreement of nonaggression. But Moscow is also demanding a large portion of Turkish territory, plus control of the Dardanelles. And, in South America, the Russians are trying to establish diplomatic missions and links to local Communist organizations. It is almost as if in whatever direction the U.S. Signals Intelligence Service turns its radio direction finders, someone, somewhere, is trying to upset the fragile, newly won peace.

✖ ✖ ✖

In Tokyo, the latest American air raids have caused various communications delays and difficulties according to the analysts in Washington.[19] This is why Foreign Minister Togo's message of June 1—sent before Togo apparently received Sato's message about his May 29 meeting with Molotov—fails to reach Marshall's desk until June 4.

The message to Sato from Togo is marked "absolutely secret" and it confirms the reason why alarm bells are ringing in Washington. Togo is trying to cut a deal with Russia. "We must realize," says Togo, "that it is a matter of the utmost urgency that we should not only prevent Russia from entering the war but should also induce her to adopt a favorable attitude toward Japan. I would therefore like you to miss no opportunity to talk with the Soviet leaders.

"As far as we here in Tokyo are concerned, I feel that there would be certain disadvantages in my talking [in Tokyo] with Soviet ambas-

---

18. SRS 1687, 3 June 1945.
19. SRS 1688, 4 June 1945.

sador Malik personally. I have therefore delegated this task to former premier Hirota, who will confer with Malik as soon as possible. Hirota will keep a close watch on Soviet tendencies and will try to lead the Russians along the lines we desire.'' The analysts in Washington comment for Marshall that it isn't clear what "disadvantages" Togo sees in talking with Malik himself. One explanation might be that the Japanese government has some sort of proposal in mind and wants to approach the Russians about it in an informal manner without making Japan vulnerable to an embarrassing rebuff.

They also point out that Hirota is the person Foreign Minister Shigemitsu had in mind the previous summer when he wanted to send a "special envoy" to Moscow. (The Russians turned down this idea.) At that time the Japanese insisted that the "special envoy" would be charged simply with improving Japan's relations with the Soviet. But there were other indications that something more was actually involved.

This will prove to be the case.

On June 3, Ken Harada, the Japanese envoy to the Vatican, advises Tokyo that he has rejected the request of an unidentified American to discuss peace terms.[20] The essence of Harada's reasoning is found when he tells Tokyo: "At the present time I believe that Japan does not seek to hasten the coming of peace. Furthermore, it goes without saying that we cannot discuss such questions with a person whose official position and identity are unknown to us."

The next day's Magic Summary contains a report of May 29 to Tokyo from Commander Mishina, the Japanese naval attaché in Stockholm.[21] Mishina claims that "according to reports obtained from reliable sources, not a few British and American diplomats serving here say that Great Britain and the U.S. would make peace if Japan were to give up all territory acquired since 1931 with the exception of Manchuria. Our informant believes that the purpose of giving Manchuria to Japan is to provide a barrier against Russia."

Mishina recommends: "Build up further the morale of the people and strengthen their determination to fight to the end, thus increasing more and more the enemy's desire for peace."

The same day's Summary contains a report from the Portuguese minister about the "disastrous" results of the most recent bombing raids on Tokyo. He then says: "A huge part of the population is trying

---

20. SRS 1689, 5 June 1945.
21. SRS 1690, 6 June 1945.

to flee, but the authorities are preventing the departure of individuals who work in war industries.

"Every day the progress of the war becomes more alarming. This has resulted in propaganda aimed at convincing the people that the effects of the deployment of the Allied troops to the Pacific will be felt only within six months, a time when Japanese military preparations will be superior to the Americans!

"The military, which has everything to lose with the end of hostilities, [intends] to continue the war at all costs, and the clear-thinking people of the country can do nothing [about it]."

✖ ✖ ✖

There is no record in Washington as to the effect such reports in the Magic Summaries have on the American leaders. But it is interesting to note that historians agree that between June 1 and 6, Secretary of War Stimson becomes convinced that the atomic bomb—if tests prove it will work—will have to be dropped on Japan. President Truman is now up to speed on developments and is also reading the Magic Summaries. A combat veteran of World War I, he agrees with Stimson.

✖ ✖ ✖

The Magic Summary of June 7 has as its first item for Marshall's attention another Japanese report of continuing Soviet military movements to the Far East.[22]

This latest report is submitted by a courier who arrives in Moscow on June 1 and sends his finding to Tokyo via Ambassador Sato on June 4. The report says flatly that "the Red Army seems to be continuing mass shipments to the Far East." Between Chita and Omsk the courier had seen—during a sixty-eight-hour period from May 26 to 29 (apparently three days without sleep)—about 200 "transport trains." They carried 1,149 trucks and other vehicles, 435 fighter planes, 98 attack bombers, 391 medium tanks, 66 light tanks, 88 field guns, and 211 small-caliber guns.

West of Omsk, the courier noted that the traffic decreases "somewhat." But all the trains moving eastward appeared to be "military

---

22. SRS 1691, 7 June 1945.

ones'' and included ''extensive shipments'' of maintenance equipment and locomotives. He also noted that few Lend-Lease goods were observed moving westward.

The Magic Summary of June 9 brings some unexpected news to Marshall's desk.[23] A few days earlier, on June 5, Captain Nishihara, the Japanese counselor for naval affairs in Bern, reports to Tokyo that he has been approached by Allen Dulles, the OSS representative in Switzerland. Nishihara says that Dulles recently proposed that a ''discussion'' between Japan and the United States be held in Switzerland and that a Japanese admiral be flown in from Tokyo ''in absolute secrecy'' for that purpose.

Only a portion of Nishihara's message is available, but it contains the ''Proposal of the American Special Presidential Representative Dulles.'' The American is identified as having been a special envoy of the ''late President Roosevelt, [and] is continuing, under Truman, his political activities, which extend throughout Europe, with Switzerland as the center. On 23 and 25 May he [Dulles] made the following proposal in strictest secrecy—through an absolutely reliable third party—to Fujimura, and sent two long dispatches of similar purport to Washington.''

The suggestion of talking in Switzerland is because ''it is the only place in the world which can provide an atmosphere in which a 'discussion' or 'talk' between Japan and the U.S. could be conducted on an equal footing. [Also,] there are no diplomatic relations between Switzerland and Russia so there would be little surveillance or meddling on the part of Russia.'' As we know, however, the Russians are fully aware of Dulles's activities.

Furthermore, it doesn't seem to matter what Dulles might or might not suggest. The real position Tokyo is taking vis-à-vis Moscow is reflected in Ambassador Sato's latest comments to Foreign Minister Togo.[24]

The analysts recap the Japanese position for Marshall, saying that, late in April and again in May, Togo instructed Sato to sound out Molotov about Russia's intentions toward Japan. Sato was to ask whether Japan ''can again achieve some suitable understanding on Russo-Japanese relations'' during the remaining year of the Neutrality Pact's existence.

However, Sato didn't follow Togo's instructions during his talk of May 29 with Molotov. Now Sato is telling Togo that in his opinion,

---

23. SRS 1693, 9 June 1945.
24. SRS 1695, 11 June 1945.

the approach Togo suggests would be "useless" since Russia has demonstrated clearly that she doesn't want to improve her relations with Japan, although she presumably intends to remain neutral in the Pacific War "for the present at least." (Sato advised Togo after his May 29 interview with Molotov that Russia would either open hostilities against Japan or seek to mediate a peace by July or August.)

The analysts now dissect Sato's views of Japan's military prospects as the Ambassador makes the following points:

1. Japan at present is at the mercy of American bombers and is in much the same position as was Germany, whose destruction in the final analysis was brought about by air attacks.

2. If Japan can continue the war, she can probably make the Americans "lose heart," but Japan has now reached the point where the "maintenance of our powers to wage war is in doubt." While this question is one for the Japanese government alone to decide, "under conditions of modern warfare it would be unthinkable to continue hostilities once our means of resistance has been crushed."

3. With the fall of Okinawa, which now appears certain, Manchukuo—"our last rear supply base"—will come under enemy air attack, and Japan will lose her last hope of maintaining the power to make war.

4. There will be "no hope at all" of saving the Empire's future if Russia should come into the war. If "by some remote chance" Russia should embark on a course of "positive intervention," Japan *"would have no choice but to reach a decision quickly and, resolving to eat dirt and put up with all sacrifices, fly into her [Russia's] arms in order to save our national structure."* (Emphasis added.)

Fly into Russia's arms!

This is the last thing that Washington wants to happen. (In retrospect, one wonders what would have happened to Japan if she had fallen under Russian domination at the war's end.)

A few days later, the Magic Summary carries another warning about

Soviet military movements to the Far East.[25] The information is reported on June 7 by Ambassador Yamada in Hsinking, and it's described as a "compilation of data obtained by the Manchukuo Government."

When summarized, the report confirms the totals of war materials being sent to the East. A courier traveling west between Kuibyshevka (northeast of Blagoveshchensk on the Trans-Siberian railway) and Chita observes, from May 11 to 13, twelve military trains among fifty-seven eastbound trains. He counts "95 cars carrying troops," 47 fighter planes, 75 ground attack planes, 130 antiaircraft guns, 5 antiaircraft machine guns, 6 cannon and 39 trucks.

Meanwhile, the Manchukuoan consulate watches the railway at Chita for twelve hours a day for fourteen days, from May 15 to 28, and observes 227 eastbound trains, of which 100 are military, 56 are passenger and 71 are unidentified. The military trains carry about 448 cannon and heavy guns, 106 tanks, 1,540 trucks and other vehicles, 34 planes and more than 34,000 troops. (But, oh, those ubiquitous trucks!)

✖ ✖ ✖

Meanwhile, the French Foreign Ministry in Paris advises its ambassadors in Moscow, London and Chungking that the French Ministerial Committee on Indochina (created to organize "all forms of French participation in the liberation of Indochina") has made certain decisions. Among them are (1) General de Gaulle should call General Sabatier, commander of the French forces in China, back to Paris "to receive instructions"; (2) the French airline (air corridor) over India must be organized and, if possible, extended as far as Chungking; (3) General de Gaulle should authorize the DGER (Direction Générale des Etudes et Recherches, the French Intelligence Agency) to requisition French and Indochinese personnel for its activities in the Far East. The analysts in Washington point out to Marshall that the Japanese may be reading this particular French code since the codebook for the system in which the message is sent is an old one used by the Vichy government.[26]

Meanwhile, in Paris, Turkish ambassador Menemencioglu reports to Ankara after meeting with French foreign minister Bidault. Apparently Bidault claims that France will make an alliance with the U.S.

---

25. SRS 1697, 13 June 1945.
26. Ibid.

much like the Franco-Soviet Alliance. Asked if this is really true, Bidault replies: "Yes, definitely and very shortly."

The Turkish ambassador finds the claim difficult to believe, because: "Should such [an alliance] come to pass, France would try (1) to play the role of a link between the U.S. and Russia, whom she considers the two bastions of the world's destiny, and (2) to win the position of spokesman of [for] the U.S. on European questions."

A few days later, the Turkish ambassador reports on June 4 that the crisis in the Levant has soured the relationship between the U.S. and France. Accordingly, "[General de Gaulle] is likely to draw closer and closer to the Soviets. . . . [In his statement of June 2] he openly declared the spite he felt against England. . . . It is impossible not to consider this statement a weakness and a product of inexperience. . . . [De Gaulle, who] is very much the slave of the desire to plunge England into difficulties by bringing forward one more element of [a] troubled world, will . . . make a mistake."

✷ ✷ ✷

The same Magic Summary contains the first of the three messages Nishihara sends Tokyo about the Dulles proposal. (The analysts note that they can't tell if Nishihara is the author of the messages or merely relaying them.) This particular message is an "estimate of the general situation since the surrender of Germany." It is notable in the way it summarizes what the Japanese mistakenly believe to be specific American policies.

First, it is believed that the present American government has lost much of the confidence of the people, particularly as a result of the failure of the San Francisco Conference. While they appear to be giving strong support to the military for the unconditional surrender of Japan, they are secretly anxious to bring about a suitable conclusion of the war as soon as possible in order to gain popularity and maintain their own position.

Next, all the circles in America want to fight the war against Japan without British or Russian assistance. As time passes, however, the chances are that the British, and even Russian forces, will be brought into the war. (According to a [Japanese] intelligence report, Russia agreed at Yalta to cooperate after a certain time in a positive way in the war against Japan; the time the Soviets will move is at the end of August.) The government, business circles, and a large part of the military in the U.S. wants to end the war against Japan quickly in order to limit Russian participation and thus prevent the postwar Bolshevization of East Asia.

The greatest concern of the Anglo-American authorities is to prevent the spread of Communism in Europe. The wishes of Eisenhower's headquarters—faced on the one hand with the request of Nimitz for more men (in the Pacific) and on the other with the heavy pressure of Russia in Europe—may bring about a speedy conclusion of the war with Japan.

Nishihara also believes there is a conviction, particularly among the leaders of the U.S. government, that America must soon clash directly with Russia in the Far East. He says there are those (unidentified) who would bring about an early cessation of the war with Japan even though that might mean conceding something (unspecified) to Japan.

He points out, however, that the American military, and particularly the Navy, want to bring about Japan's unconditional surrender and to make it impossible for her to rebuild her fighting strength. Those who hold that opinion would, in the light of the lessons learned in Europe, destroy in a short period—by repeated and relentless air attacks—Japanese factories, transportation facilities and cities and then try to effect a landing on the Japanese homeland, probably in July or August.

The last paragraph is accurate but for two aspects. The estimated date of invasion is incorrect. And it does not anticipate the totally destructive measures described earlier that the Americans are prepared to inflict by conventional means on the population of Japan if it promises lower casualties among the American invasion forces.

On June 14, Marshall learns that the Japanese definition of *unconditional surrender* is causing great problems among government officials.[27] From Moscow, Ambassador Sato sends Tokyo on June 11 a message that illustrates how the term *unconditional surrender* is viewed in the Far East.·

"What is the meaning of the phrase *unconditional surrender?*" Sato cables. "There are virtually no precedents from history to provide the answer to this question. With the hope of discovering the significance and scope of the phrase as defined in the minds of the United Nations' leaders, I have drawn up a statement of my observations on the Four-Power Declaration [with respect to Germany]."

The analysts in Washington pick out for Marshall's attention three

---

27. SRS 1698, 14 June 1945.

specific points from Sato's long report. The first one is: "The United Nations do not take the customary course of administering the occupied area through negotiations with the central government of the defeated power; . . . they issue orders unilaterally."

In other words, Sato is bluntly telling Tokyo that not only will the central government of Japan be pushed aside by the victors, but so will the Emperor. The entire structure of Japanese government will be toppled. Impossible from the Japanese point of view.

Second, Sato says: "The occupation of Germany . . . is a real and true occupation . . . but it is not what you might call a 'simple occupation' since there is also preparation for alienations of [German] territory." Again, the transfer of territory belonging to, or claimed by, Japan is unacceptable to the Japanese way of thinking.

Last, Sato points out: "[After noting the provisions dissolving all armed forces including the SS, SA and Gestapo, and the provisions requiring military, industrial and other facilities to be held in good condition at the disposal of the Allies], these points show the absolute completeness of unconditional surrender."

At last. Sato's got it! But the mind-set in the Japanese Army and Navy refuses to acknowledge that the militaristic domination of the Japanese government is about to end. Japan is a warrior nation. The militarists believe the Japanese people—all of them—should be prepared to die by the code of Bushido if it means keeping the dreaded Anglo-Americans out of Japan.

The same day's Summary also contains the third and final part of the series of messages Captain Nishihara sent Tokyo. Again the analysts say they do not know who the author of the whole message really might be, but they say this section is Nishihara's "own opinions of the Dulles proposal." The message reads in substance as follows: "*Dulles's character.* This man was the special representative in Europe of the late President Roosevelt. Truman is using him in the same capacity, and from his headquarters in the OSS [in Bern] he has continued his activities throughout Europe. Particular reliance seems to be placed upon Dulles. Not limiting himself merely to political matters, he is in direct contact with Washington on all manner of problems including military, diplomatic and economic intelligence, postwar [word missing], etc. . . . He would seem to be invested with an extremely wide range of authority. He has an excellent staff. (Dulles and a number of his staff possess special presidential affidavits giving them access to all troops and facilities of the U.S. forces in Europe, irrespective of time and place, and requiring the prompt execution of Dulles's requests for the use of planes and other communications facilities of any operational forces whatsoever. The third party who got in touch with us said he had seen this affidavit.)

"The . . . surrender of all German troops in northern Italy and in Austria stemmed from the execution of plans which Dulles had been formulating since January of this year. At that time Eisenhower was most intent on capturing the German forces about to entrench themselves in the Alps of northern Italy and southern Germany, and as a result of Dulles's rational stipulations and humane measures, it [the instrument of surrender] was signed in Caserta on 2 May [actually on 29 April, becoming effective on 2 May]. . . ." (A footnote is indicated at this point in the Magic Summary, but it is not included in the text released to date.)

"The U.S. government has great confidence in Dulles and he is said to have received secret instructions to leave soon—around the latter part of June—for a post at Frankfurt am Main as administrative head of the U.S. occupation zone in Germany.[28]

"*Essence of proposal.* The proposal [made by Dulles] is authoritative, and although we have been investigating for some ten days as to whether or not it is in full faith, we believe that it is not a stratagem but is quite trustworthy and carries full faith. Up to the present time we have discovered no evidence refuting that belief. Our judgment is based on (1) the fact that the second party [the representative of Japan] is quite aware of the identity of the first party [Dulles] and (2) the content of the previously mentioned dispatch to Washington (Dulles's staff with his permission showed the draft of this dispatch to the third party in private, and part of it was revised in accordance of the opinion of the third party). [In reporting the proposal made by Dulles on May 23 and 25, the second message from Nishihara (DS 9 June 1945) stated that Dulles had sent 'two long dispatches of similar purport to Washington.']

"The reason for the designation of the Navy [the original message (DS 9 June 45) specified that if Japan wished to enter into discussions, 'a naval officer of the rank of admiral' should be sent from Tokyo as quickly as possible]—and they can discuss this type of problem in Japan now and in the future [*sic:* 'meaning unknown,' the analysts tell Marshall]—is that in the opinion of the other party no suitable person can be found outside of the Imperial Navy.

---

28. Dulles was named Chief, OSS German Mission, which, because of Truman's dismantling of the OSS, became the SSU, or Special Services Unit. Dulles went to Berlin in July 1945.

''*Maintenance of secrecy.* Since an absolute maximum of secrecy is necessary in this matter, the other party warned us particularly on that score. As an example of the other party's maintenance of secrecy, in connection with the surrender of troops in northern Italy and in Austria, a hundred messages were sent back and forth from January on and a considerable number of round-trips were made by employees, but nothing was detected and satisfactory results were obtained.

''Naturally, absolute secrecy is demanded of us, and at present, outside of Dulles and two of his staff, the go-between, and our two men mentioned above [Captain Nishihara and his assistant, Commander Fujimura], no one is cognizant of this matter. Furthermore, if absolute secrecy is to be maintained in connection with the flight of the Japanese admiral (including a staff of three), it will be necessary to resort to some device such as the use of a Swiss plane carrying mail for British and American prisoners in Greater East Asia.

''However, since this matter is of supreme importance to the national fate of the Empire, the words of the other party have been conveyed to us through the good offices of only one third party. Not a word or an inkling of this matter has been revealed [to anyone except those mentioned].''

Could it be that the arrogance of the Japanese—in believing that their diplomatic ciphers were unbreakable—helped cause this peace-seeking effort to fail? As we know, there is no secrecy left to the matter. The program can be shot down by a hundred hidden guns with no one knowing who fires the fatal bullet. There is only the one undisputable fact: what Nishihara proposes will never be acceptable to Tokyo.

✖ ✖ ✖

The following day's Magic Summary confirms Russia's intentions of increasing her power in the Middle East.[29] An earlier Summary had mentioned discussions held in Moscow between Foreign Commissar Molotov and Turkish ambassador Sarper on the evening of June 7. Now, according to Sarper, Molotov is asking for a rearrangement of the eastern frontier between Turkey and Russia as a prerequisite to any new treaty between the two nations. Molotov also questions Turkey's ability to protect the Dardanelles and indicates that Russia wants military bases in the area.

29. SRS 1699, 15 June 1945.

In reply, Ambassador Sarper takes it upon himself to say that Turkey will not even discuss territorial concessions or the granting of bases. (This stand by Sarper is confirmed later by the Turkish Foreign Ministry.) Furthermore, there can be no revision of the Montreaux Convention without consulting other interested powers. Because of the "very grave" situation that might arise if the Russians persist in their demands, the Turkish government tells Moscow via Sarper that it is informing the British about the developments. The Magic Diplomatic Summaries are more than living up to their name in terms of defining the machinations of the Russians.

✖ ✖ ✖

Events are heating up in the Far East. The Japanese consul general in Vladivostok reports that the Russians are building up their military in the area.[30] There has also been a border incident between the Russians and the Japanese in the neighborhood of Wei-tzu-kou (about 250 miles NNE of Vladivostok). The issue involves "hot pursuit." Japanese police chase thieves across the border and they take refuge on Soviet ships.

The following day's Magic Summary carries a surprising analysis of Japanese aluminum production capabilities.[31] The "Japanese would arrive at the end of September [1945] with some aluminum to spare." This means that "if all aluminum output were stopped at once, the amount of metal then in the pipeline would be enough to keep the aircraft industry going for six months, and if aircraft production were reduced in the meantime by Allied air attacks, the supply in the pipeline would last even longer."

The same report also carries a circular issued on June 1 by the G.E.A. Ministry, describing the incendiary damage done to the Ministry's main building during the air raid of May 25–26, which says: "We are now negotiating with a view to transferring the capital [from Tokyo] altogether." The analysts note for Marshall, however, that on June 1, a broadcast from Tokyo to western North America declared that "the central government is determined to stay in the metropolis, even if the metropolis is reduced to ashes."

As for the Portuguese view of the Japanese attitude toward peace,

---

30. SRS 1701, 17 June 1945.
31. SRS 1703, 19 June 1945.

in the same Summary the Portuguese minister to Japan reports home: "With the destruction of her production centers, and military failures everywhere, all that remains for Japan is to admit the reality of her defeat. This she will not do, however, because of the well-known characteristics of the race."

With ever-increasing momentum, Japan's military leaders are bringing a terrible retribution upon the nation's ordinary citizens.

19

Within the past month, the Diplomatic Summaries reveal that the de Gaulle government has attempted to annex unilaterally a portion of northwest Italy and the Alps that its troops occupied during their advance.[1] De Gaulle stops his land grab only when President Truman threatens to cut off supplies to the French Army. As mentioned earlier, de Gaulle also tries to reclaim French control over Lebanon and Syria despite the fact that the Big Three had declared the two nations to be independent states. As a result of the French intervention, serious fighting erupts in the Middle East. Now, on June 15, French ambassador Maugras in Ankara reports that Soviet ambassador Vinogradov told him "in confidence" that Foreign Commissar Molotov is "well disposed" toward the French cause in Syria.[2]

Maugras points out that it is "obviously" because of instructions issued by the Soviets that two Turkish newspapers under the Soviet embassy's influence are adopting a pro-French editorial policy on the Lebanon problem, which contrasts with the general hostility of most of the Turkish press toward France.

No wonder then that Churchill and Truman agree to keep de Gaulle from attending the Potsdam conference.

---

1. The Summaries reveal that the French call this action a mere "readjustment of territories in the Alps and in Africa." The severity of the French behavior is pinpointed by the analysts for Marshall. They note that General Doyen, Commander of the French Army in the Alps, wrote to Major General Crittenburger, Commanding General, IV Corps, Fifth Army (U.S.), among other things, threatening "grave consequences" if any effort was made to displace French troops and French control in northwest Italy. SRS 1692, 8 June 1945; SRS 1700, 16 June 1945.
2. SRS 1703, 19 June 1945; see also SRS 1694, 10 June 1945.

✻ ✻ ✻

The month of June also sees an end to the slaughter on Okinawa. In some of the bloodiest fighting of the war, as mentioned earlier, the Americans endure 40,000 battlefield casualties as opposed to 81,000 for the Japanese. This casualty ratio of about 1 to 2 is terrifying to contemplate when the Japanese home islands are defended by 2.3 million troops, plus another 4 million Army and Navy employees and the newly created civilian militia, which numbers 28 million.

The Japanese code of Bushido is demonstrated once again for the Americans as the Marines are about to capture the Japanese command center. That night, Generals Ushijima and Sho enjoyed a special dinner. Just before daylight the next day, wearing their full dress uniforms, both men kneel on clean white sheets facing north (where the Emperor resides in Tokyo) and disembowel themselves. General Sho's last written statement is: "I depart without regret, shame, or obligations." Members of the lower ranks emulate their leaders. Only they use hand grenades held against their midsections instead of sabers. The American GIs who know that they are scheduled to invade the Japanese home islands are not pleased by the prospect.

This brings forward a controversy that has marred Washington's preparations to commemorate the fiftieth anniversary of ending the war with Japan. First comes the debate in the U.S. Congress about how the Smithsonian Museum should display its exhibits on the subject. A unanimous Senate vote rebukes the museum's politically correct curators, but a group of American scholars continues challenging the number of casualties estimated by U.S. military planners should America have had to invade Japan. Then they raise the question about whether a high-level meeting of top people discussing the atomic bomb ever took place. Last, Kai Bird writes in the *New York Times* that "... no scholar of the war has ever found archival evidence to substantiate claims that [President] Truman expected anything close to one million casualties, or even that such huge casualties were conceivable."[3] According to Kai Bird, American veterans are being fooled into believing that the atomic bomb saved them from sacrificing their lives in an invasion of Japan.

This writer telephones Samuel Halpern, who had worked in the OSS assisting War Plans in Washington during the last months of the

---

3. *New York Times* Op-Ed, Sunday, October 9, 1994, page 15. Kai Bird writes that "many well-

war, to ask what did President Truman actually know about the casualty estimates for the invasion of Japan. Halpern volunteers that in
July and August 1990, he had written and challenged Professor Bernstein, who, according to Kai Bird, ''. . . has pored over declassified
military planning documents, [and] could not find a worst-case estimate of higher than 46,000 *deaths*.'' (Emphasis added.) Halpern
makes his correspondence with Professor Bernstein available to this
writer. It is fascinating to see how two historians, one of whom actually worked in the OSS helping War Plans, view the same documents in differing ways.[4]

Halpern tells this writer that in early May 1945, he had been stationed in Kandy, Ceylon, preparing to fly ''over the hump'' [the Him-
alayas] to the OSS mission in China. Suddenly, he and three more
senior OSS people receive new orders to fly back to Washington by
the fastest route possible. To speed them on their way they are assigned
Joint Chiefs of Staff Number One Priority, which no one in OSS/Kandy
had ever heard of before, but which means they board aircraft ahead
of everyone else. Halpern arrives in Washington on VE Day, May 8,
1945, and is immediately assigned to help in the top secret planning
for the invasion of Japan. He is not told about the atomic bomb. But
when he is briefed on his duties, he is told repeatedly that the landings
in Japan will result in 500,000 casualties.

''What really struck me,'' Halpern told this writer, ''was that the
military casualty estimate was only for the *first* thirty days of fighting.
If the fighting was to continue another thirty days, double the casualties.
Multiply the figure by three for a ninety-day campaign. In those terms
it wasn't difficult to envisage 1.5 million casualties for the invasion and
occupation of Japan.''

According to Halpern, Professor Bernstein dismissed Halpern's
first letter about his experiences. ''Memory,'' Bernstein replied, ''often reflects not the distant event but intervening discussions about the
distant event.'' A trained historian, Halpern accepts the challenge and

---

known scholars—including Barton J. Bernstein, Martin J. Sherwin, Robert Messer, James Hersh-
berg, Gar Alperovitz, Melvyn P. Leffler and Stanley Goldberg—have noted that there is com-
pelling evidence that diplomatic overtures, coupled with assurances on the post-war status of
the emperor and the impending entry of the Soviet Union into the war, *probably* would have
led the Japanese to surrender long before an American invasion could be mounted. . . .'' (Emphasis added.)
4. Halpern's correspondence with Professor Bernstein is reproduced in full in the appendix so
the reader can check his careful sourcing.

goes to work, carefully reconstructing the events of the time according to archival records, and writes Bernstein about his findings. Bernstein does not respond to this letter. What did Halpern discover? On June 9, 1945, for example, President Truman transmits to the War Department former President Herbert Hoover's memo about ending the war with Japan. In his transmittal memo Truman asks Secretary Stimson for his analysis of Hoover's comments because of Stimson's personal knowledge of the Far East. Truman also requests later discussions on the matter.

It is apparent from the records on hand that the War Department had already received a copy of the Hoover memo, probably before Truman did. [It is not known how many people Hoover sent copies of his memo to Truman.] General Marshall had already passed on his staff's comments about the matter to Stimson on June 7, stating his general agreement with their findings. This paper says in paragraph VI: "What are the results to the United States and Britain? America will save 500,000 to 1,000,000 lives and an enormous amount of resources. Comment: It is obvious that peace would save lives and resources, but the estimated loss of 500,000 lives due to carrying the war to conclusion under our present plan of campaign [underlining in the original] is considered to be entirely too high." This document indicates that the staff working for War Plans was considering a 500,000 casualty estimate and that Halpern's memory is not faulty.

Halpern also points out that the Hoover memo Truman sent on to Stimson for analysis on 9 June contained on page 2 the statement: "Beyond this point there can be no objectives worth the expenditure of 500,000 to 1,000,000 American lives." Later, on page 4, Hoover says: "We would have saved the lives of 500,000 to 1,000,000 American boys, the loss of which may be necessary by going to the end." This demonstrates that from the outset Truman was aware of the possibility of huge casualties in invading the home islands of Japan.[5]

---

5. Halpern's account is confirmed by David Holloway in his epochal book *Stalin and the Bomb*. In an incredible investigation describing how Stalin failed to comprehend the significance of atomic warfare until after Hiroshima, Holloway confirms that (1) the Americans already knew that Roosevelt's agreement with Stalin at Yalta, giving Russia territory in the Far East in return for Russian entry into the war, would never be acceptable to the Chinese, yet Truman would honor the agreement with Russia; (2) the Russians believed it would be too costly for them to invade the home islands of Japan; and (3) "the primary motive for using the [atomic] bomb against Japan was to bring the war to a speedy end." David Holloway, *Stalin and the Bomb*, Yale University Press, 1994, pages 121–31.

On 14 June, Admiral Leahy arranges a meeting at the White House for 18 June to discuss the defeat of Japan. Halpern notes that in his invitational cover memo about the meeting Leahy says the President wants to have "an estimate on killed and wounded resulting from the invasion of Japan." The Admiral also says: "The President will make a decision on the campaign with the purpose of economizing to the maximum extent possible in the loss of American lives." From the President's point of view, Leahy says, "time and money are relatively unimportant."

The casualty figures discussed with Truman at the meeting of 18 June range all over the lot, starting with a low estimate of 31,000 from General MacArthur based on his campaign in retaking the island of Luzon. According to Halpern's reading of the extracts of this meeting, Admiral Leahy is not satisfied with similar low estimates. He points out that in seizing Okinawa the U.S. forces suffered 35 percent casualties. [Leahy's figure is only slightly higher than the actual figures: Tenth Army casualties were 39,413 and the Navy's 17,700.] And prior to the attack on Iwo Jima, the Marines had estimated 31 percent casualties out of a force of 61,000, while the actual figures were 32.8 percent, or 19,969. Leahy also says: "If this percentage were applied to the number of troops to be employed in [invading] Kyushu, he thought that from the similarity of fighting to be expected that this would give a good estimate of the casualties to be expected. He was interested therefore in finding out how many troops are to be used in Kyushu."

Later in the meeting, Marshall says the invasion force for Kyushu will number 766,700 men. This means, Halpern says, that, "if Truman, following Leahy's suggestion, took 30 percent of 766,700 he would arrive at the figure of 230,010 casualties, and 268,345 if he used 35 percent. If Truman later added the same percentages for the invasion of the Tokyo plain (CORONET), he would get the figure of 600,000 casualties out of 2 million [the total number of troops to be committed by May 1946], or 700,000 casualties using 35 percent.

Speaking for the Army Air Forces, General Eaker added that "present air casualties are averaging 2 percent per mission, about 30 percent per month." He gave no total figures.

Truman is obviously concerned about the casualty estimates. Halpern says: "At the meeting he [Truman] is said to have said that Kyushu was 'practically creating another Okinawa closer to Japan, to which the Chiefs of Staff agreed.' And on giving the go ahead on the plan to invade Kyushu, the President said, 'He hoped that there was a possibility of preventing an Okinawa from one end of Japan to the other.' It must have been a question to which he returned.'' Halpern also told this writer that this meeting was immediately followed by another from which everyone not cleared for Magic/Ultra, or the atomic bomb, was excluded; no minutes of this meeting have been released.

According to Halpern, Truman gives the go ahead for OLYMPIC, the first of the two invasions of Japan, on 18 June, and the debate about casualties continues. On 2 July 1945 Stimson sends a memo to Truman saying in part:

''2. There is reason to believe that the operation for the occupation of Japan following the landing may be a very long, costly and arduous struggle on our part.

''3. If we once land on one of the main islands and begin a forceful occupation of Japan, we shall probably have cast the die of last ditch resistance. . . . Once started in actual invasion, we shall in my opinion have to go through with an even more bitter finish fight than in Germany. We shall incur the losses incident to such a war and we shall have to leave the Japanese islands more thoroughly destroyed than was the case with Germany.''

Or, as Robert Crowley noted earlier, America is preparing to destroy by conventional means the very civilization of Japan if it means saving a million American casualties.

This writer has not been able to determine if the safety of Allied prisoners of war was discussed with Truman. The Magic Diplomatic Summaries released to date do not mention this specifically. Nor could this writer confirm if other Japanese military intercepts reveal what follows: On the island of Java, the Japanese are holding some 300,000 prisoners, both military and civilian. As the war ends, the Japanese field marshall stationed in Saigon issues orders to ''eliminate these useless consumers of scarce food supplies.'' The prisoners are told to dig their own graves and nearly complete the job when the first atomic bomb is dropped on Hiroshima. Emperor Hirohito now commands the field marshall to rescind his order. The field marshall does not wish to comply. Hirohito sends his brother, Prince Chichibu, to Saigon to dissuade the field marshall. The second atomic bomb is dropped; the 300,000 prisoners are spared.[6]

---

6. Frederick K. Bauer, *Wall Street Journal,* Letter to the Editor, 7 October 1994, page All.

✼ ✼ ✼

The next significant report of Soviet military movement in the Far East occurs on June 23.[7] Again Ambassador Sato forwards to Tokyo the report of two Japanese couriers who have just made the railroad trip from Man-chou-li, a border town in Manchukuo, to Moscow. The couriers count a total of 171 military trains moving eastward during the period of June 9 through 16, and they carried "about 120,000 troops." They also bore self-propelled guns, rocket launchers, 1,600 trucks, 30 tanks of American origin, and 19 [or 30] "Joseph Stalin" heavy tanks. The couriers also spotted about 250 tank cars, and a "great deal" of lumber, coal, iron and steel.

During the middle of June, there is considerable turmoil within the Japanese diplomatic group in Stockholm.[8] Japanese minister Okamoto accuses his military attaché, Major General Onodera, of engaging in unauthorized peace maneuvers with "foreigners," including Eric Erickson, a Swedish oilman. Swedish diplomats warn Okamoto about the unauthorized dialogue, and he immediately asks the Foreign Office to take steps at once to see that such activity is prohibited "regardless of whether or not Onodera was acting on orders from Army headquarters." The Minister adds: "A dual diplomacy at the present time would be disastrous and I feel very strongly that the Foreign Office must take a firm attitude." The Japanese Army apparently had not authorized the talks.

On June 24, the Vice Chief of the Army General Staff in Tokyo sends Attaché Onedera a stiff, cover-your-flanks message: "As we have said before, Japan is firmly determined to prosecute the Greater East Asia war to the very end. There is a report, however, to the effect that some Japanese official stationed in Sweden is making peace overtures to America. That is demagoguery pure and simple, and if you have any idea as to the source of those reports, please inform us."[9] There is no record of a reply from Onodera. But no more rumors about peace proposals come from Sweden.

---

7. SRS 1707, 23 June 1945.
8. SRS 1709, 25 June 1945.
9. SRS 1711, 27 June 1945. SRS 1725 of July 11, 1945, reports further on this incident. After Ambassador Okamoto complained to Tokyo, Togo called the matter to the attention of the War and Navy Ministers and the Chiefs of the Army and Navy General Staffs, and "the leaders of both Army and Navy" were "in agreement" that such activity should be stopped. Warning

✖ ✖ ✖

The Magic Diplomatic Summaries of July 1945 are the fateful documents that condemn the Japanese people to nuclear attack. They prove beyond reasonable doubt that the Japanese military leaders will never accept "unconditional surrender." They also prove that the Japanese military leaders, in order to protect their way of life, are willing to strike a last-minute deal with the Russians that would drastically alter the balance of power in the Far East. Above all, they indicate that the only way the Japanese might be considered a "peace-loving nation" in the future will be for the Americans to seize total control of the Japanese government and install democracy.

In the Magic Summary of July 3, the first item marked for Marshall's attention is headlined: *"Japanese attempt to win over Russia."*[10] The text of the Summary is crucial to the fate of Japan and is printed in full. It begins with a reprise prepared by the analysts in Washington:

"Early last month Foreign Minister Togo advised Ambassador Sato that it was a matter of the 'utmost urgency' not only to prevent Russia from entering the Pacific war but to induce her to adopt a favorable attitude toward Japan. Togo continued that he had accordingly asked former premier Hirota[11] to confer with Soviet ambassador Malik 'as soon as possible' and that 'Hirota will keep a close watch on Soviet tendencies and will try to lead the Russians along the line we desire' [DS 4 June 1945].

"It now appears that during the period 3–14 June, Hirota had four conversations with Malik. A 28 June message from Togo to Sato describing the talks is set forth as Tab A; it discloses that:

"a. The first conversation—on 3 June—consisted largely of an exchange of amenities in the course of which Hirota assured Malik that it was 'the universal desire' of both the Japanese government and the Japanese people to have friendly relations with Russia.

---

that the Attaché might be recalled home, Togo is mollified when the Army Chief of Staff says he will "immediately have this man given strict warning."
10. SRS 1717, 3 July 1945.
11. According to MacCormack's analysis, "Koki Hirota was Premier from March 1936 to February 1937 and had also been Ambassador to Russia (1930–32) and Foreign Minister (1933–36, 1937–38). He was the man Foreign Minister Shigemitsu had in mind last summer when he wanted to send a 'special envoy' to Moscow, ostensibly to improve Japan's relations with Russia (a proposal that was turned down by the Russians—DS 20 September 1944.)"

"b. The next day Hirota was invited to supper by Malik and took the opportunity to state that Japan specifically hoped to 'achieve a means of maintaining peaceful relations between the two countries over a rather long period, say twenty or thirty years.' Malik made no answer on this point but mentioned that, although Russia had tried to pursue a peaceful policy in the Far East, past events had produced 'a feeling of distrust and lack of safety.'

"c. At the third interview—on 14 June—Hirota pressed Malik for a statement of Russia's reaction to his previous proposal, but without success; he then stated that Japan wished to iron out all sources of friction with Russia and specifically was willing to:

"**1.** reconsider the Russo-Japanese political and economic relations in Manchukuo;

"**2.** arrive at some agreement on the question of China and;

"**3.** supply Russia with commodities from the southern areas.

"Hirota then inquired directly whether 'Russia will consent to reach some agreement with Japan more favorable than the Neutrality Pact, or will improve its currently good relations with Japan.'

"Malik replied: 'Until the expiration of the Neutrality Pact, we shall continue to play the role we have been playing. I can well understand that you would like to exchange views with me regarding our future relations even before the Pact expires. However, our future relations will have to be based on concrete actions.'[12]

"d. At their last conference the same evening, Hirota stated: '*Japan will increase her naval strength in the future, and that, together with the Russian Army, would make a force unequaled in the world.* In this connection, Japan would like to have Russia provide her with oil, in return for which Japan would provide rubber, tin, lead, tungsten and other commodities from the south (transport would be up to the Russians).' [Emphasis added.]

"Malik replied that Russia had no oil to spare but that he would study the proposal.

"In conclusion, Hirota stated that Japan hoped for an early peace

---

12. To cancel the Neutrality Pact one of the two parties is required to serve notice of its intent to cancel one year before the Pact actually expires. In other words, the Pact is still in force when Russia attacks Japan in 1945.

but the reply was that 'since Russia was not a belligerent in the East, His Excellency Mr. Hirota must be well aware that peace there did not depend on Russia.' "[13]

The idea that Japan is willing to join militarily with the Soviet Union to *"make a force unequaled in the world"* at this late stage in the war presents Washington with an entirely new set of problems. First, the Japanese offer sounds very much like the scenario that Tokyo painted for Berlin just before Stalingrad. (Back then the idea was for the Germans and the Japanese to join hands in the Middle East, create two economic spheres and control the world.) The bloody battle of Stalingrad had prevented this projection from occurring. What will be needed to prevent the new Japanese proposal from becoming reality?

Second, at the time Hirota makes the incredible offer to Malik, the Japanese still have several million soldiers under arms. They control, besides the Japanese home islands (including the southern half of Sakhalin), all of Korea, all of Manchukuo, some of the richest parts of China, including Peking, Nanking, Shanghai, Hangchow, Hong Kong, plus the island of Formosa. They also control French Indochina, Thailand, Malaya, Sumatra, Borneo and the Celebes.

The economic potential of the territories Japan occupies is almost beyond comprehension. If she divides China with the Soviet Union, which would settle the so-called "China Question," and if Japan protects the mainland with its navy, the balance of power will have shifted dramatically in favor of Moscow. Perhaps this is what Ambassador Sato meant when he said that the Japanese should throw themselves into the arms of the Russians. Perhaps not. Because the proposal unravels when one realizes that the Japanese Navy is no longer a viable military threat. Then there is the Allied knowledge that Stalin has promised to attack Japan in August.

Nevertheless, the idea of a union between Russia and Japan, which might forestall the Russians from attacking Japan as her diplomats have warned, is enough to make Washington and London prepare for truly desperate measures to end the war. Perhaps that is why the British government, on the Fourth of July, or the day after Hirota makes his breathtaking offer to Malik, consents to the use of atomic weapons against Japan.

---

13. The conversation between Malik and Hirota as revealed by Magic can be found in the appendix (see page 579).

✖ ✖ ✖

The day after Hirota makes his offer to Ambassador Malik, the Magic Summary prepared for Marshall has as its first item of business the most recent Japanese peace feelers in China.[14] Chiang Kai-shek is telling the Japanese that it is "very difficult for Chungking to make any answer to the peace terms offered [by the Japanese], which dealt only with peace between the two Chinas, since there now had come into being a new relationship with the United States." Accordingly, Chiang instructed the Japanese agent brokering the negotiations to find out if the Japanese had any new proposal based on the new situation, "find out about it and come back to Chungking."

Although Chiang Kai-shek is being faithful to his American ally, Japanese ambassador Tani reports that Chungking fears that "an incursion of Soviet power into China is inevitable." He also notes that there is no hope for a general peace "except through the settlement of the Pacific problem" that would involve "an acceptance of all Chinese and Anglo-American demands." Furthermore, "by continuing her indomitable fight," Japan may bring "even the Americans" to realize that the "continued existence of the Empire in the long run gives the only assurance of the stability of East Asia [without which] there can be no security for their interests and economic schemes."

The headline information for the next day's Magic Summary is that on June 25, some 4,000 troops of the Chinese Communist Eighth Route Army invaded Manchukuo.[15] Captured documents reveal there are some 364,500 "effective" troops in the Eighth Route Army and they are planning to invade the provinces of Jehol and Lianing. The Japanese in Manchukuo warn Tokyo that the situation must be watched closely vis-à-vis the strengthening of the Soviet military to the north.

With the all-important Potsdam Conference about to begin between the Big Three—Great Britain, America and Russia—on June 30, Foreign Minister Togo instructs Ambassador Sato to see Foreign Commissar Molotov before the conference and to "do everything in your power to lead the Russians along the lines we desire."[16]

The offer Sato is to make to Molotov reads as follows:

---

14. SRS 1718, 4 July 1945.
15. SRS 1719, 5 July 1945.
16. SRS 1723, 9 July 1945.

"Firm and lasting relations of friendship shall be established between Japan and Russia and they shall both cooperate in the maintenance of peace in East Asia. . . . A treaty shall be concluded between the two countries which shall assure mutual assistance on problems involving the maintenance of peace in East Asia and relations based on the principle of nonaggression."

This is the basic concept dressed up in diplomatic language as proposed by Hirota to Ambassador Malik in Tokyo a few days earlier. Now Tokyo adds some sweeteners: "We have no objections to an agreement involving Manchukuo's neutralization. . . . We have no objection to renouncing our fisheries rights provided that Russia agrees to supply us with oil (the basic necessity that caused Japan to attack Pearl Harbor). . . . We have no objection to discussing any matter which the Russians would like to bring up for discussion."

Ambassador Sato, however, isn't impressed by Togo's offerings to the Russians. In the same Magic Summary he makes his beliefs clear: Togo's foreign policy is misguided. According to Sato: "If the purpose of this interview [with Molotov] is merely to sound out Russia's attitude, that . . . is one thing. If, however, we desire something more, I cannot help feeling that we will be going against the general worldwide trend—particularly in the matter of Russia's relations with England and America. . . . They have been steadily improving—witness, for example, the establishment of the United Nations Charter and the reform of the Provisional Government in Poland—and I personally believe that this trend will continue. . . . [Today] Japan [is] considered by world opinion as the one obstacle to the restoration of world peace.

"From these facts, it seems extremely unlikely that Russia would flout the Anglo-Americans and the opinion of the entire world by supporting Japan's war effort with either moral or material means. . . . I believe that the conference [with Molotov] will have to be limited to the settlement of issues in dispute between Russia and Japan. If it should go beyond such minor questions, the reaction of the Anglo-Americans and of the entire world would be tremendous. I believe that the Russians would feel absolutely unable to consent to that."

✖ ✖ ✖

In the days to come, reading the Magic Diplomatic Summaries in chronological order, in exactly the same way they cross the desks of the few American leaders in Washington privileged to see them, one begins to believe that the Japanese are seeking their own destruction. One can sense the frustration that must have gripped Marshall, Stimson, Truman and King as they witness the Japanese employing their desperate strategy with the Russians and the world, hour by hour, day by day.

Aside from the fact that the Summaries contain messages that are decrypted out of the order in which they are sent, which means that the readers must do some careful interpretation on their own, they prove beyond a doubt that the Emperor of Japan is personally involved and committed to seeking a new order in Asia based on a military/economic alliance with Russia. The Emperor also wants peace. But the Emperor—as represented by the Army and the Navy—also refuses to accept unconditional surrender and relinquish his feudal power.

Thus the coming month's Magic Summaries read like a macabre study of national insanity. Tokyo cooks up foreign policy, but is afraid to put it in writing. Every statement made by Foreign Minister Togo bears the stain of deceit and mendacity. To those in the American government who know Japan well, it is obvious that the Japanese military control the Emperor, the government, and are determined to fight to the end. Diplomats such as Ambassador Sato may rage against the "bureaucrats" who run Japan, just as his successors will rage against the same type of bureaucrats half a century later, but the fact is the Japanese have no leader strong enough to force them to the peace table. Such decisions are reached by consensus in Japan. They always have been. They probably always will be. Since the Japanese Army and Navy control the government in 1945, and the military are willing to sacrifice the lives of 70 million innocent civilians, studying the Magic Summaries in the days to come is like slipping into the waters of a great whirlpool whose vortex sucks the viewer ever downward to the ultimate blossoming of nuclear death.

The pigheadedness, incompetence and stupidity born of arrogance that the Japanese military leaders display at this crucial moment in history leads the men reading these intercepts to only one conclusion: the atomic bomb must be used. As proven by the Magic Summaries, if blame for unleashing nuclear warfare is to be apportioned, the Japanese military must bear the full burden of responsibility for the event and, worse, making Japanese civilians the tragic victims of their hubris.

As demonstrated in the pages that follow, the record clearly shows that, prior to the Allied dropping of the bomb, the Japanese military refuse every opportunity to negotiate a surrender. Even when the Emperor reaches his inevitable decision to end the war, but only after *two* nuclear weapons are exploded over the cities of Hiroshima and Naga-saki, and while the Russians seize much of Manchuria, the militarists will then revolt, try to seize the Imperial Palace and prevent Japan from surrendering.

✖ ✖ ✖

The Magic Summary of July 10[17] presents some problems for the analysts in Washington. They note that, on June 30, Foreign Minister Togo sent Ambassador Sato a message (No. 853) containing what appear to be the essential points of a proposal to be made to Russia (a mutual assistance and nonaggression treaty, and stating Japan's willingness to arrange for the "neutralization" of Manchukuo, to renounce her fisheries rights—in return for oil—and to discuss any other matters).

After decoding other messages, it now turns out that the proposal as outlined in message No. 853 has already been conveyed to the Russians. Former premier Hirota handed it to Ambassador Malik in Tokyo on June 29 saying it represented "Japan's views on future relations between the two countries." In turn, Malik promised to transmit it to his government.

The analysts conclude: "It also now appears that the Japanese government has unceremoniously overridden Sato's repeatedly expressed doubts about the wisdom of the move and has renewed its instructions to him to make every effort to see Foreign Minister Molotov about the proposal before the Big Three Conference (Potsdam)."

Sato objected to Togo's strategy, apparently reading the Russians better at this time than his compatriots in Tokyo. "Yesterday," the analysts note, "Foreign Minister Togo sent the following brief communication to Sato, referring to the Ambassador's two messages of protest, and his own previous instructions [saying]: 'Your opinions notwithstanding, please carry out my orders.' Shortly thereafter, Togo sent this follow-up message to Sato: 'Russia is now reaching the point where she will give basic consideration to her relations with Japan and is particularly concerned about Japan's policy toward Manchukuo either because of her own interest in that area or because of her relations with China and America. Therefore, bringing up the matter of Manchukuo's neutralization may draw the Russians out and induce them to carry on

---

17. SRS 1724, 10 July 1945.

conversations with us. In any case our proposal is not confined to this problem alone, and we are willing to discuss other matters as well, if the Russians wish it. Please bear this in mind, do your best to carry out our plans and reply as to the results.' "

Two days later, the first item in the Magic Summary is headlined: *"Japanese peace move."* On July 11, Togo sends Sato an "extremely urgent" message, saying: "We are now secretly giving consideration to the termination of the war because of the pressing situation which confronts Japan both at home and abroad. Therefore, when you have your interview with Molotov (in accordance with previous instructions) you should not confine yourself to the objective of rapprochement between Russia and Japan but should also sound him out on the extent to which it is possible to make use of Russia in ending the war.

"As for our proposal that we pledge mutual support in the maintenance of peace over a long period [this is in reference to the proposal made by ex-premier Hirota to Ambassador Malik on June 29], that should be put forward in conjunction with sounding out Russia's attitude toward Japan; in connection with the abrogation of Japan's fishing rights, we are prepared to seek Russia's favor through amendment to the Portsmouth Treaty. Note also the fact that we will consent to discuss other matters and will meet Russia's wishes on a broad scale. While we naturally hope to obtain a treaty through negotiations between Hirota and Malik, those talks are also intended to find out the extent to which it is possible to make use of Russia in ending the war.

"We would like to know the views of the Russian government on this subject with all haste. *Furthermore, the Imperial Court is tremendously interested in this matter.* Furthermore, so please have an interview with Molotov . . . attempt to sound out the Russians' views and reply at once. While there is no question as to your skill, please be careful in your conference to avoid giving the impression that our plan is to make use of the Russians in ending our war." (Emphasis added.)

Rarely has a diplomat been given a more demanding assignment of finding out a lot of information while giving only a little. And, for the first time, the Imperial Court is injected into the proceedings. But overall, Togo's strategy of leading from weakness to strength is the complete opposite of how successful negotiations are handled. It is also an act of folly. Sato recognizes this. Why cannot Togo see the same?

A little later on the same day, Togo sends Sato another "extremely urgent" message, reading: "Despite the last statement in my previous message, it would appear suitable to make clear to the Russians our general attitude with regard to the termination of the war. Therefore, please tell them that: 'We consider the maintenance of peace in East Asia to be one aspect of world peace. Accordingly, Japan—as a proposal for ending the war and because of her establishment and maintenance of lasting peace—has absolutely no idea of annexing or holding the territories she occupied during the war.'

"We should like you to have the interview with Molotov in a day or two. Please reply at once as to his answer."

Reading this message from the vantage point of those in Washington, the Americans would be bound to ask: Who the heck does Togo think he is? His nation is defeated. He's taking his population over the cliff down the abyss with him. Yet here he is demanding that Molotov dance a ballet for him. . . .

Meanwhile, the analysts note that this series of messages is the closest that Japan has come to saying that it hopes to obtain Russia's good offices in arranging a peace. Even though the Japanese diplomats are not supposed to say this. . . . The analysts seem to appreciate the subtle humor of Malik's earlier statement to Hirota when the Russian ambassador says: "Since Russia is not a belligerent in the East, His Excellency Mr. Hirota must be well aware that peace there does not depend on Russia."

The same day's Magic Summary contains the report Ambassador Sato makes late on the night of July 10 about his conversation with Vice Commissar Lozovsky. (Sato doubted he could see Molotov before he left for Potsdam.) Sato says he urged an "immediate reply" to the proposal former premier Hirota had made to Ambassador Malik. The reply from Lozovsky is: "It is naturally difficult to predict what my government's reply will be, but we shall do our best to comply with your wishes."

For the moment, then, Russia will say nothing.

✖ ✖ ✖

There are certain elements of black humor in the Magic Summaries. One occurs at this point when Turkish ambassador Menemencioglu reports on a conversation held in late June with General Catroux, the French ambassador to Russia.[18] According to Catroux: "Stalin himself is the most moderate element in Russia." (One imagines the hollow laughter from the millions of victims of his purges.)

---

18. Ibid.

According to the French ambassador the real problem is that "very ambitious men are grouped around [Stalin], and the future frontier which those men want to draw around Russia is so wide it could not be effaced. . . . Only the existing military equilibrium is protecting Europe today from the worst consequences. That equilibrium results from (1) the air superiority of the Americans and the British and (2) the 5.5 million experienced German troops who are in their hands. The Russians well know that these prisoners, together with the great material potential of the Americans, constitute a reserve of strength. However, if the Far Eastern war lasts very long—as it unfortunately will—one must assume that the Americans and the British, especially the Americans, will send a greater force to the Far East and that will cause the Russians to cast off their comparative moderation.

"Stalin proposed the Soviet-French alliance and got General de Gaulle and M. Bidault to accept the text prepared by the Russians, word for word, without discussion of a single point. The alliance may be considered a success of Soviet policy and no credit is due the French government."

✖ ✖ ✖

The following day, Foreign Minister Togo sends another "very urgent" message to Ambassador Sato that increases the stakes in the Japanese peace move.[19] In an imperious tone, Togo says: "I have not yet received your wire about your interview with Molotov. Accordingly, although it may smack a little of attacking without adequate reconnaissance, we think it would be appropriate to go a step further on this occasion and, before the opening of the Three Power Conference, inform the Russians of the Imperial will concerning the ending of the war. We should, therefore, like you to present this matter to Molotov in the following terms:

" 'His Majesty the Emperor, mindful of the fact that the present war daily brings greater evil and sacrifice upon the peoples of all belligerent powers, desires from his heart that it may be quickly terminated. But so long as England and the United States insist upon unconditional surrender, the Japanese Empire has no alternative but to fight on with all its strength for the honor and existence of the Motherland. His Majesty is deeply reluctant to have any further blood lost

---

19. SRS 1727, 13 July 1945.

among the people of both sides, and it is his desire for the welfare of humanity to restore peace with all possible speed.'

"The Emperor's will, as expressed above, arises not only from his benevolence toward his own subjects but from his concern for the welfare of humanity in general. It is the Emperor's private intention to send Prince Konoye to Moscow as a Special Envoy with a letter from him containing the statements made above. Please inform Molotov of this and get the Russians' consent to having the party enter the country. (I shall telegraph the names and members of the party later.)

"Although it will be impossible for this delegation to get there before the big men in Moscow leave for the Three Power Conference, we must arrange for a meeting immediately after their return. Accordingly, I should like to have the trip made by plane, if possible. Please try to arrange for a Russian plane to go as far as Man-chou-li or Tsitsihar [in northwest and north-central Manchukuo respectively]."

If the Emperor is really this interested in peace, why is the offer being made via the back door in Moscow? Why not go directly to the Americans? Conversely, if the Americans possess this knowledge—that the Emperor wants peace but not unconditional surrender—how should they act vis-à-vis Stalin at Potsdam about the matter?

Should the Americans take it upon themselves to offer, say via Switzerland, the possibility that there is a way around the problem about the Emperor's postwar role? Cool thinking prevails. First, the atomic bomb hasn't even been tested. It might not work. What happens then? Second, if the Americans even hint at the discussions being held between Japan and Russia, the word will get out that the Japanese ciphers have been compromised. America will lose the most vital secret of the war. (It would appear that the Russians do know about the breaking of the Japanese ciphers, but the U.S. at this point has no clear evidence that they do.) We also need to know if the Russians and Japanese will join forces to create a new force in Asia. Third, and most important, the invasion of Japan is yet to take place. Nothing must be done that will jeopardize our men who will hit the beaches of Japan. Their safety is paramount.

Washington is caught in a bind. It knows too much and can do too little. It is similar to Marshall's analogy of the agonies he endures knowing that he can warn an American convoy to turn away from Japanese submarines and avoid a costly attack. But he doesn't do so for fear of compromising Magic. The proper diplomatic move belongs to Japan. The ball is in her court. All Marshall and the others can do is hope and pray that the Japanese make the proper decision.

✖ ✖ ✖

The same day's Magic Summary reveals that Sato did manage to see Molotov on July 11, but at the time of the conference, he hadn't received Togo's latest instructions to find out if the Russians would help Japan make peace.

So much for the importance of timing.

This means that Sato can only ask Molotov about the proposal for improving Russo-Japanese relations that Hirota submitted to Malik. Molotov is noncommittal, saying that a detailed report on the matter has not yet been received. This is a major diplomatic warning, a solid indication that things might not be going well for Tokyo in Moscow. But it sinks like a stone in Togo's office, without leaving even a trace of a ripple.

The illogical position the Japanese are taking is reinforced the next day. Sato's replies to Togo's latest messages about the Emperor's thinking crosses Marshall's desk.[20] These messages, sent from Moscow on July 12 and 13, reveal that (a) as of the morning of July 13, Sato intended to try to see Molotov to present the Emperor's peace plea before Molotov could leave for Potsdam, and (b) Sato is pessimistic for the success of such a move unless the Japanese government is prepared to accept terms "virtually equivalent to unconditional surrender."

The analysts tell Marshall that some of Sato's message is missing. What is available says: "I received your [two] messages of 11 July immediately after I had reported to you on my July 12 interview with Molotov. I realize that the gist of your idea is a basic sounding out of the Russians on the possibility of using them in ending the war.

"In my frank opinion, it is no exaggeration to say that the Russians are not attracted by the proposals which former premier Hirota made to Ambassador Malik and that there is no hope that they will meet our terms. [Such proposals] run completely counter to the Russians' foreign policy, as I have explained in detail on numerous occasions. Moreover, if I were to try to find out to what extent the Russians could be used in ending the war on the basis of your proposals, it should be clear from the report of my interview with Molotov that I would be unable to achieve such a purpose.

"Furthermore, the reasoning in your messages of 11 July consists

---

20. SRS 1728, 14 July 1945.

of nothing more than academic fine phrases. With regard to your reference to 'the maintenance of peace in East Asia [as] one aspect of the maintenance of world peace,' it is indeed unfortunate that Japan is no longer in a position where she can be responsible for peace in East Asia—now that the Anglo-Americans may be about to wrest from us the power to maintain this peace and even the Japanese mainland has been reduced to such a critical state.''

The next section of the message is missing. But one has to admire Sato. He may have made an error of judgment earlier about Russia's being friendly to Japan. Now, when the real crunch of diplomacy counts every second, he doesn't hesitate to tell his superior, Foreign Minister Togo, that the Government's plan ''consists of nothing more than academic fine phrases.'' Which brings up yet another point. If the best of the Japanese diplomats abroad cannot comprehend what the Japanese government intends to do, or even what it wishes to do, how can anyone else, such as the Americans and the British, figure out what the Japanese government is really thinking? It looks as if the war will have to be played out to the bitter end.

Sato's next words drop some important information on Washington about the internal problems in Japan. He says to Togo: ''Having no accurate information about the present state of our military operations, I am in no position to reach any definite conclusions about these vital problems; not to mention the fact that I have learned that positive plans were resolved upon at the conference in the Imperial Presence during the early part of June.''

At this point, the analysts in Washington prepare an extremely important note for Marshall. They point out that ''the Japanese phrase for 'conference in the Imperial Presence' is *Gozen Kaigi,* which is used by the Japanese to refer to that type of Imperial Conference which is convoked only during periods of serious crisis in foreign affairs. Such conferences were held before Japan's entrance into the Russo-Japanese and the First World War, before her adherence to the Tripartite Pact and probably also before Pearl Harbor;[21] others have been concerned with the China Incident, and with Japan's policy toward Russia in 1941 and 1942. *There has been no previous indication that such a conference was held early in June.*'' (Emphasis added.)

This final statement is most important. Historians have claimed for

---

21. If it could be proven that a similar Imperial Conference was held prior to Pearl Harbor, then Emperor Hirohito would have to be called a "war criminal," because he would then have agreed to the sneak attack and the waging of war in the Pacific.

many years that the Allies knew on June 22 that Emperor Hirohito told the Supreme Council that steps must be taken that would lead to peace. In real time, however, the information is not revealed by Magic until July 14, and Sato pinpoints the exact date of the Imperial Conference as being June 8 (SRS 1730, 16 July 1945), which is more than a month earlier.

Contrary to what historians have claimed, all the Americans know is that during this time the government of Japan has offered to align itself militarily with Russia to create *"a force unequaled in the world."* Also, one of the most senior diplomats in service, Ambassador Sato, is telling the Japanese government that its statements about seeking peace resemble only "academic fine phrases."

Therefore, historians who claim that America knew a month earlier, i.e., on June 22 or earlier, that the Japanese intended to seek peace have had their claims disproved by the war's most accurate record: the Magic Diplomatic Summaries as they cross the desk of Chief of Staff Marshall in chronological order.

Sato's message to Togo continues: "Assuming that since that [Imperial] conference the course of the war has brought us to a real extremity, the Government should make that decision. Once that resolve has been taken, there may be some hope of getting the Russian Government into motion and obtaining its good offices in terminating the war. There can be no doubt, however, that the situation which we would face in that event would be virtually equivalent to unconditional surrender.

"I have expressed my views frankly, and I fear that I must apologize for the unceremoniousness of my words. I am filled with thoughts of fear and heartbreak at the knowledge that even the Imperial Court is concerned with this, but we must face the facts of the international situation without flinching and I have therefore reported these facts as they are. I send this message in the belief that it is my first responsibility to prevent the harboring of illusions which are at variance with reality. I beg your indulgence."

With these words Sato proves himself one of Japan's most devoted and clear-thinking servants. If only the Japanese military possessed the same acumen and understanding.

The analysts again point out to Marshall that early the next day—yesterday [the thirteenth]—Sato advised Togo that his message conveying the Emperor's plea had been received at 1 A.M. (Moscow time) and went on to say: "Although the date of Molotov's departure for Berlin is drawing extremely close, I shall do my best to fulfill your instructions. If, by any chance, I cannot get an interview, I will convey the Emperor's wishes before Molotov's departure for the Three Power Conference.''

Later on the thirteenth, note the analysts, Sato sends an additional message of comment to Togo, the first half of which reads: "Although I imagine that the Russians will agree to our proposal to send a Special Envoy [Prince Konoye] to Moscow, it is difficult to say anything until we actually receive their reply. However, if they should agree to this, it is entirely out of the question to limit the functions of the Special Envoy to sounding out the extent to which we might make use of the Russians in ending the war or to presenting an abstract exposition—as suggested in your message of 11 July.

"I kneel in veneration before the exalted solicitude of His Majesty for the restoration of peace as conveyed in your message of 12 July, and I resign myself to his will with deep feelings of awe. Nevertheless, if the proposal of the Japanese Government, brought by a Special Envoy at the Emperor's particular desire, goes no further than we have gone in the past, if it is to be a proposal that contains only abstract words and lacks concreteness—we shall uselessly disappoint the expectations of the authorities in this country. More than that, we shall generate feelings of dissatisfaction at our Government's lack of good faith and thus bring evil even upon the Imperial Household. I feel very serious anxiety on this point.'' (The second part of the message is missing, say the analysts.)

✖ ✖ ✖

On July 15, two days before the Potsdam Conference is to begin, the Magic Diplomatic Summary reveals that, on the thirteenth, Sato advises Tokyo that he tried to meet with Molotov to transmit the Emperor's plea for peace.[22] He was told, however, that Molotov "simply could not manage it.'' Instead, Sato should confer with Vice Commissar Lozovsky. The Ambassador's message goes on to say:

"I therefore went to see Lozovsky at 5 P.M. on the thirteenth. I had previously translated the Imperial instructions into Russian and had included them in a confidential letter from me to Molotov, in which I also mentioned His Majesty's private intention of sending Prince Konoye [to Moscow]. I presented this letter to Lozovsky and asked him

---

22. SRS 1729, 15 July 1945.

to convey it to Molotov at once. I also requested that the Russian Government consent to the Prince's coming and asked in that event the Russians provide an airplane and other facilities. The conversation then proceeded as follows—

"*Sato:* I should like the Russian Government to bear particularly in mind the fact that the present Special Envoy will be of an entirely different character from the Special Envoy I have discussed with Molotov in the past; this time the Envoy will be sent at the particular desire of His Majesty."

The analysts in Washington note for Marshall the significance of Sato's words in reference to special envoys in the past: "On the first two of these occasions—in the fall of 1943 and in April 1944—the Japanese were apparently attempting to bring about a German-Russian peace. On the third occasion—in September 1944—the ostensible purpose of the Japanese move was to improve Russo-Japanese relations, although there were some indications in the traffic that the Japanese hoped to obtain a general world peace. Each of the three overtures were rejected by the Russians." (MS 20 April 1944; DS 20 September 1944.)

"*Sato:* The Japanese Government wishes to know with all speed of the Russian Government's agreement to this proposal, even if it only an agreement in principle. I should, therefore, like to have an answer before Molotov's departure, if that is possible. We wish to arrange things so that the Special Envoy can meet with the Russian authorities as soon as possible after their return from Berlin.

"*Lozovsky:* To whom in the Russian Government is the Japanese Emperor's message addressed?

"*Sato:* The message communicates His Majesty's private intentions and is not addressed to anyone in particular. However, we should like to have Mr. Molotov communicate it to Mr. Kalin, the head of the Soviet Union, and to Mr. Stalin, the Chairman of the Council of People's Commissars.

"*Lozovsky:* I can understand that the Japanese Government is in some haste about this matter and I should like to satisfy your desire for a speedy reply. The fact is, however, that some members of the Government are supposed to be leaving this very night, so it will really be impossible to make any reply before Molotov's departure.

"*Sato:* We shall have to think about making preparations for the Special Envoy's party. If we are too late to get a reply before Molotov's departure, then I should like you, if possible, to get in touch with Berlin by telephone or the like, and give us an answer.

"*Lozovsky:* I will certainly try to do this, and in any event will forward your letter to Molotov without loss of time."

Early in the morning of July 14, Sato sends a further report to Tokyo saying: "In the dead of night on the thirteenth, Generalov, the head of the Japanese Section of the Foreign Commissariat, sent the following message to me from Lozovsky—'Because of the departure of Stalin and Molotov a reply will be delayed. Therefore, please understand.' "

✖ ✖ ✖

On July 16, the day before the Potsdam Conference begins, the Magic Summary notes for Marshall that on the previous day, Foreign Minister Togo asked Sato to "please send us a reply message as to when Stalin and Molotov left." Apparently Sato reports everything to Togo before receiving Togo's request, because he says: "It appears that Stalin and Molotov left Moscow for Berlin on the evening of the fourteenth. Therefore, so far as I can surmise, despite the fact that they probably had at least half a day remaining before their departure, they avoided making any reply other than the tentative statement that they were delaying their answer. . . . It therefore appears doubtful that we will be able to obtain a prompt reply."

Sato goes on to list four "probable" reasons for hesitation on the Russians' part.

They don't know if the Special Envoy will present "a concrete plan for ending the war."

They worry that Japan seeks a "negotiated peace."

They don't want to hurt their Anglo-American relations "at a critical moment when cooperation between the three countries is needed more than ever."

Last, they may have to get the agreement of the British and the Americans to allow the Special Envoy to come to Moscow. Sato says: "Perhaps Stalin believes that it will be impossible to determine the Russian attitude until he has informed the British and American authorities of the recent Japanese communications and has learned their views."

At this point the analysts in Washington note for Marshall the sticky point about whether or not the Russians will mention their discussions with the Japanese. The analysts stress that "on 12 July, Tokyo instructed Sato to ask the Russians to 'maintain absolute secrecy' in connection with the peace move, but it was not clear whether Tokyo wanted secrecy maintained on all aspects of the matter, nor did it appear whether Tokyo wanted the Russians to keep the matter secret from Anglo-American officials as well as from the general public. Sato's report of his 13 July conference with Lozovsky did not specify what, if anything, he said about maintaining secrecy; and the above remarks suggest that he may not have said anything to discourage the Russians from mentioning the subject to the Anglo-Americans.''

This perceptive comment by the analysts in Washington underlines what a huge burden of disclosure has effectively been placed on the shoulders of the Russians. How will they play their hand at Potsdam? For on this day, in Alamogordo, New Mexico, under the code name TRINITY, the Americans explode the first nuclear bomb in an awesome test that signifies the downfall of the Japanese Empire.

✖ ✖ ✖

As if to highlight the sense of impending doom facing Japan, on this same day Sato continues his report to Tokyo saying: ''In connection with the subject of a 'negotiated peace' mentioned above, we must remember that the Americans and the British—particularly the for-mer—have always opposed the making of a negotiated peace in both the European and Pacific wars. Furthermore, since Russia herself in-sisted upon the unconditional surrender of Germany—spurring on the Anglo-Americans to open the second front and finally defeating Ger-many with their cooperation—it will obviously be extremely difficult to obtain Russia's support for any proposal concerning negotiation of a peace treaty.

''Leaving aside Japan's sincere desire for the termination of the war, I believe that in the long run she has no choice but to accept unconditional surrender or terms closely equivalent thereto.

''I would like to point out, however, that even on the basis of your various messages I have obtained no clear idea of the recent situation. Nor am I clear about the views of the Government and of the military with regard to the termination of the war. Moreover, I have been of the opinion that, if it were finally decided to bring the war to an end, it would be necessary to obtain a new formal resolution which would be sufficient to overrule the decision reached at the conference held in the Imperial Presence on 8 June, but this has not been done.''

The analysts break in here to point out to Marshall that ''in his

12 July message (DS 14, 15 July 1945), Sato had referred to 'positive plans' which he understood had been 'resolved on at the conference during the early part of June.' In that message—as above—his remarks seem to imply that the 'plans' did not contemplate making an unconditional surrender.''

Sato goes on to tell Tokyo: "Now, if the Special Envoy does not bear concrete terms as mentioned above, I am fearful lest he should be dispatched with the approval of the Russians only to achieve unsatisfactory results in the end. Please consider the facts presented in this wire along with those in my previous messages, and if it is formally decided to send the Envoy, I sincerely pray that resolution be passed by the Cabinet to have the Envoy take with him a concrete plan for the termination of the war.''

It is now painfully clear to the British and the Americans that the peace feelers the Japanese have been floating toward Moscow in the last month, and the mind-set revealed by them, fall dismally short of what the Allies believe is necessary to end the war in a way that will insure peace in the Far East.

As the Potsdam conference opens, a quick summary of what has been learned from the Magic Diplomatic intercepts is in order. In no particular order, the list shows:

1. The Japanese are trying to make a deal with Russia. The most extreme element of the proposal is the linkage of Russo-Japanese military strength to create "a force unequaled in this world.''

2. At the same time Ambassador Sato has been pressing the Japanese case in Moscow, Foreign Commissar Molotov has also been meeting with Chinese Communist leaders in the Kremlin. Sato has been pointing out in his messages to Tokyo that one of the greatest dangers facing Japan is the possibility of Russia signing a pact of "friendship'' with the Chinese Communists.

3. Besides meeting with Chinese Communist leaders, Molotov has also been meeting with Communists from Manchukuo. No one knows, however, what the substance of the talks with the latter two groups has been.

4. Studies prepared at this time by the U.S. Navy's experts point out that the Soviet military buildup in the Far East is creating a huge military force far superior to what the Japanese have in the area. The Navy studies also state that Russia has the "legal right'' to attack Japan

whenever she wishes, because Japan has consistently violated the Russo-Japanese Neutrality Agreement throughout the war by helping the Germans. Thus, the U.S. Navy
predicts that Russia will attack Japan in the Far East seeking to right the many humiliations the Japanese have inflicted on the Soviet Union over the course of history.[23]

The Navy strategists also point out that Japan has consistently been
trying to push Russia's borders westward so that she could not threaten
Japan's three-hundred-year-old dream of driving through Korea and
Manchuria for the ultimate conquest of China. According to the Navy,
the "Divine Mission" of Japan is contained in two simple words:
"Conquer barbarians (foreigners)." By evolution this became the
"Continental Policy" (the conquest of Asia via Korea and Manchuria)
and, eventually, the "Tanka Memorial" (world domination). The U.S.
Navy determines that at this point in history the Japanese military is
firmly in control of the Japanese government. No diplomatic negotiations will be allowed by the Japanese military that will change the way
the military controls Japan—and the Emperor. To put it bluntly: Japan
will fight to the end.

On this pessimistic note, the Americans go to Potsdam.

✖ ✖ ✖

According to historical records, Secretary of War Stimson is the American at Potsdam who receives the first word that the test of the atomic
bomb in New Mexico is successful. At lunch the next day, Stimson
breaks the news to Churchill, who wants the news kept from Stalin.
Later the same day, it is alleged that Stalin tells Churchill that he has
received a message from the Japanese, supposedly from the Emperor,
about the possibility of surrender, but that there has been no mention
of unconditional surrender.

At this time, the invasion of Japan is still scheduled for November
1, which is about three and a half months away. The first American

---

23. SRH-077 Sino-Soviet Relations (1 June 1945), Publication of Pacific Strategic Intelligence
Section; SRH-078 Russo-Japanese Relations (April–May 1945); SRH-079 Russo-Japanese Rela-
tions (June 1945) dated 2 July 1945; SRH-071 Abrogation of the Soviet-Japanese Neutrality
Pact; SRH-075 Japanese Reaction to Germany Defeat, 21 May 1945.

troops from the European theater have boarded troop ships and sailed for the Far East. Meanwhile, the discord between the Big Three erupts.

Truman is meeting Stalin for the first time. It is also the American president's introduction to the postwar problems inherent in agreements reached between America, England and Russia during the war. There are problems between the Big Three as regards to Vienna, Austria, Berlin, Poland, Greece, the Balkans, Hungary, Rumania and Bulgaria. Agreement for wartime reparations from Germany cannot be reached. Each power will handle the matter differently within its own zone of occupation. Stalin is also making demands for major concessions in Manchuria and the Chinese have told Washington that these demands are not acceptable. Some Americans want the Soviets to intervene there against Japan, others do not. (This split among the Americans is exacerbated by the fact that hardly anyone in the American delegation knows the whole picture of the Magic Diplomatic Summaries, or about the atomic bomb.)

By July 21, a full report of the awesome power of the bomb is given to Secretary Stimson. He then gives the report to Marshall, then to Truman and his adviser, James F. Byrnes. The bomb is far, far more powerful than anyone had imagined. The following day, Churchill notes that "Truman had been much fortified by something that had happened and that he stood up to the Russian in a most emphatic and decisive manner."[24]

Later, after reaching agreement with the British on the matter, Truman gives Stalin a camouflaged description of the new weapon. According to witnesses, including Churchill, Stalin doesn't blink an eye at the news and says merely that he hopes America uses it well. Onlookers cannot tell whether or not Stalin is surprised. Fifty years after the fact, however, one can safely say that from his spy network, Stalin is already fully briefed about the bomb, but he fails to comprehend its diplomatic significance until after Hiroshima.

On July 24, 1945, still at Potsdam, Stimson reports to Truman that, after further conversations with General Marshall, the Chief of Staff now believes there is no need to request Russian aid against Japan. The two men discuss the date for which the first atomic bomb might be dropped on Japan (they agree that it will be after about August 3), also the question of warning Japan about her fate and the possibility of reassuring the Japanese that the role of the Emperor might be continued

---

24. Henry L. Stimson, *Diary*, 21 July 1945.

if Japan were willing to surrender. Meanwhile, Stalin's advice is to reject the peace proposal the Japanese have floated via Moscow.

Churchill, Truman and the representative of China now agree to send a message to Japan. (Russia is not involved in this exchange, because she is not a "belligerent" in the Far East.) The Allies warn Japan that the Japanese will suffer what happened to Germany unless Tokyo takes this opportunity to end the war. If the Japanese cannot follow "the path of reason," it will mean "the inevitable and complete destruction of the Japanese forces, and just as inevitably the utter devastation of the Japanese homeland."

The Allies say "we shall brook no delay" and that there are no alternatives. Those who have "deceived and misled" the people of Japan will have to be "eliminated for all time." The military will be disarmed, Japanese sovereignty will be restricted to the four main islands of Japan, the four freedoms of the Atlantic Charter will be established (freedom of speech, freedom of worship, freedom from fear, freedom from want). The message ends: "We call upon the Government of Japan to proclaim now the unconditional surrender of all the Japanese armed forces, and to provide proper and adequate assurances of their good faith in such action. The alternative for Japan is complete and utter destruction."

The following day, Prime Minister Churchill and Clement Attlee, his deputy in the wartime government and head of the British Labor Party, go home to England for the general election. In a bizarre quirk of fate, the man who led England through the war is defeated in a landslide victory for Labor. Attlee returns to Potsdam; Churchill does not.

Roosevelt is dead. Churchill is voted out of power. The Empire of Japan is about to vanish. The age of nuclear politics is born.

✖ ✖ ✖

Unaware of the atom bomb, but alerted by Magic/Ultra intelligence to the build-up of the Japanese defenses for the home islands during June, MacArthur's medical staff now revises its need for hospital beds upward by 300 percent. Brig. Gen. Guy Denit, MacArthur's chief surgeon, estimates that for the invasion of Kyushu *alone* that in 60 days there will be 56,000 battle casualties and 121,000 nonbattle casualties. For 120 days, Denit estimates a total of 395,000 casualties (126,000 battle casualties and 269,000 nonbattle casualties). Similar estimates for Navy and Marine Corps casualties are unavailable. (It is understood that Japanese casualties, military and civilian, would have been higher.) All told there is little difference between a man's being mangled in combat or mangled when freight shifts aboard a landing craft—except for the Purple Heart.[25]

---

25. Via Sam Halpern courtesy of Stanley L. Falk, former historian for the Army/Defense Department, who had access to the unpublished *U.S. Army Medical History,* Pacific.

20

ith a preliminary date of August 3, 1945, set for the dropping of the first nuclear weapon against mankind, with the knowledge that the Japanese have been warned that the alternative to surrender is "complete and utter destruction" of their homeland, only one question remains: Do the Japanese ever give any indication that they will accept the Allies' terms? We know from the historical record that, on July 28, Premier Susuki of Japan tells the press in Tokyo that the ultimatum issued at Potsdam is to be ignored. But what about the secrets hidden in the Japanese diplomatic traffic?

Let us examine this secret record, beginning on the first day of the Potsdam Conference, up until the dropping of the bomb. For here is the ultimately damning testimony, as presented in the Magic Diplomatic Summaries, and spoken by the Japanese themselves, proving that Japanese intransigence leads to the tragedy of Hiroshima and Nagasaki.

The first page of the Magic Diplomatic Summary for July 18, 1945,[1] has as its headline: *"Tokyo says no to unconditional surrender."* "On 17 July, Foreign Minister Togo sent the following message to Ambassador Sato:

" 'We have been fully aware from the outset that it would be difficult under existing circumstances either to strengthen the ties of friendship between Japan and Russia or to make effective use of Russia in ending the war. The present situation, however, is such that we have no recourse but to make efforts along those lines, and we cannot be satisfied merely with keeping Russia from entering the war against Japan. We have therefore decided to recognize the Russians' wishes on a broad scale in order to obtain their favor. Negotiations for that pur-

---

1. SRS 1732, 18 July 1945.

pose are necessary [word uncertain, possibly "prerequisite"] for soliciting Russia's good offices in concluding the war and also for improving the basis for negotiations with America and England.

" 'Although the directing powers, and the Government as well, are convinced that our war strength can still deliver considerable blows to the enemy, we are unable to feel an absolutely secure peace of mind in the face of an enemy who will attack repeatedly. If, today, when we are still maintaining our strength, the Anglo-Americans were to have regard for Japan's honor and existence, they could save humanity by bringing the war to an end. If, however, they insist unrelentingly upon unconditional surrender, the Japanese are unanimous in their resolve to wage a thoroughgoing war.

" 'The Emperor himself has deigned to express his determination and we have therefore made this request of the Russians. Please bear particularly in mind, however, that we are not asking the Russians' mediation in anything like unconditional surrender.

" 'It is extremely vital that we obtain the Russians' consent in the sending of a Special Envoy as quickly as possible; so please endeavor through Lozovsky to obtain that consent.' "

It is difficult to believe that the Japanese military—and the Emperor—can delude themselves so thoroughly that, at this point in the war, they believe they are in a strong enough position to propose peace terms to the Allies. But this is the case. No wonder then that Stalin tells the Allies to forget the peace overtures floating toward Moscow from Tokyo. "Use the bomb well," Stalin is reported as saying. He might well have added that the leaders of Japan are not living in the real world.

As for the historians who go around protesting that the Allies should take the word of the Japanese that "if . . . when we are still maintaining our strength [which is a lie], the Anglo-Americans were to have regard for Japan's honor and existence, they could save humanity by bringing the war to an end," there is only one response. The only people who now should be worried about Japan's honor and existence are Emperor Hirohito and his military leaders. It is they who have put Japan in the position where unconditional surrender is being demanded by the Allies. If these leaders cannot comprehend this, they are beyond hope. And as for those who claim it is up to the Allies to offer terms acceptable to the Japanese, one can only point out that you can only deal with an enemy such as Japan by the ruthless application of power. During four long years of fighting in the Pacific, the Japanese themselves taught the Americans how to negotiate surrender. A lot of green

American troops were killed by Japanese pretending to surrender or pretending to be wounded or dead. The survivors have learned their lessons well.

They have good reasons to believe the Japanese are not going "to lose face" by acknowledging to the Anglo-Americas that they cannot win. It is the Japanese themselves who make this all too clear. If the Japanese had legitimately approached the western Allies seeking peace at this time, or even after the Potsdam declaration, it is the author's conviction that they would have been spared nuclear destruction. But, as we will see, the Japanese military will continue to refuse to acknowledge reality.

Meanwhile the same day's Diplomatic Summary shows that the Chinese Communists have begun operating more openly in Manchukuo and are increasing their guerrilla activities in north China. And the economic specialists in Washington are predicting that the Japanese home island of Honshu is about to be cut off from its supply of coal by virtue of American submarine and bomber attacks. The specialists conclude this will bring "munitions and rail production on Honshu to a virtual standstill."

It is not for several days that the British and Americans learn Moscow's answer to the latest peace proposal floated by Tokyo.[2] On July 19, Ambassador Sato informs his government that "on the evening of the eighteenth, I received a personal letter from Lozovsky, the content of which is as follows. . . . 'In the name of the Soviet Government I have the honor to call Your Excellency's attention to the fact that the intentions expressed in the Japanese Emperor's message are general in form and contain no specific proposals. It is the Soviet Government's view that the mission of Prince Konoye, the Special Envoy, is in no way made clear and that it is impossible for the Soviet Government to give a definite reply to the Japanese Emperor's message or in regard to the [proposed mission of the] Special Envoy, Prince Konoye, mentioned in your letter of 13 July.' "

This causes Sato, later on July 19, to send a "very urgent" follow-up message saying: "It is extremely regrettable that the Russian Government has expressed its disapproval of the plan for dispatching a Special Envoy on the ground that the Envoy's mission has not been made concrete. This, however, confirms my humble opinion that we have no alternative but to present the Russians with a concrete plan. I have given consideration to your views outlined in your 17 July mes-

---

2. SRS 1734, 20 July 1945.

sage [which, the analysts point out to Marshall, said that if the Anglo-Americans 'insist unrelentingly upon unconditional surrender, the Japanese are *unanimous* in their resolve to wage a thoroughgoing war']. It is nevertheless hard to deny that *the Japanese authorities are out of touch with the atmosphere prevailing here.* In any event the rejection of the plan in question indicates that we cannot thus accomplish the desired objective of winning over the Russians.'' (Emphasis added.)

Also available in the same Magic Summary is Sato's reply of July 18 to Togo's message of July 17 that said that Japan would not accept unconditional surrender. Sato's reply is ''obscurely worded,'' the analysts note for Marshall. But the essence is this: ''Except for the matter of maintenance of our national structure, I think we must absolutely not propose any conditions. The situation has already reached the point where we have no alternative but unconditional surrender or its equivalent.''

Nothing could make things clearer for the British and the Americans. The debate about unconditional surrender is being blocked at the highest levels of the Japanese government by the military, and they are supported by the Emperor. For the Allies to suggest any weakening of terms at this time would be poor negotiating strategy. At times such as these, the weaker party must make the first move. Anything else might allow the military to remain in control of Japan.

Meanwhile, in Switzerland, Japanese minister Kase is already planning for the future. He suggests that one way to protect the large amount of Japanese money in Swiss banks from possible postwar restrictions is to make payments on goods—such as machine tools and diesel engines—that will be delivered in from two to five years' time. Captain Nishihara, the Japanese counselor for naval affairs in Bern, has apparently gone ahead with negotiations for such ''peacetime'' items. He believes that even if the facts come out later about the buying spree, ''the Swiss firms will think only of their obligation to make delivery to Japan.''

One of the problems of dealing with the Magic Summaries becomes apparent on this same day in Washington with more information about the peace negotiations in Bern being uncovered too late for anything to be done by the Americans.

As the analysts note for Marshall, ''in the first week of June, Captain Nishihara, the Japanese Counselor for Naval Affairs in Bern, advised the Navy General Staff in Tokyo that Allen Dulles, OSS representative in Bern, had proposed that a 'discussion' between Japan and the U.S. be held in Switzerland and that a Japanese admiral be flown from Tokyo for that purpose.[3] Nishihara further stated that he believed the proposal was 'quite trustworthy and carries full faith.' (DS 9, 13, 14 June 1945.)

"A 6 July message from Nishihara has now been received which indicates that the Navy General Staff sent Nishihara a reply expressing its 'misgivings' because of the 'possibility of a good deal of stratagem in the other party's proposal' and ordering Nishihara *to make no reply to Dulles.* [Emphasis added.]

"In response, Nishihara states that an 'exacting investigation' has revealed 'no trace of enemy stratagem' and goes on to make the following points:

"a. 'On or about 20 May—before the proposal was made to us [on 23 and 25 May]—Dulles asked Washington for instructions as to the advisability of trying to get in touch with the Japanese naval officials in Switzerland. About 10 June, after we had been approached indirectly, Washington replied that "in principle it approves; no objections." On two subsequent occasions were told that the other party's preparations were completed and were asked whether a reply had come from Tokyo. *However, in obedience to your orders, we made no reply.'* [Emphasis added.]

"b. 'Next, Dulles returned to Washington at the President's request, probably for various preliminary arrangements, remaining there from 15 to 25 June, returning to Bern on the twenty-sixth. [According to the go-between], Dulles had [words uncertain, probably "encouraging news"] tempered with seriousness. He frankly recognized the danger of Russia becoming involved and had hopes for an early end to the war.'

"c. 'The other party, in view of the war situation, seems dumbfounded by our obstinate silence. While we cannot be sure that some enormous ruse is not involved, [we believe that] there is too much encouraging news, frankness and sincerity for this to be an enemy stratagem.' "

The analysts in Washington conclude that "Nishihara appears to ask the Tokyo authorities to reconsider or at least send him any information they might have pointing to an enemy trick.

"On 14 July Nishihara advised Tokyo that Dulles had recently left Bern to take up his duties in Germany but before going had made

---

3. Ibid. The references in the margin of the Magic messages released in 1993 indicate the problem Washington has had breaking Nishihara's communications. They are in the difficult JN cipher and the marginal references for these messages are JN-5 8859-G and JN-5 8565-G.

arrangements whereby Nishihara could 'get in touch with him at any time.' "

The analysts then add a special "Note," reminding Marshall that in "yesterday's Summary, on 19 June, Chinese Minister Liang in Bern reported that, as one peace maneuver, the Japanese had arranged for 'a certain Swiss' to inquire of 'Paul Blum of the American Legation' what the Anglo-American peace terms might be. After Foreign Minister Togo had sent to Minister Kase in Bern an intercept of Liang's message, Kase denied the truth of the Japanese report and commented: 'According to our investigation, Blum is a subordinate of Dulles . . . who is searching out our activities.' "

The analysts conclude: "Nishihara has apparently told Kase nothing about his alleged contacts with Mr. Dulles."

Why, at this time, do the analysts use the term "alleged contacts" in reference to Nishihara and Dulles? Given the fact that Marshall knows that Dulles's communications are being read by the Russians, and given Stalin's anger about the earlier Dulles negotiations with the German forces in Italy, a scene Washington does not want replayed about Japan, the obvious answer is that Dulles's conversations with the Japanese are unauthorized by the American Chief of Staff. After all, Dulles is supposedly doing "secret" work. The problem is that his work isn't "secret." Too many nations know about it.

The next day's Magic Summary contains comments by Ambassador Sato on Allied strategy.[4] Sato warns that the enemy will not only bombard our shores, "but will also attempt to deprive our people of the very means of subsistence." He warns that the Allies understand the value of the coming autumn rice harvest. He says: "The enemy may well ascertain when the rice fields throughout Japan are dry . . . and devise a scheme for reducing these fields to ashes in one fell swoop. . . . If we lose this autumn's harvest, we will be confronted with absolute famine and will be unable to continue the war."

The analysts note for Marshall's attention that "rice fields in Japan are normally drained three or four weeks before harvesting. The stalks are cut when still green and are then left in the fields to dry for about a week before being threshed." Harvesting will not begin until mid-September.

The same Summary contains another message from Captain Nishihara.[5] In a message of July 16, the analysts note that Nishihara "now

---

4. SRS 1735, 21 July 1945.
5. Ibid. This JN reference is JN-5 9319-G CCG.

states that the go-between in this affair had a talk with Geron von Gaevernitz—described as Dulles's 'private secretary,' and an American of German origin, and a close friend of the go-between since 1940— just before von Gaevernitz accompanied Dulles to his new post in July." (A footnote identifies von Gaevernitz as having worked closely with Dulles in the negotiations for the surrender of the German forces in Italy.) The message appears to quote von Gaevernitz substantially as follows:

" 'With the turn in the war situation, the Government and people of Japan face critical times which may affect Japan's national structure. The matter was apparently discussed when Dulles returned to Washington in June in response to Truman's summons. It appears that the U.S. leaders are of the opinion that the Japanese national structure is not to be upset. However, in view of the necessity for consulting with Great Britain and China, no secret agreement or communication appears possible at the present time.

" 'Although discussions between Dulles and General Wolff with regard to the surrender of the German forces in North Italy extended over a period of several months, the negotiations advanced as far as the signing [on 29 April] without Hitler's cognizance. Furthermore, although the surrender terms were unconditional, covertly they contained mitigating conditions.' "

Nishihara goes on to say that Dulles believes his security is airtight.[6] The Japanese naval captain says he will send Tokyo his interpretation of von Gaevernitz's statement in a separate message. (The analysts note the message is not yet available for Marshall to read.)

Apparently, up to three days before the orders are cut to drop the atomic bomb on Japan, the Americans are attempting to negotiate a peace with Japan. Whether or not these negotiations are officially sanctioned or not becomes irrelevant. Because the Diplomatic Summaries prove that the Americans are rebuffed at every turn.

It is also on this day that a special courier from Washington arrives in Potsdam with a special report for Secretary of War Stimson. The test of the atomic bomb in New Mexico proves that it has the force of fifteen thousand to twenty thousand tons of TNT, the brightness of several suns and the destructive force to level everything for a mile around it. The only question for the Americans now is this: Can the bomb be employed in time to speed up the surrender of Japan before American lives are lost in an invasion?

---

6. Robert T. Crowley rebuts Dulles's belief in his security, saying: "That's what killed the dog."

✖ ✖ ✖

With the atomic bomb's ushering in the era of nuclear diplomacy, the Magic Diplomatic Summary of July 22, 1945, seals Japan's fate.[7]

So important is this document that six pages of it are reproduced in the appendix, pages 585–90. And once again the first item marked for the attention of Chief of Staff Marshall is headlined: *"Tokyo again says no unconditional surrender; Sato pleads for peace."*

Foreign Minister Togo, upon receiving Ambassador Sato's communication with the Russian rejection of a Special Envoy's trip to Moscow, replies in haughty tones on July 21, saying:

"Special Envoy Konoye's mission will be *in obedience to the Imperial Will.* He will request assistance in bringing about an end to the war through the good offices of the Soviet Government. In this regard he will set forth positive intentions, and he will also negotiate details concerning the establishment of a cooperative relationship between Japan and Russia which will form the basis of Imperial diplomacy both during and after the war. [Emphasis added.]

"Please make the above representations to the Russians and work to obtain their concurrence in the sending of a Special Envoy.

"Please understand exactly my next wire."

Sent the same day, Togo's "next wire" reads: "With regard to unconditional surrender (I have been informed of your 18 July message[8]) *we are unable to consent to it under any circumstances whatever.* Even if the war drags on and it becomes clear that it will take much more bloodshed, the whole country as one man will pit itself against the enemy in accordance *with the Imperial Will* so long as the enemy demands unconditional surrender. It is in order to avoid such a state of affairs that we are seeking a peace which is not so-called unconditional surrender through the good offices of Russia. It is necessary that we exert ourselves so that this idea will be finally driven home to the Americans and the British. [Emphasis added.]

"Therefore, it is not only impossible for us to request the Russians to lend us their good offices in obtaining peace without conditions, but it would also be disadvantageous and impossible, from the standpoint

7. SRS 1736, 22 July 1945.

8. In this message, Sato advocated unconditional surrender provided the Imperial House is preserved (DS 20 July 1945). Togo's language in his reply to Sato is a personal rebuke in that Togo is saying that he refuses to read such defeatist words.

of foreign and domestic considerations, to make an immediate declaration of specific terms. Consequently, we hope to deal with the British and the Americans after first [a] having Prince Konoye transmit to the Russians our concrete intentions as expressed *by the Imperial Will* and [b] holding conversations with the Russians in the light of their demands in regard to East Asia. [Emphasis added.]

"In view of the fact that this is a grave matter which will decide the fate of the nation, please ask the Russians to give a full explanation of their reply, as contained in Lozovsky's letter, so as to make sure we grasp its real meaning."

Togo's imperious manner, his outrageous demands that Russia bow to Japan, his chutzpah is wrongly displayed at an inappropriate moment in history. Japan is about to be flattened by the steamroller of history. Time is running out for the Empire.

The true tragedy of Togo's messages is his undisputed confirmation that Emperor Hirohito *(the Imperial Will)* and the heads of the Japanese Army and Navy, plus Foreign Minister Togo, are so unaware of the true status of the war—whether it be conventional or atomic—that they are blindly condemning hundreds of thousands of their civilians to a horrific, unnecessary death. Fifty years after the end of World War II, it is terrifying to contemplate that the only way the German or Japanese peoples could be liberated from Nazism and militarism is that both nations and their leaders first had to be totally defeated.

Consider the difference of opinion as expressed by Togo in Tokyo as related above with the reflective words of Sato in Moscow, who now tells Togo: "In my message of 8 June, I pointed out that it would be unthinkable for us to continue the war once our fighting strength has been destroyed [DS 11 June 1945]. In the absence of Supreme Orders, our Imperial Army and the people as a whole will not, of course, lay down their arms until the last mile has literally been reached. Nevertheless, all our officers, soldiers, and civilians—who have already lost their fighting strength because of the absolute superior incendiary bombing of the enemy—cannot save the Imperial House by dying a glorious death on the field of battle. When we consider how the Emperor's mind must be disturbed because 70 million people are withering away, we must recognize that the point of view of the individual, the honor of the Army and our pride as a people must be subordinated to the wishes of the Imperial House. I have therefore come to the conclusion that there is nothing else for us to do but strengthen our determination to make peace as quickly as possible and suffer curtailment."

The same day's Magic Summary contains the final plea from Captain Nishihara to the Navy in Tokyo.[9] The Naval Counselor in Bern sees events in much the same light as does Sato, which Nishihara makes clear when he sends his "opinions" concerning the "peace" conversation with von Gaevernitz. The analysts note the two most important items Nishihara tells Tokyo as being: "Von Gaevernitz stated that (a) 'the U.S. leaders are of the opinion that the Japanese national structure is not to be upset' in the event of a surrender, and (b) 'if Japan has any request to make, [Dulles] can return to Switzerland [from Germany] at once.'"

The basic message that Nishihara wants Tokyo to hear includes the following points:

1. Russia will cooperate with America;
2. "If things progress in their present fashion, Japan will ultimately be torn asunder just as Germany is now. The populace will probably be reduced by half (35 million people) as a result of the difficult struggle for life and of food shortages";
3. "American military men and businessmen have complete self-confidence about the war against Japan and the people they are cheerfully supporting the government policy in a sporting frame of mind. Among the politicians many are of the opinion that the outcome of the war against Japan is already evident and the earlier it ends the better."

It is Nishihara's belief that Dulles wanted to "establish a liaison channel between Japan and the U.S. and to bring about peace quickly. There is no information to indicate the proposal is a stratagem of the U.S. . . . Consequently, I believe that, without breaking off our liaison along the present line, it is absolutely necessary for the sake of Japan to open—no matter how the war situation develops—a [new] channel. I would like to know your opinion. . . . I would like to do something about this, but only in accordance with your instructions, so please reply immediately."

As we will see, no constructive reply from Tokyo will be forthcoming.

---

9. Ibid. The JN reference is JN-5 9519-G CRN.

✳ ✳ ✳

It is not until July 23 and 24 that the Magic Summaries reveal that peace talks other than the ones Captain Nishihara has described to Tokyo have also been taking place in Switzerland.[10]

The Summary of July 23 presents a partial report from Japanese minister Kase, dated July 21, describing recent conversations in Basel between Kojiro Kitamura of the Yokohama Specie Bank and the Bank of International Settlements, one of Kitamura's subordinates (as yet unnamed), and Dr. Per Jacobson, formerly attached to the Bank of International Settlement.

The Summary of July 24 includes the portions missing from the previous day's Summary, and the analysts in Washington conclude that, on July 13, Kitamura told Jacobson "that some assurance from the Allies with respect to the future of the Japanese 'Imperial House and the national structure' could be 'the greatest and most effective inducement for ending the war.' "

Apparently the three men met on July 10 and 13, and a third talk was held on the sixteenth. In the latter meeting Jacobson described his conference with Mr. Dulles, which he said had taken place in Wiesbaden on July 14 and 15.

The Summary continues: "According to Jacobson, Mr. Dulles had told him that (1) 'the only way for Japan to save anything is for her to accept at once "unconditional surrender" as defined in [Under Secretary] Grew's statement of 10 July,' (2) the Berlin Conference provided a good opportunity for arranging surrender talks, and (3) 'once Russia joins England and the U.S. [against Japan], it will by no means be so simple to end the war.' "

It is important to note that on the dates these conversations are reported to have taken place, neither the Japanese nor Dulles knew of the existence of the atomic bomb. The conventional wisdom of the moment is that Japan will be destroyed by naval bombardment and massive bomber raids that would create up to 150,000 civilian casualties per day, if not more.

The Summary of July 24 also contains a Japanese intelligence report from Harbin that the Russians intend to invade South Sakhalin

10. SRS 1737, SRS 1738; 23 and 24 July 1945.

and that they have assembled an occupation force in North Sakhalin. Administrative staff are currently being trained in Vladivostok to administer the occupied territory.

It is on this day, July 24, that General Marshall decides America does not need any help from the Soviet Union to end the Pacific war. And while Truman gives the bare details of the bomb's existence to Stalin, Secretary of War Stimson approves the fateful orders for the 509th Composite Bomb Group, which is gathering at Tinian Island under the command of Gen. Carl Spaatz. The order reads:

To General Carl Spaatz, CG, USASTAF

1. The 509 Composite Group, 20th Air Force will deliver its first special bomb as soon as weather will permit visual bombing after about 3 August 1945 on one of the targets: Hiroshima, Kokura, Niigata and Nagasaki. . . .
2. Additional bombs will be delivered on the above targets as soon as made ready. . . .
3. Dissemination of any and all information concerning the use of the weapon against Japan is reserved to the Secretary of War and the President of the United States. . . .
4. The foregoing directive is issued to you by direction and with the approval of the Secretary of War and the Chief of Staff, USA.

It is agreed and understood between Truman and Stimson that this order will stand unless Truman notifies Stimson that "the Japanese reply to our ultimatum was acceptable."[11]

The major news of July 25 is the defeat of Prime Minister Churchill in the British general election.

The following day, July 26, America, Great Britain and China issue the Potsdam proclamation. As the declaration regards Japan, according to British historian Charles Messenger, the "authority and influence of all those who had led the Japanese on their march of conquest had to be eliminated; Japan itself was to be occupied and was to evacuate all territories outside the mainland islands. Finally, it called upon the Japanese Government to 'proclaim now the unconditional surrender of all Japanese armed forces, and to provide proper and adequate assurance of their good faith in such actions. The alternative for Japan is

11. *Years of Decision: 1945,* vol. 1 of *Memoirs* by Harry Truman (New York: Da Capo [QPB Series], 1986, 419–21.

prompt and utter destruction.' ''[12] How this destruction would be achieved is not explained.

The clock is ticking down for Japan. The Magic Summaries now reveal a weakness in the intercepting, decrypting and translating. When it comes to minute-by-minute developments, the system has difficulty keeping up to events. For example, the Summary of the twenty-seventh can only report in the first instance on Japanese diplomatic maneuvers that are "out of sync" in terms of real-time necessities. The first item marked for Marshall's attention goes back to July 21 when Japanese minister Kase in Switzerland continues to bombard Tokyo with "all kinds of material obviously designed to persuade the [Japanese] Government of the need for an early peace."[13]

This delay in up-to-the-minute information causes a supplemental Diplomatic Summary to be issued later in the day. The supplement is more timely, noting that Tokyo's latest instructions to Sato in Moscow have been delayed in transmission. On July 25, Togo instructed Sato to take advantage in the lull (for the general election in Britain) to try to obtain an interview with Molotov at "a place of the Russian's own choosing."

The analysts report that it now appears that as of late in the night of the twenty-sixth (Moscow time), Sato has not yet seen these instructions. Shortly after midnight (in the early hours of the twenty-seventh) he complains to Tokyo that he cannot read the first and last part of Togo's message. It was the first part of the message that contains Togo's order to set up a meeting with Molotov.

Sato has complained previously about a delay in receiving Tokyo's instructions. Togo is concerned, and in what the analysts call "a somewhat obscure message" sent on the twenty-sixth, he tells Sato that when it appears messages are delayed, Sato is to make an immediate request for a retransmission of same. Togo also lets slip that Sato's messages—especially the one that was received today (the twenty-sixth) "was placed before *the Imperial Court.*" Togo also reveals that Emperor Hirohito is asking specifically about Sato's messages. (Emphasis added.)

This gives Marshall and Stimson conclusive evidence that Emperor Hirohito is personally involved in trying to set up a deal with

---

12. *The Chronological Atlas of World War II* by Charles Messenger (New York: Macmillan, 1989), 223.
13. SRS 1741, 27 July 1945.

Russia that may not lead to peace in the Pacific as envisaged by Washington, London and Chungking.

The full text of the meeting between Sato and Lozovsky reveals for the first time Sato's belief that the Russians are beginning to show interest in the Japanese proposals.

✖ ✖ ✖

On July 28, in Tokyo, Premier Susuki tells the Japanese press that the Potsdam Declaration is to be ignored.

The Magic Summary of July 29[14] demonstrates that Tokyo is *not* ignoring the Potsdam Declaration, but is trying to figure out how to use it to its advantage.

Togo cables Sato and tells the Ambassador in Moscow: "What the Russian position is with respect to the Potsdam Joint Declaration made by England, America and Chungking is a question of extreme importance in determining our future counterpolicy. . . . Moreover, since as it happened we were awaiting the Russian answer in regard to sending a Special Envoy, the question arises as to whether there is not some connection between this Joint Declaration and our proposal. Obviously we are deeply concerned as to whether there is such a connection, that is to say, whether the Russian government communicated our proposal to the English and the Americans, and [we are also concerned] as to what attitude the Russians will take toward Japan in the future.

"As a countermeasure in response to the Joint Declaration, we are adopting a policy of careful study (while waiting for the Russian answer to our proposal). So we should like Your Excellency to have an interview with Molotov as quickly as possible and, in addition to driving home the ideas expressed to you in our No. 944 [this relates to Togo's instructions to see Molotov during the lull in the Potsdam Conference], to attempt to sound out the Russian attitude toward the Joint Declaration."

Meanwhile Sato cabled Tokyo on July 27, and apparently he had still not read Togo's message No. 944, reinforcing his previous arguments that the Japanese government must make concrete proposals for peace "without circumlocution." In his view, "the joint ultimatum to Japan . . . seems to have been intended as a threatening blast against us

---

14. SRS 1743, 29 July 1945.

and as a prelude to a Three Power offensive. As might have been expected, any aid from the Soviet Union has now become extremely doubtful and there can be little doubt that this ultimatum was meant to serve as a counterblast to our peace feelers." (The analysts note that Togo is "not convinced of any such relation between the two moves.")

Sato continues, saying: "According to a BBC broadcast of the twenty-sixth, before Lord [Louis] Mountbatten returned to Great Britain he stopped off at Potsdam in order to report to the leaders of Great Britain, the United States and the Soviet Union on the war situation in the Far East. The broadcast added that Stalin has, for the first time, participated in the discussions of the Anglo-American leaders regarding the war in the Far East. I think that this point is particularly worth noting. I cannot help being afraid that this development may influence the attitude of the Soviet Government on the question of aiding in effecting our plan."

The following day finds the Magic Summary split in two, with the Japanese section being added after the initial report.

Now Sato reports to Togo in a wire dated July 29,[15] in which he says: "The repeat wire was received and read on the twenty-eighth. On the same day Mr. Attlee, the new Prime Minister, returned to Potsdam and immediately participated in the Conference. As a result it is no longer possible for me to comply with your instructions to seek an interview with Molotov; furthermore, if I were to seek such an interview and the Russian officials were to find no reason to approve my trip [to Berlin], we would only have betrayed our feelings of uneasiness.

"You also direct me to request Russia's good offices [in ending the war] and to advise the Russians that if they show a cold attitude, we will have no choice but to consider other courses of action. You evidently feel that we can achieve a satisfactory result by either lifting Russia up or taking her down, but, in view of the general situation, I believe that such an approach is unsound.

"Although the American 'spokesman' [word in English] spoke firmly for an unconditional surrender, he certainly hinted that if we were to agree to this, the terms would in actual practice be toned down; indeed if we assume this to be his true meaning, the situation is as I stated in my message of 20 July [in which Sato urged that Japan should surrender provided she was permitted to retain the Imperial House— DS 22 July 1945]."

---

15. SRS 1744, 30 July 1945. It is obvious that the Pentagon is doing everything possible to get the Japanese messages to Marshall and Stimson as quickly as possible.

For the first time, and it has been confirmed by Togo's previous messages on the subject, the Americans and British know that the hints of better terms than unconditional surrender are being placed before Emperor Hirohito by his most trusted diplomats. This should end the debate as to whether or not the message ever got through to the Japanese leaders. It got through. They simply didn't want to pay any attention to it.

Sato drives his point home even more deeply when he next refers to the broadcasts, asking the Japanese to come to the peace table, that were made by U.S. naval captain Zacharias. These broadcasts have caused much controversy among historians. It is interesting, therefore, to see how the Japanese view them at the time. As Sato says: "I don't know to what extent the statement of Captain Zacharias in his recent broadcast were authoritative; the principle enunciated by him—that Japan can reap the benefits of the Atlantic Charter—differs from the attitude which the Allies took toward Germany before her capitulation.

"While no reason is apparent why the Allies—in contrast to their treatment of Germany—are softening their attitude toward Japan, our position is different from Germany's in that [as you say] we have no objection to the restoration of world peace on the basis of the Charter. This raises the question of whether the Imperial Government is prepared to accept [the principle of] disarmament[16] and will so inform the Russians at the outset in making any representations—regardless of whether or not we send a Special Envoy. There is also the similar question of whether we are now prepared to recognize the independence of Korea."

Another element in Sato's remarks that should be addressed at this point concerns racism. And it cuts both ways. The Americans believed themselves superior to the Japanese at the outset of the war, and this stupidly complacent outlook was one of the reasons the Japanese attack on Pearl Harbor was so successful. Now, at the end of the war, the Japanese military believe that the Japanese race is superior in every way to the white Anglo-Americans. It isn't polite to say so, but the truth is that Japan's racist attitude of the time, the belief in the infallibility of the Emperor, prevents them from negotiating with the *gaijin* (foreigners) and leads to the nuclear devastation of Japan.

Sato concludes his remarks to Togo saying: "According to the

---

16. The eighth "principle" enunciated in the Atlantic Charter provides for the disarmament of aggressor nations "pending the establishment of a wider and permanent system of general security."

BBC, Your Excellency has issued a statement that the Japanese Government has decided to ignore the Three Power ultimatum of the twenty-sixth, but I have as yet received no official message on the subject. Nevertheless, whether we treat this ultimatum with silent contempt or publicize it in our ordinary reports, the fact remains that it is a public expression of the intention of England, America, and China and is the basis of the statement made by Captain Zacharias. It is true that there are discrepancies in some of the important points in the ultimatum [presumably between it and the Atlantic Charter]. (In the ultimatum it is understood that, while Japan's territory is to be limited to Honshu, Shikoku, Kyushu, and Hokkaido, America will keep Okinawa.)''

Now Sato really lets Togo have it. One can sense the Ambassador's belief that Togo—and his fellow militarists—have betrayed Japan when he says: ''In your July 12 message you merely informed me of Japan's desire to send a Special Envoy [to Moscow]; then in a message dated 21 July, you instructed me to seek the good offices of the Russian Government; now in your 25 July message, I am directed to make clear that the purpose of sending a Special Envoy is to induce Stalin to become a peace advocate. I regret that our plans have been doled out this way. . . .

''I am now waiting for a reply to the representation which I made to Lozovsky on 25 July [in which Sato again urged the Russians to receive Prince Konoye—DS 26, 27 July 1945], and if no reply arrives by the thirtieth (Monday), I will press for one without delay.

''I had no sooner finished drafting this report when I received your message of 28 July [urging Sato to have an interview with Molotov as quickly as possible—DS 29 July 1945]. As for seeing Molotov, I would particularly like to be informed whether our Imperial Government has a concrete and definite plan for terminating the war; otherwise I will make no immediate request for an interview.''

And there it is, in simple black and white. As of July 30, 1945, the Japanese government has no plan for ending the war.

✖ ✖ ✖

From this point on, one reads the Diplomatic Summaries with an ever increasing sense of impending doom.

The Magic Summary of July 31[17] reveals that Sato has done as

---

17. SRS 1745, 31 July 1945.

he promised. On the thirtieth he goes to Lozovsky and asks that the Russians reply to his renewed plea. Lozovsky promises to relay the message to Stalin and Molotov this very day, but, he points out, they are in Berlin and an answer may not be possible. Once senses the tragedy Sato feels when he ends his report to Tokyo saying: "Lozovsky promised once again to communicate what I had said and I withdrew."

And from Bern, Switzerland, Japanese naval captain Nishihara acknowledges his latest instructions.[18] The taut words of the analysts in Washington describe the situation: "As previously noted . . . Nishihara . . . has been unable to persuade the Tokyo Navy General Staff to follow up an earlier 'alleged' proposal of OSS representative Allen Dulles that a Japanese admiral come to Switzerland for a 'discussion' with representatives of the United States. On July 22 he was finally told that (a) 'this question has been transmitted to the Foreign Office,' and (b) 'after getting in touch with the Foreign Office representative in Bern,' he was to 'take, at least outwardly, no further part in the matter' (DS 28 July 1945)."

Nishihara acknowledges receipt of these orders on July 26, saying: "I am fully aware of the established policy of the Empire and the stand of the Navy."

✖ ✖ ✖

It is the first of August 1945. The atomic bomb will be dropped on Japan in five days.

From Bern, Switzerland, Minister Kase sends a long message to Tokyo analyzing the Three Power Proclamation at Potsdam.[19] He points out specifically that "the Proclamation states that after the Japanese forces are disarmed the Japanese people will be given an opportunity to lead a peaceful and productive life." He also comments on the fact that Japan can preserve her peacetime industry. (The actual terms are that Japan would be allowed to maintain "such industries as will sustain her economy" and she would be permitted "eventual participation in world trade relations," which seems rather ironic fifty years after the event.) Needless to say, Kase is recommending that Tokyo accept the terms.

---

18. Ibid. The reference is JN-5 1204-H CRN.
19. SRS 1746, 1 August 1945.

Meanwhile, in Tokyo, Foreign Minister Togo is still worrying the Potsdam Proclamation to death like a small terrier throwing itself upon a large beef bone. Togo can see more robbers under the bed than can fifty spinsters. Obviously the Russians were involved in all this, he believes, but what does it mean?

Sato spells it out for Togo, saying: "However much we may exert ourselves to prevent Stalin from entering the war, and even though we exalt him as an advocate of world peace, we shall have no particular success [vis-à-vis the Special Envoy]. There is no alternative but immediate unconditional surrender if we are to try and make American and England moderate and to prevent [Russia's] participation in the war.

"Moreover, immediately after Japan's surrender, Stalin will bring full and heavy pressure on America, England, and China with regard to Manchukuo, China and Korea, and will proceed in the hope of achieving his own demands. Since he actually possesses the real power [to do this], there is no reason why he should now want to make a treaty with Japan. Your way of looking at things and the actual situation in the Eastern Area may be seen to be absolutely contradictory.

"Furthermore, it is worthy of note that Evatt, the Australian foreign minister, has stated that he is opposed to the tendency of the Joint Proclamation to show greater leniency toward Japan than the United Nations showed Germany."

Not only is Sato telling Togo that his view of events contradicts reality, but the Ambassador is also pointing out that Australia—one of the most powerful forces in the Allied operations during the Pacific war—is saying that Japan deserves everything she is going to get. (One should also note that after the war, the Australians wanted Emperor Hirohito tried as a war criminal.)

At this point in the Magic Summaries, the analysts in Washington make an important notation for Marshall. A careful review of Sato's messages reveals that "the request for Russia's good offices was not explicitly made until Sato's second conference with Lozovsky on 25 July. Accordingly, the Soviet note of 18 July (stating that a definite reply could not be made to the Emperor's message or to the proposal that Japan send a Special Envoy) was not a rejection of such a request." No, the Russian response is the proper reply to an inadequate request made as the result of a clumsy Japanese foreign policy.

The Magic Diplomatic Summary for August 2 begins with the views of Naval Counselor Nishihara in Bern that he sends to Tokyo on July 22 in which he points out that British and American authorities are "unofficially" expressing respect for the Imperial Household.[20] This means the Allies might not meddle "with our national structure . . . in order not to incite our people needlessly. There is danger that if we [continue to] rattle the saber, it will be all over, and a stain will appear on the structure of our country, which has never been tainted by foreign invasion."

He goes on to recommend surrender and the preservation of "our national structure," and he paints a gloomy view of Japanese prospects to achieve any military gains. The enemy has total superiority, Japan stands alone against the world, and it is clear that Russia is preparing "to enter the war immediately."

Meanwhile the first and third parts of Japanese minister Kase's message of July 29 has been retrieved. He tells Togo that the Allies seem to be offering Tokyo a better deal than Germany, which "has been handled as a country without a ruler or a government." He goes on to point out that if the "American military authorities have actually moderated their war terms a little without dropping the guise of unconditional surrender and have [put forth a hand] much sooner than expected, I believe such a step is based on American initiative." This, Kase goes on to say, is a sign of American strength "rather than of war weariness."

A special supplement of the same day carries the first half of a message that Togo sends to Sato on August 2. (Now we are reading the diplomatic correspondence in same-day time.) Referring to Sato's comments of July 30 about the Three Party Proclamation, Togo reveals that Tokyo is still studying the surrender terms.

"I have been fully apprised of Your Excellency's views by your successive wires," Togo says, "and am well able to understand them as the opinions of the Ambassador on the spot. However, it should not be difficult for you to realize that, although with the urgency of the war situation our time to proceed with arrangements for ending the war before the enemy lands on the Japanese mainland is limited, on the other hand it is difficult to decide on concrete peace conditions here at home all at once. At present, in accordance with the Imperial Will, there is unanimous determination to seek the good offices of the Russians in ending the war, to make concrete terms a matter between Japan and Russia, and to send Prince Konoye, who has the deep trust of the Emperor, to carry on discussions with the Russians. . . . It has been decided at any rate to send a Special Envoy in accordance with the

---

20. SRS 1747, 2 August 1945.

views of the highest leaders of [this] Government, and along with this [decision] we are exerting ourselves to collect the views of all quarters on the matter of concrete terms. (Under the circumstances there is a disposition to make the Potsdam Three Power Proclamation the basis of our study concerning terms.)''

The significance of Togo's words are not lost on Washington, where the power resides to end the war quickly and decisively. First, the Emperor is *not* going to offer concrete terms with the British, Americans and Chinese. But he will do so with the Russians. The Emperor will not concede the point that the Russians may not want to accept a Special Envoy but, instead, will attack Japan. It appears that the Emperor mistakenly believes he can manipulate the Russians—as the Japanese have done in the past—and can ignore the other Allies.

Meanwhile, the same day's Summary also reveals the latest machinations of the Soviets in regard to the Mediterranean area. At issue are items such as the award of the Dodecanese, and possibly Cyprus, to Greece; the ceding to Bulgaria of the Turkish port of Enez [on the Aegean at the mouth of the Maritsa River]; and the partitioning of Albania between Greece and Yugoslavia. According to French ambassador Catroux in Moscow, the Russians ''are now working toward the Mediterranean—to which they have recently shown their firm desire to have access. In order to realize that plan, it is to their advantage to gain [general] acceptance of the claims of the states which are in their sphere in influence, that is the claims of the Yugoslavs [with respect] to the Adriatic and that of the Bulgars [with respect] to the Aegean.''

Even though the war has not come to an end, the goals sought by Stalin are clear: expand the Russian borders as far as possible in real geographic terms and export Communism to every country in the world.

The containment of Russia by the Western powers—and the Russian creation of the Iron Curtain—is well under way.

✖ ✖ ✖

The first item marked for Marshall's attention in the Magic Diplomatic Summary of August 3 is headlined: *''Further Japanese reports of Soviet military movements to the Far East.''*[21] The analysts point out that

---

21. SRS 1748, 3 August 1945. See also the Magic Diplomatic Summaries for 23 April, 19 and 28 May, 7 and 13 June 1945.

the Diplomatic Summary for June 23 noted 173 troop trains moved east in the middle of the month carrying an "estimated total of 120,000 troops." This rate has been stepped up in July with the observation of 202 eastbound trains with "2,932 cars carrying troops" (a total of 117,280 troops at the normal rate of 40 men to a car). Many of the mechanized and artillery units appeared to be front-line units, and a number of vehicles "were considerably damaged," suggesting they had been transferred directly from the western front.

On July 28, from Moscow, Sato cables another report by Japanese diplomatic couriers traveling westward on the Trans-Siberian Railway from Man-chou-li to Moscow. The report says "the impression was received that the Russians were reinforcing their troops on the Outer Mongolian frontier."

Between Chita and Yaroslavl (about 165 miles northeast of Moscow) the couriers noted 381 eastbound trains, which they estimated to be carrying 170,000 troops, 9,800 motor vehicles, 60 tanks, 200 self-propelled guns, 450 antitank guns, 89 rocket guns, 220 airplanes, 300 barges for crossing streams, 83 pontoon bridges, and 2,900 horses.

The couriers arrived in Moscow on July 25. They estimated that "present eastbound military shipments have apparently reached the maximum capacity of the Trans-Siberian Railway." The construction of sidings and the expansion of rail facilities were observed to be going on "everywhere."

The second item in the Summary is an intelligence report from Captain Nishihara in Bern, which he attributes to "a British informant." According to Nishihara, "American preparations for a landing on Japan will not be completed as soon as American military authorities secretly gave Great Britain and Russia to understand they would be. That is why the U.S., just before the Potsdam Conference, made a great deal of propaganda about Japanese unconditional surrender—without, however, [achieving any] result.

"The Americans, it seems, had decided upon September or October [for a landing], but British military authorities warned them (1) that military preparations were not yet sufficient to take the decisive step of a landing on the Japanese mainland, and (2) that they [the Americans] could not succeed by their own power alone—although from an operational standpoint they could, of course, establish a beachhead on the Japanese mainland and throw the populace into confusion.

"The present American offensive is manifestly based on political and diplomatic considerations."

It is impossible to tell how this report—which contradicts Nishi-hara's report of the previous day advising Japan to stop the war immediately in order to save her "national structure"—is accepted in Japan. But if it gives the Japanese the idea that an Allied invasion is not immediately imminent, then it gives Tokyo a false sense of security and support in thinking that the greatest danger Japan faces is Russia.

✖ ✖ ✖

The only Japanese message concerning the negotiations for peace comes from Sato on August 3. It appears in the Magic Diplomatic Summary of August 4, two days before the atomic bomb is dropped.[22] Sato first acknowledges Togo's impatient wire of the previous day, saying that he will "naturally attempt to have a conference with Molotov immediately upon his return." Unfortunately two parts of Sato's message are missing, but the analysts conclude that the entire message "seems to consist of a review of his [Sato's] arguments that Japan must decide upon a 'concrete proposal' for ending the war in order to have any chance of obtaining Russia's 'good offices.' "

✖ ✖ ✖

On August 5, the Magic Diplomatic Summary reveals that Japan is evacuating a number of strategic areas in Korea, but Washington believes that the evacuation can only be a partial one in view of the large numbers of people involved.[23]

A special supplement prepared the same day carries the full text of Sato's message to Togo of the previous day. It contains nothing new or noteworthy. The latest message from Sato is sent August 4, and it concerns the Russians yet again.

"As for the peace terms which would [ultimately] be worked out," says Sato in an ironic and prophetic statement, ". . . if one looks at the terms for the handling of Germany decided upon at Potsdam, it is not far-fetched to surmise that a certain amelioration [of conditions for Ja-

---

22. SRS 1749, 4 August 1945.
23. SRS 1750, 5 August 1945.

pan] would be possible. Moreover, if communication to the United Nations of Japan's resolution to seek peace is *speeded up even by one day,* the degree of amelioration will be [affected] to that extent. However, if the Government and the Military dillydally in bringing this resolution to fruition, then all Japan will be reduced to ashes and we will not be able [to avoid] following the road to ruin. [Emphasis added.]

"Even though there may be some amelioration, it is already clear, even without looking at the example of Germany, what the peace terms will be, and we must resign ourselves beforehand to ——— [words uncertain, probably: "giving up"] a considerable number of [so-called] war criminals. However, the state is now [on the verge of] ruin, and it is wholly inevitable that these war criminals [must] make the necessary sacrifice to save their country as truly patriotic warriors."

Thus, on the day before the atomic bomb is dropped, Washington and London know the suggestion has been made to Emperor Hirohito that if Japan should appeal to the United Nations and says she seeks peace, there is every chance that the terms of the Potsdam Declaration can be ameliorated.

This Magic Summary destroys the argument used by historians who contend that the leaders of Japan did not have adequate warning that immediate surrender was required, or that further negotiations with the Japanese were needed, or that the atomic bomb should have been demonstrated for the Japanese military. The Magic Diplomatic Summaries themselves, and this one in particular, prove beyond reasonable doubt that adequate warning is given the Japanese and that they comprehend it. They also understand that the faster they surrender the better the terms might be.

As Sato has pointed out, all it would take to end the war at this moment is a simple radio message to the United Nations.

The Japanese government refuses Sato's advice.

And now the civilians of Japan will pay the price.

✖ ✖ ✖

On August 6, 1945, the first atomic bomb explodes two thousand feet above the city of Hiroshima. It destroys forty-two square miles of the metropolis, kills 80,000 people, wounds another 37,000, and leaves missing another 10,000 souls. Untold thousands more will die later from radiation sickness.

The Magic Diplomatic Summary for the day[24] does not contain a single mention of the event. It does, however, note the "Japanese reaction to [the] announcement of future B-29 targets." The Intelligence Circular of the Vice Chief of the Japanese Army General Staff, dated August 4, states: "It is particularly alarming that since July 27 [the enemy] has been carrying out threatened bombings aimed at arousing a general antiwar feeling among the people and at dividing the Army and the people."

✖ ✖ ✖

Unbelievably, in the Magic Summary of August 7,[25] there is no mention by the Japanese of a nuclear explosion or any news about Hiroshima.

✖ ✖ ✖

On August 8, yet again, there is no mention by the Japanese of the fate of Hiroshima in the Magic Summary.[26] The latest information from Japan focuses in a different direction and is revealed in a special supplement that is headlined: *"Tokyo impatient for action."* "Yesterday," the analysts note for Marshall's attention, "some thirty-four hours after the atomic bomb attack on Hiroshima, Foreign Minister Togo sent the following message to Ambassador Sato:

"Re your message No. 1519 [not available in Washington];

"The situation is becoming more and more pressing, and we would like to know at once the explicit attitude of the Russians. So will you put forth still greater efforts to get a reply from them in haste."

The analysts also point out for Marshall: *Sato to see Molotov today.* "Also on August 7," the analysts say, "but presumably before he had received Togo's message, Ambassador Sato reported as follows:

"Re my No. 1519;

"As soon as Molotov returned to Moscow, I immediately requested an interview, and as I had asked Lozovsky for his good offices

---

24. SRS 1751, 6 August 1945.
25. SRS 1752, 7 August 1945.
26. SRS 1753, 8 August 1945.

in this matter on numerous occasions, I received a notice from Molotov on the seventh that he would be able to see me at 5 P.M. tomorrow, the eighth.'' Sato (and the Americans) do not know it, but Molotov is going to tell Sato that Russia is declaring war on Japan as of August 9.

The next morning Russian troops pour across the Manchurian border. Because Tokyo has ordered large numbers of its troops back to Japan for defense against an American invasion, a troop movement that Washington did not know about via the usual signals intelligence intercepts, the Russians' manpower is greater than that of the Japanese by 3:2. The Russians also have a 5:1 superiority in artillery, 5:1 in tanks and 2:1 in aircraft. So instead of putting up a fierce resistance against the Russian troops invading Manchuria, which Washington expected them to do, from the outset the Japanese are routed. Now the Japanese endure their own form of Pearl Harbor. Not only have they badly deceived themselves into believing that they were maneuvering the Russians into helping them negotiate a peace favorable to Tokyo, the Russian Foreign Office has made fools of the Japanese.

At the same time, on the morning of 9 August, not having heard any response to the demands that Japan surrender unconditionally or face total destruction, the Americans drop a second atomic bomb on the city of Nagasaki. This bomb kills 35,000 Japanese civilians, wounds another 6,000 and causes 5,000 to be listed as missing. Yet the Magic Diplomatic Summaries say nothing about the nuclear disasters in Japan. Instead, the Magic Summary for this day[27] lists as its primary concern a series of reports about Manchurian border violations by the Russians. The Japanese Supreme Council is being overtaken by events. As the analysts note for Marshall: ''Yesterday—presumably before Tokyo had heard of Russia's declaration of war—Foreign Minister Togo sent the following 'urgent' message to Ambassador Sato. According to a report from military sources here, at about 6 A.M. on the 6th twenty Soviet soldiers crossed the Manchukuo-Soviet border near our position (held by 30 men) at Wu-chiang-t'un [unidentified] north of Lake Khanka [about 100 miles north of Vladivostok].'' What Togo wants Sato to do about the matter is unclear. Other Japanese intelligence reports for the day hint that the Russo-Manchurian border is about to explode.

The Magic Summaries cannot reveal, since no advisories are being sent out by Tokyo, this day's convening of an emergency session of the Japanese Supreme Council for the Conduct of the War to review

---

27. SRS 1754, 9 August 1945.

the situation. The story of what happens at this meeting is not made public for years. But historians are amazed to learn that even though the Russians have broken their pledge of nonaggression and invaded territory controlled by Japan, and the Americans have dropped two atomic bombs on Japanese cities, on 9 August the Supreme Council cannot bring itself to vote for surrender. The Minister of War, General Anami, tells his fellow council members: "It is far to early to say that the war is lost. That we will inflict severe losses on the enemy when he invades Japan is certain, and it is by no means impossible that we may be able to reverse the situation in our favor, pulling victory out of defeat. Furthermore, our Army will not submit to demobilization. And since they know they are not permitted to surrender . . . there is really no alternative for us but to continue the war." General Anami is ready to sacrifice his army, plus any number of Japanese cities, to nuclear or conventional destruction in total disregard of civilian casualties. Since Anami controls the Japanese war effort, the Supreme Council vote on whether Japan should continue fighting or surrender is evenly split. The deadlock is broken only later in the day when Foreign Minister Togo and Admiral Suzuki meet secretly with Emperor Hirohito and persuade the Emperor to convene another Council. This time the Emperor will preside, not Anami.

The second meeting takes place that night in the Emperor's bomb shelter. For another two hours, the all-powerful General Anami argues for continuing the fighting, adamantly refusing to surrender. Finally, Hirohito assumes the role he should have taken earlier. He defies the militarists on the Council to say: "Continuing the war can only result in the annihilation of the Japanese people and a prolongation of the suffering of all humanity. It seems obvious that the nation is no longer able to wage war, and its ability to defend its own shores is doubtful."

It is time, Hirohito declares, "to bear the unbearable."

He approves a proposal made by Togo to accept the Allied demand of unconditional surrender.[28]

As so often happens, momentous events are explained in simple terms. Without fanfare, the Magic Diplomatic Summary, SRS 1755 of August 10, 1945, notes as its primary heading: *"MILITARY 1. English text of Japan's surrender offer:"* Early today (Greenwich time) the

---

28. American intelligence specialists recommend *The Fall of Japan* by William Craig (New York: The Dial Press, 1967) as being the most authoritative book on the subject. Later, the author commissioned Mr. Craig's next work, a miniclassic called *Enemy at the Gates: The Battle of Stalingrad.*

Japanese Foreign Ministry instructed its representatives in Stockholm and Bern to transmit Japan's surrender offer to the four principal belligerent countries, stating that it was sending an English, as well as a Japanese, text. . . . ''

Thus ends the narrative about how the Japanese unwittingly helped Germany lose World War II, allowed the Allies to give Berlin to the Russians, and brought nuclear devastation upon themselves.

EPILOGUE

Japan surrenders on August 15, 1945, and the Foreign Ministry in Tokyo sallies forth to rebuild from the ashes of defeat. Overnight new alliances are created throughout the Far East; Tokyo requires the Empire be maintained. We are witness to this maneuvering because the U.S. Army has continued to be successful in making the Japanese think their diplomatic Purple codes are secure. The proof of this comes on September 6, four days after the formal documents of surrender are signed on board the battleship *Missouri,* when Foreign Minister Shigemitsu sends a message to Minister Kase in Bern, Switzerland, asking that Kase pass the information to Japanese diplomats in Sweden and Portugal.[1]

"Since we have received no orders whatsoever from the Allied Supreme Commander [MacArthur] regarding code communication," declares Shigemitsu, "it will be our policy for the time being to continue to use the remaining cipher machines and codebooks. (We are making preparations so that we can dispose of the cipher machines and codebooks at any time.) Depending on the situation at your place, take whatever steps are necessary with the above. In the event that code communications are suspended, I shall report that fact to you."

As Henry Clausen explained to the writer: "The U.S. Army was absolutely brilliant when it convinced the Japanese that their codes were secure. It gave MacArthur an incredible advantage in the early days of governing Japan." Reading the files of Diplomatic Summaries that have been declassified to date, from mid-August until November 3, 1945, one is struck by how much of these particular Diplomatic Summaries remains classified today. But given the behavior of our former allies of

---

1. SRS 1783, 7 September 1945.

World War II, some of whose selfish "colonial" behavior has been revealed earlier in the narrative, this censorship is understandable. Hopefully the U.S. State Department will release these Summaries in the near future. Intelligence experts say that none of their secrecy requirements applies to these documents. Meanwhile, from the decrypts that *have* been released, one can see the seeds being sown that will create one of America's saddest military endeavors: Vietnam.

Day after day, the Japanese report on the activities of the French, British, Cambodians and Chinese regarding this vital section of Asia. "Even if you can succeed in reestablishing a French administration here, it would no longer be obeyed," the Annamese emperor Bao Dai cables General de Gaulle in Paris on August 20. "I beg you to understand that the sole means to salvage French interests in Indochina is to recognize openly the independence of Vietnam."[2]

The problems regarding independence in Vietnam worsen quickly.[3] The analysts note that on September 23, liberated French prisoners of war in Saigon seized the local headquarters of the Annamese Provisional Government. On September 26, the Japanese embassy in Saigon reports its version of events to Tokyo, saying: "[Although] local French circles take an extremely grave view of the recent activities of the Indochina Independence League . . . the more radical [French] faction decided to take advantage of the ostensible indifference of the British military authorities. . . . They forced through a restoration of the [French] administrative and police apparatus in utter disregard of the views of the Annamese. This in turn caused the Annamese to further resistance, and clashes between the French and the Annamese have been taking place throughout the city. Up until the twenty-fifth, a state of siege existed in various parts throughout the city. The markets are closed and the populace is panic-stricken. . . . The British forces seem to have adopted the view that the responsibility for maintaining order in the country still belongs to the Japanese forces and have ordered the Japanese to disarm the Annamese." The Japanese maintain that "they cannot undertake the responsibility of maintaining order and have asked the British to recon-

---

2. SRS 1770, 25 August 1945. The analysts note for Marshall that, on the previous day, Bao Dai sent a similar cable to President Truman saying: "The day of colonial conquest is gone, and a people, especially the people of Vietnam [the Annamese name for their country], who have twenty centuries of history and a glorious past—can no longer be placed under the guardianship of another people. May France bow to this truth, proclaimed and upheld by the noble American nation." Bao Dai's plea for American help falls on deaf ears.
3. SRS 1812, 6 October 1945.

sider.... However, the British have been supporting the French and refuse to compromise.... We expect the situation to grow more difficult.''

The stage is being set for another tragic war.

✖ ✖ ✖

As for China, Japanese diplomats report almost daily on the increasingly violent struggle between the Communists and the Nationalists, noting that the Communists are making ever-increasing gains in popular support. This leads an anti-Communist Foreign Ministry to decide that it is in Japan's best interest to strike a deal with the Chungking government of Chiang Kai-shek, a move abhorrent to a great many Chinese citizens. The Japanese Foreign Ministry also instructs its diplomats in neutral countries not to surrender their custody of diplomatic and consular property, or archives, because ''this demand is not covered by any of the stipulations of the Potsdam Declaration.''[4] Japanese diplomats in Europe, notably Switzerland and Sweden, take extraordinary measures to protect their nation's financial assets from being frozen by the Allies.[5] Similar financial transactions are carried out throughout the Far East as Tokyo restructures formerly government-owned businesses and transfers them to Japanese nationals living in countries such as Burma, Thailand, Indochina, Malaya, China, Formosa. The most important financial operations involve China, where Tokyo pays off its war debts to puppet Chinese banks with tons of gold. The analysts note for Marshall that because of the violent inflation in China, ''Japanese expenditures of puppet [government] currencies has continued to soar and Japanese indebtedness to the Chinese banks has accordingly reached astronomical totals.''[6]

The analysts also report that by Tokyo's creating a new linkage with China, ''the obvious long-run aim of the [Japanese] 'measures' . . . is the creation of a Japanese-Chinese bloc.'' Thus, one sees that according to ''the Supreme Council for Economic and Political Guidance,'' which is Japan's top control group operating in China, and which consists of representatives of the War, Navy and GEA ministries, the overall plan is: ''In order to assist in China's development, we will dispatch Japanese

4. SRS 1762, 17 August 1945.
5. SRS 1764, 19 August 1945.
6. SRS 1768, 23 August 1945.

technical experts to China on a large scale. In particular we will develop widely in China those branches of industry prohibited [by the Supreme Commander] in Japan, as well as mining and agricultural techniques."[7]

Another facet of the plan is for Tokyo to protect from postwar retribution those who ran the puppet Nanking government, the North China Political Council, the Mongolian Autonomous [Menchieng] Government, and "other Chinese who have cooperated with Japan." Foreign Minister Shigemitsu also tells his diplomats in Asia that he wants them to make every effort to ensure that the Chungking government of Chiang Kai-shek "will ultimately come to realize the necessity of a coalition with Japan." What also interests Washington is Shigemitsu's attitude toward Korea. He tells his diplomats that "we still cherish the desire to see Korea revert to the Empire."[8] The lack of Japanese understanding of how the occupied, exploited, brutally treated people of China, Korea and other countries taken over by Japan for inclusion in the Greater East Asian Co-Prosperity Sphere feel about Japan and the Japanese is incredible.

By the first of September, or only three weeks after the first atomic bomb exploded above Hiroshima, we witness the resilience of the secret government that controls Japan. The Emperor may have surrendered his nation to the Allies, but the government is planning to keep as much of the Far East as possible under Japanese influence. This brings us to the Japanese view of the atom bomb.

It is Minister Okamoto in Stockholm who first suggests an effective strategy about the atomic bomb that Japan will employ for the next fifty years. His concept is classic jujitsu, the Japanese form of wrestling that allows one to use the strength and weight of an opponent against him. On August 29, Okamoto sends a message to Tokyo in which he analyses Anglo-American public opinion garnered from reading magazines and newspapers. He tells Tokyo that the distrust of Japan is widespread and, according to the analysts in Washington, that "the people of England and America were deeply shocked at the use of the atomic bomb, of which on the whole they disapprove." Thus, says Okamoto: "In my opinion, we should judge [and make use of] the condition of enemy public opinion on the subject of the atomic bomb. Since it is difficult to justify the heavy damage inflicted and the massacre of hundreds of thousands of innocent people, there is the oppor-

---

7. SRS 1769, 24 August 1945.
8. SRS 1774, 29 August 1945.

tunity—by making use of the Diet, the radio, the various other means—
to play on enemy weakness by skillfully emphasizing the extreme
inhumanity of the bomb. I also think that we should expose the bad
faith of Russia, with whom we had neutral relations, in ignoring Japan's
request to mediate for peace and in entering the war."[9]

Two weeks later, Foreign Minister Shigemitsu begins Tokyo's exploitation of the issue. The analysts note for General Marshall that "the
Japanese leaders intend to play up the atomic bombings not only to
explain Japan's surrender [to an army that does not believe it was defeated in combat], but to offset publicity on Japan's treatment of Allied
prisoners [of war] and internees [plus countless other atrocities]." On
September 13, Shigemitsu sends a message to the Japanese legations
in Sweden, Switzerland and Portugal, saying: "The newspapers have
given wide publicity to the Government's recent memorandum concerning the atomic bomb damage in Hiroshima and Nagasaki, the sending of an Imperial messenger, the daily rising count of the dead, and
the like. Also an American investigating party went to Hiroshima on
the eighth, part of the group having gone previously to Nagasaki,
and the head of the group, Brigadier General [Thomas F.] Farrell, is
reported to have said: 'We knew from aerial photographs that the damage at Hiroshima was tremendous, but, having visited the scene, we
know now that the damage was beyond description. So horrible a
weapon must never be used again.' His statement attracted considerable
attention." (The analysts point out in a footnote that "American press
dispatches on the findings of the preliminary survey of Hiroshima contain no such statement by General Farrell.")

Shigemitsu continues, saying: "All these reports have been sent
abroad by Domei [the Japanese news service] in full detail. To what
extent have they been carried by the newspapers and other media at
your place? Since the Americans have recently been raising an uproar
about the question of our mistreatment of prisoners, I think we should
make every effort to exploit the atomic bomb question in our propaganda. If necessary, we shall telegraph further details. Please let me
know by wire whether that would be desirable."

The last sentence of this portion of the Diplomatic Summary is
for Marshall: "Note: General MacArthur today issued an order restrict-
ing Domei to the distribution of news inside Japan."[10]

---

9. SRS 1777, 1 September 1945. These recommendations by Okamoto are listed under the
heading "Psycological and Subversive."
10. SRS 1791, 15 September 1945.

Two days later, it appears that Shigemitsu's message about propaganda regarding the atomic bomb was given additional impetus by Minister Morishima in Lisbon.[11] The analysts note that he has been speculating to Tokyo about how far the Allies will go in prosecuting war criminals and has forwarded reports to Tokyo that even the Emperor and Premier Higashi-Kuni were being mentioned as possible defendants. On September 10, Morishima told Tokyo of his own suggestion: "As I have previously pointed out, the question of war criminals is coming more and more to the fore. Leaving aside for a moment the question of 'international crime' [presumably the 'crimes against peace' defined in the charter of the Four Power International Military Tribunal], it stands to reason that, if those who have violated the regular laws of warfare are to be punished, no distinction should be drawn between the victors and the vanquished.

"In particular, it is inescapable that using the atomic bomb was a crime against humanity unparalleled in the pages of history. It is quite clear from Churchill's 16 August speech in Parliament that the decision to use the bomb was arrived at by Truman and Churchill at the Potsdam Conference. I therefore believe that Japan has adequate grounds for exposing them as violators of the laws of warfare."

In response to Shigemitsu's message about counteracting the American stressing of Japanese mistreatment of prisoners, urging that *"every effort"* should be made to *"exploit the atomic bomb question in our propaganda,"* Ministers Kase in Bern and Okamoto in Stockholm both urge Tokyo to avoid creating the impression that Japan is conducting an atomic bomb propaganda campaign—even if it's true. Okamoto's message, which was sent the day General MacArthur restricted Domei to distributing news only inside Japan, includes the following suggestions for Tokyo's unobtrusively accomplishing its desired goal.

"Have announcements made exclusively for home consumption," advises Okamoto, "and have the Anglo-American news agencies carry these announcements. [Also] have Anglo-American newspapermen write stories on the bomb damage and thus create a powerful impression abroad."

On September 17, Minister Morishima in Lisbon registers his agreement on the opinions of his colleagues, adding a number of

---

11. SRS 1793, 17 September 1945.

points.[12] As reported by the analysts, they include: (A) "Although the 'worldwide shock' occasioned by the use of the bomb was 'tremendous,' and 'neutral nations, particularly the Vatican, immediately condemned its use as inhumane,' public opinion in general tends to consider the employment of the bomb as an act of humanitarianism since it hastened the end of the war. (B) Despite the fact that Japanese reports on the bomb were published 'more or less faithfully' in various Anglo-American newspapers, 'I have the feeling that those reports have been overshadowed recently by the powerful propaganda about Japanese atrocities.''

Morishima then continues, saying: "I think it might be rather effective to supply data to the Apostolic Nuncio in Japan. Also, I should like you to telegraph me an outline of the available data to assist me in giving confidential explanations . . . to the authorities in Portugal. . . . Wide publicity has been given here to the pitiable consequences of the bomb, through reports from the Japanese side as well as from British and American correspondents in Japan, and the people in general have been deeply shocked.''

According to Karel van Wolferen, who is considered one of the best Western experts on Japan: "No country has ever spent as much on officially recorded lobbying expenses as the Japanese were spending in Washington in the mid- and later 1980s. . . . A large proportion of academic research by Western scholars who concentrate on Japan is funded by Japanese institutions. The idea that scholars and commentators can remain objective because no formal conditions are attached to what they receive is mostly an illusion when the money comes from Japan. . . . [This] has bred large numbers of Japan specialists who are in varying degrees—however unwittingly—apologists for Japan. . . . Japanese propaganda is also spread . . . by numerous newspaper and magazine articles mindful of the editorial convention of telling the imagined 'two sides' of a story . . . notwithstanding the systematic Japanese protectionism that has been staring [the writers] in the face for more than two decades.''[13] One can see how the propaganda program Morishima started in 1945 continues to reap untold benefits for Japan, and what damage has been done to a true Western understanding of Japan, its government, its objectives, and its people.

---

12. SRS 1796, 20 September 1945.
13. Karel von Wolferen, *The Enigma of Japanese Power* (New York: Alfred A. Knopf, Inc., 1989), pages 12-13. The Japanese government suppressed this book. One does not need to be told why.

✖ ✖ ✖

During the first week of November 1945, the Republican members of the Joint Committee investigating Pearl Harbor release to the press, despite the pleas of General Marshall and President Truman that they not do so, the momentous news that America broke the Japanese diplomatic ciphers prior to and during World War II. As a result, on November 3, the U.S. stops reading these Japanese messages.[14] America's most important informational source regarding Japanese intentions is destroyed. The last Diplomatic Summary concludes with a circular sent out by the Japanese Foreign Ministry on November 2 to the embassy offices at Nanking and Saigon and to the Consulate General at Tsingtao. The one-sentence announcement from Tokyo says only: "With this wire as the last, we are discontinuing radio communication *for a while* because of [Allied] radio control." (Emphasis added.)

✖ ✖ ✖

Almost fifty years to the day before this book was completed, Japanese consul general Beppu in Dublin, Ireland, sent Tokyo a long appraisal of world political affairs.[15] In concluding, he comments: "Japan has been disarmed and stands hemmed in between America and Russia. If, however, our people maintain their unity and preserve internal order, we are still capable of making use of our geographical position and our superior faculties to establish a stable and influential footing in East Asia." A few days later, Beppu sends another analysis to Tokyo, saying: "The basic policy of the United Nations is to render Japan powerless for as long a period as possible. Japan's need for overseas expansion, however, arises from her economic difficulties. We should emphasize the fact that this was the reason for the so-called rise of the military [in Japan], and thus get the Allies to concentrate their attention on economic problems."

The rebirth of Japan as a world economic power is today an accomplished fact. And the efforts begun by Shigemitsu in 1945 to make the Anglo-American alliance bear the entire burden for using atomic

---

14. SRS 1837, 3 November 1945.
15. SRS 1801, 25 September 1945.

weapons has been successful; it is being supported by certain American historians' highly selective usage of U.S. pre-invasion casualty figures to bolster their moral indictment of the men who, in the most difficult circumstances, had to rely on "real-time intelligence" in making their decision to drop the atomic bomb. Meanwhile, two generations of Japan's youth have been brought up to believe that the primary moral event of World War II occurred on August 6, 1945, when the first atomic bomb exploded over Hiroshima. Within Japan the moral questions of Japan's actions prior to, and during, World War II are still unresolved. According to recent news reports,[16] the right wing in Japan has "long opposed mixing the history of the war with the Hiroshima bombing." And for forty years that city's Peace Memorial Museum has given visitors only the slightest hint of Japan's responsibility for starting a war that the bombing ended. Museum visitors were not told that Hiroshima's factories had been converted to build military hardware in World War II, or that the city was where the Mitsubishi Heavy Industries shipyard built great warships. Nor did the visitors know that most of the workers in these industries were Koreans and Chinese who had been forcibly brought to Japan as slave labor.

Only fifty years after the fact has the museum in Hiroshima displayed items such as photographs celebrating the Japanese capture of Nanking, China, in December 1937, which was followed by six weeks of rape and pillage that shocked the world. The Japanese-language captions for these photographs carefully ignore how many Chinese were killed during those horrific days by the Japanese army. (Only an English-language caption cites the figure given by China: 300,000.)

Meanwhile, in 1994, two ministers of the Japanese government are forced to resign because they publicly tried to explain away Japan's responsibility for the war. This occurs while the Japanese government is about to acknowledge for the first time the truth about another terrible atrocity and pay a billion dollars to assuage the pain and suffering of 200,000 Asian "comfort women" (mostly South Korean) who were forced at gunpoint to become prostitutes for the Japanese military. Most recently, current pulp fiction in Japan is rewriting the history of the war so that Japan wins in battles it had actually lost.[17] And the Japanese parliament is unable to agree whether

---

16. *New York Times,* 4 August 1994, A4.
17. *New York Times,* 4 March 1995, A1.

or not Japan should apologize for invading other Asian countries and killing millions of people during the course of the war.[18].

As proven by the Magic Diplomatic Summaries, ever since August 1945, the policy of Japan has been to portray herself as a victim of the war. For how long will the Japanese government try to mislead its people and continue this propaganda campaign overseas? Can the still-powerful right-wing militarists regain control of Japanese foreign policy? One sees questions such as these raised constantly in the media. At times it makes one wish that America had never revealed its greatest secret of World War II: Magic.

18. *New York Times,* 6 March 1995, A9.

APPENDIX

President Roosevelt's memo setting forth his disagreement with the British proposal for postwar zones of occupation.

SOURCE: ABC 384 NW EUROPE, 20 AUGUST 1943, SEC. 1-B.

SECRET

WS 82
February 22, 1944.

THE WHITE HOUSE

WASHINGTON

February 21, 1944

MEMORANDUM FOR

THE ACTING SECRETARY OF STATE

I disagree with the British proposal of the occupation of boundaries which would go into effect in Germany after unconditional surrender or after fighting has stopped.

1. I do not want the United States to have the postwar burden of reconstituting France, Italy and the Balkans. This is not our natural task at a distance of 3,500 miles or more. It is definitely a British task in which the British are far more vitally interested than we are yet.

2. From the point of view of the United States, our principal object is not to take part in the internal problems in southern Europe but is rather to take part in eliminating Germany at a possible and even probably third World War.

3. Various points have been raised about the difficulties of transferring our troops, etc., from a French front to a northern German front— that is called a 'leap-frog'. These objections are specious because no matter where British and American troops are on the day of Germany's surrender, it is physically easy for them to go anywhere—north, east or south.

4. I have had to consider also the ease of maintaining American troops in some part of Germany. All things considered, and remembering that all supplies have to come 3,500 miles or more by sea, the United States should use the ports of northern Germany—Hamburg and Bremen—and the ports of the Netherlands for this long range operation.

5. Therefore, I think the American policy should be to occupy northwestern Germany, We, British and other occupying the area from the Rhine south, and also being responsible for the policing of France and Italy, if this should become necessary.

6. In regard to the long range security of Britain against Germany, this is not a part of the first occupation. The British will have plenty of time to work that out, including their holding, air fields, etc. The Americans by that time will be only too glad to retire all their military forces from Europe.

7. If anything further is needed to justify this disagreement with the British lines of demarcation, I can only add that political considerations in the United States make my decision conclusive.

You might speak to me about this if the above is not wholly clear.

F. D. R.

SECRET

On 13 April 1944, the Working Security Committee instructs Ambassador Winant in London to adhere to Roosevelt's wishes regarding the American zone of occupation.

SOURCE: ABC 384 NW EUROPE, 20 AUGUST 1943, SEC. 1-B.

- 2 -

2. Ambassador Winant should be instructed that, in his discretion, he may concur in a recommendation by the Commission that the boundary between the northwestern zone and the southern zone be defined as proposed by the British Delegation.

3. With respect to the zones to be occupied by the United Kingdom and the United States, Ambassador Winant should be instructed to adhere to the directives which were given him under date of February 25, 1944 (EACOM 7) setting forth the decision of the President that American forces should occupy the northwestern zone. This Government is of the opinion that the southern zone and Austria should be occupied by British forces.

WS- 134
April 13, 1944

ZONES OF OCCUPATION

It will be recalled that the War Department, under date of February 25, 1944, transmitted a copy of CCS 320/4 (Revised) setting forth the views of the United States Chiefs of Staff with respect to the zones of occupation of German and Austrian territory with the recommendation that these views be transmitted to Ambassador Winant for negotiation in the European Advisory Commission. Ambassador Winant, pending consideration of his recommendations in this matter, did not present these views to the European Advisory Commission and informed the Department of State that his recommendations would be presented by Mr. George F. Kennan, Counselor of the American Delegation to the European Advisory Commission, who was returning to Washington. These recommendations were transmitted to the War Department under date of April 5, 1944 together with the information that Mr. Kennan had discussed this problem with the President, and that the President had expressed himself as being favorably inclined to an acceptance of the western border of the Russian zone of occupation as proposed by the British and Russian Delegations. By letter of April 10, the War Department took note of these developments and of its expectation that the Working Security Committee would now prepare new instructions to Ambassador Winant, for clearance with the Joint Chiefs or Staff in the usual manner.

The recommendations of the Working Security Committee on this question or zones of occupation are as follows:

1. Ambassador Winant should be instructed that, in his discretion, he may concur in a recommendation by the Commission that the boundaries of the Soviet zone of occupation be defined as proposed by the Soviet Delegation.

2. Ambassador Winant

Eisenhower's letter to Generals Bradley, Montgomery, and Devers of 15 September 1945. Eisenhower says, "Berlin is the main prize. . . . Our strategy, however, will have to be coordinated with that of the Russians."

SOURCE: POST OVERLORD PLANNING 381, VOL. 1.

The order of 29 March 1945 that sent the Second Armored Division racing to the river Elbe.

S E C R E T

```
!:::::::::::::::::!!!
:   S E C R E T   :
: AUTH: CG 2 AD   :
: INIT:  Bil       :
: DATE:   29 Mar 45
!:::::::::::::::::!!!
```

Hq 2d Armd Div
APO 252
F323341
290400A Mar 45

───────────────────────────────────────

FO NO 5

MAPS: GSGS, 4416, 1/100,000 GERMANY

1. a. See current G-2 Per Rpt and Estimate of situation, 28 Mar.
    b. 8th Armd Div and 30th Inf Div on right continue adv to E.
        17 A/B Div and Gds Armd Div (Br) continue adv to E and N.
        83 Inf Div (Mtz) will follow 2 AD closely, prepared to take
        over objs gained, clean out pockets of resistance by-pass-,
        ed, and secure lines o f com unications. (See ovly).

2. a. 2d Armd Div:
        (1) Atk 30 Mar through XVIII Corps from line HALTERN-
             DULMEN.
        (2) Atk E, N of the LIPPE Canal, to seize LUDINGHAUSEN
             and secure crossings over the DORTMUND-EMS Canal.
        (3) Continue atk to cut communications E of HAMM.
        (4) Be prepared to immediately continue atk to E on
             BERLIN.
    b. Routes, objs, boundaries: See ovly.
    c. Time of attack 300600A Mar 45.
    d. TROOP LIST:

CCA	CCB
Brig Gen J H Collier, Cmdg	**Col Sidney R Hinds, Cmdg**
66th AR	67th AR (-3 Bn)
2d Bn, 41 AIR	1st & 3d Bn, 41 AIR
377 RCT (- reinf Bn)	Co D, 17 Engr Bn
Co A, 17 Engr Bn	Co C, 702 TD Bn
Co A, 702 TD Bn	Co B, 48 Med Bn
Co A, 48 Med Bn	78th FA w/dets 195 AAA Bn
14 FA w/dets 195 AAA Bn	92nd FA w/dets 195 AAA Bn
65 FA w/dets 450 AAA Bn	Det Maint
Det Maint Bn	

Eisenhower's order to his field commanders telling them to advance on the river Elbe "and be prepared to conduct operations beyond. . . . "

HQ TWELFTH ARMY GROUP

AG CABLES
INCOMING CLASSIFIED MESSAGE

ORIG: 021444A APR 45   R

TOP SECRET-URGENT

FROM   : SHAEF FORWARD signed EISENHOWER cite SHGCT

ACTION TO   : C in C EUR, CO TWELFTH ARMY GROUP, CG SIXTH ARMY GROUP.

INFO TO   : AGWAR for COS, AMSSO for BCOS, CG FIRST ALLIED A/B ARMY, CG USSTAF,
                AMCIF, CIC in C 2ND TAF, CG NINTH AIR FORCE, FIRST TACAF, CG CONT ZMT,
                SHAEF MAIN.

REF NR   : FWD 18475

S.S.M. SHAEF 22/6/45.

1. Limit distribution of this message to absolute minimum, deliver only to addressee or his appointed representative.

2. Operations to isolate the Ruhr as directed in my Forward 18179 (SCAF 247) of 25 March 1945 having been completed, it is my intention to divide and destroy the enemy forces by launching a powerful thrust on the axis Kassel-Leipzig. It is hoped that this advance will make a junction with the Soviet forces in that area.

3. Effective 040000B April, Ninth United States Army will revert to operational command Twelfth Army Group.

4. Northern Group of Armies:

    A. Will continue, without pause, its advance to the general line Hanover-Bremen (SEE para 5A)

    B. Will, thereafter, launch a thrust to the River Elbe in conjunction with and protecting the Northern flank of Central Group of Armies (see para 5B)

    C. Will seize any opportunity of capturing a bridgehead over the River Elbe and be prepared to conduct operations beyond the River Elbe.

    D. The question of opening the port of Bremen will have to be decided as the situation develops.

5. Central Group of Armies will:

    A. Mop up encircled enemy forces in the Ruhr. During this phase it will protect the southern flank of Northern Group of Armies so as to ensure the latter's advance, without pause, to Hanover. It will firmly establish its left flank in the Hildesheim area for this purpose. (see para 4A).

REF NR: FWD 18475   TOP SECRET-URGENT   W-42439

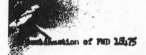

...uation of FWD 18475   Page 2.

    B. In conjunction with Northern Group of Armies, launch a thrust with
        its main axis: Kassel-Leipzig, establishing the right flank of its
        advance on the line: Erz Gebirge mountains-Bayreuth (see Para 4D)

    C. Seize any opportunity of capturing a bridgehead over the River Elbe
        and be prepared to conduct operations beyond the Elbe.

6. Southern Group of Armies:

    A. Will protect the right flank of Central Group of Armies west of the
        Bayreuth area, where it will connect up with Central Group of Armies;

    B. Will, without prejudice to 5A above, be prepared to launch a thrust
        on the axis: Nurnburg-Regensburg-Linz, to prevent consolidation of
        German resistance in the south.

    7. Boundaries: Subject to adjustment in detail by Commanders concerned, effective
010001B April:

    A. Between Northern and Central Groups of Armies: Present boundary between
        Ninth Army and Second Army as far as Alpen thence Wesel-Brunen-Coesfeld-
        Halden-Valen-Coesfeld-Munster-Halle (all to Group of Armies) thence
        (all inclusive to Northern Group of Armies) Lubecke-Minden-Stadthagen-
        Hanover-Uelefelde-Stendal. Running rights to Central Group of Armies
        on Autobahn North of Hanover.

    B. Between Central and Southern Groups of Armies: Present boundary extended
        from Heidingen-Coburg-Bayreuth (all to Central Group of Armies).

8. Acknowledge

9. For CCS and BCOS this is SCAF Number 261.

REFERENCE: FWD 18179 SCAF 247   (TOP SEC)   (M-44945)

TWELFTH ARMY GROUP DISTRIBUTION: ACKNOWLEDGED BY Q-28644

ACTION TO: 1. G-3

COPIES TO   2. G-2
          3. G-4
          4. File
          5565

Copy: 4

REF NR: FWD 18475   TOP SECRET-URGENT   M-44939

Letters written by Samuel Halpern to Professor Barton Bernstein sourcing the archival documents proving that President Truman was fully aware of the high casualty estimates involved in the invasion and occupation of Japan. The handwritten note on the last page says: "Prof. B.B. never commented on this last letter. S.H. 10/19/94."

2202 Popkins Lane
Alexandria, VA 22307
July 16, 1990

Prof. Barton Bernstein
Dept. of History
Stanford University
Stanford, CA 94305-2024

Dear Professor Bernstein,

This letter comments on two points you made during your talk on July 12, 1990 at the Strategic Bombing Symposium on the Atomic Bombing of Japan. One point had to do with the number of American casualties that U.S. military planners expected when the U.S. invaded Japan. The other point had to do with your questioning whether a meeting of top-level people discussing the use of the atomic bomb ever took place.

My comments are based on my background. I was trained as an historian in the City College of the City of New York (CCNY), 1938-1942, under Professors Oscar I. Janowsky, Michael Krauss, Nelson P. Mead, Richard B. Morris, J. Salwyn Shapiro, Louis L. Snyder, and Joseph Wisan; and in Columbia University, 1942-1943, under Professors Allan Nevins, Nathaniel Pfeffer, and Robert Schuyler. In early 1943 I joined the Office of Strategic Services (OSS) and remained in the intelligence profession, occupying positions of increasing responsibility, until retiring from CIA at the end of 1974.

Regarding the question of the number of American casualties expected in the invasion of Japan, I strongly support the figure of 500,000 casualties as stated by General Andrew Goodpaster during the discussion period of the symposium session. This was the operative figure among the military planners preparing the plans for the invasion of Japan, one landing to be on the island of Kyushu, and one to be on the main island, Honshu, near Tokyo, involving either the Kanto plain area or Tokyo Bay itself.

Even before the battle of Okinawa, which resulted in some 49,000 American casualties, ended in June 1945, plans for invasion of the main islands of Japan were being developed. In early May 1945 I was stationed with an OSS unit in Kandy, Ceylon. I, a junior officer, and three, more senior of my colleagues (two geographers and one cartographer) were suddenly ordered back to Washington from Ceylon. We had, previously received orders to go to China, "over the hump." Neither we, nor our superiors at the base in Ceylon, had any idea of why our orders had been changed. Everyone was surprised too at the fact that our orders stated that we were assigned Joint Chiefs of Staff No. 1 priority,

-2-

the highest possible, for travel by air via the fastest, most direct, route back to Washington. We reported for duty on VE day, May 8, 1945.

The four of us were assigned to help in the then top secret planning for the coming invasion of Japan. We were to provide a variety of data for use by the military planners and to provide answers to questions posed by them. No, we were not told about the "special weapon", the atomic bomb. When we were briefed on our duties, it was repeatedly stressed that the U.S. forces could expect to suffer some 500,000 casualties. That figure has stayed with me ever since early May, 1945, before the atomic bomb was used.

That is why I strongly support Gen. Goodpaster's statement on July 12, 1990. In addition, given the figure of some 49,000 casualties to take Okinawa alone, reason alone says that the number of casualties to take the main islands of Japan would have to be several times that of the Okinawa figure.

Notwithstanding the figures one might find in declassified planning documents, the figure of 500,000 American casualties was the operative one at the working level. As a veteran of some 32 years in the government bureaucracy, I can assure you that numerous planning documents, signed by a variety of authorities can be found, many of which did not become final action directives. The mere existence of planning documents does not mean that they are definitive and represent final approval positions. In addition, if possible, one needs to know who actually drafted the papers and their level of competence. One is reminded of the many officers on the staff of Field Marshal Haig in World War I who drafted all sorts of military plans while stationed in England without ever once setting foot on the actual battlefield in France. They never saw, and therefore never appreciated, the actual conditions of trench warfare. Is it possible that the officers who prepared the documents, with the expected low casualty figures you used, suffered from similar inexperience?

You somewhat jokingly doubted that a high-level meeting about the atomic bomb prior to its use ever actually took place. Your reason was that not one of the five or six high level persons ever mention it in their diaries. I put it that because of the high level of secrecy surrounding the atomic bomb that one should not be surprised that no mention is found in the diaries. Take the case of the high level of secrecy surrounding another sensitive activity during World War II, namely the breaking of enemy codes and ciphers, namely ULTRA and MAGIC. Even though some 30,000

2202 Popkins Lane
Alexandria, VA 22307
August 27, 1990

Dear Professor Bernstein,

Thank you for your letter of July 31, 1990 which I received on August 11, 1990. It has taken me the intervening time to find a copy of your article in the Bulletin of the Atomic Scientists (June/July 1986) and then to consult, at the National Archives, the documents you cite.

I found the documents quite interesting and revealing but not necessarily leading to the same conclusions as yours. For example: your footnote 7 states "Marshall to secretary of war, June 7, 1945, with Handy to Hull, June 1, 1945, and attachment, file OPD 336 TS; Truman to secretary of war, n.d., with Herbert Hoover, 'Memorandum for Ending the Japanese War,' file OPD 704 TS, Records of War Department General Staff, Record Group 165, National Archives." In fact the Truman transmittal note to the secretary of war is dated June 9, 1945 and asks for Stimson's analysis because of his Far Eastern knowledge and asks for later discussions. The note also refers to the attached paper by a "Mr. Hoover". Truman does not say Herbert Hoover. The War Department stamp on the transmittal note is clearly stamped "Received War Department Secretary's Office 1945 JUN 9 PM 2129." (S/W Safe File (Stimson) "Japan")

But this was not the first time the Hoover memorandum reached the War Department, although in a slightly different version. In OPD 336 TS Sect. IV, Case 119, 1945, Box 143, is a Memorandum for the Record dated 11 June 1945 with the signature block having the initials H.P.T. This memorandum states that Gen. Handy sent a memo dated 1 June 1945 directing OPD to prepare a study for the Secretary of War showing the War Department General Staff reaction to a

"...paper prepared by an economist (name unknown) which was furnished to General Handy by the Secretary of War.

"2. A study was prepared in the Strategy and Policy Group on 4 June, cleared with General Hull and hand-carried to General Handy. On 7 June the original was dispatched to the Secretary of War by memorandum signed by the Chief of Staff." Obviously the General Staff did not know the memo came from Mr. Hoover, let alone from the former President Herbert Hoover.

It is clear that the War Department had a version of the Hoover paper before Truman did. The Chief of Staff (Marshall) transmitted the staff's comments to Stimson on 7 June 1945 stating his General agreement with the staff's comments. The economist's paper had said in paragraph VI:

"What are the results to the United States and Britain? "America will save 500,000 to 1,000,000 lives and an enormous loss of resources.

"Comment: It is obvious that peace would save lives and resources, but the estimated loss of 500,000 lives due to

-3-

people worked on various phases of ULTRA for example, there was no mention of it in people's diaries or published works for almost 30 years, or until Group Captain Winterbotham published "The Ultra Secret" in 1974, the first book on the subject in English. (The first book to reveal that the German codes and ciphers had been broken appeared in 1967 in Polish and in 1973 a book on the subject appeared in French.) Following that, the military histories of World War II which had been published had then to be seen in a new light. None of them had mentioned ULTRA, especially the official military histories and those by the military commanders such as Eisenhower, Bradley, Montgomery, etc. It shows that secrets can be kept when people realize their importance.

It should not be surprising therefore, to find that in view of the extreme sensitivity of the subject matter, none of the "participants" at the "meeting" ever made any note of it. Having worked in an atmosphere of security classifications and classified activities for my entire adult life, I have seen that mere absence of a record document does not mean that something did not happen. It is a version of Sherlock Holmes's "The Hound of the Baskervilles" where the clue was that the dog did not bark.

I hope the above is helpful and useful.

Sincerely yours,

[signature]

Samuel Halpern

P.S. I am sending a copy to Ms. Tami Biddle at the National Air and Space Museum for her use.

As to the numbers game itself, the June 18, 1845 meeting with Truman, where he gave the go ahead for Olympic, is a good place to begin.

According to Adm. Leahy's memo of 14 June 1945 (later identified as JPS 697/D, 14 June 1945) stating to the JCS that the "President wants to meet 18 June 1945" to discuss the defeat of Japan, Adm. Leahy said that, among other things, the President wanted to have an "estimate on killed and wounded resulting from the invasion of Japan." Adm. Leahy also said "The President will make a decision on the campaign with the purpose of economizing to the maximum extent possible in the loss of American lives." Adm. Leahy indicated that from the President's viewpoint, "Time and money are relatively unimportant."

This shows Truman's concern about casualties and indicates that he would seek information wherever he could find it. True, Truman liked and trusted Marshall. But he disliked and distrusted staffs and bureaucracy in general, remembering his World War I experience in the artillery. He also disliked MacArthur, then as well as later in the Korean War. Truman also liked and had a high regard for Adm. Leahy. And Leahy was closer at hand in the White House than was Marshall who was at the Pentagon or even if he was at the War Department offices at 21st and D streets, northwest, the area of the current State Department. How often did Truman consult with others, such as Leahy or Stimson?

The extracted items from the minutes of the meeting with Truman at the White House on 18 June 1945 give some flavor of the discussion about casualties. Marshall apparently did not give JCS 1388 to Truman (JCS 1388 was the paper asked for by Leahy in his 14 June 1945 memorandum), but discussed it verbally in briefing Truman (25 June 1945 memo for Asst. Secy WDGS--ABC 384 Japan (31 May 1944) TS Sec 1B). He pointed out that "our experience in the Pacific war is so diverse as to casualties that it is considered wrong to give any estimate in numbers." Marshall then went on into the numbers game using JCS 1388 as amended as his text, including the latest figures from MacArthur, who had disagreed with an earlier estimate from his own staff. No one knows how much of this oral briefing and its detailed statistics Truman retained. It is reasonable to assume that he may have retained the summation line "there is reason to believe that the first 30 days (underlining added) in Kyushu should not exceed the price we paid for Luzon." That figure was used in JCS 1388 as revised (JPS 697/2, 9 July 1945) was 31,000 casualties (killed, wounded and missing in action).

But not all present at the meeting with the President were satisfied or agreed with the casualty figures discussed. Adm. Leahy recalled that the President was interested in the price for Kyushu. He pointed out that the troops in Okinawa had lost 35 percent in casualties. (The Tenth Army casualties were 39,413 and the Navy 9,700.) (The 35 percent

-3-

carrying the war to conclusion under our present plan of campaign (underlining in original) is considered to be entirely too high." (Stimson)

In the National Archives file entitled "S/W Safe File (Stimson) 'Japan'." is found additional data on the Hoover paper attached to Truman's transmittal note to Stimson. In the version given to Truman, Hoover, on page 2 after listing his views of six American objectives, states "Beyond this point there can be no American objectives that are worth the expenditure of 500,000 to 1,000,000 American lives." Again in paragraph 10 (b) on p.4, Mr. Hoover says "We would have saved the lives of 500,000 to 1,000,000 American boys, the loss of which may be necessary by going to the end."

The military staff comments on this version of the Hoover paper were apparently prepared by GAL (probably George A. Lincoln) on 14 June 1945. This staff paper again denigrated the large casualty figures. The comments were sent to Stimson by Marshall on 15 June 1945. On the side of the file copy are notes which indicate that Stimson was not in agreement with all the staff comments.

In the same National Archives file are copies of memos to Truman from "Acting Secretary" (agency not shown, but probably State Department),commenting on the Hoover paper. One such memo, 5 pages, from Acting Secretary to the President is dated June 13, 1945, referring to the Hoover paper attached to a June 9, 1945 transmittal note from the President. This is the same date Truman sent a note with the Hoover paper to Stimson. A second memo, 1 page, from Acting Secretary, dated June 16, 1945 refers to a June 12, 1945 memo analyzing the Hoover paper (probably June 13, 1945 was meant or the June 13, 1945 memo transmitted the analysis which was done on June 12, 1945).

My reason for going into so much detail on the Hoover paper is to indicate that the 500,000 figure was not "a postwar creation" as you say. It had obviously been bruited about at least by the end of May and early June 1945 by no less a figure than former President Hoover and by both State and War Departments at some levels had considered and discussed the matter. Hoover had distributed the paper to more than just to Truman. It would be interesting to know to whom else he had given it. But it is clear that the 500,000 figure was not made up after the event.

I still do not know where the people who briefed me and my colleagues in early May 1945 got the figure of 500,00 casualties. I only know that it was the figure used and it made a deep indelible impression on a young man, 23 years old. It is something I have never forgotten, even though I never kept a diary which was against strict security regulations.

It may be possible that General Goodpaster may have additional data on Secretary of War Stimson's use of the 500,000 figure when the general was assigned to OPD in 1945 as a lieutenant colonel. You may recall that Gen. Goodpaster said that Stimson used the 500,000 figure regularly.

-4-

figure used by Leahy was high, but not that much off. For example, the Marines at Iwo Jima had estimated 31 percent or 18,190 out of a force of 61,000 prior to the attack and the actual figures were 32.8 percent or 19,969. /See RG 319 Records of the Army Staff, OLMH Manuscript "HL Stimson on the War Years" folder marked Surrender of Japan draft Bx 68 in letter D--Rudolph A. Winnacker to Henry L. Stimson, 12 Nov. 1946./

Leahy went on to point out that "If this percentage were applied to the number of troops to be employed in Kyushu, he thought from the similarity of the fighting too be expected that this would give a good estimate of the casualties to be expected. He was interested therefore in finding out how many troops are to be used in Kyushu."

At the meeting Adm King, CINCUS (COMINCH) and CNO, who had not agreed with an early estimate of casualties by the planners (PFI/Ad-3, 2 May 1945), gave as his opinion "that a realistic casualty figure would lie somewhere between the number experienced by General MacArthur in the operations on Luzon and the Okinawa casualties." (Adm. Nimitz, CINCPAC and CINCPACPOA; sent in his estimate later, JCS 1388/1, 20 June 1945, of casualties for the first 30 days of Olympic alone as 49,000; he did not give any estimates for Coronet. It is not known whether this figure was ever given to Truman.)

Later at the 18 June 1945 meeting, Marshall said that the total of assault troops for Kyushu (Olympic) was 766,700. If Truman, following Leahy's suggestion, took 30 percent of 766,700 he would arrive at the figure of 230,010 casualties and 268,345 if he used 35 percent. If Truman later added the same percentages for the invasion of the Tokyo plain (Coronet), he would get the figure of 600,000 casualties using 30 percent out of 2,000,000 or 700,000 casualties using 35 percent. Plans for Coronet called for the use of 375,000 as the assault force followed by an additional 1,625,000 troops for a total of 2,000,000 troops by May 1946.)

Gen. Baker., speaking for the Army Air Force, added air casualties to the discussion by pointing out that "Present air casualties are averaging 2 percent per mission, about 30 percent per month." Baker gave no total figures.

It was clear that Truman was concerned about the casualty figures. At the meeting he is said to have said "Kyushu was "practically creating another Okinawa closer to Japan, to which the Chiefs of Staff agreed." And on giving the go ahead on the plan to invade Kyushu, the "President said "He hoped that there was a possibility of preventing an Okinawa from one end of Japan to the other." It must have been a question to which he returned.

-5-

As the figures above show, it would not be difficult for Truman to arrive at a 500,000 and more casualty figure for the invasions of Japan, both Kyushu and the Tokyo Plain. The June 18 meeting was not the end of Truman's concern about the costs involved in invading Japan. He knew from that meeting that his military advisers were not fully agreed on the subject. At least one item appears in the National Archives files I consulted, and there may be more scattered in other files. The one item consulted was a memorandum for the President sent by Stimson on 2 July 1945. (The file, S/W Safe File (Stimson) "Japan", has the second draft of a June 26, 1945 memo with the notation that it was sent on 2 July 1945.) Stimson says in part:

"2. There is reason to believe that the operation for the occupation of Japan following the landing may be a very long, costly, and arduous struggle on our part.

"3. If we once land on one of the main islands and begin a forceful occupation of Japan, we shall probably have cast the die of last ditch resistance...Once started in actual invasion, we shall in my opinion have to go through with an even more bitter finish fight than in Germany. We shall incur the losses incident to such a war and we shall have to leave the Japanese islands even more thoroughly destroyed than was the case with Germany."

I do not know how many more similar memos were sent to Truman by others, both in and out of government; nor do I know how many people spoke with Truman along the same lines, people such as Adm.Leahy for example. But clearly the June 18, 1945 meeting with the JCS was not the end of the discussion.

To all this we must add the information available to Truman, et al. obtained from intercepted Japanese radio messages and decrypted by U.S. cryptanalysts. These Japanese messages revealed in late June and July 1945 that the Japanese military high command were preparing for a fight to the finish including massive suicide attacks by aircraft and ships and men and an armed civilian populace. It would be one thing to receive "guesstimates" of casualties from military planners, among which there was not complete agreement, and to contemplate total losses after months of a fight to the finish to subdue and occupy Japan.

In sum, the 500,000 casualty figure was no myth then or now. It was real and plausible, as Adm. Leahy could have shown (and may have) by merely multiplying the total number of American forces to be used by a 30 percent casualty rate. As for the semantic view of the word "lives" referring only to dead and the word casualties including dead, wounded, and missing, I believe that Truman and others, particularly the average layman, the word lives would include all categories.

-6-

Truman was not writing a staff study nor talking to professional soldiers. People's lives are very much affected by being wounded or missing. The fine points can be argued by professionals and academics, but the average person does not make such fine distinctions.

As to the high-level meeting at Potsdam, I suppose we will have to agree to disagree. There is no way either you or I can prove our respective thesis.

Thank you for getting me interested enough to do some historical research again. It was fun, despite the amount of time it took. I'm sure I have not changed your mind, but I know I have been strengthened in my view and that of General Goodpaster.

Sincerely yours,

Samuel Halpern

cc: Tami Biddle, NASM

Prof. E.S. never commented on that last letter.
SH
10/14/94

Archival documents exchanged between the Joint Chiefs, Secretary of War Stimson, and President Truman demonstrating the discussion of casualty figures involved in the invasion and occupation of Japan.

MEMORANDUM
ON
ENDING THE JAPANESE WAR

I believe there is just a bare chance of ending the Japanese war if an adequate declaration of Far Eastern policy be made by the United States and Britain jointly, and if possible with China. The President has already taken an admirable step in this direction which might now be no further advanced.

The following is my own view of American objectives and the interpretation of them into such a declaration

1. As this war arose fundamentally over Japanese invasion of Manchuria, the first point in such declaration is the restoration of Manchuria to China. It is an essential step to the establishment of the sanctity of international agreements.

2. For reparations to China, it should be declared that all Japanese Government property in China must be handed to the Chinese.

3. As the militarist party in Japan has proved a menace to the whole world, a third point in such a declaration should be to insist upon the unconditional surrender of the whole Japanese Army and Navy and their equipment.

4. In view of the military caste by inheritance among the Japanese people which even assassinates Japanese opposition, they cannot be trusted with a military establishment. Therefore, the third point is continued disarmament for a long enough period (probably a generation) to dissolve the whole military caste and its know-how.

THE WHITE HOUSE
WASHINGTON

June 9, 1945

MEMORANDUM FOR THE SECRETARY OF WAR

FROM: Harry S. Truman

The attached paper was submitted to me by Mr. Hoover and I should like for you to submit to me your analysis of it. After you have done so, we can discuss it.

In view of your long experience in far eastern affairs, I should especially value your judgment.

5. As certain Japanese officers are charged with violation of the rules of war and human conduct, they should be surrendered for fair trial by the Allies.

6. As certain islands held by Japan are necessary protection against the future and to enforce disarmament, the next point of declaration could be the ceding of these islands to the Allies.

Beyond this point there can be no American objectives that are worth the expenditure of 500,000 to 1,000,000 American lives.

7. Encouragement to Japan to accept such points and a part saving of face could be had by further necessary points in the declaration.

(a) That the Allies have no desire to destroy either the Japanese people or their government, or to interference in the Japanese way of life; that it is our desire that the Japanese build up their prosperity and their contributions to the civilised world.

(b) That the Japanese retain Korea and Formosa as trustees under the world trustee system. The Koreans and Formosans are today incapable of self-government, they are not Chinese, and the Japanese have proved that under the liberal elements of their country that they are capable administrators. These countries have been Japanese possessions for over fifty years and their annexation has been admitted by treaties of America, Britain and China.

(c) A further point in declaration should be that except as above mentioned we wished no reparations nor indemnities.

8. A final declaration could be added that if the Japanese Government is not prepared to accept these terms it is evidence that they are unfit to remain in control of the Japanese people and we must need proceed to their ultimate destruction.

9. That the Japanese would accept these terms and end the war cannot be stated with any assurance. The factors favorable to its acceptance are:

(a) The appointment of Suzuki, a one-time anti-militarist elder-statesman, as Prime Minister;

(b) The desire of the Japanese to preserve the Mikado who is the spiritual head of the nation;

(c) The sense they showed after the Russo-Japanese war of making peace before Russia organised her full might;

(d) The fear of complete destruction which by now they must know is their fate;

(e) The fact that there is a large middle class in Japan which was the product of industrialization, who are liberal-minded, who have in certain periods governed Japan and in these periods they gave full cooperation in peaceful forces of the world. That this group again exert itself is the only hope of stable and progressive government.

10. From an American point of view, if such a declaration were successful, we would:

(a) Have attained our every objective except perhaps the vengeance of an excited minority of our people;

(b) We would have saved the lives of 500,000 to 1,000,000 American boys, the loss of which may be necessary by going on to the end.

(c) We would have saved the exhaustion of our resources to a degree that otherwise will make our own recovery very, very difficult and our aid to the rest of the world of little consequence;

(d) We will save ourselves the impossible task of setting up a military or civil government in Japan with all its dangers of revolutions and conflicts with our allies.

11. If Japan does not accept, the essence of such a declaration still has advantages:

(a) It will clarify the world's understanding that Manchuria is to be returned to China;

(b) It again demonstrates that America is not in war for any purpose but to establish order in the world.

C070234

C070233

THE WHITE HOUSE
WASHINGTON

14 June 1945

URGENT - IMMEDIATE ACTION

MEMORANDUM FOR   THE JOINT CHIEFS OF STAFF:

The President today directed me to inform the
Joint Chiefs of Staff that he wishes to meet with the
Chiefs of Staff in the afternoon of the 18th, in his office,
to discuss details of our campaign against Japan.

He expects at this meeting to be thoroughly informed of our intentions and prospects in preparation for
his discussions with Churchill and Stalin.

He will want information as to the number of men
of the Army and ships of the Navy that will be necessary
to defeat Japan.

He wants an estimate of the time required and an
estimate of the losses in killed and wounded that will
result from an invasion of Japan proper.

He wants an estimate of the time and the losses
that will result from an effort to defeat Japan by isolation,
blockade, and bombardment by sea and air forces.

He desires to be informed as to exactly what we
want the Russians to do.

He desires information as to what useful contribution, if any, can be made by other Allied nations.

It is his intention to make his decisions on the
campaign with the purpose of economizing to the maximum
extent possible in the loss of American lives.

Economy in the use of time and in money cost is
comparatively unimportant.

I suggest that a memorandum discussion of the
above noted points be prepared in advance for delivery
to the President at the time of the meeting in order that
he may find time later to study the problem.

WILLIAM D. LEAHY

RETURN TO JOINT CHIEFS OF STAFF
R4R4 SECTION, ROOM 2-0-934
THE PENTAGON

J. C. S. FILE COPY

Minutes of Meeting held
at the White House
on Monday, 18 June 1945 at 1530

PRESENT

The President

Fleet Admiral William D. Leahy

General of the Army G. C. Marshall

Fleet Admiral E. J. King

Lieut. General I. C. Eaker
   (Representing General of the
   Army H. H. Arnold)

The Secretary of War, Mr. Stimson

The Secretary of the Navy, Mr. Forrestal

The Assistant Secretary of War, Mr. McCloy

SECRETARY

Brig. General A. J. McFarland

JUN 20 45

DISTRIBUTION   COPY NO.

Admiral Leahy   1
General Marshall   2 & 5
Admiral King   3 & 6
General Arnold   4
Secy, JCS   7

Casualties. Our experience in the Pacific war is so diverse as to casualties that it is considered wrong to give any estimate in numbers. Using various combinations of Pacific experience, the War Department staff reaches the conclusion that the cost of securing a worthwhile position in Korea would almost certainly be greater than the cost of the Kyushu operation. Points on the optimistic side of the Kyushu operation are that: General MacArthur has not yet accepted responsibility for going ashore where there would be disproportionate casualties. The nature of the objective area gives room for maneuver, both on the land and by sea. As to any discussion of specific operations, the following data are pertinent:

Campaign	U.S. Casualties Killed, wounded, missing	Jap Casualties Killed and Prisoners (Not including wounded)	Ratio U.S. to Jap
Leyte	17,000	78,000	1:4.6
Luzon	31,000	156,000	1:5.0
Iwo Jima	20,000	25,000	1:1.25
Okinawa	34,000 (Ground) 7,700 (Navy)	81,000 (not a complete count)	1:2
Normandy (1st 30 days)	42,000	- - -	- - -

The record of General MacArthur's operations from 1 March 1944 through 1 May 1945 shows 13,742 U.S. killed compared to 310,165 Japanese killed, or a ratio of 22 to 1.

[Author's note: MacArthur's kill ratio figures as presented to President Truman are misleading. They were restated in JCS 1388/4 of 11 July 45 to include other casualties. The revised JCS paper states: "During this same period (for MacArthur's operations from 1 March 1945 to 1 May 1945) the total U.S. casualties, killed, wounded and missing, were 63,510 or a ratio of approximately 5 to 1." It would be fair to say, then, that the lowest casualty estimate for the first thirty days of an invasion would be 20 percent while the highest estimate would be 33 percent based on experience.]

- ᴄ -

THE PRESIDENT then asked Admiral Leahy for his views of the situation.

ADMIRAL LEAHY recalled that the President had been interested in knowing what the price in casualties for Kyushu would be and whether or not that price could be paid. He pointed out that the troops on Okinawa had lost 35 percent in casualties. If this percentage were applied to the number of troops to be employed in Kyushu, he thought from the similarity of the fighting to be expected that this would give a good estimate of the casualties to be expected. He was interested therefore in finding out how many troops are to be used in Kyushu.

ADMIRAL KING called attention to what he considered an important difference in Okinawa and Kyushu. There had been only one way to go on Okinawa. This meant a straight frontal attack against a highly fortified position. On Kyushu, however, landings would be made on three fronts simultaneously and there would be much more room for maneuver. It was his opinion that a realistic casualty figure for Kyushu would lie somewhere between the number experienced by General MacArthur in the operations on Luzon and the Okinawa casualties.

GENERAL MARSHALL pointed out that the total assault troops for the Kyushu campaign were shown in the memorandum prepared for the President as 766,700. He said, in answer to the President's question as to what opposition could be expected on Kyushu, that it was estimated at eight Japanese divisions or about 350,000 troops. He said that divisions were still being raised in Japan and that reinforcement from other areas was possible but it was becoming increasingly difficult and painful.

THE PRESIDENT asked about the possibility of reinforcements for Kyushu moving south from the other Japanese islands.

GENERAL MARSHALL said that it was expected that all communications with Kyushu would be destroyed.

ADMIRAL KING described in some detail the land communications between the other Japanese islands and Kyushu and stated that as a result of operations already planned, the Japanese would have to depend on sea shipping for any reinforcement.

ADMIRAL LEAHY stressed the fact that Kyushu was an island. It was crossed by a mountain range, which would be difficult for either the Japanese or the Americans to cross. The Kyushu operation, in effect, contemplated the taking of another island from which to bring increased air power against Japan.

THE PRESIDENT expressed the view that it was practically creating another Okinawa closer to Japan, to which the Chiefs of Staff agreed.

- 4 -

MEMORANDUM FOR THE PRESIDENT.

Proposed Program for Japan

1. The plans of operation up to and including the first landing have been authorized and the preparations for the operation are now actually going on. This situation was accepted by all members of your conference on Monday, June 18th.

2. There is reason to believe that the operation for the occupation of Japan following the landing may be a very long, costly, and arduous struggle on our part. The terrain, much of which I have visited several times, has left the impression on my memory of being one which would be susceptible to a last ditch defense such as has been made on Iwo Jima and Okinawa and which of course is very much larger than either of those two areas. According to my recollection it will be much more unfavorable with regard to tank maneuvering than either the Philippines or Germany.

3. If we once land on one of the main islands and begin a forceful occupation of Japan, we shall probably have cast the die of last ditch resistance. The Japanese are highly patriotic and certainly susceptible to calls for fanatical resistance to repel an invasion. Once started in actual invasion, we shall in my opinion

2.

have to go through with an even more bitter finish fight than in Germany. We shall incur the losses incident to such a war and we shall have to leave the Japanese islands even more thoroughly destroyed than was the case with Germany. This would be due both to the difference in the Japanese and German personal character and the differences in the size and character of the terrain through which the operations will take place.

4. A question then comes: Is there any alternative to such a forceful occupation of Japan which will secure for us the equivalent of an unconditional surrender of her forces and a permanent destruction of her power again to strike an aggressive blow at the "peace of the Pacific"? I am inclined to think that there is enough such chance to make it well worthwhile our giving them a warning of what is to come and a definite opportunity to capitulate. As above suggested, it should be tried before the actual forceful occupation of the homeland islands is begun and furthermore the warning should be given in ample time to permit a national reaction to set in.

We have the following enormously favorable factors on our side - factors much weightier than those we had against Germany:

Japan has no allies.

Her navy is nearly destroyed and she is vulnerable to a surface and underwater blockade which can deprive her of sufficient food and supplies for her population.

4.

effective national finance and respected position in many of the sciences in which we pride ourselves. Prior to the forcible seizure of power over her government by the fanatical military group in 1931, she had for ten years lived a reasonably responsible and respectable international life.

My own opinion is in her favor on the two points involved in this question.

a. I think the Japanese nation has the mental intelligence and versatile capacity in such a crisis to recognize the folly of a fight to the finish and to accept the proffer of what will amount to an unconditional surrender; and

b. I think she has within her population enough liberal leaders (although now submerged by the terrorists) to be depended upon for her reconstruction as a responsible member of the family of nations. I think she is better in this last respect than Germany was. Her liberals yielded only at the point of the pistol and, so far as I am aware, their liberal attitude has not been personally subverted in the way which was so general in Germany.

3.

She is terribly vulnerable to our concentrated air attack upon her crowded cities, industrial and food resources.

She has against her not only the Anglo-American forces but the rising forces of China and the ominous threat of Russia.

We have inexhaustible and untouched industrial resources to bring to bear against her diminishing potential.

We have great moral superiority through being the victim of her first sneak attack.

The problem is to translate these great advantages into prompt and economical achievement of our objectives. I believe Japan is susceptible to reason in such a crisis to a much greater extent than is indicated by our current press and other current comment. Japan is not a nation composed wholly of mad fanatics of an entirely different mentality from ours. On the contrary, she has within the past century shown herself to possess extremely intelligent people, capable in an unprecedently short time of adopting not only the complicated technique of Occidental civilization but to a substantial extent their culture and their political and social ideas. Her advance in all these respects during the short period of sixty or seventy years has been one of the most astounding feats of national progress in history - a leap from the isolated feudalism of centuries into the position of one of the six or seven great powers of the world. She has not only built up powerful armies and navies. She has maintained an honest and

5.

On the other hand, I think that the attempt to exterminate her armies and her population by gunfire or other means will tend to produce a fusion of race solidity and antipathy which had no analogy in the case of Germany. We have a national interest in creating, if possible, a condition wherein the Japanese nation may live as a peaceful and useful member of the future Pacific community.

5. It is therefore my conclusion that a carefully timed warning be given to Japan by the chief representatives of the United States, Great Britain, and, if then a belligerent, Russia, calling upon Japan to surrender and permit the occupation of her country in order to insure its complete demilitarization for the sake of the future peace.

This warning should contain the following elements:

The varied and overwhelming character of the force we are about to bring to bear on the islands.

The inevitability and completeness of the destruction which the full application of this force will entail.

The determination of the allies to destroy permanently all authority and influence of those who have deceived and misled the country into embarking on world conquest.

6.

The determination of the allies to limit Japanese sovereignty to her main islands and to render them powerless to mount and support another war.

The disavowal of any attempt to extirpate the Japanese as a race or to destroy them as a nation.

A statement of our readiness once her economy is purged of its militaristic influences, to permit the Japanese to maintain such industries, particularly of a light consumer character, as offer no threat of aggression against their neighbors, but which can produce a sustaining economy, and provide a reasonable standard of living. The statement should indicate our willingness, for this purpose, to give Japan trade access to external raw materials, but no longer any control over, the sources of supply outside her main islands. It should also indicate our willingness, in accordance with our now established foreign trade policy, in due course to enter into mutually advantageous trade relations with her.

The withdrawal from their country as soon as the above objectives of the allies are accomplished, and as soon as there has been established a peacefully inclined government, of a character representative of the masses of the Japanese people. I personally think

7.

that if in saying this we should add that we do not exclude a constitutional monarchy under her present dynasty, it would substantially add to the chances of acceptance.

6. Success of course will depend on the potency of the warning which we give her. She has an extremely sensitive national pride and, as we are now seeing every day, when actually locked with the enemy will fight to the very death. For that reason the warning must be tendered before the actual invasion has occurred and while the impending destruction, though clear beyond peradventure, has not yet reduced her to fanatical despair. If Russia is a part of the threat, the Russian attack, if actual, must not have progressed too far. Our own bombing should be confined to military objectives as far as possible.

Sgd Henry L Stimson

The conversation between Malik and Hirota as revealed by Magic showing that Japan seeks to align itself with Russia and divide Asia between them. Hirota stated, "Japan will increase her naval strength in the future, and that, together with the Russian army, would make a force unequaled in the world."

SOURCE: SRS **1717**, 3 JULY 1945.

ULTRA
Copy No. ___ Mt-1

TOP SECRET SRS-1717

(Incl. TAB A)

Total pages—20

No. 1195 - 3 July 1945

WAR DEPARTMENT
Office of A. C. of S., G-2

By Auth. A. C. of S., G-2
Date 3 July 1945
Initials C. W. C.

"MAGIC"—DIPLOMATIC SUMMARY

NOTE: No one, without express permission from the proper authorities, may disseminate the information reported in this Summary or communicate it to any other person.

Those authorized to disseminate such information must employ only the most secure means, must take every precaution to avoid compromising the source, and must limit dissemination to the minimum number of secure and responsible persons who need the information in order to discharge their duties.

No action is to be taken on information herein reported, regardless of temporary advantage, if such action might have the effect of revealing the existence of the source to the enemy.

The enemy knows that we attempt to exploit these sources. He does not know, and must not be permitted to learn, either the degree of our success or the particular sources with which we have been successful.

DECLASSIFIED per Part 3, E. O. 12356
by Director, NSA/Chief, CSS 2 5 JAN 1993
_____ Date: _____

MILITARY

1. **Japanese attempt to win over Russia:** (194426 WIAR)
Early last month Foreign Minister Togo advised Ambassador Sato that it was a matter of the "utmost urgency" not only to prevent Russia from entering the Pacific War but also to induce her to adopt a favorable attitude toward Japan. Togo continued that he had accordingly

---

TOP SECRET

ULTRA

asked former Premier Hirota to confer with Soviet Ambassador Malik "as soon as possible" and that "Hirota will keep a close watch on Soviet tendencies and will try to lead the Russians along the lines we desire" (DS 4 Jun 45).

It now appears that during the period 3-14 June Hirota had four conversations with Malik. A 28 June message from Togo to Sato describing the talks is set forth as TAB A; it discloses that:

a. The first conversation—on 3 June—consisted largely of an exchange of amenities in the course of which Hirota assured Malik that it was "the universal desire" of both the Japanese Government and the Japanese people to have friendly relations with Russia.

b. The next day Hirota was invited to supper by Malik and took the opportunity to state that

-2-

TOP SECRET

ULTRA

*Koki Hirota was Premier from March 1936 to February 1937 and has also been Ambassador to Russia (1930-1932) and Foreign Minister (1933-1936, 1937-1938). He was the man Foreign Minister Shigemitsu had in mind last summer when he wanted to send a "Special Envoy" to Moscow, ostensibly to improve Japan's relations with Russia (a proposal which was turned down by the Russians—DS 20 Sept 44).

TOP SECRET
ULTRA

Japan specifically hoped to "achieve a means of maintaining peaceful relations between the two countries over a rather long period, say 20 or 30 years." Malik made no answer on this point but mentioned that, although Russia had tried to pursue a peaceful policy in the Far East, past events had produced "a feeling of distrust and lack of safety."

c. At the third interview—on 14 June—Hirota pressed Malik for a statement of Russia's reaction to his previous proposal, but without success; he then stated that Japan wished to iron out all sources of friction with Russia and specifically was willing to (1) reconsider Russo-Japanese political and economic relations in Manchukuo, (2) arrive at some agreement on the question of China and (3) supply Russia with commodities from the southern areas. Hirota then inquired directly whether Russia "will consent to reach some agreement with Japan more favorable than the Neutrality Pact, or will improve its currently good relations with Japan," but Malik replied:

"Until the expiration of the Neutrality Pact, we shall continue to play the role we have been playing. I can well understand that you would like to exchange views with me regarding our future relations even before the Pact expires. However, our future relations will have to be based on concrete action."

g. At their last conference that same evening, Hirota stated: "Japan will increase her naval strength in the future, and that, together with the Russian Army, would make a force unequalled in the world. In this connection, Japan would like to have Russia provide her with oil, in return for which Japan would provide rubber, tin, lead, tungsten, and other commodities from the south (transport would be up to the Russians)." Malik replied that Russia had no oil to spare but that he would study the proposal. In conclusion, Hirota stated that Japan hoped for an early peace but "the reply was that, since Russia was not a belligerent in the East, His Excellency Mr. Hirota must be well aware that peace there did not depend on Russia."

Ref. DS Item MIL-1

28 June Message from Foreign Minister Togo to
Ambassador Sato Describing Hirota-Malik
Conversations

I

On 3 June former Premier Hirota called on Ambassador Malik at the Gora Hotel. Hirota opened the conversation by saying:

"It is particularly fortunate that in the course of the present great war Japan and Russia have not gone so far as to hurl defiance at one another, and Russia is deeply to be congratulated that, notwithstanding colossal losses, she finally won her fight [in Europe].

"As far as Japan is concerned, she hopes to maintain the security of Asia in the shifting situation, and is seeking to found this [security] on cooperation with Russia."

Malik replied:

"I am happy that I have been able to carry out my mission under peaceful circumstances in the midst of the present war.

"There used to exist in Japan powerful political forces which were under the influence

of many foreign quarters. How is the situation in that respect at present?"

The former Premier answered that [the Japanese] people had been aroused by the arguments for cooperation with Russia—which date back to the time of Prince Ito*—and that at present it was the universal desire among both Government and people to have friendly relations with Russia. In meeting Malik's question, he alluded also to the idea of sending a Special Envoy [to Russia], which had been suggested last year.

II

Malik invited Hirota to supper the next day, the 4th, and on that occasion the conversation was as follows:

Hirota: It would seem that Russia, in addition to devoting every effort to postwar reconstruction and to regaining lost territories in Europe, plans to improve her

*Presumably a reference to Prince Hirobumi Ito, a leading Japanese statesman who at the turn of the century was an advocate of friendly Russo-Japanese relations. In 1901 Ito advocated a settlement with Russia which would give the latter a free hand in Manchuria in return for recognition of Japan's liberty of action in Korea. He did not participate in the negotiations leading up to the Portsmouth Treaty (1905) but was blamed by certain Japanese circles for what they regarded as the too lenient terms of that treaty.

TOP SECRET
ULTRA

relations with —— [word missing] countries. I feel that her views with regard to us here are the same.

In this connection, while there is no question about the observance of the Russo-Japanese Neutrality Pact, Japan hopes for the improvement of relations within the remaining period of the treaty and is, I know, giving thought to the question of what form this should take. I should like to inquire as to what the Russian Government's views on this are, in general.

Malik: Notwithstanding the fact that Russia had consistently and at all times pursued a peaceful policy [in Europe], the recent occurrences took place because Germany was the sort of state she was. Although we have done our best to follow a similar policy in the East, with reference to Japan particularly, we have not been able to achieve our hopes, because there has been a strong opposition of forces. Accordingly, a sort of irreducible sense [of hostility] has remained, and a feeling of distrust and lack of safety has been

-A3-
TOP SECRET
ULTRA

-A5-
TOP SECRET
ULTRA

TOP SECRET
ULTRA

produced. Is there any concrete plan to dispel this?

Hirota: Since the whole Japanese nation has finally succeeded in interpreting the Russian attitude correctly, it has striven for the basic improvement in the relations between the two countries which is its heart's desire. However, as you have said, in the past feelings have not been good, so that we must —— [word missing] Russia's intentions as to dispelling this.

At the San Francisco Conference, Russia insisted on independence for India, etc. I wish to point out that this and other [similar] points are in the last analysis what Japan is working for. Japan would like to achieve a means of maintaining peaceful relations between the two countries over a rather long period, say 20 or 30 years, while —— [words missing] but [she is not much concerned] about such formalities as treaties, etc.

Malik then asked whether this was merely Hirota's own view or that of the Government, to which the former Premier replied that he wished it to be regarded as the

-A4-
TOP SECRET
ULTRA

view of the Japanese Government and people, and went on to say:

"In continuing yesterday's preliminary conversation with you today, I have learned your views more or less concretely. I shall express my own views after studying yours carefully, both as a whole and individually, and I should like to take some time to do this."

Hirota also reiterated that, if the basic questions were settled, naturally other trivial matters would find a solution and that he felt the present to be a golden opportunity for the settlement of basic problems.

III

Because of various circumstances, the next conference was put off from day to day. It finally took place on the afternoon of the 14th.

On that occasion Hirota several times asked about the Soviet views on the proposal he had made during the last interview, but Malik merely kept repeating that he would pass on the proposal made by the former Premier to his Government and ask for its views. Hirota then said:

"The Japanese Government is quite ready to consider the wishes of the Soviet Government with regard to all problems which might in any way prove a barrier to the improvement of Soviet-Japanese relations. To be specific, we are quite willing to consider [a] a modification of Japanese-Soviet political and economic relations in Manchukuo, [b] the arrival at a common point of view on the question of China, and [c] the supply of materials to the Soviet Union from the south.

"It seems to me that, if the Orient is ever to enjoy a genuine peace, our two countries will have to achieve relations based on mutual understanding. If the Soviet Government shares my views on this question, I think that we can easily arrive at an agreement on all problems at stake between us.

"As you know, throughout the world there are those who have no faith in the continued friendship of the Soviet Union for Japan. I would therefore very much like to know if, at this time, the Soviet Union will consent to reach some agreement with Japan more favorable than the

"Neutrality Pact or will improve its currently good relations with Japan."

Hirota went on in this vein and repeatedly asked Malik about the views of the Soviet Government. The latter part of the conversation was as follows:

Malik: Until the expiration of the Neutrality Pact, we shall continue to play the role we have been playing. I can well understand that you would like to exchange views with me regarding our future relations even before the Pact expires. However, our future relations will have to be based on concrete actions.

Hirota: By concrete actions, do you mean settling our present problems or drawing up specific agreements and pacts?

Malik: Both.

Hirota: My Government will /be glad/ to look into any problem at stake between us ---- /words missing/.

IV

During a dinner party given by Hirota on the evening of the same day, he said:

"Japan will increase her naval strength in the future, and that, together with the Russian Army, would make a force unequalled in the world. In this connection, Japan would like to have Russia provide her with oil, in return for which Japan would provide rubber, tin, lead, tungsten, and other commodities from the south (transport would be up to the Russians)."

Malik replied that he would study the proposal although Russia had no margin as far as oil was concerned, and although he assumed the Japanese Army would be opposed to the plan, since it reflected the views of the Navy. (Hirota explained that it was the common view of both Army and Navy and that in matters of national defense there was unanimity of views.)

Since Malik had spoken repeatedly of the fact that Russia was in the process of returning to peace, the former Premier said that Japan too, like Russia, wished to revert to peace quickly. The reply was that, since Russia was not a belligerent in the East, His Excellency Mr. Hirota must be well aware that peace there did not depend on Russia.

Tokyo again rejects the concept of unconditional surrender. This crucial Magic intercept helps doom Hiroshima and Nagasaki to nuclear devastation.

SOURCE: SRS 1736, 22 JULY 1945.

ULTRA Copy No. MI-3

TOP SECRET

Total pages--29
(Incl. TABS A and B)

SRS-1736

No. 1214 - 22 July 1945

By Auth.   A. C. of S., G-2
Date   22 July 1945
Initials   C. W. C.

WAR DEPARTMENT
Office of A. C. of S., G-2

"MAGIC"–DIPLOMATIC SUMMARY

NOTE: No one, without express permission from the proper authorities, may disseminate the information reported in this Summary or communicate it to any other person.

Those authorized to disseminate such information must employ only the most secure means, must take every precaution to avoid compromising the source, and must limit dissemination to the minimum number of secure and responsible persons who need the information in order to discharge their duties.

No action is to be taken on information herein reported, regardless of temporary advantage, if such action might have the effect of revealing the existence of the source to the enemy.

The enemy knows that we attempt to exploit these sources. He does not know, and must not be permitted to learn, either the degree of our success or the particular sources with which we have been successful.

DECLASSIFIED per Part 3, E. O. 12356
by Director, NSA/Chief, CSS 2 5 JAN 1993
Date:

MILITARY

1. <u>Tokyo again says no unconditional surrender; Sato pleads for peace:</u> On 19 July Ambassador Sato forwarded to Tokyo a letter from Vice Commissar Lozovsky which stated that since "the mission of Prince Konoye, the Special Envoy, is in no way made clear" the Russian Government could not give a "definite reply" to the Japanese proposal (DS 20 Jul 45).

(197837
197845
WLMR)

TOP SECRET
ULTRA

ULTRA

In a message of 21 July, Foreign Minister Togo
has now replied as follows:

"Special Envoy Konoye's mission will be
in obedience to the Imperial Will. He will
request assistance in bringing about an end to
the war through the good offices of the Soviet
Government. In this regard he will set forth
positive intentions, and he will also negotiate
details concerning the establishment of a cooperative relationship between Japan and Russia
which will form the basis of Imperial diplomacy
both during and after the war.

"Please make the above representations to
the Russians and work to obtain their concurrence
in the sending of the Special Envoy.

"Please understand especially my next wire."

Togo's "next wire", sent the same day, reads
as follows:

"With regard to unconditional surrender (I
have been informed of your 18 July message*) we

---

*In that message Sato advocated unconditional sur-
render provided the Imperial House was preserved (DS 20
Jul 45).

—2—

ULTRA

ULTRA

are unable to consent to it under any circumstances
whatever.   Even if the war drags on and it becomes
clear that it will take much more bloodshed, the
whole country as one man will pit itself against
the enemy in accordance with the Imperial Will so
long as the enemy demands unconditional surrender.
It is in order to avoid such a state of affairs that
we are seeking a peace which is not so-called unconditional surrender through the good offices of
Russia.   It is necessary that we exert ourselves
so that this idea will be finally driven home to
the Americans and the British.

"Therefore, it is not only impossible for us
to request the Russians to lend their good offices
in obtaining a peace without conditions, but it
would also be both disadvantageous and impossible,
from the standpoint of foreign and domestic considerations, to make an immediate declaration of specific
terms.   Consequently, we hope to deal with the
British and Americans after first /a/ having Prince
Konoye transmit to the Russians our concrete intentions as expressed by the Imperial Will and /b/ holding conversations with the Russians in the light of

-3-

ULTRA

ULTRA

their demands in regard to East Asia.

"In view of the fact that this is a grave matter which will decide the fate of the nation, please ask the Russians to give a full explanation of their reply, as contained in Lozovsky's letter, so as to make sure that we grasp its real meaning.

"The Government's sole responsibility in this case is limited to advising /the Emperor/ that a Special Envoy should be sent. The Envoy will be sent as a special emissary representing the Imperial Will as it is directed toward mundane affairs in particular. Please make both these points clear to the Russians, if necessary. Please also bear in mind the necessity of sufficiently impressing them with the fact that Prince Konoye enjoys the confidence of the Imperial Court and holds an outstanding position in the political circles of our country.

"Since it is not absolutely necessary, please avoid stating in writing what was said in my preceding message."

Togo concluded by saying that he had read a long message of 20 July from Sato, but that the decision

-4-

ULTRA

ULTRA

he was communicating had been made by the Cabinet and
that Sato should proceed accordingly.

The long message of 20 July from Sato to which
Togo was referring is set forth in full as TAB A.*   It
constitutes an impassioned plea to the Japanese Government to surrender to the Allies with the sole reservation
that Japan's "national structure"---i.e., the Imperial
House--be preserved.   Speaking as he himself says entirely "without reserve", Sato includes in his argument
such extraordinary statements as the following:

 a. "Since the Manchurian incident Japan has
followed a policy of expediency.   When it came
to the East Asia war, we finally plunged into a
great world war which was beyond our strength."

 b. "Ever since the conclusion of the Anti-
Comintern Pact /in 1936/ our foreign policy has
been a complete failure."

 c. "While it is a good thing to be loyal
to the obligations of honor up to the very end of
the Greater East Asia war, it is meaningless to

---

*A portion of this message dealing with the danger
of Allied air attacks on Japanese crops was contained in
yesterday's Summary.

--5--

ULTRA

prove one's devotion by wrecking the State."

<u>d</u>. "I think that we have the inescapable
and fundamental obligation to resolve as quickly
as possible to lay down our arms and save the
State and its people."

<u>e</u>. "Our people will have to pant for a
long time under the heavy yoke of the enemy . . .
/but/ after some decades we shall be able to
flourish as before."

<u>f</u>. "Immediately after the war ends, we must
carry out thoroughgoing reforms everywhere within
the country. . By placing our Government on a more
democratic basis and by destroying the despotic
bureaucracy, we must try to raise up again the
real unity between the Emperor and his people."

INDEX

Kathryn   Brzgan
Donna
Marlene